LIBERTINES AND THE LAW

A British Academy Monograph

The British Academy has a scheme for the selective publication of monographs arising from its British Academy Postdoctoral Fellowships, British Academy Newton International Fellowships and British Academy / Wolfson Fellowships. Its purpose is to assist individual scholars by providing a prestigious publishing opportunity to showcase works of excellence.

Adam Horsley is currently a British Academy Postdoctoral Research Fellow in French at the University of Exeter. He studied for his PhD at the University of Nottingham, one year of which was spent in Paris whilst teaching at the Université Paris-Diderot (Paris VII). He subsequently taught at Nottingham for three years as an Honorary Visiting Research Fellow. He is the author of a number of studies on seventeenth-century French libertine literature, criminal history, and material bibliography.

LIBERTINES AND THE LAW

Subversive Authors and Criminal Justice in Early Seventeenth-Century France

Adam Horsley

Published for THE BRITISH ACADEMY
by OXFORD UNIVERSITY PRESS

Oxford University Press, Great Clarendon Street, Oxford OX2 6DP

First edition published 2021

British Library Cataloguing in Publication Data
Data available

Library of Congress Cataloging in Publication Data
Data available

Typeset in the offices of The British Academy
by Portia Taylor

Printed and bound by CPI Group (UK) Ltd, Croydon, CR0 4YY

ISBN 978–0–19–726700–4

In loving memory of
Joyce Mary Wing

Contents

List of Illustrations

List of Abbreviations

ADHG: Archives départementales de la Haute-Garonne.
AMT: Archives municipales de Toulouse.
AN: Archives Nationales (Paris).
APP: Archives de la Préfecture de Police (Paris).
BMT: Bibliothèque Municipale de Toulouse.
BNF: Bibliothèque Nationale de France (Paris).
BNF Est: Bibliothèque Nationale de France Cabinet des Estampes.
BNF MS Fr: Bibliothèque Nationale de France Manuscrits Français.
BNF MS NAF: Bibliothèque Nationale de France Nouvelles Acquisitions Françaises.

A Note on Translations, Style, and References

English translations of quotations in foreign languages are provided in the main body. On a small number of occasions where the meaning of short phrases is clear to non-French speakers, English translations have not been deemed necessary. All translations are my own unless otherwise stated, though I refer the reader to my acknowledgements for the assistance I have received in translating from Latin. I have used early modern spelling conventions as they appear in primary sources. The uses of i, j, u, and v have been modernised where appropriate. Accents have been preserved as they appear in the original, with a minimal number of interventions where the meaning would otherwise be unclear. Translations give limited additional punctuation, including the beginning of new sentences, in instances where comprehension would otherwise be impeded; though with archival material in particular it has often been more instructive to preserve the original at the expense of fluency. Ampersands have been resolved in the main body and longer titles shortened in the footnotes.

The contents of certain archive series are not always clear from their titles. In such cases, the catalogued title of a series appears in the bibliography, whereas relevant footnotes refer to its content for the sake of clarity. For example, the source referenced in the bibliography as 'AN X 2B 1185: 'Minutes d'instruction' (janvier – juin 1624)' is given as 'AN X 2B 1185, first interrogation (22 March 1624)' in footnotes on Théophile's trial. When discussing the sovereign law courts, I distinguish between a generic or abstract 'parlement' and a specific 'Parlement', which is given as a compound noun in French (e.g. 'by the Parlement de Paris'). Illustrations are referenced and tabulated as figures, whilst their numbers indicate the chapter followed by the sequence in which they appear.

Acknowledgements

The criminal trials and executions of authors, resulting from meticulous analyses of their writing by learned judges, is not the best subject to inspire self-confidence in writing one's first book. Thankfully, I have benefited from the encouragement and advice of many of my peers, colleagues, mentors, and friends. It has been my great pleasure to incur such debts of gratitude and to record them at the beginning of this study.

My thanks are owed first to those who have been closely involved in the various phases of writing this book. My doctoral supervisors, Stephen Bamforth and James Helgeson, provided invaluable encouragement and guidance in the formative stages of this project. I hope that they will find the following pages to be worthy reflections of their support and their inspiring examples. My external examiner, Richard Maber, was the first to suggest that I write a book on the criminal trials of authors studied in my thesis. My British Academy mentor Hugh Roberts, and my monograph mentor Neil Kenny, helped me to develop my ideas into their present form with their patient advice, and encouraged me to share my findings with other colleagues and audiences. The anonymous readers for OUP offered meticulous and thought-provoking comments on drafts which have undoubtedly strengthened the present work.

In addition to those mentioned above, several other colleagues were generous enough to offer comments on draft chapters and their earlier incarnations: Catherine Attwood, Robin Briggs, Rebecca Ford, Mark Greengrass, Tom Hamilton, Nick Hammond, Jan Machielsen, John O'Brien, Jonathan Patterson, Michèle Rosellini, and Julian Swann. Further thanks are due to Tom Hamilton for sharing his invaluable expertise on navigating the criminal archives and his help with transcriptions. Helena Taylor kindly offered comments on my English translations of Latin quotations. I am also grateful to Didier Foucault and Francesco Paolo Raimondi for their encouragement, generosity, and hospitality both during and after my visit to Toulouse in 2019, which included a tour of its Grand' Chambre to mark the 400th anniversary of Vanini's trial.

I have been fortunate enough to have benefited from supportive and encouraging colleagues at my host institutions. I should like to thank the Department of Modern Languages and Cultures at the University of Nottingham, where I completed my degrees and with which I will always feel a close bond, for providing such a stimulating environment for discovering the early modern period as well as for postgraduate research and development. I am also grateful to the former Université Paris-Diderot (Paris VII, now incorporated into the Université de Paris) for a one-year teaching position which allowed me to explore the great libraries of Paris. More recently, the Department of Modern Languages and Cultures at the University of Exeter welcomed me not only as a British Academy Postdoctoral Fellow, but as a colleague, teacher, and friend. I hope that the laughter has at least partially recompensed my colleagues and students for being such generous hosts. I have also gained much from the comments, suggestions, and friendships to have emerged over the years from my activities with the Society for Early Modern French Studies (SEMFS). I hope that colleagues from all of these institutions will understand if I am not able to name them all here. For their advice on specific points in the present study, however, I should like to record my thanks to Melanie Bhend, Mette Birkedal Bruun, Zoe Boughton, Boris Donné, R. Margarita Escobar H., Claire Faure, Christine Göttler, Jenny Horsley, Marie Houllemare, Yuliya Kostyuk, Ian Maclean, Samuel Matuszewski, Michael Moriarty, Jean-Christophe Sanchez, Marc Schachter, and Martina Williams. Any remaining faults in the following pages were committed without accomplices.

The archivists at the Archives départementales de la Haute-Garonne, the Archives municipales de Toulouse, the Archives de la Préfecture de Police, and the BNF Richelieu were only too happy to offer their assistance and insights. The staff at the Archives Nationales deserve especial mention for helping me to locate certain items, for quite literally running after the occasional returns trolley when I neglected to set items aside for the next day, and for their patience when I repeatedly took closing time to refer to the closing of manuscripts rather than of doors. I am also grateful to these institutions for permission to reproduce the images included in the following chapters. Equally deserving of thanks for their patience are my BA publications manager Geetha Nair, and my BA production editor Portia Taylor, for being flexible and understanding when COVID-19 repeatedly moved the goalposts in all of our home and work lives. Due to these same circumstances, I was unable to take planned trips to Paris and Toulouse in the summer of 2020 to photograph my remaining archival sources and to follow up new leads. Michel Ollion (Archives Nationales), Pierre Amilhauld (Archives départementales de la Haute-Garonne), Géraud de Lavedan (Archives municipales de Toulouse), and Nga Bellis-Phan were generous enough with their time to indulge my hunches and to photograph some of the results.

This book could not have been completed without funding from the British Academy, as well as PhD funding from the AHRC, and was further aided by research allowances from the Universities of Nottingham and Exeter. Chapter 3 includes research published in 'Remarks on subversive performance at the trial of Giulio Cesare Vanini (1618–1619)', *Modern Language Review*, 110: 1 (2015), 85–103; whilst Chapter 5 incorporates work published in 'Strategies of Accusation and Self-defence at the Trial of Théophile de Viau (1623–25)', *Papers on French Seventeenth-Century Literature*, 44: 85 (2016), 157–77. I am grateful to these journals for permission to reproduce this research in the present work.

Finally, I should like to thank my parents, without whose many forms of support this work could not have been undertaken.

Adam Horsley
February 2021

Introduction

ORGON
Mon frère, ce discours sent le libertinage.
Vous en êtes un peu dans votre âme entiché;
Et comme je vous l'ai plus de dix fois prêché,
Vous vous attirerez quelque méchante affaire.

CLÉANTE
Voilà de vos pareils le discours ordinaire.
Ils veulent que chacun soit aveugle comme eux.
C'est être libertin que d'avoir de bons yeux;
Et qui n'adore pas de vaines simagrées,
N'a ni respect, ni foi, pour les choses sacrées.

ORGON
Brother, your words smack of libertinism.
Your soul is somewhat tainted with it;
And as I have warned you a dozen times,
You will bring trouble upon yourself.

CLÉANTE
That is what people like you usually say.
They would have everyone be as blind as they are.
To be clear-sighted is to be a libertine,
And whoever does not worship vain theatrics
Neither respects nor has faith in sacred things.

[Molière, *Le Tartuffe ou l'Imposteur* (1664)[1]]

In Molière's *Le Tartuffe ou l'Imposteur*, Orgon confesses his admiration for Tartuffe, the false man of piety whom he has invited to live in the family home. When Orgon's brother-in-law Cléante refuses to join him in taking Tartuffe's hypocritical façade at face value, he provokes a curious reaction: Cléante is accused of *libertinage*, and

[1] Molière, *Le Tartuffe*, Act I Scene 5, ll. 315–23, in Molière, *Œuvres complètes*, ed. by Georges Couton, 2 vols (Paris: Gallimard, Bibliothèque de la Pléiade, 1971), I, pp. 907–8.

warned of the dire consequences of continuing in his scepticism. What exactly is Cléante suspected of here, and what might Molière's intended meaning have been in evoking this term which, by the late seventeenth century, had come to denote excessive moral, religious, or sexual licence? On the one hand, Orgon may be accusing Cléante of refusing to follow the social norm of respecting those who have dedicated their lives to serving the Church, and of instead wishing to emancipate himself from any form of dogmatic constraint, including religion. On the other hand, Orgon could be using *libertinage* to refer more specifically to the disobedience of religious authority embodied by Tartuffe. In this case, Orgon's threat of a *méchante affaire* could well allude not only to social ostracism and spiritual danger, but to the serious legal repercussions of blasphemy or atheism. Cléante had previously criticised Tartuffe for his exaggerated acts of piety in front of Orgon and others, and now retorts that for Orgon, anyone who is clear sighted must be a libertine. In doing so, Cléante plays on the flexible and ambiguous nature of the term, and criticises the wielding of *libertinage* as an accusation against a wide variety of targets, many of whom are possessed of more common sense than the accuser himself. This might in turn allude to a refutation of blind faith that is rationally unjustifiable, a plea for us to draw upon experience and reason in the search for universal truths, or it may constitute an indirect reference to Tartuffe's blatant impiety and gluttony observed by the *bons yeux* of the majority of the play's characters. These distinctions were not mere topics of intellectual conversation, and such *méchantes affaires* were treated with often deadly seriousness by the legal authorities. Cléante's reply recalls the trial and grisly execution of the Italian philosopher Giulio Cesare Vanini, who was left quite literally clutching at straws when, during an interrogation by the Parlement de Toulouse in 1619, he tried to prove the existence of God using a piece of straw he had spotted on the floor. For not only was much of Vanini's supposed libertinism born of rational observation and attempts to demystify organised religion, but the criminal investigation into his conduct demonstrated the considerable difficulty the authorities faced in pinning down the precise nature of his crimes.

Orgon's and Cléante's conflicting perspectives on *libertinage*—the rational and the profane, the challenging and the subversive, the vocal and the silent—also echo the slippery nature of the very definition of a libertine. What exactly did it mean to be a libertine, or to be called a libertine, and how might the term's use be understood? In seeking to answer this question, one immediately runs into difficulty in establishing the composite elements of libertinism. We might, for example, distinguish between the philosophical, social, and psychological aspects of *libertinage*. Individual writers might be separated between those who indulged in sensual pleasures—which we might call *libertinage de mœurs* (*libertinage* in one's behaviour or morals)—and a more intellectual, philosophical class of free-thinkers: the *libertins érudits*.[2] In terms of public and private spaces of reading and debate, we might also speak of libertines who provoked scandal and those who were able to remain hidden beyond the reach of legal reprisal.[3] Some scholars have suggested dividing libertine authors between those at the royal court and a second generation of bourgeois libertines; or between individuals who simply refused to submit to religious dogma, and those who demonstrated a wider state of freedom.[4] In terms of engagement with the world, distinctions might be made between those identified as libertines through their social behaviour and their literary outputs; or between those who entertained unorthodox ideas and those who put such thoughts into action. Finally, we might simply track the linear progression of the term's meaning over time, taking as a guide contemporary commentaries on subversive authors as well as a broader corpus of theological texts.[5]

The inevitable problem with the development of such classifications is that so many seventeenth-century authors appear more at home within their borderlands. René Pintard asserts, for example, that the *libertins érudits* were particular to a period in the seventeenth century beginning in the early 1630s, at which point 'se forme le premier groupe érudit où se puisse constater, active, la présence de l'esprit libertin' ('the first erudite group was formed which actively demonstrated the presence of the libertine spirit').[6] Such a rigid chronology does not afford space for the early works of Gabriel Naudé—one of the central members of the *Tétrade* of *libertins érudits*—including his *Le Marfore ou discours contre les libelles* (Paris: Louis Boulenger, 1620) and the *Instruction à la France sur la verité de l'histoire des Freres de la Roze-Croix* (Paris: François Julliot, 1623). In juxtaposing learned men with those of the tavern, Pintard's system does not allow for authors whose literary production and biographies extend into both of these

[2] René Pintard, *Le Libertinage érudit dans la première moitié du XVIIe siècle* (Geneva: Slatkine, 2000), p. xix.

[3] See Antoine Adam, *Les Libertins au XVIIe siècle* (Paris: Buchet-Chastel, 1964), p. 7.

[4] Maurice Lever, *Les bûchers de Sodome* (Paris: Fayard, 1985), p. 105; Louise Godard de Donville, *Le Libertin des origines à 1665: un produit des apologètes* (Paris, Seattle and Tübignen: Papers on French Seventeenth-Century Literature (Biblio 17), 1989), p. 27.

[5] Françoise Charles-Daubert, *Les Libertins érudits en France au XVIIe siècle* (Paris: Presses Universitaires de France, 1998), p. 11; Pierre Caye, 'Libertinisme et théologie: considérations sur une expérience de pensée singulière et perdue', in *La Question de l'athéisme au dix-septième siècle*, ed. by Pierre Lurbe and Sylvie Taussig (Turnhout: Brepols, 2004), pp. 11–29 (pp. 17–18). For Marcella Leopizzi, *libertin* was a religious term in the sixteenth century, a philosophical term in the seventeenth century, and a 'moral' term to denote hedonists in the eighteenth century. See Marcella Leopizzi, *Les Sources documentaires du courant libertin français—Giulio Cesare Vanini* (Fasano: Schena; Paris: Presses de l'université de Paris-Sorbonne, 2004), pp. 532–3. For a recent study which argues against such a linear evolution of the term's meaning, see Jean-Pierre Cavaillé, 'Les Usages polémiques des termes «*libertine*», «*libertinism*» en Grande-Bretagne aux XVIe et XVIIe siècles', in *Libertin! Usage d'une invective aux XVIe et XVIIe siècles*, ed. by Thomas Berns, Anne Staquet and Monique Weis (Paris: Classiques Garnier, 2013), pp. 51–79. Cavaillé suggests that the English terms *libertine* and *libertinism* denoted at the same time moral freedom, religious disobedience, and political disobedience (p. 56).

[6] Pintard, *Libertinage*, p. 127.

worlds. Théophile de Viau had clearly received an education in the classics—from Ovid's *Metamorphoses* to Lucretius's *De rerum natura*—but was also known to frequent Parisian taverns and to compose sexually explicit verse.[7] François Maynard produced a considerable corpus of lewd and irreligious verse, but was also well-acquainted with the poetry of Martial and Juvenal, and had a successful albeit brief legal career. In his *Confessions* (*c.*1631–2), Jean-Jacques Bouchard describes his numerous sexual encounters with maids, childhood friends, and even fellow male parishioners in Church.[8] Yet he does so under the pseudonym of Oreste (inspired by the Atreidae), whilst both his sexual experiments and his literary documentation of these encounters are very much those of a scientific investigator, inspired in part by the authoritative Latin medical textbooks of his age.[9] An alternative approach to the libertine phenomenon, conceived to overcome the problems of cogent categorisation, is to embrace the macroscale and the vague nature of the term, whether this was born out of an amalgamation of different accusations, or from the duplicitous nature of certain writers' strategies of simulation and dissimulation.[10]

This leads us to evaluate the benefits and limitations of considering *libertinage* as a literary or even philosophical classification.[11] Isabelle Moreau has suggested that the best way forward might be 'abandonner un vocable qui finit par perdre de sa pertinence, ou d'en préciser étroitement les caractères définitoires' ('to abandon a term which ends up losing its relevance, or to specify its defining characteristics

[7] François Garasse, for example, described Théophile in 1623 as a one of 'nos yvrognets, mouscherons de tavernes [...] qui n'ont autre Dieu que leur ventre, qui sont enroolez en cette maudite confrérie, qui s'appelle la *Confrerie des Bouteilles*' ('our drunkards, tavern flies [...] who have no other god than their bellies, and who have enrolled themselves in that cursed *Brotherhood of Bottles*': François Garasse, *La Doctrine curieuse des beaux esprits de ce temps* (Paris: Sebastien Chappelet, 1623), p. 37). On Théophile and Ovid, see Helena Taylor, *The Lives of Ovid in Seventeenth-century French Culture* (Oxford: Oxford University Press, 2017), pp. 107–40.

[8] See Jean-Jacques Bouchard, *Confessions*, ed. by Patrick Mauriès (Paris: Le Promeneur, 2003), pp. 11–15.

[9] Having secured the sexual favours of a milkmaid, for example, Oreste does not limit himself to the sexual exploitation of the girl, but furthermore uses her to acquire scientific knowledge: 'Et ayant été quérir à Paris quantité de livres de médecins traitants *de generatione* et choses appartenantes, il se mit à faire sur cette fille les expériences des choses plus rares qu'il trouvait écrites' ('and having sought a number of medical books on *de generatione* and related matters from Paris, he began to perform experiments on this girl on the rarest things which he had found in print': Bouchard, *Confessions*, p. 19). The link between sexual exploration and science is common in libertine literature. See James Grantham Turner, *Schooling Sex: Libertine Literature and Erotic Education in Italy, France and England 1534–1685* (Oxford: Oxford University Press, 2009), p. 19.

[10] Sophie Gouverneur, *Prudence et Subversions Libertines: La Critique de la raison d'État chez François de la Mothe le Vayer, Gabriel Naudé et Samuel Sorbière* (Paris: Honoré Champion, 2005), p. 10; Bruno Roche, *Le Rire des libertins dans la première moitié du XVIIe siècle* (Paris: Honoré Champion, 2011), p. 573.

[11] On *libertinage* as a philosophy, see Antony McKenna and Pierre-François Moreau (eds.), *Libertinage et philosophie au XVIIe siècle, 12: Le libertinage est-il une catégorie philosophique?* (Saint-Étienne: Presses Universitaires de Saint-Étienne, 2010).

precisely'),[12] whereas Alain Mothu provides an even less favourable appraisal of the term's suitability in modern literary studies:

> Par quel miracle la catégorie controversée échappe-t-elle donc à l'éviction pure et simple du champ historiographique? [...] que reste-t-il des «libertins» et du «libertinage» quand on constate, d'une part, que nulle personne *a priori* concernée ne se définissait sérieusement ainsi (au moins en France et à l'époque qui nous intéresse), et quand d'autre part échouent tous les critères pour définir ces notions avec un minimum de rigueur conceptuelle?
>
> How is it that, by some miracle, this controversial category has escaped being purely and simply removed from the historiographical field? [...] What remains of 'the libertines' and of '*libertinage*' when we consider that, on one hand, none of those concerned seem to have defined themselves as such (at least in France and in our period of interest), and that on the other hand, there has been a failure to define these terms with the slightest degree of conceptual rigour?[13]

Mothu's proposed solution is to exclude the term *libertin* from modern literary studies entirely, in favour of terms including atheism, religious scepticism, irreligion, impiety, indifference, and heterodoxy.[14] But what do we stand to lose in rejecting a concept that already existed in our period of study for the sake of expediency in modern criticism? Such an approach would, for example, distort our understanding of the creative potential of the fear of being labelled a libertine. This 'crisis' was responsible for the covert writing strategies of the *libertins érudits*, and for the striking shifts in tone in the works of authors such as Maynard, Antoine Girard de Saint-Amant, and Charles Sorel.[15] It created a climate of self-censorship in which a number of bold poetic voices dared to appear above the parapet of simulation:

> Vous qui violentez nos volontés sujettes
> Oyez ce que je dis, voyez ce que vous faites,
> Plus vous la forcerez, plus elle aura de force

[12] Isabelle Moreau, *«Guérir du sot»: Les Stratégies d'écriture des libertins à l'âge classique* (Paris: Honoré Champion, 2007), pp. 13–14. The image of the libertines created by Garasse is also seen as a major obstacle for Godard de Donville: 'il est temps de nous affranchir des pièges où nous prend encore l'illusionniste Garasse, de sa représentation du libertin' ('it is time that we freed ourselves from the traps in which the illusionist Garasse still snares us with his representation of the libertines': Godard de Donville, *Libertin*, p. 410).

[13] Alain Mothu, 'Pour en finir avec les *libertins*', *Les Dossiers du Grihl*, online since 09/09/2010, http://dossiersgrihl.revues.org/4490?lang=en [accessed 20 September 2011]: para. 1–2. See also Cavaillé's positive response to Mothu: Jean-Pierre Cavaillé, 'L'histoire des «libertins» reste à faire', *Les Dossiers du Grihl*, online since 18 October 2010, http://dossiersgrihl.revues.org/4498?lang=en [accessed 20 September 2011].

[14] Mothu, 'Libertins': para. 6.

[15] Moreau speaks of a 'crise' in 1626 following Théophile's trial (see Moreau, *Guérir*, pp. 87–148). I have analysed Maynard's fear of falling foul of anti-*libertin* polemicists in Adam Horsley, '*Le Président libertin*: The Poetry of François Maynard after the Trial of Théophile de Viau', *Early Modern French Studies*, 37: 2 (2015), 93–107.

Plus vous l'amortirez, plus elle aura d'amorce
Plus elle endurera, plus elle durera.

You who assault our subjected wills
Listen to what I am saying, look at what you are doing,
The more you constrain it, the more strength it will have
The more you destroy it, the more alluring it will be
The longer it will endure, the longer it will last.[16]

To gloss over the lexicon of libertinism in this way surely risks distorting, where it does not disguise outright, both the individual experiences of those identified by their contemporaries as libertine authors, as well as the texts that such associations engendered; from the vitriolic polemical texts of Catholic apologetics, to militant reactionary verse, to the serious undercurrents of Molière's comic characters. Given this, a potential way forward might be to focus more specifically not on cogent definition or vague and often contradicting intended meanings, but on specific individuals who were linked to the libertine phenomenon. This approach would thus embrace the fluidity of the term and its conceptual background as another means of understanding early modern thought and society.

The present study offers a new contribution to the field of libertine literature. It privileges individual cases in which authors were associated with a range of intellectual, religious, or social deviances broadly identified in their time as *libertinage* over retrospective attempts to define this accusation cogently. As such, it does not propose its own watertight definition of a libertine text or author, nor does it aim to identify rigid consistencies in meaning across multiple sources and periods. This approach allows us to avoid the pitfalls of retrospective classification, and of joining the early modern judges in condemning our subjects of study for failing to meet our own expectations of brave, unorthodox writers whose free-thinking might be recognised as 'modern'.[17]

The wealth of studies on libertinism from literary, religious, and philosophical perspectives has already been alluded to. The present work aims to shed light on the history of libertine authorship from a surprisingly underexplored critical angle: the criminal justice system. Libertine authors are intrinsically linked to the legal policing of texts and their ideological sympathies in early modern France. Their texts were often written in reaction to the stifling of free-thinking, which was carried out in the interest of maintaining dominant socio-religious norms imposed by both Church and State. As physical objects, texts were subjected to a number of legal regulations. These pertained to the granting of a royal privilege for the work to be printed, the publishers who were permitted to print and sell the work, the

[16] Mathurin Régnier, 'Complainte', in *La Quint-essence Satyrique, ou Seconde partie du Parnasse des Poètes Satyriques de notre temps* (Paris: Antoine de Sommaville, 1622), p. 200.
[17] On these issues see especially the seminal work by Quentin Skinner, 'Meaning and Understanding in the History of Ideas', *History and Theory*, 8: 1 (1969), 3–53 (particularly 6–30).

length of the text, and even the quality of the paper and typeface. The contents of certain religious texts were submitted for the approval of two doctors of Theology from the Sorbonne. It was illegal to treat a number of themes in print during our period, ranging from certain questions of religion and astrological predictions, through to regicide and the limits of papal authority. As such, the law courts had close links with the book trade on two levels: in regulating a commercial industry, and in examining works carrying intellectual and ideological currency which, if deemed appropriate through the critical readings of the magistrates, could be used as material evidence in a criminal trial.[18] Magistrates held considerable influence over the reception and legacy of libertine literature, not least the power to condemn a text (and often its author) to the flames. Free-thinking was encouraged by the crumbling of old-world views; from Aristotelianism and Biblical literalism, to the image of the king of France as the first son of the Catholic Church following the accession of the sometimes-Protestant Henri IV.[19] The ensuing religious and political conflicts inevitably led to a growth in the policing of the literary sphere as the authorities became increasingly aware of the power of the printing press.

A consequence of this nascent absolutism was the development of 'libertine strategies' in order to dissimulate unorthodox ideas in print.[20] Whilst a number of studies have rightly considered specific examples and overarching trends in these writing strategies, relatively little has been said about the legal consequences that such strategies were intended to avoid. This is all the more notable given that a number of those writers associated with the libertine genre had in fact failed in their attempts at simulation and dissimulation, leading them to appear in court to answer for the perceived criminal content of their works. As such, these persecuted (or rather, prosecuted) writers have to an extent fallen through the cracks between two distinct yet complementary disciplines. Literary studies provide illuminating explorations of the lives and works of those libertine writers who faced criminal charges for their works. However, they present their trials as an extension of the writers' biographies, or as an afterword to the critical reception of their texts, whilst understandably focussing on the judges' engagement with these texts as if they were casual readers. This results in a tendency to speak of these legal proceedings in generic terms without fully explaining the legal mechanisms at work. What does it mean to speak of a writer's 'judges', their 'investigation', or even the 'trial'?

[18] J.H. Shennan, *The Parlement of Paris* (Stroud: Sutton, 1998), pp. 94–5.

[19] Joseph Bergin, *The Politics of Religion in Early Modern France* (New Haven, CT, and London: Yale University Press, 2014), pp. 5, 11.

[20] On this important aspect of libertine literature, see especially Joan DeJean, *Libertine Strategies: Freedom and the Novel in Seventeenth-century France* (Columbus, OH: Ohio State University Press, 1981); Christian Jouhaud, *Les Pouvoirs de la littérature: histoire d'un paradoxe* (Paris: Gallimard, 2000); Gouverneur, *Prudence et Subversions Libertines*; Moreau, *Guérir*; and Jean-Pierre Cavaillé, *Dis/simulations: Jules-César Vanini, François La Mothe Le Vayer, Gabriel Naudé, Louis Manchon et Torquato Accetto. Religion, morale et politique au XVII*e *siècle* (Paris: Honoré Champion, 2008).

Where did the hearings take place, in whose presence, and which of the actors in these legal dramas were given speaking parts?[21] To answer these questions one has to turn to historical studies on the various and complicated judicial institutions of early modern France, as well as wider works on political history and the history of crime and punishment. Whereas the former are able to provide an awareness of the institutional framework of criminal courts, the latter are largely concerned with the trials of political actors, or with overviews of crimes such as murder, theft, or sexual infractions, rather than crimes committed through writing.

The following chapters are a step towards bridging this gap between literary and legal historical disciplines, by focussing on the legal consequences of failed attempts to deploy covert libertine strategies. In order to avoid repeating work already undertaken on the literary outputs of the three authors considered in this book, we will focus largely on their strategies of self-defence at trial rather than their texts, though literary criticism will nonetheless feed into the following analyses. This is not to say that the cross-disciplinary nature of this study is itself a justification of its approach. As I shall argue, the criminal trial of an author has a sizeable contribution to make to the study of libertine literature. The judges who assembled for the final deliberation on a case constituted a gathering of critical thinkers possessed of a solid classical education.[22] Whether the alleged crime pertained to the religious or moral transgressions that a text was deemed to represent, or to the act of having the work printed (*faire imprimer*), the criminal trial was an arena for the critical reading of both printed texts and witness statements recorded by court scribes. Their very purpose was to define cogently the issues at hand and the likelihood of criminal culpability; to decide on truth or falsehood, licence or censorship, guilt or innocence, life or death.

An engagement with these author trials, in which the accused were forced to defend their lives before a foreboding and learned body of magistrates, is therefore more than a chapter of an author's biography, or an example of the socio-political climate in which their texts were engendered. It is a valuable source of contemporary critical reactions to unorthodox writers (akin in this sense to epistolary exchanges between members of the lettered classes), from educated readers who were simultaneously the embodiment and mouthpiece of the state's political and spiritual ideologies.[23] This book will also determine the extent to which the trials of libertine authors might inform our understanding of the stages

[21] On the analogy of the law court as theatre, see Marie Houllemare, *Politiques de la parole: le Parlement de Paris au XVIe siècle* (Geneva: Droz, 2011), pp. 439–86: 'Le parlement comme théâtre au XVIe siècle.'

[22] On the libraries and education of magistrates, see Shennan, *The Parlement*, pp. 127–37 and Tom Hamilton, *Pierre de L'Estoile and his World in the Wars of Religion* (Oxford: Oxford University Press, 2017), pp. 166–94.

[23] On the expectation that the magistrates should be embodiments of model piety, see Robert A. Schneider, *Public Life in Toulouse 1463–1789: From Municipal Republic to Cosmopolitan City* (Ithaca, NY, and London: Cornell University Press, 1989), p. 28; Houllemare, *Politiques de la parole*, pp. 511–24.

of criminal procedure, as well as the discrepancies between the idealised theory of criminal justice in print and its practical application in the law courts. These will be born out of differences between pedagogy and practice, between legislative acts and the norms of criminal procedure, and between the specificity of legal statutes and the ambiguous role of the magistrate in their implementation.[24]

For such a cross-disciplinary approach to be fruitful, it is necessary to contextualise the extant trial documentation with early modern legislative acts and legal manuals. French law was largely inherited from the Emperor Justinian's *Corpus Juris Civilis*, comprised of the *Codex*, the *Digest*, and the *Institutes*. The early modern French justice system was far from an exact replica of the law courts of Antiquity. Prospective *conseillers* (councillors, the rank of regular magistrates) were made to select a passage from the *Corpus Juris Civilis* at random. They were then given a matter of hours to prepare an explanation of their passage, before the *présidents* (higher ranking judges) and *conseillers* interrogated them on laws and royal ordinances. Yet as early as the Edict of Moulins (1566, article 10), it was claimed that these examinations had lost their original rigour.[25] The favouritism shown towards applicants with family members serving in a given parlement, combined with the number of applicants who received dispensations for taking up their posts under the stipulated minimum age (as low as twenty-one under Henri IV), led to legislation demanding that new recruits be sufficiently learned in the law and of a certain age.[26] Even a working knowledge of the Justinian *Corpus* did not guarantee sufficient competence in the administration of justice. Ian Maclean provides a helpful outline of how the need for interpretation stemmed from the asymmetrical nature of the law:

> The written law is, on the one hand, not the law; rather it embodies more or less directly and successfully the norms and force of the law; as a long series of jurisprudential texts have warned the student, to know the words of the law is not to know the law. The law, on the other hand, *is* the spoken or written law; no matter how much jurists might wish to invoke non-verbal controls on the law such as legal

[24] On the differences between the pedagogical and legal functions of renaissance magistrates, see Ian Maclean, *Interpretation and Meaning in the Renaissance: The Case of Law* (Cambridge: Cambridge University Press, 1992), p. 62. On the tension between legislators and the habitual applications of law by the criminal justice system, see Jean-Philippe Schreiber, 'La criminalisation du péché', in *Le blasphème: du péché au crime*, ed. by Alain Dierkens and Jean-Philippe Schreiber (Brussels: Éditions de l'université de Bruxelles, 2012), pp. 11–20 (p. 15). On tensions between 'textual specificity' and 'the ambiguity surrounding the judge's role in implementing the law', see Nora Martin Peterson, *Involuntary Confessions of the Flesh in Early Modern France* (Newark, DE: University of Delaware Press, 2016), p. 49.

[25] Charles Desmaze, *Le Parlement de Paris* (Paris: Cosse, Marchal et Billard, 1860), p. 101.

[26] See Shennan, *The Parlement*, pp. 136–7. For legislation on the age, education, and conduct of prospective magistrates, see for example articles 105–7 of the May 1579 'Ordonnance sur les états généraux de Blois' (1576), in *Recueil général des anciennes lois françaises, depuis l'an 120, jusqu'à la révolution de 1789*, ed. by François-André Isambert and others, 29 vols (Paris: Belin-Leprieur, 1822–33), XIV ii — juillet 1559–mai 1574 (1829), pp. 107–8.

> norms or equity, or custom, in the end, the *ius non scriptum* is only known because it can be translated into the medium of speech or writing.[27]

An exclusive focus on Roman law does not take into consideration the idealised nature of the law. Nor does it include localised legal custom born from habitual application of the law—'the regulation of everyday life through a multiplicity of local codes'—or legal precedent.[28] Jurists were aware of the problems which accompanied the application of Roman law in their own day. On the one hand, there was a concern that Roman law might become fallible if its words were too greatly refracted through the prism of historical or linguistic interpretation. This led some jurists to consider Roman law in its purest possible form to be supreme over French custom. Others, inspired by this purist attitude, sought instead to determine a similar legal system based on the ancient law of the Gauls. Alternatively, attempts were made to apply Roman law to 'modern' situations; to use it primarily as a historical context for French customary law; or to replace it with either a universal science of law based on history, or with a national law based on custom.[29] The physical traces of the judges' erudition offer a revealing reflection of these concerns. Magistrates' libraries generally contained an increasingly larger number of works on customary law than on Roman law, whereas volumes of royal ordinances and decrees produced by the parlements were also popular.[30] This trend was arguably encouraged by article 3 of the Ordinance of Villers-Cotterêts (1539), which stipulated that all legal judgements and procedures were to be recorded in French in order to avoid ambiguity in Latin.[31] Besides the distinction between contemporary and Roman law, Houllemare has observed that jurists' libraries in the late sixteenth and early seventeenth centuries also had a marked interest in legal precedent. The *Corpus Juris Civilis* and the *Corpus Juris Canonici* of Catholic canon law accounted for less than 5% of the books in their libraries, whereas greater space was afforded to collections of royal ordinances (16%) and *arrêts* (sentences or final judgements, 20%).[32] Part II of the present study will illustrate this point further, by showing how the magistrates in our case studies made explicit reference to the examples set out for them by recent legal precedent rather than by Antiquity.

Given these factors, and given that the development of French law at the turn of the seventeenth century was increasingly influenced by contemporary

[27] Maclean, *Interpretation and Meaning*, pp. 87–8.

[28] Robin Briggs, *The Witches of Lorraine* (Oxford: Oxford University Press, 2007), p. 22.

[29] On the problems and schools of thought outlined above, and for examples of their proponents, see Maclean, *Interpretation and Meaning*, pp. 16–17; Schneider, *Public Life*, pp. 52–3. For a wider historical approach, see Donald R. Kelley, *Foundations of Modern Historical Scholarship: Language, Law, and History in the French Renaissance* (New York and London: Columbia University Press, 1970).

[30] Shennan, *The Parlement*, p. 134.

[31] See John Lough, *Writer and Public in France: from the Middle Ages to the Present Day* (Oxford: Clarendon, 1978), p. 34; Shennan, *The Parlement*, p. 65.

[32] Houllemare, *Politiques de la parole*, p. 347.

political events (with the study of Roman law beyond academic purposes being overtaken by local interests), this study will predominantly take early modern French legislation and legal manuals as its benchmark for criminal procedure.[33] Our focus on the criminal justice system will centre primarily on the *practice* of serving justice through the various stages of a trial, rather than the manifestations of written law as expounded in legal theory. Legal manuals should not be taken at face value as inflexible legal blueprints that were followed to the letter in legal practice. Rather, they were idealised notions of criminal procedure, inspired by a search for 'la norme derrière l'exercice de la justice parlementaire' ('the norm behind the exercising of parliamentary justice'), which were to be imitated in order to lay a solid base for a legal trial.[34] Nevertheless, these texts—written by those experienced in administering justice for the benefit of their peers and often their family successors—serve as a useful point of reference for understanding a number of aspects of criminal procedure. Beyond the categorisation and definition of crimes and their respective punishments, they also include the stages of a trial and the roles of its actors, the complex categorisation of proof and valid refutations of evidence, and even the characteristics deemed necessary for a competent judge. Although clear communications of the sovereign's will (or as Alfred Soman describes it, the intention of censorship),[35] the various royal ordinances and edicts in these texts do not reveal how justice, as the king's pleasure, was carried out through criminal procedure in which the judge 'performs the law by deciding its relationship to an individual case'.[36] Finally, the use of texts published in the early modern period—both official legislation and independently published legal treatises—allows us to track changes in perceived attitudes to crimes, their punishments, and the wider socio-political conditions of our period, all of which are explored in Chapter 2.

It is not the aim of this book to provide a comprehensive legal history of the suppression of dissident ideas in print for the entire seventeenth century. Such an undertaking would need to consider the literary and legal implications of the dispute surrounding Henri IV's coronation (1594) and his numerous religious conversions. It would also require an analysis of the changes brought about by the ministry of Cardinal Richelieu (1624–42), the regulation of the book trade prescribed by the Code Michaud (1629), and the formation of the police under Louis XIV, which was typified by the creation of the *lieutenant général de police*

[33] Maclean, *Interpretation and Meaning*, p. 18.

[34] Houllemare, *Politiques de la parole*, p. 24; see also pp. 25–6. I have recently explored this tension in a blasphemy trial at the Parlement de Toulouse. See Adam Horsley, 'Blasphemy Hunters: Nicolas de Verdun and the Punishment of Criminal Speech in Early Bourbon France', *French Studies*, 75: 2 (2021), 145–62.

[35] Alfred Soman, 'Press, Pulpit and Censorship in France before Richelieu', *Proceedings of the American Philosophical Society*, 120: 6 (1976), 439–463 (439); Houllemare, *Politiques de la parole*, p. 39.

[36] Maclean, *Interpretation and Meaning*, p. 177.

in 1667.[37] Such a wide-ranging study would also need to make allowances for the considerable shifts in literary tastes, as well as in the limits of public acceptability with regards to subversive texts, between the Wars of Religion and the age of Versailles. It has therefore been necessary to limit the scope of this book to a relatively short chronological period, spanning roughly from the accession of Henri IV to the late 1620s, which for Soman saw the beginning of systematic censorship following the advent of Richelieu's ministry in 1624.[38]

A striking number of political and legal events relative to the policing of literature, as well as the wider link between literature and politics, took place during this 'crucial phase' for French absolutism.[39] The death of the first Bourbon monarch was followed by the unstable regency of Marie de Médicis (1610–14), during which tensions between aristocratic and confessional factions—which had been left simmering in the uneasy peace afforded by the Edict of Nantes (1598)—boiled to the surface once more.[40] Further friction occurred between the predominantly Gallican Parlement de Paris and the hotly contested Jesuit presence in France, whose influence on our trials and the wider policing of literature will be considered in Chapters 2 and 5. The princes of the blood revolted in an attempt to hand power to Henri II Prince de Condé, whilst France's Huguenot leaders were left anxious by Marie's apparent attempts to ally with Catholic Spain.[41] The consequences of these revolts for literature and our case studies were twofold. First, they led to a significant use of the printing press to rally public support through pamphlet literature.[42] Second, the new wave of tensions between Catholics and Huguenots

[37] See Isambert, *Recueil général*, XVI — mai 1610–mai 1643 (1829), pp. 225–342.

[38] Soman, 'Press, Pulpit and Censorship', 463.

[39] A.D. Lublinskaya, *French Absolutism: The Crucial Phase, 1620–1629*, trans. by Brian Pearce (Cambridge: Cambridge University Press, 1968).

[40] Soman has observed how the regicide led the law courts to focus heavily on crimes pertaining to lese-majesty. See Alfred Soman, 'Les procès de sorcellerie au Parlement de Paris (1565–1640)', *Annales: Économies, Sociétés, Civilisations*, 32 (1977), 790–814 (796).

[41] In 1615, Louis XIII was married by proxy to the Spanish princess Anne of Austria, whilst his sister Elisabeth was married by proxy to Philip IV of Spain. Many interpreted these marriages as signs of the Guises' influence over the queen regent. On reactions to these marriages, see in particular the essays which form *Dynastic Marriages 1612/1615: A Celebration of the Habsburg and Bourbon Unions*, ed. by Margaret M. McGowan (Farnham: Ashgate, 2013). On Marie de Médicis's relations with the Huguenot leaders at this time, see Jean-François Dubost, *Marie de Médicis: La reine dévoilée* (Paris: Payot et Rivages, 2009), pp. 450, 496, 649.

[42] On this subject (which will be explored in Chapter 2), see especially the following studies by Hélène Duccini: 'Regard sur la littérature pamphlétaire en France au XVIIe siècle', *Revue historique*, 260: 2 (1978), 313–39; *Concini: Grandeur et misère du favouri de Marie de Médicis* (Paris: Ablin Michel, 1991), pp. 139–273; *Faire voir, faire croire: l'opinion publique sous Louis XIII* (Seyssel: Champ Vallon, 2003). See also Jeffrey K. Sawyer, *Printed Poison—Pamphlet Propaganda, Faction Politics, and the Public Sphere in Early Seventeenth-century France* (Berkeley, Los Angeles, CA, and Oxford: University of California Press, 1990); *Histoire de l'édition française*, ed. by Roger Chartier and Henri-Jean Martin, 4 vols (Paris: Promodis, 1982–5), I: Le livre conquérant (1982), pp. 374–407; and Caroline Bitsch, *Vie et carrière d'Henri II de Bourbon, Prince de Condé (1588–1646)* (Paris: Honoré Champion, 2008), pp. 127–96. For the sixteenth-century context to the pamphlet wars of Marie de Médicis's regency, see Luc Racaut, *Hatred in Print. Catholic Propaganda and Protestant Identity during the French Wars of*

not only inspired a renewed interest in repressing Huguenot ideology (including in print), but furthermore caused Louis XIII to be absent from his capital during our authors' trials whilst he led military campaigns against the Huguenot rebels. As one early 1620s satire suggests, this royal absence had a direct effect on Parisians' respect for the rule of law: 'O Dieu! quel desordre! Je ne croy pas que le roy sçache la moitié de ce qui se passe, car, s'il le sçavoit, il y mettroit ordre: il feroit observer les loix' ('Oh God, what disorder! I do not think that the king knows half of what is going on, because if he knew, he would put everything in order and ensure that the law was respected').[43]

Our period of interest encompasses other historical events which influenced the policing of print culture. The Estates General of 1614 contained a number of articles pertaining to the printed and spoken word. The short-lived government of the *garde des Sceaux* (keeper of the seals) Claude Barbin and the *secrétaire d'État* (secretary of state) Claude Mangot, from November 1616 to April 1617, was unable to police the pamphlet market effectively. Despite being in charge of policing the book trade, Mangot was confounded by the fact that the Parlement de Paris—which was predominantly Gallican against the perceived papal influence of Marie de Médicis—was quietly content to turn a blind eye to those pamphlets which cast the queen regent in a poor light.[44] In 1617, the assassination of Marie's favourite—her fellow Italian Concino Concini—plunged France into a further crisis of leadership. Culminating with *les guerres de la mère et du fils* (the wars between the mother and the son, March 1619–April 1620), the abrupt transition from regency to direct rule changed the political landscape overnight. Those leading political figures (and the writers they patronised) linked to the queen mother's Italian influence at court suddenly found themselves in the opposing camp to Louis XIII's personal reign.[45] So too did those who had rebelled against the regency, whose disobedience could no longer be excused as patriotic duty against a foreign, female head of government. As we shall see in Chapter 2, the king's anxiety to secure the throne was reflected in a plethora of wide-ranging legislation, including a number of laws passed on the book trade, on the thematic content of printed works, and on irreligious speech acts. These reflected the wider political transition which sounded the death knell for neo-feudal and Huguenot resistance to absolutism. This shift is neatly encapsulated by a curt exchange between the king and the duc de Longueville at Poitiers in 1620. Longueville had been granted an audience with the king in order to ask forgiveness for having joined first Condé then Marie de

---

Religion (Aldershot: Ashgate, 2002) and Emily Butterworth, *Poisoned Words: Slander and Satire in Early Modern France* (Oxford: Legenda, 2006).

[43] *Les Caquets de l'Accouchée*, ed. by Édouard Fournier and Antoine Le Roux de Lincy (Paris: P. Jannet, 1855), p. 37.

[44] See Dubost, *La reine devoilée*, pp. 510–25.

[45] Pintard, *Libertinage*, p. 31.

Médicis in rebelling against him. 'Sire, je trouve que Votre Majesté a bien grandi' ('Sire, I see that you have grown considerably'), said the duke awkwardly. 'Et vous, mon cousin, je trouve que vous avez bien diminué' ('and I see that you, my cousin, have diminished considerably'), came the reply.[46]

The chronological span of this study ends roughly in the mid-1620s. Our author trials took place during a period in which the king and his agents of justice, who in the preceding era of political instability were seemingly reticent in enacting legislation to regulate the printing industry, were beginning to flex their muscles with increasingly repressive legal statutes. This began very shortly after Concini's assassination with the *Lettres-patentes sur les nouveaux statuts des libraires, imprimeurs et relieurs de la ville et université de Paris* (*Letters patent on the new status of booksellers, printers and binders in the city and university of Paris*, June 1618, passed by the Parlement on 9 July). By 1624, the disgraced Richelieu had been named a member of the *conseil du roi* (the king's council).[47] The vogue for collections of sexually obscene and impious poetry, known collectively as the *recueils satyriques* (satirical anthologies), came to an end with *Le Parnasse satyrique* ([n.p.]: [n. pub.], 1622) and the trial of our third author, Théophile de Viau (1623–5). The Huguenot party had suffered its decisive defeat with the signing of the Treaty of Alès in 1629, allowing Louis XIII and Richelieu to turn to the consolidation and centralisation of royal power. For Dubost, the freedom of expression for which France had hitherto been famous was intended to facilitate the coexistence of the two faiths, and thus found itself severely out of step with the absolutist direction of political travel after the 1620s.[48] The trial and execution of the popular and influential Henri II duc de Montmorency in 1631, who served as a protector to several libertine authors including Théophile, was a similar milestone in the repression of dissidence within the Catholic fold.[49]

Alongside the extensive Code Michaud (1629), Richelieu's ambitions also included an attempt to secure control over the great literary talents of the age. The poet and playwright François le Métel de Boisrobert had told Richelieu of a weekly gathering at the home of Valentin Conrart. This literary circle included Antoine Godeau, Nicolas Faret, Claude Malleville, and Jean Chapelain.[50] Concerned that this group might facilitate resistance to his grand designs for the kingdom, the cardinal agreed to host and to patronise these writers (somewhat against their will) with a view to transforming them into a more official collective entity at the

[46] Quoted in Jean-Christian Petitfils, *Louis XIII*, 2 vols (Paris: Perrin, 2014), I, p. 373.

[47] On events leading up to Richelieu's appointment as *premier ministre*, see Petitfils, *Louis XIII*, pp. 425–52; Philippe Erlanger, *Richelieu* (Paris: Perin, 2004), 261–90; and Michel Carmona, *Richelieu* (Paris: Tallandier, 2013), pp. 549–82.

[48] Dubost, *La reine devoilée*, p. 549.

[49] On this point see Duccini, 'La littérature pamphlétaire', 334.

[50] Émile Magne, *Le Plaisant Abbé de Boisrobert, fondateur de l'Académie Française* (Paris: Mercure de France, 1909), p. 212.

service of the state.[51] In doing so, he laid the groundwork for the founding of the *Académie française*, which received its official letters patent in 1635.

The mid-1620s were also a key turning point in the history of another serious crime purportedly committed by those living on the margins of society, and which might be included under the umbrella term of crimes against the Church: witchcraft. The criminal justice system had already begun to treat supposed cases of witchcraft and possession with increasing scepticism at the turn of the century. The mid-1620s saw the automatic granting of appeal to those condemned to death for sorcery (decades before this was the case for other crimes), as well as the final instances of torture and execution for this same crime.[52] The chronological scope of this book therefore covers a key period in French legal history in general, as well as in the development of the institutionalisation, censorship, and legislation of literature.

Beyond the temporal scope of the present study, it is also useful to delineate what appeared to constitute a libertine author in the early seventeenth century in relation to other forms of dissent. Louys Le Roy provides an example of such distinctions:

> Or est Sedition, dissention des citoyens, ainsi appellee, selon Cicero, par ce qu'ils vont les uns vers les autres, se separent en parties. Si elle est des sujects envers leurs superieurs et seigneurs, se nomme Rebellion: entre esgaux, faction.
>
> Sedition is the dissension of citizens, and is given this name, according to Cicero, because they act against one another and divide themselves into groups. If it is a question of subjects against their superiors and lords, it is called rebellion; if between equals, it is a faction.[53]

Seditious texts encourage rebellion against the sovereign, whereas subversive texts prescribe the rejection of a wider variety of power structures and social codes, for example the Church as well as accepted social and sexual norms. Given the fluid, catch-all nature of the term *libertin* alluded to earlier, such texts could all reasonably be considered to be of a libertine nature insofar as their central tenets are an emancipation from authority and servitude, with a potential if not intrinsic rejection of organised religion. Yet several texts which fell foul of French censorship in the early seventeenth century, such as works written in support of Gallicanism or justifiable regicide, fit into Le Roy's classifications without being recognised today as part of the canon of libertine texts. Before turning to our author trials, then, it will first be necessary to address the associated meanings

[51] On the initial scepticism towards the embryonic *Académie française*—from its founding members, the Parlement de Paris, and even from Louis XIII—see Magne, *Plaisant abbé*, pp. 215–21.

[52] See Alfred Soman, 'La Décriminalisation de la sorcellerie en France', *Histoire, économie et société*, 4 (1985), 179–203 (196–7).

[53] Louys Le Roy, *Exhortation aux Francois pour vivre en concorde, et jouir du bien de la paix* (Paris: Jacques du Puis, 1570), p. 8. I am grateful to John O'Brien and Marc Schachter for this reference.

and historical precedents of the word *libertin*, in addition to the political and legal contexts in which our authors were put on trial.

This book is therefore divided into two parts. Its opening chapter provides a word history of the term *libertin* and its cognates from its biblical and judicial roots in Antiquity through to the early seventeenth century. In doing so, it offers a solid understanding of the ways in which the term's use varied through the ages, and how these variants nonetheless came to contribute to the amalgamated image of the libertine in our period of interest. This methodology will also allow us to mitigate the imprecise nature of the term which continues to preoccupy modern scholars, whilst providing a solid base for studying the criminal prosecution of libertine authors in Part II. The end of Chapter 1 pays particular attention to the Jesuit father François Garasse. Though Garasse has rightly received much negative criticism in modern scholarship, he had an undeniable influence on the uses and intended meanings of the term *libertin* in the early 1620s and beyond, as well as on the views of the *procureur général du roi* (king's attorney general) Mathieu Molé. Given the influence of his anti-*libertin* writings, a focus on Garasse will show him to be both a fine example of the vague nature of *libertinage*, whilst also very much a catalyst for broadening this term of accusation to encompass a range of crimes both real and imagined.

Chapter 2 complements this word history by outlining the political and legal context of our author trials. The religious polemics and unstable regency of the first two decades of the century led to a number of legislative acts which sought to clamp down on subversive words in their written and spoken forms. These gave a clear indication of the king's attitude towards the under-regulated pamphlet market, towards the Jesuit and Gallican factions within the Parlement de Paris, as well as towards a range of themes from frivolous printed material through to blasphemy. Furthermore, such legislation provided the magistrates with the opportunity to compare their cases with recent precedents. Not all of the writers who appear in this chapter were considered libertines, though the authors which form our three substantial case studies repeatedly attracted this term of opprobrium. Rather, in imitation of the fluid definitions of *libertin* outlined in the first chapter, Chapter 2 contextualises our libertine author trials by exploring the critical reading, prosecution, and censorship of texts whose contents were judged to be politically or theologically unorthodox. As well as providing an insight into the various climates in which our authors' texts were printed and read, this approach will also ground the legal proceedings against them within the contexts of both royal legislation and legal precedent. Finally, Chapter 2 will outline the necessary technical vocabulary for understanding the complex workings of the French criminal justice system at this time. It will be the first work on libertine authors to explain the various ranks of magistrates, the parliamentary chambers and their respective competences, the means by which a case was investigated, and the habitual stages of a criminal trial. In order to facilitate the critical readings given in Chapters 3–5 further, a glossary of key criminological and parliamentary vocabulary is provided at the end of this book.

Part II consists of three substantial case studies of libertine author trials. In order to stay as close as possible to the concept of *libertinage* as it existed at the time, we shall focus on authors who feature prominently in Garasse's influential *Doctrine curieuse*: the Italian philosopher Giulio Cesare Vanini, the likely Jewish convert Jean Fontanier, and the poet Théophile de Viau. To be sure, Garasse's polemical texts cannot automatically be considered as accurate accounts of a given author's beliefs or biography. Nevertheless, they are valuable examples of the ways in which texts by so-called libertine authors were read critically by their adversaries, as well as the kinds of accusations that these readings provoked. I take my cue here from scholarship on witch trials. The varied, contradictory, and often nonsensical corpus of witchcraft accusations is embraced as part and parcel of the sociology of the witch-hunt, rather than being seen as an insurmountable obstacle to its validity as a category for modern scholarship. In examining a specific corpus of trials, this book will avoid anachronistically projecting modern judgements of what constitutes a *libertin* text onto a wider selection of authors. Instead, we shall privilege maintaining as close a proximity as possible to authors who were demonstrably targeted as libertines, both prior to and immediately following their trials, by the most influential anti-*libertin* polemicist of their day.[54]

This is not to say that these trials affected Vanini, Fontanier, and Théophile alone. As will become clear in the following pages, their ordeals were repeatedly depicted in seventeenth-century sources as milestones in the history of free-thinking, of the book trade, or of wider political change. Théophile's trial in particular served as a watershed moment for other authors, whilst the wider reading public was clearly aware of the consequences of his sensational imprisonment and lengthy trial for literary freedoms. Not all writers who observed the prosecution of our authors—whether in printed accounts or as eyewitnesses—did so from an entirely external vantage point. For despite the many literary 'schools', *querelles* (literary debates), and powerful protectors that it was able to sustain, the Parisian literary world remained a small one, engendering complex networks of mutual friends, distant relatives, professional connections, and shared patrons.[55] As Part II will

[54] Our three authors are also mentioned together as epicureans and atheists ('Epicuri discipuli, athei detestabiles') in Pierre de L'Escalopier, *M.T. Ciceronis de natura Deorum libri tres, cum Petri Lescaloperii argumentis, expositionibus et illustrationibus* (Paris: Sebastien Cramoisy, 1660), p. 181. For Pintard, the persecution of these same three authors demonstrates the considerable efforts to re-establish moral discipline, whereas for Melaine Folliard, Pierre Ronzeaud, and Mathilde Thorel, our three authors were used to enforce the social reality of *libertinage*. See Pintard, *Libertinage*, p. 31; Melaine Folliard, Pierre Ronzeaud and Mathilde Thorel, *Théophile de Viau, la voix d'un poète. Poésies 1621, 1623, 1625* (Paris: Presses Universitaires de France, 2008), p. 39.

[55] For a recent study on familial ties in writing communities, see Neil Kenny, *Born to Write: Literary*

show, criminal investigations into a writer could dictate the immediate actions, and sometimes the subsequent literary careers, of authors within their social circles as well as the aristocratic patrons they shared. In selecting a small corpus of writers, we will furthermore be able to provide more than a brief vignette of their respective trials, and to afford space to explore a number of pertinent historical contexts. These include a pre-history of Vanini's trial from his arrest and interrogation in England; the surprisingly influential status of Jews in France in the years leading up to Fontanier's trial; and the subtle yet crucial distinctions made between imitation and translation by Théophile and his judges, derived from their similar experiences in the learning of rhetoric.

Our authors were tried in three different judicial arenas. Vanini—an enigmatic tutor who had wandered across Italy, England, and France—was arrested in Toulouse in 1618 for allegedly having expressed blasphemous and impious views in private conversation. Although Garasse's *Doctrine curieuse* has become synonymous with the persecution of Théophile de Viau, the greater part of the Jesuit's text was in fact written against Vanini. His case became famous in France, and was described in a number of *canards* and printed accounts. Having initially been arrested by the municipal arm of justice in Toulouse—the *capitouls*—Vanini's subsequent execution at the hands of the Parlement de Toulouse in 1619 has largely eclipsed other aspects of his life. His only surviving texts, which were both written in Latin and published in France, have yet to be translated into English or fully into French.[56] According to his *arrêt de mort* (death sentence), the records of his trial were to be burned along with his body, though there is no definitive proof that this part of his sentence was carried out. A number of contemporary sources (some of which were written by magistrates), as well as a recent archival discovery, allow us to shed new light on the initial criminal investigation against Vanini. Although we do not have access to his trial records, we are nonetheless able to discern unrecorded elements of the trial from the shadows that these have cast on extant contemporary sources and the wording of the *arrêt*. Chapter 3, which is the most comprehensive study of Vanini's trial in English, begins with a brief introduction to his early biography, his interrogation by the ecclesiastical authorities in England, and his texts.[57] It then proposes a new

Families and Social Hierarchy in Early Modern France (Oxford: Oxford University Press, 2020). For a table illustrating circles of literary patronage, see Stéphane Van Damme, *L'épreuve libertine: Morale, soupçon et pouvoirs dans la France baroque* (Paris: CNRS Éditions, 2008), p. 165. For lists of scientific and literary circles, as well as their patrons and members, see Robert A. Schneider, *Dignified Retreat: Writers and Intellectuals in the Age of Richelieu* (Oxford: Oxford University Press, 2019), pp. 13, 30–6.

[56] Giulio Cesare Vanini, *Amphitheatrum aeternae providentiae* (Lyon: Antoine de Harsy, 1615); *De admirandis nature regine deaeque mortalium arcanis* (Paris: Adrien Perier, 1616).

[57] The two authoritative studies on Vanini are Didier Foucault, *Un Philosophe libertin dans l'Europe baroque: Giulo Cesare Vanini (1585–1619)* (Paris: Honoré Champion, 2003) and Francesco Paolo Raimondi, *Giulio Cesare Vanini Nell'Europa del Seicento, seconda edizione aggiornata* (Rome: Aracne, 2014).

evaluation of the efforts to bring him to justice in Toulouse and the role played by rumour and reputation at his trial. It ends by positing that Vanini's final moments at his execution were themselves daring acts which subverted the expected public performance of repentance.

In 1621 Jean Fontanier suffered the same fate as Vanini, for having advertised clandestine lessons in how to obtain boundless riches through readings of his enigmatic text: the *Trésor inestimable*. Although initiates were first made to swear an oath of secrecy, two of his students experienced a crisis of conscience and denounced Fontanier to the authorities. As the lengthy oath sworn by his students reveals, Fontanier's 'lessons' led his listeners dangerously far from Catholic orthodoxy. Influenced by his own conversion to Judaism following sojourns in Constantinople, Italy, and Cambrai, Fontanier's teachings were judged to be a mixture of atheism and Judaism. As one contemporary source demonstrates in summing up its account of Théophile's trial, the perceived boundaries between these two crimes could often be quite fluid:

> Puisque nous sommes entrez sur des punitions d'Athées, nous mettrons d'une suitte ce qui se voit aussi imprimé en ceste année, d'une Juive bruslee le 20 Mars, par le peuple de S. Jean de Lus.
>
> Seeing as we have gotten onto the subject of punishing atheists, we shall follow on from this with something else which has been printed this year, about a Jewish woman burned on 20 March by the people of Saint-Jean-de-Luz.[58]

Although judges were in little doubt of how to punish atheists, the legal status of Jews in France was a very recent concern at this time. Fontanier's trial took place at almost the precise midpoint between those of our other authors. He was first tried and sentenced to death by the Paris Châtelet. He then exercised his right to appeal his execution (enshrined in law since the 1530s, though such appeals were not made automatic until after 1670) by bringing his case before the Parlement de Paris as the final court of appeal, which confirmed his original sentence.[59] As such, his trial provides a bridge between the trials of Vanini—who shared the same fate as Fontanier, but at the hands of a royal court outside of Paris and without appeal—and Théophile, whose definitive sentence was passed by the same legal body as Fontanier (the Parlement de Paris), but which sentenced the poet to a loosely-enforced banishment from France. Fontanier's trial has not been analysed since the discovery of the magistrate Nicolas de Bellièvre's personal

[58] *Le Mercure françois, ou suite de l'histoire de notre temps*, 25 vols (Paris: Jean Richer, 1613–43), V — 1617–19 (1619), p. 65.

[59] See Alfred Soman, 'Criminal Jurisprudence in Ancien-Régime France: The Parlement of Paris in the Sixteenth and Seventeenth Centuries', in *Crime and Criminal Justice in Europe and Canada*, ed. by Louis A. Knafla (Waterloo, Ontario: Wilfrid Laurier University Press, 1981), pp. 43–75 (p. 46) and Alfred Soman, 'Deviance and Criminal Justice in Western Europe, 1300–1800: An Essay in Structure', *Criminal Justice History*, 1 (1980), 3–28 (11).

notes on the case in the 1980s.[60] Yet his trial deserves attention for a number of reasons. Fontanier did not publish sizeable tomes like Vanini's philosophical treatises or Théophile's collected poetry. His subversive message instead reached a Parisian reading public first through a placard, and subsequently through clandestine gatherings at his home. Here, Fontanier read from his ninety-four-page *Trésor inestimable*. Ironically, the general contents of this text have survived solely in Bellièvre's notes, an agent of the very same legal system which sought to erase Fontanier's teachings from collective memory by burning the text at his execution. As such, his case provides an uncommon link between libertine studies and pamphlet literature, as well as oral culture and the relationship between the printed and spoken word.[61] It also represents a neglected and tragic chapter in the history of the treatment of Jews in France. Both Fontanier's illegal gathering of students, and the supposedly subversive nature of his lessons, were overshadowed by Bellièvre's aim to prove that Fontanier was a Jew through at times pitiless and humiliating means. Fontanier also appears to have been of a lower social class than the other authors of our corpus. Whilst his judges sought to determine whether he was the author of the *Trésor inestimable*, he did not therefore enjoy the same level of education as Vanini and Théophile, which would prove to be a decisive factor in the trial outcome.

Chapter 4 is only the fourth critical study on Fontanier (and the first in English), as well as the most extensive exploration of his life and trial. It comments on the ways in which his first sentence at the Châtelet was evaluated and eventually verified by the Parlement, drawing largely from the personal notes recorded by Bellièvre. Unfortunately for Fontanier, these notes demonstrate that the *président à mortier* Bellièvre (who had previously served as *procureur général du roi*, and who would also go on to play a role in Théophile's trial) was an assiduous, erudite scholar with an advanced knowledge of the curriculum for students of law. Fontanier changed his defence numerous times, encouraged by the dishonest assurances of mercy from Bellièvre. These shifting strategies will form the focus of my analysis of the trial proceedings. It posits that Bellièvre's reading of Fontanier's text constitutes an early example of forensic linguistics, by which I refer to the practice of using the vocabulary, grammar, and syntax of a text to determine the degree of confidence with which it can be attributed to a given author.[62] For it was this meticulous methodology, rather than casual

[60] Elisabeth Labrousse and Alfred Soman, 'Un bûcher pour un judaïsant: Jean Fontanier (1621), *XVIIe siècle*, 39: 2 (1987), 113–132. Alain Mothu has shed new light on Fontanier's students in his brief study on Pierre Petit. See Alain Mothu, 'Pierre Petit à l'école antichrétienne de Jean Fontanier (1621)', *La Lettre clandestine*, 23 (2015), 261–70.

[61] The link between the production of libertine texts and the spoken word will become evident in all three of our case studies.

[62] Forensic linguistics may more broadly be divided between the study of 'the language of the legal process and language as evidence'. See *The Routledge Handbook of Forensic Linguistics*, ed. by Malcolm

Garassian opprobrium or a lack of respect for legal procedure, which led to the confirming of Fontanier's death sentence.

Our final chapter focusses on the most notorious libertine author trial in the seventeenth century. Between 1623 and 1625, the poet Théophile de Viau stood trial before the Parlement de Paris accused of blasphemy and impiety, having previously been convicted *in absentia* of lese-majesty. Despite the considerable number of his poems used as evidence by his two interrogators, Théophile is the only author in our corpus to have been found innocent of the initial charges against him. Nevertheless, the impact of his trial and its resultant literary polemic marked the end of a 'first wave' of libertine writers, and ushered in a generation of *libertins érudits* who were more cautious in publishing their subversive ideas. As one of Théophile's supporters put it immediately after the poet's release:

> La liberté peut bien se retirer de France
> Puisque le Parlement,
> Par l'exemple d'un seul, nous fait à tous deffense
> De parler librement.
>
> Freedom can now well and truly leave France
> As the Parlement,
> By the example of a single person, has banned us all
> From speaking freely.[63]

Théophile's trial has also left behind a much richer corpus of archival evidence than the previous cases. A large number of his contemporaries commented on the trial in print, speaking out both for and against his cause. The complete trial records have survived in the Archives Nationales, as have a number of manuscripts detailing the pre-trial investigation. Although Lachèvre's study provides transcriptions of the trial records, these have been used almost exclusively to inform literary scholarship rather than studies on the criminal justice system. Given the wealth of interrogations, witness depositions, and confrontations between witnesses and the accused, Théophile's trial records are fertile ground for an analysis of criminal procedure as well as strategies of accusation and self-defence. Moreover, the prestige of the Parlement de Paris as the highest court in the land allows us to draw on a wider range of sources on the magistrates themselves than is possible for other courts.

Chapter 5 explores previous efforts to bring about Théophile's condemnation, as well as the *recueils satyriques* genre of poetic anthologies, before providing the first critical comment on his judges and the areas of criminal procedure relevant to his case. It then offers close readings of the trial transcripts themselves. These are

Coulthard and Alison Johnson (London: Routledge, 2010), p. 7.

63 'Élégie sur l'arrêt de Théophile' quoted in Frédéric Lachèvre, *Le Libertinage devant le parlement de Paris: Le Procès du poète Théophile de Viau*, 2 vols (Paris: Honoré Champion, 1909), I, p. 513.

augmented by several of my own discoveries of unpublished archival documents, including informative texts drawn up by the *procureur général* Mathieu Molé. These discoveries furthermore include new testimonial evidence heard during the trial from an accomplice, who was the only witness who did not seek to discredit Théophile. Using this new information, I have in turn been able to correct a number of chronological estimates in modern studies, as well as to pinpoint for the first time precisely where the poet had been hiding in an attempt to escape arrest. Chapter 5 concludes by commenting on the comparative efficacy of the prosecution's and defendant's attempts to gain rhetorical control over the hearings. In doing so, it sheds new light on a well-known author trial from the perspective of criminal history, whilst at the same time bringing to bear new critical readings of the literary evidence brought before the Parlement, particularly regarding the important distinctions that were made between imitation and translation.

It is hoped that this book will go some way to challenging the notion that the magistrates' efforts to police subversive literature in our period were scant and largely ineffective. It does so by bringing together authors from a variety of national, socio-economic, confessional, and intellectual backgrounds, who were linked by the criminal investigations brought against them as well as by the animosity of their most enduring accuser, François Garasse. It evaluates their strategies of self-defence when they had been quite literally extracted from the world of letters and placed before the scrutinising gaze of the law courts. From a legal perspective, our case studies are valuable accounts of how trial proceedings in practice could often deviate from the standards prescribed in legal manuals. The following chapters are enriched by a range of images of the surviving court records, as well as by analyses of these as legal, literary, and physical objects where appropriate. Their inclusion is intended to make a small contribution to demystifying such rich and valuable archival manuscripts whose density, relative lack of digital classification, and notorious illegibility have earned them an uninviting reputation. In these ways, it is hoped that this study of infamous author trials might prove useful for future works on literary reception, religious and political histories, as well as the history of criminology.

Part I

Libertines and the Law

1
Libertines

> Par le mot de libertin je n'entens ny un Huguenot, ny un Athée, ny un Catholique, ny un Heretique, ny un Politique, mais un certain composé de toutes ces qualités. [...] Un Libertin doncques se descouvre en ses discours et en ses actions.
>
> By the word libertine I mean neither a Huguenot, nor an Atheist, nor a Catholic, nor a Heretic, nor a *Politique*, but a certain blend of all these qualities. [...] A Libertine therefore reveals himself in his words and in his actions.
>
> [François Garasse[1]]

This well-known quotation has become an essential point of reference for any study of seventeenth-century French libertine literature. Most notably remembered as the literary adversary of Théophile de Viau and the author of the infamous *Doctrine curieuse des beaux esprits de ce temps* (1623), the Jesuit father François Garasse led a personal campaign of hatred against what he considered to be a libertine threat to the Catholic souls of France. As we shall see in Chapter 5, he also played an active role in influencing Théophile's trial and the *procureur général du roi* (king's attorney general) Mathieu Molé. As his would-be definition makes clear, the libertine menace was seemingly everywhere, and even a cursory reading of the *Doctrine curieuse*'s index reveals that it took aim at a range of authors besides Théophile. In terms of authors writing in France, Garasse primarily took issue with Pierre Charron and our three authors; referring to the latter as 'trois meschans libertins' ('three wicked libertines') to exemplify the libertine condition in relation to their treatment by the criminal justice system.[2] How did Garasse

[1] François Garasse, *Les Recherches des Recherches et autres œuvres de Me Etienne Pasquier* (Paris: Sébastien Chappelet, 1622), pp. 681, 683.

[2] François Garasse, *La Doctrine curieuse des beaux esprits de ce temps* (Paris: Sébastien Chappelet, 1623), p. 972. The pagination for pp. 971–2 is repeated in some copies of this text. Our quotation is taken from p. 971 in the first of these two sequences.

and his readers come to understand *libertinage* in the 1620s? Where did the term's various connotations come from, and how was Garasse able to produce such a seemingly incoherent definition without finding its ambiguity problematic?

This chapter offers a brief word history of the term *libertin* from its origins in Antiquity through to the early seventeenth century, in order to understand how different linguistic tributaries fed into the early modern notion of *libertinage* in theological, literary, and legal contexts.[3] It goes without saying that no such lexical tracing can claim to be exhaustive, given both the plethora of potential literary sources as well as the ephemeral nature of any oral usages of the term.[4] This chapter argues that after its use in the polemics of Jean Calvin, *libertin* was increasingly used not only pejoratively but as an accusation. It shows that by the seventeenth century the term had a wide variety of potential connotations, and that its uses in the texts of both Garasse and the Minim friar Marin Mersenne were in fact very much in keeping with other sources which refer to libertines. Garasse and Mersenne are significant for studying the persecution of libertine texts. They went beyond purely religious polemic to become adversaries of libertine writers, including those studied in Part II of this book, whilst their works offer a valuable catalogue of instances in which *libertinage* is conceived within the context of irreligious (and therefore illegal) words and deeds. Finally, this chapter posits that from a historical perspective, the semantic range of the term *libertin* can be seen in certain aspects of the legal trials considered in our subsequent chapters.

SLAVES, SLAYERS, AND TAVERN-GOERS: LIBERTINE ROOTS IN THE ANCIENT AND MEDIEVAL WORLDS

The Latin root of the word—*libertinus*—refers to a former slave freed by their master as well as the descendants of a freed slave. *The American Cyclopedia* of 1864

[3] Stéphane Van Damme, for example, claims in his study on Théophile's trial that 'le libertin est une réalité constituée dans les années 1620' ('the libertine was a reality constituted in the 1620s': Stéphane Van Damme, *L'épreuve libertine: Morale, soupçon et pouvoirs dans la France baroque* (Paris: CNRS Éditions, 2008), p. 46). The following chapter instead points to a much wider history of the term in which 'the defenders of religious orthodoxy in France invent terms like *libertin* and *libertinage* to characterise their opponents and the loose morals with which they associate them' (Richard Scholar, *Montaigne and the Art of Free-thinking* (Oxford: Peter Lang, 2010), p. 44). For an overview of the appearance of the word *libertin* in pre-seventeenth-century texts, to which this study will add a number of further examples, see Gerhard Schneider, *Der Libertin, Zur Geistes- und Sozialgeschichte des Burgertums im 16. und 17. Jahrhundert* (Stuttgart: J.B. Metzlert, 1970); Jean-Claude Margolin, 'Libertins, libertinisme et «libertinage» au XVIe siècle', in *Aspects du Libertinisme au XVIe siècle*, ed. by André Stegmann (Paris: Librairie Philosophique J. Vrin, 1974), pp. 1–34; and Didier Foucault, *Histoire du Libertinage* (Paris: Perrin, 2010), pp. 13–251.

[4] On these issues see Neil Kenny, *Curiosity in Early Modern Europe: Word Histories* (Wiesbaden: Harrassowitz Verlag, 1998), p. 33; and Richard Scholar, *The 'Je-Ne-Sais-Quoi' in Early Modern Europe: Encounters with a Certain Something* (Oxford: Oxford University Press, 2005), p. 22.

provides a detailed and useful description of this legal term, and is a source made all the more pertinent given that it was written shortly after the emancipation of American slaves:

> Freedmen (liberti libertini): the designation of manumitted slaves in Roman antiquity. They were called liberti with reference to their masters, and libertini with reference to their new rank or condition. According to various circumstances, defined by law, the freedmen became Roman citizens, Junian Latins (from the Junian law which gave them freedom, and the similarity of their status to that of Latin colonists), or dediticii. The last were neither citizens (Roman or Latin) nor slaves. The Junian Latins suffered great disabilities as to property, but could in various ways rise to citizenship. But even the freedmen of the first class were not genuine (ingenui) citizens, and remained under certain obligations to their masters. The freedmen wore a cap as a sign of freedom, and took the names of their previous owners.[5]

The invaluable research conducted by Gerhard Schneider demonstrates that *libertin* had already appeared in print in the 1520s.[6] In these early texts, the word was most commonly used in either translations of Latin texts or accounts of events in Antiquity, particularly with reference to freed slaves. A striking example given by Schneider is found in Claude Seyssel's 1544 translation of Appian of Alexandria's *Roman History*:

> Les Libertins qui avoient esté Esclaves, estoient reputez comme Citoyens [...] car les francz avoient esté contrainctz de payer la quarte partie de leur revenu: et ceulx qui estoient de condition libertine, extraictz d'Esclaves, la huictiesme.
>
> The libertines who had been slaves were known as citizens [...] as the free-born had been forced to pay a quarter of their revenue, and those of libertine condition, descended from slaves, an eighth.[7]

Libertin is used here in a strictly legal sense, in keeping with the word's original definition in ancient Rome. The Roman origin of *libertin* characterises a freed slave regarded with both suspicion and disdain by full citizens. This individual, although freed from the authority that had previously kept him or her in servitude, was still regarded as an outsider excluded from certain activities. The term *libertin* was still emerging in the middle of the sixteenth century. A 1547 edition of Guillaume Budé's posthumous *Livre de l'institution du Prince* states that 'Pompée avoit un libert, c'est-à-dire, un serviteur, qu'il avoit mis de servitude à liberté' ('Pompei had a *libert*, that is to say, a servant that he freed from servitude'), whilst *libert* is accompanied with the Latin translation *libertinus* in the margin

[5] 'Freedmen' in Charles A. Dana and George Ripley, *The New American Cyclopaedia*, 16 vols (New York: D. Appleton and Company, 1858–66), VII (1864), p. 739.

[6] Schneider, *Der Libertin*, p. 37.

[7] Appian Alexandrin, Historien Grec, *Des Guerres des Romains, livres XI, traduicts en Francoys par feu M. Claude de Seyssel* (Lyon: A. Constantin, 1544), pp. 395, 622, quoted in Schneider, *Der Libertin*, p. 37.

of this edition.[8] In the same year, however, another version of the text was edited by Jean de Luxembourg in which the word *libert* is replaced with *libertin*, and *serviteur* with *esclave* (slave).[9] It is clear that Budé considered the word *libertin* to be unknown or at least unfamiliar to readers, whereas Luxembourg judged the word to be sufficiently common in the French language for Budé's Latin translation to be omitted.

A second origin of the word *libertin* in Antiquity is to be found in the Bible. Acts 6:9 refers to the group of individuals who argue with St Stephen as the *libertinôn* in the original Greek, or *synagoga libertinorum* in Latin. This line was first translated into French by Guiars des Moulin in 1477 as follows: 'Les ungs se esleverent de la sinagogue qui estoient appelles des libertiniens et des cireneciens et dalexandriens et ceulx qui estoient de cecille et d'asie [...] disputoient avec Estienne' ('then there arose certain of the synagogue, which is called the synagogue of the Libertiniens, and Cyrenians, and Alexandrians, and of them of Cilicia and of Asia [. . .], disputing with Stephen').[10] Other translations of the Bible, in which the term *libertiniens* is replaced with *libertins,* were in circulation as early as 1480.[11] Nevertheless, *libertiniens* was still being used as late as 1541 in the *Second volume de la Bible en français.*[12] By the late sixteenth century the word *libertinien* fell out of use, and *libertin* became the translation of choice for all editions of the Bible. These contrasting translations further demonstrate that *libertin* was a word with which people were still relatively unfamiliar, even though it had existed in French vocabulary for at least a century by the 1540s.[13] Having played a part in the death of the first Christian martyr, the *libertins* of Acts 6:9 rejected the teachings of Christ. This could well have led to the term being understood to denote enemies of the Church—an element of accusation and of unbelief not to be found in the context of a freed Roman slave. The exact group of people referred to in Acts, dated to the 1st century AD, is uncertain. As Shelley Matthews remarks:

> By setting up the Stephen episode with accusations from Jews of 'Cyrene, Alexandria, Cilicia and Asia' (6.9), Acts lays his death at the feet of Jews representing

[8] Guillaume Budé, *Le Livre de l'institution du Prince* (Paris: J. Foucher, 1547), quoted in Schneider, *Der Libertin*, pp. 35–6; Margolin, 'Libertins', p. 2.

[9] Guillaume Budé, *De l'Institution du Prince, revue, enrichi, d'Arguments par Messire Jean de Luxembourg, abbé d'Ivry* (Paris: Nicole l'Arrivour, 1547), quoted in Schneider, *Der Libertin*, p. 37.

[10] Quoted in Margolin, 'Libertins', p. 3.

[11] Julien Macho, *Le vray Exposition et Declaration de la Bible, tant du Vieil que du Nouvel Testament* (Lyon: [n.pub.], [c. 1480?]), quoted in Schneider, *Der Libertin*, p. 41.

[12] *Le Second volume de la Bible en français* (Paris: [n. pub.], 1541): 'Les uns se levèrent de la synagogue qui est appelée des Libertiniens.'

[13] Some studies have asserted that in 1544 Calvin became the first person to use the word *libertin* in a French printed text (Isabelle Moreau, *«Guérir du sot»: Les Stratégies d'écriture des libertins à l'âge classique* (Paris: Honoré Champion, 2007), p. 32; Frédéric Tinguely, 'D'un usage pervers de l'analogie: libertins et protestants dans la *Doctrine curieuse* du Père Garasse', *Libertinage et philosophie*, 8 (2004), 31–46 (33)). Yet from Schneider alone we know of at least three French texts in which *libertin* had appeared prior to 1544, the earliest of which Schneider dates to 1480 (*Der Libertin*, p. 41).

> a vast expanse of territory—from the far reaches of North Africa to the provinces of Asia.[14]

This would suggest that these *libertins* are not a clearly defined group of individuals in contact with each other, but a specific faith containing an unknown quantity of followers across a wide physical area. Whereas determining the geographical origins of these individuals would go beyond the scope of this study, it is noteworthy that they are not always interpreted as belonging to several separate synagogues. Richard Pervo, for instance, has suggested that the *libertins* in Acts were a varied group of individuals that formed a single synagogue.[15] The fact that the biblical *libertins* were most probably a diverse mix of people is in keeping with the use of the term in relation to Roman slaves, who would almost certainly have originated from various conquered lands.

By the medieval period, a further meaning can be found which is not apparent in the ancient sources explored above: the primacy of sensual pleasures.[16] In the thirteenth and fourteenth centuries, wandering poets known today as the *goliards* (possibly deriving from *Golias*— the Latin form of Goliath, David's adversary in the first book of Samuel) travelled across France and Europe.[17] The *goliards* were condemned by numerous synods from the thirteenth century onwards, and were last mentioned in a theological context at the synods of Salzburg and Mayence in 1310.[18] Their poetry includes apologies for the pleasures of youth,[19] accounts of rape (in which women are left in either happy or distraught states),[20] celebrations

[14] Shelly Matthews, *Perfect Martyr: The Stoning of Stephen and the Construction of Christian Identity* (Oxford: Oxford University Press, 2010), p. 60. Notably, in this early example of the term 'libertine' denoting an opponent of the Christian Church, the libertines in Acts 6:9 wield the accusation of blasphemy against St Stephen, rather than being accused of blasphemy themselves (see Acts 6:11).

[15] Richard Pervo, *Acts: A Commentary*, ed. by Harold W. Attridge (Minneapolis, MN: Fortress Press, 2009), pp. 166–7. Hans Conzelmann shares this view: '"synagogue," means the building as well as the congregation, but here the meaning is closer to the latter. Luke is probably not thinking of several (Hellenistic) synagogues, but of one, which had a varied makeup' (Hans Conzelmann, *Acts of the Apostles: A Commentary on the Acts of the Apostles*, ed. by Eldon Jay Epp and Christopher R. Matthews, trans. by James Limburg, A. Thomas Kraabel and Donald H. Juel (Philadelphia, PA: Fortress Press, 1987), p. 47).

[16] These examples furthermore contradict Claude Reichler's assertion that there are no traces of the *libertins* before the Padouan philosophers and Calvin. See Claude Reichler, *L'Âge libertin* (Paris: Éditions de Minuit, 1987), p. 8.

[17] Olga Dobiache-Rojdesvensky, *Les poésies des Goliards* (Paris: Rieder, 1931), p. 23. For more on the history of the *goliards*, see George F. Whicher, *The Goliard Poets: Medieval Latin Songs and Satires* (Westport, CT: Greenwood Press, 1976), pp. 1–6.

[18] Dobiache-Rojdesvensky, *Poésies*, p. 22; *Carmina Burana*, ed. by Étienne Wolff (Paris: Imprimerie Nationale, 1995), p. 20. Although the *goliards* were wandering bands of men, the ecclesiastical councils considered them to be both an *ordo* and a *secta*. See Helen Waddell, *Songs of the Wandering Scholars*, ed. by Dame Felicitas Corrigan (London: The Folio Society, 1982), p. 306.

[19] Such as 'Estuans Intrinsecus', quoted and translated in Whicher, *Goliard Poets*, p. 108.

[20] Poem 72 of the *Carmina Burana*, for example, describes a woman left satisfied by her ordeal, whereas Poem 84 of the same manuscript portrays a *goliard* who leaves his rape victim in tears.

of copious eating and drinking,[21] and even satires of religious institutions.[22] The *goliards* also use the term *libertini* in their poetry. Mathias Flacius Illyricus's 'Regula beati Libertini ordinis nostri' ('The rule of our order of blessed libertines') gives a light-hearted manifesto of the *goliard* 'order':

Abbas noster tritus est cyphos evacuare,
Abbatissa nostra scit per pedem declinare.
Praepositus noster magnus est praelatus,
Septem artes perfecte scit, dum est inebriatus.
Custos noster scit res perfecte conservare,
Et omnibus superuenientibus nihil habet dare.
Canonici nostri sunt raro calceati,
Sed camisiis et retibus sunt superpelliciati.
Claviger noster semper clamat, Infunde,
Sic cyphus cyphu sequitur tanquam fluentes undae.

Our Abbot is worn out from emptying jugs,
Our Abbess knows how to bend down on her feet
Our provost is a great prelate;
He knows the "seven arts" perfectly well when drunk.
Our order knows how to preserve the estate perfectly well,
To all those who come, there is nothing to give
Our clergymen seldom wear shoes,
But they are very handsome with their albs and nets.
Always our key-bearer screams: pour in!
So that one jug follows another like the flowing river.[23]

In a carnivalesque parody of religious hierarchy and ceremonies, the poet applies the regulations of the Church to the tavern. A further poem to use the word *libertini*—'In taberna quando sumus' ('When we are in the tavern')—appears in the *Carmina Burana*:

Primo pro nummata vini;
ex hac bibunt libertini:
semel bibunt pro captivis,
post haec bibunt ter pro vivis,
quater pro Christianis cunctis
quinquies pro fidelibus defunctis.
Sexies pro sororibus vanis.

First, here's to the wine merchants;
From there on, the libertines drink

[21] Such as 'Aut Lego Vel Scribo', quoted in Whicher, *Goliard Poets*, p. 16.

[22] Such as 'Licet Eger Cum Egrotis', quoted in Whicher, *Goliard Poets*, pp. 132–4.

[23] Mathias Flacius Illyricus, 'Regula beati Libertini ordinis nostri', quoted in Dobiache-Rojdesvensky, *Poésies*, p. 146. On the carnivalesque see Mikhail Bakhtin, *Rabelais and His World*, trans. by Hélène Iwolsky (Bloomington, IN: University of Indiana Press, 1984).

One for the prisoners,
After which they drink three for the living
Fourth for all Christians,
Five for the faithful dead,
Six for the loose sisters.[24]

Significantly, *libertini* has posed problems for modern translators of this poem. Dobiache-Rojdesvensky and Godard de Donville propose *les débauchés* (the debauched ones).[25] Wolff omits *libertini* altogether and suggests 'On porte d'abord un toast à celui qui paye le vin' ('first a toast is proposed to the one who is paying for the wine'), whereas Didier Foucault proposes *affranchi* (freedman).[26] It is striking that these studies do not give *libertin* as a possible solution, perhaps owing to the numerous modern connotations of the term which might render it an anachronistic translation choice.

Nevertheless, the Latin cognates of *libertin* were used by the *goliards* to describe a group which inverts and subversively parodies religious practices. These are also the first examples of the term being used to refer to obedience to natural appetites upon which Garasse would later rely so heavily in his anti-*libertin* diatribes. Furthermore, the *goliards*' use of *libertini* is the first known example of the term's use to refer to oneself.[27] The reasoning behind their word choice is not obvious from their poetry alone. The *libertins* of the Bible, Roman Antiquity, and the *goliard* poems are all linked by the theme of displacement and their situation outside of society. In his 1644 biblical commentary, Jean Diodati writes that the sect in Acts 6:9 may have been Jews freed by the Romans, 'et qu'ils faisoyent une

[24] 'In taberna', quoted in Ludwig Laistner and Eberhard Brost, *Carmina Burana: Lieder der Vaganten* (Heidelberg: Verlag Lambert Schneider, 1961), p. 20. Comprised of 228 poems, the *Carmina Burana* was found in the abbey of Benediktbeuern in 1803. As well as *goliard* poetry, it also contains two religious dramas. Thematically similar lines can be seen in 'Bacche benevenias' in Laistner and Brost, *Carmina*, pp. 108–15, and 'Vinum bonum et suave' in Dobiache-Rojdesvensky, *Poésies*, pp. 204–6. As Louise Godard de Donville notes, Bacchus was known to the Latins as *Liber*, which Richeôme likely had in mind when writing his *L'Idolatrie huguenotte* of 1607, in which one of the chapters is entitled 'Bacchus libertin' (Louise Godard de Donville, *Le Libertin des origines à 1665: un produit des apologètes* (Paris, Seattle and Tübignen: Papers on French Seventeenth-Century Literature (Biblio 17), 1989), p. 38). It is worth noting here that for Richeôme, the terminology of *libertin* had both a moral and linguistic connection to Bacchus. See also 'Liber' in the *Dictionnaire en théologie contenant entière déclaration des mots, phrases et manières de parler de la sainte Écriture tant du vieil que du nouveau Testament* (Geneva: Jean Crespin, 1560): 'Liber: le surnom de Bacchus. [...] Il est appelé Liber, ou pour ce qu'il a mis les Grecs en liberté: ou pour ce que le vin délivre de soin et tristesse' ('Liber is another name of Bacchus. [...] He is called Liber, either because he freed the Greeks, or because wine delivers from care and sadness').

[25] Dobiache-Rojdesvensky, *Poésies*, p. 202; Godard de Donville, *Libertin*, p. 37.

[26] Wolff, *Carmina*, p. 196; Foucault, *Histoire*, p. 38.

[27] The *libertins* of the early seventeenth century very rarely referred to themselves as *libertins*, most probably due to the profession of religious disobedience that this would have entailed. Rather, as Margolin notes, it was always used by one's adversary (Margolin, 'Libertins', p. 5). See also Françoise Charles-Daubert, *Les Libertins érudits en France au XVIIe siècle* (Paris: Presses Universitaires de France, 1998), p. 5.

assemblee a part, estans detestés des autres Juifs' ('and that they formed their own assembly, as they were hated by the other Jews').[28] Furthermore, the *goliards*' lack of permanent residence, and the isolation that their beliefs and works might have caused them, link them to the two strains of *libertins* from Antiquity.[29] It therefore seems likely that these poets referred to themselves as *libertini* in order to vaunt their separation from certain religious institutions and practices identified in the poems quoted above. Blending religious and intellectual nonconformity with physical licence, through self-abandonment to sensual pleasures, it is not surprising that by the end of the fourteenth century the law courts used the term *goliard* as a synonym for a brothel-keeper.[30] A description of the *goliards* by their contemporaries at the Council of Salzburg even resembles later descriptions of the seventeenth-century *libertin*:

> They go about in public naked, lie in bake-ovens, frequent taverns, games, harlots, earn their bread by their vices and cling with inveterate obstinacy to their sect, so that no hope of their amendment remaineth.[31]

Another group calling itself the *libertini*, formed in the early 1520s to fight for the freedom of the cities of Siena and Florence, has only recently received scholarly attention in the field of *libertinage* studies.[32] As Foucault emphasises, although this political group had entirely different concerns and characteristics to the *goliard* poets, they nonetheless chose the same word to express their commitment to liberty.[33] It is therefore clear that by the early sixteenth century, *libertin* had become a word sufficiently flexible and well-known to be used to describe one's personal fight for freedom from oppression on a purely political level, in addition to much older connotations of spiritual liberty and theological dispute.[34] These are essential elements for understanding the ways in which our three authors were tried before the law courts and attacked in print. Closer to our period of study, however, Jean Calvin both popularised and weaponised the term *libertin* from a predominantly theological perspective.

[28] Jean Diodati, *La Saincte Bible* (Geneva: Pierre Aubert, 1644), quoted in Margolin, 'Libertins', p. 4.

[29] For Foucault, this separation from society extends from a physical distance to an intellectual separation (Foucault, *Histoire*, p. 24).

[30] Waddell, *Scholars*, p. 307.

[31] Quoted in Waddell, *Scholars*, p. 308.

[32] Jérémie Barthas, 'Retour sur la notion de libertin à l'époque moderne. Les politiques libertins à Florence, 1520–1530', *Libertinage et philosophie*, 8 (2004), 181–99. For a more detailed study, which includes fascinating examples of the term *libertini* being used as a self-referent in Italian poetry from the same period as Calvin's texts, see Luca Addante, 'Radicalismes politiques et religieux', in *Libertin! Usage d'une invective aux XVIe et XVIIe siècles*, ed. by Thomas Berns, Anne Staquet and Monique Weis (Paris: Classiques Garnier, 2013), pp. 29–50.

[33] Foucault, *Histoire*, p. 230.

[34] For André Stegmann, the meaning of *libertin* to refer to both religious and political liberty was established by the sixteenth century (André Stegmann, *Aspects du libertinisme au XVIe siècle* (Paris: Librairie Philosophique J. Vrin, 1974), p. i).

THE BIRTH OF AN ACCUSATION: JEAN CALVIN AND GUILLAUME FAREL

Calvin first attempted to bring the Reformation to Geneva between 1536 and 1538, upon the invitation of his fellow reformer Guillaume Farel.[35] Calvin's rigid and dogmatic approach did not remain popular for long, especially once Anabaptist preachers gradually began to arrive in Geneva in the summer of 1537. Ordered by the local government to attend a synod at Lausanne in March 1538, Calvin and Farel bitterly resisted its rulings and were soon expelled from the city. Far from relying entirely on rumour or his own imagination, by the time he came to write his anti-*libertin* texts Calvin had already had sufficient dealings with Anabaptists to be able to describe their beliefs and practices in relatively reliable detail.[36] In a letter dated 26 May 1544, father Valérand Poullain of Strasbourg complained to Calvin about two brothers who were purportedly counteracting religious orthodoxy in his city, whilst further reports told of a libertine sect that had taken root in Liège and Valenciennes.[37] Similarly, on 5 September 1544 Pierre Viret wrote a letter to Rudolph Gaulter, in which he expressed his concerns about 'une nouvelle espèce de catabaptistes qu'on appelle libertins' ('a new sect of Anabaptists called libertines').[38] Perceived by many to be *libertins spirituels*, these individuals began to spread their doctrine of religious, moral, and even sexual freedom within the Protestant Reformation. Calvin's response came in his *Brieve instruction pour armer tous bons fidèles contre les erreurs de la secte commune des Anabaptistes* (Geneva: Jehan Girard, 1544), followed one year later by his *Contre la secte phantastique et furieuse des Libertins, qui se nomment spirituels* (Geneva: Jehan Girard, 1545).

Calvin distinguishes between two types of religious adversary in his *Brieve instruction*. The more dangerous of these, the libertines, 'ne tiennent compte de la saincte parolle de Dieu, non plus que de fables' ('take no more note of the holy word of God than of fables').[39] He furthermore says of the libertines that 'si les bêtes pouvaient parler, elles parleraient plus sagement' ('if the beasts could

[35] For an overview of Calvin's life, theology, and literary output, see Bernard Cottret, *Calvin: A Biography*, trans. by M. Wallace McDonald (Edinburgh: T&T Clark, 1995) and Willem Van't Spijker, *Calvin: A Brief Guide to His Life and Thought*, trans. by Lyle D. Bierma (Louisville, KY: Westminster John Knox Press, 2009).

[36] See on this point Karl H. Wyneken, 'Calvin and Anabaptism', in *Articles on Calvin and Calvinism*, ed. by Richard C. Gamble (New York and London: Garland Publishing, 1992), pp. 18–29 (p. 22).

[37] Cottret, *Biography*, p. 277.

[38] Quoted in Henri Busson, *Le Rationalisme dans la Littérature Française de la Renaissance (1533–1601)* (Paris: Librairie Philosophique J. Vrin, 1957), p. 303. For rare examples of the theological views of these individuals as described by themselves, see Charles Schmidt, *Traités mystiques écrits dans les années 1547 à 1549, publiés d'après le manuscrit original* (Paris: Sandoz et Fischbacher, 1876) and Émile Picot, *Théâtre Mystique de Pierre du Val et des Libertins Spirituels de Rouen au XVIe siècle* (Paris: Damascène Morgand, 1882).

[39] Jean Calvin, *Brieve instruction pour armer tous les bons fidèles contre les erreurs de la secte commune des Anabaptistes* (1544), in Jean Calvin, *Œuvres*, ed. by Françis Higman and Bernard Roussel (Paris: Gallimard, Bibliothèque de la Pléiade, 2009), pp. 623–724 (p. 626).

speak, they would speak more wisely').[40] This is one of several examples where Calvin refers to the libertines as being worse than beasts.[41] The *libertins*—whom Calvin interestingly refers to in places as a *synagogue*, suggesting that his texts may have been coloured by the Jewish synagogue in Acts 6:9—believed in privileging the purity of their inner being, leading them to physical indulgence and a lack of exterior restraint.[42] It is this openness to instinctive pleasures of the flesh that leads Calvin to refer to such a group in *Contre les libertins* as 'cette secte bestiale des libertins' ('this bestial sect of the libertines').[43] If *libertinage* involves an interior, unregulated relationship with God, it is not surprising that Calvin should comment on the wider social implications of this doctrine for civil authority:

> Sans scrupule chascun vesquist a son appetit; abusans de la liberté Chrestienne pour lascher la bride à toute licence charnelle: prenans plaisir à mettre conclusion au monde, en renversant toute police, ordre et honnesteté humaine. [...] Ces phrenetiques, sans aucune distinction, abolissent toute la loy, disans qu'il n'y faut plus avoir d'esgard, pource que nous en sommes affranchis.
>
> Each lives according to his appetites without scruple, abusing Christian liberty to indulge in unbridled carnal licence of all kinds, taking pleasure in bringing the world to an end by overturning all polity, order and human decency. [...] These frenzied people abolish all of the law without distinction, saying that we must no longer have any regard for it as we are made freed of it.[44]

The *libertins* of Jean Calvin thus continue the motif of separation from authority and dogma which we observed earlier in the freed slave of Antiquity. Taking the freed slave and the rebel against Christ's Church, Calvin also accuses the *libertins* of satisfying animal impulses and of seeking to overturn all manifestations of law and order.

In 1550, Guillaume Farel published a lengthy defence of Calvin's anti-*libertin* texts entitled *Le Glaive de la parole véritable*. Farel attacks a separate, now lost work written by a Franciscan which expounded the doctrine of the *libertins spirituels*.[45] Calvin's fear of a clandestine group possessing secret knowledge, and

[40] Calvin, *Brieve instruction*, p. 674.

[41] On bestial representations of the *libertins*, see Peter A. Huff, 'Calvin and the Beasts: Animals in John Calvin's Theological Discourse', *JETS*, 42: 1 (March 1999), 67–75; Anne E. Duggan, 'Epicurean Cannibalism, or France Gone Savage', *French Studies*, 67: 4 (2013), 463–77.

[42] Jean Calvin, *Contre la secte fantastique et furieuse des libertins, qui se nomment spirituels* (1545), in Calvin, *Œuvres*, pp. 725–830 (pp. 769, 791). The term *synagogue* had also been used to denote other groups that were perceived to exist outside of the Catholic Church prior to Calvin. Stokes notes, for example, that the term was used to refer to the witches' Sabbath in texts such as the anonymous *Errores Gazariorum* (1452). See Laura Stokes, *Demons of Urban Reform: Early European Witch Trials and Criminal Justice, 1430–1530* (Basingstoke: Palgrave Macmillan, 2011), p. 21.

[43] Calvin, *Contre les libertins*, p. 742.

[44] Quoted in Schneider, *Der Libertin*, pp. 54, 64.

[45] This man is referred to only as a *Cordelier* in both Calvin's and Farel's works. We know that the man in question was a Franciscan from Calvin's sermon against him—*Contre un Franciscain, sectateur des erreurs des Libertins*—which was delivered in the Franciscan's native Rouen on 20 August 1547. The

the curiosity through which this knowledge is obtained, is also present in Farel's paranoiac belief that the *libertins* receive theological inspiration from sorcerers and astrologers.[46] Farel also went further by distorting certain images of the *libertins* as they had been described by Calvin. He distances the *libertins* from Christianity, and instead accuses them of worshipping an entirely different God in the universal spirit; a term that has strong connotations with the *anima mundi* of pantheism.[47] Calvin does not refer to the *libertins* as Epicureans in either the *Brieve instruction* or *Contre les libertins*, but claims that they seek a life without hardship and full of sensual indulgence.[48] It is therefore significant that Farel should use the word *épicurien* to denote not only *libertins* in general but also the more specific group identified by Calvin: 'toute l'hérésie de ce misérable Cordelier, et des Libertins, Anabaptistes, Papistes, Epicuriens, Athéistes, ou autres quelconques' ('all the heresy of this miserable Cordelier, and of the Libertines, Anabaptists, Papists, Epicureans, Atheists, or whatever others').[49] In situating the term *libertin* alongside *épicurien*, Farel disregards any interest in cogent definition, and instead identifies *libertin* as yet another catch-all term of abuse within the arsenal of religious polemic.[50]

Farel tailors Calvin's accusation to suit his own purposes, despite the fact that both he and Calvin were combatting the same perceived religious adversary. As stated earlier, Calvin begins his *Brieve instruction* by distinguishing two separate groups of Anabaptists, one of which 'reçoit l'Écriture sainte, comme nous' ('receives Holy Scripture, like us').[51] The second group, in an interestingly similar situation to the *libertins* of the Bible, is an extremist group of perceived 'non-believers'

lost text attacked by Calvin's sermon was entitled *Le Bouclier de defense*.

46 See Calvin, *Contre les libertins*, p. 739; Guillaume Farel, *Le Glaive de la parole véritable, tiré contre le Bouclier de défense: duquel un Cordelier Libertin s'est voulu servir, pour approuver ses fausses et damnables opinions* (Geneva: Jean Girard, 1550), p. 462.

47 'La secte Libertine, qui a la croix et tribulation en horreur' ('the libertine sect, which is horrified by the Cross and Christ's tribulations': Farel, *Glaive*, p. 290).

48 The association between Epicurean living and openness to sensual pleasures is not necessarily a *libertin* characteristic. Higman and Roussel note that for the *libertins* according to Calvin, 'plus on peut s'éloigner de la créaturalité basse de la chair et du corps et de sa servitude, plus on s'approche du royaume de l'esprit, et plus on est libre' ('the further one is able to get from the lowly, animal flesh and body, as well as servitude, the closer one gets to the kingdom of the spirit, and the more one is free': Calvin, *Contre les libertins*, p. 1306). In this sense, the doctrines of Calvin's *libertins* differ from those of the medieval Free Spiritualists, whose doctrine of Antinomianism (the belief that the soul is one with God, and that therefore moral and religious laws can be disregarded) was often interpreted by their persecutors as an autotheistic form of amoralism which excused any physical impulse as divine.

49 Farel, *Glaive*, p. 218; see also p. 222: 'Libertins, Epicuriens, et tous tels errants' ('Libertines, Epicureans, and other such wanderers'). In 1587 François de la Noue would group the *libertins* and the Epicureans within the same undesirable group of dissidents, blaming the Wars of Religion for engendering 'un million d'Epicuriens et de Libertins,' and later referring to 'certaines gens, qu'on ne peut mieux appeler qu'Epicuriens et Libertins' ('certain people, who are best described as Epicureans and Libertines': François de la Noue, *Discours Politiques et Militaires* (Basle: François Forest, 1587), pp. 34, 492, quoted in Schneider, *Der Libertin*, pp. 140, 146).

50 See Pierre Vesperini, *Lucrèce: Archéologie d'un classique européen* (Paris: Fayard, 2017), pp. 262–8. I am grateful to Hugh Roberts for pointing me towards this study.

51 Calvin, *Brieve instruction*, p. 626.

which has broken away from the larger, conventional group of religious dissidents, that is to say the wider Anabaptist movement. Farel muddies the waters here by listing the *libertins* alongside papists, Epicureans, and atheists. For Luce Albert, a distinction can be made between Calvin and later apologists in that Calvin is careful to define his terms, suggesting that it was important to him to differentiate between various theological opponents and to adopt a certain 'sobriété lexicale'.[52] We might therefore draw a parallel between Farel's use of the term *libertin* and the wider uses of the term *athée* (atheist) in the sixteenth century.[53]

Calvin's texts were more concerned with presenting clear and accurate accounts of *libertin* beliefs than Farel's *Glaive,* which links the *libertins* to other collectives outside of Farel's own denomination. In doing so, Farel does not use the term *libertin* in a precise manner. Instead, he adds weight to his accusations against theological adversaries, whilst at the same time increasing the number of potential targets of his accusation by adding new aspects to the *libertin* identity. Although Farel could potentially be but one example of this evolution in the term's use rather than its pioneer, such shifts allowed early seventeenth century conceptions of *libertinage* to include a wide range of derogatory and potentially dangerous accusations.

LIBERTINS IN EARLY SEVENTEENTH-CENTURY TEXTS

Libertin appears in few dictionaries published at the turn of the century. The 1611 edition of Cotgrave's dictionary, while not having an entry for *libertin,* describes *libertinage* as 'Epicurism, sensuality, licentiousness, dissoluteness'.[54] A French–Spanish dictionary printed in 1607 defines libertin as 'celui qui est affranchi du serf qu'il était' ('he who is freed from being the serf that he was').[55] In 1602, *libertin* was defined as an open-minded person in both a French–German dictionary ('ders mit allem Glauben halt') and a French–Flemish dictionary ('vry gheest').[56] Finally, a dictionary printed in 1625 refers to *libertin* under *liberté* as 'qui use trop de liberté, licentiosus. Libertin, licentieux, debauché' ('who enjoys too much

[52] Luce Albert, 'Jean Calvin et le libertin spirituel—de l'archétype à l'alter ego', in *Libertin! Usage d'une invective aux XVIe et XVIIe siècles*, ed. by Thomas Berns, Anne Staquet and Monique Weis (Paris: Classiques Garnier, 2013), pp. 83–99 (pp. 85–6).

[53] Although the examples given above do not explicitly equate *libertinage* with atheism, it is likely that the two words had a significant semantic overlap in the period in which Calvin and Farel were writing. On the indiscriminate use of 'atheist' as a powerful accusation in the sixteenth century, see Lucien Febvre, *Le Problème de l'incroyance au 16e siècle: La Religion de Rabelais* (Paris: Albin Michel, 1968), p. 127.

[54] Randle Cotgrave, *Dictionary of the French and English Tongues* (London: Adam Islip, 1611).

[55] *Tesoro de las dos lengua francese y espanola* (Paris: Orry, 1607).

[56] *Dictionnaire français-allemande et allemande-français* (Nuremberg: Levinus Hulsius, 1602); *Dictionnaire ou promptuaire français-flamand* (Rotterdam: I. Waesbergue, 1602).

liberty, licentiosus. Libertine, licentious, debauched'), and defines *libertinage* as 'des hérétiques, avec leur liberté de conscience' ('of heretics, with their freedom of conscience').[57] Significantly, the entry for *liberté* in the 1614 edition of this dictionary ends with 'licentiosus', whilst omitting the reference to *libertin*, suggesting that the association of the term *libertin* with debauchery was uncommon at this time. These limited examples are the result of an investigation into the word *libertin*'s presence in a much wider corpus of dictionaries from the early seventeenth century which, for the most part, do not refer to the term. Examples of *libertinage* in other texts from this period are however more numerous, and cover the full range of possible connotations in our word history so far.

The original judicial meaning from ancient Rome can still be seen in texts written on the subject of Antiquity. On the ninth emperor of the Roman Empire, Jean-Pierre Camus writes 'un sien libertin nommé Cerylus, lequel pour fuir le tribut se disoit estre né libre' ('a libertine of his named Cerylus, who said that he was born free to escape paying tribute').[58] This text is one of several to use the word *libertin* to describe the status of freed slaves in Roman Antiquity.[59] Camus's text stands out, however, in that both the author and reader are called *libertins*: 'si nous ne sommes serfs et esclaves tout à fait, du moins sommes-nous libertins, qui est tousjours une marque d'esclavage' ('if we are not entirely serfs and slaves, then we are at least libertines, which is still a mark of slavery').[60] Despite Calvin's vilification of those he had perceived to be *libertins*, the term could still therefore be used in its original legal sense from Antiquity in the early seventeenth century, as the magistrate Jacques de la Guesle further demonstrates:

> Nous répétons ce mot d'impiété, et adjoustons celuy de patronne, d'autant que si celuy qui donne la liberté, doit estre tenu pour Patron, et celuy qui la reçoit libertin on les peult justement appeler libertins de la France, comme les ayant affranchy de la cruelle servitude de ce Dom-Piètre.
>
> We repeat this word impiety, and add that of patron, particularly if the one who gives freedom must be considered a Patron, and the one who receives it [must be considered] a libertine, we can justifiably call them libertines of France, having freed them from the cruel servitude of this Don Pedro.[61]

[57] *Le Grand dictionnaire français–latin* (Lyon: C. Larhot, 1625).

[58] Jean-Pierre Camus, *Les Diversités*, 10 vols (Paris: Claude Chappelet, 1609-18), I (1609), p. 15. The following examples are intended to add to those identified by Schneider and Godard de Donville. See also Claude Seyssel's translation of Thucydides quoted in Edmond Huguet, *Dictionnaire de la langue française du seizième siècle*, 7 vols (Paris: E. Champion; Didier, 1925–67), V (1961): 'Une bende d'esclaux [sic] et de libertins qui avoient esté de servitude mis en liberté' ('a band of slaves and of libertines who had been given freedom from servitude').

[59] See also Camus, *Les Diversités*, pp. 271, 276; Jean de Montlyart, *Les Hiéroglyphiques de Jean-Pierre Valérian* (Lyon: Paul Frellon, 1615), p. 530; Claude Duret, *Histoire admirable des plantes et herbes émerveillables et miraculeuses en nature* (Paris: Nicolas Buon, 1625), 'Préface', fol. E^{r}.

[60] Camus, *Les Diversités*, p. 272.

[61] Jacques de La Guesle, *Les Remontrances de Messire Jaques de La Guesle Procureur General du Roi*

In this instance, *impiété* refers to Spain's treatment of France, and Spain is only termed *libertin* after it has been called impious. Having been freed from servitude under Pedro of Castile, the Spanish *affranchis* now owe a debt to France, that is to say the supposed *patron* (i.e., the Latin *patronus*—he who liberates a slave from servitude). *Libertin* could also refer to wider forms of freedom from servitude. In a separate text, Camus links the *libertins* to debauchery, although the main connotation remains that of a lack of respect for the rule of law:

> Pauvrets, tellement aveuglez de leurs libertinages, et de leurs desbauches (car de toutes les saisons de la vie la plus desreiglée c'est celle, pour l'ordinaire, qui se coule aux Universitez, où en apprenant les lois, on renverse toutes les lois).
>
> Poor things, so blinded by their *libertinages* and their debaucheries (for of all of life's seasons, the most dissolute is usually that which is spent at Universities, where in learning the law, all laws are overturned).[62]

For Bruscambille, actors cannot be described as *libertins* due to their rigid observance of ancient rules of rhetoric which, he implies, is not in keeping with the meaning of the term:

> Mais à propos, quelles gens sont-ce? des libertins, hé quelle liberté d'estre en une servitude perpétuelle, pour practiquer ceste partie de Rethorique, sçavoir, l'action tant vantée des Grecs et des Latins, pour laquelle Cicéron a tant peiné, et Démosthène tant sué.
>
> On that note, what people are these? Libertines? Well what kind of liberty is it to be in perpetual servitude, to practise this part of rhetoric, that is to say, the act so lauded by the Greek and Latin writers, for which Cicero worked so hard, and Demosthenes sweated so much.[63]

St François de Sales refers to libertines as those 'qui ne veulent point avoir d'autres lois que celles que la propre volonté leur dicte' ('who do not want any other laws than those given to them by their own will'); whereas Laurent de Paris's *Le Palais de l'amour divin* similarly speaks of pious individuals who seek

---

(Paris: Pierre Chevalier, 1611), p. 321. Pedro of Castile (1334–69) was murdered by his successor, Enrique II. Pedro was led to Enrique's tent by the French knight Bertrand du Guesclin which, for de La Guesle, rendered France the *patronne* of Castile.

[62] Jean-Pierre Camus, *La Sixième partie de l'Alexis de Monseigneur l'Evêque de Belley* (Paris: Claude Chapelet, 1623), p. 242. For further links between *libertinage* and those who resist order or endure rules with difficulty, see Pierre De L'Ancre, *Tableau de l'inconstance et instabilité de toutes choses* (Paris: Abel l'Angelier, 1610), pp. 24, 447. On misrule in student society, see Jean Imbert, *La Pratique Judiciaire, tant civile que criminelle* (Paris: Robert Fouet, 1616), p. 600; Natalie Zemon Davis, *Society and Culture in Early Modern France* (London: Duckworth, 1975), pp. 111–15, 183–4.

[63] Bruscambille [Jean Gracieux], 'Les Pitagoriens', in *Œuvres complètes*, ed. by Hugh Roberts and Annette Tomarken (Paris: Honoré Champion, 2012), p. 388 (first published in *Les Nouvelles et plaisantes imaginations* in 1613). This flippant use of a charged term such as *libertin* is all the more striking given that Bruscambille's text is one of the earliest defences of the theatre in early modern France. See Hugh Roberts, '"Au Diable soient donnez les Comediens": La haine dans les apologies du théâtre au début du XVIIe siècle', *Littératures classiques*, 98 (2019), 65–75 (69–70).

to avoid 'l'usage libertin de sa propre volonté' ('the libertine use of their own will').[64] De Paris then goes on to reiterate Calvin's view of the freedom preached by the *libertins* as 'une secousse du joug de toute loy pour perpétrer toute sorte de forfaits sans scrupule ni remors quelconque de conscience' ('shaking off the yoke of all laws to commit all kinds of crimes without scruple or any kind of remorse of conscience').[65] In contrast with the views of the *libertins,* however, he sees the freedom from ecclesiastic regulation prescribed by the *libertins* as a mere transferral of servitude from the Church to one's own appetites: 'cependant le libertin du monde pense être bien libre, et ne voit pas qu'il est esclave de tous ses pechez' ('yet the libertine of society believes that he is free, and does not see that he is a slave to all his sins').[66]

The link between libertines and pleasures of the flesh also appears in a number of other texts. In seeking to dismiss Epicurean materialism, Pierre Le Loyer suggests that Epicurus was 'remarqué de l'antiquité pour un libertin, voluptueux et impie' ('known in Antiquity to be a voluptuous and impious libertine').[67] The link between libertinism and depravity is likewise made by Laurent:

> Semblablement quand de vôtre vie mauvaise, dépravée, libertine, de voz aversions et distractions volontaires de Dieu, de vôtre propre volonté, propre libertinage de vie et d'esprit débandé ...
>
> Similarly when from your awful, depraved, libertine life, from your aversions and voluntary distractions from God, from your own will, your own libertine living and your unbridled spirit ...[68]

Similarly, an anonymous pamphlet describing a girl supposedly possessed by demons attributes impiety to:

> la corruption misérable de ce temps, auquel les créatures par leurs desbauches libertines, se sont en fin precipitez en tel aveuglement d'esprit, qu'à peine veulent ils recevoir, sans probation philosophique, les principes et fondements de la Religion.
>
> the miserable corruption of this age, into which creatures have thrown themselves in such a blindness of spirit by their libertine debauchery, that they scarcely

[64] St François de Sales, *Sermons recueillis* quoted in Huguet, *Dictionnaire du seizième siècle*; R.P.F. Laurent, *Le Palais de l'amour divin entre Jésus et l'âme chrétienne* (Paris: Denys de la Noüe et Charles Chastellain, 1614), p. 62.

[65] Laurent, *Le Palais*, p. 233; see also p. 232. For Pierre Milhard, those who disrespect the need for parental permission to marry are 'les enfants trop libertins' ('children who are too libertine': Pierre Milhard, *La Vraie guide des curés, vicaires, et confesseurs* (Rouen: Robert de Roues, 1610), p. 307).

[66] Laurent, *Le Palais*, pp. 234–5.

[67] Pierre Le Loyer, *Discours, et histoires des spectres, visions et apparitions des esprits, anges, démons, et âmes, se montrant visible aux hommes* (Paris: Nicolas Buon, 1605), p. 14.

[68] Laurent, *Le Palais*, p. 561. See also Jacques Tahureau's *Dialogues* quoted in Huguet, *Dictionnaire du seizième siècle*, which speaks of 'des nouvelles et abhominables sectes qui courent pour le jourd'huy à l'endroit de je ne sçai quels pernicieus et naturalistes libertins' ('new and abominable sects which can be found today around I do not know what kinds of pernicious and naturalist libertines').

> wish to receive the principles and foundations of Religion without philosophical probation.[69]

Finally, it is in the Bacchic sense of the term that *libertin* is used, in a rare self-description for the time, by an anonymous poet in *La Quint-essence satyrique* (1622). The 'Description du voyage de Saint Cloud' begins as follows:

> Quoy, veux-tu donc sçavoir nostre libertinage
> Et comme l'autre jour nous fismes le voyage
> De S. Cloud en basteau pour prendre le plaisir
> Qu'on reçoit par les champs saoulant nostre desir.
>
> So, do you want to know about our *libertinage*
> And how the other day we made the journey
> From Saint-Cloud by boat to take the pleasure
> That we get in the countryside as we glut our desires.[70]

The poem describes a large meal followed by dancing and a visit to a brothel, resulting in a fight which obliges the poet and his friends to flee the scene. The first line above disregards the irreligious connotations of the term *libertin* described earlier, and openly mocks those who might use *libertinage* as an accusation of impious living. As well as attesting to the audacious nature of the *recueils satyriques* (satirical anthologies), this poem also demonstrates that *libertinage* could be understood outside of a religious or philosophical context to refer to hedonism.

By deploring the beliefs of those he perceived to be *libertins* in his influential sixteenth-century texts, Calvin inadvertently provided his Catholic opponents with a term of insult for those of the entire *religion prétendue réformée*.[71] Jean Auvray's powerful call to arms against the French Protestant movement encourages the king's army to vanquish 'ces subjects rebelles, / Mutins, capricieux, libertins, infidelles' ('these rebellious subjects, / mutineers, capricious people, libertines, infidels').[72] Camus writes that the popularity of Protestantism in France has resulted in the nation losing its Catholic identity, 'tant le meslange de l'heresie, qui est parmy nous, et nos extravagans libertinages, ont rendu nostre foy suspecte à ceste nation' ('such has the mix of heresy among us, and our extravagant *libertinages*, made our faith suspect to this nation').[73] For Scipion Dupleix, 'la

[69] *Histoire prodigieuse nouvellement arrivée à Paris: D'une jeune fille agitée d'un Esprit fantastique et invisible* (Paris: Ducarroy, 1625), p. 4.

[70] In *La Quint-essence satyrique, ou Seconde partie, du parnasse des Poètes satyriques de notre temps* (Paris: Antoine de Sommaville, 1622), p. 120.

[71] On naming, identification, and accusation in sixteenth-century theological conflicts, see Denis Crouzet, *Dieu en ses royaumes: une histoire des guerres de religion* (Paris: Champ Vallon, 2008), pp. 174–87.

[72] Jean Auvray, 'Les guerriers volontaires' in *Le Banquet des Muses, ou les divers satires du sieur Auvray* (Rouen: David Ferrand, 1628), p. 175. On the same page Auvray accuses Calvin's reformers of 'libertine audace' ('libertine audacity').

[73] Camus, *Les Diversités*, III (1613), p. 118.

mauvaise vie des heretiques libertins' ('the wicked lives of heretical libertines') from abroad led to 'des sectes pleines d'impietés et d'irreligion, introduisant le libertinage et la sensualité au lieu de la maceration, de l'austerité et des œuvres pieuses' ('sects full of impiety and irreligion, introducing *libertinage* and sensuality instead of mortification, austerity and pious works').[74] Finally, this concern for the presence of Huguenots in France is not limited to theological texts. In *Les Caquets de l'accouchée*—a series of pamphlets satirising women's gossip in the lying-in chamber—one of the female characters attempts to defend the Protestant reformation movement against various accusations made against it: 'on nous appelle libertins, cruels acariastres, imposteurs, semeurs de zisanies, la peste des Estats, et l'origine de tous les malheurs qui ont inondé par toute la France' ('they call us libertines, cruelly cantankerous, imposters, sowers of discord, the plague of states, and the origin of all the ills which have flooded the whole of France').[75] The term *libertin* was thus closely linked to the reformed religion in France. By putting the defence of Protestantism into the mouth of a gossiping woman, the author of the *Caquets* undermines the character's arguments, whilst also insinuating that Protestantism threatens the stability of the French nation.

Denying specific tenets of the Catholic faith was also labelled *libertinage*, whereas the ultimate denial of these—atheism—was explored in particular detail in the works of Garasse and Mersenne. In his 'Satyre première contre les Simoniaques' Thomas Sonnet de Courval refers to 'les langues serpentines / des Atheistes meschans, et ames libertines' ('serpentine tongues / of wicked atheists, and libertine souls').[76] Dupleix lamented the impudence of 'aucuns heretiques libertins d'oser nier que S. Pierre ait esté à Rome' ('certain libertine heretics to dare to deny that St Peter had been in Rome').[77] Similarly, Le Loyer discusses the Sadduceans, a Jewish sect which denied the resurrection of the dead and an afterlife. He refers to their selective reading of the Bible as 'un pur Atheïsme et Libertinisme' ('pure Atheism and Libertinism'), and later describes them as 'des Juifs, non tant Heretiques, qu'Athees, et Libertins' ('Jews, not so much Heretics as Atheists and Libertines').[78]

Religious texts of this period often present *libertinage* as part of a wider vocabulary describing dissidence from Catholicism in the form of lists. According to Laurent, 'ce siècle abonde d'héretiques, de deïstes, de libertins, et mocqueurs

[74] Scipion Dupleix, *Mémoires des Gaules* (Paris: Laurent Sonnius, 1619), pp. 477, 533.

[75] *Les Caquets de l'accouchée*, ed. by Édouard Fournier and Antoine Le Roux de Lincy (Paris: P. Jannet, 1855), p. 83. A longer condemnation of the Reformation appears on pp. 84–7.

[76] [Thomas Sonnet de Courval], *Les Œuvres satyriques du Sieur de Courval-Sonnet gentilhomme virois* (Paris: Rolet Boutonne, 1622), p. 61.

[77] Dupleix, *Mémoires*, p. 448. A similar use of the term as an adjective to describe atheists appears in the title of Claude Garnier, *Le Te Deum, Contre les Atheistes Libertins* (Paris: Daniel Guillemot, 1623).

[78] Le Loyer, *Discours*, pp. 13, 478. Blaise de Monluc's *Lettres* speak vaguely of 'libertins et attaystes' ('libertines and atheists') in the kingdom of France (quoted in Huguet, *Dictionnaire du seizième siècle*).

athéïstes et de mal vivans Catholiques' ('this century is abound with heretics, deists, libertines, and atheist mockers and with loose-living Catholics').[79] According to Le Loyer, sceptics and doubting philosophers are a further category of unbelievers, 'ne différans gueres des Atheïstes et libertins' ('hardly differing from Atheists and Libertines'), whilst he later writes 'aux Athees, aux libertins, aux voluptueux, aux ignorants, aux accariastres' ('to Atheists, to libertines, to the voluptuous, to the ignorant, to the cantankerous').[80] In a text originally published in 1610, Milhard reports that 'Bogomites, Anabaptistes et libertins Heretiques' ('Bogomils, Anabaptists and heretical libertines') allowed their followers to renounce their faith in order to save their lives as long as they continued to believe in their hearts, which he describes as 'une doctrine purement hérétique, et condamnée pour telle par l'Eglise de Dieu' ('a purely heretical doctrine, and condemned as such by God's Church').[81] Not even Calvin escaped from being labelled a libertine. Jean de Benedicti refers to *libertins* as being amongst 'des anciennes hérésies' along with 'Calvinistes, Beguines et Begards, Cyriens, [et] Anabaptistes.'[82] In doing so, he tars Calvin with the same brush fashioned by the Protestant reformer himself to attack the Anabaptist movement, in a reflection of the wider tendency in theological conflicts of the time to yoke together all forms of perceived dissident heretics.

Our word history from the ancient world to the beginning of the seventeenth century does not claim to be an exhaustive list of uses of the term *libertin*. It does, however, provide a sufficient number of occurrences to draw some broad conclusions for the present study and potentially for future work. *Libertin* was rarely used by authors to refer to themselves between the early sixteenth century and the mid-seventeenth century. Unlike modern notions of *libertinage*, in early Bourbon France the term was increasingly associated with the irreligious rather than the sexual. Even in instances where indulgence of the flesh is described as libertine, it is noteworthy that such descriptions are usually given in terms of the spiritual consequences of the reveller, or in terms of the religious group to which such activities are said to pertain. The diverse range of intended meanings and

[79] 'Avis aux bénévoles lecteurs' in Laurent, *Le Palais*, n. p.

[80] Le Loyer, *Discours*, pp. 35, 923. The *approbation* for this text also refers to 'les pernicieuses et erronees opinions des anciens et modernes Atheïstes, Naturalistes, Libertins, Sorciers, et Heretiques' ('the pernicious and erroneous opinions of ancient and modern Atheists, Naturalists, Libertines, Witches and Heretics').

[81] Pierre Milhard, *La Grande guide des curés, vicaires, et confesseurs* (Lyon: François Arnoullet, 1619), p. 438.

[82] Jean de Benedicti, *La Somme des péchés et des remèdes d'iceux* (Paris: Guillaume de la Noue, 1601), p. 40. Benedicti later refers to Calvinists as 'ces libertins Epicuriens' ('these Epicurean libertines', p. 217). For an example of the Beguine heresies of the Free Spirit, see Marguerite Porete, *A Mirror for Simple Souls*, ed. by Charles Crawford (Dublin: Gill and MacMillan, 1981). See also Robert E. Lerner, *The Heresy of the Free Spirit in the Later Middle Ages* (Berkeley, Los Angeles, CA, and London: University of California Press, 1972) and Raoul Vaneigem, *The Movement of the Free Spirit* (New York: Zone Books, 1994), particularly pp. 95–232.

targets is also notable, and the works of Pierre Le Loyer particular—in which the term *libertin* is used to denote both an indulgence in physical appetites as well as atheism—demonstrate that these variations cannot be attributed solely to conflicting definitions according to different authors. Although a generalised term of abuse, *libertin* could and did serve as a background to the persecution of free-thinkers in our period of study. It is with these general remarks in mind that we can better understand the works of two apologists writing against supposedly libertine texts, and who made specific reference to our three authors: Garasse and Mersenne. These writers provide a crucial contextual backdrop for understanding the cultural, historical, and linguistic values of the accusations made against Vanini, Fontanier, and Théophile during their criminal trials.

FRANÇOIS GARASSE, MARIN MERSENNE, AND THE TARGETING OF LIBERTINE AUTHORS

The Jesuit father François Garasse has become synonymous with the persecution and subsequent trial of the *libertin* poet Théophile de Viau. Within the field of seventeenth-century *libertinage* studies, he is furthermore recognised as being instrumental in the persecution of *libertin* literature (including texts by our three authors) and the birth of modern censorship.[83] As such, his works are useful tools for understanding the mentalities which sent two of our authors to the stake, and the ways in which the texts of so-called libertine authors were read by their adversaries. I shall argue that Garasse's casual use of *libertin* to describe a variety of individuals, undeterred by the levels of overlap and indeed contradiction in his polemic, is more than a symptom of his rhetorical shortcomings. Rather, I contend that Garasse was drawing from the very rich word history of *libertin* outlined in our earlier representative examples. Garasse played a crucial role in the development of this history. For as Neil Kenny proposes, he was responsible for promulgating the libertine myth and literary category, 'giving them a collective identity—which they would not otherwise have had—by taking heterogeneous intellectual and literary figures and lumping them together as *libertins*, *athées* and *curieux*'.[84] His diatribes therefore allow us to examine the views of at least some of those who were hostile towards unorthodox views and literature, but only if we are willing to confront and embrace the ambiguity and hyperbole which clearly formed a part of such mentalities.

[83] See, amongst others, Godard de Donville, *Libertin*; and Joan DeJean, *The Reinvention of Obscenity: Sex, Lies, and Tabloids in Early Modern France* (Chicago and London: The University of Chicago Press, 2002), p. 46.

[84] Neil Kenny, *The Uses of Curiosity in Early Modern France and Germany* (Oxford: Oxford University Press, 2004), p. 114. Isabelle Moreau describes Garasse's *libertin* as a 'hybride de Théophile et de Vanini' (Moreau, *Guérir*, p. 50).

François Garasse was born in Angoulême in 1585. He entered the *Compagnie de Jésus* in 1601—seven years after the expulsion of the Jesuits from France following Jean Châtel's failed attempt on the life of Henri IV.[85] Although the Jesuits and their colleges were later allowed to return under the protection of Marie de Médicis, there is little doubt that Garasse had joined the order at a relatively low point in its reputation and influence.[86] Garasse's first attempts at writing were modest in both aim and length compared to his later works. His first known work, the *Elegiarum de funesta morte Henrici magni liber singularis* (Poitiers: Antoine Ménier, 1611) is a collection of elegies to the late Henri IV, and was quickly followed in the same year by an address to Louis XIII, *Sacra Rhemensia Carolina Heroica nomine Collegii Pictavensis oblata Ludov. XIII. Regi Christianissimo in sua inauguration* (Poitiers: Antoine Ménier, 1611).[87] Before taking his vows to become a Jesuit father in 1618, Garasse began to turn his attention to defending the Jesuits and wider Catholicism. His *Horoscopus Anticotonis* ([Antwerp (?)]: Ex officina Hieronymi Verdussii, 1614) is a short defence of the Jesuits against their adversaries. Like his subsequent work, the *Elixir Calvinisticum* (In Ponte Charentonio [Paris (?)]: Joannem Molitorem, 1615), it was published under the pseudonym André Scippius, a choice that demonstrates Garasse's awareness of his own satirical writing style.[88] The *Banquet des sages* ([n.p.]: [n. pub.], 1617) is the first of Garasse's texts to be written primarily against one person: the *avocat général* (assistant public prosecutor) Louis Servin, who was an enemy of the Jesuits.[89] All of Garasse's subsequent texts are written in French, although several anecdotes and even entire paragraphs in his later works are given in Latin or Greek. In 1619, Garasse published *Le Rabelais reformé par les Ministres* (Brussels: Christophe Girard, 1619) in response to the Huguenot pastor Pierre Du Moulin's *De la Vocation des Pasteurs* (Sedan: Jean Jannon, 1618). Although written specifically against Pierre Du Moulin, the *Rabelais reformé* is a work

[85] Châtel admitted to having studied with the Jesuits at the Collège de Clermont. See Jacqueline Marchand, 'Apologie du Père Garasse (1585–1631): Le Jésuite et les Libertins', *Cahiers laïques*, 173 (1980), 92–106 (93).

[86] Marchand, 'Apologie', 93. On the royal protection of the Jesuits in the early seventeenth century and French Jesuit colleges in this period, see Henri Fouqueray, *Histoire de la Compagnie de Jésus en France*, 5 vols (Paris: Bureaux des Études, 1910–25), III (1922) pp. 1–237; Eric Nelson, *The Jesuits and the Monarchy* (Aldershot: Ashgate, 2005).

[87] Alexander Chalmers, *The General Biographical Dictionary*, 32 vols (London: J. Nichols and Son and Bentley, 1812–17), XV (1814), p. 264. Garasse wrote a further text on the subject of Louis XIII—*Les champs Elyséens pour la Réception du Roy Louis XIII, lors qu'il entrait à Bordeaux a l'occasion de son Mariage*—in 1612.

[88] 'Niceron observes, that our author's satirical style was very like that of the famous Schioppius, which was apparently the reason of his choosing that mask, which suited him exactly well' (Chalmers, *Dictionary*, p. 265).

[89] Charles de Trooz, 'Le Père Garasse et *La Doctrine curieuse*', *Lettres Romanes*, 1: 2 (1947), 113–34 (115). A previous text, *L'Anti-Joseph* ([n.p]: [n. pub.], 1615), is a sixteen-page satire whose target is not explicitly named.

which seeks to reach a wider and possibly Protestant audience through a detailed and methodical approach.[90]

It is clear from this brief early bibliography that Garasse enjoyed a certain degree of notoriety by the time he turned his attention to libertine authors. Christian Jouhaud has pondered whether Garasse's place in the Jesuit order was as 'une sorte d'original, marginal agité, ou s'il y occupa une position centrale, engagée' ('a sort of original, agitated marginal, or whether he occupied a central, engaged position').[91] Whatever his standing may have been with the Jesuits, his numerous publications suggest that he was both a known author as well as an experienced writer when he first began to make accusations of *libertinage* through his texts.[92] The first of these came in response to Étienne Pasquier's *Recherches de la France*, which was published posthumously by his children in 1621. Pasquier had been hostile to Jesuit ambitions to extend their influence through the establishment of a new college in Paris, and had even won a case for the University of Paris against the Jesuits in 1565.[93] In his *Recherches,* Pasquier defends the freedoms and autonomies of the French crown, the French Church, the University of Paris, and French literature against papal authority, the Jesuits, and foreign literature.[94] Garasse's response, *Les Recherches des recherches et autres Œuvres de Me Etienne Pasquier*, was published anonymously on New Year's Day in 1622.[95] The text is divided into five books—'Le Libertin' being the second largest according both to number of sections and pages—and includes the famous epigraph to the present chapter.[96]

[90] Gerrit Harm Wagenvoort, 'Le Rabelais reformé (1620) du P. François Garasse, S.J.: Une réaction au traité de Pierre du Moulin, De la Vocation des Pasteurs (Style, mentalité, controverse religieuse et emploi des sources)' (unpublished Masters dissertation, Université Catholique de Nimègue, 1992), p. vii).

[91] Christian Jouhaud, 'La méthode de François Garasse', in *Les Jésuites à l'âge baroque (1540–1640),* ed. by Luce Giard and Louis de Vaucelles (Grenoble: Jérôme Millon, 1996), pp. 243–60 (p. 243).

[92] On this point, see Van Damme, *Épreuve*, p. 59; Charles Nisard, *Les Gladiateurs de la république des lettres aux XVe, XVIe, et XVIIe siècles,* 2 vols (Paris: Michel Lévy Frères, 1860), II, p. 317; Chalmers, *Dictionary*, p. 264; Mathilde Bombard, 'Un antijésuitisme «littéraire»? La polémique contre François Garasse', in *Les Antijésuites: Discours, figures et lieux de l'antijésuitisme à l'époque moderne,* ed. by Pierre-Antoine Fabre and Catherine Maire (Rennes: Presses Universitaires de Rennes, 2010), pp. 179–96 (p. 179). Pascal Debailly conversely asserts that Garasse did not achieve notoriety until the publication of the *Recherches des recherches* in 1622 (Pascal Debailly, 'Le Père Garasse, critique et disciple de Mathurin Régnier', *XVIIe siècle*, 188 (1995), 431–45 (431)).

[93] Wagenvoort, *Rabelais reformé*, p. viii.

[94] See Wagenvoort, *Rabelais reformé*, pp. 5–6.

[95] Antoine Rémy claims that Garasse's *Recherches* were published on New Year's Day ([Antoine Rémy], *Défense pour Estienne Pasquier vivant conseiller du Roi, et son Avocat Général en la Chambre des Comptes de Paris, contre les impostures et Calomnies de François Garasse* (Paris: Thomas de la Ruelle, 1624), E^r^). According to the 'Avis au Lecteur' of Garasse's *Recherches des recherches*, the Pasquier children added ninety new chapters to their father's work, as well as additions to existing chapters, which together constituted over half of the posthumous edition.

[96] Garasse, *Recherches*, p. 681: 'Par le mot de libertin je n'entens ny un Huguenot, ny un Athée, ny un Catholique, ny un Heretique, ny un Politique, mais un certain composé de toutes ces qualités' ('By the word libertine I mean neither a Huguenot, nor an Atheist, nor a Catholic, nor a Heretic, nor a *Politique*, but a certain blend of all these qualities').

According to Garasse, Pasquier's dissident views render him not only a kindred spirit to the *libertin* Huguenots, but also wholly impious: 'je trouve que sans paraventure il y a du libertinage, et de l'impieté en la teste de Maistre Pasquier' ('I find without doubt that there is *libertinage* and impiety in Master Pasquier's head').[97] In Garasse's *Recherches*, a *libertin* can be any individual who is in some way perceived to be outside of the Catholic Church; that is to say, whichever of Garasse's perceived enemies is targeted by his given accusation. The distinctions between Catholics, Huguenots, heretics, and *libertins* are unclear. In Section XVII of the first book, Garasse acknowledges that Pasquier is a Catholic, thus taking a different approach to the parallels that he had earlier drawn between Pasquier's beliefs and those of the Huguenots.[98] Yet a little later, he proposes an entirely different image of Pasquier's religious position by suggesting that he is not only a Huguenot, but that he is 'LIBERTIN, qui signifie un Huguenot et demy' ('LIBERTINE, which means a Huguenot and a half'), and that 'Pasquier est Libertin, ny d'un costé ny d'autre, également ennemy des Catholiques et des Huguenots' ('Pasquier is a Libertine, on neither one side nor another, equally the enemy of Catholics and Hugeunots').[99]

Pasquier was attacked for a plethora of reasons, using a wide range of arguments and slander of which Pasquier the libertine was only a composite part. By 1622, events in the Parisian print market would lead Garasse to publish an even more frenzied attack on *libertinage*: *La Doctrine curieuse des beaux esprits de ce temps*, which carries a royal privilege dated 19 March 1623. This second tome was aimed at a much wider variety of targets, and identified their figurehead to be our final author of study, Théophile de Viau.[100] At over one thousand pages in length, the *Doctrine curieuse*—the first of Garasse's texts signed with his own name—was written with impressive speed, betraying the sense of urgency the author felt to put an end to the licence enjoyed by the authors attacked in this latest treatise.

The *Doctrine curieuse* is divided into eight books, each of which is headed by a supposed maxim of the *libertins* as conceived by Garasse. After a brief expansion on a maxim, Garasse offers a refutation rooted in Antiquity, theology, or slander. An extremely dense text in which repetitions are common, the *Doctrine curieuse* is written as a reference book for those who wish to join Garasse in the fight against *libertin* beliefs.[101] An overlooked aspect of the encyclopaedic *Doctrine curieuse* is that it is not written solely or even primarily against Théophile. Rather, it contains

[97] Garasse, *Recherches*, p. 55.

[98] Garasse, *Recherches*, p. 121. Garasse later states that when Pasquier committed errors of faith, this was because 'son esprit estoit si transporté en l'amour de Dieu qu'il ne sçavoit ce qu'il disoit' ('that his mind was so overcome by the love of God that he did not know what he was saying', p. 441).

[99] Garasse, *Recherches*, pp. 126, 692.

[100] On the context of the *Doctrine curieuse*, Théophile's obscene sonnet which inspired this text, and Garasse's prior involvement in Théophile's persecution, see Chapter 5, pp. 256–82.

[101] Jouhaud repeats this view of the text in 'Méthode', p. 52 and *Pouvoirs*, p. 51.

arguments against multiple authors (and often several works from the same author), and the collective *recueils satyriques* of sexually explicit or irreligious poetry. Unlike in the *Recherches des recherches*, Garasse attempts to offer a much clearer definition of what constitutes a *libertin* in the *Doctrine curieuse*:

> En l'eschole de nos dogmatizans il y a deux sortes de disciples, les uns sont LIBERTINS, et les autres sont tout à fait IMPIES, les uns sont commençans, les autres sont parfaicts, les uns sont chenilles, les autres sont papillons, les uns sont apprentifs et les autres sont maistres en malice. J'appelle Libertins, nos yvrongnets, mouscherons de tavernes, esprits insensibles à la piété qui n'ont autre Dieu que leur ventre, qui sont enroolez en cette maudite confrérie, qui s'appelle la *Confrérie des Bouteilles*, à laquelle nous gardons son Chapitre à part. Il est vray que ces gens ne croient aucunement en Dieu. [...] J'appelle impies et Athéistes ceux qui sont plus avancez en malice.
>
> At the school of our dogmatisers there are two types of disciples: some are LIBERTINES and others are completely IMPIOUS; some are beginners, others are complete; some are caterpillars, others are butterflies; some are apprentices and others are masters of malice. I call libertines our drunkards, tavern flies, minds untouched by piety who have no other God than their stomachs, who have enrolled themselves in that cursed fellowship which is called the *Fellowship of Bottles*, for which we will reserve a separate chapter. It is true that these people have no belief in God. [...] I call those who are more advanced in their malice impious and atheists.[102]

Libertinage is thus conceived as a developmental stage of impiety in which gluttony leads to indifference, to impiety, and eventually to atheism as the most extreme form of estrangement from the Catholic faith. On the one hand, the underlying concern here may be that straying from orthodox teaching—for example, doubting the salvific value of works—is a slippery slope which inevitably leads to the loss of one's belief in God. On the other hand, the intention may have been to assimilate a wider range of contemporary theological opponents. Recalling St Paul's Epistle to the Romans—whom Paul claims have been released from slavery to sin and are now slaves to righteousness, rather than being emancipated 'freemen'—this polysemy could have served to target both those who preached justification by faith rather than by works (Lutherans and Calvinists), and those who considered themselves to be released from moral obligations (Antinomians).[103] The satisfaction of one's natural appetites, alluded to above by the *libertins*' excessive drinking in taverns, is a recurrent accusation in Garasse's works. By claiming that the *libertins*—qualified at one point in the text as 'nos animaux de taverne' ('our tavern animals')—give into impulses without question, Garasse depicts them as resembling the brute

[102] Garasse, *Doctrine*, pp. 36–8.
[103] See Romans 6:15–19.

beasts, and therefore dismisses them as serious theological adversaries.[104] The relationship between these *libertins* and other religious dissidents does not remain constant throughout the text. Having stated that *libertinage* is a pre-atheist stage of indifference to piety, Garasse reminds the reader that:

> si je parle quelquesfois diversement des Atheistes ou Libertins [...] il doit se ressouvenir qu'il y a plusieurs degrez d'Atheisme, et que le corps de mon livre vise en general contre toutes les parties de ce monstre; mais noméement contre les LIBERTINS.
>
> if I sometimes speak indistinctly about atheists or libertines [...] he [the reader] should remember that there are several degrees of atheism and that the body of my book is generally aimed against all parts of this monster, notably against the LIBERTINES.[105]

In this instance, *libertinage* is a component, but not an independent form, of atheism. Published at a time when Paris was both severely affected by the plague and gripped by at least two apparent cases of demonic possession, the *Doctrine curieuse* seeks to capitalise on its readers' fear and concern for order.[106] The *libertins* are described as corrupting the heads of Christian nations, 'qui ont pensé ruyner les Cours des Princes Chrestiens par ces Maximes d'impieté et de libertinage' ('who thought to ruin the courts of Christian princes by these maxims of impiety and *libertinage*').[107] According to Garasse's image of the *libertins*, their Epicurean tenets—ill defined though they are in relation to atheism and Protestantism—are also seen as being against the established order: 'il faudroit, à ce conte, que nos beaux esprits prétendus fissent de nouvelles lois et renversassent tout le monde—pour establir leurs Maximes Epicuriennes ('in that case, our so-called fine wits would have to make new laws and turn the world up on its head to establish their Epicurean maxims').[108]

Some modern studies have stressed Garasse's use of the term *libertin* against Théophile in particular. For Jouhaud, the *Doctrine curieuse* depicts Théophile

[104] Garasse, *Doctrine*, p. 810; see also p. 698: 'Contenter sa nature en toutes choses, est un principe de Cannibales, et de bestes brutes' ('to satisfy one's nature in all things is a principle of cannibals and brute beasts').

[105] Garasse, *Doctrine*, p. 38.

[106] See Jouhaud, 'Methode', p. 259; Marchand, 'Apologie', p. 98, 100–01.

[107] Garasse, *Doctrine*, p. 5.

[108] Garasse, *Doctrine*, p. 729. Garasse uses several terms incorporating the word *Epicure* to designate the *libertins* throughout the text, such as *nouveaux epicuriens* (p. 962), *nos jeunes epicuriens* ('our young epicureans', p. 485) and *pourceaux d'Epicure* ('pigs of Epicurus', p. 753). As Wagenvoort explains, the *pourceau* was not only associated with excessive greed but with a lack of discipline (Wagenvoort, *Rabelais*, p. 85). In the opening scene of Molière's *Dom Juan*, the titular character's servant Sganarelle describes his master by parodying a recognisably Garassian tirade—similar to the 'lists' describing theological adversaries seen earlier—in which Dom Juan is also described as a man 'qui passe cette vie en véritable bête brute, en pourceau d'Épicure' ('who lives this life as a true brute beast, as a pig of Epicurus': Molière, *Dom Juan*, Act I Scene 1, in Molière, *Œuvres complètes*, ed. by Georges Couton, 2 vols (Paris: Gallimard, Bibliothèque de la Pléiade, 1971), II, pp. 2, 33).

as 'le chef de file et comme l'emblème du libertinage et de l'athéisme' ('as the figurehead and as the emblem of *libertinage* and atheism'); an interpretation also shared by Marchand.[109] The large number of authors referred to by Garasse calls this view into question. As early as page 19 of the original text, Garasse refutes the texts of a variety of authors including William Barclay, Raymond Lulle, Goropius Becanus, Nicolaus Copernicus, and Robert Fludd, in order to identify the possible textual inspirations of libertine beliefs.[110] Although some authors are referred to only occasionally or studied in a single section—such as Gerolamo Cardano and Pietro Pomponazzi—other authors are more significant to Garasse's strategy. One such author is Pierre Charron, whose three levels of spirits in the natural world are equated with those of Vanini and Cardano.[111] In doing so, Garasse proposes a continuation of the teachings of a supposed *libertin* sect which can be discerned in several texts written by different authors. Both Charron's texts and his character are repeatedly attacked by his Jesuit accuser:

> Pour Charron, je suis marry que je n'en puisse faire un plus favorable jugement; ma conscience m'oblige à dire de luy que ce fust un tres pernicieux ignorant, qui a voulu parler de ce qu'il n'entendoit pas. [...] il se glisse insensiblement dans le cœur des lecteurs, avec un tel ascendant sur leur esprit qu'il y en a qui ne jurent que par luy. Et je confesse que je me suis trouvé en peine de persuader à quelques jeunes Seigneurs de tres grande qualité, que Charron fust un livre dangereux, car pour eux ils le prenoient en qualité de livre spirituel, sans s'apercevoir des impietés qui luy sont, ou par ignorance, ou par malice eschappées de la plume.
>
> As for Charron, it aggrieves me that I am not able to pass better judgement on him. My conscience obliges me to say of him that he was a very pernicious and ignorant man, who wanted to speak of things he did not understand. [...] He slips imperceptibly into the hearts of readers, with such power over their minds that there are some that swear only by him. And I confess that I have found myself struggling to persuade a number of young lords of very high birth that Charron's book was dangerous, because for them, they took it as a spiritual book, without perceiving the impieties which, out of ignorance or malice, have escaped his quill.[112]

Although feeling a certain obligation to be lenient with his fellow Catholic priest, Garasse nonetheless sets out to discredit Charron's texts both by refuting the maxims they contain and attacking their author personally.[113] In doing so, Garasse was also reflecting a wider tendency of the time to distinguish between Michel

[109] Jouhaud, 'Doctrine', p. 245; Marchand, 'Apologie', p. 95.

[110] Garasse, *Doctrine*, pp. 19–22.

[111] Garasse, *Doctrine*, pp. 31–2.

[112] Garasse, *Doctrine*, p. 1015. Garasse and others also depict Vanini and Théophile as dangerous authors who seduced impressionable youths.

[113] See also Garasse, *Doctrine*, p. 27, in which Charron is accused of writing 'sans voir bonnement ce qu'il faisoit; car c'estoit un franc ignorant' ('without really seeing what he was doing, because he was clearly ignorant').

de Montaigne's *Essais* and Charron's *De la Sagesse*. Montaigne presented himself as a lay commentator who defended freedom of judgement without Parisian patronage or religious office. Charron, on the other hand, was a man of the Church who presented himself as a priest, a theological scholar, and a doctor of the laws. His text, which sought ecclesiastical and aristocratic patronage, preached secular wisdom through a professional public personae of both a theologian and a jurist.[114] Garasse's dual attack on Charron, which is not seen in the Jesuit's response to every author whom he considers to have inspired the *libertins*, is but one example of how he did not envisage Théophile as the sole target of this text.

Garasse's treatment of our first author demonstrates this point further. He repeatedly uses Vanini, rather than Théophile, as an illustration of the *libertin* beliefs that he aims to refute. Towards the end of the text, he gives an important insight into his ranking of *libertin* source texts in his metaphorical *bibliothèque des libertins* ('library of the libertines'): 'Le premier rang contient le Pomponace, le Paracelse, et Machievel. [...] Le second rang de la Bibliotheque de nos Atheistes, contient Hierosme Cardan, Charron, et Lucilio Vanini' ('The first row contains Pomponazzi, Paracelsus, and Machiavelli. [...] The second row of our atheists' library contains Gerolamo Cardano, Charron, and Lucilio Vanini').[115] It is only on the third 'row' that Garasse includes the *Parnasse satyrique* and *Quint-essence satyrique* anthologies of obscene poetry. In doing so, he places free-thinking and subversive philosophers on a higher level of impiety than the *recueils satyriques* anthologies in which a number of Théophile's incriminating poems were printed. It is therefore unsurprising that in the index of the *Doctrine curieuse*, the fifteen entries for Théophile across eighteen pages are surpassed by twenty-two entries, covering fifty-seven pages, for Vanini.

Garasse was therefore unlikely to have written the *Doctrine curieuse* solely in order to secure Théophile's condemnation. Rather, the appearance of a poem attributed to Théophile in *Le Parnasse satyrique* both hastened its publication, and provided in him a living embodiment of this supposed threat to Catholic orthodoxy which served as a lightning rod for the Jesuit's vitriol. Garasse's long-standing interest in defeating the perceived *libertin* threat attests to this, as does the large number of works and authors attacked in the *Doctrine curieuse*. Again,

[114] These differences between Montaigne's and Charron's texts, their contents, and their authorial identities are explored in Warren Boutcher, *The School of Montaigne in Early Modern Europe*, 2 vols (Oxford: Oxford University Press, 2017), II, pp. 428–31. A further comparison can be drawn with Garasse's dual attack on Charron's text and character. In the posthumous revised edition of *De la Sagesse* (1606), Charron's literary testator Rochemaillet included an elegy to Charron in which he sought 'to defend Charron's works, and especially *De la sagesse*, by means of a defence of his character and conduct' (Boutcher, *School of Montaigne*, p. 426). For a more detailed comparison see Jean-Pierre Cavaillé, 'Pierre Charron, "disciple" de Montaigne et "patriarche des prétendus esprits forts"', *Les Dossiers du Grihl* (2009), http://journals.openedition.org/dossiersgrihl/280 [accessed 4 March 2020].
[115] Garasse, *Doctrine*, pp. 1013–14.

this was a significant departure from the Jesuit's writing strategy in his previous works which sought to refute a single adversary. It was the creation of a menacing collective identity, rather than the vilification of Théophile, that Garasse sought to achieve with the *Doctrine curieuse*. Notably, and notwithstanding the criticisms made of the *Doctrine curieuse*'s tone in its day, it is only in seeking a consistent and precise definition of the *libertin* in Garasse's works that this rhetorical strategy becomes problematic.[116] Within the context of accusation and fearmongering, Garasse was able to bring more authors under the term *libertin* by loosely defining his adversary, allowing him in turn to present a more vivid image of a libertine menace that was partly of his own confection. In doing so, he increased the size of both the supposed *libertin* community and the extent of their purported infiltration into pious society. Such lax control over the nature of his accusation may frustrate modern attempts to delineate a cogent definition. But within the original contexts of religious polemic and slander, Garasse's seemingly confused explanations were perfectly at home in an often violent literary arena in which ambiguity favoured the accuser.

Whilst Garasse's vitriolic polemic raged on, quieter and more measured reflections were being formed from the Minim convent behind the Place Royale (known today as the Place des Vosges). The two anti-libertine texts of Marin Mersenne had no evident influence on the persecution of authors in the early 1620s, and lacked the profuse hyperbole of his Jesuit counterpart.[117] This said, they nonetheless provide us with further examples of contemporary anxieties towards

[116] Garasse's *Doctrine curieuse*—particularly its use of humour, the potentially subversive detail in which it described libertine beliefs, and its aggressive tone unbecoming of a priest—created a literary polemic in its own right: 'la Querelle de la raillerie chrétienne' ('the quarrel of Christian mockery': Marc Fumaroli, *L'Âge de l'éloquence—Rhétorique et «res literaria» de la Renaissance au seuil de l'époque classique* (Geneva: Droz, 2002), pp. 327–8; see also Bombart, 'Antijésuitisme'). It would require a separate chapter to do justice to this subsequent literary debate, as a mere chronology of its composite texts demonstrates: Guez de Balzac, *Lettre à Hydaspe* (1624), quoted in Frédéric Lachèvre, *Le Libertinage devant le Parlement de Paris: Le Procès du poète Théophile de Viau*, 2 vols (Paris: Honoré Champion, 1909), II, pp. 189–92 (with a further four texts engendered from Balzac and Garasse's dispute: see pp. 194–206); François Ogier, *Jugement et censure du livre de la Doctrine Curieuse, de François Garasse* (Paris: [n. pub.], 1623); François Garasse, *Apologie du Père François Garassus, de la Compagnie de Jésus, pour son livre contre les Athéistes et Libertins de notre siècle* (Paris: Sebastien Chappelet, 1624); [Rémy], *Défense pour Etienne Pasquier* (1624); [Geoffrey Guay?], *Nouveau jugement de ce qui a été dit et écrit pour et contre le livre de la Doctrine Curieuse des beaux esprits de ce temps* (Paris: Jacques Quesnel, 1624); François Garasse, *La Somme théologique des vérités capitales de la Religion Chrétienne* (Paris: Sébastien Chapelet, 1625); Jean du Vergier de Hauranne de Saint-Cyran, *La Somme des fautes et faussetés capitales, contenues en la Somme théologique du Père François Garasse de la Compagnie de Jésus* (Paris: J. Boüillerot, 1626); François Garasse, *L'Abus découvert en la censure prétendue des textes de l'Ecriture sainte* (Paris: [n. pub.], 1626).

[117] For Richard Popkin, Marin Mersenne is 'one of the most important and most neglected figures in the history of modern philosophy', whereas Robert Lenoble has described him as as 'éminemment représentatif de la pensée moyenne du public instruit de son temps' ('eminently representative of the average thoughts of the educated public of his time'). See Richard Popkin, 'Father Mersenne's War Against Pyrrhonism', *The Modern Schoolman*, 34 (1957), 61–78 (61); Robert Lenoble, *Mersenne ou la naissance du mécanisme* (Paris: Librairie Philosophique J. Vrin, 1943), p. 4.

unorthodox literature, justified in polemical texts by a purported concern to defend the minds of impressionable youths and the faithful. Like Garasse, Mersenne was educated at La Flèche, and was one of its first students after Henri IV entrusted the college to the Jesuits in 1604.[118] Having subsequently completed his theological studies at the Sorbonne, Mersenne received the habit of the Minim friars on 17 July 1611. Between 1611 and 1618, he taught at the convent of Saint François de Paule in Nevers before returning to the Minim convent overlooking the Place Royale in Paris, where he would remain until his death on 1 September 1648.

Mersenne wrote a Latin commentary on the Book of Genesis in 1623—the *Quaestiones celeberrimae in Genesim*—in which he refuted the pantheistic and animistic ideas attributed to authors including Marsilio Ficino, Martin Delrio, and Robert Fludd. The work's main target, however, was our first author Vanini.[119] William L. Hine has meticulously and convincingly demonstrated how 'Mersenne summarises chapters, or portions of chapters, from Vanini's books, and then follows the summary with lengthy discussions examining, and usually refuting, the basic point which Vanini raised.'[120] As we will explore further in Chapter 3, the vast majority of contemporary sources on Vanini report on his activities in Toulouse. Mersenne provides an unusual account of his alleged teachings in Paris, which reflect his later strategy of simulating Catholic piety in order to dissimulate atheism:

> Sic enim Lutetiae Vaninum aiunt fuisse conatum ut Atheismum proseminaret, quippe qui vehementer in atheos prius insurgere et eos summopere detestari videbatur, id enim verbis acrioribus simulabat.
>
> They say that Vanini stayed on in Paris so that he could try to disseminate atheism, since to start with he appeared to attack atheists violently and to execrate them heartily, for he made a show of doing so in the harshest terms.[121]

Mersenne subsequently turned his attention to a different kind of threat to Catholicism. In the early 1620s a manuscript circulated in Paris entitled *L'Antibigot,*

[118] Hilarion de Coste, *La Vie du R. P. Marin Mersenne, théologien, philosophe et mathématicien de l'Ordre des Pères Minimes* (Paris: Sébastien Cramoisy et Gabriel Cramoisy, 1649), p. 8. This text, written by Mersenne's fellow Minim friar, is the closest contemporary account we have of Mersenne's life.

[119] Francesco Paolo Raimondi, 'Vanini et Mersenne', in *Kairos*, 12 (1998): *Vanini—Libertinage et philosophie à l'époque moderne*, ed. by Jean-Pierre Cavaillé and Didier Foucault (Toulouse: Presses Universitaires du Mirail, 1998), pp. 181–253 (p. 186).

[120] William L. Hine, 'Mersenne and Vanini', *Renaissance Quarterly*, 29:1 (1976), 52–65 (56), which presents passages from Mersenne's text referring to Vanini alongside matching lines in Vanini's texts (56–9). Hine also offers evidence to suggest that Mersenne was advised to conceal his references to such subversive material in a work concerned chiefly with analysing a Biblical text (in Renato Thuillier, *Diarium partum et sororum ordinis minimorum provinciae Franciae sive Parisiensis qui religiose abierunt ab anno 1506 ad annum 1700*, 2 vols (Paris: Petrus Gissart, 1709), I, p. 95).

[121] Marin Mersenne, *Quaestiones celeberrimae in Genesim* (Paris: Sebastien Cramoisy, 1623), col. 671, quoted and translated in Raimondi, 'Vanini et Mersenne', p. 225.

ou le faux dévotieux, more commonly known as *Les Quatrains du déiste*.[122] Comprised of 106 quatrains, the anonymous *Antibigot* is written in such a way that the arguments it contains can be easily committed to memory and repeated in conversation. Its primary argument is that the attribute of omnipotent goodness and perfection associated with deity is incompatible with the God of the Old Testament. Typically written in the form of a thought-provoking question, each quatrain is designed to lead the *bigot* reader to question their beliefs and to reject the notion of deity as proposed by organised religion. Instead, the deistic message within the text suggests the presence of the divine in all aspects of the natural world; a philosophical position that might be compared to the *anima mundi* (world soul) seen in Ficino and Fludd which Mersenne had previously attacked in his *Quaestiones celeberrimae in Genesim*. According to Lachèvre, this pamphlet had already been in circulation for some time, based on Mersenne's own claim that the text was only passed between trusted friends.[123] If Lachèvre's assertion is correct, then it is possible that Mersenne may have been aware of the *Quatrains* much earlier in life. During the construction of the college of La Flèche, Jesuit students were dispersed temporarily across several buildings in the city for both their education and lodgings. This caused a lack of discipline amongst the students, and also exposed them to social circles perceived to be undesirable. This threat to the Jesuit students was considered so serious that in 1605 a royal edict was enacted to protect them from the influences of tavern-goers, prostitutes, and charlatans, who were reputed to be teaching them unchristian beliefs and practices.[124] It is therefore likely that if *L'Antibigot* was circulating at this time, Mersenne would have been aware of its existence, and may even have known students at La Flèche who had read the work.

Mersenne appears to have been motivated to write his first work against the *libertins*—*L'Impiété des déistes, athées, et libertins de ce temps* (Paris: Pierre Bilaine, 1624)—by two factors. First, the 'Préface au lecteur' relates that having acquired a copy of *L'Antibigot* (which suggests that he had no first-hand knowledge of the text before the early 1620s), Mersenne felt compelled to combat 'ces impies qui [...] veulent persuader aux ignorants, et aux libertins qu'il n'y a point d'autre religion qui soit véritable, que celle des Déistes' ('these impious people who want to persuade the ignorant and libertines that there is no true religion other than

[122] The complete version of the *Quatrains* was lost until being discovered by Lachèvre in the early twentieth century. It was published, with several errors, in both Lachèvre, *Procès*, II, pp. 93–126, and Antoine Adam, *Les Libertins au XVIIe siècle* (Paris: Buchet-Chastel, 1964), pp. 88–109. For an accurate critical edition of the text, reproduced under its original title—*L'Antibigot*—see Alain Mothu, '*L'Antibigot* ou les «Quatrains du Déiste»', *La Lettre Clandestine*, 21 (2013), 23–68. Though referred to as the *Quatrains* in almost all of the relevant secondary literature, I take my cue from Mothu's recent edition by referring to the text as *L'Antibigot*.

[123] Lachèvre, *Procès*, II, p. 98.

[124] Lenoble, *Mersenne*, p. 18.

that of the deists').[125] According to de Costes, Mersenne was also inspired by a wider concern at the rise in *libertinage*: 'voyant que l'impiété s'augmentait en ce malheureux siècle, et que Dieu était grandement déshonoré par quelques jeunes libertins' ('seeing that impiety was growing in this wretched age, and that God was greatly dishonoured by a few young libertines').[126] If we are to accept Descotes's reasonable assertion that *L'Impiété* was written between 1620 and 1624, then these *jeunes libertins* may well have been those who allegedly led the same lifestyle of frequenting taverns and blaspheming in intimate groups as Théophile.[127]

Finally, for Mersenne the sources of *libertinage* also include recently deceased writers whose works purportedly continued to spread ideas contrary to the Catholic faith, such as Bruno, Cardano, Vanini, and Charron.[128] *L'Impiété* was therefore written with both a single, unidentified author in mind—the author of *L'Antibigot*—as well as an emerging Parisian social class of young, free-thinking *libertins*. They appear to have formed part of the same demographic alluded to in Garasse's texts, thereby betraying the two Catholic apologists' concern for the ideological sympathies of young men of high status who might have gone on to have influence at court.[129] The two theologians' motivations were furthermore in keeping with those of the magistrates, who had an interest in localising the supposed libertine threat, rather than confining such matters to the regulation of the print industry or by 'preserving the almost "exotic" nature of the threat.'[130]

L'Impiété begins with a series of conversations between the Deist and the Theologian (Mersenne) in which the reader witnesses the gradual conversion of

[125] Marin Mersenne, *L'Impiété des déistes*, ed. by Dominique Descotes (Paris: Honoré Champion, 2005), p. 63. According to Descotes, Mersenne did not acquire a copy of *L'Antibigot* in time to refute it in the *Quaestiones celeberrimae in Genesim* (p. 13). The detailed verse-by-verse refutation of the work in *L'Impiété* demonstrates that Mersenne had a copy of the text to hand by this time.

[126] De Coste, *Vie*, p. 17.

[127] Mersenne, *L'Impiété*, p. 8. Mersenne's text refers to the second part of Théophile's *Œuvres*, which was granted its royal privilege on 18 April 1623 and published the following month. *L'Impiété* received its royal privilege on 8 May 1624.

[128] Mersenne, *L'Impiété*, pp. 410–11. The popularity of some of these authors can be seen in publishing records in the first quarter of the seventeenth century, which for example saw three editions of Cardano's *Hieronymi Cardani Mediolanensis Medici De Subtilitate* (Basil: Sebastianum Henricpetri, 1611; Rome: J.B. Roblettum, 1617; and Geneva: P. et J. Chouët, 1624). Pierre Charron was by far the most read of these authors. Excluding the original Bordeaux edition of 1601, Charron's *De la Sagesse* was reprinted twenty-one times by fourteen different publishers operating from Paris, Rouen, and Lyon between 1604 and 1623 alone. The years 1606, 1614, 1618, 1621, and 1623 saw *De la Sagesse* published by three different publishers (all of which were located in Paris in 1621 and Rouen in 1623), further attesting to the popularity and influence of Charron's work. Comparatively, Montaigne's *Essais* were reprinted seventeen times during this period.

[129] As De Waard remarks, the religious scepticism within *L'Antibigot* also had negative implications for the status of the mathematical sciences as undisputed truths, 'car la plupart des «libertins» du XVIIe siècle [...] englobaient dans le même scepticisme la science et la religion' ('as the skepticism of most 'libertines' in the seventeenth century encompassed both science and religion': De Waard, *Correspondance*, p. xlv).

[130] Stéphane Van Damme, 'Libertine Paris', in *The Cambridge Companion to the Literature of Paris*, ed. by Anna Louise Milne (Cambridge: Cambridge University Press, 2013), pp. 34–51 (36).

the Deist to Catholic orthodoxy. In significant contrast to Garasse's method, those who hold beliefs contrary to those of the Catholic faith are permitted to speak for themselves in Mersenne's text. This said, his Deist already appears repentant and to an extent appalled by libertine practices, allowing him and the Theologian to condemn a third and silent party—unrepentant libertines—together. The text thus aims to address the *libertin* threat through dialogue, and to vanquish the threat of *libertinage* alongside those who might already have taken their first steps towards religious nonconformity. Gone are the vitriolic tirades to be found in Garasse's texts, which are replaced with a purportedly benign desire to save libertine souls as equals:

> Les Déistes, et toutes sortes de Libertins; desquels je désire, et recherche le salut avec affection, et sincérité, comme ils verront dans ces dialogues, que je leur adresse. [...] Pour moi je ne désire rien davantage que ta conversion, et ta pénitence.
>
> The Deists, and all sorts of Libertines, whose salvation I desire and seek with affection and sincerity, as they will see in these dialogues that I address to them. [...] I personally desire nothing more than your conversion and your penitence.[131]

Far from condemning his interlocutor with the kind of derogatory accusations seen in Garasse, the Theologian encourages his ever-astute student—and his reader—to join him in the privileged position of Catholicism from which all parties are able to deride the *libertins*. Mersenne is also capable of using the term *libertin* as an accusation against others. The works of Charron and Cardano are identified by the Deist as the cause of his deviation from the Catholic faith.[132] The Theologian describes Charron's words in his *De la Sagesse* as 'fort libertines, et ressentaient souvent l'Athéisme [...] les maximes y sont drues, et fréquentes, et ceux-là sont ordinairement libertins' ('most libertine, and often smack of Atheism [...] the maxims it contains are dense, numerous and usually libertine').[133] As well as connoting the atheistic, the term *libertin* is also used to describe general deviations from the Catholic Church and impious attitudes.[134] Further on in the text, the word is used in a different context. When the Deist claims that it is sufficient to believe in God, and that all other aspects of the Christian faith are man-made, the Theologian's reply strongly suggests that the political power of the Catholic Church as an institution is an essential ingredient for godly living:

131 Mersenne, *L'Impiété*, pp. 63–4. A similar note of compassion is struck in one of Mersenne's subsequent texts, *La Vérité des sciences* (1625): 'Or je supplie l'éternel qu'il lui plaise guérir la manie de ces esprits Libertins' ('Now I implore the Everlasting that it may please Him to cure the compulsion of these libertine spirits': Marin Mersenne, *La Vérité des sciences*, ed. by Dominique Descotes (Paris: Honoré Champion, 2003), p. 254). Again, it is difficult to determine whether such lines attest to Mersenne's more benevolent character, or simply towards his less aggressive rhetorical style.

132 Mersenne, *L'Impiété*, p. 151. Chapter 9 of *L'Impiété* is devoted to Charron's supposedly irreligious beliefs.

133 Mersenne, *L'Impiété*, p. 154.

134 See Mersenne, *L'Impiété*, p. 177.

> Il y a longtemps qui j'ai ouï parler de cette secte, mais assurez-vous qu'elle ne vient que d'un pur libertinage, lequel a pris pied en France, lorsque les maudites hérésies de Calvin, Luther, et des autres hérétiques y ont entré. S'il y eut jamais une grande porte ouverte à toutes sortes de débauches, d'impiétés, et de trahisons, c'est celle-ci.
>
> I heard about this sect a long time ago, but be assured that it comes from pure *libertinage*, which gained a foothold in France when the cursed heresies of Calvin, Luther, and other heretics came here. If there were ever a great open door to all sorts of debaucheries, impieties and treacheries, it is this one.[135]

Libertinage clearly does not denote atheism in this instance, but serves as a general term to refer to multiple 'sects' that appeared in the wake of the Reformation, and which Mersenne identifies as non-Catholic. In the conclusion to this volume, Mersenne provides summative comparisons between different forms of unbelief including *libertinage*. For Mersenne, *libertinage* can be a general term encompassing atheism and deism, or it can be a developmental stage of unbelief that leads to impiety, as observed earlier in Garasse's text.[136] Alternatively, it may be seen as a separate sect that inspires the abhorrence of Catholics in the same way as atheism or deism;[137] or it may be a deviation from Catholicism that does not necessarily imply any specific theological practices:

> Aujourd'hui ils se tournent vers le Calvinisme, demain vers le Luthéranisme, puis après vers le Mahométisme, une autre fois vers le Judaïsme, et quand ils ont quelques bons intervalles, vers la religion Catholique; bref ils ne cessent de chercher, tourner, et rôder jusques à ce qu'ils soient tombés dans l'impiété, dans l'Athéisme, et dans le Libertinage.
>
> Today they turn towards Calvinism, tomorrow towards Lutheranism, and then towards Islam, another time towards Judaism, and during a few good intervals, towards the Catholic faith. They do not cease to search, to turn and to roam until they have fallen into impiety, into Atheism, and into *Libertinage*.[138]

The second volume of *L'Impiété* continues to use the term *libertin* in a variety of different contexts. Tellingly, it is dedicated to Mathieu Molé, the *procureur général* who was instrumental in Théophile's trial. In stating to Molé that 'votre zèle à la

[135] Mersenne, *L'Impiété*, p. 149. *Libertinage* is also used as a synonym for excessive freedom on p. 229, where Mersenne asserts that learning of God's goodness 'servira de bride à vos libertinages' ('will reign in your *libertinages*').

[136] See Mersenne, *L'Impiété*, pp. 395–6: 'plusieurs jeunes folâtres, qui ont déjà l'esprit disposé au Libertinage, se laissent aller à l'impiété' ('several young fools, whose minds are already disposed towards *Libertinage*, allow themselves to move on to impiety').

[137] See Mersenne, *L'Impiété*, p. 400 on Reformers: 'lesquels au lieu de faire des Chrétiens réformés, engendrent des Déistes, des Athées, et des Libertins. [...] les malheureuses opinions des Athées, des Déistes, et autres Libertins' ('who instead of making reformed Christians, engender Deists and Libertines. [...] the wretched opinions of Atheists, Deists, and other Libertines').

[138] Mersenne, *L'Impiété*, p. 399; see also p. 635: 'ceux qui se sont éloignés de la créance de l'Église, tels que sont vos Libertins' ('those who have strayed from the beliefs of the Church, as your Libertines have').

recherche des Libertins de notre siècle, ayant éveillé le mien' ('your zeal in hunting the Libertines of our time, having awakened my own'), Mersenne openly lends his support to the persecution of the authors published in the *recueils satyriques* such as Théophile, who had already been interrogated six times over the course of his ongoing trial when Mersenne wrote his dedication on 9 July 1624.[139] In this second part, the Theologian and the Deist reflect on how people become *libertins*. In these concluding remarks, a distinction is made between those who are *libertin* through their beliefs on one hand, and by virtue of their actions on the other. The Theologian describes youths who 'après avoir été Calvinistes, deviennent Athées, et Libertins' ('after having been Calvinists, become Atheists and Libertines').[140] *Libertins* are young, weak-minded seekers of novelty who have progressed from a less-serious state of irreligion—Calvinism—to more serious deviations towards atheism and *libertinage*. Far from being a primary stage of impiety as seen above, *libertinage* is described as a final, advanced state of separation from Catholic orthodoxy. The Deist's response, however, shifts the focus of the term to locate their misdemeanours within the literary sphere:

> Cela est très véritable, car j'avais été Calviniste avant que de me jeter dans le Libertinage; j'en connais aussi plusieurs autres qui s'amusent à faire des tragédies, et diverses sortes de vers pour attraper la pièce d'argent, ou les bonnes grâces de quelques Seigneurs avec leurs Sonnets, et leurs Odes.
>
> That is very true, as I had been a Calvinist before throwing myself into *Libertinage*. I also know several others who amuse themselves by writing tragedies, and several sorts of verse to earn a little coin, or the good graces of a few lords, with their Sonnets and their Odes.[141]

Although this could be interpreted as referring to several individual poets of the time, including the collective contributors to the *recueils satyriques*, it is likely that Mersenne had Théophile in mind when writing this passage. As well as being the defendant in a sensational trial that had not yet concluded at Mersenne's time of writing, Théophile had published his tragedy *Les Amours tragiques de Pyrame et Thisbé* in 1621, and had enjoyed the protection and patronage of several *seigneurs* including Candale, Liancourt, and Montmorency by the time *L'Impiété* was written.

[139] Mersenne, *L'Impiété*, p. 410. Armand Beaulieu contends that Mersenne dedicated part of his *Impiété* to Molé because the latter was known for his piety and his defences of orthodoxy, without making any connection to Théophile's trial. See Armand Beaulieu, *Mersenne: Le Grand Minime* (Brussels: Fondation Nicolas-Claude Fabri de Peiresc, 1995), p. 43.

[140] Mersenne, *L'Impiété*, pp. 588–9.

[141] Mersenne, *L'Impiété*, p. 590. On the commercial aspect of the *Parnasse satyrique* see Michèle Rosellini, 'Risques et bénéfices de la publication d'un "mauvais livre": la stratégie commerciale des libraires-éditeurs du Parnasse satyrique (1622–1625)', in *Les arrière-boutiques de la littérature: auteurs et imprimeurs-libraires aux XVIe et XVIIe siècles*, ed. by Edwige Keller-Rahbé (Toulouse: Presses Universitaires du Mirail, 2010), pp. 185–208.

Mersenne was already working on his second text against sceptics–*La Vérité des sciences, contre les Sceptiques ou Pyrrhoniens* (Paris: Toussaint Du Bray, 1625)–whilst writing *L'Impiété*.[142] In a departure from the focus of *L'Impiété*, the primary aim of *La Vérité* is not to convert *libertins* to the Catholic faith, but to use them as examples of what can happen to individuals who allow new, intriguing, or appealing theological or philosophical schools to draw them away from Catholicism.[143] It is this aim that explains the text's curious dedication to the seventeen-year-old brother of Louis XIII, Gaston d'Orléans. It would be wrong to assume that Mersenne sought the protection of Louis XIII's brother who, as Émile Roy reminds us, was still a child subjected to a strict disciplinarian upbringing in the early 1620s.[144] As his recent biographer notes, Gaston's tutor—the duc d'Ornano—was keen to surround the young prince with men of letters including Tristan L'Hermite, Vincent Voiture, Antoine Girard de Saint-Amant, and François de Malherbe, as well as scientific innovators of the day.[145] Whilst it is likely that Mersenne sought to associate himself with the prince's fine education through the dedication of his *Vérité des sciences*, he might also have been encouraged by contemporary events. In the same year that *La Vérité* was published, Gaston hosted 'Le Ballet du monde renversé' ('The Ballet of the World Turned Upside-down'), in which a madman instructed a philosopher and a schoolboy whipped his master.[146] Although these role reversals were a long-established tradition in the history of carnival, it is possible that the ballet was perceived by Mersenne, or by others, as sufficiently alarming to merit the warnings given in *La Vérité*.

The dedication claims that the *libertins* 'tâchent de faire glisser dans l'esprit de certains jeunes hommes qu'ils connaissent pour être portés au libertinage, et à toute sorte de voluptés, et de curiosités' ('work their way into the minds of certain young men known to them to be led into *libertinage*, and into all sorts of delights and curiosities').[147] Like the *libertins* of the tavern in Garasse's texts, Mersenne's sceptical *libertins* evade all confrontation and public declaration of their beliefs through fear of persecution. Against the light of truth 'se bandent un tas de libertins lesquels n'osant faire paraître leur impiété de peur qu'ils ont d'être châtiés, s'efforcent de persuader

[142] On scepticism in early modern France, see Richard Popkin, *The History of Scepticism: From Savonarola to Bayle* (Oxford: Oxford University Press, 2003). For an overview within the context of *libertinage*, see Isabelle Moreau, 'Sceptics and Free-thinkers', in *The Cambridge History of French Thought*, ed. by Michael Moriarty and Jeremy Jennings (Cambridge: Cambridge University Press, 2019), pp. 110–23.

[143] Descotes in Mersenne, *La Vérité*, pp. 8, 34.

[144] See Émile Roy, *La Vie et les œuvres de Charles Sorel, sieur de Souvigny (1602–1674)* (Geneva: Slatkine, 1970), p. 78.

[145] Jean-Marie Constant, *Gaston d'Orléans: Prince de la liberté* (Paris: Perrin, 2013), p. 60.

[146] Claude Kurt Abraham, *Gaston d'Orléans et sa cour: étude littéraire* (Chapel Hill, NC: The University of North Carolina Press, 1964), p. 44.

[147] Mersenne, *La Vérité*, p. 111. This description recalls Gaston's early education, his wide reading, his early pastimes at court, and the variety of *curiosités* that he likely encountered under Ornano's instruction.

aux ignorants qu'il n'y a rien de certain au monde' ('a rabble of libertines are in league together who, not daring to show their impiety through fear of being punished, strive to persuade the ignorant that there is nothing certain in the world').[148] As with Garasse, Mersenne attempts to play on a culture of fear in contemporary society. By suggesting that not all *libertins* are overt nonbelievers, he allows other forms of unbelief to be susceptible to accusations of *libertinage*. At the same time, he impresses on his reader the large number of *libertins* potentially living amongst them, having previously estimated in the *Quaestiones celeberrimae in Genesim* that 'unicam Lutetiam 50 saltem Atheorum millibus onustam esse' ('Paris alone is filled with at least fifty thousand atheists').[149] Claiming to disprove the foundations of scepticism in a refutation of Pyrrho and Sextus Empiricus, Mersenne concludes that both sceptics and the *libertins* grapple with concepts beyond their comprehension:

> C'est en quoi je les trouve semblables aux libertins de ce siècle, qui sont Athées, Déistes, hérétiques, Schismatiques, ou qui font quelqu'autre bande à part, car ne plus ne moins que ceux-là manquent d'esprit, et de jugement pour reconnaître le véritable d'avec le faux, de même ceux-ci manquent d'affection, et de bonne volonté envers Dieu.
>
> In this way I find them to be similar to the libertines of our time, who are Atheists, Deists, heretics, Schismatics, or who form some other kind of separate group, for just as some of them lack the spirit and judgement to recognise the true from the false, so others lack affection and good will towards God.[150]

Once again, *libertin* is used indiscriminately to describe varying degrees of non-Catholic belief, from a philosophical belief in an abstract divinity (deism) to an utter rejection of belief in God (atheism). In referring to *quelqu'autre bande à part,* Mersenne may simply be claiming that a *libertin* subscribes to other forms of non-belief, or that a *libertin* must be in some way separated from the collective whole, meaning that any individual who emancipates themselves from socio-religious norms can legitimately be classed as *libertin*. *La Vérité des sciences* would be the last of Mersenne's texts written to convert libertines. The remainder of his literary career was dedicated to works on harmonics, astronomy, and mathematics, as well as to corresponding with the leading scientific minds of his day including Gassendi and Descartes. This change in Mersenne's scholarly interest allowed him to remain a respected figure in Parisian society and to avoid the disgrace which later befell Garasse.[151]

[148] Mersenne, *La Vérité*, p. 110.

[149] Mersenne, *Quaestiones celeberrimae in Genesim*, pp. 669–74, which was removed in subsequent editions of the text. This estimate is misattributed to Garasse in Elisabeth Labrousse and Alfred Soman, 'Un bûcher pour un judaïsant: Jean Fontanier (1621)', *XVIIe siècle*, 39: 2 (1987), 113–132 (129).

[150] Mersenne, *La Vérité*, p. 252.

[151] This is not to say that Mersenne was met with universal approval from his correspondents. Robert Fludd, for example, would strongly defend his position against Mersenne in his *Sophiae cum moria certamen* ([Frankfurt (?)]: [n. pub.], 1629) and *Summum Bonum* ([Frankfurt (?)]: [n. pub.], 1629). On

This chapter has outlined an increased tendency, from the works of Calvin onwards, to use the term *libertin* as an accusation within a religious context. It was not predominantly used to emphasise one's own positive emancipation, but the destructive and irreligious disobedience of an individual or group identified as a religious 'other'. This notion of the other allowed the term to be used quite loosely when applied to a theological or philosophical opponent, and although we tend to identify the image of a *libertin* as an atheist, the accusation was often exchanged between Catholics and Protestants. Neither Garasse nor Mersenne provides a consistent image of their adversaries, and the relationship between *libertinage*, atheism, Calvinism, scepticism, and debauchery alters depending on the context in which the term *libertin* is used, the individual being described, or the author's aims in any given passage. As our word history has shown, this was not necessarily a poor reflection on their abilities as authors. Given that ambiguous accusations serve to the advantage of those wielding the accusation, it was surely central to their ambitions that the descriptions of their enemies should have been applicable to as broad a range of non-believers as possible, whilst sparing no detail in describing their offences against God.

Garasse's and Mersenne's texts prey upon fears of a *libertin* contagion within the walls of Paris, upon the threat of chaos and of the invisible. It is worth recalling that in the early 1620s Paris was affected by the plague, which at the same time spread fears of contamination and suspicions of potentially magical origin. Furthermore, Paris was the reported destination for two 'invisible' cabalistic sects at this time: the Rosicrucians, who had authored placards announcing their arrival in the streets of the capital, and the lesser known 'illuminated' Alumbrados from Seville.[152] Along with Mersenne's declared desire to convert as many *libertins* as possible (an evangelism that is noticeably absent in Garasse), this context of multiple targets of accusation also explains the apparently confused state of Mersenne's method of defence identified by Pintard.[153] The frequent listing of the enemies of Catholicism serves to demonstrate further that the term *libertin* was understood to refer to any individual who deviated either from specific Catholic doctrine, or who was seen as

this point, see Frances A. Yates, *Giordano Bruno and the Hermetic Tradition* (Chicago: The University of Chicago Press, 1964), pp. 432–9. On Mersenne's exchanges with Descartes—for which Mersenne is most often remembered in modern studies—see most recently Emma Gilby, *Descartes's Fictions: Reading Philosophy with Poetics* (Oxford: Oxford University Press, 2019), pp. 121–37.

[152] On the Alumbrados in France during the reign of Louis XIII, see Sophie Houdard, *Les Invasions mystiques: Spiritualités, hétérodoxies et censures au début de l'époque moderne* (Paris: Les Belles Lettres, 2008). Houdard notes that the *Mercure françois* also attests to a preoccupation with various forms of invasion at this time (pp. 32–3). On the Rosicrucians and their relation to Fontanier's trial, see Chapter 4 of the present study, pp. 177–9.

[153] René Pintard, *Le Libertinage érudit dans la première moitié du XVII*[e] *siècle* (Geneva: Slatkine, 2000), p. 63: 'Sa méthode est étrange, mais c'est aussi qu'il ne sait, pour défendre le christianisme, de quel côté se tourner. [...] À tous, Mersenne s'efforce de répondre' ('his method is strange, but it is also that he does not know which way to turn in order to defend Christianity. [...] Mersenne tries his hardest to respond to all').

abandoning orthodoxy by virtue of their actions. In the case of Garasse, it may be tempting to identify ambiguity and self-contradiction as proofs of his buffoonery, alongside his hyperbole, crude humour, and anger. Whilst this study does not seek to defend Garasse's ideas or conduct, it is clear that his uses and conceptions of *libertinage* are neither absurd nor exceptional. His various proposed images of libertines instead had their antecedents in the word history of this term, whilst his tone reflected rather than pioneered these linguistic trends. In this sense too, as Robert A. Schneider has recently argued, the dissimilarities in tone between Garasse and Mersenne stemmed from their differing conceptions of their roles in the fight against impiety, as well as religious doubts, within the context of the Counter-Reformation:

> What separated them, then, was not so much their beliefs as the fact that one, recognizing that the age of confessional combat was over, understood that discretion must govern public discourse, while the other, for whom the religious wars had not ended, deployed language as a weapon to injure and inflame.[154]

Garasse and Mersenne also comment on contemporary literature in their descriptions of *libertins*, and it is only natural that Garasse in particular should have sought to capitalise on as many of the possible faces of *libertinage* as possible in order to condemn Vanini, Théophile, and to a lesser extent Fontanier. Garasse's polemic evolved from strictly theological concerns in his earlier texts to condemning purportedly libertine writers. Mersenne's more measured and conciliatory rhetoric makes particular reference to the poets of the *recueils satyriques* and to impressionable youths in the upper echelons of the social and political hierarchy. It also explicitly acknowledges Mersenne's debt to Mathieu Molé, whose legal actions inspired Mersenne to fight against *libertinage* through his writing. Having established the linguistic, historical, theological, and ideological contexts of libertine literature, we will now turn to the legal and political climate in which our authors were writing, as well as the criminal justice system which scrutinised their texts.

[154] Robert A. Schneider, *Dignified Retreat: Writers and Intellectuals in the Age of Richelieu* (Oxford: Oxford University Press, 2019), p. 153.

2

The Law

Ce prince donne de très grands témoignages qu'un jour il saura se faire obéir et qu'il aime la justice.

This prince is showing very great signs that he will one day know how to make himself obeyed, and that he loves justice.

[François de Malherbe on Louis XIII (1614)[1]]

L'impunité des crimes bien souvent les augmente, et semble que les voir et les laisser sans châtiment c'est désirer le désordre et la confusion. Le bon prince est tenu d'empêcher telles actions.

The impunity of crimes most often causes them to increase, and it seems that allowing them to be seen and to go unpunished is to invite disorder and confusion. A good Prince is expected to prevent such actions.

[Louis XIII to Mathieu Molé (1620)[2]]

One of the central roles of the kings of France was to guarantee justice for their subjects; from the preliminary investigation into a suspect prior to arrest, to the preservation of the prisoner's life so that they might be judged by the agents of the king's justice: the magistrates.[3] What were the powers and jurisdictions of these magistrates in policing dissident literature, and in what ways was our period of study significant in the evolution of censorship? This chapter begins by outlining

[1] 'Malherbe à Peiresc' (17 October 1614), in *Lettres de Malherbe* (Paris: J.J. Blaise, 1822), p. 413.

[2] 'Lettre du roi à Mathieu Molé' (31 March 1620), in Mathieu Molé, *Mémoires de Mathieu Molé*, ed. by Aimé Champollion-Figeac, 4 vols (Paris: Jules Renouard, 1855), I, p. 235.

[3] Yves-Marie Bercé and Alfred Soman, 'Les archives du Parlement dans l'histoire', *Bibliothèque de l'école des chartes*, 153: 2 (1995), 255–73 (255, 265). On magistrates as representatives of both royal and divine justice, see Jacques Krynen, 'De la représentation à la dépossession du roi: les parlementaires «prêtres de la justice»', *Mélanges de l'école française de Rome*, 114: 1 (2002), 95–119.

the historical and political contexts of this aspect of criminal justice, with a particular emphasis on the regency government of Marie de Médicis. Drawing from general legislative acts as well as specific examples of censored books in this period, it explores how the political turmoil following the assassination of Henri IV (14 May 1610) led to a gradual expansion of the state's interest in regulating the printing industry. Much of the legislation pertaining to literature at this time was concerned with the production of texts as material commodities. This should not, however, be dissociated from the regulation of subversive content. As Henri-Jean Martin and Roger Chartier observe, the surveillance of such texts was intrinsically linked to the ability of the courts to control the agents of their dissemination, and such powers therefore served as a further filter capable of detecting and prohibiting the diffusion of subversive content.[4] The following comments on the regulation of the book trade therefore offer a broad historical context in which our authors were writing, as well as outlining an increasingly oppressive legal apparatus intended to address the potential dangers of seditious ideas in print. The second part of this chapter provides an overview of the criminal institutions relevant to our case studies, followed by an explanation of the habitual stages of a criminal trial, in order to inform the critical readings of the author trials in Part II.

EARLY MODERN REGULATION OF THE PUBLISHING INDUSTRY

The authors studied in our subsequent chapters were not prosecuted for having taken part in the commercial production of subversive texts as was the case, for example, with those responsible for the publication of *L'École des filles* in 1655.[5] This is not to say that a writer was considered to be entirely divorced from the preparation of a text for printing. The *arrêts* (sentences or final judgements) against authors often found them guilty of *avoir écrit et fait imprimer* (having written and had printed) the work in question. The decision to print a text—a separate enterprise from *publishing* a work (for example, via handwritten letters or manuscripts)—was legally seen as a conscious decision to contribute a title to the book trade and therefore to a reading public.[6] An outline of the regulation of this market, along with a non-exhaustive survey of the various legislative acts passed on this subject, provides a context for the reception of libertine texts as well as to the criminal investigations against their authors.

[4] *Histoire de l'édition française*, ed. by Roger Chartier and Henri-Jean Martin, 4 vols (Paris: Promodis, 1982–5), I: Le livre conquérant (1982), p. 405.

[5] On this trial, which centred on the collaboration between Michel Millot, Jean L'Ange, and the printer Louis Piot, see Frédéric Lachèvre, *Le Libertinage au XVIIe siècle: mélanges* (Paris: Honoré Champion, 1920), pp. 82–126.

[6] On early modern distinctions between published and printed texts, see Harold Love, *Scribal Publication in Seventeenth-century England* (Oxford: Clarendon Press, 1993), p. 36.

The Wars of Religion had motivated French authorities to tighten their grip on the growing book market, in order to avert the reading public's eyes from the works of Calvin, Luther, and their supporters. A significant example of this can be seen in the Edict of Châteaubriant (27 June 1551). Sixteen of its forty-six articles pertained to the regulation of the printing press, marking 'the apogee of the collaboration between the king, the Parlement, and the Sorbonne regarding censorship'.[7] Henri II sought to ban the printing of any text without his royal privilege (*privilège du roi*) and the approval of the university's Faculty of Theology. Taking inspiration from Italy, where privileges were used to limit the financial damage of counterfeit editions to the legitimate publishers, in France the use of privileges moved from economic to increasingly censorial motives.[8] When these efforts were flagrantly ignored, Charles IX's edict of 10 September 1563 decreed that those who printed books without a privilege would be 'pendu et étranglé' ('hanged and strangled').[9] Repeated in later legislation (in 1566 and 1571), the 1563 edict included a requirement for publishers to display both their royal permission and the chancellor's seal in their texts.[10] The Edict of Moulins (February 1566) makes it clear that such legislation was passed with the welfare of the reading public in mind:

> Tous imprimeurs, Libraires, ou relieurs qui imprimeront, ou feront imprimer livres, ou libelles diffamatoires, seront punis comme perturbateurs du repos public, et en ce faisant privez et deschevez de tous leurs privileges et immunitez, et declarez incapables de pouvoir jamais exercer l'Art d'Imprimerie ou Libraire.
>
> All printers, booksellers, or binders who print, or cause to be printed, either books or defamatory pamphlets, will be punished for disturbing the public peace, and as such will have their privileges and immunities stripped from them and terminated, and they will be declared unable to trade in the printing or selling of books ever again.[11]

[7] Roger Chartier, *The Order of Books: Readers, Authors, and Libraries in Europe between the Fourteenth and Eighteenth Centuries*, trans. by Lydia G. Cochrane (Cambridge: Polity Press, 1994), p. 49. See also Alfred Soman, 'Press, Pulpit, and Censorship in France before Richelieu', *Proceedings of the American Philosophical Society*, 120: 6 (1976), 439–63 (441).

[8] Laurent Pfister, 'Author and Work in the French Print Privileges System: Some Milestones', in *Privilege and Property: Essays on the History of Copyright*, ed. by Ronan Deazley and others (Cambridge: Open Book Publishers, 2010), pp. 115–36 (p. 119).

[9] André Chevillier, *L'Origine de l'imprimerie de Paris: Dissertation historique et critique* (Paris: Jean de Laulne, 1694), pp. 395–6. The phrase 'hanged and strangled' was intended to prevent the executioner from delivering a quick death by allowing the criminal to fall from a great height, thereby breaking their neck (see Freddy Joris, *Mourir sur l'échafaud: Sensibilité collective face à la mort et perception des exécutions capitales du Bas Moyen Age à la fin de l'Ancien Régime* (Liège: Éditions du Céfal, 2005), p. 16). This should not be confused with the *retentum* in some death sentences for the condemned to be strangled before burning at the stake, which conversely sought to spare them the pain of the flames.

[10] For a recent discussion of this practice and statistics on the number of privileges granted over the course of the sixteenth century, see Tom Hamilton, *Pierre de L'Estoile and his World in the Wars of Religion* (Oxford: Oxford University Press, 2017), pp. 56–68.

[11] 'Édit de Moulins' (1566), article 78, quoted in M.L. Bouchel, *Recueil des status et reglemens des marchands, libraires, imprimeurs, & relieurs de la ville de Paris* (Paris: François Julliot, 1620), p. 60. See also the 'Édit sur la pacification des troubles du royaume, les protestans, les religionnaires fugitifs, la convocation des États Genéraux, etc.', article 5, in *Recueil général des anciennes lois françaises, depuis*

The phrasing of this statute echoes sentences pronounced against authors, who were directly implicated in the production of the offending text as a material object as much as a work of literature or thought.[12] As Pfister has succinctly explained, the inclusion of the author's name in a text made it easier for them to be held accountable for their actions. This requirement was intended to facilitate further legal action against authors and their texts, and as such it is unsurprising that the granting of a royal privilege did not require the author's permission.[13] As Soman observes, the repetition of these stipulations across numerous legislative acts proves that the authorities were unable to enforce them effectively, not least as there was a degree of overlap in the jurisdictions of legal bodies. Given the rivalry that existed between these, we might well speak of competition between the chancellor and the parlements (both of which could grant privileges), and the Faculty of Theology which could grant its own approbations. Writers and even printers could evidently capitalise on the situation by quite literally choosing their own critics.[14] One of our authors, Vanini, is a case in point. Although both of his surviving texts clearly manifest religious beliefs that are at the very least pantheistic in nature if not atheistic, both received the necessary legal and theological seals of approval. His second text, *De admirandis*, was censored one year after having been approved by two doctors of theology, though such retractions of official approval were not uncommon. Early attempts to regulate the book trade had therefore proved ineffective. By the beginning of the seventeenth century, the repeated threats of harsh punishment in legislation from the preceding decades had also failed to deter uncooperative printers. This led to a less repressive publishing climate reflecting the relative political stability established in the years following the Edict of Nantes (1598).[15] The reign of Louis XIII during which our authors were writing, however, saw an initial struggle for political dominance and legitimacy in which the print market would play a significant role.

THE GROWING ARM OF THE LAW: THE PARLEMENT DE PARIS AND CENSORSHIP

The assassination of Henri IV by François Ravaillac (14 May 1610) removed the central pillar upon which the coexistence of France's leaguer, *politique*, and Huguenot partisans had cautiously been constructed.[16] Although Henri IV's reign

l'an 420, jusqu'à la révolution de 1789, ed. by François-André Isambert and others, 9 vols (Paris: Belin-Leprieur, 1822–33), XIV ii — juillet 1559–mai 1574 (1829), pp. 282–3, which banned 'l'impression, publication et vendition de tous livres, libelles et escrits diffamatoires' ('the printing, publishing and sale of all defamatory books, pamphlets and writings').

[12] On this point see Chartier, *The Order of Books*, p. 50.

[13] Pfister, 'Author and Work', pp. 120–2.

[14] See Soman, 'Press, Pulpit, and Censorship', 454–5; and p. 122 of the present work.

[15] J.H. Shenann, *The Parlement of Paris* (Stroud: Sutton, 1998), p. 95.

[16] On Henri IV's assassination, see especially Roland Mousnier, *L'Assassinat d'Henri IV: 14 mai 1610*

took a relatively lax attitude towards policing the print industry, the market saw an explosion in increasingly audacious pamphlet literature following the regicide.[17] As Jacques Auguste de Thou lamented in a speech to the Parlement de Paris's Grand' Chambre on 15 June 1610:

> Impunement sont exposez en vente des livres contenants des propositions schismatiques et pleines d'impieté, entre autres que ceux qui ont le charactere clerical sont exempts non seulement de toute jurisdiction seculiere mais de puissance souveraine.
>
> Books are displayed for sale with impunity containing propositions that are schismatic and filled with impiety, among others, that 'those who bear the clerical character [ordained clergy] are exempt not only from all secular jurisdiction but also from the authority of the sovereign'.[18]

Broadly speaking, there were two themes in pamphlet literature which particularly preoccupied the authorities in the second decade of the seventeenth century: religious and political commentaries, though these were not of course mutually exclusive.[19] Henri IV's death provoked a wave of anti-Jesuitism in the capital, though in certain years the pro-Jesuit cause was able to dominate the market.[20] As the title of one manuscript collection of trial records suggests, the Parlement de Paris was especially active in censoring Jesuit texts, including those published abroad.[21] This was because the question of Henri IV's successor had rekindled a debate that had played no small part in his journey to the throne: the extent of the pope's authority in France's state affairs. The pope had previously opposed Henri IV's coronation and was confounded by France's increasing hostilities against Catholic Spain. To make matters worse, the French king was apparently willing

(Paris: Gallimard, 1964). For a more recent study see Michel Cassan, *La Grande peur de 1610: Les français et l'assassinat d'Henri IV* (Paris: Champ Vallon, 2010).

[17] Chartier and Martin, *Histoire de l'édition française*, p. 374; Henri-Jean Martin, *Le Livre français sous l'ancien régime* (Paris: Promodis, 1987), p. 133. When one foreign visitor complained of too many prohibited books criticising the pope in 1608, he reported that 'the ministers excuse themselves for not doing more, on the grounds that there are too many private presses, that there is a tradition of freedom in the book trade, and that Paris is too populous a city' (Ubaldini to Borghese (5 February 1608) quoted in Soman, 'Press, Pulpit, and Censorship', 457).

[18] BNF MS Dupuy 90, fol. 42^r.

[19] A third genre of concern, which somewhat amalgamated the political and religious, were astrological predictions or other prognostications on the coming of natural disasters, or on the deaths of leading members of the royal family. On this point see Soman, 'Press, Pulpit and Censorship', 447. Several legislative acts against defamatory texts or subversive pamphlets also referred to such *almanachs*. For examples of these, see [Pierre Guénois], *Le corps du droict françois* (Geneva: Pour Jean de Laon, 1600), pp. 521–2.

[20] See Hélène Duccini, *Faire voir, faire croire: l'opinion publique sous Louis XIII* (Seyssel: Champ Vallon, 2003), pp. 88–102 and Jean-François Dubost, *Marie de Médicis: La reine dévoilée* (Paris: Payot et Rivages, 2009), p. 453.

[21] BNF MS Fr 15734: 'Censures d'un certain nombre d'ouvrages, principalement d'ouvrages de Jésuites du XVIIe siècle' ('Censorship of a certain number of works, principally works by Jesuits in the seventeenth century').

to risk a European war by marching his forces into the Spanish Netherlands to retrieve the beautiful Charlotte de Montmorency.[22] Enamoured with Charlotte, the king had married her off to Henri II de Bourbon, Prince de Condé in order to keep her away from prying eyes and hands (particularly those of François de Bassompierre). Unfortunately for Henri IV, the reputedly homosexual Condé had become rather more taken with Charlotte than expected, and had moved his wife out of the king's reach to Brussels. Ravaillac thus sank his dagger into Henri IV's chest during a period of political tension and dread which is often understated in *le bon roi Henri*'s glorious posthumous reputation. These events also set the scene for the censorship of texts which explored the legality of committing regicide, as well as those which discussed the deaths of Henri IV or the nine-year-old Louis XIII, and the ensuing debates between proponents of papal and Gallican authority.

Faced with a regency government, the Parlement de Paris asserted its duty to protect the king's law, as well as to ensure that his powers were not eroded before he could exercise them personally. Religious and political pamphlets were weaponised by two factions who had the potential to diminish royal authority: the advocates of papal authority (including the Jesuits), and those princes of the blood who were dissatisfied with the new structures of government. In addition to these, there was also the influence of the Parlement's magistrates to contend with. The respective interests of these political actors were not always distinct from one another. The Parlement included supporters of the Jesuits, as well as those of the Gallican doctrines on the supremacy of French monarchs over papal interference.[23] It was prepared to condemn both Condé's attempts to fan the flames of civil war against Marie de Médicis, as well as his arrest at the queen's command. Condé vacillated between seeking parliamentary support for his cause, and producing pamphlets against official *arrêts* which were published by the magistrates in the king's name. The Jesuits were keen to advance their mission in France at a time when their status in the kingdom was far from secure, and mindful to avoid being dragged into debates on their role in the promotion of regicide. Finally, the queen regent's behaviour towards Condé oscillated from hostile condemnation (both in print and in court) to inviting him to reconciliation as circumstances dictated. Though she chose to support the Jesuits against waves of hostile propaganda, she was also conscious of the importance of the Parlement. Marie went beyond the

[22] On Henri IV's ambitions to make a credible challenge to the Habsburg dominance of European politics at this time, see Caroline Bitsch, *Vie et carrière d'Henri II de Bourbon, prince de Condé (1588–1646): Exemple de comportement et d'idées politiques au début du XVIIe siècle* (Paris: Honoré Champion, 2008), pp. 52, 80, 94.

[23] On the rivalry between Gallican and Jesuit factions, see Marc Fumaroli, *L'Âge de l'éloquence—Rhétorique et «res literaria» de la Renaissance au seuil de l'époque classique* (Geneva: Droz, 2002), pp. 223–57, 326–42. For a political history of Gallicanism in this period, see especially Joseph Bergin, *The Politics of Religion in Early Modern France* (New Haven, CT, and London: Yale University Press, 2014), Chapter 3: 'Gallican stirs', pp. 64–85.

usual protocol of announcing her regency to the magistrates by letters patent, choosing instead to hold a *lit de justice* in the very heart of the Parlement in person. In doing so, she sought both to bring the magistrates on side, and to install the necessary mechanisms of her regency government, before Condé could return to Paris and exert his influence.[24]

Significantly, the Parlement's assertion of its duty to protect royal authority, as well as its efforts to expand its legal jurisdiction to this end, was manifested in its rulings pertaining to the print industry. On 28 May 1610, the *premier président* Achille de Harlay gave a speech before the Parlement and delegates from the Sorbonne's Faculty of Theology, which was headed by the Gallican Edmond Richer. Acknowledging that texts of a clerical nature were outside the jurisdiction of a secular law court such as his Parlement, Harlay urged the Faculty to be proactive in condemning texts advocating regicide. The Parlement proposed that the Faculty reaffirm the decree of the Council of Constance (6 July 1415), which denied that it was licit for a private party to kill a tyrant. Some members of the Faculty questioned the Parlement's competence in such matters, whilst others advocated a rival legal mechanism allowing the pope to free the faithful from heretical tyrants. Richer nevertheless prevailed, and was able to convince the Faculty to reissue its compliance with the Council of Constance on 4 June 1610.[25]

The Parlement subsequently made a series of attempts to censor texts which refuted the Gallican supremacy of French kings, or which advocated regicide with papal support, both of which were associated with the Jesuits.[26] Just four days after Richer had secured the Faculty's renewed commitment to the Council of Constance, on 8 June 1610 the Parlement declared it a crime to own or sell copies of three specific Jesuit texts, on the grounds that they violated the Faculty's decree which the Parlement had just registered. Copies of Charles Scribani's *Amphitheatrum honoris* (Palæopoli Advaticorum [Anvers]: Alexandrum [Plantin Moretus], 1605), Manuel de Sá's *Aphorismi confessariorum* (Venice: [n. pub.], 1595), and Juan de Mariana's *De rege et regis institutione* (Toledo: Petrum Rodericum, 1598) were seized and thrown to the flames.[27] Although the *premier président* Harlay had recently acknowledged the Parlement's inability to judge clerical texts,

[24] Eric Nelson, *The Jesuits and the Monarchy: Catholic Reform and Political Authority in France (1590–1615)* (Aldershot: Ashgate 2005), p. 155.

[25] Nelson, *The Jesuits and the Monarchy*, p. 157. On the Jesuit texts which follow, see BNF Dupuy 90, fols. 41^{v} – 45^{r}.

[26] Although Ravaillac's actions naturally fuelled this debate, the question of legitimate regicide had first been raised by Henri IV's apparently cavalier actions on the European political stage (see Bitsch, *Condé*, pp. 97–101). On the Jesuit take on legitimate regicide, see Harro Höpfl, *Jesuit Political Thought: The Society of Jesus and the State, c.1540–1630* (Cambridge: Cambridge University Press, 2004), pp. 314–38.

[27] An overview of the Parlement's collaboration with the Faculty of Theology in renewing the Edict of Constance is given in the *Arrest de la Cour de Parlement, ensemble la censure de la Sorbonne, contre le livre de Jean Mariana, intitulé De Rege & Regis Institutione* (1610). For this *arrêt*, see BNF MS Fr 15734, fol. 78.

the magistrates were able to turn international politics to the advantage of state censorship. Their legal strategy was twofold. First, these authors were writing with foreign monarchs in mind who were tied to a less absolutist concept of monarchy than France. From a French critical perspective, then, some of their arguments strayed into the secular domain of constitutional rights over which the Parlement de Paris could claim jurisdiction. Second, the Parlement based its condemnation on legal precedent; namely the *arrêt* passed against Jean Petit for having supported John the Fearless in the assassination of Louis d'Orléans in 1407.[28] The Parlement's deliberations on this matter speak volumes about the delicate tensions between religious factions at the time, as well as the division of opinion on the Jesuits between magistrates in the chamber:

> La matiere fut mise en deliberation en laquelle se vit grande diversité du discours et d'opinions, les uns ne pouvants condamner ces bons Peres Jesuites, ny aussi soustenir ceste mechante et impie doctrine de tuer les Rois, et ce seul respect les retenoit de dire beaucoup de choses pour les excuser et defendre leur innocence, neantmoins les louoient fort comme compagnie desirée par toute la France, et necessaire pour l'instruction de la Jeunesse, d'autres disoient que s'il falloit brusler Mariana il falloit aussi brusler les livres de Calvin, Luther, Buchanan qui avoient dit la mesme chose que Mariana ainsy qu'ils disoient avoir appris et oui dire sans le savoir pourtant autrement, d'autres craignoient que le Pape trouvast mauvais ce jugement et qu'il s'en offensast.

> The matter was deliberated in the Parlement, over the course of which a great diversity of speeches and opinions were observed. Some were unable to condemn these good Jesuit fathers, yet were equally unable to support this wicked and impious doctrine on the killing of kings, and it was only because of this that they were able to hold themselves back from saying many things to excuse them and defend their innocence. They nonetheless praised them highly as being a religious order which all of France supported, and necessary for the education of the young. Others said that if Mariana's texts were to be burned, then books by Calvin, Luther, and Buchanan should be burned too, as these had said the same thing as Mariana, or so they said they claimed to have learned and heard said without otherwise being sure. Others feared that the pope would not approve of this judgement and that he would be offended by it.[29]

Other observers were also mindful of how the pope might react to the Parlement's censoring spree. The verdict on Mariana's text had led to the condemnation of Cardinal Roberto Bellarmino's *Tractatus de potestate summi pontificis in rebus temporalibus* (Rome: B. Zannetti, 1610) on 26 November 1610, due to its discussions of political authority during a regency and the limited temporal authority of kings. The papal Nuncio considered the judgement to 'fait un grand

[28] Nelson, *The Jesuits and the Monarchy*, p. 162.

[29] BNF MS Dupuy 90, fols. 43^{r} – 43^{v}. The unnamed proponent of burning other books was likely Guillaume Deslandes (see Chapter 5, pp. 315).

prejudice à l'auctorité du Pape' ('be an act of great prejudice against the pope's authority'), not least as Bellarmino's arguments were more theological in nature than Mariana's legal claims had been.[30] Once again, and this time without prior condemnation by the Faculty of Theology, the Parlement was able to legislate against what it considered to be a seditious text which treated religious themes. In this instance, the Parlement claimed that although the offending text was largely theological, it nonetheless represented an attack on secular laws pertaining to the king's sovereignty which were within its jurisdiction.[31]

As Nelson observes, the Jesuits had sought to distance themselves from these condemnations by denying the link, asserted by writers such as Father Pierre Coton, between the Jesuit order and individual authors who had published their own views abroad.[32] The censoring of a range of Jesuit texts in the early years of the regency presented the Parlement with two distinct though not unrelated issues. On the one hand, there was the question of whether the Jesuits bore collective responsibility for texts attacking the absolute authority of French monarchs—be it through regicide or papal supremacy in the face of tyrants—in the wake of Henri IV's assassination. On the other hand, it was unclear to what extent the Parlement, especially during regencies, could extend its secular powers to condemn texts of a theological nature which advocated for an erosion of the king's absolute authority. Given the political situation, and support for the Jesuits from the queen regent as well as from a number of its own magistrates, the Parlement chose to focus on its ability to defend the king's law by expanding its juridical reach in the censorship of literature. Thus, when Francisco Suárez's *Defensio fidei* (Conimbriga: Gomez de Loureyro, 1613) was brought before the Parlement by the Gallican *avocat général* (assistant public prosecutor) Louis Servin on 26 June 1614, the Parlement was quick to dismiss Servin's attempts to conflate Suárez's ideas with those of the Jesuits more widely. Instead, it ordered that Suárez's text should be condemned by the Jesuits themselves, who were quick to oblige.[33]

[30] BNF MS Dupuy 90, fol. 58^{r}. On this case see also fols 57^{r} – 63^{v}. Fol. 193^{r} gives the printed *arrêt* which declares it a crime of lese-majesty to 'recevoir, retenir, communiquer, imprimer, faire imprimer, ou exposer en vente ledict livre' ('to receive, keep, pass on, print, have printed, or display for sale the aforementioned book'). See also Duccini, *Faire voir, faire croire*, p. 92. On the diplomatic correspondence between France and the papacy, see Sylvio Hermann de Franceschi, *La Crise théologico-politique du premier âge baroque. Antiromanisme doctrinal, pouvoir pastoral et raison du prince: le Saint-Siège face au prisme français (1607–1627)* (Rome: École française de Rome, 2009).

[31] On Bellarmino's own career as a censor, see Piet van Boxel, 'Robert Bellarmine, Christian Hebraist and Censor', in *History of Scholarship: A Selection of Papers from the Seminar on the History of Scholarship Held Annually at the Warburg Institute*, ed. by Christopher Ligota and Jean-Louis Quantin (Oxford: Oxford University Press, 2006), pp. 251–75.

[32] Nelson, *The Jesuits and the Monarchy*, pp. 167–8, 174.

[33] See Nelson, *The Jesuits and the Monarchy*, pp. 210–15. The *arrêt* against Suárez's text, dated 27 June 1614, can be found in BNF MS Fr 15734, fol. 31 (handwritten) and fols. 40–1^{v} (printed). An annotation on fol. 31 accuses Suárez's text of encouraging 'la subversion des Estats' ('the subversion of states'), and explicitly links the court's decision to register the Faculty of Theology's renewed commitment to the

The Jesuits were not the only religious faction to feel the force of the Parlement's growing confidence in censoring theological texts. Caspar Schoppe's *Ecclesiasticus auctoritati Jacobi regis oppositus* (Hartberg: [n. pub.], 1611) was condemned by the Parlement on 24 November 1612, as it was deemed to contain 'plusieurs blasphemes et diffamations execrables contre la tres-heureuse et loüable mémoire du feu Roy Henri IIII (que Dieu absolve) et aultres propositions tendantes à troubler le repos de toute la Chrestieneté' ('several blasphemies and execrable defamations of the most happy and laudable memory of the late King Henri IV (may God absolve him) and other propositions leading to a breach of the peace of all Christendom').[34] Philippe Duplessis-Mornay, the *gouverneur* of the Protestant Académie de Saumur, saw his *Mystère de l'iniquité, c'est à dire, l'Histoire de la papauté* (Saumur: T. Portau, 1611) banned for critiquing the overreaching powers of the pope.[35] Beyond questions of regicide, the Protestant historian Louis Turquet de Mayerne's *La monarchie aristodémocratique* (Paris: J. Berjon and J. le Bouc, 1611) could scarcely have been more inflammatory towards Marie de Médicis. Spanning over 1500 pages, it attacked queens, foreigners, the absolute power of kings, and the very concept of hereditary monarchy, as well as suggesting that the nobility should be allowed to work in all trades.[36] Turquet de Mayerne was arrested and interrogated by the *lieutenant civil* Nicolas Le Jay on 22 June 1611. Although his book was banned, copies continued to circulate in Paris and Mayerne was soon released, ironically at the personal request of his queen.[37] Even Richer, who had persuaded the Faculty of Theology to comply with the Parlement's request in 1610, was to fall victim to his own success. In that same year Marie de Médicis had appointed Nicolas de Verdun, who would go on to play an important role in the trial of Théophile de Viau, as the new *premier président* of the Parlement due to his reported sympathies for the Jesuits. Verdun, however, wasted little time in adopting the predominant Gallicanism of the Parlement, and encouraged Richer

Council of Constance on 8 June 1610. A letter from John Chamberlain to Dudley Carleton reveals that a number of Suárez's books were publicly burned in England on 1 December 1613. See Francesco Paolo Raimondi, *Giulio Cesare Vanini Nell'Europa del Seicento, seconda edizione aggiornata* (Rome: Aracne, 2014), pp. 655–6. On Suárez's thought, see John P. Doyle, *Collected Studies on Francisco Suárez*, ed. by Victor M. Salas (Leuven: Leuven University Press, 2010).

[34] BNF MS Fr 15734, fols. 10^{r} – 10^{v}. See also BNF MS Dupuy 90, fol. 271^{r}.

[35] See Armand Jean du Plessis, Cardinal de Richelieu, *Mémoires du Cardinal de Richelieu*, ed. by Horric de Beaucaire and others, 10 vols (Paris: Librairie Renouard, 1907), I (1600–15), pp. 153–4.

[36] On this text see Roger Soltau, 'La Monarchie aristo-démocratique de Louis Turquet de Mayerne', *Revue du seizième siècle*, 13 (1926), 78–94 and Mark Greengrass, 'The Calvinist and the Chancellor: The Mental World of Louis Turquet de Mayerne', *Francia. Forschungen zur Westeuropäischen Geschichte*, 34 (2007), 1–23. Louis should not be confused with his son, Sir Theodore Turquet de Mayerne, a successful physician who spent much of his life in the service of English royalty and aristocrats.

[37] Hélène Duccini, *Concini: Grandeur et misère du favori de Marie de Médicis* (Paris: Albin Michel, 1991), pp. 144–5. Le Jay later served as one of Théophile's judges. According to Richelieu, Marie decided on clemency in order to avoid offending the Huguenots (Richelieu, *Mémoires*, I, p. 154). For Turquet de Mayerne's interrogation, see BNF MS Dupuy 558, fols. 20–66.

to publish his *Libellus de Ecclesiastica et Politica Potestate* ([Paris (?)]: [n. pub.], 1611). Yet so radical was the Gallicanism proposed by Richer's text that it too was judged to be in opposition to the concept of absolutist monarchy, and his book was promptly condemned the following year.[38]

Leaving aside the public burning of books, debates on the secular criminality of Jesuit texts were relatively private affairs between lawyers and theologians, and were more concerned with questions of institutional jurisdiction than with political events and public opinion. During this same period, however, Marie de Médicis found herself embroiled in a literary and political battle with much higher stakes. The volatile years of her regency brought with them an extraordinary outpouring of pamphlet literature which reached far beyond the debating chambers of the Parlement and the Sorbonne. Consequentially, the crises of the first seven years of Louis XIII's reign led to a concerted effort to control both public opinion and the influential power of the printing press.

PAMPHLET WARS AND THEIR AFTERMATHS DURING THE REGENCY OF MARIE DE MÉDICIS

As Marie de Médicis sought to buy the support of powerful noblemen, few represented a greater threat to her authority than the Prince de Condé. The nephew of Henri IV was widely seen as a steadier hand to guide the state through what many judged to be an illegitimate regency, headed by a foreign woman, and declared through the Parlement rather than through the usual means of an Estates General. When the queen regent arranged the unpopular Spanish marriages (between Louis XIII and the Spanish Infanta Anne of Austria; and between her daughter Elizabeth of France and Phillipe IV of Spain), Condé requested in print that these procedures be suspended.[39] This was to be the first of a great many pamphlets written between the queen regent and a rebel prince—not to mention others written by their respective supporters—in which conflicting policies were tried in the court of public opinion. The urgency of these debates is evinced by the speed with which they appeared in print. Condé, for instance, published his *Lettre de Monseigneur le Prince de Condé à la reine* on 18 February 1614. The queen's response and counterarguments were available in print the very next day, and went through fourteen reprints in 1614 alone.[40] A comparison between a quantitative

[38] Dubost, *La reine dévoilée*, pp. 454–6; Philippe Denis, *Edmond Richer et le renouveau du conciliarisme au XVIIe siècle* (Paris: Éditions du Cerf, 2014). For manuscript sources detailing the condemnation of Richer's text, see BNF MS 15734, fols. 1–8^{v}, 15–27. For further legal action against authors during this period, see the *arrêts* which form BNF MS Fr 22087.

[39] *Discours sur les mariages de France & l'Espagne contenant les raisons qui ont meu Monseigneur le Prince à en demander la surséance* ([n.p.]: [n. pub.], 1614).

[40] *Lettre de Monseigneur le Prince de Condé à la reine* ([n.p]: [n. pub.], 1614); *Response de la Reyne*

analysis of these pamphlets—made possible by the invaluable research conducted by Hélène Duccini—and the increased regulation of the printing presses at this time allows us to form an image of the legal and cultural context in which our authors were writing.

The rebellion led by Condé and other influential aristocrats brought with it a number of peaks in pamphlet production which were usually reflective of particularly tense moments of conflict. These pamphlet wars were an important period in the history of public opinion. Both factions clearly recognised the value of public support, and that a primary means of obtaining this support was by dominating political discourse through the mass-produced printed word.[41] The regency saw 1107 pamphlets and defamatory texts in all, involving at least sixty-one Parisian publishers.[42] A notable peak in these coincided with the calling of the Estates General from 27 October 1614 to 23 February 1615. Having delayed this event until after Louis XIII had attained his majority (on 27 September), Marie de Médicis had hoped to strengthen the royal government's hand following Condé's first revolt between January and May 1614.[43] According to Duccini, the Estates General led to the printing of 779 texts during this period (a substantial proportion of the 806 published 1614–17). At least 386 of these appeared in 1615 alone, some of which went through as many as twelve reprints.[44] Having failed to gain the support of the nobility, Condé turned to the Parlement de Paris. As Sawyer observes, 'both major factions in the 1614–17 conflict were competing for the loyalty or cooperation of large political interest groups', including 'the magistrates of the sovereign courts'.[45] The nobility had attempted to instigate reforms to the venality of offices within the Parlement, and Condé went beyond supporting the magistrates' right to transfer offices to their male heirs through the

---

Régente, Mère du Roy à la lettre escrite à sa Majesté par Monseigneur le Prince de Condé ([n.p.]: [n. pub.], 1614). See Bitsch, *Condé*, p. 187.

[41] For Jeffrey K. Sawyer, 'From the perspective of the later sixteen-hundreds, we can see that France entered the century with a relatively open public sphere that was free from direct state control. [...] Before the 1630s the institutional means for comprehensive state control of the press and public political discourse simply did not exist' (Jeffrey K. Sawyer, *Printed Poison: Pamphlet Propaganda, Faction Politics, and the Public Sphere in Early Seventeenth-century France* (Berkeley, Los Angeles, CA, and Oxford: University of California Press, 1990), p. 134). Luc Racaut concurs that 'In France, 'public opinion' emerged during the Wars of religion as a political force to be reckoned with [...] At the beginning of the French Wars of Religion, however, 'public opinion' was not wholly recognised as either a legitimate or desirable political force' (Luc Racaut, *Hatred in Print: Catholic Propaganda and Protestant Identity during the French Wars of Religion* (Aldershot: Ashgate, 2002), p. 48). See also Tatiana Debbagi Baranova, *A coups de libelles: Une culture politique au temps des guerres de religion (1562–1598)* (Geneva: Droz, 2012).

[42] Duccini, *Concini*, p. 142; Sawyer, *Printed Poison*, p. 54.

[43] On this revolt see Bitsch, *Condé*, p. 133.

[44] Duccini, *Concini*, pp. 142–3; Hélène Duccini, 'Regard sur la littérature pamphlétaire en France au XVIIe siècle', *Revue historique*, 260: 2 (1978), 313–39 (336, 321). Chartier and Martin have conversely identified 858 pamphlets, with a total of 1425 reprints (*Histoire de l'édition française*, p. 407).

[45] Sawyer, *Printed Poison*, p. 32.

payment of the royal tax on offices (*la paulette*).[46] Conscious of the fact that senior magistrates were less open to change, Condé's charm offensive included inviting young *conseillers* (councillors) to a ballet at his *hôtel* on 23 February 1615.[47] The Parlement's response was also publicised in print. In the *Remonstrances présentées au roy par noseigneurs du parlement le vingt-uniesme may 1615*, it made its views on Marie's politics, particularly regarding her favourite Concini, crystal clear. It advised the king:

> retenir en vostre Conseil les Princes de vostre sang, les autres Princes et Officiers de la Couronne, et les anciens Conseillers d'Estat [...] extraits de grandes maisons et familles anciennes [...] et en retrancher les personnes introduites depuis peu d'annees, non pour leurs merites et services rendus à vostre Majesté, mais par la faveur de ceux qui en veulent avoir des creatures.
>
> to keep the Princes of your blood in your council, as well as the other Princes and Officers of the Crown, and the long-serving Councillors of State [...] taken from great houses and ancient families [...] and to remove those who have been brought [into the council] in recent years, not for their talents and services rendered towards Your Majesty, but by the favour of those who wish to have servants there.[48]

The Parlement's plea, which also advised curbing the payment of *pensions* and maintaining the venality of offices, was banned from print the very next day by royal decree. As the king himself was said to have reacted, 'il avoit entendu les Remonstrances, desquelles il n'estoit pas bien satisfaict' ('he had heard the *Remonstrances* of the Parlement, and was little satisfied with them').[49] Whilst the magistrates were keen to exercise their authority at this time—both as agents of textual censorship and as protectors of royal supremacy—their reactions to political events were at times reflected in the administering of justice. Pamphlets written against Marie de Médicis reached the very heart of royal government. The *Mercure françois* relates how Concini brought one such work, written in criticism of the Spanish marriages, to a meeting of the *Grand Conseil* in which Louis XIII and his mother discussed their reactions to the Parlement's *remonstrances*. The queen regent complained that 'on souffre vendre des libelles diffamatoires, contre l'honneur du Roy, et le mien, sans en faire justice. Tenez, voyez ce livre intitulé, *La Cassandre*' ('we are allowing defamatory pamphlets to be sold which are written against the king's honour and mine, without bringing the guilty parties to justice.

[46] See Bitsch, *Condé*, pp. 152–3.

[47] Dubost, *La reine dévoilée*, pp. 444–5. Condé had first attempted to win the support of the Parlement by addressing them in print in his *Lettre de Monsieur le prince de Condé au Parlement de Paris, présentée par le sieur de Fiefbrun, le vingt-deuxiesme février 1614* ([n.p]: [n. pub.], 1614).

[48] *Remonstrances présentées au roy par noseigneurs du parlement le vingt-uniesme may 1615* ([n.p.]: [n. pub.], 1615), p. 14.

[49] *Le Mercure françois, ou suite de l'histoire de notre temps*, 25 vols (Paris: Jean Richer, 1613–43), IV – 1615–17 (1617), p. 74. See Dubost, *La reine dévoilée*, p. 446.

Take this book, *La Cassandre*, for example').[50] Given the short shrift that his Parlement had just received, it is little surprising that the *premier président* Nicolas de Verdun responded that 'il y avoit trois jours qu'il en faisoit faire une exacte perquisition chez les imprimeurs, et qu'il n'avoit encore sçeu rien descouvrir' ('after three days of carrying out thorough raids on printers, he had not yet been able to discover anything on the matter').[51] The duc d'Épernon, however, took the view that 'ce n'estoient ces pauvres gens là qu'il falloit punir, qui ne cherchoient qu'à gagner leur vie, mais les autheurs' ('that it was not these poor people who should be punished, who were only trying to make a living, but the authors').[52] A copy of an *arrêt* dated 27 May 1615 shows that the *conseiller* François Courtin was instructed to investigate this case by the *procureur général du roi* (king's attorney general) Mathieu Molé.[53] Molé's own *Mémoires*, whilst omitting the name of the *conseiller* selected to carry out the criminal investigation, reveal that Servin saw the legal proceedings against *La Cassandre française* as a pretext to push further against such libellous texts:

> M. Servin eut dit que lorsqu'il plut au Roi leur faire bailler ce libelle, ils lui avoient répondu qu'il étoit necessaire, pour le bien de son service, que la justice fût faite également de tous autres mauvais écrits [...] Que tels libelles et écrits ne pouvoient apporter que des troubles et partialités au royaume par la semence de mauvaise opinions.
>
> Monsieur Servin had said that as it pleased the king to entrust them with the matter of this pamphlet, they had replied that it was necessary, for the good of his service, that justice be served against all other harmful writings [...] That such pamphlets and writings could bring nothing but trouble and partiality to the kingdom by spreading false opinions.[54]

Such incidents were not however representative of the wider picture, which clearly shows that the regency was generally able to dominate the pamphlet market. With 331 pamphlets written in the king's favour between 1610 and 1617, almost half of this corpus supported the royal cause. This compared with 125 texts (around 20%) for the princes and the Protestants combined, whereas 6% were written in support of reforms without attacking Marie de Médicis directly.[55] A more microscale analysis tells the same story in terms of both the number of titles and the total number of reprints. In the wake of the first revolt, sixteen pamphlets supported the queen regent across sixty-one reprints between 12 February and the end of March 1614, whereas the princes garnered support in ten pamphlets

[50] *Mercure françois*, p. 80.
[51] *Mercure françois*, p. 80.
[52] *Mercure françois*, p. 80.
[53] BNF MS Fr 15734, fol. 154.
[54] Molé, *Mémoires*, p. 106.
[55] Duccini, *Concini*, p. 143.

reprinted in forty-three editions. By June 1614, only four texts supported Condé compared to thirteen in favour of Marie de Médicis. Not even the controversial Spanish marriages were able to prise the pamphlet market from the royal grasp. Whilst 106 pamphlets were written in support of Marie's policy between 1614 and 1615, there were only thirty-six which condemned her actions.[56]

Louis XIII took over the successful propaganda campaign led by his mother, who in turn discarded her strong hand in spectacular fashion. Between late June and early July 1615, Condé and other rebel princes began to leave the royal court. The young king addressed Condé in his *Lettre du Roy à Monsieur le Prince de Condé*, who responded in turn in the *Response de Monsieur le Prince de Condé au Roy* and his *Declaration et Manifeste de Monsieur le Prince de Condé présenté au Roy.*[57] Despite failing to find support for his uprising, and an *arrêt* from the Parlement condemning his actions, Condé was able to negotiate a seat for himself at the king's council in the Peace Treaty of Loudun (3 May 1616).[58] Yet as of August that year Marie de Médicis began to plan Condé's arrest, which was carried out on 1 September 1616.[59] Her actions provoked an outcry of protest, and proved strikingly effective in uniting an often factional aristocracy squarely against her.[60] Louis XIII made his intentions quite clear, however, in his *Declaration du Roy* following a *lit de justice* on 7 September. Through thirteen editions (including in Latin for the benefit of foreign dignitaries), his *Declaration* justified the imprisonment. Condé would not emerge from the Bastille until 1619, after the last great obstacle to the king's personal rule, Concini, had been eliminated.[61]

Notwithstanding Condé's arrest and the queen's liberal spending of the reserves left by Henri IV and Sully, the greatest criticism levelled against Marie de Médicis was that the royal favourite Concino Concini, along with his wife Léonora Galigaï, had been elevated to a seemingly unchallengeable position of power at court.[62] The influence of the Concinis had led to a rise in anti-Italian

[56] Duccini, *Concini*, pp. 148, 156, 181; Bitsch, *Condé*, pp. 195–6.

[57] *Lettre du Roy à Monsieur le Prince de Condé* ([n.p.]: [n. pub], 1615); *Response de Monsieur le Prince de Condé au Roy, de Coucy, 27 juillet 1615* ([n.p.]: [n. pub], 1615); *Declaration et Manifeste de Monsieur le Prince de Condé présenté au Roy, etc., de Coucy, 9 août 1615* ([n.p.]: [n. pub.], 1615).

[58] See Bitsch, *Condé*, pp. 158–64. This peace settlement cost the royal coffers some four million *livres*, whereas Condé's gratifications since the regicide had already reached 3.4 million *livres* by January 1616 (Jean-Christian Petitfils, *Louis XIII*, 2 vols (Paris: Perrin, 2014), I, pp. 233–4, 249).

[59] See Duccini, *Concini*, pp. 232–7.

[60] See Dubost, *La Reine Dévoilée*, p. 509; Duccini, *Faire voir, faire croire*, pp. 236–7; Bitsch, *Condé*, pp. 184–7.

[61] *Declaration du roy, sur l'arrest fait de la personne de Monseigneur le Prince de Condé, & sur l'eslongnement des autres Princes, Seigneurs & Gentils-hommes. Publiée en Parlement le Roy y seant le septiesme jour de Septembre 1616* (Paris: Fed. Morel & P. Mettayer, 1616); Duccini, *Concini*, p. 238. The inclusion of a Latin translation was a clear and extraordinary declaration of Louis XIII's intention to justify Condé's arrest to a wide audience: only 1% of the pamphlets published between 1614 and 1617 were in Latin, compared to around 20% for all texts printed in Paris (Sawyer, *Printed Poison*, p. 68).

[62] As both Dubost and Duccini make clear, Léonora was far from a domestic double to her husband's political ascension. With her own favourites and political plans, Léonora used her sway over the queen

sentiment in Paris, during the same period in which Vanini abandoned the capital following the condemnation of his final publication, *De admirandis*.[63] Only 223 anti-Concini pamphlets (30.8% of the considerable total corpus) defended Marie de Médicis. Moreover, although the princes of the blood were supported in only 116 pamphlets (16%), these pamphlets went through more reprints than those in favour of the queen regent which, for Duccini, helped to pave the way for Concini's assassination on 24 April 1617.[64]

These events had consequences for the regulation of the printing press. The flurry of texts commenting on the often sensational chains of political events encouraged a wider use of pamphlets and chapbooks. As Richelieu lamented on the state of affairs in February 1614, 'force livrets séditieux couroient entre les mains d'un chacun. Les almanachs, dès le commencement de l'année, ne parloient que de la guerre' ('a considerable number of seditious booklets were freely passed from one pair of hands to another. As of the beginning of the year, the almanacs talked only of war').[65] The royal government made a clear link between serious crime and an excessive licence in publishing 'libelles diffamatoires qui contiennent autant de crimes capitaux que de parolles, et dont les Autheurs, gens execrables et maudits, ne meritent pas moins que le feu' ('defamatory pamphlets which contain as many capital offences as words, and whose execrable and cursed authors deserve nothing less than the fire').[66] Though legislation dating from the preceding decades had largely proved ineffective, the evident importance of pamphlet literature, coupled with the high stakes of Condé's rebellion against the policies of a vulnerable regency, left a clear mark on the history of French law.[67]

There was a discrepancy between the official (that is to say the legal) ideals of the printing industry and the practical reality of the market. Lacking a legal status in its own right, the Parisian publishing sector fell under the jurisdiction of an ineffective corporation of printers and the Sorbonne, which was tasked with authorising twenty-four booksellers in the capital. In reality, there were at least sixty booksellers (the majority of which lay beyond the university's direct jurisdiction), whose activities and professional qualifications eluded both the

---

regent to influence appointments to positions of high office and even to guide state policy.

[63] See Chapter 3, p. 122–3.

[64] Duccini, *Concini*, p. 144.

[65] Richelieu, *Mémoires*, p. 265.

[66] *Advertissement a la France touchant les libelles qu'on seme contre le gouvernement de l'Estat* ([n.p.]: [n.pub], 1615), p. 6. Gabriel Naudé used similar language in decrying 'libelles dignes du feu plustot que de la veüe des hommes, [...] lesquels se tirent de la poche, ne se donnent qu'entre amis, se vendent en secret, s'achètent bien cher, ne vallent rien' ('pamphlets more worthy of the flames than the sight of men [...] which are slid out of a pocket and only passed between friends; which are sold in secret, cost a great deal, and are worth nothing': G.N.P. [Gabriel Naudé Parisien], *Le Marfore ou discours contre les libelles* (Paris: Louis Boulenger, 1620), p. 6).

[67] For Sawyer, 'The concern with pamphlets suffuses the wording of censorship legislation of the 1610–1618 period' (Sawyer, *Printed Poison*, p. 25).

corporation of booksellers, printers, and binders, as well as the legal authorities.[68] The University and corporation thus found that their role in controlling printed material was surpassed by that of the law courts.[69] As we saw earlier, the Crown had attempted to introduce a range of measures which sought at the very least to monitor the literary output of its subjects if not to control them outright.[70] These were the stated aims of various legal statutes passed during the regency, such as a declaration passed on 11 May 1612 which noted that 'il est assez notoire combien peut causer de mal la licence que plusieurs se donnent d'escrire' ('it is quite well-known just how much harm can be done by those who grant themselves the licence to write').[71] A spate of legislation, spanning between the princes' rebellions and the true beginning of Louis XIII's personal rule in 1618, suggests a strong desire to curtail printing freedoms in the wake of the regency pamphlet wars. The 1616 Edict of Pacification, written as a direct response to the Estates General of 1614, made it clear that not only was the tide of seditious texts published during the regency to remain illegal, but that subsequent such infringements of the law would be punishable by death:

> Tous mémoires, libelles diffamatoires, lettres, escrits et livrets injurieux et scandaleux demeureront supprimez: et sont faites défenses très expresses à tous libraires et imprimeurs d'en imprimer ny exposer en ventre cy après, et à toutes personnes d'en escrire et composer, sur peine de la vie. Enjoignant à tous nos juges et officiers de faire leur devoir à la recherche et punition des autheurs d'iceux.
>
> All memoirs, defamatory pamphlets, letters, writings, as well as abusive and scandalous booklets will remain outlawed. Furthermore, all booksellers and printers are most expressly banned from printing them and from displaying them for sale hereafter, as are all individuals from writing and composing them, on pain of death. All our judges and officers are ordered to carry out their duty in seeking out and punishing the authors of these texts.[72]

An ordinance from the *lieutenant civil* in May 1616 ordered all booksellers and printers to relocate to the University quarter ('au destroit de l'Université') within twenty-four hours, after which their stock would be seized.[73] An edict enacted on 7 September 1617, which had first appeared as a sentence by the Châtelet on 17 June

[68] An *arrêt* from 26 May 1615, for example, banned booksellers, printers, and binders from taking on apprentices who could not read or write, suggesting that this was a recognised problem in the trade. See Bouchel, *Recueil des status et reglemens*, p. 20.

[69] Alfred Soman, 'Press, Pulpit, and Censorship', 453; Sawyer, *Printed Poison*, p. 60.

[70] For an early seventeenth-century collation of such legal measures, see Antoine Fontanon and Gabriel Michel, *Les édicts et ordonnances des rois de France*, 4 vols (Paris: [n. pub.], 1611), IV, pp. 467–81.

[71] 'Déclaration qui défend d'imprimer aucun livre sans nom d'imprimeur et sans permission', 11 May 1612, in Isambert, *Recueil général*, XVI, p. 26.

[72] 'Édit de pacification contenant des dispositions générales sur l'administration du royaume en conséquence des états de 1614' (13 May 1616), in Isambert, *Recueil général*, XVI, pp. 89–90.

[73] 'Ordonnance du Lieutenant Civil', 19 May 1616, quoted in Bouchel, *Recueil des status et reglemens*, p. 8. This page also gives examples of individuals prosecuted for disobeying such laws in the summer of 1617.

that year, declared that a royal privilege would not be granted until two copies of a text had been received for the king's library.[74] The printed word was thus intended to be brought squarely under the watchful eyes of the royal and learned authorities, from its inception at the printers to its public display as a commodity.

The notion of the print market as a physical space was more than a metaphor for the authorities' desire to survey the full process of literary production. One of the key concerns for jurists was the policing of peddlers and hawkers known as *colporteurs*. The *colporteurs* earned their name from selling cheap texts of only a few pages in length from trays worn around their necks (*porter au col*), which would in fact become a legal requirement in 1618.[75] Legislation dating between 1578 and 1594 shows that *colporteurs* were permitted to sell almanacs, edicts, ordinances, court sentences, and short texts which had not been the subject of censorship, though such a crowded market inevitably led many to sell texts beyond these parameters.[76] Although *colporteurs* were to be found both in the university quarter as well as in the vicinity of the Parlement, their numbers spilled beyond the physical and legal confines of the authorities. As Sawyer has shown, despite the legal limit of twelve *colporteurs* in Paris, the true number in 1615 may have surpassed one thousand if we include all hawkers of printed material.[77] In an attempt to regulate their considerable commercial activity, on 29 April 1613 the *lieutenant civil* banned *colporteurs* from keeping their own bookshops as well as from printing material themselves. Their texts, of no more than eight sheets, were instead to bear the name of a Parisian bookseller or master printer, including their name and the permission they had obtained to publish the work, on pain of confiscation of their merchandise and a fine of ten écus. Moreover, in 1616 an *arrêt* renewed letters patent passed by Henri III on 12 October 1586, stipulating that *colporteurs* could not sell books that had not been granted a royal privilege.[78]

The importance of the printing press in the regency pamphlet wars, combined with the lack of an effective legal mechanism to police the considerable commercial activity which took place beyond official regulations, presented a potential danger to Louis XIII following Concini's assassination. Consequentially, 1618 saw

[74] 'Déclaration portant qu'il sera remis à la bibliothèque du roi deux exemplaires de tous les ouvrages qui seront imprimés', 7 September 1617, quoted in Isambert, *Recueil général*, XVI, p. 106; Bouchel, *Recueil des status et reglemens*, p. 10.

[75] See article 26 of the 'Lettres-patentes sur les nouveaux statuts des libraires, imprimeurs et relieurs de la ville et université de Paris' (June 1618) in Isambert, *Recueil général*, XVI, p. 123.

[76] See Henri-Jean Martin, *Livre, pouvoirs et société à Paris au XVIIe siècle*, 2 vols (Geneva: Droz, 1999), I, p. 358; Henri-Jean Martin, *Le Livre français*, p. 133.

[77] See Sawyer, *Printed Poison*, pp. 55–6. A 'sentence du Prevost de Paris' passed on 1 August 1594 restricted where these twelve sanctioned *colporteurs* were allowed to trade, with two tradesmen permitted at six different locations in Paris. See Bouchel, *Recueil des status et reglemens*, p. 50.

[78] Bouchel, *Recueil des status et reglemens*, pp. 47–9. One of Théophile de Viau's judges, Henri II de Mesmes, has left a fascinating account of his investigations into illegal *colportage* in 1615 in his role as *lieutenant civil*. See Chapter 5, pp. 316–7.

something of a legal turn for the printing market: the 'Lettres patentes sur les nouveaux statuts des libraires, imprimeurs et relieurs de la ville et université de Paris' ('Letters patent on the new statutes for booksellers, printers, and binders of the city and University of Paris'). Consisting of thirty-eight articles, these letters patent strike the tone of a modern political manifesto, with a strong contrast between the failings of the disordered past and the promise of a peaceful and ordered future brought about by the king's personal reign:

> C'est chose assez notoire que la licence qui s'est glissée entre nos subjects pendants les guerres qui ont eu cours en cestuy nostre royaume, tant du règne du défunt roy Henry le Grand, nostre très honoré seigneur et père, que, à l'occasion des mouvemens derniers, a apporté un tel désordre en tous les estats, offices, arts et métiers. [...] Mais Dieu nous ayant fait la grâce d'affermir cet estat par une profonde paix [...] nostre principal soin a esté de réformer toutes choses en mieux, chasser les abus et désordres qui se sont rencontrés en chacune vacation [...] ayant trouvé les recteurs et suppôts d'icelle disposés entièrement à contribuer au retranchement des abus, désordres et mépris de ses anciens statuts et règlements, que la malice des guerres passées y avoit introduits.
>
> It is quite well known that the licence that has crept into the conduct of our subjects during the wars which have taken place in this our kingdom, both during the reign of the late king Henri the Great out most honoured lord and father, as well as during recent troubles, has brought such disorder to all the states, offices, arts and professions. [...] But as God has given us the grace to strengthen this state with a deep peace [...] our principal aim has been to reform everything for the better, to bring an end to the abuses and disorders which are to be found in each profession [...] having found the rectors and their colleagues entirely disposed to contribute to the removal of the abuses, disorders and contempt towards its former statutes and rules, which had been introduced by the evils of the past wars.[79]

In a *sentence* passed on 24 May 1617, the corporation of booksellers, printers, and binders had already been asked to elect eighteen of their own to draw up a list of statutes.[80] They then submitted their recommendations to the king, who judged the book merchants to be so disordered 'en sorte qu'il est besoin d'y interposer nostre auctorité pour les faire vivre en une bonne reigle, qui soit stable et perdurable à l'advenir' ('that there is a need for our authority to intervene so that they may live according to sound law, in a manner which is stable and durable for the future').[81] These statutes were first scrutinised by the king's council, the *lieutenant civil*, the

[79] 'Lettres patentes sur les nouveaux statuts des libraires, imprimeurs et relieurs de la ville et université de Paris', 9 July 1618, in Isambert, *Recueil général*, XVI, pp. 117–18. The articles of these letters patent quoted hereafter are given on pp. 117–25. For comparison, see the previous attempts to reform the printing industry by François I (1544), Charles IX (1571, 1572), Henri III (1583), and Henri IV (1594, 1595) in Fontanon and Michel, *Les édicts et ordonnances*, IV, pp. 470–80. Louis XIII's reforms largely surpass those of his predecessors in terms of their number of composite articles.

[80] Bouchel, *Recueil des statuts et reglemens*, p. 18.

[81] Isambert, *Recueil général*, XVI, p. 119.

procureur général, and subsequently the chancellor, before receiving approval from the king himself as ratified by the Parlement de Paris. The 1618 letters patent brought together the principal agents of literary dissemination as well as those of state censorship in an attempt to create a solid legal apparatus for the print market, and placed a great emphasis on collaboration between the printing and legal spheres. The state's interests in controlling the print market, particularly the trade in subversive and defamatory pamphlet literature, are obvious. Those involved in the material production of these texts, however, were motivated by profit. When an author obtained a privilege for their work, they were unable to exercise these rights without first selling them to a bookseller.[82] An author's text was therefore a commodity before it had even made it to the printing press. The regulation of both the industry and the commercial market, though perhaps at first glance a self-defeating objective for those in the trade, was therefore a potentially lucrative means of exploiting their commercial rights fully in the face of pirated editions.[83]

Article 17 of the 1618 letters patent stipulated that the corporation of booksellers, printers, and binders was to meet on 8 May each year, in the presence of the *lieutenant civil* and a *substitut du procureur général*, in order to elect a *syndic* (a representative of their professional community) and four *adjoints* (deputies). Those elected to the new Printers' Guild were then to carry out inspections of premises and report any infractions to the *lieutenant civil* (article 18). With such a localised and meticulous approach to policing the printing industry, the writing was well and truly on the wall for those who sought to print audacious material: illustrators, upholsterers, and even wallpaper manufacturers ('dominotiers') were to be inspected to ensure that they were not producing dissolute merchandise (article 23). Printed texts were to be produced in clear characters on quality paper, with the name of the author, the bookseller, and the work's privilege clearly displayed (article 12). Those who produced defamatory works were to be charged with breaching the public peace, stripped of their privileges, and declared unfit to trade in the future (article 13). With the explicit aim of suppressing scandalous books printed without the name of their authors, article 16 only permitted one bookseller, printer, and binder to be admitted to the corporation per year, who were to present their candidature a year in advance so as to be registered officially. Booksellers were only to trade within the University, the *Palais*, and the area surrounding the chapel of Saint-Yves (a longstanding locus for printing activity, article 30). No unauthorised parties were to open bookshops (article 29), and even authorised merchants were banned from operating mobile businesses ('tenir boutique portative', article 31).[84] In accordance

[82] Pfister, 'Author and Work', p. 123.

[83] On this point see Chartier and Martin, *Histoire de l'édition française*, p. 369; Henri-Jean Martin, *The History and Power of Writing*, trans. by Lydia G. Cochrane (Chicago, IL, and London: The University of Chicago Press, 1994), pp. 271–2.

[84] Isambert, *Recueil général*, XVI, p. 124.

with legislation quoted earlier, *colporteurs* were restricted to selling edicts, almanacs, and small books of no more than eight sheets bearing the name of a master printer (article 26); whereas preference in granting licences to would-be *colporteurs* was given to former booksellers, printers, and binders who were too old to continue in their previous trade (article 27). This considerable attempt to regulate the printing industry did not of course spell the end for the covert activities which it sought to curtail. In early 1619, for example, the Paris *lieutenant civil* Henri de Mesmes received complaints from *colporteurs* that unlicensed competitors had been trading illegally, 'ce qui pourroit apporter des seditions' ('which could lead to seditious acts').[85] On 15 March, de Mesmes responded by announcing in the streets of Paris that no books were to be published by booksellers or printers without his permission, and that guilty parties would be beaten naked with canes ('fustigez nuds de verges').[86]

Our three authors wrote at a time of increased regulation and surveillance of literary production. These legislative acts were inspired by international politics following the death of Henri IV, the political stakes of the ensuing pamphlet wars, and a growing awareness of the power of the printing press over public opinion. Vanini published his two surviving texts in Lyon (1615) and Paris (1616).[87] Théophile's reputation as a writer was in the ascendant in the second half of 1618. By 14 June 1619 he had been temporarily banished from France (potentially for his reputed atheism), yet his name nonetheless appeared in poetic anthologies in the late 1610s and early 1620s. Fontanier was in Paris between 1614 and 1617, before returning again from travels across Europe in 1621, and therefore had only a sporadic experience of the shifting sands of censorship explored above. Having established how the king and the agents of his royal justice legislated on literature, let us now consider the mechanics of the criminal trials of those unfortunate enough to have fallen foul of the law.

LAW COURTS AND CRIMINAL PROCEDURE[88]

The early seventeenth-century criminal justice system was comprised of a complex structure of law courts; or as Charles de Figon's illustration would have it, the intricate and interwoven 'branchage de la justice' ('branches of justice')

[85] BNF MS Fr 22115, fol. 26.

[86] See Bouchel, *Recueil des status et reglemens*, p. 4; Martin, *Livre, pouvoirs et société*, p. 463.

[87] Giulio Cesare Vanini, *Amphitheatrum aeternae providentiae* (Lyon: Antoine de Harsy, 1615); Giulio Cesare Vanini, *De admirandis nature regine deaeque mortalium arcanis* (Paris: Adrien Perier, 1616).

[88] The following section is not intended to serve as an exhaustive explanation of the early modern French judiciary, but to cover elements of the criminal justice system relevant to our trials of study. Many of the following explanations may be self-evident to readers familiar with the modern French justice system. On the differences between European courts and courts based on English common law, see John H. Langbein, *The Origins of Adversary Criminal Trial* (Oxford: Oxford University Press, 2005), pp. 1–9. For convenience, a glossary of legal terms relevant to our period can be found at the end of this book (see pp. 355–363).

stemming from the tree of French government.[89] Its jurisdictions and privileges were meticulously codified and zealously protected, whilst also presenting a considerable degree of overlap. It is worth mentioning two particularities of this system from the outset. First, the royal ordinances and contemporary legal manuals to which we shall often refer describe how the courts were intended to work in theory. The publication of these texts proves that generations of magistrates were mindful of such laws and precedents in exercising their craft. It was perhaps inevitable, however, that the application of such rigid codifications was doomed to a level of interpretation, and therefore inconsistency, in practice. Second, this system did not allow for a neat compartmentalisation of crimes between given legal institutions. No single law court was solely competent in judging crimes related to author trials such as blasphemy, heresy, impiety, or publishing defamatory works, not least as these crimes were themselves difficult to distinguish from one another. Instead, the legal arena in which our three authors were forced to defend themselves depended on other factors, including the circumstances surrounding the opening of an investigation against them, the social status of the accused, and the severity of their purported crimes. It would therefore be difficult to explain, for example, *why* Théophile de Viau was tried by the Parlement de Paris, whereas Jean Fontanier was first judged by the Châtelet, with reference to jurisdiction alone. Rather, it is both more feasible and more useful to consider the precise events and individuals involved in the early stages of our trials, and to situate these in relation to the law courts and the habitual stages in which they tried a case.

The upper echelon of the law court hierarchy was occupied by the seats of royal justice: the sovereign law courts known as parlements, which judged all three of our authors. The oldest and by far the most influential of these was the Parlement de Paris, which was also a political entity passing legislation in the king's name.[90] Other parlements were later established which replicated the Paris Parlement's structure of chambers. The oldest of these, the Parlement de Toulouse (established in the 1440s) held jurisdiction over one eighth of France, and passed the death sentence against Vanini in 1619. The original function of the Parlement de Paris was to serve as the king's court; a non-stationary body which followed the king's person throughout the land until it was fixed in Paris by

[89] Charles de Figon, *Discours des estats et offices, tant du gouvernement, que de la justice et des finances de France* (Paris: Galiot Corrozet, 1608), p. 15.

[90] For an introduction to the Parlement de Paris, as well as lower courts within its jurisdiction, see Alfred Soman, 'La justice criminelle, vitrine de la monarchie française', *Bibliothèque de l'école des chartes*, 153: 2 (1995), 291–304; and Michel De Waele, *Les Relations entre le Parlement de Paris et Henri IV* (Paris: Publisud, 2006), pp. 13–190. For more in-depth discussions, see Marie Houllemare, *Politiques de la parole: le Parlement de Paris au XVI*e *siècle* (Geneva: Droz, 2011); and Françoise Hildesheimer and Monique Morgat-Bonnet, *Le Parlement de Paris: Histoire d'un grand corps de l'État monarchique, XIII*e*-XVIII*e *siècle* (Paris: Honoré Champion, 2018).

Philippe le Bel in 1302.[91] The Parlement was not an exclusively oppressive body used to exert the king's will upon the populace. It saw itself as an institution at the service of the people, dispensing justice for the king's subjects in his name.[92] The Parlement de Paris wielded considerable power in this judicial capacity. It served as the Supreme Court for almost half of the kingdom (roughly eight to ten million inhabitants). It was the final court of appeal for cases judged by lower courts within its appellate jurisdiction, including for death sentences, corporal punishment, or banishment, in accordance with the Edict of Crémieu (1536) and the ordinance of Villers-Cotterêts (1539).[93] In this capacity, for example, it dealt with roughly 590 cases on appeal between 1609 and 1610.[94] The prestige of the Parlement (alongside the financial value of its offices) attracted the most experienced and knowledgeable men the legal profession had to offer, equipping it with magistrates who were particularly assiduous in the examination of evidence in criminal trials.[95]

As early as the late thirteenth century, the Parlement was divided into three main chambers: the chambres des enquêtes (for written cases, small criminal matters, and the preparation of investigations); the chambres des requêtes (which responded to petitions to the Parlement and its judges for justice, as well as private cases involving members of the royal household); and the Grand' Chambre.[96] Staffed by the Parlement's most senior magistrates, the Grand' Chambre was originally used as the sole chamber for judging crimes carrying capital or corporal punishment, as well for plenary sessions and special events such as *lits de justice*. It judged cases deemed to be of particular importance, due either to the gravity of the crime or the social rank of the parties, including princes of the blood, high-ranking magistrates, and the city of Paris. Over time, the Parlement de Paris became increasingly specialised in jurisprudence and attracted a growing number of cases. In order to alleviate the workload of criminal cases, a new chamber was created which would play a role in the trials of Vanini and Théophile: the Tournelle.

[91] Constantin Gérard, *Histoire du Châtelet et du Parlement de Paris* (Paris: Cognet, 1847), p. 75.
[92] Houllemare, *Parlement*, p. 19. For De Waele, the magistrates were keen to stress to the king that their opinions should be listened to carefully, as theirs was the voice of the people (De Waele, *Relations*, p. 89).
[93] Monique Langlois, 'Parlement de Paris', in Michel Antoine and others, *Guide des recherches dans les fonds judiciaires de l'ancien régime* (Paris: Imprimerie Nationale, 1958), pp. 67–139 (pp. 69, 77–8); Alfred Soman, 'Criminal Jurisprudence in Ancien-Régime France: The Parlement of Paris in the Sixteenth and Seventeenth Centuries', in *Crime and Criminal Justice in Europe and Canada*, ed. by Louis A. Knafla (Waterloo, Ontario: Wilfrid Laurier University Press, 1981), pp. 43–75 (p. 46).
[94] Bercé and Soman, 'Les archives du Parlement dans l'histoire', 268. See also Alfred Soman, 'Les Procès de sorcellerie au Parlement de Paris (1565–1640)', *Annales: Economies, Sociétés, Civilisation*, 32 (1977), 790–814 (790).
[95] Sylvie Daubresse, *Le Parlement de Paris ou la voix de la raison (1559–1589)* (Geneva: Droz, 2005), p. 11; Shennan, *The Parlement*, p. 32.
[96] Julian Swann, *Exile, Imprisonment, or Death: The Politics of Disgrace in Bourbon France, 1610–1789* (Oxford: Oxford University Press, 2017), p. 176. These divisions are visible in legislation enacted by Philip III in 1278 (Shennan, *The Parlement*, p. 17).

The Tournelle appears in legislation dating back to 1446, according to which only the Grand' Chambre could pronounce death sentences at that time.[97] The Tournelle's competences grew to that of a fixed chamber (in 1515) and to judging cases carrying corporal punishment, to the extent that even small criminal cases—habitually tried in the chambres des enquêtes—were sent to the Tournelle if the purported crime carried a physical punishment.[98] Here, clergymen were required to step outside of the chamber when it came to vote, as they were not permitted to take part in judgements that led to the shedding of blood.[99] The Tournelle was not staffed by a permanent, dedicated body of magistrates as was the case for the other chambers. Instead, it was comprised of magistrates operating on a rota system (from which it may have derived its name), 'afin que l'habitude de condamner et de faire mourir des hommes n'altère la douceur naturelle des juges' ('so that the repeated habit of condemning men to death does not alter the judges' natural gentleness').[100] The Tournelle comprised five of the most junior *présidents à mortier* (a high legal office in the Parlement) and eight *conseillers* from the Grand' Chambre, as well as two members from each of the five chambres des enquêtes. The *présidents à mortier* served for the judicial year, the *conseillers* of the Grand' Chambre for six months, and those from the *enquêtes* for three months.[101] It is this peculiarity of the Tournelle that likely explains why the two judges originally charged with investigating Théophile's trial were replaced over the course of the proceedings. Rather than indicating dissatisfaction with their work, or a desire to replace them with magistrates who were more likely to return a desired verdict, the replacement of André Charton and Gabriel Damours with François de Verthamon and Jacques Pinon was a normal part of the working rhythms of the chamber to which they had been assigned. The Tournelle was a chamber for the criminal trials of the unprivileged. Cases involving either particularly serious crimes—including those of Vanini and Théophile—or parties of higher social standing were therefore tried by an 'assembly' of the Tournelle and the Grand' Chambre in the latter chamber, as alluded to in *arrêts* which described such court sessions as *les Grand' Chambre et la Tournelle assemblées*.[102]

[97] 'Ordonnance du 28 octobre 1446', articles 10–13, 25, quoted in Charles Desmaze, *Le Parlement de Paris* (Paris: Cosse, Marchal et Billard, 1860), p. 31.

[98] Gérard, *Histoire du Châtelet*, pp. 120–3; Desmaze, *Le Parlement*, p. 16.

[99] Desmaze, *Le Parlement*, p. 28; Adhémar Esmein, *Cours élémentaires d'histoire du droit français, à l'usage des étudiants de première année* (Paris: L. Larose, 1898), p. 378.

[100] Ferrière quoted in Desmaze, *Le Parlement*, p. 32. An alternative derivation of 'Tournelle' was its location in the tower holding the king's former robing room at the current *Palais de la cité*: the *tour de César*.

[101] Shennan, *The Parlement*, p. 41; Diane C. Margolf, *Religion and Royal Justice in Early Modern France: The Paris Chambre de l'Édit, 1598–1665* (Kirksville, MO: Truman State University Press, 2003), p. 37.

[102] Shennan, *The Parlement*, p. 41; Langlois, 'Parlement de Paris', pp. 70–1. See, for example the two *arrêts* from Théophile's first trial *in absentia* in August 1623 in Frédéric Lachèvre, *Le Libertinage devant le parlement de Paris: Le Procès du poète Théophile de Viau*, 2 vols (Paris: Honoré Champion, 1909), I, pp. 141–2. In 1566, Charles IX decreed that *grands criminels*, as well as noblemen, men of the Church,

The most senior member of a Parlement was its *premier président*. He was appointed by the king, served as a permanent member of the king's council, and shared the royal privilege of receiving the relic of the true cross upon his death.[103] The *premier président* often sat in judgement over the most serious of criminal cases, including the trials of Vanini (presided over by Gilles Le Mazuyer) and Théophile (presided over by Nicolas de Verdun, who had previously served as *premier président* of the Parlement de Toulouse). Next came the *présidents* of the Grand' Chambre. These were visually distinguished from the *présidents* of other chambers by their mortarboards from which they derived their name: the *présidents à mortier*. Any of the *présidents à mortier* were able to take the place of an absent *premier président*, including in order to preside over *les chambres assemblées*.[104] Then came the *présidents* of other chambers, and finally the *conseillers*, who also sat in a specific chamber (except if drafted for service in the Tournelle). In *La Crucifixion* (*c.*1449)—an oil on wood panel painting which hung in the Grand' Chambre in order to remind senior magistrates of their Christian duty—God Himself is depicted above the crucified Christ dressed in the red raiment of a *président* of the Parlement.

Both the parlements and prévôtés (provostships: inferior royal courts) included another group of magistrates of relevance to our author trials: *les gens du roi* (the king's men). The precursors of the *parquet* in the modern French legal system, the *gens du roi* consisted of the *procureur général du roi*, his *subsituts du procureur général*, and *avocats généraux*. As the head of the *gens du roi*, the *procureur général*—from the Latin *procurator*, he who represents another in matters of criminal justice—was originally tasked with investigating cases in advance of trials in the fourteenth century. As the number of trials requiring royal justice increased through the ages, the *procureur général* came to be a representative of the king serving as public prosecutor in his name.[105] As we shall see, his jurisdiction in defending the king's interests grew to considerable proportions by the early seventeenth century. As such, one of the ways in which a criminal investigation could be triggered was at the request of the *procureur général* or one of his *substituts*, described in court records as being 'à la requête du procureur général'. Whilst he did not sit in judgement of serious criminal trials, he did offer his opinions (termed *conclusions*) based on the points of law relevant to the case in question, which would subsequently be considered in the final deliberations.[106]

---

and military officers should be tried in the Grand' Chambre (Gérard, *Histoire du Châtelet*, p. 120).

103 Shennan, *Parlement*, pp. 45, 33–5; Desmaze, *Le Parlement*, pp. 191–2.

104 Desmaze, *Parlement*, p. 197.

105 Esmein, *Cours élémentaires*, p. 400; Shennan, *The Parlement*, pp. 41–5. On *procureurs* outside of Paris, see Claire Dolan, *Les Procureurs du Midi sous l'Ancien Régime* (Rennes: Presses Universitaires de Rennes, 2012), particularly Chapters 1–3.

106 Due to the number of cases heard, the *procureurs* were in turn reliant on their *substituts* to present them with their own views, which they could then use to inform their *conclusions*. See Langlois,

It is therefore significant that Théophile attracted not only the legal attention, but also the personal animosity, of the powerful *procureur général du roi au Parlement de Paris* Mathieu Molé.

The two other law courts relevant to our author trials—the Paris Châtelet and the Capitoulat of Toulouse—were municipal courts subordinate to the royal parlements of their respective appellate jurisdictions. Although both were exceptional judicial bodies for different reasons, they held in common a general competence in what is broadly referred to in legal manuals as the 'police' of their respective cities. This regulation of the community included the day-to-day maintenance of order and the settling of minor disputes, whereas *la haute police* (high policing) of the population, provided by the parlements, pertained more to defending the interests of the Catholic faith.[107]

As a result of its history of relative autonomy, seventeenth-century Toulouse included a form of law court found nowhere else in France: the Capitoulat.[108] Unusually, the eight magistrates who comprised this tribunal—who were known as *capitouls*, and who judged cases in a court building known as a the Capitole—were elected for just one year. They therefore depended on an annual register of events, written by their predecessors, to replace the experience and knowledge of legal precedents which would otherwise have been gained from a lengthy legal career. The *capitouls* were divided between four different areas of local government with two *capitouls* responsible for each: the maintaining of discipline and order (*la police*), hospitals, infrastructure and repairs, and justice, which was the most prestigious jurisdiction of the four.[109] Having affirmed in 1600 that it was their duty to hear all of Toulouse's criminal cases *en première instance* (as a court of the first instance), the *capitouls* held jurisdiction over the most serious of crimes including blasphemy and lese-majesty.[110] For reasons that will be discussed in Chapter 3, the *capitouls* handed Vanini's case to the Parlement de Toulouse which, like its Parisian counterpart, served as a final court of appeal with its own Grand' Chambre, Tournelle, as well as chambres des enquêtes and chambres des requêtes.

'Parlement de Paris', p. 72. On the role of *substituts* see Isabelle Storez-Brancourt, 'A l'ombre de Messieurs les Gens du Roi: le monde des substituts', in *Histoire du Parquet*, ed. by Jean-Michel Carbasse (Paris: Presses Universitaires de France, 2000), pp. 157–204.

[107] Roland Mousnier, *Les Institutions de la France sous la monarchie absolue*, 2 vols (Paris: Presses Universitaires de France, 1980), II, p. 258. 'Police' is defined as 'reglement d'un estat et communauté' ('the regulation of a state and community') in Jean Nicot, *Thrésor de la langue françoyse* (Paris: David Douceur, 1606); whereas Furetière speaks of 'loix, ordre et conduite [...] l'ordre qu'on donne pour la netteté et seureté d'une ville' ('laws, order and conduct [...] the order provided for the cleanliness and security of a city': Antoine Furetière, *Dictionnaire universel*, 3 vols (The Hague and Rotterdam: Arnoud et Reinier Leers, 1690), II).

[108] Further particularities of the Capitoulat are discussed in Chapter 3.

[109] Claire Faure, *La justice criminelle des capitouls de Toulouse (1566–1789)* (Toulouse: Presses de l'Université Toulouse 1 Capitole, 2017), pp. 29–30.

[110] See Faure, *Capitouls*, pp. 38, 162–3, 275–7. For a detailed list of such crimes under their jurisdiction, see pp. 277–315.

The jurisdictions of the Paris Châtelet are particularly difficult to define cogently, not least because its archives have not survived substantially prior to the eighteenth century. The Châtelet was the *prévôté* for Paris of the same level as a *bailliage* or *sénéchaussée* (a bailiwick or the jurisdiction of a seneschal, in the North and South of France respectively). The unique status of the capital as a centre for justice, however, gave added importance to the Châtelet. When Henri II created *présidial* law courts to judge minor civil cases and appeals in 1552, the *présidial* of Paris merged with the *prévôté*.[111] The Châtelet was therefore the seat of the *prévôt de Paris* (the Paris Provost, a sovereign judge in common law) as well as serving as a court of appeal for cases judged in seigneurial courts; whilst its own judgements *en première instance* were themselves subject to appeal by the Parlement de Paris.[112] The official head of the Châtelet, the *prévôt*, was a largely ceremonial role in our period of study. The real power behind this law court lay with its *lieutenant civil*—who was the true head of the Châtelet and particularly the policing of the city—and the *lieutenant criminel*, who presided over the criminal chamber. It is noteworthy that two of Théophile's judges were former *lieutenants civils*: Nicolas Le Jay (1609–13), and Henri II de Mesmes (1613–21) who vacated his position in the same year as Fontanier's execution in December 1621.[113] The Châtelet judged a range of cases including counterfeiting, public disorder, illegal literature, murder, witchcraft, and lese-majesty, as well as other crimes judged to be *cas royaux* (royal cases), where a crime was committed against the king's person or the state.[114]

The prosecution of crimes pertaining to the book trade did not fall within the jurisdiction of a single tribunal. As we saw earlier, in the wake of Henri IV's assassination it was the Parlement de Paris which passed a wave of legislation condemning books perceived to be hostile towards the French monarchy, particularly by Jesuit authors. Yet it was the Châtelet which banned the Jesuit Thomas Sanchez's *Disputationum de Sancto Matrimonii Sacramento Tomi Tres* (Antwerp: M. Nutium, 1607) for obscene content in 1611.[115] It was at this same court where Geoffroy Vallée (the great-uncle of Théophile's close friend and

[111] Charles Desmaze, *Le Châtelet de Paris: son organisation, ses privilèges* (Paris: Didier, 1870), pp. 22–3, 56. The *prévôts* were originally officers who served justice on behalf of the king in places where feudal lords did not fulfil this role. See Esmein, *Cours élémentaires*, p. 350.

[112] See Desmaze, *Châtelet*, pp. 7–15; Mousnier, *Les Institutions de la France*, pp. 252, 259, 269–70; Yvonne Lanhers, 'Châtelet', in Michel Antoine and others, *Guide des recherches dans les fonds judiciaires de l'ancien régime* (Paris: Imprimerie Nationale, 1958), pp. 163–220 (pp. 163–6).

[113] Desmaze, *Châtelet*, p. 104. De Mesmes was succeeded by Nicolas de Bailleul in February 1621.

[114] Michèle Bimbenet-Privat, 'Série Y: Châtelet de Paris, répertoire numérique détaillée', http://www.archivesnationales.culture.gouv.fr/chan/chan/pdf/sa/Y-0-Intro.pdf [accessed 8 October 2019], pp. 9, 19–20. For a list of the competences of *baillis* and the large number of crimes which could be considered *cas royaux*, see Mousnier, *Les Institutions de la France*, pp. 265–7. Even regicide could involve an investigation by multiple courts: after his attempt on Henri IV's life, Jean Châtel was interrogated by the *prévôt de Paris* as well as by the Parlement (Desmaze, *Châtelet*, p. 61).

[115] See Soman, 'Press, Pulpit, and Censorship', 446–7. On the Châtelet and illegal print material see also Sawyer, *Printed Poison*, pp. 60–3.

potential lover, Jacques Vallée Des Barreaux) was condemned to death in 1573, after his *La béatitude des chrestiens, ou Le fléo de la foy* ([Paris (?)]: [n. pub.], 1572) was found to contain blasphemous tenets.[116] Parisian booksellers and printers were summoned to the *lieutenant civil*'s home in 1594, where they were ordered not to produce texts written by members of the Catholic League against Henri III or Henri IV.[117] In mid-March 1619, the *lieutenant civil* Henri de Mesmes took to the streets of Paris to proclaim a ban on booksellers and printers from printing books without his permission ('publier à son de trompe et cry public par les carrefours ordinaires de Paris').[118] De Mesmes even received letters directly from the king, commanding him 'de proceder extraordinairement contre les autheurs, Imprimeurs, et colporteurs des livretz et libelles diffammatoires qui s'impriment et se vendent à Paris' ('to proceed extraordinarily against authors, printers, and hawkers of defamatory booklets and pamphlets which are being printed and sold in Paris').[119]

Théophile's case is a fine example of the range of legal avenues available to those seeking to censor literature through the law courts. In April 1623, he attempted to distance himself from his inclusion in an incriminating anthology of poetry, *Le Parnasse satyrique*, by reporting it to the *lieutenant civil*. He then sought the suppression of the Jesuit François Garasse's *La Doctrine curieuse* by bringing his case before both the Châtelet and the *procureur général du roi* Mathieu Molé.[120] Molé then exercised his power in the Parlement to order a criminal investigation against the poet on 11 July. After Théophile had fled Paris, his whereabouts were reported to the Parlement de Paris by the *lieutenant criminel de robe courte* of Saint-Quentin. Here, the poet was imprisoned at the hands of a *prévôt des maréchaux* (provost marshal, a royal bailiwick magistrate whose jurisdiction chiefly included vagrants and crimes committed on the king's roads), before being transported to stand trial before the Parlement de Paris. Thus, there was no single court to which a seditious, defamatory, or irreligious text was expected to be referred for criminal investigation. Despite the parlements' prerogative to overturn the verdicts of lower courts as final courts of appeal, the lack of appetite for reform suggests that the complex hierarchy and competing jurisdictions of the law courts were not seen to be as problematic as they might appear by modern standards.[121]

[116] This sentence was confirmed by the Parlement on appeal in 1574. See Lachèvre, *Mélanges*, pp. 30–44.

[117] Desmaze, *Châtelet*, p. 96.

[118] Bouchel, *Recueil des status et reglemens*, p. 4.

[119] BNF MS Dupuy 91, Louis XIII to Henri de Mesmes (18 September 1615), p. 212^{r}.

[120] Lachèvre, *Procès*, pp. 119–21; Stéphane Van Damme, *L'épreuve libertine: Morale, soupçon et pouvoirs dans la France baroque* (Paris: CNRS Éditions, 2008), p. 53.

[121] Only 5–10% of original sentences were confirmed unaltered by the Parlement de Paris in the early seventeenth century. See Soman, 'Criminal Jurisprudence', 47. As Esmein observes, reforming the criminal justice system did not form part of the États de la Ligue (1593) or the *assemblée des notables* at Rouen (1596) (Adhémar Esmein, *Histoire de la procédure criminelle en France, et spécialement de la*

Two of the trials examined in this book were partly concerned with subversive texts as physical objects. Fontanier had unwisely posted placards in the streets of Paris advertising clandestine lessons of a vaguely esoteric nature. His students in turn became accomplices in the physical dissemination of his ideas by penning dictated copies of Fontanier's text. Théophile, on the other hand, publicly argued with the printers of *Le Parnasse satyrique*, and was reproached by the Parlement for having contributed to the material production of obscene and irreligious poetic anthologies. The ideological and even linguistic content of these texts (in the case of sexually explicit or sacrilegious vocabulary, for example) also contributed to the prosecution of these authors. As such, the trials of Fontanier and Théophile were particularly concerned with authorial identity. In Fontanier's case, this was viewed from a mechanical but nonetheless literary perspective. The *président à mortier* Nicolas de Bellièvre was predominantly concerned with proving beyond reasonable doubt that Fontanier had composed the incriminating text seized from his home during his arrest. In doing so, he sought to demonstrate that Fontanier had not only produced the text as a material pedagogical tool, but that he also bore legal responsibility for the teaching of what Bellièvre considered to be a belief system contrary to Catholic teaching. Théophile's case is more nuanced, and reveals a greater emphasis on the ownership of ideas rather than a printed commercial product. For whilst parts of his interrogations centred on the drafting and printing of texts, Théophile's strategy often focussed on distinguishing himself as a defendant from the *je poétique* (the poetic 'I') of his works. In doing so, he aimed to reject ownership of, and thus legal culpability for, their sexually or theologically unorthodox content.

As we saw in the previous chapter, the predominant accusations made against our authors—blasphemy, atheism, and impiety—were often described as *libertinage* in literary texts. Within the legal sphere, however, they were recognised as lese-majesty, which was in turn identified as a *cas royal*. Originally denoting a case which could only be heard by the royal law courts (the parlements), by the end of the sixteenth century lese-majesty had come to refer more generically to any serious criminal offence. This is because infractions against the king's interest—'crimes that threatened the peace, the person, the property, and the rights of the king'—extended to cover the protection of his subjects and thereby to conflate with the public interest.[122] A consequence of this was that the magistrates within

procédure inquisitoire (Paris: L. Larose et Forcel, 1882), p. 171). Mousnier furthermore remarks that the method of gathering witness testimony and 'confronting' these with the accused was not criticised at the Estates General (1614–15) or the *assemblées des notables* of 1617–18 and 1626–27 (Mousnier, *Les Institutions de la France*, p. 393).

[122] Lisa Silverman, *Tortured Subjects: Pain, Truth, and the Body in Early Modern France* (Chicago, IL: University of Chicago Press, 2001), p. 39. See also Esmein, *Cours élémentaires*, pp. 400, 420–1. Soman describes *cas royaux* as being 'treason and plotting against the most prominent figures of the socio-political hierarchy; also, by extension, crimes which directly affronted the dignity or financial resources

a parlement were at the same time defenders of the royal cause whilst also serving as public prosecutors. The Toulouse jurist Gabriel de Cayron is explicit on this point: 'le [crime] public est comme de leze-majesté, heresie, simonie, homicide, trahison, faussеté et semblables, l'accusation desquels est commune, et appartient à un chacun, pour utilité publique' ('public crimes include lese-majesty, heresy, simony, murder, treason, counterfeiting and other such things. Accusations of such crimes are common and fall to everyone for the public good').[123]

Lèse-majesté was the subject of at least nine separate legislative acts between 1562 and 1593.[124] For Claude Le Brun de La Rochette, *lèse-majesté divine*—'le plus grand et enorme de tous les crimes' ('the biggest and greatest of all crimes')—encompassed sorcery, simony, heresy, apostasy, and blasphemy. Blasphemy in turn included questioning the justice, goodness, or power of God, denying the Immaculate Conception and virginity of the Virgin Mary, and irreverence towards images of the Saints.[125] This is to be distinguished from *lèse-majesté humaine*, which covered crimes against the sovereign or his councillors of state, treason, counterfeiting, and sedition through the carrying of firearms or through *assemblées illicites*.[126] Cardin Le Bret divides lese-majesty between speaking out against the sovereign's actions, making an attempt on their life, and conspiring against the state.[127] Finally, Vouglans gives a more granular explanation by defining *lèse-majesté au premier chef* (lese-majesty in the first degree) as encompassing atheism, apostasy, heresy, schisms between adherents of the same religion (which could be

of the sovereign—armed rebellion, brigandage, highway robbery, counterfeiting of the coinage, smuggling of goods important to royal revenues (e.g., salt), occasional large-scale outbreaks of heresy. Also prosecuted at public expense were "horror crimes" (*cas énormes*) such as parricide, multiple murders or rapes, and sexual offenses such as sodomy or incest within the nuclear family' (Alfred Soman, 'Deviance and criminal justice in Western Europe, 1300–1800: An essay in structure', *Criminal Justice History*, 1 (1980), 3–28 (9)). Finally, Faure notes that for the *capitouls* in Toulouse, lese-majesty could be considered a crime against public order (Faure, *Capitouls*, p. 309).

[123] Gabriel Cayron, *Stil et forme de proceder, tant en la cour de Parlement de Tolose, et chambre des requestes d'icelle, etc.* (Tolose: Jean Boude, 1611), p. 154.

[124] For details on these see Jean Imbert, *La Pratique Judiciaire, tant civile que criminelle* (Paris: Robert Fouet, 1616), pp. 700–1 and Pierre François Muyart de Vouglans, *Institutes au droit criminal, etc.* (Paris: Le Breton, 1757), pp. 459–60. For sources describing the legal context of *lèse-majesté* in the late Renaissance, see BNF MS 4745, fols. 143, 152–3; and BNF MS Dupuy 558, fols. 5–39, 81–119. For modern studies of this term, see G.A. Kelly, 'From Lèse-Majesté to Lèse-Nation: Treason in Eighteenth-century France', *Journal of the History of Ideas*, 42: 2 (1981), 269–86; Ralph E. Giesey, Lanny Haldy and James Millhorn, 'Cardin Le Bret and Lese Majesty', *Law and History Review*, 4 (1986), 23–54; and Jacques Chiffoleau, 'Le crime de lèse-majesté, la politique et l'extraordinaire. Note sur les collections érudites de procès de lèse-majesté du XVIIe siècle français et sur leurs exemples médiévaux', in *Les procès politiques (XIVe-XVIIe siècle*, ed. by Yves-Marie Bercé (Rome: École française de Rome, 2007), pp. 577–657.

[125] Claude Le Brun de La Rochette, *Les Procès civil, et criminel, contenans la methodique liaison du droit, et de la practique judiciaire, civile et criminelle* (Rouen: Pierre l'Oyselet, 1619), 'Le Proces criminel', I, pp. 132–3.

[126] La Rochette, *Les Procès civils*, p. 140.

[127] See the section on lese-majesty in Cardin Le Bret, *De la souveraineté du roy* (Paris: Toussaint Du Bray, 1632), pp. 527–55 (p. 528).

tried as breaching the public peace), blasphemy, perjury, and sorcery. Examples of *lèse-majesté au second chef* include sacrilege, interrupting Divine service, failing to observe religious festivals, and crimes against clergymen.[128] Théophile was convicted of *lèse-majesté divine* at his first trial *in absentia*. Whereas the *arrêts de mort* (death sentences) for Vanini and Fontanier did not specifically refer to *lèse-majesté divine*, Vanini was nevertheless convicted of blasphemy and atheism, whilst Fontanier's *arrêt* refers to blasphemy and abominations against God. The various crimes of which our three authors were accused thus clearly situated them at this apex of the early modern French criminal hierarchy for which the punishment was death, as well as within the wider polemical connotations of *libertinage* with which all three were tarnished in print.

Criminal trials could be instigated by the discovery of a criminal *in flagrante delicto* by a magistrate, by denunciation, by a collective report (for example, by a crowd of witnesses in a public space), or at the request of a king's attorney general or one of his *substituts* (*à la requête du procureur général*). Vanini appears to have been denounced by young gentlemen to whom he had revealed his irreligious beliefs in private. Fontanier was first denounced by a number of the 'students' who had attended his private lectures, before being caught in the act of dictating his unorthodox lessons by the *lieutenant criminel* Antoine d'Aguesseau in person. The *arrêt* from Théophile's first trial *in absentia* (19 August 1623) shows that proceedings had been carried out 'sur la plaincte faicte par le Procureur général du roy et livres par luy représentez' ('on a complaint filed by the king's attorney general and books produced by him for the court').[129]

Following a denunciation, the Tournelle or the Grand' Chambre would decide whether to appoint *commissaires* (commissioners) to gather evidence against the accused. According to one contemporary legal manual, the choice of *commissaires* would usually be a pairing of 'un des anciens avec un des jeunes' ('one of the elder and one of the younger magistrates').[130] This gathering of evidence, in a process similar to a modern-day police investigation, was termed the *instruction,* and those selected to carry out this task were said to *instruire* (to instruct) the trial. It is worth noting a distinction from the modern understanding of a 'trial' in certain countries. We might consider that a modern trial begins with the defendant appearing in court, in a series of 'hearings' in front of a jury, and that the prior gathering of evidence to build a case constitutes the pre-trial preparations of a police investigation. In the early modern French system, however, this gathering of evidence through interrogations of the accused and the hearing of oral witness

[128] Vouglans, *Institutes*, pp. 430–54. For further distinctions, see for example Joos de Damhouder, *Practique judiciaire des causes criminelles* (Anvers: Jehan Bellere, 1564), pp. 58–63.

[129] AN X 2A 217 quoted in Lachèvre, *Procès*, p. 143.

[130] See E. Girard, *Trois livres des offices de France* (Paris: Estienne Richer, 1638), p. 304, which dates this regulation to Charles VII's ordinance of 1446, article 20.

testimony was considered part of the trial itself (*le procès*). The results of these investigations—which were written in French rather than Latin owing to an ordinance by Louis XII in 1510—were the *informations* on the case, whilst the dossiers that these formed were sometimes termed *sacs* (sacks) in reference to the sealed sack bags in which they were kept.[131]

The *information* largely took the form of gathering witness testimony in private, the collation of which was known as the *recollement*.[132] The accused would be presented with witnesses in order to hear the testimonial evidence against them, in a form of court hearing termed a *confrontation*. As we shall see in more detail with Théophile's trial, these confrontations were heavily weighted against the accused. Testimony could only be rejected by the accused as invalid (termed a *reproche*) for a small number of reasons. The defendant was required to make these objections without legal counsel, before the witness's statement had been read out, and without the defendant even being informed of the crime for which they were on trial.[133] The secrecy surrounding the Parlement's business was not without its critics in the early modern period. The magistrates Jean Constantin, Pierre Du Moulin, and Pierre Ayrauld, for example, were vocal opponents of the secrecy surrounding criminal trials and the accused's limited ability to claim *reproches* against the witnesses.[134] Yet as Houllemare has demonstrated, this secrecy could also protect the accused against the danger of external pressure being placed on witnesses, whilst also allowing the Parlement 'à renforcer la distance entre la justice du roi et le monde profane' ('to reinforce the distance between the king's justice and the world of the profane').[135] In order to maintain a record of due process, written witness depositions as well as transcripts of the *confrontations* were read back to both parties, who then signed these in order to validate their accuracy. This final stage in the collation of oral testimony is signified by the typical closing line of trial transcripts of the period: *lecture faite, a persisté* ('after the reading, persisted').

[131] As stated earlier, several of these elements still exist in the modern French criminal justice system. An engraving by Abraham Bosse—'L' Étude du procureur'—shows these *sacs* hanging from the wall of a lawyer's office (BNF Est., Ed 30).

[132] Esmein, *Histoire de la procédure*, p. 140; *Cours élémentaires*, p. 417; Arlette Lebigre, *La Justice du Roi: La vie judiciaire dans l'ancienne France* (Paris: Albin Michel, 1988), p. 186.

[133] Shennan, *The Parlement*, p. 67; Lebigre, *La Justice du Roi*, p. 191. In practice, however, defendants of high social standing could hire a *procureur* to assist in their case, whereas defendants might learn of the charges against them through earlier sentences or simply through gossip. According to Guillaume Jaudin, 'le stille le plus ordinaire est, que le criminel ne soit averty des tesmoings jusques à ce que la confrontation, d'iceulx se face contre luy' ('the most common means [of confronting witnesses with the accused] is for the criminal not to be informed about the witnesses until they are face to face in the confrontation': Guillaume Jaudin, *Traité de tesmoings et d'enquestes* (Paris: La veuve Françoys Regnault, 1555), pp. 25–6). See also Bernard Automne, *La Conference du droict francois avec le droict romain* (Paris: Nicolas Buon, 1610), p. 445.

[134] See Esmein, *Histoire de la procédure*, pp. 159–65.

[135] Houllemare, *Parlement*, p. 122.

The hearing of witnesses and *confrontations* marked the end of a trial's *instruction*. Throughout this phase, the trial's actors were limited to the prisoner, the two magistrates designated as *commissaires* to carry out the *instruction* and to interrogate the accused, and any witnesses called for a deposition or a *confrontation*.[136] At this point there were two distinct transitions in the trial: from oral to written evidence, and from two *commissaires* to a full panel of judges. The mass of written evidence—which even in the trial of an author of multiple texts such as Théophile was largely comprised of testimony and interrogation records—was collated in the trial's *sac*. A magistrate who had not taken part in the interrogations, *information*, or *recollement* (owing to an ordinance from May 1579) was selected to serve as the *rapporteur* (reporter). His task was to organise a presentation of the documents, to guide the judges through the findings of the *information*, and to offer his opinion on the value of each piece of evidence.[137] Crucially, he was expected to perform these tasks without revealing his own judgement on the case as a whole.[138] When Théophile's *arrêt* states that a verdict was reached 'sur le rapport de M. Deslandes' ('on the report of Guillaume Deslandes'), this merely confirms that Deslandes had been tasked with presenting the contents of the *sac* to his colleagues, rather than indicating that the judges were persuaded by Deslandes's own views which, at least in theory, he was not supposed to reveal.

As early as July 1490, an ordinance by Charles VIII had decreed that during deliberations over a verdict, judges were to be heard in silence by their peers. The only two individuals who were allowed to interrupt proceedings were the *premier président* and the *rapporteur* who, with his superior knowledge of the evidence, was permitted to alert the assembly to an *erreur de fait* (a factual error) committed by a judge during his speech, following an ordinance by Charles VII in 1446.[139] The *rapporteur* also spoke first during the deliberations, thereby detracting somewhat from his impartiality in presenting the evidence.[140] According to the Edict of

[136] On the analogy of the Parlement as a theatre, see Houllemare, *Parlement*, pp. 439–86. On theatrical representations of sovereign judgement, see Hélène E. Bilis, *Passing Judgement: The Politics and Poetics of Sovereignty in French Tragedy from Hardy to Racine* (Toronto, Buffalo, NY, and London: University of Toronto Press, 2016).

[137] See Henri III's 'Ordonnance sur les états généraux de Blois' (1576), article 130, in Isambert, *Recueil général*, XIV, p. 413. It would require a separate study to confirm to the extent to which norms such as these were respected. On 11 May 1605, for example, the *procureur général* Jacques de La Guesle wrote a letter to chancellor Pomponne de Bellièvre regarding an upcoming trial, and noted that 'le rapporteur et jusqu'à ceste heure Instructeur du proces est Monsieur Scarron' ('the reporter and up until now the instructor of the trial is Mr Scarron': BNF MS Fr 15898, p. 39^{r}).

[138] 'Ordonnance sur les états généraux de Blois' (1576), article 130, in Isambert, *Recueil général*, XIV, p. 413. See also Esmein, *Histoire de la procédure*, p. 149; Margolf, *Religion*, p. 153; and Shennan, *The Parlement*, pp. 64–70.

[139] Desmaze, *Le Parlement*, p. 507; Girard, *Trois livres*, p. 26.

[140] The *rapporteur* habitually spoke last until the sixteenth century. From this period onwards, he was more likely to speak first, and the order in which the wider panel of judges spoke was at the discretion of the *président* (Shennan, *The Parlement*, p. 65). Furthermore, in the Parlement de Toulouse the *rapporteur* was allowed to interrogate the accused. See Silverman, *Tortured Subjects*, pp. 38–9.

Moulins (1566), the *rapporteur* could also stand in for the *greffier* (the court clerk) in writing down the judgements and *arrêts* of the courts when these were read aloud, and an *arrêt* was not considered valid without the signature of the *rapporteur* and one of the *présidents*.[141] In addition to the *rapporteur*, the *procureur général* or one of his *substituts* could also present their views (*leurs conclusions*), which consisted largely in the points of law they considered to have been raised during the case. The opinions which held particular sway in the outcome of a trial were therefore those of the *rapporteur*, the *procureur général*, and in Vanini's and Théophile's trials, the *premier président du parlement* due to his seniority in the court.

Before considering their verdict based on these various forms of evidence and legal counsel, the full complement of judges assigned to a case could assemble for a final interrogation of the defendant, which was termed an *interrogatoire sur la sellette*. It was this final questioning of the accused, in front of a panel of individuals tasked with voting on a verdict, which perhaps most closely resembles our modern image of a criminal trial. The judges then reached their verdict, and the *arrêt* was read out to the accused. Taking place shortly before the judges' deliberations, the final *interrogatoire sur la sellette* was usually the first time that the defendant was brought before his or her judges. Prior to this, they would have been examined by the two *commissaires* in charge of the *instruction*, and any witnesses summoned for a *confrontation*. The type of legal and performative arena in which a defendant was examined, relative to the stage of the criminal process, thus serves as a useful context for evaluating an author's rhetorical strategies and wider forms of self-defence. For as we have seen, a typical early modern French criminal 'trial' (*procès*) included the *commissaires*' initial gathering of written and testimonial evidence, as well as their interrogations of the accused and confrontations with witnesses, and not solely the final hearing (the *interrogatoire sur la sellette*) in which the accused had the opportunity to defend themselves before their judges.[142] For the most part, then, the trial transcripts analysed in Part II more closely resembled the modern questioning of a suspect by the police, rather than the dramatic appearance of a prisoner before an imposing panel of judges in a courtroom.

This in turn leads us to outline the definition of 'trial records' in this study.[143] Arrivals at the Paris Conciergerie prison were recorded in the *registres d'écrou* (registers of incarceration), which are the only records in our Parisian corpus held

[141] See the 'Édit de Moulins' (1566), articles 63 and 65, in Isambert, *Recueil général*, XIV ii, p. 206.

[142] To give a recent example illustrating this perhaps pedantic yet significant conceptual difference: Harold J. Cook's illuminating study on Descartes asserts that 'Théophile de Viau's trial occurred in 1625.' This claim only describes the final stages of the trial (the *interrogatoire sur la sellette* and the deliberations on the verdict), whilst ignoring the majority of the *instruction* which began on 4 October 1623 (Harold J. Cook, *The Young Descartes: Nobility, Rumour, and War* (Chicago, IL: University of Chicago Press, 2018), p. 154).

[143] On the following remarks, see Alfred Soman, 'Petit guide des recherches dans les archives criminelles du Parlement de Paris à l'époque moderne', *Histoire et Archives*, 12: 1 (2002), 61–79.

by the Archives de la Préfecture de Police as opposed to the Archives Nationales. The *écrous* provide a number of details including the prisoner's name, their address, their crime, the sentence passed against them (for appeal hearings), the Parlement's verdict, and the date of the *arrêt*. The transcripts of the defendant's interrogations, as well as those of witnesses and the defendant during *confrontations*, constitute the *minutes d'instruction*. The final *interrogatoires sur la sellette* were kept in a separate register, known as the *plumitifs du conseil de la Tournelle*.[144] Both of these interrogation series were recorded in notoriously difficult handwriting which, for Soman, may have been a deliberate attempt to maintain the secrecy of the Parlement's records.[145] In addition these sources outlined by Soman, I have also utilised another series—the *conclusions du procureur général du roi*—to shed new light on Théophile's trial including the discovery of a new witness. Although largely written according to a standard template, the resultant *arrêt* provides an overview of the case in question, a summary of the defendant's crimes, a description of their punishment, and the signature of both the *rapporteur* and the leading *président* judging the case. Finally, the Toulouse Capitoulat kept a register of significant cases tried in the city for the benefit of future *capitouls*: the *Annales des capitouls de la ville de Toulouse*. Although not strictly trial records (as they were neither produced by the trial process, nor did they feed into or influence the verdict), they are nonetheless legal records, kept by the city's magistrates, which constitute one of the few remaining archival sources on Vanini's trial.

In the previous chapter we noted that a word history of *libertin* could make little gains into the oral history of the term's use. The trial records outlined above, however, offer a comparatively larger array of sources on the reception of libertine authors spanning the literary and the legal, the textual and the oral. On the one hand, the initial and final records of a trial—the *écrou* and the *arrêt*—provide textual manifestations of the law courts' engagement with authors according to a relatively inflexible template of standard phrases. On the other hand, the transcripts which form the investigative element of the trial provide valuable records of the oral cultures inhabited by the defendants. Our corpus includes authors' responses to questions on their texts, their rhetorical strategies when faced with witnesses and the conversational tones set by these (including records of laughter, shouting, mumbling, tears, and even body language), as well as verbal accounts of gossip and the sharing of audacious texts in the streets and taverns of Paris. Thus, from a literary perspective, the 'allure of the archives' derives from their potential as repositories of 'auditory memory' and 'captured speech' relative to the commercial

[144] The *minutes* are held in AN X 2B 1174–1318; whereas the *plumitifs* can be found in AN X 2A 907–1154 (Soman, 'Petit guide', 61). For clarity, this study will differentiate between these two series by referring to the *minutes d'instruction* as interrogations and confrontations, and the *plumitifs du conseil de la Tournelle* as *interrogatoires sur la sellette*.

[145] Soman, 'Petit Guide', 72.

and social lives of texts, their writers, and their readers, all of which can often prove more elusive than those of later historical periods.[146]

Our authors' interventions into the world of literature were brave steps into a minefield of impassioned conflicts between Jesuits and Gallicans; between supporters of Louis XIII's new reign and Condé's grievances as expressed through pamphlet literature; between the emerging Concini faction and those loyal to the marginalised king; and even between proud chambers of justice with rival institutional jurisdictions. As will become clear, none of our three authors could escape being situated within this fractured political landscape through their literary production; whether it be Vanini's Italian origins, Fontanier's link to the Concinis through his apparent Judaism, or Théophile's Huguenot origins, his choice of patrons, and the ideological sympathies of his judges. The courts in which they were tried were more than mere extensions of an absolutist royal prerogative to suppress dissidence through exemplary punishment. The jurisdictions and competences of individual courts may not have been cogently or exclusively defined, but they were a highly organised, professional, and erudite body of magistrates. Their task was to judge the criminal culpability of a subversive author in terms of the intellectual content of the work, the means through which the text was disseminated, and the extent to which its authorial identity could be equated to (and therefore punished through) the writer stood before them. Yet for all their elevated social status and advanced learning, the magistrates were no less fallible than the idealised mechanisms of criminal procedure to which they looked for guidance. Using extant court records, private letters, memoirs, and printed pamphlets, Part II will explore how the criminal trials of subversive authors were not only the legal interpretations of philosophical, theological, and social concepts as embodied by literary texts. They were also emotionally charged and often politicised arenas, in which the decision between life and gruesome death was decided through intellectual, rhetorical, and personal contests between human wills.

[146] On these notions of the archives as auditory memory and captured speech, see Arlette Farge, *The Allure of the Archives*, trans. by Thomas Scott-Railton, with a foreword by Natalie Zemon Davis (New Haven, CT: Yale University Press, 2013), pp. 61–3; and in particular Chapter 6: 'Captured Speech' (pp. 79–113). For a more recent study of these sonic perspectives on literature, see Nicholas Hammond, *The Powers of Sound and Song in Early Modern Paris* (University Park, PA: Pennsylvania State University Press, 2019).

Part II

Libertine Author Trials

3

Hiding in Plain Sight: The Trial of Giulio Cesare Vanini (1618–19)

La parole découvre le cœur pour si fort qu'on veuille le cacher.

Words betray the heart no matter how much we wish to hide it.

[Nicolas de Saint-Pierre[1]]

S'il y avoit un Dieu je le prierois de lancer un foudre sur le Parlement comme du toute injuste et inique; et s'il y avoit un diable, je le prierois aussi de l'engloutir aux lieux sous terrains: mais parce qu'il n'y a ny l'un ny l'autre, je n'en feray rien.

If there were a God I would pray to Him to throw lightning down on the Parlement for its injustice and iniquity; and if there were a Devil I would also pray that he would swallow it up beneath the Earth. But because neither of them exists, I shall do nothing.

[Giulio Cesare Vanini[2]]

[1] AMT MS BB 278: *Annales des capitouls de la ville de Toulouse*, vol. VI, 'chronique 290' (Nicolas de Saint-Pierre, 1618), fols. 13–14 quoted in Marcella Leopizzi, *Les Sources documentaires du courant libertin français—Giulio Cesare Vanini* (Fasano: Schena; Paris: Presses de l'université de Paris-Sorbonne, 2004), p. 101. The quotations in this chapter from archival documents also are referenced with transcriptions in modern sources where available. I am grateful for permission to reproduce in this chapter material previously published in Adam Horsley, 'Remarks on subversive performance at the trial of Giulio Cesare Vanini (1618–1619)', *Modern Language Review*, 110: 1 (2015), 85–103, and to Géraud de Lavedan of the Archives Municipales de Toulouse for allowing me to consult his transcriptions of the *capitouls' chroniques* for 1618 and 1619.

[2] *Le Mercure françois, ou, La Suite de l'histoire de la paix*, 25 vols (Paris: Jean Richer, 1613–43), V (1619), p. 65.

In late October 1619, the printers and booksellers of Toulouse were paid an ominous visit, the likes of which the city had not seen for over seventy years. Following legislation by the Parlement de Toulouse against prohibited books, the stock found on their premises was meticulously examined by theologians headed by the *vicaire général* (vicar general) Jean de Rudèle. Ninety books were confiscated from twelve different booksellers, before being purged from the city by fire on 12 and 19 November.[3] The seized books ranged from Protestant Bibles and Pierre Charron's *De La Sagesse*, to the works of François Rabelais and Mathurin Régnier. Rudèle was soon to return to the book merchants with more specific prey in mind.[4] The Parisian authorities had alerted him to a dangerous Italian author of atheistic texts condemned by the Sorbonne. This author had since taken flight from Paris, after anti-Italian sentiment had reached fever pitch prior to Concini's assassination. His name was Giulio Cesare Vanini. Having sought the learned views of a number of theologians on the matter, Rudèle passed an ordinance banning the sale of Vanini's texts on 16 July 1620, before ordering all booksellers and printers to surrender their remaining copies on 13 August.[5] The critical judgements of the theologians concurred on both the criminal content of his texts, as well as the dangerous means through which their author's views were disseminated:

> Monsieur, j'ai parcouru Jules Caesar. C'est un livre très pernicieux: il enseigne l'athéisme, en faisant semblant d'estre un grand protecteur de l'honneur de Dieu.
>
> Sir, I have looked over Jules Caesar's work. It is a most pernicious book, in which he teaches atheism by pretending to be a great protector of God's honour.[6]

> Monsieur, en ce que j'ay peu veue de ce livre, je le juge fort dangereux et pernitieux; en iceluy sont subtilement enseignés les principes de l'athéisme.
>
> Sir, from what I have been able to see of this book, I find it to be extremely dangerous and pernicious, for it cunningly teaches the principles of atheism.[7]

Their conclusions painted a worrying picture of a deceitful atheist, capable of donning the mask of outward Catholic orthodoxy in order to spread an insidious message. Echoing later criticisms of the credulous Sganarelle in Molière's *Dom*

[3] Didier Foucault, *Un Philosophe libertin dans l'Europe baroque: Giulio Cesare Vanini 1585–1619* (Paris: Honoré Champion, 2003), p. 488.

[4] For more detail on these printers and booksellers, see Francesco Paolo Raimondi, *Giulio Cesare Vanini Nell'Europa del Seicento, seconda edizione aggiornata* (Rome: Aracne, 2014), pp. 777–808.

[5] See these legislative acts in Raimondi, *Vanini Nell'Europa del Seicento*, pp. 834–8. On Rudèle and a second text sought in the raids of August 1620—Jacques Ferrand's *Traicté de l'essence et guérison de l'amour ou de la mélancholie érotique* (Tolose: Jacques Colomiex et Raymond Colomiez, 1610)—see Didier Foucault, 'Jacques Ferrand, la 'mélancolie érotique' et la censure des théologiens toulousains', *Cahiers du Centre d'étude d'histoire de la médecine*, 17 (2009), 39–61.

[6] ADHG MS 1 G 410, Jean Dupuy to Jean de Rudèle (July 1620) quoted in Raimondi, *Vanini Nell'Europa del Seicento*, p. 819.

[7] ADHG MS 1 G 410, Nicolas de Mauléon to Jean de Rudèle (July 1620) quoted in Raimondi, *Vanini Nell'Europa del Seicento*, p. 820.

Juan, another theologian summarised Vanini's work to Rudèle thus: 's'agit-il de confirmer la foi orthodoxe, il n'emploie que les arguments les moins forts, il néglige et réfute les meilleurs' ('when it comes to confirming the orthodox faith, he [Vanini] only uses the weakest of arguments, whilst neglecting and refuting the strongest').[8] It was not without irony that the theologians were struck by both Vanini's potentially subversive message and the duplicitous nature of his rhetoric. For less than two years previously, this most evasive figure had resided in Toulouse, rubbing shoulders with a number of high-ranking magistrates, aristocrats, and in particular their adolescent children. Not only this, but he had been burned alive and his ashes thrown to the wind by the Parlement de Toulouse on 9 February 1619, without any of the magistrates realising who he really was.

Although his texts remain relatively understudied, the figure of Vanini as a philosopher and teacher has become synonymous with the current of *libertinage érudit* prevalent in early seventeenth-century France, as have the numerous contemporary descriptions of his gruesome death.[9] The courage with which he defended himself at trial, and the reported audacity with which he subverted the expected performance of repetence at his execution, have earned this 'prince des libertins' a firm place in the company of 'les martyrs de la libre pensée' ('martyrs of free-thinking').[10] Like the ghost whom Rudèle was unknowingly chasing in the printshops of Toulouse, much of Vanini's story remains in shadow. His very identity escaped precise definition in contemporary accounts: he is described variously as Pompeo, Pomponio, or Pompinio Usciglio; Pomponier Usciglior; Lucilio or Luciolo Cesare; Giulio or Jules Cesare; not to mention the Latin name under which his two surviving works were published—Julius Caesar Vaninus—and his identity whilst a Dominican friar: brother Gabriele. His crimes provoked fear and loathing rather than a search for clarity from the authorities. The records of the wood purchased for the execution of this convicted atheist and blasphemer, for instance, describe its intended purpose as 'brusler Lucilio magissien et sorcier' ('to burn the magician and sorcerer Luciolo').[11] Vanini's journey across Europe was characterised by evasion from hostile and oppressive situations. By the age of

[8] Pélissier to Rudèle (July 1620) quoted in Foucault, *Vanini*, p. 489.

[9] See René Pintard, *Le Libertinage érudit dans la première moitié du XVIIe siècle* (Geneva: Slatkine, 2000). The most recent studies to associate Vanini with *le libertinage érudit* and other writers of the genre are *Giulio Cesare Vanini dal Tardo Rinascimento al Libertinisme érudit, Atti del Convegno di Studi (Lecce – Taurisano, 24–26 ottobre 1985)*, ed. by Francesco Paolo Raimondi (Galatina: Congedo, 2003); Foucault, *Vanini*; Jean-Pierre Cavaillé, *Dis/simulations. Jules-César Vanini, François La Mothe Le Vayer, Gabriel Naudé, Louis Manchon et Torquato Accetto. Religion, morale et politique au XVIIe siècle* (Paris: Honoré Champion, 2008); and Jean-Pierre Cavaillé, *Les Déniaisés: Irréligion et libertinage au début de l'époque moderne* (Paris: Classiques Garnier, 2013).

[10] Émile Namer, *La Vie et l'œuvre de J.C. Vanini: Prince des Libertins* (Paris: Vrin, 1980); Jules Barni, *Les Martyrs de la libre pensée* (Geneva: Les Principaux Libraires, 1862).

[11] AMT CC 216: 'Pièces à l'appui des comptes, 1618–1619' (26 March 1619), quoted in Raimondi, *Vanini Nell'Europa del Seicento*, p. 772.

thirty-three, he had disobeyed his superior in the Carmelite Order by refusing to abandon his studies at Padua; passed himself off as an Anglican convert whilst a guest of the Archbishop of Canterbury, only to escape imprisonment once his ruse had been discovered; published a pantheistic text in Paris at the very moment when anti-Italian sentiment was building up to the assassination of Concini; and had purportedly used his position as a tutor to corrupt young noblemen in Toulouse.

The legal documentation relative to Vanini's trial is limited to his *arrêt de mort* (death sentence) and brief notes made on the trial by pronvincial magistrates (the *capitouls*). The trial records themselves—witness depositions, interrogations of the accused, and confrontations between witnesses and the accused—have not been found. Émile Namer asserts that these were likely to have been burned in accordance with an edict enacted in 1614. Yet Pierre de L'Estoile's *Journal* reveals not only that this procedure was already practised as early as 15 October 1601, but that judges regularly decided to burn only part or none of the records of a given trial.[12] Furthermore, Vanini's *arrêt de mort* does not mention such a procedure, whereas those of the libertine writers Jean Fontanier and Claude Le Petit refer to this practice explicitly.[13] It is therefore possible that Vanini's trial transcripts may one day be discovered in the some 80,000 *sacs à procès* (trial sacks) of the Parlement de Toulouse which still remain to be catalogued.[14] Nevertheless, a careful and critical engagement with second-hand accounts written shortly after the trial allows us to comment on the legal procedures involved in Vanini's case.

This chapter begins by considering Vanini's daring misadventure in England, which itself ended in a form of trial before the Anglican authorities. The English investigations into Vanini's activities have survived in a much larger corpus of archival material than for his stay in Toulouse. As such, they are extremely useful sources with which to construct a picture of Vanini's conduct, his character, and his strategies of self-defence under interrogation. These can subsequently be used to evaluate extant and often second-hand accounts of his trial in France. To this same end, the present chapter will offer a flavour of Vanini's philosophy in relation to Catholic teaching as evinced in his texts; not least as these are relatively little known having yet to be translated into English or fully into French. Finally, we will consider the trial itself in terms of the nature of the accusations made against Vanini, and the abnormalities of the subsequent legal proceedings, using new conspiracy theories based on archival material previously unknown to scholars of Vanini.

[12] Namer, *Vie et l'œuvre*, pp. 199–200; Pierre de L'Estoile, *Journal de L'Estoile pour le règne de Henri IV*, ed. André Martin, 3 vols (Paris: Gallimard, 1958), II (1601–9), pp. 45, 155, 273; III (1610–11), p. 121; Francesco Paolo Raimondi, 'L'arrêt "de mort" contro Vanini: un documento enigmatico', *Bruniana & Campanelliana*, 17: 2 (2011), 585–96 (590).

[13] For writing his *Bordel des muses*, for example, Le Petit was sentenced to be 'bruslé vif avec son procès' ('burned alive along with his trial documents': Claude Le Petit, *Les Œuvres libertines de Claude Le Petit*, ed. by Frédéric Lachèvre (Geneva: Slatkine Reprints, 1968), p. L).

[14] Boris Donné, *Vanini: portrait au noir* (Paris: Allia, 2019), p. 17.

VANINI IN ENGLAND: A PRELUDE OF POLITICS AND DECEPTION

Vanini was born in Naples in 1585.[15] His meanderings across Europe began with him leaving his comfortable familial environment in order to study for his doctorate in civil and canon law. He took holy orders with the Carmelites under the name of brother Gabriele in 1603, and received his doctorate on 1 June 1606. Vanini's thirst for knowledge took him to Venice and Padoua, where he studied alongside a fellow Carmelite named Giovanni Ginocchio from 1608 to 1612. The Paduan *studio* had produced great proponents of natural philosophy such as Gerolamo Cardano and Pietro Pomponazzi, whose beliefs were considered to be irreligious by authors such as Garasse.[16] So great was the influence of such thinkers on Vanini that Guy Patin would later claim that 'tout son livre *De Arcanis naturae Dialogi* est dérobé de Scaliger *in Cardanum*, de Fracastor, et de Pomponace. Je vous assure que cela est très vrai, car je l'ai moi-même vérifié' ('all of his book *De Arcanis naturae Dialogi* is stolen from Scaliger's *in Cardanum*, from Fracastoro, and from Pomponazzi. I assure you that this is very true, as I have checked it myself').[17] Having been influenced by these writers, Vanini and Ginocchio ironically proved themselves to be more adept in the arguments of their theological adversaries.[18] Their Carmelite General Enrico Silvio, who shortly prior to Vanini's arrival had removed Paolo Antonio Foscarini from the Carmelite order, was hardly a sympathetic character for such free-thinking.[19] By 28 January 1612, Silvio had ordered Vanini and Ginocchio to leave Venice.

[15] For a condensed early biography on Vanini, see Didier Foucault, *1619: Vanini, un libertin sur le bûcher* (Portet-sur-Garonne: Éditions Midi-Pyrénéennes, 2018), pp. 6–14. For a more detailed account of this period of Vanini's life, see Foucault, *Vanini*, pp. 61–75, 92–5, 252–350.

[16] In his three levels of *libertin* books, Garasse places Pomponazzi on the first level and Cardano on the second (François Garasse, *La Doctrine curieuse des beaux esprits de ce temps* (Paris: Sebastien Chappelet, 1623), pp. 1013–14). On the influence of sixteenth-century rejections of scholasticism on Vanini, and traces of the Paduan school in his philosophical development, see Mark Bannister, 'Vanini and the development of seventeenth-century thought', *Seventeenth-Century French Studies*, 19 (1997), 25–36.

[17] [Guy Patin], *Patiniana* in [Gabriel Naudé and Guy Patin], *Naudaeana et Patiniana* (Paris: Florentin et Pierre Delaulne, 1701), p. 31.

[18] The English ambassador to Venice, Dudley Carleton, describes how 'They came now from Padoa from whence they are both removed by the Generall of their order the one to Naples the other to Pisa, and upon this reason because in questions of controversy they were growen to perfect on the opposite part, and were more industrious in confuting of Bellarmin though *disputative* only then [sic] was thought fitt for the liberty of this people' (Dudley Carleton to George Abbot (17 February 1612) in Raimondi, *Vanini Nell'Europa del Seicento*, p. 590).

[19] Francesco Paolo Raimondi, 'Filosofia della libertà e libertà del filosofare in Vanini. Dal Rinascimento all'Età moderna', in *Giulio Cesare Vanini: Filosofia della libertà e libertà del filosofare. Atti del terzo convegno internazionale di studi Vaniniani (Lecce – Taurisano, 7–9 febbraio 2019)*, ed. by Francesco Paolo Raimondi (Rome: Aracne, 2019), pp. 157–83 (p. 165). Foscarini's attempt to refute Copernicanism with Holy Scripture (*Lettera sopra l'opinione de' Pittagorici e del Copernico* (Napoli: Lazaro Scoriggio, 1615)) was added to the *Index Librorum Prohibitorumin* in 1616.

It was at this point that Vanini demonstrated a presence of mind and a political awareness which he would later employ in Paris, before fatally disregarding it in deciding to travel to Toulouse. Rather than return to the confines of their monastery, Vanini and Ginocchio looked to England as a potential shelter from Catholic oppression. As Francesco Paolo Raimondi observes, Franco–English relations had reached a Cold War climate in which both sides of the confessional divide were 'trincerati dietro le rispettive cortine di reciproca impermeabilità e di intolleranza, diffidenti l'uno verso l'altro, [e] impegnati in una guerra di prestigio' ('entrenched behind their respective curtains of mutual impermeability and intolerance, distrustful of one another, [and] engaged in a war of prestige'). In such conditions, large-scale military hostilities had been replaced by mutual surveillance and the clandestine encouragement of respective faiths behind enemy lines, with an aim to erode the opposing camp's image of superiority and unity.[20] Fortunately for historians, Vanini's actions in England also engendered a considerable corpus of candid and often ciphered letters in England, Venice, and Rome.[21] It is also possible that Vanini hoped to find a greater level of freedom of expression in Protestant England than he had hitherto found in the Papal States. The two Italians offered their services to the Venetian ambassador Dudley Carlton, as well as the Archbishop of Canterbury George Abbot. In what Raimondi has termed the 'clima di contrapposizione ideologica tra mondo riformato e mondo cattolico' ('climate of ideological opposition between the reformed world and the Catholic world'), Vanini and Ginocchio were to be small victories in a propaganda war against the papists, and potentially active combatants.[22] Impressed by their learning, eloquence, and the apparently sincere motives for their conversion, Carleton facilitated the Italians' voyage to England via Holland. By 15 June 1612 the pair had arrived in London, where on 28 June:

> [the] two Carmelites made a publike confession of theyre fayth and conversion, with an abjuration of theyre former errors [...] at the Italian Church, in the

[20] Raimondi, *Vanini Nell'Europa del Seicento*, p. 264, which alludes to this need to 'presentare di se un'immagine di compattezza e di superiorita'. Foucault also compares this situation to the Cold War in *1619*, p. 8.

[21] Letters pertaining to Vanini's brief flirtation with Anglicanism were originally published in a number of nineteenth-century journal articles. The first study offering a collation of these, and which is most often cited in modern studies, is Émile Namer, *Documents sur la vie de Jules-César Vanini de Taurisano* (Bari: Adriatica Editrice, 1965). Namer's valuable contribution to the field, however, is neither complete nor free from transcription errors. The definitive collation of archival documents pertaining to Vanini, containing 206 archival documents from 23 institutions, is the 'appendice' in Francesco Paolo Raimondi, *Giulio Cesare Vanini Nell'Europa del Seicento, seconda edizione aggiornata* (Rome: Aracne, 2014). This second edition augments the original 2005 edition by over three-hundred pages.

[22] Raimondi, *Vanini Nell'Europa del Seicento*, p. 259. According to a letter from Guido Bentivoglio, 'il Re gli vuole applicare a scrivere contro i Cattolici' ('the king [James I] wishes to set him to writing against the Catholics': Guido Bentivoglio to Scipione Borghese (1 August 1612) in Raimondi, *Vanini Nell'Europa del Seicento*, p. 618).

> presence of a great assemblie whereof Sir Francis Bacon was the man of the most marke.[23]

It is from this stay in England, between 1612 and 1614, that we encounter the earliest first-hand testimony to Vanini's simulated piety and his attempts to dissimulate critiques of religious belief. As well as being provided with lodgings at Lambeth Palace, Vanini was granted the freedom to visit other English cities and to preach at the Italian church in London, Mercer's Chapel. The Archbishop attested that:

> In the time of his abiding with mee, hee frequented prayers, received the Communion twise or thrice in my Chappell, preached diverse times at the Italian Churche in London, especially at his first coming.[24]

As time went on, Vanini's attitude appears to have changed. If Dudley Carleton is to be believed, Vanini's disenchantment with England was a gradual process which began with a sincere desire to convert to Anglicanism, rather than being a strategic ruse from the beginning. Abbot, for his part, claimed to 'have reason to suspect that some Instrument of a forraigne Ambassador hath ben tampering with them, and hath both with money and faire promises corrupted them'.[25] The death in September 1612 of Vanini's former Carmelite superior Enrico Silvio—whose 'hard measure' and 'fury' Vanini accredited as his reason for fleeing to England—may have led him to reconsider his self-imposed exile.[26] Another possible explanation may simply have been the relatively mediocre situation in which Vanini found himself. As he made the transition from an honoured guest to an indebted member of Abbot's entourage, he was now shocked to find himself 'faine to make his owne bed and sweep his chamber, things he was never put to in

[23] John Chamberlain to Dudley Carleton (12 July 1612) in Raimondi, *Vanini Nell'Europa del Seicento*, p. 610.

[24] George Abbot to Dudley Carleton (16 March 1614) in Raimondi, *Vanini Nell'Europa del Seicento*, p. 704. Carleton elsewhere described Vanini early in his stay as 'less papal than any other Italians' (Dudley Carleton to George Abbot (25 May 1612) in Raimondi, *Vanini Nell'Europa del Seicento*, p. 603).

[25] George Abbot to James Montagu (4 February 1614) in Raimondi, *Vanini Nell'Europa del Seicento*, p. 661.

[26] George Abbot to James Montagu (4 February 1614) in Raimondi, *Vanini Nell'Europa del Seicento*, pp. 660–1: 'He now also sayeth, that he was never otherwise then a Papist in his faith; and that there comming into England was for nothing but to avoyd the hard measure which their Generall used to them'; George Abbot to William Trumbull (30 March 1614) in Raimondi, *Vanini Nell'Europa del Seicento*, p. 695: '[they] confess that they were always Papists, and that they came from Italy to escape the fury of their Generall, which lay very hard on them'. Vanini himself makes a similar claim in the *Amphitheatrum*: 'fatale mihi fuit ut ab Henrico Sylvio injustissime laesus Britaniam inviserem' ('My fate was that, most unjustly betrayed by Henricus Silvius, I should be obliged to visit Britain': Giulio Cesare Vanini, *Amphitheatrum aeternae providentiae* (Lyon: Antoine de Harsy, 1615), p. 285 quoted in Richard Copley Christie, 'Vanini in England', *The English Historical Review*, 10 (1895), 238–265 (244)). See also Raimondi, *Vanini Nell'Europa del Seicento*, p. 306.

the place whence he came'.[27] Chamberlain had predicted as early as June 1612 that the novelty of the two Italian converts would soon wear off:

> To tell you freely my opinion as far as I understand this busines, thought yt cannot be denied but that you have don a very goode and charitable worke in reducing these straying sheep, yet I doubt you will reape no great thanks on either side, for I find our bishops here not very fond of such guests, and thincke they might have enough of them, yf they could provide them maintenance, so that unles they be very eminent, and men of marke, they shall find little regard after a small time.[28]

Morover, in a letter to Carleton's secretary Isaac Wake, Vanini suggests that he had high hopes of trading the crumbs from Abbot's table for a more stable and prestigious position which failed to materialise:

> Le do nova di me come, lodato il sig[no]re, sto bene, et allegro, accarezzato dall'Ill. mo Mons.re Archiv[escovo] che di continuo mi tiene nella sua tavola, dandomi speranza, ch'un giorno ricapiterà bene la mia persona.
>
> I am well and happy, thanks be to God, and am treated most affectionately by my lord the most illustrious archbishop, who constantly entertains me at his table and gives me hope that one day he will confer some office upon me.[29]

Vanini may have had other reasons for developing misgivings towards Abbot, who did not turn out to be the liberal Protestant patron he had hoped for. Rather, as Raimondi notes, he was a 'puritano radicale, intransigente e fanatico [...] egli era l'esponente piu radicaledell'ala puritana' ('a radical, intransigent and fanatical puritan [...] he was the most radical exponent of the Puritan wing').[30] Despite his tolerance of moderate nonconformity within the Anglican fold, Abbot had sought 'to deflect the attention of those who were critical of his tolerance of non-schismatic nonconformity and also to assure the king of his orthodoxy and zeal' by obtaining the death sentence against the heretics Edward Wightman and Bartholomew Legate in 1612, immediately prior to Vanini's arrival.[31] He even

[27] John Chamberlain to Dudley Carleton (14 January 1612) in Raimondi, *Vanini Nell'Europa del Seicento*, p. 638.

[28] John Chamberlain to Dudley Carleton (17 June 1612) in Raimondi, *Vanini Nell'Europa del Seicento*, p. 609.

[29] Vanini to Isaac Wake (9 October 1612), quoted in Raimondi, *Vanini Nell'Europa del Seicento*, p. 629, translated in Christie, 'Vanini in England', 247. Christie is a little too confident in Vanini's religious belief in blaming Abbot for his subsequent actions: 'it is by no means improbable that, had [Vanini's and Ginocchio's] expectations been fulfilled, their faith would have been confirmed, and that Vanini, instead of perishing at the stake at Toulouse, might have lived and died a member of the Church of England, and might probably have persuaded himself and his patrons that he was actuated by no other motive than that of zeal for the truth. But the benefices did not come' (248).

[30] Raimondi, *Vanini Nell'Europa del Seicento*, p. 261.

[31] Susan Holland, 'Archbishop Abbot and the problem of puritanism', *The Historical Journal*, 37:1 (1994), 23–43 (36). See also David Como and Ian Atherton, 'The Burning of Edward Wightman: Puritanism, Prelacy and the Politics of Heresy in Early Modern England', *English Historical Review*, 120: 489 (2005), 1215–50; and Foucault, *Vanini*, p. 292.

wished to be informed of those who attended multiple places of worship in order to learn from different preachers, 'since this absence was suggestive of subversive tendencies'.[32] Such actions give credence to the subjective description of Abbot by the Ambassador Extraordinary to London, Pedro de Zúñiga, to Philip III of Spain:

> The Archbishopp of Canterburie is the greatest persecutor that ever hath bine here amongst the Catholikes, and the most zealous in his sect and because hee seeth that hereby hee well pleaseth the kinge his master he useth much diligence to make his obstinacie more appeare.[33]

It was whilst lodging with this 'persecutor', who 'above all [...] believed in order and due respect for authority',[34] that Vanini began to let slip his mask of pious simulation and to contemplate offering himself once again as a repentant convert, this time to the Catholic Church in Rome. A certain Ascanio Baliani da Palermo, the lay reader of Mercer's Chapel who had previously been investigated for plotting against the crown, attested to Vanini's and Ginocchio's good conduct to Isaac Wake in December 1612.[35] By March 1614, however, Ascanio had prevented Vanini from preaching at Mercer's Chapel. Although professional rivalry and a need to redeem himself in the eyes of his Anglican hosts were likely to have influenced his actions, it is notable that Ascanio, according to the Archbishop, 'hath long kept Julius Caesar from preaching in his Churche, as taking him to bee of no religion, but a profane person, a filthy speaker, and a grosse fornicatour'.[36] Though perhaps merely a fictitious catalogue of sins of thought, word, and deed, this association of impiety with sexual immorality was common in the early modern period, from descriptions of purported witches through to libertine authors. The first recorded accusations against Vanini, then, were both situated within a historically recognised trend in early modern thought, as well as largely concerned with his speech acts. These recriminations were soon followed by others. The watchful eyes of the Archbishop began to see Vanini for who he really was. He later informed the Bishop of Bath James Montagu how:

> About 3 moneths since I by a secret meanes understood that the elder of them [Vanini] had written to Rome and I had cause to conjecture that it was for an

[32] Susan Holland, 'George Abbot: The Wanted Bishop', *Church History*, 56:2 (1987), 172–87 (174–5).

[33] Pedro de Zúñiga to Philip III of Spain, 10 August 1612 in Raimondi, *Vanini Nell'Europa del Seicento*, p. 620.

[34] Holland, 'The Wanted Bishop', 174.

[35] See Isaac Wake to Dudley Carleton (5 December 1612) in Raimondi, *Vanini Nell'Europa del Seicento*, p. 634: '[Ascanio] in the name of the whole congregation acknowledged unto me the obligations that they all had unto your L[ordshi]p for the 2 Carmelites, whose good behaviour hath got them much credit and donne your L[ordshi]p as much honour.' On Ascanio, whom Raimondi describes as being a 'figura losca, priva di scrupoli e di dubbia moralità' ('a shady, unscrupulous character of dubious morality'), see Raimondi, *Vanini Nell'Europa del Seicento*, pp. 271–3.

[36] George Abbot to Dudley Carlton (16 March 1613) in Raimondi, *Vanini Nell'Europa del Seicento*, p. 706.

> absolucion for their departure from their Order. I caused one to speake with him thereabout; and hee gave such an answeare, as I cold not contradict; but yet thought fitt to carrye an eye over them.[37]

In this instance, Vanini's request for an absolution from the Catholic Church was made within the apparent safety afforded by the secrecy of private written correspondence. With the aid of his spies, Abbot was able to infiltrate this hidden sphere of communication which had hitherto managed to exist outside of the control of the Anglican authorities. Writing of Vanini's visit to Oxford, which began on 19 January 1614, Abbot added in the same letter that:

> There to one or twoe who had ben in Italy he lett fall divers wordes declaring his dislike to our religion [...] together with divers other both unfit and untrue speeches without honesty or shame. And divers intimacions he gave of his purpose to withdrawe himself out of England with all speed.[38]

It is striking that the true nature of Vanini's beliefs appears to have been relatively undetectable to the English. It was the Italian lay reader at Mercer's Chapel who noticed Vanini's questionable views. It was in the company of *one or two who had been in Italy* that Vanini dared to reveal his private thoughts. Finally, Abbot describes to Carleton how 'to one who had formerly bene a Roman Priest, and lived much in Italy, hee opened himselfe that hee was in hart a Papist'.[39] Whatever his outward marks of piety may have been, Vanini was reluctant to conform to the religious orthodoxy of his environment, and felt comfortable revealing his inner thoughts when in private conversation with his fellow countrymen. These are significant traits of Vanini's character from a well-documented period of his life, whilst the scant surviving documentation from his final years suggest that he repeated these same social patterns in his relationships with the upper classes of Toulouse.[40]

The sequence of events leading to Vanini's and Ginocchio's escape from England remains unclear. Did Vanini begin to arouse suspicion amongst his hosts and fellow Italians, thereby tipping the balance in his own mind towards a tactical flight back into the Catholic fold? Or, did he first decide to leave the disillusionment of England behind him, which subsequently led him to be more careless in his

[37] George Abbot to James Montagu (4 February 1614) in Raimondi, *Vanini Nell'Europa del Seicento*, p. 659.

[38] George Abbot to James Montagu (4 February 1614) in Raimondi, *Vanini Nell'Europa del Seicento*, p. 660.

[39] George Abbot to Dudley Carleton (16 March 1614) in Raimondi, *Vanini Nell'Europa del Seicento*, pp. 705–6.

[40] On Vanini's dissimulation of atheism according to contemporary sources, see Mario Carparelli, *Il più bello e il più maligno spirito che io abbia mai conosciuto. Giulio Cesare Vanini nei documenti e nelle testimonianze* (Padova: Il Prato, 2013), pp. 321–47; Francesco Paolo Raimondi, '*Simulatio* e *dissimulatio* nella ecnica vaniniana della composizione del testo', in *Giulio Cesare Vanini e il libertinimso*, ed. by Francesco Paolo Raimondi (Galatina: Congedo, 2000), pp. 77–126; Cavaillé, *Dis/simulations*, pp. 39–66.

speech within private conversation? Whatever the case may have been, by 31 January 1614 Vanini had quite literally packed his bags—stealing two suitcases in order to sell their contents to raise funds, before discarding them into the Thames instead.[41] Before he could escape, Vanini was detained, imprisoned at the Lambeth Palace Gatehouse for forty-nine days, and subjected to three interrogations on 2 and 3 February. As Cavaillé remarks, there is a curious contradiction in Vanini's defence during his interrogations at the hands of the English.[42] In his first interrogation, Vanini donned the the mask of outward conformity, and performed according to the anticipated tenets of his hosts by assuring them of his loyalty to the Anglican faith. Yet in the second interrogation Vanini abandoned this defence, instead revealing what Abbot termed his 'strange dissimullation'.[43] According to Abbot, Vanini brazenly admitted that in renouncing the papacy ('quod Papatui renunciasset') he had merely meant that he renounced any interest in becoming the pope; and that in vowing to embrace the faith of the Church of England, he had meant 'the same faith which the Church of England possessed a hundredth or two hundredth years ago'![44] Vanini quickly revealed his conversion to have been motivated by personal and political gain, leading Abbot to seek an exemplary punishment for his relapsed convert by sending him to Virginia, or 'into the Barmudes, there to digge for his living'.[45]

What could have led Vanini to reveal himself so readily, as one church historian described him later in the century, to be 'neither good dough nor good bread'?[46] Cavaillé has proposed that such a volte-face may have been situated within the wider context of equivocation, when used as a rhetorical strategy of self-defence in trials for crimes against religion in England.[47] The answer may alternatively be found by constructing a profile of Vanini's character through a comparison between these events and his later conduct in Toulouse. In the

[41] On this incident and for a wider analysis of Vanini's subsequent interrogations, see Francesco Paolo Raimondi, 'Le Retour de Vanini dans le monde catholique à la lumière de nouveaux documents londoniens', *La Lettre Clandestine*, 11 (2001), 135–55.

[42] See Cavaillé, *Dis/simulations*, pp. 60–2. For the records of Vanini's interrogations, see pp. 673–7.

[43] George Abbot to James Montagu (4 February 1614) in Raimondi, *Vanini Nell'Europa del Seicento*, p. 661.

[44] For Abbot's account of Vanini's interrogations, see George Abbot to Dudley Carleton (16 March 1614) in Raimondi, *Vanini Nell'Europa del Seicento*, p. 706. Due to the crudeness of such wordplay, lacking the subtlety of Vanini's refined writing style, Raimondi suspects that this account may be 'inquandro in realtà nelle strategie d'attacco del Primate e sono il prodotto delle sue elucubrazioni mentali' ('in fact contaminated with Abbot's attack strategies, and the product of his mental reflections', p. 296).

[45] George Abbot to Dudley Carleton, 16 March 1614 in Raimondi, *Vanini Nell'Europa del Seicento*, p. 707.

[46] Thomas Fuller, *The Church History of Britain from the birth of Jesus Christ until the year 1648*, ed. by J.S. Brewer, 6 vols (Oxford: Oxford University Press, 1845), V, p. 531 quoted in Calvin F. Senning, 'Vanini and the Diplomats, 1612–1614: Religion, Politics, and Defection in the Counter-Reformation Era', *Historical Magazine of the Protestant Episcopal Church*, 54: 3 (1985), 219–39 (232).

[47] See Cavaillé, *Dis/simulations*, pp. 63–4.

Lambeth Palace Gatehouse in which he was a prisoner, as later at the Place du Salin in Toulouse, Vanini simply saw no point in continuing his performance when reports of his private conversations had reached the Archbishop, or when his plans to flee England and to seek a pardon from Rome—which the Holy Office was aware of as early as April 1613—were so close to coming to fruition.[48] The 'mocking impertinence'[49] with which Vanini responded to the questions put to him by his captor is entirely in keeping with one observer's description of him as 'è prigione pronto (dice) al Martirio' ('in prison, and ready (so he says) for martyrdom').[50] The pleasure he took in his audacity, and the boldness with which he was able to abandon his *strange dissimullation* as Abbot's prisoner, bear a striking resemblance to the end of Vanini's story. At his final trial in Toulouse, Vanini would again spectacularly throw down the mask of conformity once the death sentence had been read against him. His almost jovial demeanour on his way to the stake strongly mirrors his conduct in England, and his alleged readiness to die a martyr's death at Abbot's hands foretold his final mockery to the crowds gathered for his execution: 'allons, allons allaigrement mourir en Philosophe' ('come, come, let us die joyfully as a Philosopher').[51] The time had not yet come, however, for Vanini to face justice with such subversive gaiety. Between 5 and 10 March 1614 he was able to escape the Gatehouse, leaving works by Machiavelli and a pornographic text by writer Aretino as a final calling card to be found by Abbot.[52] As Chamberlain related to Carleton:

> I heard lately that the two friers you sent over are returned to theire vomit and prove notable knaves, professing now that they were never other than Romish catholikes wherin they will live and die. [...] They have solicited theyre return, and to be receved again into theyre mother church by the Venetian Ambassador here and other meanes at Rome.[53]

48 See 'Congregazione del Santo Uffizio' (11 April 1613) in Raimondi, *Vanini Nell'Europa del Seicento*, p. 645: 'Apostatarum ordinis Carmelitarum fugitivorum Londini petentium absolutionem in foro fori dari facultatem confessario ipsos absolvendi a quibusvis casibus, liberari a votis religionis at subijci ordinario ut vivere possint in habitu presbiteri secularis' ('Apostates of the Carmelite Order who are fugitives in London, seeking absolution and the opportunity to confess, to be exempt from any reprisals, to be freed from religious vows in order to lead decent lives as secular priests'). By October, Vanini was informed that he would be allowed to return to the Catholic fold (see Senning, 'Vanini and the Diplomats', 228–9; Foucault, *Vanini*, p. 310).

49 Senning, 'Vanini and the Diplomats', 221.

50 Giovanni Francesco Biondi to Dudley Carleton (18 February 1614) in Raimondi, *Vanini Nell'Europa del Seicento*, p. 681, translated in Christie, 'Vanini in England', 260.

51 *Histoire véritable de tout ce qui s'est faict et passé depuis le premier Janvier 1619 jusques à present, tant en Guyenne, Languedoc, Angoulmois, Rochelle, qui Limousin & autres lieux circonvoisins* (Paris: Nicolas Alexandre, 1619), p. 10.

52 'And I do finde both by the books themselves, and by their owne confession, that the greatest matter which they have studyed for many months past, were the workes of Petrus Aretinus, and of Macciavelli in Italian. So virtuous was their disposition' (George Abbot to Dudley Carleton (16 March 1614) in Raimondi, *Vanini Nell'Europa del Seicento*, p. 707). See also Raimondi, 'Le Retour de Vanini', 140.

53 John Chamberlain to Dudley Carleton (3 February 1614) in Raimondi, *Vanini Nell'Europa del*

Having fled England, Vanini ignored calls from the pope to return to Italy.[54] He instead sojourning briefly in Genoa (late October 1614–19 January 1615), before arriving in Lyon in March 1615, attracted either by possible family connections to the area or having noted a strong Italian presence when passing through the city in 1614.[55] It was there, in June of that same year, that he published the first of his two texts that have survived to the present day: the *Amphitheatrum*.

THE *AMPHITHEATRUM AETERNAE PROVIDENTIAE* (1615) AND *DE ADMIRANDIS* (1616)

Vanini's two surviving texts have not been translated into English and are thus far less studied than his trial.[56] Given that these nonetheless constitute the most credible testimonies to his thought in the absence of surviving trial records, it is worth considering these texts briefly in order to contextualise Vanini's subsequent actions as a legal defendant. It seems likely that Vanini hoped to publish the *Amphitheatrum* in England. He fled Lambeth Palace in March 1614, yet his 300-page text consisting of fifty philosophical exercises had already been read and approved for print in Lyon by 6 June 1615. The *Amphitheatrum* outwardly seeks to defend Catholic orthodoxy by refuting the tenets of atheists, epicureans, and the stoics.[57] According to the *Amphitheatrum*, the pursuit of knowledge of Divinity is akin to Divinity itself:

Seicento, p. 671. Abbot, for his part, wrote bluntly of the two relapsed converts in June 1614 'it is well we are rid of them' (George Abbot to William Trumbull (17 June 1614) in Raimondi, *Vanini Nell'Europa del Seicento*, p. 738).

[54] See 'Congregazione del Santo Uffizio' (28 August 1614) in Raimondi, *Vanini Nell'Europa del Seicento*, p. 740, which states that the pope 'suadeat dictum Julium Cesarem, ut redeat in Italiam'. For details on Vanini's movements between England and Lyon, see Raimondi, *Vanini Nell'Europa del Seicento*, pp. 341–66.

[55] Foucault makes the case for a branch of Vanini's family in Lyon in *Vanini*, pp. 350–73. Raimondi, however, more cautiously suggests that in the absence of evidence tying Vanini's family to this branch, we can only assume that he returned to Lyon having encountered networks of Italians there in 1614 (see Raimondi, *Vanini Nell'Europa del Seicento*, pp. 360–1).

[56] Vanini's texts have been translated into Italian in the following critical editions: Giulio Cesare Vanini, *L'anfiteatro dell'eterna provvidenza*, ed. by Francesco Paolo Raimondi and others (Galatina: Congedo, 1981); Giulio Cesare Vanini, *I meravigliosi segreti della natura*, ed. by Francesco Paolo Raimondi (Galatina: Congedo, 1990); and Giulio Cesare Vanini, *Tutte le opere*, ed. by Francesco Paolo Raimondi and Mario Carparelli (Milan: Bompiani, 2010). The only translation of Vanini's texts into French—*Œuvres philosophiques de Vanini*, ed. by Xavier Rousselot (Paris: Charles Gosselin, 1842)—is both incomplete and inaccurate.

[57] Cavaillé and Foucault have suggested that the title of this work was inspired by that of another Latin text which claimed to combat atheism: Lenaert Leys, *De providentia numinis et animi immortalitate* (Antwerp: Ex officina Plantiniana, 1613) ('Introduction', in *Kairos*, 12 (1998): *Vanini: Libertinage et philosophie à l'époque moderne*, ed. by Jean-Pierre Cavaillé and Didier Foucault (Toulouse: Presses Universitaires du Mirail, 1998), p. 16). For Hubert Dethier, however, Vanini took inspiration from Heinrich Khunrath's *Amphitheatrum sapientiae oeternae solius verae etc.*, which was first published in 1609 (See Hubert Dethier, 'J.-C. Vanini et *L'Amphitheatrum* de Heinrich Khunrath', in *Giulio Cesare Vanini dal Tardo Rinascimento*, pp. 75–107).

> Quaeris a me, quid Deus sit? Si scirem, Deus essem, nam Deum nemo nouit, nec quid sit quisquam scit, nisi ipsemet Deus: possumus tamen quasi per nubem solis lumen, quid ipse sit, per eius opera aliquantum cognoscere: non tamen per ea melius intelligimus, quam per ea, que negamus nos intelligere.
>
> You are asking me what is God? If I knew, I would be God himself, for no one knows God nor what he is, except God himself: we could, however, catch a glimpse of what God is somewhat through his work, like sunshine piercing through a cloud as it were. However, we do not understand [Him] better through these [His works] than through those things we say we do not understand.[58]

In alluding to the possibility of a knowledge of God through nature, Vanini's claim could be seen to assert that the nature of God is beyond mere human understanding, and that anyone who claims to possess such knowledge is by implication claiming divine intellectual status. Furthermore, in reducing humanity's understanding of God's nature to His works—that is to say His creations in nature—Vanini completely overlooks the role of Holy Scripture in human relationships with God, and suggests a dangerous similarity between the divine and the natural. The *Amphitheatrum* is a fine example of *dissimulatio*, in which the author's inner agreement with the heterodox ideas discussed in the work are disguised by outward condemnation. On Machiavelli, for instance, Vanini writes that:

> [Macchiauellus] existimat miracula excogitari, et confingi a Principibus ad subditorum informationem, et a Sacerdotibus ad lucri, honorisve aucupium. At putridum hoc mendacium est, ut ex tuo ipsius ore patefaciam serve nequam.
>
> [Machiavelli] thinks that miracles have been devised by leaders to tame their subjects and by priests for the sake of profit or honours. But this was a filthy lie from your own mouth, as I will now demonstrate, wicked slave.[59]

Vanini typically expounds subversive views on theological matters whilst taking care to attribute them to a source other than himself. He then expands on them in such a way that his own agreement with them is often evident, before condemning and insulting them in ironic and exaggerated terms. A further example of this technique, where Vanini has previously detailed Pomponazzi's theory that miracles are caused by celestial bodies, reads as follows:

> Consentit Hieronymous Cardanus, qui ab astris legum ducit originem, in lib. De supplemento Alman. Cap. 22. Ita loquitur (ô os impudentissimum, ô linguam execrandam, ô Sermones inquinatissimos, ô voces detestandas) [...] O sacrilegam doctrinam, et ex hominum consortio eliminandam: ô impietatem nefariam, et post homines natos inauditam?

[58] Giulio Cesare Vanini, *Amphitheatrum aeternae providentiae* (Lyon: Antoine de Harsy, 1615), pp. 8–9.
[59] Vanini, *Amphitheatrum*, p. 50.

> Gerolamo Cardano agrees, he who draws the origin of law from the stars, in the De supplemento Alman. 22. And so he says (oh most foolish language, detestable tongue, most corrupted speeches, loathsome words!) [...] Oh sacrilegious doctrine that men must abolish: oh criminal impiety unheard from men until now![60]

Vanini also presents the views of more ambiguous, generalised adversaries such as atheists:

> Aliqui molles Athei in dubium vocare miraculorum certitudinem non verentur, quia nullum unquam viderint, immo et maiores natu interrogarint, an de aliquo miraculo testimonium certum proferre possint: illi vero auditos, non oculatos testes esse se responderint. De visu deponunt aniculae, et de quibusdam levissimis, quae transferri ad naturalem causam commodè depossunt.
>
> A few mild atheists do not shy away from calling into question the evidence for miracles because they have never seen any. Indeed, when asking their elders whether they can provide any reliable testimony, they reply only by reporting what they heard, having not witnessed it with their own eyes. Old women report what they see, which is based on such tenuous ground that a natural cause could easily account for such miracles.[61]

Again, Vanini goes into great detail in describing the views and justifications of those he claims to be refuting in the text. In a similar rhetorical strategy to that for which Garasse would later be criticised, Vanini's official explanation of the liberal inclusion of unorthodox religious views is that he has quoted these in order to refute them:

> Sed valeant iterum abeantque Astronomorum fabulae et deliria, quae detestari me prorsus execrarique profiteor, in medium tamen adduxi, ut inertia praeceptorum ineptiaque patefieret.
>
> Be gone and farewell to all this nonsense and all these senseless tales from the astronomers, which I declare to detest and utterly abhor; even though I did bring them up, it was for the sole purpose of exposing the idleness and absurdity of their precepts.[62]

Vanini's writing strategies appear to have worked, as the *Amphitheatrum* was not condemned in his lifetime. This is all the more remarkable given the text's apparent popularity. Despite efforts by Church authorities to confiscate copies of the *Amphitheatrum* in the summer of 1620, there are at least 119 copies of this text in existence today.[63]

[60] Vanini, *Amphitheatrum*, pp. 53, 57.
[61] Vanini, *Amphitheatrum*, p. 72.
[62] Vanini, *Amphitheatrum*, p. 77.
[63] Nicholas S. Davidson, '"Le plus beau et le plus meschant esprit que ie aye cogneu": Science and Religion in the Writings of Giulio Cesare Vanini, 1585–1619', in *Heterodoxy in Early Modern Science and Religion*, ed. by John Brooke and Ian Maclean (Oxford: Oxford University Press, 2005), pp. 59–79 (p. 62).

Vanini arrived in Paris in early July 1615. By September the pope had once again given orders for the papal Nuncio Ubaldini to convince Vanini that he had nothing to fear from returning to Italy.[64] It was in Paris that Vanini met Adrien de Monluc, comte de Cramail, and the maréchal François de Bassompierre.[65] Vanini found patronage and employment as an almoner in Paris to the Swiss Guards responsible for the king's protection. These were commanded by Bassompierre, who maintained close relations with the queen mother Marie de Médicis and Concini, as well as poets including Maynard, Saint-Amant, Laugier de Porchères, Racan, and Balzac. A gallant seducer whose name was a byword for good looks, a curious mind, and a speaker of five languages, Bassompierre was an obvious source of protection for a free-thinker such as Vanini.[66] In 1616 Vanini published *De admirandis*—which he dedicated to Bassompierre—with the Lyonnais printer Adrien Périer. *De admirandis* is a more forthright publication of Vanini's beliefs, and is comprised of a series of dialogues between Julius-Caesar and his student, Alexandre.[67] At the beginning of the text, Alexandre admits his confusion regarding numerous philosophical arguments which he has studied for several years at the Sorbonne. He then asks the character Julius-Caesar (henceforth J.C. in accordance with the text's original typography) to clarify these points for him:

> Hoc igitur ipsum est, quòd etiamsi multos annos in Sorbonicis Scholis sim philosophatus, ita tamen arduis et abstrusis quibusdam difficultatibus, tanquam Chrysippeis retijs irretitus detineor, ut si me ab ijs explicueris, non recuso quin Philosophorum Deus in posterum vociteris.
>
> Therefore it is a fact that even though I have practised philosophy for so many years at the Sorbonne, I am nonetheless being held down by such laborious and intricate difficulties, as if entangled in Chrysippus's net, so that if you were to extract me from them, I would be inclined to hail you as the God of philosophers for generations to come.[68]

[64] See Raimondi, *Vanini Nell'Europa del Seicento*, pp. 367, 751 ('Congregazione del Santo Uffizio', 24 September 1615). Ubaldini's already strained ties with Vanini appear to have been severed as of August that year.

[65] Marcella Leopizzi, 'Vanini en France: perspectives de recherche', *Studi Francesi*, 168 (2012), 505–12 (505–6); Vanini, *Tutte le opera*, p. 307.

[66] 'On appeloit partout Bassompierre ceux qui excelloient en bonne mine et en propreté' ('"Bassompierre" was commonly used to refer to all those of particularly healthy complexion and cleanliness': Tallemant des Réaux quoted in Foucault, *Vanini*, p. 391). On Bassompierre see Noel H. Williams, *A Gallant of Lorraine: François, Seigneur de Bassompierre, Marquis d'Harouel, Maréchal de France (1579–1646)*, 2 vols (London: Hurst and Blackett Ltd., 1921); Paul M. Bondois, *Le Maréchal de Bassompierre* (Paris: Albim Michel, 1925); and Foucault, *Vanini*, pp. 389–402.

[67] For François Berriot, Alexandre represents Bassompierre in this text (François Berriot, *Athéismes et athéistes au XVIe siècle en France*, 2 vols (Lille: Cerf, 1984), II, p. 811). There is however no evidence to suggest this, nor that Bassompierre was Vanini's student. For Henri Busson, Alexandre represents Vanini's younger self (Henri Busson, *Le Rationalisme dans la Littérature Française de la Renaissance (1533–1601)* (Paris: Librairie Philosophique J. Vrin, 1957), p. 317).

[68] Giulio Cesare Vanini, *De admirandis nature regine deaeque mortalium arcanis* (Paris: Adrien Perier, 1616), pp. 1–2.

From the beginning, Vanini situates the arguments he is to develop as contrary to the learning of the Sorbonne, and as an alternative source of knowledge to that of widespread Catholic orthodoxy, as the overtly pantheistic title of the work suggests. An overarching concern of the work is to explain supposed miracles and supernatural occurrences. To give one example: Vanini describes a man who, unhappy with his lodgings at an inn, released certain vapours from a glass into his room and slipped away without paying. When a servant was sent upstairs to investigate he returned dancing uncontrollably, and was unable to stop even when restrained:

> Huius rei causam daemonum arti omnes referebant, non modo Catholici, sed et etiam Huguenoti. Iulius vero Caesar irridebat huius modi aniles fabellas, et naturali causae omnia adscribebat. Credendum enim est pedisequum illum exsiccati Phalangii puluerem habuisse: Eamque vino infundisse. Qui primus ascendit hospitiolum, illius vini haustum assumpsit, moxque à sede prosiluit. Si igitur Tarentulae morsus ad saltandum incitat, cur illius exusti puluis vino dilutus idem non operabitur?
>
> Everyone, not only the Catholics but also the Huguenots, would ascribe his doings to the work of demons. But Julius Caesar would laugh at these old wives tales and would regard everything as being the result of a natural cause. Indeed, it is to be believed that there was an attendant who had a venomous spider ground into powder and mixed it up with wine. He who went up first to the soldier's lodging had some of this wine and soon leapt up out of his seat. Indeed, if a tarantula's bite causes one to jump, why would some dried powder of this insect diluted in wine not produce a similar effect?[69]

No place is accorded to the supernatural or the divine in J.C.'s explanation of the servant's dancing. On the contrary, it is a subscription to the belief in demons which obscures the truth from both Catholic and Protestant perspectives. Vanini gives a similar scientific explanation for weeping statues. Having first offered scientific explanations pertaining to humidity, he then goes on to ask

> An tepidus aer, quem Notus, vel mulierculae basiolis perspirarunt, imaginibus ad hærescens, nactus superficiei frigus aliquod, in guttas, quas plebs appellat lachrymas, coactus est? [...] An depicti Deunculi cutem belvino, vel humano cruore clam tingendam? vel sanguineam undam per canaliculos ad Idoli oculos confluendam sacriocolae curarunt? mox templi ianuis apertis occurrens plebecula obstupuit, naturalemque euentus causam non agnoscens, miraculum dixit.
>
> Is it not either some mild air or some women's little kisses producing some steam which the Notus wind compels to be fixed until something cold brings it up to the surface [of the eye] in drops, recognised by the common people as tears? [...] Have priests not taken care to moisten the outer surface of the little god they have fashioned with animal or human blood, or to make blood-like liquid flow from

[69] Vanini, *De admirandis*, p. 447.

> little channels in the eyes of the idol? Whereupon the common people, rushing through the open doors of the temple, were amazed, and, unaware that the event had a natural cause, proclaimed it a miracle.[70]

Beginning with a scientific explanation devoid of any theological explanation, Vanini moves from speculation to accusation by suggesting that priests are the true mechanics behind this event, recognised by the crowd as a miracle. This opposition of religious credulity and logical explanation from the natural world would become a favourite tenet of the *libertins* as the century progressed.[71] To the contemporary reader, the consequences of such thinking would have been obvious. In expressing doubt regarding the existence of demons—that is to say the existence of supernatural, malevolent beings in the terrestrial world—Vanini implicitly contests the existence of benevolent supernatural beings such as angels.[72] As P.G. Maxwell-Stuart notes, 'the Church itself could not deny the existence of demons for to do so it would also have to deny the reality of spirits, both good and bad, upon which so much doctrine relied'.[73] To deny the existence of spirits in the world thus ran the risk of denying numerous passages in Holy Scripture as well as the coming of Christ.[74] Vanini's accusations against the priesthood are so audacious that they are not to be found in the explanation of miracles given by other *libertins* writing in the first quarter of the seventeenth century, with the exceptions of Guy Patin and the anonymous author of the *Antibigot*.[75]

This said, Vanini stresses his knowledge of the Church's official view on certain matters and, where possible, highlights that he is not infringing any ecclesiastical ban on expressing certain opinions. He asserts on the subject of oracles, using Pomponazzi as an additional means of protecting himself from accusations of impiety, that 'A Daemone haec omnia facta esse, pro certo habetur apud Christianos: Attamen inficiari nullum extat Ecclesiae decretum, non est veritus Magister meus Pomponatius id insiciari' ('All these facts proceed from spirits; this is known for certain amongst Christians. Yet because there is no existing decree from the Church confirming such a belief, my master Pomponatius was not afraid to deny this interpretation').[76] When asked whether it is true that one can be cured of rabies by walking into the Church of St Vitus, J.C. replies 'Cum tamen Romana Ecclesia nihil super hoc definierit, vereor ne conficta fabella sit' ('However, since

[70] Vanini, *De admirandis*, pp. 410–11.

[71] Henri Busson, *La Pensée religieuse française de Charron à Pascal* (Paris: Vrin, 1933), p. 316.

[72] Further such refutations of the existence of demons are given on pp. 427, 472.

[73] Martin Delrio, *Investigations into Magic*, ed. and trans. by P.G. Maxwell-Stuart (Manchester and New York: Manchester University Press, 2000), p. vii.

[74] As Garasse asserts: 'dire qu'il n'y a point de Diables au monde, c'est une proposition qui a son passe-port parmy les Libertins' ('to say that there are no devils in the world is a proposition which has credit amongst the libertines': Garasse, *Doctrine*, p. 843).

[75] Busson, *Rationalisme*, p. 318.

[76] Vanini, *De admirandis*, p. 379.

the Roman Church has not ruled on the subject, I fear it is only some forged story').[77] Finally, on the resurrection of the dead, J.C. tells Alexandre that:

> E mortuis resurrexisse credo illos duntaxat, quos sacra pagina, et Ecclesiasticae historiae Pontificiis confirmatae decretis comemorant: Cæterum quos tu supra retulisti, non verè mortuos, sed morbo aliquo correptos fuisse arbitror.
>
> I only believe in those who rose again from death if their resurrection is mentioned in Holy Scriptures or is placed on record by Pontifical decree as listed by established Ecclesiastical history: the rest of the cases to which you referred were not really dead but only seized by some illness, I think.[78]

In emphasising that his work is in line with Church legislation, Vanini provides himself with a defence against any accusations of irreligion that might be brought against him, whilst at the same time underlining the fact that the Church can act as a barrier to discussion and learning. He suggests that the Church operates in a world in which the laws of logic and science do not apply, and that its teachings are disconnected from our reality which can be better explained through scientific materialism. Vanini uses other libertine strategies to deflect criticism from his texts, particularly the discussion of the views of the other.[79] Alexandre recalls having met an atheist in Amsterdam who claimed that Christianity was designed to snare the weak-minded:

> Addebat in quacunque Religione licet absurdissima, ut Turcarum, Indorum, et nostri saeculi Haereticorum, adesse infinitum propemodum stultorum numerum, qui pro patriae Religionis tutela ultro se tormentis obijcerint: et cum plura Indorum exempla ex historicis recitasset, Anglo-Calvinistarum meminit, qui Marianis temporibus pro Calvinismo vitam cum morte commutare non exhorruerunt. Tunc ego Dei zelo inflammatus, appellavi illum Antechristum.
>
> He added that in any religion, even the most absurd one such as that of the Turks, the Indians and, nowadays, the heretics, there is a number of almost infinite measure of foolish men who subject themselves voluntarily to torture for the protection of the state religion: he started listing many examples of Indian martyrs in history, he recalled the Anglo-Calvinists, who, under Mary's reign, were not afraid to give their lives for their religion. Then I, burning with devotional spirit for God, called him the Antichrist.[80]

This atheist is mentioned again later on in the text:

> Consimilem errorem quidam Atheus Absterodami [sic] tuebatur. Has ille, nescio quo misero, funestoque fato compulsus, delvrans euomebat blasphemias. Ex

[77] Vanini, *De admirandis*, p. 450.
[78] Vanini, *De admirandis*, p. 456.
[79] A term I borrow from Joan DeJean, *Libertine Strategies: Freedom and the Novel in Seventeenth-century France* (Columbus, OH: Ohio State University Press, 1981).
[80] Vanini, *De admirandis*, pp. 356–7.

> Bibliorum contextu infertur, Daemonem Deo præualere reluctante Dei voluntate Adamum, et Evam totumque Genus humanum ad interitum duxit.
>
> In Amsterdam, an atheist upheld a similarly erroneous view. Compelled by some wretched and grim fate, he started spewing out blasphemies. From the biblical context, it can be inferred that the devil can prevail upon God since it is against God's will that he drove Adam and Eve and all humankind to ruin.[81]

Although Vanini is careful to ensure that his characters always refute the atheism they have been exposed to, these reported conversations serve as a means to disseminate criticisms of the Catholic Church. This strategy did not escape the attention of Garasse and Antoine Rémy – two enemies united in their hostility towards Vanini:

> Il seme ses impietez sous un pretexte honorable, de renverser l'Atheisme. [...] Dans ses Dialogues il discourt en parfaict Atheiste, en sorte neantmoins qu'il peut desadvoüer toutes les impietés, d'autant qu'il se couvre d'un sac mouïllé, il les fait prononcer à son disciple Alexandre, il les rapporte à quelque mal'heureux Atheiste [...] il se void que ce n'est autre que luy mesme qui nous estalle ses blasphemes sous le nom de quelque homme de paille.
>
> He sows his impieties under the honourable pretext of overthrowing atheism. [...] In his *Dialogues*, he discusses matters as a perfect atheist, yet in such a way that he can disavow all impieties, and all the more for covering himself with a wet bag: he has his disciple Alexander say them, he attributes them to some miserable atheist [...] it is evidently none other than himself [Vanini] who spreads his blasphemies before us under the name of some straw man.[82]
>
> C'est le stratageme qu'observoit Lucilio Vanino, lequel soubs le nom d'Alexandre estalloit ses maximes Impies, affin que ne les écrivant comme sortis de son fonds, on n'eut point tant de prise sur luy.
>
> This is the strategy observed by Lucilio Vanino, who under the name of Alexandre spread his impious maxims, so that not writing them as if they have come from himself, there is nothing that can be held against him.[83]

Vanini's strategy of dissemination consists in the apparent refutation of atheism which in reality, in the eyes of the supposedly wiser *libertin* reader, is an audacious

[81] Vanini, *De admirandis*, p. 420.

[82] Garasse, *Doctrine*, pp. 785, 1008. A similar remark would later be made by Jacques Gaultier: 'Aucuns de ses adherans le voulurent excuser, et rejetter ses maximes impies sur la Philosophie, qui luy servoit de pretexte, mais son impieté fut peremptoirement descouverte, quand il luy fut ordonné de faire amande honorable' ('some of his followers wanted to excuse him, and to reject his impious philosophical maxims, which served as a pretext, but his impiety was abruptly discovered when he was ordered to perform the *amende honorable*': Jacques Gaultier, *Table chorographique de l'état du christianisme* (Lyon: Pierre Rigaud, 1626), p. 878).

[83] [Antoine Rémy], *Défense pour Etienne Pasquier vivant conseiller du Roi, et son Avocat Général en la Chambre des Comptes de Paris, contre les impostures et Calomnies de François Garasse* (Paris: Thomas de la Ruelle, 1624), pp. 841–2.

lesson in atheism in which the characters' defences of Catholicism are merely packaging to be dispensed with. For Alexandre, the most intriguing of religious questions are often those which concern ancient pagan societies. Such questions are a thinly disguised encouragement for the reader to relate Vanini's views to contemporary French society. Believing himself to be protected against accusations of atheism, Vanini delivers biting condemnations of supposedly Pagan religions, describing them as:

> Sed à principibus ad subditorum paedagogiam excogitatas, et à sacrificulis, ob honoris et auri aucupium, confirmatas non miraculis, sed scriptura, cuius nec originale vllibi adinuenitur, quae miracula facta recitet, et bonarum ac malarum actionum repromissiones polliceatur, in futura tamen vita, ne fraus detegi possit. [...] Atque ita rusticana plebecula in servitio coercetur, ob metum supremi numinis, quod omnia inspiciat, et paenis, et praemijs cuncta compenset aeternis.
>
> Laws devised by princes to educate their subjects and by priests for the sake of honours and wealth, defined not by miracles but by the scriptures whose original source is nowhere to be found, listing miracles and to the good and the wicked making promises, which are yet to be fulfilled in a future life, so that the fraud can remain undisclosed. [...] And thus the common masses living in the country are coerced into servitude, through the fear of the greatest god that sees all and, with eternal punishment and reward, weighs everything in the balance.[84]

Vanini goes far beyond a mere scientific or rational explanation of supposedly divine acts, by suggesting that religions and purported evidence substantiating their claims are purely human in origin. When asked about omens and fortune tellers—again, amongst the pagans—J.C. describes them as 'fabulae sunt, sacerdotumque illusiones ad laudis et lucri aucupium, Ethnicorumque Principium figmenta ad Plebem metu superni Numinis in servitio detinendam' ('invented stories, deceitful stories devised by priests to attract praise and profit, fictions of heathen rulers concocted to hold the masses in servitude through the fear of God').[85] Continuing the similarities with the article on 'Prêtres' in the *Encyclopédie* some 150 years later, Vanini highlights that priests do not merely deceive the populace for their own personal gain. Instead, they are part of a wider conspiracy with leaders to subjugate the people.[86] If this collusion went undetected in Pagan societies, it was because 'ob publicae potestatis formidine allatrare Philosophi non audebant' ('by fear of the public, philosophers did not dare to protest').[87] Vanini's uses of the other thus demonstrate considerable

[84] Vanini, *De admirandis*, p. 366.
[85] Vanini, *De admirandis*, p. 412.
[86] See Paul-Henri Thiry, Baron d'Holbach, 'Prêtres', in *Encyclopédie, ou dictionnaire raisonné des sciences, des arts et des métiers, etc.*, ed. by Denis Diderot and Jean le Rond d'Alembert, 28 vols (Paris: Briasson, David, Le Breton et Durand, 1751–72), XIII (1751), pp. 340–1.
[87] Vanini, *De admirandis*, p. 391.

freedom of thought, and reveal an irony-laden critique of all that organised religion holds most sacred.[88]

As with the *Amphitheatrum*, the more transparent writing strategies in *De admirandis* were nonetheless effective, as the text was approved by two theologians from the Sorbonne.[89] Just one month later, the two theologians tasked with examining the text prior to its publication claimed that the published version contained dialogues other than those which they were asked to inspect. This was not in fact an uncommon occurrence of the time. It would not be until 1623 that Cardinals Richelieu and de la Rochefoucauld would attempt to install four dedicated censors—André Duval, Pierre Quedarne, Jacques Messier, and François de Saintpere—'pour dorénavant voir, lire et examiner toute sorte de Livres nouveaux concernant la Théologie, dévotion, et bonnes-mœurs' ('henceforth to see, read and examine all sorts of new books concerning theology, devotion, and moral standards').[90] Sensing a backlash against these reforms from their own university, these *docteurs* renounced their duties, and Louis XIII instead published an edict giving the power to nominate readers of such texts to the Chancellor or the keeper of the Seals in 1629.[91] When Vanini arrived in Paris in 1615, however, there was far less regulation of this aspect of the book trade. Writers and printers were free to choose which member of the Faculty of Theology read their works as *approbateurs* until 1623. As Roger Chartier and Henri-Jean Martin observe, this allowed alliances, divergent opinions, corruption, or internal rivalries within the Faculty of Theology to influence the outcome, let alone the fact that certain critical readings may have been undertaken in haste.[92] Whatever the circumstances of the initial approval of the two *docteurs*, their approbation was retracted and *De admirandis* was condemned by the Sorbonne on 1 October 1616.[93]

One contemporary source offers a further clue to Vanini's conduct in Paris. Writing slightly after the fact, in 1623 Marin Mersenne recalled the following:

> Sic enim Lutetiae Vaninum aiunt fuisse conatum ut Atheismum proseminaret, quippe qui vehementer in atheos prius insurgere et eos summopere detestari videbatur, id enim verbis acrioribus simulabat.

[88] Cavaillé and Foucault ,'Introduction', *Kairos*, p. 10.

[89] This irony did not escape the attention of Guy Patin: 'ce livre fut imprimé à Paris sans aucune difficulté, et approuvé avec éloge par deux Cordeliers Docteurs de la Faculté' ('this book was printed in Paris without difficulty, and was approved with praise by two Cordeliers who were doctors of the Faculty': *Patiniana*, p. 32).

[90] André Chevillier, *L'Origine de l'imprimerie de Paris: Dissertation historique et critique* (Paris: Jean de Laulne, 1694), p. 398. On this subject see pp. 389–406.

[91] Chevillier, *Origine de l'imprimerie*, pp. 404–6. See also Henri-Jean Martin, *Livre, pouvoirs et société à Paris au XVIIe siècle*, 2 vols (Geneva: Droz, 1999), I, p. 441.

[92] Roger Chartier and Henri-Jean Martin, *Histoire de l'édition française*, 4 vols (Paris: Fayard, 1989), I 'Le livre conquérant', p. 370.

[93] On this point, see Foucault, *Vanini*, pp. 416–19.

> They say that Vanini stayed on in Paris so that he could try to disseminate atheism, since to start with he appeared to attack atheists violently and to execrate them heartily, for he made a show of doing so in the harshest terms.[94]

This account parallels both Vanini's behaviour in England and the 'rhetoric of subversion' in his two surviving texts.[95] With anti-Italian sentiment on the rise in the months before Concini's assassination, having seen *De admirandis* condemned, and having began to let his mask of piety slip in private conversations, Vanini was forced to take flight once again.[96] Apparently undeterred from his habits by Louis XIII's ordinance against blasphemers enacted in November 1617, Vanini made the fatal mistake of choosing Toulouse as his place of refuge, though this decision may have been motivated by Bassompierre's links with this area of France.[97] It is only following the condemnation of *De admirandis*, then, that we might speak of Vanini as a persecuted author, and there is no evidence to suggest that his writings were condemned in England or Lyon. Even in Toulouse, seemingly one of the most inhospitable of environments for free-thought at the time, the defenders of religious and moral orthodoxy had difficulty in defining or even detecting Vanini's crimes.

RUMOUR, DISGUISE, AND SEDUCTION: VANINI IN TOULOUSE

Before turning to Vanini's final and fatal journey to Toulouse, it is worth outlining from the beginning the numerous early modern sources which comment on Vanini's trial and execution. These sources must be treated with varying degrees of caution. The two most reliable accounts are those written by individuals who were involved in the trial proceedings, or who clearly came into contact with someone who was. Pierre de Gramond, for example, was one of Vanini's judges. His son Gabriel-Barthélemy de Gramond refers to these events in his *Historia prostratae Ludovico XIII sectariorum in Gallia rebellionis* (Toulouse: Petrum Bosc, 1623), as well as his *Historiarum Galliae ab excessu Henrici IV libri XVIII* (Toulouse: Arnald

[94] Marin Mersenne, *Quaestiones celeberrimae in Genesim* (Paris: Sebastien Cramoisy, 1623), col. 671, quoted and translated in Francesco Paolo Raimondi, 'Vanini et Mersenne', *Kairos*, 12 (1998), 181–253 (225).

[95] Jean-Robert Armogathe, 'Giulio Cesare Vanini: una retorica della sovversione', in *Giulio Cesare Vanini: Dal testo all'interpretazione*, ed. by Giovanni Papuli (Taurisano: Edizioni di Presenza, 1996), pp. 31–44.

[96] François de Rosset claims that the Abbot of Redon had at first enjoyed Vanini's company before being scandalised by his irreligious jokes (François de Rosset, *Les Histoires mémorables, et tragiques de ce temps* (Paris: Pierre Chevalier, 1619), pp. 191–4).

[97] See the *Recueil général des anciennes lois françaises, depuis l'an 420, jusqu'à la révolution de 1789*, ed. by François-André Isambert and others, 29 vols (Paris: Belin-Leprieur, 1822–33), XVI (1829), p. 112.

Colomerium, 1643).[98] Whilst Gabriel-Bathélemy was not personally involved with the trial, his text is informed not only by his father's experiences, but by his own interactions with Vanini: 'Je l'ai vû en prison, je le vis au supplice, et je l'avois connu avant qu'il fût arrêté' ('I saw him in prison, I saw him at the stake, and I had known him before he was arrested').[99] The trial is also mentioned by the *capitoul* Nicolas de Saint-Pierre in the *Annales de la ville de Toulouse*. Other accounts are given in *Le Mercure françois*, Garasse's *Doctrine curieuse*, François de Rosset's *Histoires mémorables*—which curiously omits 'De l'execrable docteur Vanini' ('On the vile doctor Vanini') after the first edition in 1619—and an anonymous pamphlet, the *Histoire véritable*.[100] It is clear that *Le Mercure françois* merely repeats a number of claims made in the *Histoire véritable*, as the following comparison between these two sources plainly demonstrates:

> En son eloquence glissoit tellement dans l'entendement de ses auditeurs particuliers, qu'ils commençoient à balancer en la croyance de ceste faulse doctrine, laquelle vint en evidence et à la cognoissance du Parlement qui decreta contre ce nouveau Ministre: Est interrogé, soustient ses allegations veritables.
>
> By his eloquence [he] slipped into the minds of his select group of listeners, to the extent that they started to fall into believing this false doctrine, evidence of which came to the Parlement's attention, which decreed against this new Minister. He was interrogated, and showed the allegations to be true.[101]
>
> Par son eloquence il glissoit tellement sa pernicieuse opinion dans l'entendement de ses auditeurs particuliers, qu'ils commencerent à balancer en la croyance de ceste faulse doctrine; ce qu'estant venu à la cognoissance du Parlement, il decreta contre ce nouveau Ministre: Et estant pris, et interogé, il soustint ses instructions veritables.
>
> By his eloquence he slipped his pernicious opinions into the minds of his select group of listeners, to the extent that they started to fall into believing this false doctrine. Once this came to be known by the Parlement, it decreed against this New Minister, and once he was apprehended, and interrogated, he showed the findings of the investigation to be true.[102]

Given that the *Histoire véritable* does not exclusively describe Vanini's trial, and that there is no evidence to suggest that its anonymous author was present at the event, we cannot treat this text as a purported eyewitness account. Rosset's

[98] On the significance of these two editions, see p. 148.

[99] Gabriel-Barthélemy de Gramond, *Historiarum Galliae ab excessu Henrici IV libri XVIII* (Toulouse: Arnald Colomerium, 1643) translated in David Durand, *La Vie et les œuvres de Lucilio Vanini* (Rotterdam: Gaspar Fritsch, 1717), p. 194. 'Supplice' should not be understood to mean 'torture' here, as Vanini's *arrêt de mort* makes no mention of him being put to the question.

[100] *Mercure françois*, pp. 63–5; Rosset, *Histoires mémorables*, pp. 185–213; *Histoire véritable*, pp. 9–11.

[101] *Histoire véritable*, p. 10.

[102] *Le Mercure françois*, p. 63.

text, though doubtless of interest, carries a risk of unreliability by virtue of its sensationalist genre.[103] It is also unlikely that Rosset was present at Vanini's execution. Not only does he allege that this event took place at the Place Saint-Étienne instead of the Place du Salin, but he ends his text by juxtaposing his account with that of 'un de mes amis qui assista à l'execution de l'Arrest de cét execrable' ('one of my friends who was present when the *arrêt* was carried out against this wretch').[104] This said, Rosset's detailed discussion of Vanini's previous movements in Paris and Lyon, as well as the relationship between Vanini and Cramail, does not contribute to the salacious and cautionary nature of the work, and instead appears to be based on more credible information.[105] Finally, as we have already seen in Chapter 1, the hyperbolic tone and extreme bias of Garasse's *Doctrine curieuse* necessitates a degree of caution when approaching his comments on Vanini's trial. However, the fact that Garasse claims to be passing on information about Vanini from 'plusieurs qui l'ont frequenté familièrement' ('several people who were close to him'), and that he often gives specific details of certain events, means that we should not dismiss his claims out of hand.[106] The two most reliable accounts of Vanini's time in Toulouse are therefore those of Gramond and Saint-Pierre.

In November 1617 Vanini arrived in Toulouse, one of the most staunchly Catholic areas of France. Given this and the formidable reputation of its Parlement, Vanini's decision to relocate to this city, having already come very close to harsh punishment for his dangerous speech in England, appears to have been at the very least misguided. On the one hand, Vanini had already spent a brief period in Lyon—itself a centre of ultramontane Catholicism—where he was able to publish a subversive text using covert writing strategies which did not incur the wrath of the authorities. Yet Vanini was accustomed to travelling across Europe, and could have chosen any number of refuges in France if not abroad when the political climate in Paris no longer suited him. There must surely have been something, or someone, pulling him towards Toulouse either by reputation or by actively inviting him to the city. Toulouse was not, after all, devoid of free-thinkers. In addition to Bassompierre's patronage of libertine poets, the governor of Languedoc—Henri II, duc de Montmorency—was a patron to libertine writers including François Maynard, Saint-Amant, Molière d'Essertines, and Théophile de Viau. Adrien de Monluc, comte de Cramail (spelt 'Carmain' in some sources) was a *sénéchal* (seneschal) and governor of Foix, but also founded the *Académie*

[103] As Didier Foucault notes, it is quite possible that in this text Rosset 'cherche plus les effets romanesques que la vérité historique' ('seeks quixotic effect over historical truth': Foucault, *Vanini*, p. 447).

[104] Rosset, *Histoires mémorables*, pp. 207, 210.

[105] See Dietmar Rieger, '"Histoire de loi – Histoire tragique". Authenticité et structure de genre chez F. de Rosset', *XVII*[e] *siècle*, 46: 184 (1994), 461–77.

[106] [François Garasse], *Apologie du Père François Garassus, de la compagnie de Jesus, pour son Livre contre les Atheistes & Libertins de nostre siecle* (Paris: Sebastien Chappelet, 1624), p. 143.

des Philarètes and patronised writers including Maynard and Mathurin Régnier.[107] It is not therefore difficult to conclude with Schneider that 'Vanini sought refuge in Toulouse, where he was apparently assured a favourable reception by Monluc, Montmorency, *président* Bertier, and their friends.'[108]

Vanini was estranged from Bassompierre, the dedicatee of his *De admirandis*, shortly after his arrival in Toulouse. For Bassompierre's biographers, this was due to his desire to ingratiate himself with the new king and Luynes, and to avoid being associated with a heretic, though the latter part of this argument may be overly retrospective.[109] Several contemporary sources offer insights into Vanini's activities at this time. As had been the case with his time in England, Vanini's stay in Toulouse was characterised from the outset by rumour and reputation. Obliged to earn a living by offering his services as a tutor to the young men of Toulouse's upper classes, Vanini's notoriety as a man of learning is alluded to by Rosset as follows:

> Le bruit de son sçavoir l'espandit incontinent par toute ceste ville renommée, si bien qu'il n'y avoit fils de bonne mere, qui ne désirast de le cognoistre. Le premier President mesme, dont le sçavoir et la pieté ont acquis un renom qui ne mourra jamais, le voyoit de fort bon œil. [...] Monsieur le Comte de Cremail admiroit le sçavoir de cét homme, et le loüoit publiquement.
>
> Word of his learning instantly spread across this renowned city, so much so that every good mother's son wished to meet him. Even the *premier président* [Gilles Le Mazuyer], whose learning and piety have earned him a reputation which will never die, saw him in a most favourable light. [...] The comte de Cremail admired this man's learning and praised it publicly.[110]

Vanini appears to have found himself in a comfortable situation in Toulouse, acting as *gouverneur* of Cramail's nephew 'avec une honneste pension' ('with a decent stipend').[111] Again, this seems more likely to have resulted from the invitation and prior planning of powerful contacts in Toulouse, potentially via Vanini's previous encounter with Bassompierre in Paris, rather than pure chance.[112]

[107] See Véronique Garrigues, 'Adrien de Monluc et l'académie des Philarètes', *Bulletin de la Société archéologique du Gers*, 3ème trimestre (1999), 285–97; Foucault, *Vanini*, pp. 463–4; Raimondi, *Vanini Nell'Europa del Seicento*, pp. 448–9.

[108] Robert A. Schneider, *Public Life in Toulouse 1463–1789: From Municipal Republic to Cosmopolitan City* (Ithaca, NY, and London: Cornell University Press, 1989), p.153. Given the city's notorious Catholic fervour, it is more plausible that Vanini went to Toulouse on invitation than following 'les conseils de ses amis' ('the advice of his friends': Leopizzi, 'Vanini en France', 507).

[109] According to Bondois, Bassompierre had intentionally disassociated himself with Vanini following the condemnation of *De admirandis* in order to preserve his own reputation (Bondois, *Le Maréchal de Bassompierre*, p. 114). See also Leopizzi, *Sources*, p. 55. On Bassompierre's attempts to cement his position with the king and Luynes at the time of Vanini's imprisonment, see Williams, *A Gallant of Lorraine*, I, pp. 170–224.

[110] Rosset, *Histoires mémorables*, pp. 196–7.

[111] Rosset, *Histoires mémorables*, p. 197. On Cramail see Foucault, *Vanini*, pp. 461–6.

[112] Rosset's claim that Vanini was employed by the *premier président* Gilles Le Mazuyer as a tutor to

History would soon repeat itself with remarkable accuracy, for Vanini seems not to have learned the lessons from his narrow escape from England when dissimulating his unorthodox views. Just as in England, he had secured himself a comfortable social and professional postion. As in England, he began his stay as something of a model guest—in terms of his piety in England and his intellect in Toulouse—only to grow tired, perhaps even suffocated, by the mask of conformity. In both cases, Vanini found respite from his simulation not through sudden outbursts, audacious plays on words or the loosening of lips in the tavern, but by carefully revealing his inner thoughts within select, private conversations. For Vanini, the temporary discarding of his mask of piety was less of a careless or militant gasp for fresh air, and more of a pressure valve to be released in a controlled, calculated manner when he judged the conditions to be right. In England these conditions had notably included the presence of fellow Italians or those who had spent time living in Italy. In Toulouse, however, Vanini's permitted himself a greater freedom of speech 'en bonne compagnie' ('in good company')[113], but more frequently amongst the young:

> Ce malheureux faisoit le Médecin, mais en effet il étoit Séducteur de la Jeunesse [...] Il se moquoit de tout ce qui est sacré et religieux. Il avoit en exécration l'Incarnation de Notre Seigneur, il ne connaissoit point de Dieu, il attribuoit tout au hasard. Il adoroit la Nature comme une bonne Mère, et comme la cause de tous les Etres: C'étoit là son erreur principale. [...] Il attaqua d'abord les jeunes gens qui ne faisoient que sortir du Collège et qui par leur grande jeunesse, étoient le plus susceptibles de nouvelles opinions. [...] Les jeunes gens furent d'abord frappez d'une grande admiration. [...] Ils admiroient tout ce qu'il disoit, ils l'imitoient et s'attachoient à lui. Ayant été accusé de corrompre la jeunesse par ses nouveaux Dogmes, il fut mis en prison.
>
> This wretch passed himself off as a Doctor, but was in fact a seducer of youth. [...] He mocked all that is sacred and religious. He held the Incarnation of Our Lord in abhorrence, he knew no God, he attributed everything to chance. He worshiped Nature as if it were a good Mother and the cause of all things: that was his main error. [...] He first attacked the young who had only just left school and who, by their great youth, were the most susceptible to new opinions. [...] The young were first struck with great admiration. [...] They admired everything he said, they imitated him and became part of his circle. Having been accused of corrupting youths with his new Dogma, he was put into prison.[114]

Gramond's claim that Vanini was especially dangerous for the *jeunes gens* of Toulouse is repeated in multiple sources. According to Rosset, Vanini met 'deux

his children is convincingly disproved in Foucault, *Vanini*, pp. 458–61 and Leopizzi, *Sources*, p. 129, who remind us that Le Mazuyer's children were likely under two years old at the time. Guy Patin, who claims to have seen and spoken to Vanini several times, asserts that he came to Toulouse 'à l'invitation du baron de Montaut et du comte de Cramail' (*Patiniana* quoted in Foucault, *Vanini*, p. 466).

[113] Rosset, *Histoires mémorables*, p. 198.

[114] Gramond, *Historiarum* in Durand, *Vanini*, pp. 184–7.

jeunes et braves Gentils hommes qui avoient passablement estudié' ('two brave young Gentlemen who were relatively educated') on the outskirts of Toulouse.[115] Having gained their trust, and having been offered lodgings with them in return for the occasional lesson in mathematics, Vanini accompanied the young *gentilhommes* on their hunts and walks, where he began to reveal his atheism in private conversation:

> Lors que le temps luy eust acquis leur familiarité, ce dangereux homme, qui avoit caché son venin, commenca de l'espandre sur ceste jeunesse. Il les entretenoit à toute heure de l'eternité du monde, des causes naturelles, et leur preuvoit par des raisons damnables que toutes choses avoient esté faites à l'aventure. Que ce qu'on nous racontoit de la Divinité n'estoit que pour retenir les hommes soubs une forme de Police, et par conséquent que les ames mouroient avec les corps.
>
> Once he had gained their trust over time, this dangerous man, who had hidden his venom, started to infect these youths with it. At every opportunity he conversed with them about the eternity of the world, natural causes, and proved to them with damnable reasoning that everything had been created by chance. That what we were told about the Divine was only in order to keep men under a form of control, and that souls therefore died with the body.[116]

Having parted company with these two young men, Rosset continues, Vanini arrived in Toulouse where he was once again hosted by a young man, this time a 'jeune conseiller' ('a young councillor').[117] The *Histoire véritable*, whilst depicting complicit rather than innocence youths, makes a very similar claim as well as including a useful clarification of the intended meaning of 'youth':

> Il s'estoit accosté de quelques jeunes Gentils-hommes folastres de Tholoze assez desbauchez qu'il n'est besoin de nommer, on le sçait dans la ville par noms et surnoms. Et ce nouveau Prophete (privé de la grace de Dieu, et remply de l'organe du Diable) enseignoit par les maisons particulieres de ceste jeunesse (j'appelle jeunesse, en tant qu'ils n'avoient pas le jugement de cognoistre la fausseté de ce Prédicateur nouveau, encore qu'il y en eut qui avoient plus de quarante ans).
>
> He approached a few sprightly and quite debauched young Gentleman from Toulouse, who need not be named as they are known in town by both their first and last names. And this new Prophet (deprived of the grace of God, and filled with the voice of the Devil) taught in the private houses of these youths (I say youths, as they had not the judgement to recognise the falseness of this new Preacher, even though some of them were more than forty years old).[118]

Vanini is not only described as a blasphemer or a heretic, but as an insidious predator targeting the young, caught unawares, before gaining their trust and

[115] Rosset, *Histoires mémorables*, p. 194.
[116] Rosset, *Histoires mémorables*, pp. 195–6.
[117] Rosset, *Histoires mémorables*, p. 195.
[118] *Histoire véritable*, p. 9.

slowly infecting them with atheism. Just how much credence should be given to these assertions? On the one hand, as a tutor to the younger generation of Toulouse's upper classes it is only natural, if not inevitable, that those seeking to depict Vanini as a nefarious catalyst for religious scepticism should depict him in the company of youths. After all, although Vanini's relations with Cramail are described as friendly, there is no further evidence to suggest that he was hired to teach adults.[119] Yet as Foucault notes, the corruptor of youths was a common motif with a long history.[120] Within a legal context, it was futhermore a common stereotype used to vilify a feared other in the seventeenth century. Trials for witchcraft, homosexuality, and atheism, along with Garasse's anti-*libertin* texts studied in Chapter 1, all repeatedly underline the fact that youths—the most innocent and defenceless of social groups—had been targeted by the individual standing trial. The roots of this preoccupation can partly be traced to the types of crimes judged before the parlements. In his study of witch trials in Paris between 1565 and 1640, Alfred Soman has shown that witchcraft and infanticide were the two most frequent crimes brought before the Parlement de Paris: over one hundred cases of each of these crimes per year for the majority of the first quarter of the seventeenth century. Comparatively, the crimes of homicide, sodomy, and bigamy rarely exceed twenty-five cases each per year.[121] Between 1614 and 1626—the period in which Vanini published his two texts and was put on trial—infanticide was both the most common crime brought before the Parlement (almost 300 cases, compared to some 270 for witchcraft and some 40 for homicide), and was also much more likely to be punished by death (around 270 of the 300 cases resulted in the death penalty, compared to the roughly 100 accused witches executed out of the 270 brought to trial).[122] Finally, Soman offers a useful distinction regarding the outcome of trials for what he terms crimes of rage and premeditated offences:

> Les crimes violents, commis dans un état paroxystique, provoqué par la colère, la misère noire ou la faim, sont rarement punis de mort, alors que les crimes prémédités, inspirés par la ruse [...] ainsi que les abus de confiance, sont considérés comme beaucoup plus atroces. Le notaire prévaricateur, le tuteur qui abuse de sa pupille, sapent les bases de la société.
>
> Violent crimes committed in a state of paroxysm, provoked by anger, abject poverty or hunger are rarely punished by death, whereas premeditated crimes involving cunning [...] as well as abuses of trust, are considered to be far more terrible.

[119] Tallemant des Réaux's claim that Cramail was 'un des disciples de Lucilio Vanini' ('one of Lucilio Vanini's disciples') is without apparent basis (Gédéon Tallemant des Réaux, *Historiettes*, ed. by Antoine Adam, 2 vols (Paris: Gallimard, Bibliothèque de la Pléiade, 1960), I, p. 232.

[120] See Foucault, *Vanini*, p. 454.

[121] See Alfred Soman, 'Les Procès de sorcellerie au parlement de Paris (1565–1640)', *Annales. Economies, Sociétés, Civilisations*, 32: 4 (1977), 790–814 (793).

[122] These rough figures are based on the bar charts provided in Soman, 'Procès', 797.

The corrupt notary and the tutor who abuses his pupil erode the foundations of society.[123]

In repeatedly depicting Vanini as a corrupter of youths, contemporary sources aimed to situate him amongst society's most sinister and most heavily punished criminals. This furthermore adds to the image of Vanini as a man of false piety by associating him with an irreligious demographic from a legal perspective. An analysis by Alain Cabantous of fifty Parisian blasphemy cases in the seventeenth century reveals that 90% of blasphemers were under forty years old, and almost half were in their twenties.[124] When emphasising Vanini's relations with young people, then, contemporary sources were drawing from a wide sociocultural context rather than deploying a generic rhetorical strategy.[125]

A precise chronology leading to Vanini's arrest cannot be established for certain. Given the information provided in contemporary sources, however, and given that Vanini's confidence to speak freely had previously grown over time in England, it is possible to construct a credible sequence of events whilst acknowledging scope for alternative scenarios where appropriate. Let us start with the denunciation. For Rosset, Vanini's employment as tutor to Cramail's nephew served to bolster his confidence in speaking his true feelings on matters of religion.[126] With growing confidence, Vanini began to go further by making light of Catholic doctrine under the guise of trivial jokes ('par maniere de risee'): 'chacun qui entendoit ces paroles execrables, attribuoit plustost à une certaine bouffonnerie d'esprit, ce qui procedoit d'un cœur remply de toute malice' ('everyone who heard these execrable words attributed them to a kind of foolish wit, which proceeded from a heart filled with malice').[127] As in England, however, these speech acts were soon suspected to be more than mere manifestations of the plain and open speaking for which France

[123] Soman, 'Procès', 799.

[124] Alain Cabantous, *Histoire du blasphème en Occident: XVIe–XIXe siècle* (Paris: Albin Michel, 2015), pp. 141–2.

[125] This strategy would continue centuries after Vanini's death. In the 1840s, Alexandre Du Mège fabricated a manuscript account of Vanini's crimes supposedly written by one of the Parlement's scribes, Étienne Malenfant. Victor Cousin published this text as a true account in his *Fragments de philosophie cartésienne—Vanini ou la philosophie avant Descartes* (Paris: Didier, 1856). This false testimony takes inspiration from sources attesting to Vanini's corruption of youths written after his death, accusing him of the 'vilain péché de Gomorrhe; et fut arresté deux fois diverses le commettant, l'une sur le rempart de Saint-Estienne, près la porte, avec un jeune escholier angevin, et une autre [...] avec un beau fils de Lectoure en Gascogne' ('the vile sin of Gomorrah, and was arrested twice in the act, once on the Saint Stephen rampart, by the door, with a young Angevin student, and another time [...] with a handsome son of Lectoure in Gascony': Cousin, *Fragments*, pp. 77–8). On this fabricated account, see also Namer, *Vie*, pp. 221–6 and Leopizzi, *Sources*, pp. 218–21.

[126] 'Comme il se vit aymé d'un tel Seigneur, et appuyé de beaucoup d'amis, le detestable recommença petit à petit à semer sa doctrine diabolique' ('As he saw that he was liked by such a lord, and that he had the support of many friends, little by little the detestable man started to spread his diabolical doctrine once again': Rosset, *Histoires mémorables*, p. 198). The similarities to Abbot's account of Vanini's growing confidence over time are striking.

[127] Rosset, *Histoires mémorables*, p. 198.

was famous at the time, known to Italian visitors as *la furia francese*.[128] According to Rosset, Cramail was the driving force behind Vanini's arrest and served as an active agent in his capture. He had come to realise the true motivations behind the Italian's casual irreligious remarks, seemingly independently of information from third parties.[129] Cramail sought to gain proof of his suspicions by engaging Vanini in a little dissimulation of his own: 'neantmoins il dissimula quelques jours ce qu'il en pensoit, et sceut si bien tirer le ver du nez de ce meschant homme en devisant privement avec luy, qu'il l'esclarcist entierement de sa doute' ('nevertheless, he dissimulated his thoughts for a few days, and was so adept at getting the facts out of this wicked man by conversing with him in private, that he was entirely relieved of any doubt').[130] Cramail tried in vain to bring Vanini to repentence. In a final scene recalling the fate of Molière's Tartuffe, Cramail, regretting having allowed Vanini into his household, was on the verge of dismissing him when the Parlement de Toulouse intervened:

> La Court de Parlement de Tholose deputa deux de ses Conseillers vers le mesme Comte. Ce juste et Religieux Senat ayant esté informé, que Luciolo non content de mesdire publiquement de l'Eternel fils de Dieu, avoit des sectateurs en ses execrables opinions, luy eust desja fait mettre la main sur le collet; mais auparavant elle vouloit sçavoir du sieur Comte s'il avoüoit un si meschant homme. Les deux Conseillers ayant exposé leur commission au Seigneur de Cramail, ils eurent telle satisfaction de luy, que le lendemain Luciolo fut saisi, et mené en la Conciergerie.
>
> The Court of the Parlement de Toulouse sent two of its councillors to the same comte. This just and religious Senate had been informed that Luciolo, not content with speaking ill of the Eternal son of God in public, had followers of his execrable opinions. The Court would have already seized him, but it first wished to learn whether the comte recognised such a wicked man as part of his household. Having shown their warrant to Lord de Cramail, the two councillors received such satisfaction from him that the next day Luciolo was seized and led to the Conciergerie prison.[131]

Having discovered Vanini's true views, Cramail found himself having to answer for Vanini before the Parlement de Toulouse, which had received a denunciation from a witness to his criminal speech acts. This denunciation had apparently reached the Parlement a number of days prior to his arrest, as not only had the two councillors

[128] On these observations by foreign visitors to the French court, see Jean-François Dubost, *Marie de Médicis: La reine dévoilée* (Paris: Payot et Rivages, 2009), pp. 332–4. Rosset refers to 'une certaine liberté de parler, que l'on pratique en France' ('a certain freedom of speech which is practised in France') and asserts that 'la licence de parler n'est que trop grande en France, par la liberté qu'on y a introduite' ('freedom of speech is all too great in France, due to the liberties that have been introduced here': *Histoires mémorables*, pp. 192, 198).

[129] 'Ce prudent et sage Seigneur, dis-je, recognut bien tost l'intention de Luciolo, et apprit en peu de temps ce qu'il avoit dans l'ame' ('This prudent and wise lord soon recognised Luciolo's true intentions, and took little time in learning what he had in his soul': Rosset, *Histoires mémorables*, p. 201).

[130] Rosset, *Histoires mémorables*, p. 201.

[131] Rosset, *Histoires mémorables*, pp. 202–3.

first wished to speak with Cramail, but they were able to present him with their 'commission'. This was likely to have been either a document identifying the two magistrates as *commissaires* in charge of carrying out the criminal investigation (the *instruction*), or a document giving them the power to detain Vanini equating to a modern-day arrest warrant.[132]

At this point Cramail chose not to recognise Vanini as part of his clientele, which would have protected the Italian against the accusations made against him. Legal theory of the time stipulated that although one witness was insufficient to condemn a suspect, a single witness could be sufficient to merit an arrest provided that the witness was of irreproachable honour.[133] According to his modern biographer Véronique Garrigues, Cramail—a member of the *Pénitents Bleus* who encouraged the establishment of new monastic orders on his lands—was a model Catholic with no inclination towards *libertinage*. On the contrary, Cramail's defining feature as a staunch Catholic was precisely his role in Vanini's arrest.[134] Garrigues goes on to suggest that Cramail was merely associated with *libertinage* by surrounding himself with libertines such as François Maynard and Charles Sorel, and that although he had met Vanini, he was not his protector.[135] These claims ignore the fact that there are more early modern testimonies to Cramail's libertinism than there are to his religious fervour.[136] They also present a slightly idealised image of Cramail which does not allow for the possibility that he, like many others of his time, was capable of manifesting Catholic piety (superficial or sincere) along with light-hearted, bawdy, or irreligious tendencies. This is not to say that Cramail, repulsed by his recent discoveries, could not in theory have been Vanini's denouncer who subsequently arranged for the councillors to interrogate him prior to the arrest. Nevertheless, a lack of supporting hard evidence does not allow us to push this hypothesis beyond a mere possibility.

Whatever Cramail's motives may have been, and whether or not Rosset's laudatory claims of Cramail's pious indignation were true, Cramail was not in

[132] See 'commission' in Claude-Joseph de Ferrière, *Dictionnaire de droit et pratique*, 2 vols (Paris, V. Brunet, 1769), I, p. 294: 'un pouvoir donné pour un tems [sic] à quelques personnes d'exercer quelque Charge. [...] se dit aussi de la subdélégation ou du pouvoir qu'on donne à un Juge particulier de faire quelque instruction d'un procès, quelque visite ou descente sur les lieux' ('a power given for a limited time to certain people to perform a certain task [...] is also used to describe the subdelegation or the power given to a particular Judge in order to carry out a criminal investigation for a trial, to visit or to travel to the place where a crime may have been committed').

[133] See *Le Procès criminel* in Claude Le Brun de La Rochette, *Les Procès civil, et criminel, contenans la methodique liaison du droit, et de la practique judiciaire, civile et criminelle* (Lyon: Pierre Rigaud, 1622), p. 84.

[134] Véronique Garrigues, *Adrien de Monluc (1571–1646)—d'encre et de sang* (Limoges: Presses Universitaires de Limoges, 2006), pp. 54, 88–90, 199.

[135] Garrigues, *Monluc*, pp. 355–6.

[136] On this point see Giovanni Dotoli, *Temps de Préfaces—Le débat théâtral en France de Hardy à la Querelle du «Cid»* (Paris: Klincksieck, 1996), pp. 127–8; Jean-Pierre Cavaillé, 'Adrien de Monluc, dévot ou libertin?', *Les Dossiers du Grihl*, online since 10/11/2011, http://dossiersgrihl.revues.org/1362 [accessed 15 May 2019].

fact Vanini's denouncer, and Rosset offers no details as to who this party may have been. Records show that Vanini was first arrested not by *conseillers* of the Parlement as Rosset claims, but by *capitouls* of the Capitoulat. As we saw earlier, the *Histoire véritable* ignores Cramail's role in Vanini's arrest entirely, and merely states that the Italian's dangerous doctrine 'vint en evidence et à la cognoissance du Parlement' ('evidence of his doctrine came to the Parlement's attention').[137] Only one source—Garasse's *Doctrine curieuse*—ventures to name Vanini's supposed denouncer, le sieur de Francon. Francon's apparent contribution to the trial was so crucial and controversial, however, that we will turn to him later in our chronology of events in order to propose his true role in light of a recent manuscript discovery. The results of the two *commissaires*' preliminary investigations were enough to merit further legal proceedings. Writing in the *Annales de la ville de Toulouse*, and allowing us to date the *commissaires*' visit to Cramail to 1 August 1618, Nicolas de Saint-Pierre recorded that Vanini was arrested on 2 August 1618. After an initial denunciation and a *subsequent* encounter between Cramail and the *commissaires*, the wheels of the criminal justice system were set in motion to drag Vanini on his final journey: to the Parlement de Toulouse.

PROVINCIAL JUSTICE: THE CAPITOULAT AND THE PARLEMENT DE TOULOUSE

Seventeenth-century Toulouse retained an important working vestige of its historical political autonomy in its criminal justice system: the Capitoulat. Assembling at the official building for local administration, le Capitole, it served as a municipal court until the French Revolution. Vanini was arrested by two of the magistrates serving in this court, who were known as *capitouls*.[138] The *capitouls* had a number of particularities which distinguished them from magistrates of the royal parlements. Each of the eight *capitouls*, representing the eight parishes of Toulouse, served a one-year term of office which ended in the election of their successors every 25 November. Each *capitoul* would nominate six candidates, who were then whittled down from forty-eight to twenty-four by the outgoing *capitouls* and sixteen former *conseillers des capitouls*. These were in turn passed on to the royal representative—the *viguier*—and the *sénéchal* who chose the final eight. As well as obtaining noble status from their office, each *capitoul* was given responsibility for a specific area of local government, so that *la justice*, *la police*, *les réparations*

[137] *Histoire véritable*, p. 10; *Mercure françois*, p. 63.

[138] On the Capitoulat and the *capitouls* who served there, see Henri Ramet, *Le Capitole et le Parlement de Toulouse* (Cressé: Éditions des Régionalismes, 2008) and Claire Faure, *La justice criminelle des capitouls de Toulouse (1566–1789)* (Toulouse: Presses de l'Université Toulouse 1 Capitole, 2017). The following remarks on the *capitouls* are taken from Faure, *Capitouls*, pp. 20–99.

(repairs), and *les hôpitaux* (hospitals) were each overseen by two *capitouls*.[139] The most prestigious of these areas was justice. The *capitouls* had the right to try any crime *en première instance* (first instance cases), including crimes which carried the death penalty. Although only two *capitouls* were charged with this area of local government, all of the *capitouls* were expected to sit in judgement of criminal trials, specifically on Wednesdays and Fridays from 7 to 10am.[140] Priding themselves on both the speed and the severity with which they dealt with criminal cases—the vocabulary of severity appearing frequently in their court records—the *capitouls* saw themselves as the protectors of all aspects of public life in the city.[141]

There were four means by which the Capitoulat addressed the limited experience that a *capitoul* could gain in the space of one year of office. First, one could be elected a *capitoul* more than once. Second, the 'first' *capitoul* responsible for justice, known as the *chef du consistoire* (the head of the consistory) had to have already served a previous term as a *capitoul*, whereas other more senior *capitouls* could pass on their experience to younger colleagues. Third, as a municipal court the Capitoulat was in any case subject to the judgements of the Parlement de Toulouse, staffed as it was by professionally trained career magistrates.[142] Finally, and most importantly for the Vanini affair, each year the *chef du consistoire* would write a brief account of the previous year's business—the *chroniques de l'année*—which formed part of the *Annales de la ville de Toulouse*. Beginning with the list of elected *capitouls* and their allotted roles, these extraordinary documents were careful to paint the Capitoulat's actions in the most favourable light possible, as well as to provide solid lessons in local government for future *capitouls*. The *chronique* for 1618, written by the *chef du consistoire* of that year Nicolas de Saint-Pierre, constitutes one of the very few surviving legal documents pertaining to Vanini's trial.

On Thursday 2 August 1618, the *capitouls* Jean d'Olivier and Paul Virazel arrested 'un jeune homme soy disant aagé de trente quatre ans, natif de Naples en Italie, se faisant nommer Pomponio Usciglio, deferé d'enseigner l'atheisme, duquel il estoient en queste il y avoit plus d'un mois' ('a young man around thirty-four years old, from Naples in Italy, going by the name of Pomponio Usciglio, accused of teaching atheism, who had been under investigation for more than a month') (Figure 3.1).[143] It is notable that 'Vanini' the author of the censored *De admirandis*

[139] For examples of the specific areas of competence for each of these, see Faure, *Capitouls*, pp. 29–38.
[140] Faure, *Capitouls*, pp. 78, 135.
[141] Faure, *Capitouls*, pp. 137, 124–5.
[142] This is not to say that the *capitouls* were laymen who enjoyed a temporary taste of political power. Only *avocats* (lawyers), *écuyers* (equerries), *procureurs* (prosecutors), or merchants could be elected to the Capitoulat, whereas at least three of the eight nominees had to hold a *licence* (bachelor's degree) or *doctorat* in law, who were the only candidates allowed to oversee justice. See Faure, *Capitouls*, pp. 69–72.
[143] AMT MS BB 278, *Annales*, Saint-Pierre (1618), fols. 13–14; Leopizzi, *Sources*, p. 101. D'Olivier was the second *capitoul* for justice, whereas Virazel was a *capitoul* for the hospitals. I take 'more than a month' here to refer to no more than a month and three weeks (longer than which would likely have

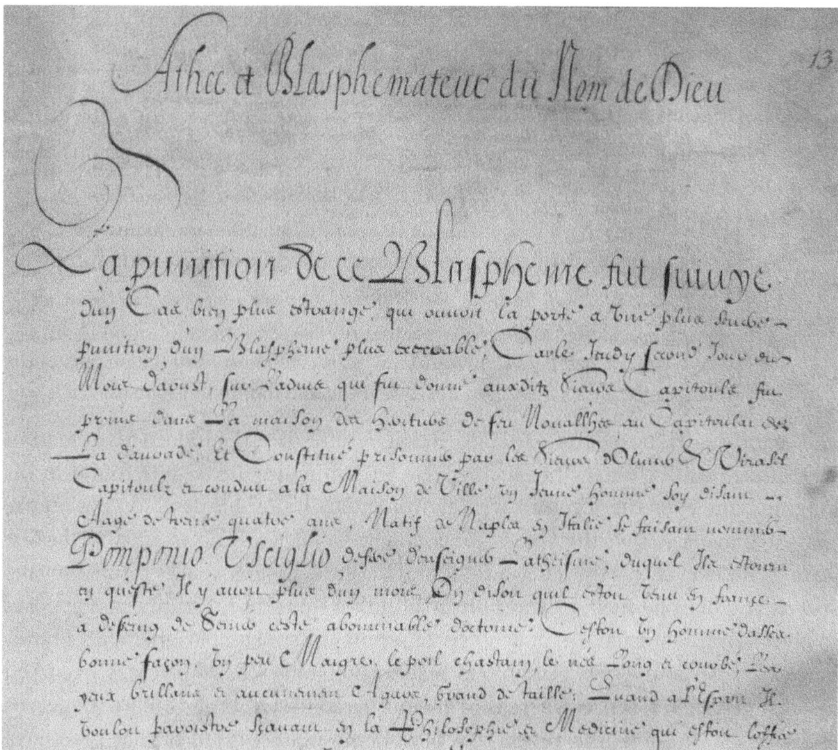

Athee et Blasphemateur du Nom de Dieu

La punition de ce Blaspheme fut suivye

Figure 3.1 AMT MS BB 278: *Annales des capitouls de la ville de Toulouse*, vol. VI, 'chronique 290' (Nicolas de Saint-Pierre, 1618), fols. 13–14, in which Nicolas de Saint-Pierre describes the arrest made by the his fellow *capitouls* d'Olivier and Virazel of 'un jeune homme soy disant aagé de trente quatre ans, natif de Naples en Italie, se faisant nommer Pomponio Usciglio, deferé d'enseigner l'atheisme, duquel il estoient en queste il y avoit plus d'un mois' ('a young man around thirty-four years old, from Naples in Italy, going by the name of Pomponio Usciglio, accused of teaching atheism, who had been under investigation for more than a month'). By permission of the Archives municipales de Toulouse.

was not under arrest, as the magistrates were not aware of his true identity. Living under an assumed name, Vanini had instead been arrested for his irreligious teachings and for being what Foucault has termed a 'passeur d'idées' ('a spreader of ideas'), thereby adding further weight to the characterisations of him as a dangerous corruptor of youths as discussed earlier.[144] As well as being unaware of who he was, the authorities even struggled to define who he was not. In addition to Saint-Pierre's

been referred to as 'nearly two months'), meaning that the investigation alluded to in Rosset had been underway since early to mid-June.

[144] Didier Foucault, *Histoire du libertinage* (Paris: Perrin, 2010), p. 282.

spelling given above, Vanini's eventual *arrêt de mort* condemned 'Pompée ~~Usiglio~~ Ucilio [sic]', whereas Rosset asserts that 'ce méchant homme quittant le nom de Vanini, se faisait appeler Luciolo' ('this wicked man abandoned the name Vanini and called himself Luciolo').[145] Thus, in seeking to define Vanini's crimes, the justice system also struggled to determine the very agency of the heterodoxy in question. Soon after his arrest, Vanini was moved to the Conciergerie prison:

> Le parlement, adverty et très asseuré de ses secretes intentions et maxims damnables qu'il avoit tenues en particulier [...] se fit remetre le cinquesme du dit moys d'aoust, des prisons de la maison de ville a la conciergerie.
>
> The Parlement, alerted and greatly assured of his secret intentions and damnable maxims which he had held in private [...] transferred him from the prisons of the town hall to the Conciergerie on the fifth of the said month of August.[146]

Again, there is no evidence to suggest that Vanini's arrest or indeed his execution were linked to his literary production. No incriminating texts were found in his lodgings, and even the accounts written immediately after his death do not accuse him of sharing his writings with his students or of teaching from unorthodox texts.[147] Rather, as was the case in England, Vanini's dissidence was limited to free speech and blasphemy in private conversation. In this sense, Vanini's case appears to be relatively unusual. In an analysis of reports of spoken blasphemy in France between 1656 and 1671, Cabantous asserts that only 24.2% of cases occurred inside a private residence, whereas 51.6% occurred in streets and 14.8% in taverns (*cabarets*).[148] These figures reveal that blasphemy was reported primarily to have taken place within public rather than private spaces. Even if this was due to a lack of reliable witnesses to blasphemy that had occurred within private spaces, the fact that Vanini's trial relied on precisely this form of testimonial evidence is nonetheless remarkable.

Saint-Pierre is unequivocal: the Parlement was responsible for taking over Vanini's case, as opposed to the *capitouls* deciding that they were unable to take the case and referring it up to the Parlement. The Parlement de Toulouse was the second oldest royal court in the kingdom, having been established on 4 June 1444.[149] Its jurisdiction covered an eighth of France, though with the help of lower

[145] See Leopizzi, *Sources*, pp. 93, 294–5, 101; Rosset, *Histoires mémorables*, p. 190.

[146] AMT MS BB 278, *Annales*, Saint-Pierre (1618), fols. 13–14; Leopizzi, *Sources*, p. 103.

[147] The *capitouls* only found 'une Bible non defendue, et de plusieurs sien escriptz, qui ne marquoient que des questions de philosophie et de theologie' ('a copy of the Bible from a permitted edition, and several of his own writings which only considered philosophical and theological questions': Leopizzi, *Sources*, p. 101).

[148] Cabantous, *Blasphème*, p. 143.

[149] On the Parlement de Toulouse, see Jean Baptiste Dubédat, *Histoire du Parlement de Toulouse*, 2 vols (Paris: Arthur Rousseau, 1885); Ramet, *Le Capitole et le Parlement*; Samuel J. Pollack, *The Crown and Judicial Venality in the Parlement of Toulouse, c.1490–1547* (unpublished doctoral thesis, Christ Church Oxford, 2016); Guillaume Ratel, *Between Facts and Faith: The Judicial Practices of the Conseillers of the*

provincial courts including the Capitoulat its litigation never surpassed ten cases per 10,000 inhabitants.[150] Like its Parisian counterpart, the Parlement de Toulouse included a Tournelle and a Grand' Chambre, the latter of which was staffed by four *présidents à mortier* and thirty-two *conseillers*, headed by the *premier président* Gilles Le Mazuyer.[151] The Parlement de Toulouse was known for its harsh punishment of religious deviance. In 1508, the city began the use of *la cage de fer* (the iron cage) to submerge blasphemers in the Garonne, a practice revived in the very same year as Vanini's arrest. This was not applied to suspects as a means of establishing culpability, as was the case with the ducking stool that often awaited suspected witches, but was used as a form of corporal punishment.[152] As the poet François Maynard's father Géraud remarks, '[ils sont] plongez par trois fois au profond par certain intervalle pour chacune desdites fois accoustumé' ('they are plunged down to the bottom three times, and left there for a certain period for each of the customary number of times').[153] Toulouse had recognised Henri IV as king in the 1596 Edict of Folembray in exchange, amongst other things, for the right to host Jesuits who were otherwise banned in France. Until the French Revolution, on May 17 it celebrated its deliverance from the Reformed Church following the expulsion of hundreds of Protestants from its walls in 1562.[154] As Gramond proudly boasted:

> Il n'y a point de ville en France où la loi soit plus sévère envers les hérétiques; et quoique l'édit de Nantes ait accordé aux calvinistes une protection publique, et les ait autorisés à commercer avec nous et à participer à l'administration, jamais ces sectaires n'ont osé se fier à Toulouse.
>
> There is no city in France where the law is more severe towards heretics. And even though the Edict of Nantes has granted public protection to the Calvinists, and has authorised them to trade with us and to participate in administrative affairs, these sectarians have never dared to trust Toulouse.[155]

Surrounded by a sea of Protestantism, the Parlement saw itself as the defender of Toulouse, itself a bastion of staunch Catholic orthodoxy.[156] Given this, Patin

Parlement de Toulouse (1550–1700) (unpublished doctoral thesis, Cornell University, 2017).

150 Bruce Lenman and Geoffrey Parker, 'The State, the Community and the Criminal Law in Early Modern Europe', in *Crime and the Law: The Social History of Crime in Western Europe since 1500*, ed. by V.A.C. Gatrell, Bruce Lenman and Geoffrey Parker (London: Europa Publications, 1980), pp. 11–48 (p. 16); Roland Mousnier, *Les Institutions de la France sous la monarchie absolue*, 2 vols (Paris: Presses Universitaires de France, 1980), II, p. 261.

151 See Mousnier, *Institutions*, p. 298.

152 See Bernard de la Roche-Flavin and François Graverol, *Arrests notables du Parlement de Toulouse* (Toulouse: Guillaume-Louis Colomiez et Jerôme Posuel, 1682), pp. 39–40; Schenider, *Public Life*, p. 68.

153 Géraud de Maynard, *Notables et singulieres questions du droit escrit*, 4 vols (Paris: Robert Foüet, 1628), I, p. 674.

154 Schneider, *Public Life*, pp. 93–8, 136.

155 Gramond, *Historiarum* in Durand, *Vanini*, p. 186.

156 As Cyrano de Bergerac would recall later in the century in his *États et Empires du Soleil*, in which Dyrcona is arrested after Cartesian diagrams found in his possession are mistaken for witchcraft. See Cyrano de Bergerac, *Les États et Empires de la Lune et du Soleil*, ed. by Madeleine Alcover (Paris:

can hardly be accused of exaggeration in asserting that Vanini 'fut despourveu de sens de quitter Paris ville pleine de libertins pour s'en aller à Toulouse ville toute bigote' ('took leave of his senses by leaving Paris, a city full of libertines, to go to the bigoted city of Toulouse').[157] There is no evident legal reason why the Parlement should have wished to take responsibility for Vanini's trial.[158] Although the *capitouls* lost the right to try civil cases in article 71 of the 1566 Edict of Moulins, they maintained the competence to judge both *petit criminel* (for example, insults and bodily harm) and *grand criminel* cases (ranging from theft and counterfeiting to rape, murder, witchcraft, blasphemy, and *lèse-majesté divine*).[159] The *capitouls* had conducted the trials of a number of blasphemers in the early seventeenth century, and the punishments they prescribed were either confirmed or hardened by the Parlement.[160] Furthermore, as Foucault has argued, the *capitouls* serving in 1618 had declared it their aim to suppress crimes against religion during their term of office.[161]

A more tactical motive may have guided the Parlement's decision to act. The Capitoulat had the judicial power to try cases *en première instance*. However, this meant that those condemned to death would have a right to appeal before the Parlement de Toulouse. In 1554, Henri II had stipulated that the Parlement would no longer be able to overturn the *capitouls*' judgements unless they were found to be 'contre les formes de droit' ('against legal procedure').[162] As we shall see, Vanini's harsh punishment at the hands of the Parlement was very much out of keeping with legal statutes. Had the *capitouls* conducted the trial, before passing a more lenient and non-lethal sentence against Vanini, the Parlement would have found itself on shaky ground in attempting to upgrade his punishment to the death sentence. But if the Parlement were to take on the case straight away, neglecting even to mention that the case had first been processed by the *capitouls* in the final *arrêt de mort* as if to suppress the fact, its royal magistrates would be able to keep a closer eye on the entirety of the investigation and to control its eventual outcome.[163]

This becomes even more significant when we consider that men of high status in Toulouse had been implicated in the Vanini affair, as shown both in contemporary

Honoré Champion Classiques, 2004), pp. 179–85.

[157] Quoted in Foucault, *Vanini*, p. 407.

[158] Raimondi finds it a 'procedura per la verità assai singolare' ('a truly peculiar procedure') that Vanini's trial should have been upgraded to the Parlement despite the lack of incriminating textual evidence found against him (Raimondi, *Vanini Nell'Europa del Seicento*, p. 460). Without full knowledge of the denunciation made against Vanini or initial testimonial evidence pertaining to his speech acts, however, we cannot say to what extent this referral was unfounded.

[159] See Faure, *Capitouls*, pp. 38, 276–7, 315. Foucault conversely claims that the *capitouls* were not able to try blasphemy cases (Foucault, *1619*, p. 3).

[160] See the cases given in Faure, *Capitouls*, pp. 311–13.

[161] On this point see Foucault, *Vanini*, pp. 467–70; Foucault, *1619*, pp. 27–8; Schneider, *Public Life*, pp. 63–92.

[162] Quoted in Faure, *Capitouls*, p. 315.

[163] On this point see Raimondi, 'Un documento enigmatico', 589.

accounts and by the shroud of secrecy hanging over much of the trial proceedings. Unlike the trial of Jean Fontanier, whose defendant and witnesses were all of non-aristocratic status, the trial of Vanini reached the upper echelons of Toulouse's legal and noble classes. In taking Vanini's case, the Parlement may have sought to ensure damage limitation through a swift and harsh judgement. It may have wished to place the building of a difficult case against him, lacking hard evidence, in the hands of more experienced professional judges. Alternatively, magistrates in the Parlement may have been acting on pressure from one of the noble families whose reputations had become compromised by their association with the accused. Those hoping for a quick and clean end to the scandal of Vanini's impious teachings were in for a disappointment, as Vanini was not about to reveal his true beliefs as easily as he had to George Abbot in England. According to Gramond, during his detention Vanini:

> se porta d'abord pour Catholique et contrefit l'Orthodoxe. [...] Dans sa prison il fut Catholique [...] il s'approchoit souvent des Sacrements pendant sa prison et cachoit adroitement ses principes.
>
> first behaved as if he were a Catholic and feigned to be orthodox. [...] In prison he was a Catholic [...] he often received the Sacraments during his imprisonment and adroitly hid his beliefs.[164]

Rosset and the *Histoire véritable* paint a less credible picture of Vanini's defence, in which he openly admitted his atheism to his accusers before he had been found guilty:

> La première chose qu'il [le sieur de Bertrand, commissaire] luy demanda, après s'estre informé de son nom, et de ses qualitez, et autres formes ordinaires, *S'il ne croyoit point en Dieu:* Luciolo avec une effronterie la plus grande que l'on sçauroit imaginer, luy respondit, *Qu'il ne l'avoit jamais veu, et par consequent qu'il ne le cognoissoit nullement.*
>
> The first thing that he [the sieur de Bertrand, *commissaire*] asked him, after his name and status, and other ordinary formalities, was *whether he believed in God.* Luciolo answered, with scarcely imaginable impudence, *That he had never seen him, and that therefore he did not know him at all.*[165]

It is hard to believe that these are the words of a man who managed to avoid prosecution by the Parlement de Toulouse for six months. Some of the atheistic assertions attributed by Rosset to Vanini's verbal defence also bear a strong resemblance to claims that Vanini had made in his texts. According to Rosset, for example, when Vanini was asked whether we can know God through his works, he replied:

[164] Gramond, *Historiarum* quoted in Durand, *Vanini*, pp. 187, 195, 196.
[165] Rosset, *Histoires*, p. 203.

> que tout ce qu'on nous publioit de la creation du monde, n'estoit que mensonge, et invention, et que tous ces Prophetes avoient esté atteints de quelque maladie d'esprit, qui leur avoit fait escrire des extravagances.
>
> that everything that we have been taught about the creation of the world is but a lie, and an invention, and that all of these prophets had been suffering from some kind of mental illness, which led them to write such extravagant claims.[166]

In *De admirandis,* Vanini's mouthpiece J.C. had described the tenets of religion and divine action over the bodies of prophets in a very similar way:

> à principibus ad subditorum paedagogiam excogitatas, et à sacrificulis, ob honoris et auri aucupium, confirmatas non miraculis, sed scriptura, cuius nec originale ullibi adinvenitur. [...] Veteres cum proxime adstantes tam subito miseros conuelli, prosternique viderent, in peculiares Diuos morbum comitialem, feu Herculeum, reluctante Hippocratem referebant. Apud Christianissimum etiam populum haec inoleuit persuasio.
>
> but these are laws devised by princes for the instruction of their subjects, and by priests on account of their obsession with honours and with gold, confirmed not by miracles, but by Scripture, of which the original is not in any place to be found [...] When the ancients saw pitiable wretches standing alongside them fall into spasms, they used to attribute this epilepsy, or malady of Hercules (although Hippocrates denies this), to particular Gods. Even among the most Christian peoples this opinion has taken root.[167]

Considering that *De admirandis* had been condemned before Vanini was arrested, and that he had managed to keep his true identity from being discovered, it is doubtful that he would have quoted his own arguments from this text during his trial. It is far more likely that Rosset had either read Vanini's texts after his execution, or that he had heard of the arguments made in these from others. Even Garasse was forced to concede that up until this point Vanini's self-defence had largely been effective, due not only to a lack of evidence but to Vanini's convincing performance at trial in the eyes of some of his judges:

> Il fut ouy et examiné publiquement, et quoy que son esprit remuant lui fournist des deffaictes assez plausibles en apparence, et que quelques-uns des Juges ne pensassent pas avoir des preuves suffisantes...
>
> He was heard and examined publicly, and even though his restless spirit provided him with artificial excuses which appeared quite plausible, and that some of the judges did not believe that they had sufficient proof...[168]

Without the trial transcripts from individual hearings, it is not possible to know how well Vanini defended himself for certain. Gramond asserts that Vanini maintained

[166] Rosset, *Histoires*, pp. 203–4.
[167] Vanini, *De admirandis*, pp. 366, 460–1.
[168] Garasse, *Doctrine*, p. 146.

his outward mask of Catholic faith even in the final *audience* with his judges:

> Vanini fut conduit à l'audience, et étant sur la sellette, on l'interrogea sur ce qu'il pensait de l'Existence de Dieu. Il répondit qu'il adoroit avec l'Eglise un Dieu en trois personnes, et que la Nature démontroit évidemment l'existence de la Divinité. Ayant par hasard aperçu une paille à terre, il la ramassa, et, étendant la main, il parla à ses juges en ses termes: Cette paille me force à croire qu'il y a un Dieu. [...] Il concluoit de tout ce discours que Dieu étoit Auteur de toutes choses. [...] Il prouva ensuite fort au long que la Nature étoit incapable de créer quelque chose, d'où il conclut que Dieu étoit l'Auteur et le Créateur de tous les Etres. Vanini disoit plutôt tout cela par vanité ou par crainte que par une persuasion intérieure.
>
> Vanini was brought to his *audience* [*sur la sellette*], and once he had taken his seat, he was interrogated on what he thought of the existence of God. He answered that he worshipped the Holy Trinity along with the Church, and that Nature clearly proved the existence of the Divine. Having spotted a piece of straw on the floor by chance, he picked it up, and stretching it forth he spoke to the judges thus: this straw forces me to believe that there is a God. [...] He concluded from his speech that God was the Author of all things. [...] He then proved at great length that Nature was incapable of creating anything, from which he concluded that God was the Author and Creator of all beings. Vanini said all this through vanity or fear rather than by inner conviction.[169]

This account is in keeping with Vanini's performative skills of outward conformity, as well as with the considerable length of the trial. According to the *Histoire véritable*:

> Pour parfaire son procés on envoya à Castres querir des principaux de la Religion pretendue reformee, pour sçavoir d'eux s'ils approuvoient ce qu'il disoit, et respondirent sagement que non, et que cet homme-là, estoit le plus abominable que l'on vit jamais. En leur presence l'Arest fut donné.
>
> In order to complete the trial, those of the supposedly reformed faith in Castres were asked whether they approved of what he said. They wisely answered that they did not, and that this man was the most abominable man they had ever seen. The *arrêt* was given in their presence.[170]

If we are to accept Gramond's claim that Vanini sought to defend himself until the end, it is not clear why the Parlement de Toulouse should have asked for expertise from Protestants at Castres, which hosted a bipartisan law court staffed by both Catholic and Protestant judges in order to provide justice for Protestants. After all, these courts (including the Paris Chambre de l'Édit, in reference to the Edict of Nantes) existed to allow Protestants to be judged by their peers as opposed to by hostile Catholics.[171] Although blasphemy cases against Protestants could not

[169] Gramond, *Historiarum* in Durand, *Vanini*, pp. 188–91.

[170] *Histoire véritable*, p. 10.

[171] See Diane C. Margolf, *Religion and Royal Justice in Early Modern France: The Paris Chambre de*

be tried by the authorities in Toulouse, there is no evidence to suggest that Vanini responded to allegations made against him by claiming to be a Protestant.[172] There are further flaws in this hypothesis. First, multiple sources agree that Vanini maintained a mask of *Catholic* orthodoxy throughout his trial. If Vanini's reported speech acts were so offensive to the ears of his interrogators, why would they seek to label these as crimes of confession, rather than crimes of *lèse-majesté* and blasphemy which they had recently been so adept at punishing? Second, the theory that Vanini might have claimed to hold Protestant beliefs is surely to be excluded. After all, Vanini really *was* a former member of the Protestant Church, and had fled the authority of both the Church of England and the Carmelites in order to publish a dangerous book subsequently censored by the Sorbonne. It is inconceivable that Vanini, who lived and indeed died in Toulouse under an assumed name, would risk exposing his true identity and recent Anglican past by bringing the question of Protestantism into his interrogations. Finally, this scenario also appears incredible from the perspective of the judges themselves. It is difficult to believe that the staunchly Catholic magistrates of Toulouse did Vanini the courtesy of comparing his views to the doctrines of non-Catholic faiths, in order to check that they had the legal authority to try his case. Foucault, who does not challenge the *Histoire véritable*'s account relating to Castres, nonetheless describes the historical period in which Vanini lived in Toulouse thus:

> Une période trop courte pour que les plaies de trente-six ans de déchirements fratricides soient complètement cicatrisées. [...] En 1618–1619, non seulement toutes les haines accumulées dans le passé n'étaient pas éteintes, mais encore des évènements récents et préoccupants étaient en train de les rallumer.
>
> Not enough time had passed for the wounds of thirty-six years of fraternal infighting to have completely healed. [...] In 1618–1619, not only had all the hatred from the past failed to dissipate, but recent, worrying events were even in the process of causing them to flare up again.[173]

As we saw earlier, Gramond explicitly states that those of the reformed religion mistrusted the people of Toulouse. They feared entering Toulouse and participating in its administration, despite officially being allowed to do so. It is thus counterintuitive that the *Histoire véritable* should place Protestants from Castres at the very heart of hostile enemy territory—the Grand' Chambre of the Parlement de Toulouse—for the reading of Vanini's death sentence. When considered alongside the *premier président* Gilles Le Mazuyer's well-known hatred of the Protestants, it therefore seems likely that the author of the *Histoire véritable* fabricated the Parlement de Toulouse's discussions with the Protestants

l'Édit, 1598–1665 (Kirksville, MO: Truman State University Press, 2003).

[172] See Faure, *Capitouls*, p. 313.

[173] Vanini, *1619*, pp. 21, 24.

at Castres. In doing so, he perhaps sought to accentuate Vanini's supposed impiety by sensationally depicting him as too heretical for the heretics.

As Gramond relates, 'comme les preuves étoient convainquantes contre lui, il fut condamné à mort par arrêt du Parlement' ('as the evidence against him was convincing, he was condemned to death by a judgement from the Parlement').[174] The *arrêt de mort* and the lack of trial transcripts make it extremely difficult to understand how the judges reached their gruesome verdict. The predominant view in modern studies is that a new witness—Francon—came forward in time to seal Vanini's fate. Upon closer inspection, however, this hypothesis is in fact highly problematic. Before turning to Vanini's execution, let us first reconsider Francon's supposedly crucial role as described in available sources, before evaluating new archival evidence offering fresh perspectives on witness testimony at the trial.[175]

A STAR WITNESS THAT NEVER WAS? LE SIEUR DE FRANCON AND THE SHADOW OF CONSPIRACY

Despite the authorities' initial efficiency in investigating and arresting Vanini, his case subsequently grew cold. It was precisely as the legal proceedings against him began to grind to a halt that the Vanini affair took one of its most enduringly enigmatic twists: the sudden appearance of damning witness testimony by a certain Francon. On this matter Rosset proves to be less reliable. According to his *Histoires mémorables*:

> On ne manqua pas de tesmoins pour la prevue de son impieté. [...] Les deux Gentils-hommes, à qui il avoit appris la Philosophie, le neveu du Comte, et plusieurs autres personnes honorables, deposerent contre luy.
>
> There was no shortage of witnesses to prove his impiety. [...] The two Gentlemen, to whom he had taught Philosophy, the comte [Cramail]'s nephew, and several other honourable people testified against him.[176]

The two noblemen alluded to here, who had delayed Vanini's arrival in Toulouse by taking him as their tutor just outside of the city, should not be confused with the *Histoire véritable*'s young gentlemen who were reputed to be libertines, and whom Vanini had met once he had arrived in Toulouse. There is no evidence to suggest that Francon was one of the two libertine noblemen alluded to in the *Histoire*

[174] Gramond, *Historiarum* in Durand, *Vanini*, p. 191.

[175] Certain critics have posited that the poet Balthazar Baro, who was also part of Cramail's circle, was an additional witness at Vanini's trial (including Namer, *Vie et l'œuvre*, p. 178; Schneider, *Public Life*, p. 154). As Foucault points out, this is based on a single piece of retrospective evidence: Joannes Bisselius's *Ætatis nostrae eminentium septenii III* (Hamburg: J. Burger, 1677) mentions 'Barones' in the accusative plural as playing a role in the trial (see Foucault, *Vanini*, p. 476).

[176] Rosset, *Histoires mémorables*, p. 205.

véritable, or indeed that he was one of Vanini's early students outside of Toulouse alluded to by Rosset. It is perfectly plausible that Rosset's two noblemen could have testified against him, as the jurisdiction of the *capitouls* included crimes that had occurred on the outskirts of Toulouse, as well as crimes committed elsewhere in cases where the culprits had been arrested within the city's walls. For Garasse, however, 'le premier qui fit la descouverte de ses horribles impietez, fut le sieur de Francon, gentilhomme de bon esprit, et de tres-grand courage' ('the first person to discover Vanini's horrible blasphemies was the sieur de Francon, a gentleman of fine wit and very great courage').[177] Garasse describes Francon as a visitor to Toulouse towards the end of 1618 who, being a *brave gentilhomme*, found himself in demand by a 'bonne et agreable compagnie' ('good and agreeable company').[178] One such admirer was Vanini, who counted on his reputation as a wise philosopher to permit him entry into this private social circle. Garasse's description of Vanini's interactions with Francon alludes to his role as a tutor, and depicts the Italian as something of a local sensation. As such, the vocabulary of the spoken word is heavily present in the Jesuit's account of events:

> Cet homme disoit de si belles curiositez, des propositions si nouvelles, des pointes si agréables qu'il s'attacha aisement à Francon [...] peu à peu il laschoit des Maximes ambiguës [...] et prononce de si étranges blasphèmes contre la sacree humanité de Jesus Christ que Francon confessa depuis, que les cheveux lui herissoient en teste, et qu'il mit deux fois la main sur son poignard pour luy plonger dans le sein. [...] Il prit un meilleur expedient, car il defera cet impie au premier President, lequel ayant consulté l'affaire, le fit saisir sur d'autres depositions secrettes.
>
> This man spoke of such fine and curious things, such novel propositions, such agreeable arguments that it was easy for him to enter into Francon's confidence [...] little by little, he let slip ambiguous maxims [...] and said such strange blasphemies against the sacred humanity of Jesus Christ that Francon since admitted than his hairs stood on end, and that on two occasions he reached for his dagger to sink it into Vanini's chest [...] He found a better solution, as he referred this impious man to the *premier président*, who having looked into the affair, had Vanini arrested on the basis of other secret depositions.[179]

Contrary to Rosset, Gramond's account of events claims that the trial was very much suffering from a lack of witnesses, and places an even stronger emphasis on Francon's testimony than Garasse:

> Il étoit même sur le point d'être élargi, à cause de l'ambiguité des preuves, lorsque FRANCONI, homme de naissance et de grande probité, comme cette seule circonstance le prouve suffisamment, déposa que VANINI lui avoit souvent nié l'existence de Dieu et s'étoit moqué en sa présence des mysteres de la Religion

[177] Garasse, *Doctrine*, p. 145.
[178] Garasse, *Doctrine*, p. 145.
[179] Garasse, *Doctrine*, pp. 145–6.

> Chrétienne. On confronta le témoin et l'accusé et celui-là soutint ce qu'il avoit avancé.
>
> He [Vanini] was even on the verge of being released, due to the ambiguous nature of the evidence against him, when Franconi, a man of high birth and of great integrity, as this matter alone demonstrates, testified that Vanini had often denied the existence of God to him and had mocked the mysteries of the Christian Faith in his presence. The witness was confronted with the accused, who maintained what he had said.[180]

For Gramond, ambiguity was replaced with solid evidence from a source of integrity. In stressing Francon's high birth, Gramond alludes to the fact that the justice system of the time took social rank into consideration when analysising testimonial evidence. Danty's translation and commentary of Jean Boiceau's 1582 *Ad Legem regiam Molinaeis habitam de abrogata testium a libra centena probatione commentaries* offers some pertinent remarks on how judges were to distinguish between different types of witnesses. These could be divided:

> soit par la consideration qu'ils sont élevez en dignité, ou qu'ils sont riches, ou qu'au contraire ce sont personnes pauvres et viles; car il doit ajoûter plus de foy à la déposition d'un homme noble, sage, riche et puissant [...] qui sont d'une probité reconnuë, ou qui sont élevez en dignité, qu'à ceux qui sont du menu peuple. [...] Il fera plus de cas même du témoignage d'un homme du commun du peuple que de celuy des personnes les plus viles.
>
> either by considering whether they are of elevated position, or if they are rich, or if on the other hand they are poor and vile persons, for a judge must give more weight to the deposition of noble, wise, rich and powerful men [...] who are recognised for their integrity, or who are of an elevated position, than to those who are of the common people. [...] The judge will even accord greater importance to the testimony of a man of the common people than that of the vilest of people.[181]

Furthermore, Le Brun de La Rochette notes under the subheading 'prudentes remarques du Juge' that 'Cependant remarquera à part soy prudemment la qualité et condition des tesmoins, et leur contenance' ('similarly a judge will remark to himself prudently the rank and social condition of the witnesses, and their countenance').[182]

[180] Gramond, *Historiarum* quoted in Durand, *Vanini*, pp. 187–8.

[181] Jean Boiceau, *Traité de la preuve par témoins en matière civile*, ed. by M. Danty (Paris: Guillaume Cavelier, 1697), pp. 18–19. On early modern vileness, see the contributions to *Early Modern French Studies*, 39: 2 (2017)—'Variations of Vileness', ed. by Jonathan Patterson and Emilia Wilton-Godberfforde; and Jonathan Patterson, *Villainy in France (1463–1610): A Transcultural Study of Law and Literature* (Oxford: Oxford University Press, 2021).

[182] La Rochette, *Les procès civil*, p. 136. For an analysis of Montaigne's views on witnesses in *Des Cannibales*, according to which simple men are preferable witnesses to men of intelligence in order to obtain unaltered testimony, see Andrea Frisch, *The Invention of the Eyewitness: Witnessing and Testimony in Early Modern France* (Chapel Hill, NC: The University of North Carolina Press, 2004), pp. 102–7.

Francon's identity has divided opinion amongst modern scholars. For Foucault and Garrigues, this star witness against Vanini was a fellow member of Cramail's entourage—Jean-Louis de Mauléon, sieur de Francon—who died whilst fighting alongside Cramail at the siege of Montauban in 1621.[183] His father, Jean de Mauléon seigneur de Francon, is unlikely to have been the Francon referred to by Garasse due to his age. Raimondi has equally speculated in favour of Jean-Louis, whilst also proposing Francon de Tersaac de Montbéraut as another potential candidate.[184] The latter is supported by Leopizzi, whereas other modern studies have simply settled for 'Francon' without commenting further on the identity of this crucial witness.[185] Recently however, Jean-Christophe Sanchez has made a convincing and detailed argument in favour of Jean-Louis.[186] Surprisingly few studies have called into question Francon's decisive contribution to the Vanini affair, or indeed his involvement at any level. Namer asserts that the practice of using *monitoires*—whereby witnesses were encouraged to come forward in church on pain of excommunication—resulted in Francon's deposition, whom he declares responsible for the opening of the investigation against Vanini.[187] Foucault also describes Francon's involvement as a 'témoignage décisif' ('decisive witness testimony'), though without suggesting the use of *monitoires* as more than a possibility.[188] Cavaillé names Francon as 'le témoin accusateur lors du procès' ('the accusing witness during the trial'), whilst Leopizzi acknowledges the unreliable nature of sources relating to the trial without questioning Francon's involvement.[189]

There is no evidence linking Francon's deposition to a *monitoire*. Furthermore, the sequence of events outlined in sources of the time is both sensational and a little too convenient. The sudden appearance of first one then several witnesses took place at the end of a period of apparent inactivity, when there was a very real

[183] Foucault, *Vanini*, p. 474; Garrigues, *Monluc*, p. 143.

[184] In Vanini, *Tutte le opere*, p. 310.

[185] Leopizzi, *Sources*, p. 67.

[186] Jean-Christophe Sanchez, 'Deux nobles commingeois dans l'entourage de Vanini: le baron de Montaut et le sieur Francon', in *L'esprit de liberté à Toulouse au temps du parlement (1443–1790), actes du colloque de Toulouse à l'occasion du 400e anniversaire du bûcher de Vanini (18–19 avril 2019)*, ed. by Didier Foucault, Olivier Guerrier and Yves Le Pestipon (Toulouse: Presses universitaire du Midi, forthcoming). I am grateful to the author for an advanced copy of this article.

[187] Namer, *Vie et l'œuvre*, pp. 173–4. These *monitoires* or *monitions* appear in article 21 of the 'Édit de Blois' (1579). See Isambert, *Recueil général*, XIV i, p. 387. For a comprehensive discussion on the regulations pertaining to *monitoires*, see Jean-Pierre Gibert, *Usages de l'Eglise Gallicane, concernant les censures et l'irregularité* (Paris: Jean Mariette, 1724), pp. 336–423. See also Fabrice Vigier, 'En quête de preuves! La publication de monitoires ecclésiastiques dans le diocèse de Poitiers à l'époque moderne', in *La Preuve en justice de l'antiquité à nos jours*, ed. by Bruno Lemesle (Rennes: Presses Universitaires de Rennes, 2003), pp. 171–89; and Eric Wenzel, 'Forcer les témoignages: le délicat recours au monitoire sous l'Ancien Régime', in *Les témoins devant la justice: Une histoire des statuts et des comportements*, ed. by Benoit Garnot (Rennes: Presses Universitaires de Rennes, 2003), pp. 83–90.

[188] Foucault, *Vanini*, pp. 475–6.

[189] Cavaillé, *Dis/simulations*, p. 55; Leopizzi, *Sources*, p. 68.

possibility that Vanini could be released. The textual evidence, and indeed the lack thereof, demands that we at least entertain the possibility of an alternative scenario: that Francon's decisive contribution to Vanini's trial is a total fabrication. My following hypothesis both explains a number of facts that simply do not add up in the broadly accepted version of events, and traces a more plausible silhouette of truth in an aspect of the trial described by Raimondi as shrouded in fog.[190]

Raimondi has proposed a convincing argument which casts doubt on Garasse's depiction of events, describing Francon's purported testimony 'una pura invenzione del gesuita' ('a pure invention of the Jesuit [Garasse]').[191] According to Garasse, Francon encountered Vanini towards the end of 1618, when Francon was serving as part of Montmorency's troops. The *Annales de la ville de Toulouse* confirm that Montmorency returned to the city on Saturday 20 October 1618, and it is perfectly plausible that upon his return, Francon's company was sought due to his reputation as a *brave gentilhomme* following his recent military exploits.[192] Despite this, Vanini could not have been among those who came to visit Francon. By this time he was already into his third month of imprisonment, following accusations supposedly made by the same recently returned Francon.

This chronology becomes even more illogical if, taking Garasse at his word, Francon was the *first* person to report Vanini's blasphemous speech to the authorities. The *Annales* state that Vanini had been under investigation for over a month when he was arrested on 2 August 1618.[193] As well as contradicting the *Annales*, Garasse's version of events would push the arrest to the beginning of 1619. This would leave barely one month in which to fit Francon's testimony, those of others that his deposition supposedly inspired, confrontations with the witnesses described in the *arrêt de mort*, as well as an impossibly long period of inactivity. What is more, the magistrate who received Francon's complaint according to Garasse—the *premier président* Gilles Le Mazuyer—was not available at this time either, as he had yet to return from the *Assemblée des notables* in Rouen (on 6 August).[194] The scene described by Garasse thus presents us with the shadowy figure of Francon on an otherwise empty stage.

The obstacles do not end here, for Garasse's claims are also suspect from a legal perspective. Francon simply could not have been both the accuser who *first* denounced Vanini to the authorities and triggered his criminal investigation, and the new witness who *eventually* testified against him after the case had begun to go cold. The legal terminology used by Garasse further betrays his ignorance of

[190] In Vanini, *Tutte le opere*, p. 310; Raimondi, *Vanini Nell'Europa del Seicento*, p. 484: 'avvolta nella nebbia'.
[191] Raimondi, *Vanini Nell'Europa del Seicento*, pp. 484–5.
[192] AMT MS BB 278, *Annales*, Saint-Pierre (1618), fol. 6.
[193] AMT MS BB 278, *Annales*, Saint-Pierre (1618), fols. 13–14; Leopizzi, *Sources*, p. 101.
[194] Foucault, *Vanini*, pp. 459–60.

the facts. We know that Vanini was investigated and subsequently arrested not by the Parlement de Toulouse but by the *capitouls*. According to Garasse however, it was the *premier président* who first learned of Vanini's impious speech, and who was responsible for the Italian's arrest. Granted, the two *capitouls* who were designated to oversee justice in the city during any given year were considered to hold the most prestigious positions of the Capitoulat, to the extent that the first of these—the *chef du consistoire*—could sometimes be referred to as the *président des capitouls*.[195] Nevertheless, the Capitoulat had no concept of a *premier président*, and Garasse could only therefore be alluding to the *premier président du Parlement de Toulouse* Gilles Le Mazuyer who, as we saw earlier, was absent from Toulouse in the months leading up to Vanini's arrest.

Now that we have sufficiently dismantled Garasse's claims, Francon's role in Vanini's trial encounters a further, fundamental problem: writing in late 1622, Garasse was the first author to allege Francon's testimony. How could any, let alone all of the earlier literary sources which mention Vanini—the *Mercure françois*, the *Histoire véritable*, and Rosset's *Histoires mémorables*—have resisted including the virtuous actions of the pious, heroic Francon in their sensational narratives? They are not the only texts with such a glaring omission. Turning to the legal sources, there is no mention of Francon in either Saint-Pierre's *Annales* or the final *arrêt de mort*. Gramond, for his part, seemingly presents an irrefutable obstacle to our hypothesis by making specific reference to Francon's role in the trial. However, this reference is only found in the revised edition of Gramond's text, published twenty-four years after the fact in 1643. Crucially, the original 1623 edition makes no connection between Francon and Vanini's trial whatsoever.[196] Given the irregularity of Vanini's trial, Raimondi finds it plausible that Garasse sought to fill the void of incriminating evidence against the Italian. Francon was of respectable character and rank. Having died at the siege of Montauban on 10 October 1621, he furthermore suited Garasse's purposes as 'un comodo testimone che non era più in grado di parlare' ('a convenient witness who was no longer able to speak').[197] Moreover, it is not in fact the case that Garasse wrote his *Doctrine curieuse* two years after Francon's death in October 1621 as Raimondi has claimed.[198] Having received its *approbation* from two theologians of the Sorbonne on 8 March 1623, Garasse's anti-*libertin* text was written following the publication of the *Parnasse satyrique* in November 1622.[199] In other words, Francon died a little over one

[195] See Faure, *Capitouls*, p. 72.

[196] I am grateful to Francesco Paolo Raimondi for pointing me towards this significant variant between the two editions of Gramond's text.

[197] Raimondi, *Vanini Nell'Europa del Seicento*, p. 489.

[198] Raimondi, *Vanini Nell'Europa del Seicento*, p. 489.

[199] Antoine Adam notes that, in the first book of the *Doctrine curieuse*, Garasse expresses his desire to see the *libertins* put to use aboard galleys wintering at the mouth of the Garonne (Antoine Adam, *Théophile de Viau et la libre pensée française en 1620* (Geneva: Slatkine Reprints, 1966), p. 333). The

year before the *Parnasse*'s publication. As such, it is all the more likely that Francon's death could have been a recent and convenient inspiration for Garasse to conjure up his account of a star witness that never was. It was only after having been influenced by Garasse, then, that Gramond subsequently added Francon's contribution to Vanini's trial in order to present a façade of due legal diligence during its proceedings.

There is certainly strong evidence to suggest that a young nobleman by the name of Francon was in Toulouse at roughly the same time as Vanini, and that they may have frequented the same group of aristocrats. But the evidence stops there. None of the contemporary sources prior to Garasse's *Doctrine curieuse* mentions Francon at all. Garasse's text was published four years after Vanini's execution, and suffers from errors ranging from the time and place of Francon's meetings with Vanini through to impossibilities in legal procedure. If it were the case that Francon had in fact been one of Vanini's early 'victims', and that he had subsequently repented of his poor judgement by contributing evidence at Vanini's trial, then surely contemporary sources prior to the *Doctrine curieuse* would have extoled Francon's virtuous actions as Garasse later would. After all, this is precisely how Rosset described Cramail's noble actions when the scales supposedly fell from his eyes in the very same way. Raimondi surmises whether Garasse could have been motivated by a desire to conceal his fellow Jesuit Pierre Coton's potential influence on the trial.[200] The royal confessor to Henri IV and Louis XIII, Coton was at court during Vanini's stay in Paris. He was likely to have encountered Vanini prior to the assassination of Concini, and may well have expressed his disdain for Vanini's thought in his posthumously published notes against free-thinkers at court.[201] For Raimondi and Godard de Donville, a passage in Garasse's *Doctrine curieuse* describing John Chrysostom's dealings with a fourth-century Théophile is a thinly disguised allusion to Coton.[202] This said, Garasse's description resembles both Théophile de Viau's banishment from court in 1619, as well as Vanini's later relations with George Abbot and Cramail:

> [Théophile], voyant que S. Jean Chrysostome estoit en grande reputation comme de raison, pour sa saincte vie et pour son eloquence merveilleuse, le redoubtoit, et se frottoit quelquesfois à sa robe avec une hypocrisie si bien couverte, que saint Jean

reference in question is found in Garasse, *Doctrine*, p. 70.

200 Raimondi, *Vanini Nell'Europa del Seicento*, pp. 483–4, 487–8.

201 [Pierre Coton], *Le Théologien dans les conversations avec les sages et les grands du monde* [ed. by Michel Boutauld] (Paris: Sebastien Marbre-Cramoisy, 1683). On attacks against Vanini in this text, where Vanini is named in contrast with other grandees targeted by this work, see Louise Godard de Donville, 'Théophile et son milieu dans les années précédant son procès', in *Théophile de Viau: Actes du colloque du CMR 17 offerts en hommage à Guido Saba*, ed. by Roger Duchêne (Paris, Seattle and Tübingen: Biblio 17, 1991), pp. 31–44 (pp. 35–6). For Godard de Donville, it is likely that Coton shared these notes with Garasse (p. 34).

202 Raimondi, *Vanini Nell'Europa del Seicento*, pp. 487–8; Godard de Donville, 'Théophile et son milieu', p. 33.

> Chrysostome commença à le prendre en affection et gouster son esprit. [...] Il ne pût pas si long temps couvrir son jeu que S. Jean Chrysostome n'eust cognnoissance de ses deportemens secrets, laquelle fit aussi tost que ce saint homme changea toute son affection en haine.
>
> [Théophile], seeing that St John Chrysostom enjoyed a great reputation as much for his saintly living as for his marvelous eloquence, feared him and would sometimes cosy up to him with such well-hidden hypocrisy that St John Chrysostom started to care for him and to appreciate his wit. [...] He could not hide his hand for long before St John Chrysostom learned of his behaviour in private, which instantly turned this saintly man's affection into hatred.[203]

Banished from Paris following Concini's assassination, Coton would once again find himself in the same city as Vanini during his stay in Toulouse between October 1618 and January 1619. Though Vanini was in prison by this time, the *Histoire véritable* claims that Vanini's impious words to the youths of Toulouse 'prend pour tesmoin le R.P. Cotton, qui preschoit le Caresme à S. Sernin ou S. Saturin dudit Tholoze, qui a veu et parlé au personnage' ('was witnessed by the Reverend Father Coton, who was preaching during Lent at Saint Sernin or Saint Saturnin in Toulouse, and who saw and spoke to the man [Vanini]').[204] Raimondi is tempted to derive from this that Coton confronted Vanini in prison, and that he may even have played a role in the later stages of the criminal investigation against him, whilst stopping short of coming to a conclusion due to a lack of supporting evidence. There is a further weakness in this hypothesis. As outlined earlier, the authorities did not realise Vanini's true identity until after his execution. If Coton had used his knowledge of Vanini's philosophy to guide the Parlement de Toulouse's line of questioning—based on his unhappy encounter with the author of *De admirandis* in Paris (first-hand or otherwise)—it is surely inconceivable that he would not have informed the Parlement of Vanini's true identity as a censored author. If, conversely, Coton did *not* meet Vanini in Paris, then any potential role he may have had in Vanini's downfall in Toulouse would have been due to his wider aversion to religious heterodoxy, rather than a desire to settle scores from Paris, and Garasse's motives for wishing to hide Coton's influence on the trial would be less clear.

There are two further possible scenarios. First, Garasse may have sought to glorify Francon posthumously by linking him to the downfall of a dangerous blasphemer after he fell at the siege of Montauban. Alternatively, alarmed by the audacious wave of *libertinage* exemplified by obscene poetic anthologies such as *Le Parnasse satyrique*, Garasse weaponised Francon's memory by fabricating a contest between noble virtue and dangerous impiety embodied by Francon's depositions at Vanini's trial. In doing so, he furthermore created the illusion of a

[203] Garasse, *Doctrine*, pp. 10–11.
[204] *Histoire véritable*, p. 9.

more conventional trial from a legal perspective, as appears to have been the case for Gramond's curiously belated recollection of Francon's decisive testimony in 1643. Garasse's true motives cannot be deduced from the available evidence. It is however my contention that the accepted narrative, according to which Francon was responsible for bringing Vanini's trial to its brutal conclusion, is almost entirely unfounded.

The tantalising void created by a seeming lack of evidence proving Vanini's culpability, mirrored by a lack of surviving interrogation transcripts with which to track the trial's progress, has shrouded the judges' journey to a guilty verdict in mystery. A recent archival discovery, however, goes at least some way to filling this gap in Vanini's story when viewed through the lens of contemporary legal practice.

WHAT THE SERVANTS SAW: FORGOTTEN WITNESSES AND FORCED TESTIMONY

Having been locked up on the basis of a private accusation to the authorities, Vanini appears to have languished in his cell for six months whilst the *commissaires* tried to construct a case against him.[205] Not only did the law state that Vanini should have been released in the absence of tangible evidence to justify his detention, but the authorities ought surely to have been able to bring the case to a close much more quickly given Vanini's notoriety in Toulouse.[206] This six-month period of inactivity should first be considered in light of the parliamentary semesters. Regular sessions of the courts were suspended for the *vacation* lasting from 15 August until the end of the feast of St Martin, on 11 November.[207] Furthermore, the absence of extant trial transcripts should not be equated with an absence of due diligence or even the identification of leads on the part of the *commissaires.*

Didier Foucault has recently uncovered archival testimony from Vanini's trial thanks to modern research into another libertine author. Previously unknown to scholars on Vanini, it sheds new light on the months leading up to his execution.[208] In her preface to the definitive edition of Cyrano de Bergerac's voyage narratives, Madeleine Alcover repeatedly refers to Marguerite de Jésus who, according to

[205] Namer, *Vie et l'œuvre*, p. 179.
[206] On the need for magistrates to judge criminal trials quickly, see for example article 6 of the Declaration by Charles IX (10 July 1566), as well as articles 139 and 140 of the 'Ordonnance sur les États Généraux de Blois' (May 1579) in Isambert, *Recueil général,* XIV ii, pp. 214, 415.
[207] Namer, *Documents*, p. 182.
[208] Foucault's analysis of this document is to be published in the forthcoming conference proceedings in *L'esprit de liberté à Toulouse au temps du parlement (1443–1790), actes du colloque de Toulouse à l'occasion du 400e anniversaire du bûcher de Vanini (18–19 avril 2019).* I am very grateful to Foucault for generously sharing his findings and page references with me ahead of his own more exhaustive exploration of the Senaux manuscript.

one of the many theories on Cyrano's death, cared for him in his final days and ensured that he died a repentant Christian.[209] In her introduction, Alcover makes a fleeting reference to a text by Thomas Souèges which suggests that Marguerite was involved in Vanini's trial.[210] Before taking holy orders, the nun who provided Cyrano with both medical and spiritual care in his dying days had been known as Marguerite de Senaux, the daughter of a family of magistrates who was married to a councillor of the Parlement de Toulouse, Raymond de Garibal.[211] Souèges gives an overview of their extraordinary involvement in the trial:

> Monsieur de Garibal ayant gagné deux de ses serviteurs, ils déposaient contre leur impie maître tant de choses de sa doctrine et de ses mœurs, qu'on n'eut que trop de preuves pour lui faire son procès. [...] Mais parce que plusieurs se trouvaient embarrassés à sa condamnation, à cause de l'appui et de la croyance qu'ils avaient donné à sa doctrine, et qu'ainsi ils auraient pu faire quelque tort à ces deux serviteurs, lesquels, pour ne pas manquer à la fidélité qu'ils devaient à Dieu, avaient déféré à la justice l'irréligion et l'infidélité de leur abominable maître, Mr de Garibal et Madame sa femme les firent évader en Espagne, où ils les entretinrent libéralement de leurs besoins.
>
> Once Mr de Garibal had won over two of [Vanini's] servants, they testified against their impious master, including so many things about his teaching and his behaviour that there was only too much evidence to put him on trial. [...] But because several people found themselves compromised by his condemnation, due to the support and credence which they had given to his doctrine, and that as such they might have taken some form of action against these two servants who, in order to do their duty to God, had reported their abominable master's irreligion and infidelity to the courts, Mr de Garibal and Madame his wife helped them to flee to Spain, where they liberally saw to their needs.[212]

A manuscript held in the archives of the Monastère de la Croix et de la Miséricorde d'Évry, written by Senaux's great-grand-nephew in 1790 based on her papers, allows us to fill in some of the gaps that have long pervaded the *instruction* of Vanini's trial.[213] Senaux and Garibal had a pious marriage to the point

[209] Cyrano's lodgings may have been set alight by Jesuits, leading him to be struck by a falling wooden beam. Alternatively, he could have been the unidentified man who was mortally wounded when the carriage of Cyrano's protector, the duc d'Arpajon, was attacked in the road. Finally, he could simply have died of a venereal disease evinced by surviving receipts for medical expenses.

[210] Cyrano, *États et Empires*, p. LXXI. See also Madeleine Alcover, *Cyrano relu et corrigé* (Geneva: Droz, 1990), pp. 35–8.

[211] This couple is also mentioned briefly in Schneider, *Public Life*, p. 174. On Senaux, see Marjorie Dennequin, *Les 'Dévotieuses': dévotion et préciosité à Grenoble au XVIIe siècle: la Congrégation de la Purification* (unpublished doctoral thesis, Université Grenoble Alpes, 2015), pp. 41–50.

[212] Thomas Souèges, *Vie de la vénérable Mère Marguerite de Jésus* (1790) quoted in Cyrano, *États et Empires*, p. LXXI.

[213] *Vie de Mère Marguerite de Jésus de Senaux o.p. Fondatrice des Monastères de Saint-Thomas et de la Croix à Paris, 1589–1667*, Monastère de la Croix (Évry). I shall refer to this document as being written by Senaux throughout. The two sets of Roman numerals in the following references indicate the part (*partie*) and chapter respectively.

of providing a Catholic education to their servants. Having lost four children by the age of twenty-one, Senaux began to consider entering a convent. Eventually, she and her husband both agreed to take holy orders together following the loss of Senaux's ninth pregnancy.[214] Before devoting their lives fully to serving God, these pious members of parliamentary families had a final piece of business to take care of. Vanini had for some months been biding his time in the Conciergerie whilst the Parlement struggled to build a case against him. In accordance with other sources relating to the trial, the Garibals had grown concerned that Vanini might walk free:

> On commençait à sentir le mal, plusieurs en étaient atteints; mais il n'y avait point d'accusateur, et ce défaut d'accusateur faisait qu'on ne se mettait nullement en peine d'arrêter le cours de cette impiété.
>
> The evil began to make itself felt, several had been touched by it, but there was no accuser, and this lack of an accuser meant that no effort was made to stop this impiety in its tracks.[215]

It would be short-sighted to attribute this concern solely to the couple's devout abhorrence of blasphemers, or indeed to a desire to combat irreverent speech as a prelude to taking holy orders. There was also a social factor at work. Senaux's decision to enter a convent was met with an unexpected reaction from the inhabitants of Toulouse:

> On donnait un tour ridicule et malin à tout ce qu'elle faisait de plus saint et de plus édifiant; on tournait en dérision tout ce que sa piété avait de plus solide et de plus exemplaire, sans épargner ni son assiduité à la prière qu'on traitait de fainéantise et d'oisiveté, ni son commerce de miséricorde et de charité, qu'on disait tout haut lui être très utile pour mieux venir à ses fins, ni ses communions fréquentes dont on disait qu'elle couvrait adroitement un grand fond d'hypocrisie, ni ses confessions qu'on taxait d'amusement, de perte de temps, de faiblesse ou de légèreté d'esprit: enfin cette femme, qui avait été longtemps l'objet de l'admiration de toute cette ville quand elle semblait pencher vers le monde, devient l'objet de ses mépris et de la censure quand elle se donne à Dieu.
>
> Her most saintly and edifying actions were treated as ridiculous and cunning; the most solid and exemplary marks of her piety were mocked. This included her diligent prayer which was treated as laziness and idleness; her works of mercy and charity which were openly said to have been very useful for her to achieve her ends more easily; her frequent receiving of communion with which she was said to hide her great hypocrisy; her confessions which were accused of being for her amusement, to pass the time, out of weakness or light spiritedness. Thus this woman, who had long been the admiration of the entire city when she occupied

[214] Garibal entered La Chartreuse Saint-Sauveur in Villefranche-de-Rouergue, whereas Senaux entered the Monastère de Sainte Catherine de Sienne in Blagnac. She would later be sent to Paris to establish the Couvent des Filles de la Croix, whose members would include Cyrano de Bergerac's sister Catherine, thus bringing her into contact with the author of *États et Empires de la Lune du Soleil.*

[215] *Vie de Marguerite de Jésus*, I, pp. XXXIII, 66.

> herself with worldly concerns, became a figure of contempt and censure when she gave herself to God.[216]

Senaux was accused of being a Tartuffe *avant la lettre*: of laziness, of overt acts of charity, of scheming, and of hypocrisy. Worse still, she was not judged to have sought a life of devotion in order to escape these pre-existing rumours surrounding her motives. Rather, she had paradoxically lost her original reputation for piety precisely for having chosen to abandon worldly concerns in order to serve God in an official capacity. There is thus an interesting duality to her involvement in Vanini's trial. Senaux's and Garibal's machinations can be seen as being in keeping with their strong Catholic faith. They can also be interpreted as a means of demonstrating the sincerity of that faith to their critics by playing a final, legal role—reflecting their family histories—in helping to punish irreligious speech in the world (*le monde*) where Senaux's piety had been looked upon more favourably. During this transitional period in their lives, Senaux and Garibal decided that Vanini could not remain unpunished. Having asked God to illuminate their judgement 'par des prières ferventes, par des jeûnes et des aumônes, et par des austérités extraordinaires' ('by praying fervently, by fasting and giving alms, and by extraordinary acts of austerity'), the couple set to work:[217]

> ils encourageaient les juges contre les sollicitations des personnes de crédit, et leur représentaient fortement l'importance de la cause de Dieu, dont le jugement qui était entre leurs mains méritait bien qu'on employât toute sorte de moyens pour le bien éclaircir.

> they encouraged the judges against the requests of respected persons, and made a strong case to them of the importance of God's cause, of which the decision in their hands was worth elucidating through the use of all manner of means.[218]

Once again, Senaux's account shows that Vanini's trial had stalled and that the judges (perhaps influenced by Vanini's protectors such as Cramail) were not inclined to pursue the case. But who were these *personnes de crédit*, and are we to interpret this line as referring to individuals who discouraged Senaux and Garibal from attempting to influence the judges, or to parties who had themselves been urging the judges to abandon the case against Vanini? The latter would appear unlikely. There is no evidence that Vanini received support from aristocratic protectors upon his imprisonment, whereas Cramail is attributed by some sources as contributing to his arrest. Given that the judges did not unanimously find

[216] *Vie de Marguerite de Jésus*, I, XXXIII, p. 47.

[217] *Vie de Marguerite de Jésus*, I, XXXIII, p. 65.

[218] *Vie de Marguerite de Jésus*, I, XXXIII, p. 65. Moréri makes no reference to Vanini's trial in his entry on Marguerite de Senaux, and limits his remarks on 1618 to the end of her childless marriage to Garibal by a 'commun consentement' (Louis Moréri, *Le Grand dictionnaire historique*, 10 vols (Paris: Les libraires associés, 1759), 9, p. 335, col. 1).

Vanini guilty, however, it is possible that other parties could have pressured certain magistrates into concluding that Vanini had no credible case to answer. The *Vie de Marguerite de Jésus* is explicit in linking Senaux and Garibal to the appearance of two witnesses which have yet to be discussed in modern studies on Vanini:

> Enfin à force de chercher des preuves contre Vanini, qui se défendait fort bien, on trouva deux de ses domestiques si bien instruits des intrigues de leur maître, qu'on ne douta point, qu'ils ne découvrissent bien des affaires mais ils le craignaient beaucoup; et avant de pouvoir les obliger à parler contre lui, il fallut leur permettre de les mettre à couvert de son ressentiment, et de tous ceux qui pourraient se trouver impliqués dans son affaire: enfin convaincus du zèle et de la charité de M. et de Madame de Garibal, ils espérèrent de trouver en eux une protection assez bonne, pour pouvoir déclarer sans crainte ce qu'ils savaient de leur misérable maître, dont jusqu'alors ils n'avaient osé parler. Ils dirent en particulier à M. et Madame de Garibal tout ce qu'ils en savaient: et ceux-ci les ayant engagés à dire la vérité, et à rendre témoignage contre Vanini, ils furent ouïs en justice, et découvrirent des choses si surprenantes et si horribles touchant sa doctrine et ses mœurs, que chacun fut convaincu de son impiété, et surtout de l'athéisme dont il était accusé; et ce malheureux lui-même ne pouvant plus s'en défendre, fut forcé d'avouer son crime.

> Finally, the search for evidence against Vanini, who defended himself very well, led to the discovery of two of his servants who were so well informed of their master's intrigues that no one doubted that they would reveal much on the matter. Yet they feared Vanini greatly, and before being able to make them speak against him, it was first necessary to allow them to hide from his resentment, and from all those who might find themselves implicated in the affair. Finally, convinced of the zeal and charity of Mr and Madame de Garibal, they hoped to find secure enough protection in them to be able to declare what they knew about their miserable master without fear, of which they had hitherto not dared to speak. They told Mr and Madame de Garibal all that they knew in private, who persuaded them to tell the truth and to provide witness testimony against Vanini. They were heard by the court, and revealed such surprising and horrible things relating to his teaching and his behaviour, that everyone was convinced of his impiety and especially of the atheism of which he was accused. The wretch himself, no longer able to defend himself, was forced to admit to his crime.[219]

These machinations must have taken place in September, as Senaux and Garibal entered holy orders in October 1618. This chronology would allow enough time after Vanini's arrest in early August for Senaux to have become concerned about the length of the *instruction*. The text does not state clearly how these witnesses were found. Given that they were at first fearful of providing testimony until they had received reassurance, it seems unlikely that Garibal and Senaux were responsible for finding the two servants in the first place. Rather, the *commissaires* in charge

[219] *Vie de Marguerite de Jésus*, I, XXXIII, p. 67. It is notable that Senaux again refers to other implicated parties here.

of the *instruction* may have looked to Vanini's household in search of witnesses. It could have been these judges, and not Garibal and Senaux themselves, who first came across the servants, before Garibal and Senaux later persuaded them to testify after guaranteeing their safety. To have refused the Parlement de Toulouse's request to provide evidence against Vanini is no small testament to how much they feared their master.

The couple could have learned of these potential witnesses through a number of means. For one, Senaux and Garibal prepared for their new life of spiritual contemplation under the guidance of a priest named Étienne Virazel.[220] One of the *capitouls* who arrested Vanini, Paul Virazel, was likely to have been a relation to this priest. Alternatively, the testimony of Vanini's servants may not have been uncovered by the Parlement at all, but by the Church in a *monitoire*. In this case, the servants would have been obliged to reveal what they knew to the Church on pain of excommunication, but may still have refused to testify for the judicial authorities without assurances of their safety. Marguerite de Senaux was known for her piety, specifically for treating her servants well and encouraging the development of their Catholic faith, and had made it her mission to bring about Vanini's condemnation before devoting her life to God. She would therefore have been ideally placed to coerce these servants into fulfilling their own duty to the faith, as well as to provide for their subsequent material needs in Spain from her own worldly goods which she surrendered before entering a convent. Garasse's allusion to the 'autres depositions secrettes' which supposedly came after Francon's testimony could well refer to a *monitoire*, and would explain why none of the contemporary sources mentions them by name.[221] After relating the servants' decisive contribution to the trial, the *Vie de Marguerite de Jésus* paints a familiar portrait of Vanini's conduct in his final days:

> Quand la procédure contre cet athée fut finie, on le garda encore du temps pour tirer de lui des éclaircissements, et prévenir les maux que ses complices, et ses disciples, pourraient faire après lui.
>
> When the legal proceedings against this atheist had come to an end, he was kept a little while longer in order to gain some clarifications from him, and to learn of the damage that his accomplices and his disciples could cause in the future.[222]

[220] 'Il y avait déjà longtemps que M. et Madame de Garibal travaillaient aux préparatifs de leur retraite; et dans cette veine ils s'étaient mis tous deux sous la conduite de Monsieur Virasel ecclésiastique fort éclairé et d'une rare mérite' ('Mr and Madame de Garibal had already been working for some time on preparations for their retreat. In doing so, they had both placed themselves under the direction of Mr Virasel, a most knowledgeable clergymen of rare merit': *Vie de Marguerite de Jésus*, II, I, p. 71).

[221] A possibility entertained in Foucalt, *Vanini*, pp. 475–6. Raimondi suggests that any *monitoire* used to instruct Vanini's case would have taken place in January (Raimondi, *Vanini Nell'Europa del Seicento*, p. 483).

[222] *Vie de Marguerite de Jésus*, I, XXXIII, p. 67.

This would have been entirely in keeping with contemporary legal practice. Known as the *question préalable*, this procedure allowed the magistrates to use torture in order to uncover the identity of any accomplices before the execution of a condemned criminal.[223] In Vanini's case however, torture was not needed to extract this additional information from him: 'comme il se vit convaincu et perdu sans ressource, il n'attendit pas qu'on employât les tortures pour tout avouer' ('as he saw that he had been convicted and that all was now lost, he did not wait to be tortured before admitting everything').[224] This account also tallies with other sources which note the striking shift in Vanini's behaviour once he had been condemned, including Abbot's account of his interrogations in England. Referring to Vanini's ordeal in Toulouse, Garasse in turn notes: 'voyant qu'il n'y avoit plus d'esperance pour lui, dit et publia que pour luy il estoit en cette creance, qu'il n'y avait point d'autre Dieu au monde que la nature' ('seeing that there was no longer any hope for him, he said and proclaimed that he was of the belief that there was no other god in the world than Nature').[225] Finally, Senaux makes a likely reference to the futile efforts of priests who attended Vanini in the moments before his execution:

> On fit tout ce qu'on put pour le retirer de son aveuglement; mais sa malice avait écarté de lui toutes les grâces de Dieu, on ne put jamais vaincre son obstination; les plus savants personnages s'y employèrent en vain; l'endurcissement de son cœur l'emporta sur tous les efforts de leur charité.
>
> Every effort was made to bring him out of his blindness, but his malice had set him beyond all the graces of God, and it was never possible to overcome his obstinacy. The most learned of men worked to this end in vain; the hardening of his heart overcame all their charitable efforts.[226]

Again, Senaux's text agrees with other accounts which claim that Vanini repelled the crucifix and the assistance of priests at his execution.[227] Those who had been instrumental in bringing him to the stake—his own servants—were well looked-after by their pious protectors:

> Dès qu'ils eurent fait leur déposition et consommé toutes les autres formalités de la procédure, ils se virent en grand danger de leur vie à cause de plusieurs personnes notables qu'ils avaient été obligés de charger pour les avoir vus prendre des leçons et tenir des conférences chez leur maître. Mais M. et Madame de Garibal eurent soin de pourvoir à leur sûreté [...] ils les envoyèrent secrètement en Espagne après leur avoir donné une somme considérable pour leur voyage et pour s'entretenir

[223] See Faure, *Capitouls*, pp. 118, 183.
[224] *Vie de Marguerite de Jésus*, I, XXXIII, p. 67.
[225] Garasse, *Doctrine*, p. 146.
[226] *Vie de Marguerite de Jésus*, I, XXXIII, p. 67.
[227] See Saint-Pierre quoted in Leopizzi, *Sources*, p. 103; Gramond, *Historiarum* in Durand, *Vanini*, pp. 191, 192–3.

> durant le séjour qu'ils seraient obligés d'y faire, jusqu'à ce qu'ils pussent revenir en toute sûreté.
>
> As soon as they had given their statement and completed all the other formalities of legal procedure, they saw that their lives were in great danger, due to several notable people whom they had been obliged to mention for having seen them take lessons and attend meetings at their master's house. But Mr and Madame de Garibal took care to see to their safety [...] they sent them to Spain in secret, after having given them a considerable sum of money for their journey and to sustain them during the stay that they would be obliged to make there, until they were able to come back safely.[228]

Several of the details in the *Vie de Marguerite de Jésus* provide new information on the stages of Vanini's trial. On more than one occasion, the text refers to the servants' fear of the consequences of having implicated important local figures in the affair. All of the contemporary accounts of Vanini's arrival in Toulouse note that he frequented the upper echelons of Toulouse society. The servants' misgivings invite a new, darker interpretation of the *Histoire véritable*'s reference to debauched young gentlemen 'qu'il n'est besoin de nommer' ('who need not be named').[229] Perhaps some of these, compromised by Vanini's trial, were coerced into serving as witnesses against the Italian's irreligious speech. According to Senaux, Vanini's former students were far from the bashful, innocent sheep who scolded him for his impiety before returning to the Catholic flock. These implicated parties judged that their involvement with him was sufficiently incriminating to ruin their reputations. The names of those incriminated have not survived in witness interrogation records, the final *arrêt de mort,* or in contemporary accounts with the exception of Cramail. This surely supports our earlier hypothesis regarding Francon. As the only one of Vanini's young aristocratic students to be named, his death provided powerful families in Toulouse with an ideal, silent scapegoat to conceal their implication in the Vanini affair. Senaux's account also goes some way to filling the void in the *instruction* of the trial. Far from keeping Vanini out of sight and out of mind in his cell, the Parlement de Toulouse clearly put more effort into constructing a case against him than scholars of Vanini have hitherto realised. A likely *monitoire*, the Garibals' coercion of the servants, their preparations to send them to Spain, and the witness confrontations themselves would all have taken place prior to Vanini's final audience with his judges before his sentence was passed.

As welcome as this new archival evidence may be, certain elements of Senaux's account nonetheless urge us to approach this source with some caution. First, some of her assertions are not in keeping with those made in relatively reliable contemporary sources. According to Senaux, it was the servants' testimony that

[228] *Vie de Marguerite de Jésus*, I, XXXIII, p. 66.
[229] *Histoire véritable*, p. 9.

finally disarmed Vanini and left him unable to maintain his innocence. Gramond, however, relates Vanini's demonstration of the existence of God using a piece of straw during his *interrogatoire sur la sellette*.[230] As Foucault remarks, this suggests that 'Vanini semble donc jusqu'au bout essayé de défendre l'idée que sa doctrine n'était pas impie' ('Vanini therefore seems to have tried to defend the idea that his doctrine was not impious until the very end').[231] A problem presents itself here. In criminal investigations of the time, the accused could be interrogated at the beginning of the investigation (known as the *instruction préparatoire*), or in a final *interrogatoire sur la sellette* before the judges deliberated a verdict. It was only before the final deliberation in criminal cases which had followed a *voie extraordinaire* that the accused would take the stand in front of the full panel of judges for the first time.[232] In other words, Gramond's account involving the piece of straw can *only* refer to Vanini's final, pre-verdict interrogation, at which point he still protested his innocence. Given Gramond's position in the legal sphere, his account must be taken to disprove Senaux's claim that the testimony of Vanini's servants, which came before the *interrogatoire sur la sellette* in which he picked up a piece of straw, led him to abandon his strategy of self-defence.

A second note of caution stems from a contrary observation: a number of Senaux's claims agree with those made in the years following Vanini's death just a little too well. She claims, for instance, that Vanini:

> dit qu'ils étaient sortis de la ville de Naples au nombre de douze imbus d'une même doctrine pour l'aller répandre par tout le monde, se proposant en cela d'imiter la mission et les voyages des douze apôtres.
>
> said that twelve of them had left the city of Naples, filled with the same doctrine, to go out and spread it across the world, with the intention of imitating the mission and travels of the twelve Apostles.[233]

None of the sources claiming to have witnessed the trial, or published shortly after Vanini's execution, refers to these disciples. This claim does, however, bear a striking resemblance to those made by authors hostile towards Vanini who wrote after the fact. Mersenne claims that 'Vaninum dixisse ferant, se cum 13 Neapoli discesisse, ut per totum Orbem terrarum Atheismum propogarent' ('Vanini declared that he had moved away from Naples with 13 of his companions to spread atheism throughout the world').[234] Jacques Gaultier in turn asserts that 'il adjousta qu'on n'avançoit guere, de le faire mourir, d'autant qu'ils estoient douze en nombre

[230] See Gramond quoted in Durand, *Vanini*, p. 188.
[231] Foucault, *Vanini*, p. 478.
[232] See Marie Houllemare, *Politiques de la parole: le Parlement de Paris au XVIe siècle* (Geneva: Droz, 2011), p. 42.
[233] *Vie de Marguerite de Jésus*, I, XXXIII, p. 67.
[234] Marin Mersenne, *Quaestiones Celeberrimae in Genesim* quoted in Raimondi, 'Vanini et Mersenne', p. 225.

sortis de Naples, qui s'estoient espanchez par l'Europe pour enseigner la mesme doctrine' ('he added that they gained nothing by putting him to death, as twelve of them had left Naples and had spread across Europe to teach the same doctrine').[235] As with Garasse's account of Francon's involvement, we find ourselves confronted with what at first appears to be a reliable detail, as confirmed by multiple texts, but which is not mentioned by authors who either published their accounts at the time or who claimed to rely on first-hand knowledge of the case. Senaux's text also joins many others in claiming that Vanini 'continuait toujours de séduire et de corrompre la jeunesse la plus qualifiée de la ville' ('still continued to seduce and to corrupt the most noble of the city's youths').[236] Here again, the language used in the Évry manuscript is very similar to that of other sources. Vanini's actions prior to his arrest, for example, are described by Senaux thus: 'il trouva le moyen de persuader à quelques libertins, que nos âmes ne sont pas immortelles, que ce monde est éternel, que tout périt à la mort avec le corps' ('he found the means to persuade a few libertines that our souls are not immortal, that the world is eternal, that all of us perishes along with the body after death').[237] The linguistic resemblance to accounts given by Rosset, the *Histoire véritable*, and the *Mercure françois* is obvious:

> Que le monde est eternel, et que les ames des hommes, et celles des bestes n'ont rien de different, puis que les uns et les autres meurent avec le corps.
>
> That the world is eternal, and that the souls of men and those of the beasts are in no way different, as both of them die with the body.[238]

> Il soustenoit que nos corps estoient sans ame, et que mourans tout estoit mort pour nous.
>
> He argued that our bodies are without a soul, and that in dying all came to an end for us.[239]

Finally, the *Vie de Marguerite de Jésus* implicitly refers to Francon. Her account would greatly undermine our earlier argument refuting Francon's role in the trial, were it not for the fact that Senaux's version of events is clearly coloured by Garasse's *Doctrine curieuse*:

> Celui n'eut pas plutôt entendu un tel discours, que saisi d'horreur et d'indignation, ne pouvant retenir son zèle comme un autre Phinéas, mit subitement la main sur la garde de son épée contre ce blasphémateur: mais le respect du bien ayant un peu retenu sa colère, il se contenta de le remarquer, de le faire suivre, et le fit ensuite dénoncer.

235 Gaultier, *Table chorographique*, p. 875.
236 *Vie de Marguerite de Jésus*, I, XXXIII, p. 66.
237 *Vie de Marguerite de Jésus*, I, XXXIII, p. 64.
238 Rosset, *Histoires mémorables*, p. 201.
239 *Histoire véritable*, p. 9; *Mecure françois*, p. 64.

No sooner had he heard such discourse that, seized with horror and indignation, and unable to temper his zeal like a second Phineas, he quickly put his hand on the hilt of his sword against this blasphemer. Yet once his respect for good had calmed his anger a little, he was happy simply to take note of Vanini's words, to have him followed, and later on, to denounce him.[240]

Francon confessa depuis que les cheveux luy herissoient en teste, et qu'il mit deux fois la main sur son poignard pour luy plonger dans le sein; mais qu'il fut retenu par une forte consideration, voyant que l'affaire s'estant passée sans tesmoings, il pourroit estre en peine apres le meutre. Il prit un meilleur expedient, car il deffera cet impie au premier President, lequel ayant consulté l'affaire, le fit saisir sur d'autres depositions secrettes.

Francon since admitted than his hairs stood on end, and that on two occasions he reached for his dagger to sink it into Vanini's chest. But he was prevented from doing by the very good reason of a lack of witnesses, which could have led him into difficulty after the murder. He found a better solution, as he referred this impious man to the *premier président*, who having looked into the affair, had Vanini arrested on the basis of other secret depositions.[241]

The *Vie de Marguerite de Jésus* should therefore be approached carefully. Although it clearly offers new and insightful material on the final stages of Vanini's trial, it also appears to have been influenced by later sources, which may even have been researched by Senaux's great-grand-nephew in order to contextualise his relative's otherwise independent recollection of events. It is not the only early modern source to borrow from earlier texts, of course, and the notes of caution sounded above should not therefore discredit the new information that this account brings to our understanding of the trial.

THE VERDICT AND EXECUTION: A FINAL ACT OF SUBVERSION

On 9 February 1619, Vanini was found guilty of atheism, blasphemy, and impieties by the assembled chambers of the Grand' Chambre and the Tournelle of the Parlement de Toulouse. Although succinct, his *arrêt de mort* is the most reliable document detailing the stages of the trial. It states that Vanini was found guilty following 'confrontements' (*confrontations*) with witnesses, as well as 'objetz par luy propouses [sic] contre les Tesmoigns a luy confrontez' ('objections proposed by him against the witnesses with whom he was confronted') and the 'conclusions du procureur general du Roy'.[242] It is notable that 'witnesses' appears in the plural here, as expected in a capital offence trial where the Biblical adage against

[240] *Vie de Marguerite de Jésus*, I, XXXIII, p. 66.
[241] Garasse, *Doctrine*, p. 146.
[242] ADHG MS B 382 (1619), fol. 153: 'Arrêt de mort de Vanini'; Leopizzi, *Sources*, p. 71.

conviction on the basis of a single witness—*unus testis, nullus testis*—came into play.[243] We can therefore say with certainty that Vanini's trial officially satisfied the need for at least two witnesses.[244]

Foucault asserts that Vanini's naturalist ideas probably came to the Parlement's attention through witnesses, and that he would not have rejected such testimony through fear of appearing imprudent before his judges.[245] This view is open to challenge. First, given that Vanini seems to have defended himself both consistently and effectively for the greater part of his trial until witness testimony had been uncovered, it would have been perfectly logical for him to refute the claims of those who testified against him. Second, the wording of the *arrêt* makes it likely that Vanini made *reproches* against witnesses and that these objections were then dismissed by the court, thereby maintaining the testimony as admissible. Although the accused could only object to witness testimony before this was read out to him, his *reproches* were invited *after* he had been confronted with the witness and both parties had confirmed that they knew each other.[246] Given Vanini's education, he would likely have known that far from being imprudent, rejecting the evidence given by his own servants based on their social rank would, as we saw earlier, have been a possible legal defence.[247] Finally, Senaux's and Garibal's promise to send the servants to Spain and to fund their exile at their own expense could, if known, have been considered a valid reason to object to the servants' testimony.[248]

There is a sense of urgency and even frustration in the wording of the *arrêt*: remarkably, it declares that the trial 'est en estat pour estre jugé diffinitivement sans informer de la verite desdicts objectz' ('is at a sufficient stage to be judged definitively without clarifying whether the aforementioned matters are true').[249] Raimondi suggests that this may simply have meant that no further information

[243] See Deuteronomy 9:15, 17:6; Numbers 35:30; 2 Corinthians 13:1; Matthew 18:16. On the legal term, see Antonino Metro, 'Unus testis, nullus testis', in *Critical Studies in Ancient Law, Comparative Law and Legal History: Essays in Honour of Alan Watson*, ed. by John Cairns and Olivia Robinson (Oxford and Portland, OR: Hart Publishing, 2001), pp. 108–116.

[244] See Christian Biet, *Droit et littérature sous l'Ancien Régime: Le jeu de la valeur et de la loi* (Paris: Honoré Champion, 2002), p. 135. It is curious that in transcribing this document, Leopizzi should claim that 'on ne peut pas dire si, outre à Francon, une autre personne témoigna contre Vanini' ('we cannot say whether, apart from Francon, another person testified against Vanini': Leopizzi, *Sources*, p. 68).

[245] Foucault, *Vanini*, p. 478.

[246] Owing to an ordinance published in 1539. See Aldémar Esmein, *Histoire de la procédure criminelle en France* (Paris: Larose et Forcel, 1882), p. 145.

[247] Mousnier notes how in Roman and Cannon law, the social condition of witnesses was one of seven elements that judges had to take into account (Mousnier, *Institutions*, p. 384).

[248] The fourth *reproche de fait* noted by La Rochette describes 'celuy qui a esté suborné et corrompu par argent ou autres presents, qui luy ont esté donnez ou promis, pour deposer' ('he who has been induced to commit perjury and corrupted by money or other presents, which have been given or promised to him, in return for testifying': La Rochette, *Les Procès civil*, p. 85).

[249] ADHG MS B 382 (1619), fol. 153: 'Arrêt de mort de Vanini'; Leopizzi, *Sources*, p. 71.

was required to be sure of Vanini's guilt of atheism.[250] Another explanation may be found by situating this extraordinary clause within its contemporary legal context. As Guillaume Ratel reminds us, the seventeenth-century meaning of a *fait* (fact) here is not one of scientific epistemology. It referred to the judges' tactics and arguments during the deliberation and the legal grounds that they quoted in support of their preferred verdict. A distinction must therefore be made between the modern notion of empirical fact and the early modern intended meaning of subjective opinion within a deliberative context.[251] Thus, this line in Vanini's *arrêt* does not reveal the judges' unwillingness to uncover whether certain aspects of the investigation were true (for example, the veracity of witness testimony). Rather, it betrays the haste with which the verdict was reached by privileging the judges' own impressions on the case over due reflection in light of specific points of law. Further on, the *arrêt* relates that the opinions of the *procureur général du roi* (king's attorney general) were heard along with 'aultres productions sur ces faictes' ('other evidence produced on these matters').[252] The wording of the text, and in particular a number of omissions pertaining to legal procedure, make Vanini's *arrêt* an exceptional and problematic document.[253]

The judges' verdict was largely influenced by one magistrate in particular: Guillaume de Catel, a man of great learning and a pioneer in the study of local history.[254] Whether or not Catel developed a strong abhorrence to Vanini's purported crimes, the punishment meted out against him would have been seen in his own time as in no way contradicting Catel's sense of justice or indeed piety. As such, Catel's role in the verdict must be evaluated from a legal perspective rather than attributing his actions to personal motives. We might well read Catel's description of Vanini in a letter to Peiresc as 'le plus beau et le plus meschant esprit que jaye cogneu' ('the finest and most wicked mind I have ever known') as a succinct encapsulation of this multifaceted nature of the mentalities of early modern judges.[255]

Although Catel's role at Vanini's trial was pivotal, the ambiguity of extant documentation has led it to become the subject of both speculation and distortion.

[250] Raimondi, 'Un documento enigmatico', 590.
[251] Ratel, 'Between Facts and Faith', pp. 305–8.
[252] ADHG MS B 382 (1619), fol. 153: 'Arrêt de mort de Vanini'; Leopizzi, *Sources*, p. 71.
[253] Raimondi has provided a meticulous analysis of this document in Raimondi, *Un documento enigmatico*.
[254] Guillaume Catel, *Histoire des comtes de Tolose* (Tolose: P. Bosc, 1623) – dedicated to none other than the liberal patron of libertine writers, Henri II de Montmorency –; Guillaume de Catel, *Mémoire de l'histoire du Languedoc* (Tolose: P. Bosc, 1633). Schneider asserts that Catel was 'the man responsible for pursuing the case against Vanini' and that he '[took] it upon himself to initiate the proceedings' against Vanini (*Public Life*, p. 154). Although Catel argued for the death sentence in the final deliberations, Vanini's case was 'initiated' by denunciation and initially investigated by the Capitoulat rather than the Parlement, whereas the 'pursuing' of the case was the responsibility of the *commissaires*.
[255] BNF MS Dupuy 688, Guillaume de Catel to Peiresc (February 1619), fol. 77v.

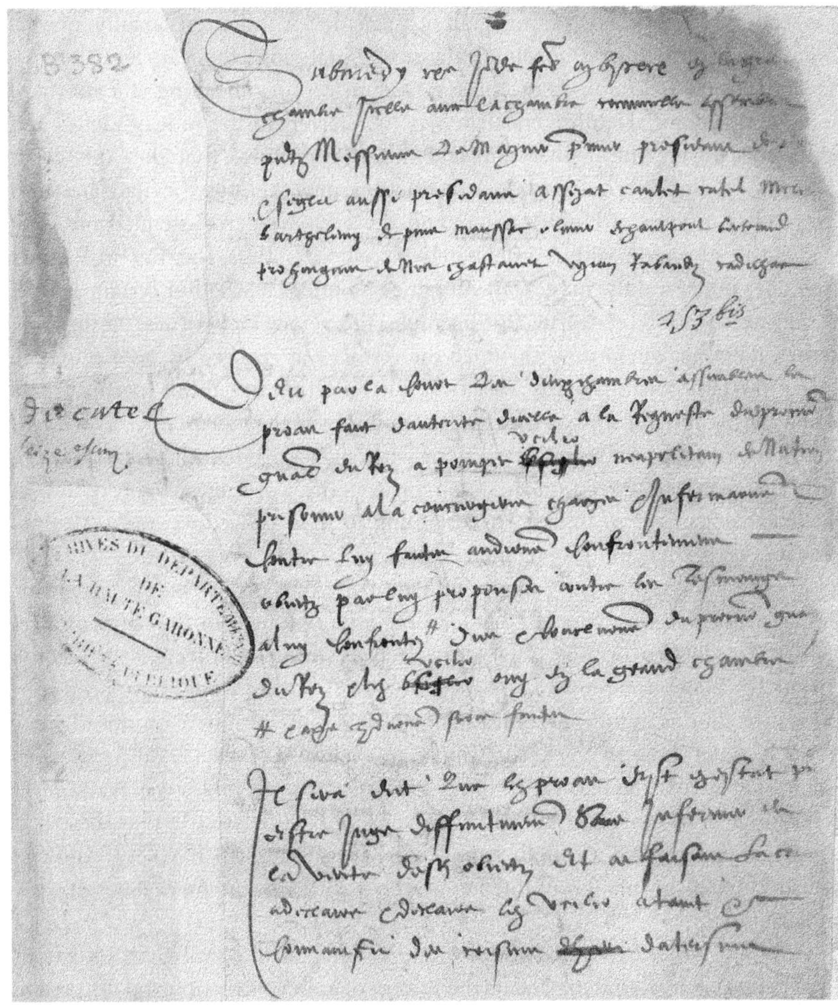

Figure 3.2 ADHG MS B 382 (1619), fol. 153: the beginning of the three-page 'Arrêt de mort de Vanini'. The marginal annotation shows that Guillaume de Catel received 'seize escus' ('sixteen écus') in *épices* for his services as *rapporteur*. © Conseil départemental de la Haute-Garonne / Archives 31 / B 382.

Catel is credited for having served as the *rapporteur* (reporter) for the trial.[256] The *Annales de la ville de Toulouse* state that '[en] la grande-chambre de la Tournelle assemblées, fut donné arrest au rapport de Monsieur de Catel, conseilier [sic] au parlement, par lequel il fut condamné' ('[in] the assembled chambers of the

[256] Foucault, *Vanini*, p. 477, who alludes to this role in identifying Catel as being in charge of the closing speech—the *réquisitoire*— in *1619*, p. 5; Raimondi, *Vanini Nell'Europa del Seicento*, p. 498.

Grand' Chambre and the Tournelle, the sentence was read out condemning Vanini to death, on the report of Mr de Catel, *conseiller* in the Parlement').[257] Catel himself proudly alluded to his decisive role in Vanini's trial in his letter to Peiresc, describing in the margin 'un insigne ~~Ph~~ athée, philosophe, et medecin fils de Naples; lequel a este sur mon raport les deux chambres condampne et ~~exec~~ brullé' ('an extraordinary son of Naples who was an ~~Ph~~ atheist, philosopher, and doctor, and who was condemned by the two chambers to be ~~exec~~ burned on my report').[258] Furthermore, Vanini's *arrêt* bears both Catel's and the *premier président* Le Mazuyer's signatures, as the signatures of a trial's *président* and *rapporteur* were required for an *arrêt* to be legally binding.[259] Yet as well as acting as the *rapporteur* for this case, Catel is credited by some critics as having stood in for the *procureur général du roi*, that is to say as a legal *substitut*, due to a marginal annotation in the *arrêt* detailing the fee that Catel received for his service, known as the *épices*: 'de Catel / seize escus' ('de Catel, sixteen écus') (Figure 3.2).[260] From a legal perspective however, Catel's service in both of these roles would have been at least highly irregular if not impossible.

Close attention to the administrative procedure in producing a verdict allows us to dispel at least some of the mystery surrounding this document. First, the *épices* were payment for Catel's services as *rapporteur*, in recognition of the time he spent sifting through the evidence in order to present a summary to his fellow judges, as well as his task of drafting the *arrêt*.[261] Charles Loyseau is unequivocal in explaining that the *épices* were reserved 'seulement pour salarier le rapporteur du labeur qu'il a pris à voir et extraire le procez en sa maison: aussi par les anciennes Ordonnances sont-elles attribuées au Rapporteur seul' ('only as the *rapporteur*'s

[257] AMT MS BB 278, *Annales*, Saint-Pierre (1618), fols. 13–14; Leopizzi, *Sources*, p. 103.

[258] BNF MS Dupuy 688, fols. 76–7. The scored-out words in the letter are significant, as they show that Catel thought it important to describe Vanini first and foremost as an atheist rather than a philosopher, and that the punishment for his crimes should be described (perhaps even savoured) in greater detail.

[259] See article 65 of the 'Édit de Moulins' (1566), in Isambert, *Recueil général*, XIV i, p. 206: 'Aucuns arrests ne seront reçus aux greffes, ni prononcéz, qu'ils ne soient signez de l'un des présidens des chambres de nosdites cours avec le rapporteur' ('no *arrêt* will be received by the court administration, or proclaimed, unless it is signed by one of the *présidents* of the chambers of our courts along with the *rapporteur*'). On the legality of *arrêts* in relation to these signatures, see also the 'Arrêt de Paris' (17 December 1555) in Bernard de La Roche Flavin, *Treize livres des parlemens de France* (Geneva: Mathieu Berjon, 1621), p. 1083.

[260] Foucault, *Vanini*, p. 478, note 2; Raimondi, 'Un documento enigmatico', 588–9; Raimondi, *Vanini Nell'Europa del Seicento*, p. 498, which speaks of 'De Catel, che aveva le funzioni della pubblica accusa' ('De Catel, who had the role of public prosecutor').

[261] Raimondi contemplates whether Catel's fee proves that he was Vanini's denouncer, as denouncers were entitled to a third of any fine levied against subsequently convicted criminals. He then highlights that the *arrêt* makes no mention of Vanini having been fined, and that it would be extraordinary for Catel to have been both Vanini's denouncer and public prosecutor, before concluding that the marginal annotation is 'un rebus' ('a mystery'). See Raimondi, 'Un documento enigmatico', 588–9. On the duties of the *rapporteur* see Chapter 2, pp. 95–6. On the *épices* see Pierre Guénois, *Le corps du droict françois* (Geneva: Pour Jean de Laon, 1600), pp. 245–8; Ratel, 'Between Facts and Faith', pp. 214–50.

salary for the work he has undertaken in working on the case at his home, and according to past ordinances they are given solely to the *rapporteur*').[262] As the ability to serve in this capacity was one of the ways in which a magistrate's skills were judged, it was desirable for each magistrate to *rapporter* for at least one trial per year.[263] The role of *substitut du procureur général*, however, was a formally recognised rank within the legal system, more specifically as one of the *gens du roi* (the king's men) tasked with defending royal interests.[264] First created by Henri III's royal edict of May 1586, there were initially to be sixteen *substituts* in the Parlement de Paris and ten in the Parlement de Toulouse. There was therefore a difference between the role of *rapporteur*—assigned to a specific case with a preference for all judges to gain experience in this role in return for commensurate remuneration—and the permanent role of *substituts*, whose numbers were limited. Given that *substituts* were considered part of the *gens du roi* who were not linked to a single given chamber in the Parlement, it might also be argued that had Catel held this position, he would have referred to himself as a *substitut du procureur général* rather than a 'conseiller du Roy' in his will.[265]

One of the *rapporteur*'s responsibilities was to draft the *arrêts*, although the number of legislative acts demanding that the *rapporteurs* write these in their own hand suggests that many delegated this onerous task to scribes. The third and final draft, termed a *dictum*, was passed to the *président* of the chamber. He would then instruct the *greffier* to write the value of *épices* to be given to the *rapporteur* in the margin. Finally, it was a legal requirement for both the *président* and *rapporteur* to sign this document, which was subsequently deposited in the *registres d'arrêts*.[266] The fact that the marginal record of the *épices* happens to appear alongside a reference to the *procureur général du roi* in the main body in no way indicates a link between the two pieces of information. Its location on the document, as well as the fact that it is written in a different hand to the main body, corresponds both

262 Charles Loyseau, *Cinq livres du droit des offices* (Paris: Abel d'Angelier, 1614), p. 96.

263 On the perceived need for a judge to be an effective *rapporteur*, see Ratel, 'Between Facts and Faith', pp. 298–301.

264 See on this point Houllemare, *Parlement*, p. 184. On the creation of this role, see the 'Édit d'érection en tiltre d'office, des Substituts des Procureurs generaux du Roy' (May 1586) in Étienne Girard, *Trois livres des offices de France* (Paris: Estienne Richer, 1638), pp. 65–6. The approval of a *procureur général* or his *substituts* was legally required in order to 'conclure à peine afflictive' ('to pass a sentence of afflictive punishment': Ferrière, *Dictionnaire*, I, p. 392, col. 2).

265 Monique Langlois, 'Parlement de Paris', in Michel Antoine and others, *Guide des recherches dans les fonds judiciaires de l'ancien régime* (Paris: Imprimerie Nationale, 1958), pp. 67–139 (p. 71); Célestin Douais, 'Le Testament de Guillaume de Catel', *Revue des Pyrénées*, 9 (1897), 497–507 (507).

266 On the drafting of *arrêts*, see Ratel, 'Between Facts and Faith', pp. 303–4, 357–66. The scored-out phrases and other peculiarities in this document, so meticulously analysed in Raimondi's article, can also be found in other such documents in the *registres d'arrêts*. As Ratel states, one of the differences between an archived *dictum* and a printed *arrêt* is that the *arrêt* omitted the allocation of *épices* found in the margin of the *dictum* (Ratel, 'Between Facts and Faith', p. 358). The fact that this document bears the signatures of Le Mazuyer and Catel, as well as the *épices*, proves that it is the definitive *dictum* rather than an earlier draft.

with other *arrêts* for similar crimes tried by the Parlement de Toulouse and with standard administrative procedure.[267]

The stages of criminal procedure also make it highly unlikely that Catel would have performed these two separate roles. On 13 June 1587, the assembled chambers of the Parlement de Toulouse decided that judges who carried out the *instruction* of a criminal case could not then serve as its *rapporteur*.[268] The Parlement was therefore mindful to compartmentalise the different roles involved in a criminal trial. Once the *commissaires* in charge of the *instruction* had completed their gathering of evidence, their documents were examined by the *procureur général*, who would give his opinion (*ses conclusions*) on the matter. He would then pass these on to the *rapporteur* in order to be sifted and synthesised for the other judges.[269]

There are three technical obstacles here to Catel serving as a *substitut* as well as the *rapporteur*. First, a *substitut* presented his views on a given case to his fellow *gens du roi*, and not to the *commisaires* in charge of the *instruction* or the wider panel of judges, so that the *procureur général* could give his conclusions on the case. It would therefore have been tenuous for Catel to claim responsibility for Vanini's death through his report to the *procureur général*, who then used this report to prepare his own *conclusions* which in turn informed, rather than dictated, the judges' decision.[270] Second, there is a conflict between personal recommendation and impartial summary which would have made the fulfilment of these two roles somewhat confusing. If Catel had served as both *substitut* and *rapporteur*, he would first have had to submit his individual opinion on the case as a *substitut*. He would then have needed to prepare an *impartial* synthesis of evidence as the *rapporteur*, without revealing his own voting intention, whilst at the same time incorporating his own personal recommendations previously formulated in his *conclusions* as the *substitut*. Finally, *arrêts* for trials in which a *substitut du procureur général* served as the public prosecutor were equally explicit in this distinction. To stay with the crime of blasphemy as a case in point, in 1599 Nicolas le Mesle was tried by the Parlement de Paris 'à la requeste du Substitut du procureur General du Roy' ('at the request of the king's attorney general's *substitut*').[271] Or to give another example within the

[267] Such as the death sentence against Blaise Vitalis for blasphemy on 21 April 1603 (ADHG MS 1 B 3548). See Adam Horsley, 'Blasphemy Hunters: Nicolas de Verdun and the Punishment of Criminal Speech in Early Bourbon France', *French Studies*, 75: 2 (2021), 145–62.

[268] La Roche Flavin, *Treize livres*, p. 1161.

[269] J.H. Shenann, *The Parlement of Paris* (Stroud: Sutton, 1998), p. 70; Margolf, *Religion and Royal Justice*, pp. 41–2.

[270] As we will see in Chapter 5, the judges did not always return the same verdict as recommended in these *conclusions*.

[271] [Vincent Mussart], *Le Fouet des jureurs et blasphemateurs du nom de Dieu* (Troye: Nicolas Oudot, 1614), pp. 47^{v} – 48^{r}. It should be added that the *substitut*'s presentation to the *gens du roi* was also termed a *rapport*, and that a *rapporteur*'s speech could also be referred to as an *opinion*. Catel's allusion to *mon rapport*, then, is in fact flimsy evidence of his role in Vanini's case.

field of *libertinage* studies: Geoffroy Vallée was burned alive on 9 February 1574 for having written the *La Béatitude des Chrestiens ou le Fléo de la Foy*, following his trial 'à la requeste du substitut du Procureur général du Roy au Chastellet' ('on the request of the *substitut* of the king's attorney general at the Châtelet').[272]

There is therefore considerable archival evidence, legal theory, and precedent in related cases to exclude Catel as the public prosecutor for Vanini's trial. As Raimondi observes, the *procureur général* François de Saint-Félix d'Aussargues was not present in Toulouse for Vanini's arrest and subsequent transfer from the Capitoulat to the Parlement.[273] Nevertheless, he had returned to Toulouse some six months prior to Vanini's condemnation. It is therefore perfectly reasonable to assume that if Vanini's *arrêt* describes his trial being 'à la requeste du procureur general du Roy' ('at the request of the king's attorney general'), and not by a *substitut* as seen in similar documents, it is because Saint-Félix had returned in time to serve as public prosecutor. Guillaume de Catel did not therefore serve as a *substitut du procureur général du roi* at Vanini's trial, and his official role was limited to the nonetheless influential and decisive role of *rapporteur*.

The *premier président* Gilles Le Mazuyer was the other authoritative voice in the deliberations. Having taken up his role as the head of the Parlement de Toulouse in December 1616, Le Mazuyer had previously served in the Parlement de Paris as a *conseiller* (as of 7 August 1596), then *maistre des requestes* (as of 18 November 1604), and was a loyal servant of Marie de Médicis.[274] He was also loyal to the Catholic cause and possessed of a particular zeal against the Protestants.[275] Whilst attending the 1617 *Assemblée des notables* in Rouen, for example, he had found time to visit Paris, where he purchased a large amount of weapons with which to fight the Protestants in the wars that he was convinced were coming.[276] Stockpiled in Toulouse, these armaments proved to be sound investments when Louis XIII began his suppression of Protestant rebels in 1620, including at the siege of Montauban where Vanini's reputed witness, Francon, lost his life. Seven years after Vanini's death, Le Mazuyer went as far as to conceal the Edict of Pacification from the Parlement in order that he might first execute one of the duc de Rohan's body guards, Campredon, for political crimes.[277] Le Mazuyer ended his days a dutiful and selfless protector of the Catholics of Toulouse. He remained in the city after the

[272] AN X 2B 78: 'Arrêt de mort contre Geoffroy Vallée' (8 February 1574) quoted in Frédéric Lachèvre, *Mélanges sur le libertinage au XVIIe siècle* (Paris: Honoré Champion, 1920), p. 44.

[273] Raimondi, *Vanini Nell'Europa del Seicento*, p. 474.

[274] Michel Popoff, *Prosopographie des gens du Parlement de Paris (1266–1743)* (Paris: Le Léopard d'or, 2003), p. 714; Foucault, *1619*, p. 5. On Mazuyer see also Foucault, *Vanini*, pp. 458–61; Raimondi, *Vanini Nell'Europa del Seicento*, pp. 475–6.

[275] Raimondi speaks of Le Mazuyer's 'odio religioso contro ogni forma di protestantesimo' ('religious hatred against all forms of Protestantism': Raimondi, *Vanini Nell'Europa del Seicento*, pp. 474–5).

[276] Foucault, *Vanini*, p. 459.

[277] On 6 April 1626. See Jack Alden Clarke, *Huguenot Warrior: The Life and Times of Henri de Rohan, 1597–1638* (The Hague: Martinus Nijhoff, 1966), p. 138.

plague struck in 1628, caring personally for those infected before succumbing to the disease himself in 1632.[278] When it came to what he considered to be spiritual maladies, Le Mazuyer showed equal devotion and determination. It could have been no comfort to Vanini that he found himself on trial under the presidency of 'un des plus ardens persécuteurs dont on ait jamais parlé [...] et cruel au dernier point. [...] Il ne connaissoit ni justice ni bonne foy, quand il s'agissoit de religion' ('one of the most ardent persecutors that was ever heard of [...] and cruel to the bone. [...] When it came to matters of religion, he had no concept of justice or good faith').[279]

Signed by Catel and Le Mazuyer, the *arrêt* spares no detail in describing Vanini's punishment. Dragged through the streets of Toulouse, he was to be publicly identified and then punished as an enemy of God:

> Portant sur ses esplaulses ung cartel contenant cez motz ateiste et blasphemateur du Nom de dieu et le conduyra audevant de la porte principale de leglise metropolitaine sainct Estienne et estant illec a genoulz Teste et piedz nudz tenant en ses mains une Torche de cire ardante demandera pardon a dieu au Roy et a Justice desdicts blasphemes et aprez ladmenera en la place du Salin et attachera à ung poteau que y sera plante luy coupera la langue et lestranglera et aprez sera son corps brusle au bucher que y sera aपresté et les cendres jettees au vent.
>
> With a sign reading 'atheist and blasphemer of the name of God' on his shoulders, he will first be brought to the main door of the Church of Saint Étienne where, on his knees, with his head and feet bare and a burning candle in his hands, he will ask forgiveness of God, the King and the judiciary for these blasphemies. Afterwards he will be brought to the Place du Salin and tied to a stake which shall be placed there. His tongue will be cut out, he will be strangled, after which his body will be burned at the stake which will be prepared there, and his ashes thrown to the wind.[280]

The dramatisation of power relations represented by the burning of a deviant thinker at the stake is a prime location for what Michel Foucault would recognise as the demonstration of sovereign power.[281] Beyond the spoken word, the mutilation of the criminal's body is also symbolic of their failed attempt to escape, the superior force of the agent of dominant orthodoxy (that is to say the dispensers of justice), and of the blasphemer's ugly difference from the rest of the God-fearing community. As Michel Foucault observes:

> Du côté de la justice qui l'impose, le supplice doit être éclatant, il doit être constaté par tous, un peu comme sa triomphe. L'excès même des violences exercées est une

[278] Schneider, *Public Life*, p. 40.

[279] Elie Benoist, *Histoire de l'édit de Nantes, etc.*, 5 vols (Delft: Adrien Beman, 1693), II, p. 317 quoted in Raimondi, *Vanini Nell'Europa del Seicento*, p. 476.

[280] ADHG MS B 382 (1619), fol. 153: 'Arrêt de mort de Vanini'; Leopizzi, *Sources*, p. 73.

[281] On this dramatisation of power relations, see James C. Scott, *Domination and the Arts of Resistance* (New Haven, CT, and London: Yale University Press, 1990), p. 66. For Michel Foucault, executions also act as a political ritual serving as one of several ways in which power is able to manifest itself. See Michel Foucault, *Surveiller et punir* (Paris: Gallimard, 1975), p. 58.

pièce de sa gloire: que le coupable gémisse et crie sous les coups, ce n'est pas un à-côté honteux, c'est le cérémonial même de la justice se manifestant dans sa force.

For the prevailing justice system, the torment must be awe-inspiring, it must be seen by everyone, almost as its triumph. The very excess of violence used against the condemned is part of its glory: if the criminal groans and cries out as the execution is carried out, this is not a shameful side issue. Rather, it is the very ceremony of the justice system showing itself through its strength.[282]

Vanini's words and actions during the moments leading up to his execution are charged with the politics of power relations. Yet for the magistrates present—including the *capitouls*, two of whom were obliged to attend every execution in the city—Vanini had a final card to play in his subversion of the pious norm.[283] Several sources affirm that a priest was on hand to offer solace to Vanini for the sake of his state of mind, the salvation of his soul, and the public spectacle in which he was to be the star performer. And perform he did:

Je le vis dans le Tombereau, lorsqu'on le menoit au supplice se moquant d'un Cordelier qu'on lui avoit donné pour le consoler et le faire revenir de son obstination. [...] Vanini farouche et opiniâtre refusa les consolations du Cordelier qui l'accompagnoit.

I saw him in the cart as he was brought to the stake, mocking a Cordelier who had been given to him to console him and to make him repent of his obstinacy. [...] Vanini, savage and obstinate, refused the consolations of the Cordelier who accompanied him.[284]

Le bon père religieux qui l'assistoit estimoit, en lui montrant le crucifix et lui représentant les sacrés mystères de l'incarnation et passion admirable de notre Seigneur, l'esmouvoir à ce qu'il recognût. Mais ce tigre enragé et opiniastré en ses faulses maximes meprisoit tout, et ne le voulut jamais regarder.

The good priest who accompanied him thought that he had moved Vanini in showing him the crucifix and in telling him of the sacred mysteries of the incarnation and admirable Passion of our Lord. But this tiger, furious and obstinate in his false maxims, held it all in contempt, and at no point wished to look upon it.[285]

Le père religieux quy l'acistoit luy monstrant le crusifix pour luy faire souvenir des souffrances de Jesus Christ. Ce tigre le mesprisoit destournant la teste pour ne le vouloir regarder mourant athee.

The priest who accompanied him showed him the crucifix to make him remember Christ's suffering. This tiger scorned it by turning his head away, not wanting to look at it, and died an atheist.[286]

282 Foucault, *Surveiller*, p. 44.
283 See Faure, *Capitouls*, p. 72.
284 Gramond, *Historiarum* in Durand, *Vanini*, pp. 91, 192–3.
285 AMT MS BB 278, *Annales*, Saint-Pierre (1618), fols. 13–14; Leopizzi, *Sources*, p. 103.
286 BMT 696: *Extrait des Annales de Toulouse de 1295 à 1633* (1618–1619); Leopizzi, *Sources*, p. 147. On

Vanini's act of repelling the crucifix is both symbolic and highly subversive. Michel Foucault refers to several *manifestations de la vérité* at executions, the second of which serves to:

> Instaurer le supplice comme moment de vérité. Faire que ces derniers instants où le coupable n'a plus rien à perdre soient gagnés pour la pleine lumière du vrai. [...] Le vrai supplice a pour fonction de faire éclater la vérité.
>
> Establish the execution as a moment of truth. To ensure that these final moments when the guilty party has nothing left to lose are won for the cause of the clear light of truth. [...] The true execution serves to expose the truth.[287]

In the case of Vanini, the execution serves to affirm the power and reason of both Catholic and royal agents of authority over the subversive deviant.[288] In refusing to accept the symbol of Christian salvation, Vanini disrupted the public transcript of sovereign power, according to which the enforcement of a subscription to Catholic doctrine must be accepted by the subjugated due to the perils associated with a refusal to comply, that is to say eternal damnation. As well as failing to conform, Vanini's action also represents a direct attack on Catholic orthodoxy. For as Scott notes, 'when a practical failure to comply is joined with a pointed, public refusal it constitutes a throwing down of the gauntlet, a symbolic declaration of war'.[289] Beyond refusing the crucifix, Vanini was also reported to have made various declarations of irreligion, atheism, and defiance against the symbolic violence and censorship to which he was subjected as a condemned man. Gramond claims that Vanini compared himself favourably to Christ in approaching the scaffold: '[il] insulta à Notre Sauveur par ces paroles: "Il sua de crainte et de faiblesse, en allant à la mort, et moi je meurs intrépide"' ('he insulted Our Saviour with these words: "He was sweating with fear and weakness as he was led out to die, and I am dying audaciously"').[290] Rosset also attributes these words to Vanini, though during the trial itself:

---

the exchanges between the condemned and their confessors at executions, see Paul Bastien, 'La parole du confesseur auprès des suppliciés (Paris, XVIIe–XVIIIe siècle)', *Revue Historique*, 2: 634 (2005), 283–308.

[287] Foucault, *Surveiller*, pp. 54–5.

[288] As Paul Friedland observes, 'In an age when one's obedience to and honour of God were being increasingly likened to the respect that one owed the king, the public performance of the *amende honorable* was meant to pay one's debt to both' (Paul Friedland, *Seeing Justice Done—The Age of Spectacular Capital Punishment in France* (Oxford: Oxford University Press, 2012), p. 98).

[289] Scott, *Domination*, p. 203.

[290] Gramond, *Historiarum* in Durand, *Vanini*, p. 193. Vanini had made a similar comparison in *De admirandis*. When asked by Alexandre whether he is God or Vanini, Jules-César replies 'Hic sum' ('I am he'; Vanini, *De admirandis*, p. 409). Cavaillé has remarked that as Jules-César is abbreviated to J.C. in the original Latin text, Vanini could be read as implicitly comparing himself to Jesus Christ. See Jean-Pierre Cavaillé, 'Une pensée de la transgression. Politique, religion et morale chez Jules-César Vanini', *Kairos*, 12 (1998): *Vanini: Libertinage et philosophie à l'époque moderne*, ed. by Jean-Pierre Cavaillé and Didier Foucault (Toulouse: Presses Universitaires du Mirail, 1998), pp. 99–141 (p. 133).

> [Vanini disait] que lors que nostre Seigneur estoit prest d'aller souffrir la mort ignominieuse de la Croix, il suoit comme un homme sans courage, et luy ne suoit nullement, quoy qu'il vist bien qu'on le feroit bien tost mourir.
>
> [Vanini said] that when our Lord was ready to go out and suffer the ignominious death of the Cross, he was sweating as a man without courage, whereas he was not sweating at all, even though he could clearly see that they would soon put him to death.[291]

The *Mercure françois* takes Vanini's audacity before the stake one step further, reporting him to have declared:

> S'il y avoit un Dieu je le prierois de lancer un foudre sur le Parlement comme du toute injuste et inique; et s'il y avoit un diable, je le prierois aussi de l'engloutir aux lieux sous terrains: mais parce qu'il n'y a ny l'un ny l'autre, je n'en feray rien.
>
> If there were a God I would pray to Him to throw lightning down on the Parlement for its injustice and iniquity; and if there were a Devil I would also pray that he would swallow it up beneath the Earth. But because neither of them exists, I shall do nothing.[292]

Finally, the *Histoire véritable* recounts how Vanini died:

> avec autant de constance, de patience, et de volonté qu'aucun homme que l'on aye veu, car sortant de la Conciergerie comme joyeux et allegre, il prononça ces mots en Italien; allons, allons allaigrement mourir en Philosophe.
>
> with as much firmness, patience and will as any man you had ever seen, for as he was brought out of the Conciergerie in a joyous and cheerful mood, he said these words in Italian: 'come, come, let us die cheerfully as a Philosopher.'[293]

The outward joy with which Vanini approached the stake was not unheard of at this time. Lutherans and Protestants had displayed similar subversions of the anticipated public performance of repentance by appearing cheerful at their executions as early as the 1520s.[294] Although the precise words that Vanini supposedly used vary between sources, it is clear that he used his execution as a means of publicly discarding his mask of conformity to Catholicism. Instead, he chose to disseminate his true views, hitherto restricted to private conversations, in the public sphere as a final act of free-thinking before the crowd, the most important actor in the ceremony of executions.[295]

Beyond the struggle between the dominant Catholic orthodoxy embodied by the judiciary, and the dominated speaker of subversive atheist discourse, the spectator

[291] Rosset, *Histoires*, pp. 204–5. Rosset later claims that Vanini shouted out to the crowd 'un miserable Juif est cause que je suis icy' ('I am here because of a miserable Jew', p. 209).

[292] *Mercure françois*, p. 65.

[293] *Histoire véritable*, pp. 10–11.

[294] See Friedland, *Justice*, pp. 124.

[295] 'Dans les cérémonies du supplice, le personnage principal, c'est le peuple' (Foucault, *Surveiller*, p. 69).

also played a role in the maintenance of power relations. The symbolic physical destruction of a deviant thinker and author had the potential to shock observers into submission. As well as serving a social and legal function as a deterrent, such solemn rituals of punishment also provided any injured or implicated parties with a clear, strong display of public justice which would deter any private quests for vengeance.[296] Friedland has posited an alternative function of the execution for spectators: not as a deterrent, but as a collective act of atonement through which people felt that both they and their communities had been purified.[297] Despite Friedland's strong denial of Foucault's claim, these two opposing views may well have coexisted in the minds of Vanini's contemporaries. It seems entirely possible that the lower classes, the magistrates, and the elites were all aware of the potential of capital punishment as both spiritual cleansing and a legal deterrent, and that motives for attending such spectacles may have varied between individuals. The very date of Vanini's execution appears to have been timed to accentuate its effectiveness as a deterrent to spectators. In early February 1619, the duc de Montmorency was present in Toulouse for the arrival of his wife, whose sister was to marry the duc de Savoie. The resultant festivities included a carnival and a ballet, *Le Ballet des Inconstants*.[298] These celebrations were timed so as not to clash with Vanini's trial or his execution.[299] As Garrigues reminds us, the festivities took place during the sober period of Lent. As well as representing an opportunity for self-reflection, Vanini's death also counteracted the pomp and abundance of the marriage festivities, and may even have constituted an opportunity for spiritual cleansing for the spectators.[300]

Despite his bravery, the strength of his convictions, and the efficacy with which he had for several months been able to maintain the upper hand at his trial, Vanini finally succumbed to the gruesome royal justice meted out by the Parlement which would do much to assure his legacy in the history of free-thought:

> Avant qu'on mît le feu au bûcher, on lui ordonna de présenter sa langue pour être coupée. Il le refusa; le Bourreau ne put l'avoir qu'avec des tenailles dont il se servit et pour la saisir et pour la couper. On n'a jamais entendu un cri plus effroyable; vous l'auriez pris pour le mugissement d'un bœuf; le reste de son corps fut consumé au feu et ses cendres jetées au vent. Tel fut la fin de Lucilio Vanini.

[296] See Alfred Soman, 'Sorcellerie, justice criminelle et société dans la France moderne (l'ego-histoire d'un Américain à Paris)', *Histoire, Économie et Société*, 12: 2 (1993), 177–217 (202).

[297] 'The inhabitants of medieval and early modern France did not attend public executions so that they could be the object of the government's didactic lesson; rather, they attended for many of the same reasons that people had taken part in earlier rituals of public penance: to witness an act of atonement and to take part in an act of collective healing' (Friedland, *Justice*, p. 91).

[298] An account of these festivities was printed in the *Relation de ce qui s'est passé à Toulouse le 3.10. & 11. Février; pour le mariage de Madame sœur du Roy avec le Prince de Savoye* (Toulouse: Raymond Colomiez, 1619), which was dedicated to Vanini's former protector Bassompierre.

[299] Foucault, *Vanini*, p. 485.

[300] Garrigues, *Monluc*, pp. 121, 134.

> Before they lit the fire, they ordered him to present his tongue to be cut out. He refused. The executioner could only get to it with the help of pliers which he used both to get a hold of it and to cut it out. Never was such a dreadful cry heard, you would have mistaken it for the lowing of a cow. The rest of his body was consumed by the fire and his ashes thrown to the wind. Such was the end of Lucilio Vanini.[301]

In evaluating Vanini's punishment by the magistrates of Toulouse, one is confronted by a striking disparity between theory and practice. As alluded to earlier, the legal position on blasphemy was in fact more lenient than cases such as Vanini's might lead us to believe. Fifteenth-century legislation had merely prescribed the pillory and fines for blasphemers, including recidivists.[302] Though sixteenth-century legislation included scope for corporal punishment—often reserved for repeat offenders—none of the laws from this period went as far as capital punishment.[303] In practice, however, the Parlement de Paris could pass the death sentence against blasphemers.[304] Specifically in Toulouse, the *cage de fer* remained in use to punish blashphemers long after it had disappeared from other provincial courts. In 1618—the year of Vanini's arrest in which the *capitouls* were so eager to stamp out irreligious speech acts—the Capitoulat re-established its use in the punishment of blasphemers specifically with reference to its historic use in Toulouse.[305] It also passed a number of death sentences against blasphemers; including Jehan Lecasse in 1580, Jehan Dufour in 1591, and two soldiers who had their togues ripped out before being burned alive on the same spot as Vanini in 1542.[306] There was thus scope—in practice but not in legal theory—to stray from legal statues in favour of historical tradition when dealing with blasphemy cases; one of the few crimes for which, occasionally, 'les capitouls ignoraient la loi du roi' ('the *capitouls* ignored the king's law').[307]

The judges at Vanini's trial seem to have ignored far more. They were ignorant of Vanini's true identity and unaware that he was a censored author. They were

301 Gramond, *Historiarum* in Durand, *Vanini*, pp. 193–4.

302 See Nicolas Delamare, *Traité de la police*, 4 vols (Paris: Michel Brunet, 1722), I, p. 547.

303 See for example the 'Édit de Moulin' (1566, article 86), 'Déclaration contre les blasphémateurs' (1572), and 'Ordonnance sur les États Généraux de Blois' (1576, article 35) in Isambert, *Recueil général*, XIV i, pp. 212, 259, 390; 'Déclaration pour la punition des blasphémateurs' (1594), in Isambert, *Recueil général*, XV, p. 87; 'Declaration contre les blasphémateurs' (1617) in Isambert, *Recueil général*, XVI, p. 112. Schneider therefore generalises in claiming that the removal of Vanini's tongue was 'the prescribed treatment for blasphemers' (Schneider, *Public Life*, pp. 154–5).

304 Gilles Fremond, for example, was executed for blasphemy by the Parlement de Paris in 1611. See Gabriel Cayron, *Stil et forme de proceder, tant en la cour de Parlement de Tolose, et chambre des requestes d'icelle, etc.* (Tolose: Jean Boude, 1611), p. 573.

305 See AMT MS BB 278, *Annales*, Saint-Pierre (1618), fols. 11–12; Leopizzi, *Sources*, pp. 97–9; Faure, *Capitouls*, pp. 311–12.

306 Faure, *Capitouls*, pp. 313, 558; La Roche-Flavin and Graverol, *Arrests notables*, p. 19. I consider this disparity between theory in practice in the conclusion of Horsley, 'Blasphemy Hunters'.

307 Faure, *Capitouls*, p. 357. For an example where corporal punishments prescribed by legal statutes led to *arrêts* passing the death sentence for blasphemy, see Jean Papon and others, *Recueil d'arrests notables des cour souveraines de France* (Paris: Robert Fouet, 1621), pp. 12–20.

unable to find witnesses to Vanini's alleged crimes, despite the assurance in contemporary sources that Vanini had blasphemed in the company of a number of impressionable young noblemen. As I have argued, the social rank of those involved appears to have affected the diligence of other areas of the trial. An impenetrable cloud of secrecy hangs over the Vanini affair. None of the available sources names any of the witnesses produced following Vanini's six-month imprisonment. Garasse's account of Francon's involvement, whose influence extends beyond subsequent early modern accounts through to present-day scholarship, has been shown to lack both foundation and credibility. Catel's intervention in the trial was crucial, though it should be remembered that his role— as *rapporteur*, as *procureur général du roi*, or an unorthodox blend of the two—meant that his views and those of the *premier président* Le Mazuyer would inevitably have carried particular weight. With an explicit disregard for learning the truth of the matters brought before them, the magistrates hurriedly executed Vanini following an unusually long period of captivity. In light of new evidence pertaining to forgotten witness testimony, this period included more leads in the investigation than scholars have previously realised.

Further discoveries may yet shed more light on what the 'verite desdicts objectz' really was.[308] Had Vanini admitted his guilt when confronted with his servants, as Senaux claims, then it stands to reason that the *arrêt* would mention this, or that it would at least place greater emphasis on decisive witness testimony. The truth of the matter appears to have been silenced from the very day that the *arrêt* was drafted, whether to shield irregularities in the criminal proceedings or the identities of powerful families implicated in Vanini's downfall. Vanini's case was consigned to the shadows and to the whim of popular news sources almost immediately upon its entry into the history books. In 1619, Pierre de Carrière, who had taken over from Saint-Pierre as the first *capitoul* responsible for writing the annual *chronicles* of the Capitoulat, made a tantalising and cryptic remark regarding:

> une notable execution qui sy debvoit faire [à Toulouse] d'un italian homme philosophe appellé Luciolo de laquelle estant faict mention en l'annale precedente, nous passerons soubs filtre plusieurs particularites desquelz nous estions instruicts.
>
> A notable execution which was to take place there [in Toulouse] of an Italian philosopher named Luciolo. As this execution was mentioned in the previous annal, we will leave out several details of which we were informed.[309]

If Vanini's trial remains shrouded in mystery and secrecy, and if we continue to suffer from a lack of official legal documentation to inform our own judgements on the case, the unsettling truth is that many of the trial's agents of justice wished it so.

[308] ADHG MS B 382 (1619), fol. 153: 'Arrêt de mort de Vanini'; Leopizzi, *Sources*, p. 71.
[309] AMT MS BB 278, *Annales*, Pierre de Carrière (1619), fol. 44; Leopizzi, *Sources*, p. 117.

4

Authorial and Confessional Identity: The Trial of Jean Fontanier (1621)

Hic scelerum Pœnæ ultrices posuere tribunal.
Sontibus unde timor, civibus inde salus.

Here the avenging punishments have established their tribunal,
Bringing fear to the guilty, and safety to the people.

[Inscription at the entrance to the Chambre criminelle du Châtelet[1]]

La main me tremble, la plume me tombe des mains

My hand trembles, the quill falls from my hands

[Jean Fontanier's last words before his arrest by the *lieutenant criminel du Châtelet*[2]]

In the summer of 1623, Parisians awoke to the news that their city had been invaded. Their uninvited guests were disciples of a German spiritual order who claimed to wield a frightening weapon: they were invisible. They had announced their arrival in two short placards posted at various crossroads in the capital, the first of which read:

> Nous deputez du College principal des Freres de la Roze-Croix, faisons sejour visible et invisible en cette ville, par la grace du Tres-haut, vers lequel se tourne le cœur des Justes. Nous monstrons et enseignons sans livres ny marques à parler toutes sortes de langues des pays où voulons estre, pour tirer les hommes nos semblables d'erreur de mort.

[1] Quoted in Pascal Bastien, *Une histoire de la peine de mort: Bourreaux et supplices 1500–1800* (Paris: Seuil, 2011), p. 65.
[2] BNF MS Fr 18319, fol. 225^{v}.

> We deputies of the principal college of the Rosicrucian Brothers are making our visible and invisible stay in this city, by the grace of the Most High, towards which turns the hearts of the Just. We show and teach people, without books or signs, to speak all kinds of languages of the countries where we wish to be, to deliver our fellow men from the error of death.[3]

News of their arrival spread quickly. The *Mercure françois* attests to the impact of this event on the print market:

> En France aussi il se vit plusieurs livrets contre une Fraternité pretenduë, appellee de la Rose-Croix, que l'Allemagne a produitte depuis quelques annees, les Confreres de laquelle furent appellez les *Invisibles*, par les faiseurs de nouvelles qui se vendent sur le pont neuf à Paris.
>
> France has also seen several booklets against a supposed Fraternity, called the Rosicrucians, which originated in Germany a few years ago. The Brothers of this order were named the *Invisibles* by the news hawkers trading on the Pont Neuf in Paris.[4]

Despite strong evidence to suggest that the placards were written by Étienne Chaume as a mere hoax, with no other aim than to laugh at those who took them seriously, the Rosicrucian placards of 1623 caused quite a stir in both literary and social spheres.[5] One pamphlet attacked the Rosicrucians for having made a pact with the devil, and described how the placards 'firent reveiller les esprits des plus curieux, tant des doctes que des ignorans' ('had awoken the most curious of minds, both learned and ignorant').[6] The preface of Gabriel Naudé's more measured response claims that Paris was 'toute esmeue et pantelante par le venin d'une fausse et ridicule opinion' ('utterly disturbed and gasping with emotion from the venom of a false and ridiculous opinion'). The need to calm panicked readers was so urgent, Naudé adds, that he hurriedly wrote his text in just fifteen days.[7] The fact that texts commenting on this event from June or July 1623 were still being published in early 1624 demonstrates just how strong the reactions to these placards had been.

[3] Quoted in Gabriel Naudé, *Instruction à la France sur la verité de l'histoire des Freres de la Roze-Croix* (Paris: François Julliot, 1623), p. 27. On this late-Medieval order founded by Christian Rosenkreuz, see Frances A. Yates, *The Rosicrucian Enlightenment* (London: Routledge and Kegan Paul, 1972).

[4] *Le Mercure françois, ou suite de l'histoire de notre temps*, 25 vols (Paris: Jean Richer, 1613–43), 9 (1622–24) (1624), p. 371. For a full transcription of the second placard, see p. 373.

[5] On the authorship of the placards see François Secret, 'Notes sur quelques alchimistes', *Bibliothèque d'Humanisme et Renaissance*, 33 (1971), 625–40 (625–6).

[6] *Effroyables pactions faictes entre le diable & les pretendus invisibles. Avec leurs damnables Instructions, perte déplorable de leurs Escoliers, & leur miserable fin* ([n.p]: [n. pub], 1624), p. 17. See also the *Examen sur l'inconnue et nouvelle caballe des freres de la Rozee-Croix, habituez depuis peu de temps en la ville de Paris* (Paris: [n. pub], 1623); [Claude Malingre], *Traicté des Atheistes, Deistes, Illuminez d'Espagne et nouveaux pretendus Invisibles, dits de la Confrairie de la Croix-Rosaire*, in Raemond Florimond, *Histoire générale du progrèz et décadence de l'hérésie moderne*, 3 vols (Paris: Pierre Chevalier, 1624), II, pp. 13–55.

[7] Naudé, *Instruction à la France*, 'au lecteur', n.p.

The Rosicrucian hoax was also associated with *libertinage*. The *Effroyables pactions* describes the philosophy of the Invisibles as 'Epicurienne, enseignent la mesme leçon et la mesme methode que ce Philosophe Italien qui fut brulé à Thoulouze en la place du Salin par Arrest du Parlement dudit lieu, en l'année 1619' ('Epicurean, teaching the same lesson and method as the Italian philosopher [Vanini] who was burned at the Place du Salin in Toulouse by a sentence of the Parlement of that place in 1619').[8] François Garasse alleged a number of similarities between the Rosicrucians and the libertines targeted in his texts. The *Doctrine curieuse*, which was written and published at around the same time as the Rosicrucian placards, asserts that both groups appeared respectable in public, yet spoke blasphemies and impieties whilst drunk in taverns.[9] His *Apologie* (which bears a privilege dated 10 January 1624) links Vanini's atheism and Théophile's private indulgence of vices to the Rosicrucians.[10] One pamphlet even went as far as to implore the magistrates to punish them for the crime of divine lese-majesty.[11]

The Rosicrucian placards would have reminded many readers of a similar occurence two years earlier in 1621, when Rosicrucianism had already caused some panic in France following the publication of pamphlets in Germany (as early as the autumn of 1620) under the name of Johann Valentin Andreae.[12] This 1621 placard equally pertained to a secret gathering with a claim to powerful arcane authority—one which did not offer invisibility, but a *Trésor inestimable* (inestimable treasure) of abundant riches acquired without effort or risk. The so-called Invisibles were supposedly able to appear to those who truly wished to join them in order to arrange their induction into the brotherhood.[13] The author of the *Trésor inestimable*, however, had to take the more practical step of giving both his name and address at the bottom of his placards: Jean Fontanier, rue de Béthisy. Those who took up Fontanier's invitation to his home were first asked to sign an oath of secrecy before God, and were then asked to attend lessons read from Fontanier's *Trésor inestimable* which, in the eyes of his judges, blended impiety, atheism, and crucially, Judaism. Horrified by where their curiosity had

[8] *Effroyables pactions*, p. 6.

[9] François Garasse, *La Doctrine curieuse des beaux esprits de ce temps* (Paris: Sebastien Chappelet, 1623), pp. 84–5. On Garasse's links between Rosicrucians and the *libertins*, see Bruno Roche, *Le rire des libertins dans la première moitié du XVIIe siècle* (Paris: Honoré Champion, 2011), p. 113.

[10] [François Garasse], *Apologie du pere François Garassus, de la Compagnie de Jésus, pour son Livre contre les Atheistes & Libertins de nostre siecle* (Paris: Sebastien Chappelet, 1624), pp. 5–6.

[11] *Examen sur l'inconnue et nouvelle caballe*, p. 8. Didier Kahn sees a parallel between these placards and 'the libertine hunt': see Didier Kahn, 'The Rosicrucian Hoax in France (1623–24)', in *Secrets of Nature: Astrology and Alchemy in Early Modern Europe*, ed. by William R. Newman and Anthony Grafton (Cambridge, MA, and London: The MIT Press, 2006), pp. 235–344 (pp. 236, 311).

[12] On the influence of German Rosicrucianism in other European countries, see Donald R. Dickson, *The Tessera of Antilia: Utopian Brotherhoods and Secret Societies in the Early Seventeenth Century* (Leiden: Brill, 1998). I am grateful to Mark Greengrass for this information.

[13] *Effroyables pactions*, p. 18.

led them, two of Fontanier's students denounced him to the legal authorities. Having initially been tried and condemned by the Châtelet as the court of first instance on 26 November 1621, Fontanier's case was subsequently heard on appeal by the Parlement de Paris where his death sentence was quickly confirmed. Like the fictitious Rosicrucians, the Jewish doctor who had taught, assisted, and paid Fontanier for his efforts seemingly vanished from France before he could suffer the same tragic consequences as his student. By the time Naudé came to write his *Instruction à la France* towards the end of 1623, he was able to refer to Fontanier and Vanini together as notorious examples of burnings at the stake, an association which continued to be made between the two authors in 1627:

> Nous avons veu depuis peu de temps les cendres d'un Lucilio Vaninio, et d'un Jean Fontanier piroüetter dans le vague de l'air, ayans esté condamnez par Arrests des parlemens de Tholoze et de Paris à estre bruslez pour leur impieté.

> Not long ago, we saw the cinders of one Lucilio Vaninio and of one Jean Fontanier twirling in the air currents, having been condemned by sentences of the Parlements of Toulouse and Paris to be burned for their impiety.[14]

Jean Fontanier has been relatively neglected in modern scholarship on libertine authors, and has yet to form the subject of a dedicated study in English. Yet his trial and execution in 1621 merit closer attention for a number of reasons. His trial is chronologically central between those of Vanini and Théophile, thereby serving as a useful bridge for understanding the treatment of subversive authors in the early years of Louis XIII's personal rule. In addition to the texts quoted above, he also appears in the works of Garasse and Mersenne, as well as forming the subject of two anonymous pamphlets, thereby attesting to the interest and notoriety of his case in the eyes of both the declared enemies of libertine authors and wider Parisian society. Fontanier was found guilty and executed by the Parlement de Paris on appeal. As such, his trial holds traits in common with those of both Théophile, who also appeared before the Parlement de Paris, but as a court of first instance from which he escaped with his life; and Vanini, who was also executed by a royal Parlement, but in Toulouse and without appeal.

His case is furthermore illuminating for scholarship on the law, the history of Jews in Europe, and literary criticism. The records of Fontanier's initial trial at the Châtelet have not survived, and may have been destroyed in accordance with the original sentence against him. Upon appeal, however, he was interrogated twice by the Parlement whose short transcripts have survived. This trial on appeal also

[14] Naudé, *Instruction à la France*, p. 16 (which bears a privilege dated 1 December 1623); Sébastien Hardy, *Dix sermons de Theodoret, evesque de Cyr. De la Providence de Dieu. Contre les Athees & Libertins* (Paris: Robert Estienne, 1627), fol. A iii quoted in Alain Mothu, 'Pierre Petit à l'école antichrétienne de Jean Fontanier (1621)', *La Lettre clandestine*, 23 (2015), 261–70 (264). Mothu erroneously attributes this text to 'Étienne Hardy'.

inspired a much longer and rarer document. The magistrate who oversaw the appeal hearings was the *président à mortier* Nicolas de Bellièvre. Whether due to curiosity, a professional interest in the legal issues at hand, or pride in his erudition evinced by the interrogations, Bellièvre wrote a considerable private memoir on Fontanier's case which was not discovered until the 1980s.[15] This manuscript provides a page-by-page summary of the *Trésor inestimable*, which must also have been handwritten given that none of the extant legal documents refers to culpable printers. As such, it constitutes the sole record of Fontanier's incriminating text which was thrown into the flames at his execution. Bellièvre's account goes much further, by outlining the events which led to Fontanier's denunciation and arrest as well as detailing the questions put to the defendant at the Parlement. Fascinatingly, when read alongside the official trial transcripts, Bellièvre's first-hand account at times confirms, develops, or nuances the questions and responses in the official court records, as well as alleging certain questions and answers of which no record appears in the Parlement's transcripts. Bellièvre offers a privileged account of the deliberations leading to Fontanier's guilty verdict—a legal process which had become a matter of secrecy by the early seventeenth century. He also provides us with a rare glimpse into the mind of a senior magistrate when preparing a criminal case, a line of questioning, and a wider strategy in bringing a defendant to justice, particularly in terms of the legal status of Jews in France.

Fontanier was accused primarily of being a Jewish proselyte (*un judaïsant*) and of teaching others about his new faith. As Bellièvre's account makes clear, the problem for the magistrates was that this did not appear to be a crime in France according to royal ordinances and legal precedent. The chief concern of Fontanier's judges was therefore to determine whether he was a Jew or a man of no religion. In turn, they sought to establish a link between his case and either the expulsion of the Jews from France, or the preaching of irreligious doctrines which could be prosecuted under the loose terms of blasphemy, impiety, or atheism. Such legal strategies therefore have much to tell us about the status of Jews and the reception of their faith in France during the turbulent early years of Louis XIII's reign.

This leads us to the value of the trial from a literary perspective. Although much of this chapter focusses on Fontanier's supposed Jewish identity and

[15] BNF MS Fr 18319: Nicolas de Bellièvre, *Remarques de monsieur le président de Bellièvre, sur ce qui s'est passé au Parlement de Paris (1607–1627)*, 2 vols, I, fols. 220^{v} – 230^{r} (henceforth 'Bellièvre'). Nineteen of the twenty-four pages of Bellièvre's memoir are transcribed in Elisabeth Labrousse and Alfred Soman, 'Un bûcher pour un judaïsant: Jean Fontanier (1621)', *XVIIe siècle*, 39: 2 (1987), 113–32, which therefore omits several details on the trial. This chapter will reference the original manuscript throughout, as well as providing the corresponding page references for all quotations appearing in Labrousse and Soman for the reader's convenience. To this same end, quotations from Fontanier's surviving trial transcripts will likewise be referenced with both the original unpaginated documents from the Archives Nationales and Lachèvre's transcriptions.

teaching, of the five activities listed in his *arrêt de mort* (death sentence) initially pronounced by the Châtelet, four refer to acts of writing: 'il a fait, écrit, composé, enseigné et dicté le livre intitulé *Trésor inestimable*' ('he has produced, written, composed, taught and dictated the book entitled *Trésor inestimable*').[16] Fontanier's case is unusual in its association of *libertinage* with more ephemeral literature than the audacious short stories or poems by *libertin* authors which appeared in print.[17] His placard was a privately produced, handwritten advertisement. Like the Rosicrucians, Fontanier extended a public invitation to his readers to share in his arcane knowledge within the confines of a subsequent, private sphere of readership at his own home.[18] His initiates were not given copies of his text, but took dictation from Fontanier's oral dissemination of its content. Fontanier's scribal, literary subversion was thus a private enterprise in which his listeners were invited to join him in the act of authorship and arguably of textual interpretation. These questions of authorship would prove to be key issues for the magistrates assigned to judge his appeal. The main aim of Bellièvre's questioning was to establish that Fontanier was the author of the text from which he was teaching. Fontanier, however, claimed that Daniel Montalto—a Jewish teacher whom he had met on his travels through Europe—was the true author, and that he was merely disseminating the text on his instruction. In addition to the legal question of Jewish teaching in France, the crux of the matter was a literary one, in which the relationship between the personal identity of the defendant and the literary identity of the poetic 'I' (*le je poétique*) was paramount in deciding legal culpability. With this aim in mind, Bellièvre adopted a mode of critical reading, which I shall propose as an early precursor to modern forensic linguistics, with which he was able to determine beyond reasonable doubt that Fontanier, and not his Jewish associate, was the true author of the incriminating text.

This chapter begins with an outline of Fontanier's biography prior to his trial in order to clarify how his *Trésor inestimable* came into being. This will also allow us to construct a profile of his character and his apparently troubled state of mind, and to provide a useful outline for future work on this neglected libertine author. This is followed by a contextualisation of Fontanier's ordeal by exploring the status of Jews in France at the time, as well as the career of Nicolas de Bellièvre, before moving to the trial itself. I will argue that recent political events involving

[16] *Arrêt de mort* pronounced by the Châtelet, 26 November 1621, quoted in Frédéric Lachèvre, *Mélanges sur le libertinage au XVIIe siècle* (Paris: Honoré Champion, 1920), p. 66.

[17] An obvious exception to this generalisation are drinking songs or '*cabaret* poetry' exemplified by certain poems by Saint-Amant, Théophile, or Maynard, which were nonetheless often printed.

[18] Although the Rosicrucian placards were also displayed in such public spaces, the *Mercure françois* notably suggests that their dissemination, and even their display in public, was a private affair between curious individuals who 's'adviserent d'y faire trotter de main en main plusieurs petits billets manuscrits, et en afficherent aux Carrefours' ('decided to pass several little notes from one hand to another, and posted them at crossroads': *Mercure François*, p. 371).

Jews at the royal court are a neglected aspect of this trial, and that Fontanier's meeting with Daniel Montalto would have linked him to these controversies. For as will become clear, Bellièvre's interrogation sought not only to demonstrate that Fontanier was the author of the offending text, but that the author could not have been either Daniel Montalto or his brother Isaac. The chapter ends by considering the respective strategies of the magistrates and the defendant, as well as the questions of law which influenced the trial proceedings.

In addition to the two legal sources outlined above, the following study draws from two anonymous pamphlets which were published on Fontanier's case shortly after the fact. The first—the *Discours sur la vie et mort de Jean Fontanier*—is a short, vague, and rambling work which offers no insight into the trial other than that Fontanier's sentence by the Parlement de Paris 'a esté rendu ce jourd'huy, confirmatif de son premier rendu au Chastelet de Paris' ('was passed today, confirming his first one passed by the Paris Châtelet').[19] This pamphlet inspired a second, more detailed text lamenting the uninformative nature of its predecessor. This second pamphlet—the *Histoire veritable de la vie de Jean Fontanier*—includes a copy of the *arrêt* passed by the Châtelet as well as a number of useful details on the trial and execution. It also served as the basis for Garasse's otherwise ill-informed comments on the trial, and was furthermore copied out in a surviving manuscript.[20] Besides this text, then, our analysis of Fontanier's trial will rely largely upon the surviving criminal registers of the Parlement de Paris as well as the private records and reflections of one of its leading magistrates.

JEAN FONTANIER: IDENTITY, CONFESSION, AND THE SHADOW OF DOUBT

Jean Fontanier was born in 1588 to a Protestant family in Montpellier.[21] His parents—Philippe Fontanier and Marie Amade—died when he was young. He was subsequently cared for by his uncle (another Philippe) who paid for his education in Montpellier and then in Toulouse. Having read Law in Valence, by 1608 Fontanier had become a defence lawyer (*avocat*).[22] His trial transcripts reveal the limited extent of his learning which would later be used against him:

[19] *Discours sur la vie et mort de Jean Fontanier natif de Montpellier, etc.* (Paris: Isaac Mesnier, 1621), p. 8.

[20] BNF MS Baluze 212, fols. 167^{r} - 167^{v}, which reproduces pp. 4–16 of the original pamphlet.

[21] The following chronology of Fontanier's movements prior to his trial are taken from Bellièvre; Lachèvre, *Mélanges*; and Labrousse and Soman, 'Fontanier'.

[22] Lachèvre proposes 1609 (*Mélanges*, p. 60). However, Bellièvre's memoir (which was not discovered in Lachèvre's lifetime) is clear on this point: '1608 fist le serment d'advocat en ce barreau, assisté longtemps aux plaidoiries, n'a touttesfois plaidé. Avoit estudié en droit deux ans à Tholose, Montpellier et Vallence' ('in 1608 was sworn in to the bar as a defence lawyer, attended pleas for some time but without pleading his own cases. Had studied law for two years in Toulouse, Montpellier, and Valence': Bellièvre fol. 222 ^{v}; Labrousse and Soman, 'Fontanier', 119).

> Pris ses degrez à Valance et avoit là veu les Institutes et Règles de droict *favorabiliores tali quam actori*, n'a jamais plaidé icy mais bien à Montpellier. [...] A faict son cours de philosophie et sa logique, n'entend la langue grecque et l'a apprise d'un écossois de la religion prétendue réformée. [...] N'a appris l'ébreu et en a eu quelque cognoissance par la grammaire. A veu Tite-Live, l'histoire de France, Froissart, Guichardin, Plutarque, Sénèque en latin ou françois, n'a appris les mathématiques ny en théologie, sinon par les conférences, a veu les pseaumes de David de Marot, de Bèze.
>
> Took his degrees in Valence where he saw in the *Institutes* and *Laws* 'defendants are treated more favourably than complainants'. Has never pleaded cases here [in Paris] but has in Montpellier. [...] Studied philosophy and logic, does not understand the Greek language and was taught it by a Scotsman of the so-called reformed faith. [...] Has not learnt Hebrew and has gained some knowledge of it through grammar. Has read Livy, the *History of France*, Froissart, Guicciardini, Plutarch, Seneca in Latin or French, has learnt neither mathematics nor theology, other than through discussions, has read translations of the Psalms of David by Marot and de Bèze.[23]

The resultant image is of a man with little interest in reading or erudition, and who does not appear to have been particularly enamoured with the career for which he had trained. Although this situates him in stark contrast to the erudite Vanini, both men were restless spirits. Shortly after completing his training, Fontanier embarked on travels to Venice and Constantinople in 1610. It is likely that his trip to Constantinople helped to lay the linguistic and perhaps theological foundations for his subsequent activities. Fontanier would later stress at trial that he travelled there 'en une gallère avec des françois, qu'il avoit des juifs pour truchement, ne leur a rien demandé de leur croyance' ('in a galley alongside Frenchmen, that he had Jews as translators, and asked them nothing about their beliefs').[24] Bellièvre's recollection is more selective, recording that it was 'à Constantinople où il se servit de quelques juifs pour truchement' ('in Constantinople where he used a number of Jews as translators').[25] He also pushed Fontanier's confession of his 'little knowledge' of Hebrew further when recalling his arrest: 'A l'instant visitation faicte des coffres et cabinets quelques livres Hebreux trouvés, prieres des Hebreux traduictes en Latin, confesse qu'il scait quelque chose de la langue Hebraique' ('his chests and *cabinets* were immediately searched. A few Hebrew books were found [as well as] Hebrew prayers translated into Latin, confesses that he has some knowledge of the Hebrew tongue').[26] Given that the *Trésor inestimable* was written and dictated in French, the question of whether Fontanier was conversant in Hebrew clearly had ideological and social

[23] AN X 2A 985, interrogation of 10 December 1621 quoted in Lachèvre, *Mélanges*, p. 69.

[24] AN X 2A 985, interrogation of 10 December 1621 quoted in Lachèvre, *Mélanges*, p. 69.

[25] Bellièvre, fol. 222v; Labrousse and Soman, 'Fontanier', 118.

[26] Bellièvre, fol. 218v.

implications, rather than practical applications, within the context of the trial interrogations.

On his return journey, Fontanier stopped in Verona where he claimed to have converted to Catholicism in 1611.[27] What could the Protestant Fontanier have found in the Ottoman Empire, in the company of Jews, to have motivated him to convert to Catholicism before he had even returned home? We will never know whether the seeds of doubt had already been planted before Fontanier's departure from France, whether this crisis of faith was a result of travel having broadened his horizons, or whether he had spoken of philosophical and theological matters with his Jewish translators. Notably, the *Histoire veritable* describes Fontanier's defence of his placard using the very same terms with which he had explained his conversion to Catholicism to Bellièvre: 'ce qu'il avoit affiché n'estoit que pour se resoudre de quelques doubts qu'il avoit avec ceux qui le viendroient voir qui ne pouvoient estre que gens d'esprit et de sçavoir' ('what he had advertised was only to resolve a few doubts of his with those who would come to see him, who could only be men of spirit and learning').[28]

Financial constraints were a likely factor in Fontanier's return to France in 1611. Having shown little enthusiasm for his career thus far, on 30 March 1612 he inherited his uncle's office as *notaire-secretaire du roi* (notary secretary to the king). Bellièvre reports that Fontanier's uncle 'luy donnoit argent quelques fois, l'entretenoit' ('sometimes gave him money for his keep'), and that 'pour ses debtes, il fust contreint vendre cest office' ('he was forced to sell this office in order to pay his debts').[29] Thus, by the time he sold his uncle's office on 22 March 1613, Fontanier had turned his back on two legal careers by the age of twenty-five and had demonstrated a tendency towards financial mismanagement. To add to this, the question of his religious beliefs clearly continued to weigh heavily on his mind, as in that same year he travelled to Toulouse to take holy orders with the Capuchins. Although Vanini had certainly not travelled to Toulouse with a contrite heart, it is nonetheless remarkable that these two men, who harboured sceptical if not outright heretical views in the eyes of their Catholic contemporaries, should have chosen Toulouse as a safe destination given the city's reputation for Catholic zeal.[30] Bellièvre states that Fontanier remained there for four months, 'et qu'il en estoit sorti par infirmité seulement' ('and that he only left due to illness').[31] The official trial records, however, give a more detailed and less flattering account of events:

[27] Verona was also home to a Jewish community known for its confraternities. Whether or not Fontanier really did convert to Catholicism in Verona, it is perfectly plausible that he may have come into contact with Jews, and possibly even the basic tenets of their faith, during his stay there.

[28] *Histoire veritable de la vie de Jean Fontanier* (Paris: Melchior Mondiere, 1621), p. 13.

[29] Bellièvre, fol. 222^{v}; Labrousse and Soman, 'Fontanier', 119.

[30] On this reputation see Chapter 3, pp. 125, 136–8.

[31] Bellièvre, fol. 222^{v}; Labrousse and Soman, 'Fontanier', 119.

> [a passé] 3 ou 4 mois à Thoulouse en l'année 1613 comme il pense après avoir vendu son office et en est sorty par maladie de teste et paralisie, ne se pouvoit le soir lever aux heures et qu'on luy donna congé.
>
> [spent] three or four months in Toulouse in 1613 according to his recollection, after he had sold his office. He left due to headaches and palsy, was unable to rise from his bed at night for the Liturgy of the Hours, and was sent away.[32]

Like Vanini before him, Fontanier found little comfort in the regimented and stifling environment of monastic life which contrasted so starkly with both individuals' fondness for travel. Fontanier was neither a fervent nor committed Protestant, and even his wider Christian faith was wavering. He was not therefore a sworn sceptic of the Catholic faith, nor an adherent of the forms of naturalist philosophy suggested in Vanini's and Théophile's texts. When faced with doubts, Fontanier had not only conformed to contemporary expectations by seeking guidance from theologians, but had in fact surpassed them by converting from Protestantism to the dominant Catholic Church. Although he seems to have genuinely sought to remedy his situation in an orthodox manner, his doubts would not be assuaged for long.

Fontanier's movements become harder to trace following his expulsion from the Capuchins of Toulouse. After obtaining a post as a secretary for the Council of the States General in the Netherlands later that year, his business in this capacity led him back to Paris in 1614. This was followed by a second trip to Italy then the Netherlands in April 1617.[33] Fontanier must have made his home in Paris later that year, as by December 1621 he conveyed to Bellièvre 'qu'il y avoit 4 ans qu'il demeuroit au nom de Jésus, rue de Béthisy' ('that he had resided at the house under the emblem of the Name of Jesus, on the rue de Béthisy, for four years').[34] In 1620 he visited Italy for the last time, before taking a fateful trip in August 1621 to Flanders, Brussels, and Antwerp. This would prove to be pivotal in his downfall for two reasons. First, this final journey 'fut à ses depens, que son beau-frère luy avoit baillié 50 l.t. et lors de son voyage avoit son argent de secrétaire du Roy' ('was at his own expense, his brother-in-law had given him fifty *livres tournois*, and during this time he had his money from the sale of his office of secretary to the king').[35] Given that he had suffered from 'force commoditez' ('a number of financial difficulties'), and invested some 4500 *livres tournois* in a carriage business in 1618, this would have placed Fontanier in a vulnerable financial position.[36] Second, it

[32] AN X 2A 985, interrogation of 10 December 1621, quoted in Lachèvre, *Mélanges*, p. 71.

[33] On this date, based on Fontanier's recollection of the Dutch relief of Venice (Bellièvre, fol. 222ᵛ), see Labrousse and Soman, 'Fontanier', 130, note 20.

[34] AN X 2A 985, interrogation of 10 December 1621, quoted in Lachèvre, *Mélanges*, p. 68, repeated almost word for word in Bellièvre, fol. 222ᵛ; Labrousse and Soman, 'Fontanier', 118.

[35] AN X 2A 985, interrogation of 10 December 1621, quoted in Lachèvre, *Mélanges*, p. 68.

[36] AN X 2A 985, interrogation of 10 December 1621, quoted in Lachèvre, *Mélanges*, p. 69. On Fontanier's investment, see p. 62.

was in passing through Cambrai on his return from Brussels, most likely in June 1621, that Fontanier found himself in the company of a Jewish man who sought his help in preaching Judaism in France, Daniel Montalto (or *Montalte* in French):

> Ce fut à Cambray qu'il eust cognoissance de l'escript dudit autheur et luy dit qu'il avoit un grand livre et qu'il lui monstreroit autre chose à Paris, le rencontra dans le pallais et ont conféré 7 à 8 jours en ceste ville, qu'il estoit portugais, parle bon françois et se mesle de marchandises, qu'il a estudié en sa religion et aux humanitez et disoit que ce livre estoit de son frère et croyt que c'est Montalte et que ce n'est pas de luy et que Montalte l'a faict.
>
> It was at Cambrai where he came to learn of the writings of the aforementioned author, who told him that he had a great book and that he would show him something else in Paris. He met him in the palace and held discussions with him for seven or eight days in this city. He was Portuguese, spoke good French and dabbled in trading. He studied his religion and the humanities and said that this book was by his brother [Isaac Montalto]. The accused believes that this brother was Montalto, and that it was not by him but that Montalto wrote it.[37]

Bellièvre's recollection includes additional details:

> Depuis 6 mois revenant des pais bas passant par Cambrey il y trouva Montalte frere du Medecin, avec lequel il eust conference 2 heures [...] lequel luy dit qu'ils s'entretiendroient davantage a Paris. 3 ou 4 jours apres son arrivée a Paris le rencontrerent, ont communiqué 2 mois ensemble, pendant lequel temps il avoit en douze jours coppié ce livre Montalte dictant ou quelques fois luy prestant son livre.
>
> Six months ago, returning from the Netherlands via Cambrai he found Montalto brother of the doctor, with whom he conversed for two hours. [...] Montalto told him that they would talk with each other further in Paris. Three or four days after his arrival in Paris they met up, and spent two months conversing with each other. During this time, over a twelve-day period Fontanier had copied out Montalto's book, who dictated it to him or who sometimes lent it to him.[38]

Fontanier's situation and his apparently fragile state of mind left him susceptible to the influence of learned men with an agenda, irrespective of whether or not Daniel Montalto genuinely saw him as a spiritual equal following a secret conversion to Judaism, or whether his relationship with Fontanier was one of pure manipulation. Fontanier had previously rubbed shoulders with Jews on his travels, and does not appear to have shared the anti-Semitism which plagued the minds of so many (though far from all) of his contemporaries. He was dangerously short of

[37] AN X 2A 985, interrogation of 10 December 1621, quoted in Lachèvre, *Mélanges*, p. 69. The *Histoire veritable* claims that the pair met in Calais and spent nine days together in Paris (pp. 5–6).

[38] Bellièvre, fol. 218^{v}. Six months prior to the interrogations in December brings us roughly to June 1621 for the date of Montalto's arrival in Paris. The *Histoire veritable* describes Daniel as 'frere d'Ysaac Montalto Medecin Portugais Juifs d'origine et de creance' ('the brother of Isaac Montalto the Portuguese doctor, both of them of Jewish origins and beliefs': p. 5).

money, and lacked both Théophile's lucrative protection by aristocratic grandees and Vanini's erudition with which to make a living as a tutor. The *Histoire veritable* asserts that Montalto 'luy bailla quelques commoditez et pension pour s'entretenir et enseigner ladite religion Judaïque par la communication de son livre' ('saw to certain expenses and an allowance for his training and for him to teach the Jewish religion through his book').[39] Garasse goes further by claiming that Fontanier was offered a new life abroad in return for his services:

> Daniel luy persuada de se declarer juif, luy donne un livre escrit à la main contenant plusieurs impietez; et luy promet de luy procurer quelque honorable appointement de la Synagogue d'Amsterdam, s'il s'en venoit dans Paris pour y semer ses maudites Maximes.
>
> Daniel persuaded him to declare himself a Jew. He gave him a handwritten book containing several impieties, and promised to procure him some kind of honorable position in the Amsterdam synagogue if he agreed to spread his cursed maxims in Paris.[40]

Though there is no evidence to corroborate this particular claim, for once Garasse was not far off the mark when he later observed how the Protestant-born Fontanier 'se fit Catholique, de Catholique Religieux, de Religieux Apostat, d'Apostat Huguenot pour la seconde fois, de Huguenot Turc, de Turc Juif, de Juif, Athéiste ayant roulé de pays en pays, d'une religion en l'autre' ('became a Catholic, from a Catholic to a priest, from a priest to an apostate, from an apostate to a Huguenot for the second time, from a Huguenot to a Muslim, from a Muslim to a Jew, from a Jew to an atheist, having wandered from one country and one religion to another').[41] It is perfectly plausible that Fontanier could have been coerced into assisting in the preaching of Judaism by financial incentives, though there is no evidence from our two judicial sources to prove this. Another likely motive for assisting Montalto, supported by our more reliable sources, is the return of Fontanier's doubts.

Bellièvre's memoir reveals that at some point during his time in Paris after his conversion to Catholicism, Fontanier 'confesse qu'il a eü quelques doute [sic] de la foy, pour s'instruire a affiché son Confesseur et autres Docteurs Catholiques n'ayant voulu ouyr ses doubtes' ('confesses that he has had a few doubts about his faith. He sought instruction from his confessor and other Catholic doctors who were not willing to hear his doubts').[42] The same claim appears in the trial

[39] *Histoire veritable*, p. 6. Garasse copies this claim word for word (including the claim that the two men had met in Calais rather than Cambrai) in his *Doctrine curieuse*, p. 149.

[40] Garasse, *Doctrine*, p. 149. The *Histoire veritable* similarly claims that Montalto converted Fontanier to Judaism (pp. 4–5).

[41] Garasse, *Doctrine*, p. 148. There is no evidence to suggest that Fontanier explored Islam. In his edition of Marin Mersenne's letters, however, Cornelis de Waard inaccurately paraphrases Garasse's claim without critical nuance. See *Correspondance du P. Marin Mersenne*, ed. by Cornelis de Waard, 18 vols (Paris: Presses Universitaires de France, 1945), I (1617–27), p. 112.

[42] Bellièvre, fols. 218^{r} – 218^{v}.

transcripts: 'qu'il a recherché des docteurs de Sorbonne et ne les a peu nommer qui luy dirent qu'il ne debvoit parler de cela et que estoit [sic] pour avoir plus grande certitude de ce qu'il doubtait ('that he sought doctors from the Sorbonne whom he was unable to name. They told him that he should not speak about it. This was to find greater certainty about the things that he doubted').[43] Fontanier was not the only author accused of *libertinage* in Paris to have attempted to bring his doubts to clergymen. According to Garasse, Théophile de Viau's close friend (and likely lover) Jacques Vallée Des Barreaux visited Jesuit fathers on multiple occasions in order to express his doubts, either sincerely or mockingly, over the Incarnation of Christ and the existence of the Devil.[44] With markedly greater sincerity, Fontanier was perennially unsure of his faith, and unable to dispel his doubts at the hands of his own confessor or indeed by travelling across France and Europe. Yet he now found himself in the private company of a learned man who was not only willing to discuss religious matters with him, but who trusted him with the task of joining him in the spreading of Judaism in Paris. Upon his arrest, then, he made a credible though weak claim that he had only undertaken his lessons in Paris out of curiosity and 'aussy pour s'esclaircir de ses doubtes' ('also to dispell his doubts').[45] Having prepared his text for dissemination, Fontanier was about to become a preacher in his own right to whom members of the Parisian educated classes would perhaps come with doubts of their own. The effect this must have had on Fontanier's troubled spirit would surely have left little need for financial bribery from Montalto. But as Garasse later remarked, 'quand un renard presche les poules, on ne peut attendre qu'une tres mauvaise yssue de tel presche' ('when a fox preaches to the chickens, one can only expect a very bad outcome from such preaching').[46]

BROKEN OATHS: DENUNCIATION, ARREST, AND THE SPARING OF THE LAMBS

Once Fontanier's text had been completed, Daniel Montalto adroitly left France. The die was cast on 7 November 1621 when Fontanier, now alone besides the few financial resources left for him by Montalto, advertised his *Trésor inestimable* in placards on the streets of Paris. Unlike its succinct Rosicrucian counterparts

[43] AN X 2A 985, interrogation of 10 December 1621, quoted in Lachèvre, *Mélanges*, p. 69. See also the interrogation of 4 December in Lachèvre, *Mélanges*, p. 67: 's'est rendu cathlolique et ce feu à cause qu'il ne croyoit point que la prétendue fut bonne et premièrement en ce qui estoit de la réalité et de l'invocation de la Vierge' ('made himself a Catholic and this was due to the fact that he did not believe that the Reformed faith was the right one, primarily due to the truth and the invocation of the Virgin').

[44] See Garasse, *Doctrine*, pp. 267, 835–6; Antoine Adam, *Théophile de Viau et la libre pensée française en 1620* (Geneva: Slatkine Reprints, 1966), pp. 341–3.

[45] Bellièvre, fol. 218ʳ. For an alternative reading of this line, see pp. 240-41.

[46] Garasse, *Doctrine*, p. 1004.

(which were each less than half a dozen lines in length), Fontanier's more rambling advertisement took up an entire page.[47] It began by presenting its author as different from writers who sought to con money from gullible readers:

> Au lieu de prendre de vous quelque peu d'argent (ce que à Dieu ne plaise seulement que je vous en demande) qu'au contraire c'est pour vous bailler les moyens pour en acquérir avec abondance et en user avec largesse, et ainsi dans peu de temps vous faire devenir trestous riches: et sçavez-vous comment? d'une telle façon qu'il ne sera plus nécessaire de rechercher le Perou dans un nouveau monde, ny traverser les mers, ny les montagnes, les deserts ny les campagnes pour acquerir des trésors, vostre richesse est icy presente, il ne la faudra point chercher ailleurs.
>
> Instead of taking a little money from you (which would not be pleasing to God for me even to ask of you), on the contrary it is to give you the means to acquire it in abundance and to spend it liberally. As such, in a short space of time you will become very rich, and do you know how? In such a way that it will no longer be necessary to go off in seach of Peru in a new world, nor to cross the seas, nor mountains, deserts or countryside to acquire treasures. Your riches are right here, there will be no need to go looking for them elsewhere.[48]

It ended by adding that financial gains would:

> ne mettre seulement les corps de ceux qui les possedent en joye et delices, pour la grande quantité des richesses qu'ils produisent: mais mesmes mettent leur esprit en perpétuelle tranquilité et repos, tellement que ceux qui ont cet esprit fort, et le jugement bon et solide (car ils ne conviennent pas à toutes sortes de gens) ne les voudroient eschanger avec tous autres biens du monde.
>
> not only bring joy and delights to the bodies of those who possess them, due to the great amount of riches that they produce, but they will even place their minds in perpetual peace and tranquility. So much so that those who have this strength of spirit, as well as sound and solid judgement (for they are not for every kind of person), would not wish to exchange them for all the riches in the world.[49]

With an ironic set of promises from a man who had journeyed across land and sea without finding material or spiritual contentment, the placard is a vague advertisement for material and personal well-being which shows no sign of the religious text to which it in fact refers. When considered alongside events in his life prior to the appearance of his placards, there is much evidence to suggest Fontanier's social isolation and restless spirit, and relatively little to suggest his solid

[47] A complete copy of Fontanier's placard and the oath he asked his students to swear can be found in Garasse, *Doctrine*, pp. 149–52; *Histoire veritable*, pp. 7–10; and Lachèvre, *Mélanges*, pp. 63–5.

[48] Quoted in Lachèvre, *Mélanges*, p. 63.

[49] Quoted in Lachèvre, *Mélanges*, p. 63. Here Fontanier's placard repeats the common rhetorical strategy found in other such texts, whereby riches are offered through an Arcanum accessible only to a select number of initiates. The placards displayed as part of the 1623 Rosicrucian hoax, for example, claimed that the Invisibles would appear only to genuinely interested parties, and not to the merely curious (*Effroyables pactions*, p. 18).

religious belief. He nonetheless attracted at least five interested parties. Having been enticed by what appeared to be a largely financial enterprise, Fontanier's would-be initiates were first required to swear an oath of an altogether different tone before their lessons could begin:

> Je N… promets à Dieu tout puissant et à chacune de ses Créatures et à M. Fontanier cy présent, de ne dire ny declarer à personne du monde, par signe, parolle, escrit, conjecture, ou autre demonstration que ce soit, le sujet de son Tresor inestimable […] ains de luy assister de ma personne et de mes moyens pour l'accomplissement de son œuvre, comme juste, honorable, utile, et qui ne contrevient point aux commendemens de Dieu: Et au cas que je contrevienne à ce serment, je veux que l'ire, le courroux, et l'indignation du grand Dieu tout puissant demeure éternellement sur mon corps, sur mon ame, et sur mes moyens.
>
> I [name] promise to almighty God and to each of his creations and to Mr Fontanier here present, that I will neither tell nor declare the subject of his *Trésor inestimable* to anyone in the world by sign, word, writing, conjecture, or other demonstration […] and that I will assist him personally and through my means to accomplish his work as just, honourable, useful, and without contravening God's commandments. And should I break this oath, may the wrath, anger and indignation of the almighty God most powerful rest forever upon my body, my soul, and my means.[50]

Bellièvre notes that the signed oaths of five students were found at Fontanier's home upon his arrest, that four were questioned on the premises, and that a fifth was absent.[51] Curiously, he does not provide the name of the fifth absent student, even though this would have been written on the relevant oath. Nor is there any identification of this absentee in the official trial documents. Given that those present do not appear to have been put on trial by the law courts after Fontanier's execution, the magistrates may simply not have judged that the absent student's signing of the oath, with no evidence that he ever attended his lessons, was worth their time.

Those who were found with Fontanier upon his arrest were twenty-two-year-old *avocat au Parlement* and future mathematician Pierre Petit, and twenty-two-year-old mathematics student Jehan Gaultier, who lived together on the rue des Mathurins. Petit would go on to become an eminent mathematician who corresponded with Descartes and Pascal, before eventually being named the *ingénieur et géographe du roi* (the king's engineer and geographer) in 1642.[52]

[50] Quoted in Lachèvre, *Mélanges*, pp. 64–5.

[51] Bellièvre, fols. 218^{v} – 219^{r}.

[52] On Petit see Mothu, 'Pierre Petit'. This Cartesian physicist should not be confused with another Pierre Petit (*c.*1617–87) who was a physician, scholar, and ironically an *opponent* of Cartesianism. The two men did their best to avoid confusion by referring to their professions in their published works. Our Pierre Petit, for example, published the *Dissertation sur la nature des cometes […] par P. Petit, Intendant des Fortifications* (Paris: Louis Billaine, 1664). The younger Pierre Petit, on the other hand, entitled his philological text *Petri Petiti, philosophi & doctoris medici, Miscellanearum observationum libri quatuor* (Trajecti ad Rhenum: Typis Rudolphi a Zyll, 1682). I am grateful to Richard Maber for this information.

The other two students were twenty-seven-year-old *avocat au Parlement* Michel Filassier and twenty-four-year-old doctor of medicine Rodolphe Ranchin. The Ranchins were a noble family in Fontanier's native Montpellier with links to the Montmorencys. Rodolphe had studied for a doctorate in medicine at Montpellier between 1612 and 1619, whilst his brother was one of sixteen lawyers in the family's history.[53] Bellièvre mistakenly speaks of 'Jean Filacier', whereas 'Michel' is given in the second *arrêt* (the final judgement of the Parlement) against Fontanier.[54] Bellièvre, who also confused Daniel Montalto with his father Elijah (Eliau) at one point in Fontanier's interrogation, doubtlessly had in mind the *secrétaire de la Chambre du Roy* (secretary to the king's chamber) Jean Filassier, whose name appears in a number of legal documents from 1610 to 1630 and could well have been Michel's father.[55] Finally, in dividing the students into these two pairs, Bellièvre adds that each pair comprised one Catholic and one Protestant.[56] Whereas Fontanier's doubts may have been fueled by financial, social, or even psychological instability, it is striking that his placards did not dupe impoverished members of the lower classes. They attracted a relatively well-to-do, educated class of Parisian youths who may well have been as enticed by the promise of arcane teachings as they were by financial reward.[57]

At least some of the initiates were disturbed to find that the language of ease and opulence in Fontanier's placard was replaced with a solemn vow before God, and that the lessons they were to receive should necessitate prior assurances that they were not contrary to the teachings of the Church. As Bellièvre observed, these were 'paroles par lesquelles apparoissoit l'anxieté de laquelle estoit detenu celuy qui l'avoit composé, pour s'assurer de la conscience de ceulx à qui il se communiqueroit' ('words which betrayed the anxiety of he who had written them, to assure the consciences of those to whom his words would be communicated').[58] Ranchin was the first to visit Fontanier on Monday 8 November, followed by another student on Wednesday 10 and the other two on Thursday 11.[59] By the time of his arrest on the Saturday, Fontanier had reached the so-called third lesson in his curriculum.

[53] On the Ranchin family see Louis Dulieu, 'Le chancelier François Ranchin', *Revue d'histoire des sciences*, 28: 3 (1974), 223–39; on Rodolphe, see 236–8. Dulieu offers no information between 1619 and 1632, thereby overlooking Ranchin's links with Fontanier entirely. Ranchin had a distant link to the prosecution of dangerous writers. The former Protestant Guillaume de Reboul's *La cabale des reformez* (1597) was published in Fontanier's and Ranchin's native Montpellier by Jean Gillet, under the pseudonym 'chez le Libertin'. According to Reboul's subsequent *Apologie de Reboul sur la cabale des reformez* ([n.p.]: [n. pub], 1597), pp. 92, 161, 644, a 'Monsieur Ranchin' had strongly criticised this text. Reboul was condemned to death for having written a satirical text in Rome in 1611.

[54] AN X 2A 985, 20 December 1621 quoted in Lachèvre, *Mélanges*, p. 73.

[55] Mothu, 'Pierre Petit', 267, note 3.

[56] Bellièvre, fol. 219r.

[57] The *Histoire veritable* gives an accurate description of the students as 'quelques gens d'estude et de qualité' ('a few men of study and high status': *Histoire veritable*, p. 9).

[58] Bellièvre, fol. 221v; Labrousse and Soman, 'Fontanier', 117.

[59] The following sequence of events is taken from Bellièvre, fols. 219r – 220r.

His audience realised 'a ceste derniere leçon que leur Maistre monstroit doctrine contraire au Christianisme' ('in this last lesson that their master was exposing them to a doctrine contrary to Christianity').[60] The oath they had signed was not enough to secure their silence, and Fontanier was denounced by two of his own students: the first of Bellièvre's pairs, Petit and Gaultier. The circumstances of his betrayal are best described by the man responsible for carrying out his arrest, the *lieutenant criminel du Châtelet* Antoine d'Aguesseau:

> Les deux logés rue des Mathurins [Pierre Petit et Jean Gaultier], à la plume d'or, en avoient donné l'advis à monsieur Fouquet, conseiller d'Estat, cy-devant président à Rennes, lequel en ayant adverty monsieur le chancellier et monsieur le gouverneur, ledict sieur gouverneur luy avoit faict donner [ordre]. Et d'effect, ces 2 escholiers-là attendoient dedans la maison toutte la matinée que luy lieutenant criminel vint pour luy ayder à surprendre ce judaïsant. Raison pourquoy il les auroit laissé aller à leur caution. Et d'autant qu'ils l'avoient requis de laisser aller Fillacier, il l'avoit faict. Le médecin [Ranchin] arresté presentant caution, il la receüt et le laisser aller, afin de ne luy point sujet de plaindre de luy, puisqu'il laschoit aller les autres.

> The two who lived at the Golden Feather on the rue des Mathurins [Pierre Petit and Jean Gaultier] had informed Mr Fouquet, councillor of state, previously *président* in Rennes, and having alerted the chancellor and the governor of Paris, the governor had given his orders. In fact, these two students waited all morning inside the house for the *lieutenant criminel* to arrive in order to help him surprise this Jewish proselyte. This is why he allowed them to go free on bail. Similarly, as they had asked him to let Filassier go, he had done so. The doctor [Ranchin] was arrested and granted bail, and was also released so as not to give him reason to complain, seeing as he let the others go.[61]

Bellièvre's record of d'Aguesseau's account reveals two striking details. First, it is notable just how quickly this denunciation by two young students had reached the upper echelons of the legal and political hierarchy. The councillor to whom Fontanier was denounced passed the information on to Chancellor Nicolas Brulart de Sillery, and to the governor of Paris who ordered the arrest: Hercule de Rohan, duc de Montbazon. Fontanier was therefore ambushed by d'Aguesseau—a senior magistrate of the Châtelet—on the orders of one of the king's most trusted servants, who ironically happened to serve as the *grand veneur de France* (the grand huntsman of France). The second significant detail concerns an obvious hierarchy amongst Fontanier's students. Petit and Gaultier appear to have been rewarded for manifesting their repentance through denunciation, as no further action was taken against them. It is curious that d'Aguesseau was so flexible in

[60] Bellièvre, fol. 219r.

[61] Bellièvre, fol. 228v; Labrousse and Soman, 'Fontanier', 125–6. Antoine d'Aguesseau was the grandfather of the future Chancellor of France, Henri François d'Aguesseau, whereas François Fouquet was the father of the Nicolas Fouquet, the finance minister imprisoned for embezzlement under Louis XIV (see Jean-Christian Petitfils, *Fouquet* (Paris: Perrin, 2005)).

this matter that he granted Filassier the same benefit of the doubt as a simple favour to his two informants, despite the fact that Filasser had not taken part in the denunciation. This leads us to ask why the denouncers did not seek the same clemency for Ranchin. Although there is no evidence with which to analyse the social relationships between the four students (apart from the fact that Petit and Filassier were both *avocats au parlement*), there are some clues as to the denouncers' possible motivations. After Fontanier's sentence was passed, a second *arrêt* ordered that the four students were to be interrogated again:

> Pierre Petit, advocat, et Jehan Gaultier, escollier, seront adjournez à comparoir en personne à certain jour en icelle Cour et Mes. Michel Filassier, aussy advocat, et Rodolphe Ranchins [sic], médecin, prins au corps et amenez prisonniers en la Conciergerie du Pallais pour estre ouyz et interrogez sur aulcuns faictz résultant dudit procès.
>
> Pierre Petit, a lawyer, and Jehan Gaultier, a student, will be summoned to appear in person on a certain day in this Court, and Mr Michel Filassier, also a lawyer, and Mr Rodolphe Ranchin, a doctor, will be seized and brought as prisoners to the Conciergerie of the Palace to be heard and interrogated on certain facts emerging from the trial.[62]

The *arrêt* unequivocally states that this second round of interrogations was to focus on further incriminating details to have emerged over the course of the trial. Given that there is no mention of these in either Bellièvre's memoir or the trial transcripts from the Parlement, it seems likely that these remaining questions had emerged over the course of Fontanier's trial of the first instance at the Châtelet, of which no interrogation records have survived. Yet as Mothu has observed, it is remarkable that Petit and Gaultier were *summoned* for interrogation, whereas Filassier and Ranchin were *arrested* to this same end.[63] A second issue presents itself here. Bellièvre is meticulous and explicit in recording how the four students present at the arrest had first visited Fontanier on three separate dates. How could Fontanier have been discovered on the Saturday dictating the same lesson to students who had signed up for his lessons at different times? A fleeting remark by Bellièvre allows us to propose a likely hypothesis which would explain both of these apparent anomalies.

Having related how the students had quickly realised the true nature of Fontanier's lessons, Bellièvre adds in the margin that 'deux d'entre eux disoient qu'ils n'avoient escrit que ceste fois-là mais qu'ils avoient pris 3 leçons commencées, estant venus de meilleure heure ce jour-la' ('two of them said that they had only written things down on that occasion [the day of the arrest], but that they had followed three lessons after they had already started, having arrived

[62] AN X 2A 985, 20 December 1621, quoted in Lachèvre, *Mélanges*, p. 73.
[63] Mothu, 'Pierre Petit', 266.

earlier that day').[64] This annotation betrays Bellièvre's clear interest in the extent to which the students had engaged with Fontanier's teachings. Though he does not mention names, it seems reasonable to assume that 'the two others' who were the last two students to sign their oaths, and who attended their first meeting with Fontanier together on Thursday, were the only two students who lived together: the denouncers Petit and Gaultier.[65] According to their version of events, Petit and Gaultier signed their oaths on Thursday. They arrived late to the lessons which the other students would have had in full on Thursday and Friday, possibly because they were otherwise engaged colluding with the authorities. On the Saturday of the arrest, they presented themselves at Fontanier's residence on time (*de meilleure heure* than their previous efforts), and were finally able to take dictation. If this were true, then it is possible that Petit and Gaultier had only arrived on the previous days after the lesson had moved from initial dictation to discussing any resultant questions. Hence, they were able to assert on the day of the arrest that they had not previously written anything down.

This seemingly trivial distinction clearly mattered to Bellièvre and the informants. Bellièvre's remark shows that Petit and Gaultier were keen to distance themselves from the other students by emphasising that they, presumably unlike their classmates, had not previously taken notes from Fontanier's text. Given that their oaths were seized during Fontanier's arrest, and that the other students would have witnessed them at Fontanier's home earlier in the week, they could hardly deny that they had attended three lessons. The clearly more dangerous activity of writing and thus propagating illegal views during these lessons, however, was easier for them to deny. Whilst the notes taken by the other students might be construed as complicity and approval, the two informants had listened with hostile spirits. They had only taken notes once, as part of their role as double agents for the legal authorities. Whether or not this was true turned out to be of little consequence for Fontanier's trial. What matters is that this was their legal defence, and that Bellièvre did not call their story into question.

The judges' treatment of the fifth student sheds further light on how they viewed different levels of involvement with Fontanier's text. This unnamed individual was absent on the day of the arrest, but had signed an oath which was found during

[64] Bellièvre, fol. 219^{r}. One could also interpret this ambiguous phrase to mean that the students had only been present for the start of the lessons, which were not then finished. However, the subsequent comparison with the day of the arrest (which they attended earlier than the previous lessons), implies that Petit and Gaultier missed part of the previous lessons due to their late arrival.

[65] An alternative scenario would see one of the inhabitants of the rue des Mathurins first attend on Wednesday. He would then have been shocked by Fontanier's dangerous teachings, before inviting his fellow lodger to come and judge his illicit lessons for himself on Saturday, which by coincidence would also have been Filassier's first day. Though not impossible, it seems unlikely that one of the denouncers, troubled by the content of the *Trésor inestimable*, would have invited his friend to become an accessory to Fontanier's crime and to undergo interrogation by the Châtelet.

the search of Fontanier's lodgings.[66] Once again, the act of writing proved to be a point of debate for the magistrates of the Parlement: 'nous deliberasmes encore, sçavoir si nous comprendrions au decret celuy duquel le serment signé s'estoit trouvé, bien qu'il ne fust, luy, trouvé escrivant' ('we deliberated again, to determine whether or not to order the arrest of the one whose oath had been found, even though he had not been found writing').[67] The signing of the oath was effectively a statement of intent to take part in illicit activities by agreeing to a document which, in truth, gave neither concrete examples nor direct allusions to Fontanier's unlawful teachings. To be discovered taking notes from Fontanier's *Trésor inestimable*, however, was to demonstrate acceptance of his blasphemous tenets as directly and clearly presented to them, and to join their author in the textual reproduction of these, thereby greatly increasing the potential for the subversive contagion to spread further. This explains why despite having agreed to join Fontanier, the fifth student's failure to participate in the lessons meant that he was spared any legal proceedings: 'enfin passa que nous n'en parlerions point, parce qu'il se pouvoit faire qu'ayant faict le serment, on luy descouvroit la meschanceté, laquelle il n'auroit voulu suivre' ('finally we decided that we would not speak of it, as it could have been that having sworn the oath, he came to realise the wickedness of it, which he then decided not to pursue further').[68]

When viewed in relation to the other students, the stark contrast of Ranchin's situation becomes clear. Having signed his oath five days prior to the arrest, he was the first of Fontanier's students yet did not feel compelled to denounce him. In the eyes of the judges, he had therefore suffered the longest period of exposure to Fontanier's pernicious influence with the least amount of apparent repentance. He lacked the support of d'Aguesseau afforded to Petit and Gaultier in return for their compliance, as well as the favour shown by the informants towards Filassier, who was presumably on friendly terms with his fellow *avocat* Petit. If Petit and Gaultier really were disturbed by Fontanier's lessons for religious reasons, they may well have harboured similar feelings towards their teacher's first recruit.[69]

Fontanier's prosecution thus began through a combination of two habitual means of instigation: he was denounced by private parties to the authorities, as well as being caught *in flagrante delicto* in his own home by the *lieutenant criminel* himself. The premeditated nature of Fontanier's arrest, in which his two denouncers had an active role, shows how important it was for him to be caught in the act. This is also made clear by the judges' attitudes towards an absent student

[66] See Bellièvre, fols. 219ʳ – 219ᵛ.

[67] Bellièvre, fol. 228ᵛ; Labrousse and Soman, 'Fontanier', 126.

[68] Bellièvre, fol. 228ᵛ; Labrousse and Soman, 'Fontanier', 126.

[69] Unfortunately, the surviving evidence does not offer any further explanation as to why Petit and Gaultier sought leniency for Filassier but not for Ranchin, though the trial transcripts from the original interrogations at the Châtelet could well have revealed accusations or personal animosities towards him.

who had nonetheless taken the first step towards the promised *Trésor inestimable*. Fontanier's address and signature underneath his placards, along with the signed oaths found at his residence, would have constituted quite the smoking gun on their own. Yet it is clear that the true infraction of interest to the magistrates was the dictation and dissemination of Fontanier's text, both as a material object and as an ideological weapon. D'Aguesseau's raid of the property scattered Fontanier's flock, who desperately tried to hide their notes from sight:

> Il trouve dans une chambre haulte cinq hommes assis au tour d'une table, l'un desquels tenoit une bible dictoit, les autres escrivoient, les papiers sont jectés soubs la table. Et se trouve à l'instant un livre in 4° escrite a la main intitulé Thresor inestimable. [...] Le lieutenant Criminel faict mettre les 4 escholiers en une chambre a part cependant procede à l'interrogatoire de celuy qui dictait ~~estant au bout de la table.~~
>
> In an upper room he found five men sat around a table, one of whom was holding a bible whilst dictating, the others were writing, their papers were thrown under the table. At that moment a handwritten in-quarto book was found entitled *Trésor inestimable*. [...] The *lieutenant criminel* had the four students sent to a separate room whilst he proceeded to interrogate the man who was dictating ~~from the end of the table~~.[70]

As we will soon see, the *Trésor inestimable* was of no comparable length to the Bible, meaning that d'Aguesseau was referring to two separate texts rather than initially mistaking Fontanier's text for the Bible. Fontanier was therefore either using his own text to engage with Holy Scripture directly, or he may have laid his text inside an open Bible in order to disguise his lessons as a final security measure. Almost prophetically, the students' notes reveal that the last line Fontanier had dictated to them was 'la main me tremble, la plume me tombe des mains' ('my hand trembles, the quill falls from my hands'). Bellièvre completes this sentence by adding a rare direct quotation from the *Trésor inestimable*:

> Quand je m'imagine que, si nous estions surprise, les gibbets et le feu ne seroient pas construits pour nous chastier, et encores ce qui me faict le plus de peine et apprehension que j'ay, que l'on ne me donneroit pas la liberté pour declarer la verité judaïque au peuple.
>
> When I imagine that, if we were to be discovered, neither gallows nor fire would be built to punish us, and what worries and pains me the most is the thought of not having the freedom to declare the truth of Judaism to the people.[71]

[70] Bellièvre, fol. 218^{r}.

[71] Bellièvre, fol. 225^{v}; Labrousse and Soman, 'Fontanier', 122. The trial transcript from the Parlement de Paris gives a variant here: 'le feu n'estre pas cappable de le punir, trop doux, sa plume luy tomboit des mains, il tremble' ('the fire was not capable of punishing him, too soft, his quill fell from his hands, he trembles': AN X 2A 985, interrogation of 10 December 1621, quoted in Lachèvre, *Mélanges*, p. 71). The *Histoire veritable* gives 'le cœur me tremble, la plume me tombe de la main' ('my heart trembles, the quill falls from my hand': *Histoire veritable*, pp. 11–12). Garasse repeats the *Histoire*

There was nothing unusual about d'Aguesseau's actions here. Those accused of a crime were to be interrogated at the earliest possible opportunity. For as Étienne Girard went on to record in 1638, legislation from 1466 had described how:

> quand ceux qui doivent estre interrogez, ont delay de penser ez interrogatoires qu'on leur fait, souventefois ils se conseillent et forgent leurs matieres et leurs responses, en telle manière qu'à grande peine et difficulté en peut l'on avoir la verité.
>
> when those who are to be interrogated are given time to think of the interrogations that they are to be subjected to, they often think strategically, and prepare their arguments and their answers in such a way that it becomes very difficult to get to the truth of the matter.[72]

Furthermore, those such as Fontanier who were arrested *in flagrante delicto* could be interrogated there and then at the scene of their crime.[73] Whilst no record of the students' depositions survive, Bellièvre notes that they were 'confrontés à ce Maistre non reprochés et demeure d'accord de leur deposition' ('confronted with their Master, who did not offer *reproches* against them and agreed with their deposition').[74] It might at first seem odd that Fontanier, a man who after all had legal training and experience, should fail to exploit the opportunity to discredit his students through legal *reproches*. Fontanier may have made a number of mistakes over the course of his trial and subsequent appeal, but this was surely not one of them. We cannot know to what extent Fontanier had sought to avoid incriminating his students out of regard for their safety or possibly even their friendship, though this appears doubtful given that they had known each other for only a short period of time. However, the circumstances of his arrest would have made it very difficult to propose *reproches*. Taking La Rochette's list of possible *reproches* as a benchmark, for example, Fontanier could hardly have alleged that one or more of these men were 'ennemy de la partie' ('enemies of the accused') when they were strangers who had only taken him as their tutor a matter of days ago. Nor would it have been plausible for him to have accused them of infamy, of being of a sordid social condition, or of

---

veritable and compares the incident to Sir Thomas More who, the moment before his arrest, had read the line 'iniecerunt in eum manus' ('they put their hand on him') from the *Passion of Christ* (Garasse, *Doctrine*, p. 152).

[72] Ordinance of Charles VII (1446), article 34, quoted in Étienne Girard, *Trois livres des offices de France* (Paris: Estienne Richer, 1638), p. 34.

[73] Adhémar Esmein, *Histoire de la procédure criminelle en France, et spécialement de la procédure inquisitoire* (Paris: L. Larose et Forcel, 1882), p. 140. On the need to interrogate prisoners quickly, see article 6 of Charles IX's 'déclaration' of 10 July 1566, which repeats article 36 of the Édit de Moulins (1566), in the *Recueil général des anciennes lois françaises, depuis l'an 420, jusqu'à la révolution de 1789*, ed. by François-André Isambert and others, 29 vols (Paris: Belin-Leprieur, 1822–33), XIV ii – juillet 1559–mai 1574 (1829), p. 214.

[74] Bellièvre, fol. 219^{r}.

basing their testimony on hearsay, when he had invited these lawyers, doctors, and scientists as guests into his home to train as his theological students.[75]

Fontanier attempted to defend himself during these on-the-spot interrogations by asking his students to confirm whether he had told them 'ce mesme matin-là, qu'encores qu'il leur dicta cela, touttesfois qu'il estoit chrestien et disoit Nostre Seigneur Jesus Christ' ('that same morning that, although he dictated this to them, he was nonetheless a Christian and said Our Lord Jesus Christ').[76] The vague and evasive responses from his students (who after all were at his lodgings to listen intently to his every word), along with the apparently improvised accusation by his two denouncers described as 'the two others' ('les deux autres'), seem to suggest that Fontanier was telling the truth:

> Deux declarant qu'ils ne s'en souviennent point, et les 2 autres disent qu'ils luy ont ouy dire chose approchante. Mais que l'accusé adjoustait à l'instant: 'Touttesfois les raisons du livre sont bien fort preignantes au contraire.'
>
> Two stated that they did not remember, and the other two said that they heard him say something similar to this, but that he had added straight away: 'the reasons contained in the book, however, strongly suggest the contrary.'[77]

Fontanier and Ranchin were taken to the Châtelet, though Ranchin was released shortly afterwards. Without access to Labrousse's and Soman's discovery, Lachèvre's study offers no comment on the stages of Fontanier's trial at the Châtelet, and moves swiftly from his arrest on Saturday 13 November to the sentence read against him thirteen days later on 26 November. Bellièvre's manuscript allows us to reconstitute some of the events from Fontanier's first trial of which no official records have survived. It reveals that he was interrogated on 18 November (the Thursday following his arrest) on the *Trésor inestimable*, and that 'il faict denegation de l'avoir faict persiste en son premier interrogatoire' ('he denies having written it, persists in what he said in his first interrogation').[78] A second interrogation followed on 22 November, and by 26 November the judges had reached their verdict. Bellièvre stresses that Fontanier was found guilty of 'ayant composé et enseigné son livre' ('having written and taught his book'), thereby identifying his crime as pertaining to the literary world as much as to crimes against the Church.[79] The same emphasis is made in the *arrêt* itself, which sentenced him to death for the crime of *lèse-majesté divine*. Before being

[75] *Le Procès criminel* in Claude Le Brun de La Rochette, *Les Procès civil, et criminel, contenans la methodique liaison du droit, et de la practique judiciaire, civile et criminelle* (Lyon: Pierre Rigaud, 1622), p. 85.

[76] Bellièvre, fol. 219r.

[77] Bellièvre, fols. 219r – 219v, quotation marks my own.

[78] Bellièvre, fol. 219v. Fontanier had claimed from the beginning that the *Trésor inestimable* had been written by Montalto.

[79] Bellièvre, fol. 219v.

burned alive along with his book and the trial records, he was first to declare in public that:

> Meschamment et exécrablement il a fait, écrit, composé, enseigné et dicté le livre intitulé *Trésor inestimable* mentionné au procès, rempli de blasphêmes et abominations contre Dieu, la Vierge Marie sa mère, et son Eglise.
>
> Wickedly and execrably he produced, wrote, composed, taught and dictated the book entitled *Trésor inestimable* mentioned in the trial, filled with blasphemies and abominations against God, the Virgin Mary his mother, and his Church.[80]

The criminal investigation was prompted by reports from Fontanier's students 'que l'on Judaïsoit en ceste maison-là' ('that people were teaching Judaism in that house'), whilst Bellièvre makes clear reference to Jewish teachings in his quotation from the *Trésor inestimable*. It is therefore significant that Judaism was not mentioned in the *arrêt*.[81] This omission betrays the awkward question of law which lay at the very centre of Fontanier's case. Although the Châtelet had apparently overcome this obstacle in pronouncing the death sentence, its judges were not to have the final say. As Fontanier was found guilty of a capital offence by a provostial court, his case was heard by the final court of appeal for the local jurisdiction—the Parlement de Paris—for consideration by a more senior panel of judges.[82] In an unusual move, the *procureur général* gave the trial documents directly to the judge he entrusted to carry out the Parlement's trial of appeal (Bellièvre), having received these from his *substitut* rather than from the *greffier* (court clerk) of the Châtelet.[83] Fontanier was transferred from the Châtelet to the Parlement's Conciergerie prison on Friday 26 November, as shown in the *registres d'écrou* (registers of incarceration) reproduced in Figure 4.1. Before turning to Fontanier's appeal at the Parlement, it is worth considering the social and particularly the legal situation of Jews in early modern France. As well as shedding new light on the judges' deliberations, this outline will also elucidate precisely who Fontanier had become fatally involved with in preparing his text.

[80] *Arrêt* of 26 November 1621 quoted in Lachèvre, *Mélanges*, p. 66.

[81] Bellièvre, fol. 218ʳ.

[82] As Yves-Marie Bercé and Alfred Soman observe, the appeal hearing of those sentenced to death by courts lower than a royal parlement was almost obligatory since the reign of François I, that is to say some 130 years before its official codification in criminal ordinance of 1670. See Yves-Marie Bercé and Alfred Soman, 'Les archives du Parlement dans l'histoire', *Bibliothèque de l'école des chartes*, 153: 2 (1995), 255–73 (260). This legal provision was not open to Vanini. As discussed previously, his trial was quickly upgraded from the Capitoulat (whose verdict could have been appealed) to the Parlement de Toulouse as the court of the first instance.

[83] Bellièvre, fol. 219ᵛ. For Labrousse and Soman, this was in order to avoid publicising the trial and the offending text (Labrousse and Soman, 'Fontanier', 115–16).

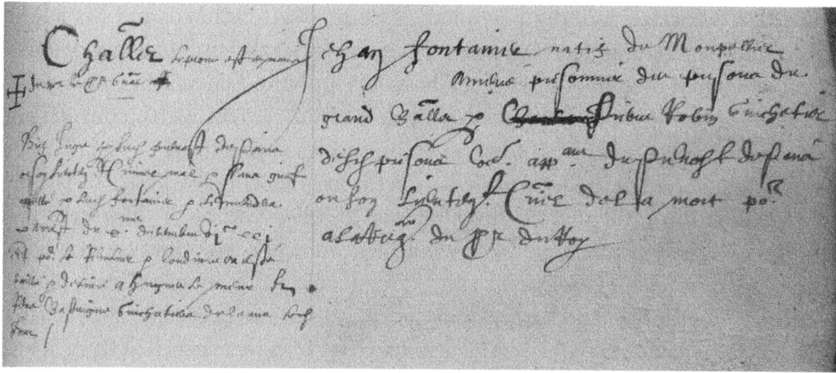

Figure 4.1 APP AB 25: *Registre d'écrou de la Conciergerie* (register of incarceration), fol. 189^{r} showing the transfer of 'Jehan Fontanier natif de Montpellier' from the Châtelet, 26 November 1621. The subsequent left-hand column notes that he was found to have been 'bien jugé par ledit prevost de Paris ou son lieutenant criminel, mal et sans grief appellé par ledit Fontanier' ('judged correctly by the *prévôt de Paris* [the Châtelet] or his *lieutenant criminel*, appealed wrongly and without grievance by Fontanier').[84]

BETWEEN THE LAW AND THE LOUVRE: THE STATUS OF JEWS IN FRANCE

The first remarks in Bellièvre's memoir leave no doubt as to the nature of his interest in the case:

> Fust traictée la question si un Juif judaisant et voulans monstrer aux chrestiens sa doctrine est punissable de mort. Et aussy la question si un chrestien faisant le semblable estoit aussy punissable de mort.
>
> [The Parlement] considered the question of whether a Jewish proselyte wishing to show his doctrine to Christians is punishable by death, as well as the question of whether a Christian doing a similar thing was also punishable by death.[85]

Despite the literary vocabulary of the *arrêt de mort* pronounced by the Châtelet as well as the Parlement's central focus on textual authorship, Bellièvre's legal concern centred on what French law had to say on the treatment of Jews. Frustratingly for Fontanier's judges, this was at the same time a relatively recent concern for the kingdom as well as an issue with little in the way of solid legal precedent on which to base a verdict. Not only did previous legislation enacted under numerous monarchs offer contradictory guidance, but the legal status of Jews also varied considerably according to their geographical location and social

[84] A full transcription of this document is given in Lachèvre, *Mélanges*, p. 66.
[85] Bellièvre, fol. 218^{r}.

status. Furthermore, judging Fontanier's case in 1621, Bellièvre and his fellow judges could only have been too aware of recent social and political manoeuvres directed against members of France's Jewish population. Given this, and given Fontanier's own links to influential Jews at the Louvre, it is worth considering the legal and social histories of Jewish communities at this time.

Officially, it had been illegal for Jews to settle in France since Charles VI passed an edict banishing them from the kingdom in 1394. Although they were not recalled on a nationwide scale by law until the French Revolution, the presence of Jews was nonetheless tolerated and even encouraged throughout subsequent centuries.[86] A significant departure from Charles VI's edict was brought about by the persecution of Jews in the Iberian Peninsula. Here, Jews were expelled from Spain in 1492 in an attempt to create peaceful religious unity, whereas the Portuguese Inquisition—along with the erosion of borders caused by the unification of these two countries between 1580 and 1650—encouraged many Portuguese Jews to flee.[87] For geographical reasons, southwest France was a natural destination in the first instance. Seizing the opportunity, in 1472 and 1474 Louis XI passed laws allowing any foreigner (except for the English) to settle in Bordeaux and Bayonne to rejuvenate these cities in the wake of the Hundred Years' War.[88]

In addition to these Sephardic Jewish refugees, some of whom may later have either converted to Catholicism or simulated Catholic faith, there were Iberian Jews who had already been forced to convert to Catholicism in their home country: the New Christians or *conversos*. Over time, these *conversos* were integrated into a number of nations (including France and the Spanish Netherlands) for economic advantages. Owing to the fact that the Netherlandish authorities were traditionally more tolerant of various Catholic and Protestant sects than their European neighbours, the cities of Amsterdam and Antwerp were particularly favoured by Jewish immigrant populations.[89] There were thus two historically

[86] Isambert, *Recueil général*, XVI, p. 76.

[87] Theodor Dunkelgrün, 'The Christian Study of Judaism in Early Modern Europe', in *The Cambridge History of Judaism*, ed. by Jonathan Karp and Adam Sutcliffe (Cambridge: Cambridge University Press, 2017), pp. 316–48 (p. 317).

[88] Esther Benbassa, *The Jews of France: A History from Antiquity to the Present*, trans. by M. B. DeBevoise (Princeton, NJ: Princeton University Press, 1999), p. 48; Jay R. Berkovitz, 'The Jews of France', in *The Cambridge History of Judaism*, pp. 923–48, (p. 924).

[89] See in particular Gary K. Waite, *Jews and Muslims in Seventeenth-century Discourse: From Religious Enemies to Allies and Friends* (London and New York: Routledge, 2019), pp. 2–37. For Berkovitz, the economic benefit of Jewish communities was surpassed only by the acquisition of new French territory—such as Metz—in accounting for increases in the French Jewish population ('The Jews of France', p. 925). On the commercial importance of Sephardic and crypto-Jewish networks, see Jonathan I. Israel, *European Jewry in the Age of Mercantilism, 1550–1750* (Oxford: Clarendon Press, 1985) and Jonathan I. Israel, *Diasporas within a Diaspora: Jews, Crypto-Jews, and the World of Maritime Empires (1540–1740)* (Leiden: Brill, 2002). For a succinct overview of Jewish migration and persecution in early modern Europe, see Evelyne Oliel-Grausz, 'Juifs, judaïsme et affrontements religieux (XVIe siècle – milieu XVIIe siècle', in *L'Europe en conflits: Les affrontements religieux et la genèse de l'Europe moderne vers 1500 – vers 1650*, ed. by Wolfgang Kaiser (Rennes: Presses Universitaires de Rennes, 2008), pp. 363–409.

distinct groups within France's Jewish community, whose growing numbers in the southern port cities would likely have been perceived as a more visible and threatening manifestation of Judaism than those French Jews whose quiet practice of their faith had been tolerated prior to 1550. On the one hand, there were the *conversos* who were officially and outwardly practising Catholics upon their arrival, having forcibly been converted before fleeing their home country, and whose true religious beliefs and practices could vary. On the other hand, there were the Sephardic Jews who maintained their faith after their arrival in France, and who had either fled from persecution in their country of origin, or who had been attracted to France by royal promises of safe haven and economic incentives.

Letters patent issued by Henri II in 1550 recognised the *conversos* as *nouveaux chrétiens* (New Christians), with a total of eight legislative acts between 1550 and 1656 subsequently granting them the right to elect domicile in France with the same status as native French subjects.[90] Preferring to be known as the Portuguese Nation, these Jews resided primarily in Bordeaux (including the mother of Michel de Montaigne), Bayonne, Biarritz, Saint-Jean-de-Luz, Bidache, and Peyrehorade, with further Jewish communities found in Avignon, Carpentras, Cavaillon, and Isle-sur-Sorgue.[91] By the time Henri IV had permitted the public practice of Judaism in 1595, Metz was home to almost three thousand Jews. This was followed by legislation in 1602 which encouraged new arrivals in the ports of southwest France to move further into the country's interior, at which point there were almost one thousand Jewish families residing between the Bay of Biscay and Bayonne.[92] It therefore comes as no surprise that in cities such as Bordeaux and Bayonne, Jews were able to live relatively peacefully alongside Christians. There was thus no single legal or even social attitude towards Jews in France, as their numbers and local rights were largely concentrated in specific parts of the kingdom. When Louis XIII attempted to expel all Jews from France on 23 April 1615, for example, the Parlement de Bordeaux—a seat of royal justice no less—refused to ratify the declaration in order to protect its Jewish residents.[93]

The *conversos* and their descendants are of relevance to Fontanier's case for two main reasons. First, the second-generation *conversos*, who had no lived experience of open Jewish worship and instead relied on an inherited oral tradition, were

[90] Benbassa, *The Jews of France*, p. 49. The following remarks are taken from Berkovitz, 'The Jews of France', pp. 924–5.

[91] On Montaigne's links to Judaism, see Harry Friedenwald, 'Montaigne's Relation to Judaism and the Jews', *The Jewish Quarterly Review*, 31: 2 (1940), 141–8.

[92] Anne Zink, 'Une niche juridique: L'installation des Juifs à Saint-Esprit-lès-Bayonne au XVIIe siècle', *Annales. Histoire, Sciences Sociales*, 49: 3 (1994), 639–69 (642–4).

[93] Berkovitz, 'The Jews of France', p. 925; Renée Levine Melammed, *A Question of Identity: Iberian Conversos in Historical Perspective* (Oxford: Oxford University Press, 2004), p. 83. On the coexistence of Christians and Jews elsewhere, see Anne Zink, 'Une niche juridique', 648 for Bayonne; and Waite, *Jews and Muslims*, p. 32 for Amsterdam.

often obliged to worship in secret as *crypto-judaïsants*.[94] In other words, the notion of Jewish worship and teaching had a strong connotation with secrecy, clandestine gatherings, and orality. Second, as Anne Zink has convincingly shown in her study of court records in Bayonne, the historical origins of this community from the Iberian Peninsula, along with their self-designation as 'the Portuguese Nation', led to the terms 'Portuguese' as well as 'Portuguese and Spanish merchants' being synonymous with Judaism.[95] The parallels with Fontanier's case are clear from the mere circumstances of his crime. He stood accused of teaching Judaism through private lessons, requiring students to swear an oath before God, on a text at least acquired if not co-written by a Portuguese contact whom he had met in Amsterdam. This strong link with Judaism was exacerbated by the content of the *Trésor inestimable*, as well as by the question of Fontanier's possible conversion and circumcision.

Given these established Jewish communities, we might well ask what Fontanier had to fear in teaching from the *Trésor inestimable*. The timing of his activities was crucial here. Had Fontanier displayed his placard in the streets of Bordeaux under Henri IV, he might well have escaped prosecution. Yet the level of tolerance towards Jews was very different in 1621 as well as in the minds of the majority. As Freddy Raphaël has extensively demonstrated, early modern anti-Semitism saw a strong correlation between Jews and witches.[96] Like witches, Jews were believed by many to be part of an international conspiracy to bring down the Christian world order. Witches and Jews—both of which could collectively be described as a synagogue—were said to worship the devil at gatherings known as Sabbaths. Hans Baldung immortalised this conflation, giving central place in his 1510 engraving 'The Witches' to a cauldron bearing pseudo-Hebraic characters; whilst Johann Fischart's translation of Jean Bodin's 1591 *Daemonomania* asserts that 'à notre époque il y a d'innombrables sorciers parmi les Juifs' ('in our time there are innumerable witches amongst the Jews').[97] However integrated Iberian Jewish

[94] See Natalia Muchnik, 'La conversion en héritage. Crypto-judaïsants dans l'Europe des XVIe et XVIIe siècles (Espagne, France, Angleterre)', *Histoire, économie & société*, 4: 33 (2014), 10–24. Similar secret acts of Jewish worship were uncovered in Amsterdam and the Spanish Netherlands. See Waite, *Jews and Muslims*, pp. 3, 25–6.

[95] This conflation between the two nations was partly encouraged by the Spanish conquest of Portugal in 1580. On the Jewish connotations of 'Portuguese' and 'Spanish', see Anne Zink, 'Être juif à Bayonne en 1630', *Annales du Midi: revue archéologique, historique et philologique de la France méridionale*, 108: 2 (1996), 44–60 (442, 458); Benbassa, *The Jews of France*, p. 49; Melammed, *A Question of Identity*, p. 82. On the wider European Jewish diaspora, see the essays which form *Jewish Culture in Early Modern Europe*, ed. by Richard I. Cohen and others (Pittsburgh, PA, and Cincinnati, OH: University of Pittsbugh Press and Hebrew Union College Press, 2014).

[96] Freddy Raphaël, 'Juifs et sorcières dans l'Alsace médiévale', *Revue des sciences sociales*, 3 (1974), 69–106. The following comparisons between Jews and witches, drawn from Raphaël's expansive list of examples, are taken from 72–83. On the perceived links between Judaism and blasphemy, see Alain Cabantous, *Histoire du blasphème en Occident: XVIe–XIXe siècle* (Paris: Albin Michel, 2015), pp. 32–5.

[97] Quoted in Raphaël, 'Juifs et sorcières', 87. See also Shelly Matthews, *Perfect Martyr: The Stoning*

immigrants may have been in the Basque region of France, and whatever legal protections they may have been offered on a local level, the prevailing stereotypes, fear, and hatred of Jews would have been familiar to those who denounced Jewish teachings on the rue de Béthisy. This said, in the years leading up to 1621 the status of integrated Jews into the highest echelons of Parisian society, with which Fontanier in fact had a personal link, was exceptional.

The question of Judaism in France served as a major catalyst to the downfall of the Concinis, and by extension to the advent of Louis XIII's personal rule, characterised as it was by the increased centralisation and censorship brought in under Richelieu's ministry. As unlikely as it may at first appear, Fontanier's contact with Daniel Montalto associated him and his purported crimes both with the Concinis' disgrace and the recently ousted government of Marie de Médicis. In order to appreciate this, we have to go back several years before Fontanier's arrest to 1606. Jewish doctors enjoyed a fine reputation in the early modern world, and as such their services were sought after by several European monarchs and aristocrats with little apparent concern for their religious beliefs.[98] One such doctor was Daniel and Isaac Montalto's father. Born in Portugal in 1567 as Felipe Rodrigués de Luna Montalto, after his conversion to Judaism in 1606 during a stay in Venice he became known as Philotheus Eliau (Elijah) Montalto.[99] As Elijah passed through Paris in 1606 en route to serve as the physician of Marie de Médicis' uncle, the Grand Duke of Tuscany Ferdinando I, he attracted the attention of Concino Concini's wife, Léonora Galigaï, who briefly sought his medical expertise. After the death of Henri IV, Marie de Médicis requested Elijah's

of Stephen and the Construction of Christian Identity (Oxford: Oxford University Press, 2010), p. 55; Norman Cohn, *Europe's Inner Demons: An Enquiry Inspired by the Great Witch-hunt* (London: Sussex University Press, 1975), pp. 100–1. On the historical context of this European phenomenon in the Medieval and early Renaissance periods, see especially Jean Delumeau, *La Peur en Occident (XIVe–XVIIe siècles)* (Paris: Fayard, 1973), pp. 273–304.

[98] Elizabeth I's physican, for example, was a Dr Rodrigo Lopez. Having fled to London from the Portuguese Inquisition in 1559, 'assisted by the wide respect that Jews had gained within aristocratic Christian circles for medicine,' he was executed in 1594 for his alleged involvement in a poisoning plot against the queen. See Waite, *Jews and Muslims*, p. 27. For Adam Shear, a distinction was made between the study of medicine by Jews—where their Jewishness was not relevant to their 'universalistic' activity—and their study of natural philosophy, which was considered as an internal theological enterprise. See Adam Shear, 'Science, Medicine, and Jewish Philosophy', in *The Cambridge History of Judaism* ed. by Jonathan Karp and Adam Sutcliffe (Cambridge: Cambridge University Press, 2017), pp. 522–49 (p. 522).

[99] I shall refer to Daniel and Isaac Montalto's father as Elijah throughout, though the French forms of his name include *Elie*, *Philotée*, and *Philotier*. As Friedenwald observes, in the first edition of Elijah Montalto's *Optica, Intra Philosophia* (Florence: Cosmum Juntam, 1606) his name is given as Philippi Montalto, whereas the second edition (Colonia Allobrogum: P. M. Marceau, 1613) reflects his conversion to Judaism: Philotheus Elianus Montalto. See Harry Friedenwald, 'Montalto: A Jewish Physician at the Court of Marie de Médicis and Louis XIII', *Bulletin of the Institute of the History of Medicine*, 3:2 (1935), 129–58 (148, and 148–56 for Montalto's bibliography). The following biographical details on the Jewish immigrants at the court of Marie de Médicis draw principally from the invaluable research conducted by Jean-Marc Pelorson, 'Le docteur Carlos García et la colonie hispano-portugaise de Paris (1613–1619)', *Bulletin Hispanique*, 71: 3–4 (1969), 518–76 (519–28).

services from the Grand Duke, on the pretext that five Parisian physicians had died in the space of as many years.[100] Elijah duly accepted on the proviso that 'il n'entendoit se desguiser et contrefaire en sa profession, ains exercer librement sa religion Judaïque' ('he intended neither to hide nor fake his religion, and as such intended to exercise his Jewish faith freely').[101] Incredibly, Elijah was granted this licence not only from Marie de Médicis but by the pope, making him the sole legally recognised Jew in the kingdom of France.[102]

By the autumn of 1612 he arrived with his wife, two of his sons, as well as his student from Amsterdam—Saul Levi Morteira—who would later publish his *Arguments Against the Christian Religion*.[103] As well as caring for Léonora, he also provided his services to Marie de Médicis, her daughter Christine, and the king himself. Montalto was not the only Jew at the royal court. During his visit in 1606 he had met the perfumer to the king and queen Manuel Mendéz, with whom he stayed in contact during his subsequent stay in Venice. In February 1610, Mendéz had presented Marie de Médicis with his niece's husband, Francisco Alvarez, who was made doctor to the queen regent (*medecin ordinaire de la Reine*). He was followed by Alonso Lopez, who came to Paris in 1612 to settle a legal dispute and to plead in favour of Jews expelled from Spain.[104] Lopez then stayed on in the city to work as a financier and a diamond merchant.[105] Finally, another doctor by the name of Carlos García was also present at the royal court, and appears to have been known to Montalto for some time by 1614. The Italian entourage of Marie de Médicis and its influence on artistic tastes has rightly led Jean-François Dubost to speak of *la France italienne*.[106] A lesser-known aspect of the regency, however, is the considerable presence of Jews around the seat of royal power just four years prior to the appearance of Fontanier's placards. This was despite the fact that these Jews—with the truly exceptional case of Elijah Montalto—were not protected by local-level legislation as was the case for certain Jewish communities in the South.

[100] Friedenwald, 'Montalto', 134.

[101] Pierre De L'Ancre, *L'incredulité et mescreance du sortilege plainement convaincue* (Paris: Nicolas Buon, 1622), p. 488.

[102] Muchnik, 'La conversion en héritage', 19–20. On Montalto's correspondence with the Jews of Rouen, see Cecil Roth, 'Les Marranes à Rouen. Un chapitre ignoré de l'histoire des Juifs de France', *Revue des Études Juives*, 88 (1929), 113–55.

[103] Pelorson, 'Carlos García', 523; Marc Saperstein, *Exile in Amsterdam: Saul Levi Morteira's Sermons to a Congregation of New Jews* (Cincinnati, OH: Hebrew Union College Press, 2005), pp. 1–35; Saul Levi Morteira, *Arguments Against the Christian Religion in Amsterdam*, trans. and ed. by Gregory Kaplan (Amsterdam: Amsterdam University Press, 2017).

[104] Hélène Duccini, *Concini: Grandeur et misère du favori de Marie de Médicis* (Paris: Albin Michel, 1991), p. 129.

[105] J.H. Elliot, *Richelieu and Olivares* (Cambridge: Cambridge University Press, 1984), p. 116. See also Henri Baraude, *Lopez: Agent financier et confident de Richelieu* (Paris: Éditions de la Revue Mondiale, 1933).

[106] Jean-François Dubost, *La France italienne: XVIe–XVIIe siècles* (Paris: Aubier, 1997).

As with Vanini and the Italians, our period of study represents a time of sudden and extreme change for what Pelorson has termed the 'Portuguese–Hispanic colony' of Jews in Paris.[107] Back in Amsterdam, a city with links to several French libertine writers of the period, Hugo Grotius had made recommendations on restricting the activities of Jews as early as 1615.[108] By 1616, one year prior to Fontanier's stay in the Netherlands in April 1617, magistrates in Amsterdam had taken up several of Grotius' suggestions. Significantly for Fontanier and Montalto, these included '1. Not to say or write anything, and also to ensure that nothing was said or written, that might in any way tend towards denigration of our Christian Religion; 2. Not to attempt to turn any Christian persons away from our Christian religion, or to circumcise them.'[109]

In France, political circumstances and a series of events linked to the royal court led to even more extreme measures being taken again Jews. By this time, Malherbe was able to lament that 'le judaïsme s'est étendu jusqu'à la Seine. Il serait à souhaiter qu'il fût demeuré sur le Jordain [sic]' ('Judaism has reached as far as the Seine. It would be more desirable for it to have stayed on the Jordan').[110] The trouble began on 28 March 1615, when a protégé of Concini, the former astrologer to Catherine de Médicis Cosimo Ruggeri, died having refused the last sacraments. Ruggeri had been gifted the Abbey of Saint-Mahé by Concini, yet on his deathbed he had claimed, with strong echoes of Vanini, that 'il n'y a point d'autres diables que les ennemis qui nous tourmentent en ce monde, ny d'autre Dieu, que les Roys et Princes, qui seuls nous peuvent advancer et faire du bien' ('there are no other devils than the enemies who torment us in this world, nor any other God than kings and princes, who are the only ones who can promote us or do good towards us').[111] Despite this final declaration of atheism, Concini demanded that Ruggeri be buried in consecrated ground, leading to public outcry and accusations of sorcery.[112] On the very same day, *remonstrances* from the Parlement de Paris lamented that Paris had become full of 'anabaptistes, juifs, magiciens et empoisonneurs' ('Anabaptists, Jews, magicians and poisoners').[113] Shortly afterwards, on 23 April Louis XIII

[107] Pelorson, 'Le docteur Carlos García et la colonie hispano-portugaise de Paris (1613–1619)'.

[108] Vanini's *De admirandis* dissimulates much of the author's more audacious views through the reported words of 'Atheus Absterodami' [sic] ('an Amsterdam atheist'). See Giulio Cesare Vanini, *De admirandis nature regine deaeque mortalium arcanis* (Paris: Adrien Perier, 1616), p. 420. Along with Guez de Balzac, two other *libertin* writers—Théophile and Tristan L'Hermite—also visited Amsterdam from 1613 to 1615. See Adam, *Pensée*, pp. 31–5.

[109] Quoted in Waite, *Jews and Muslims*, pp. 36–7.

[110] Quoted in Phillipe Bourdrel, *Histoire des juifs de France*, 2 vols (Paris: Ablin Michel, 2004), I, p. 84.

[111] *Mercure François*, 4 (1615–17: 1615), pp. 46–7. Tellingly, Garasse's account of Fontanier's crimes and punishment in his *Doctrine curieuse* is followed by a chapter on Ruggeri's fate (see Garasse, *Doctrine*, pp. 154–7).

[112] Pelorson, 'Carlos García', 532.

[113] Quoted in Jean-Christian Petitfils, *Louis XIII*, 2 vols (Paris: Perrin, 2014), I, p. 221. See also Henri Busson, *La Pensée Religieuse Française de Charron à Pascal* (Paris: Librairie Philosophique J. Vrin, 1933), p. 326.

published a declaration stipulating that all Jews were to leave France within the space of one month on pain of death, claiming that:

> lesdits Juifs se sont depuis quelques années espandus, déguisés en plusieurs lieux de cesluy nostre royaume, ne pouvant souffrir telles impiétés sans commettre une très grande faute envers sa divine bonté offensée de plusieurs blasphèmes ordinaires, nous avons advisé d'y pourvoir et remédier le plus promptement qu'il nous sera possible.
>
> the aforementioned Jews have spread themselves and disguised themselves in several places here in our kingdom in recent years. Unable to bear such impieties without committing a very great error against his divine goodness, offended by several common blasphemies, we have decided to address and to remedy this ill as quickly as possible.[114]

The *Mercure françois* adds that this legislation was enacted 'sur l'advis qu'il y eut quelques Juifs yssus de ceux de Portugal et venus de Holande se vouloient respandre et habituer à Paris' ('following reports of a number of Jews hailing from those who had come to Holland from Portugal who wished to spread and live in Paris').[115] It also refers to another event which took place in April 1615, and which directly implicated the Jewish circle at court. A number of Jews were:

> surpris en une maison qui avoient faict preparer un Agneau selon la Pasque Judaïque, lesquels l'on meit [sic] prisonniers; et leur fut enjoinct de vuider le Royaume: quelque faveur que Philotee Elian de Montalto, Medecin Portugais, qui avoit du credit en Cour, leur peut procurer. Ce Montalto estoit Juif de race, il mourut à Tours sur la fin de ceste annee.
>
> discovered in a household in which a lamb had been prepared to celebrate Passover. These individuals were taken prisoner and ordered to leave the kingdom, despite any assistance that Philotée Elian [Elijah] de Montalto, a Jewish doctor who had favour at Court, could procure them. This Montalto was of Jewish origins, and died at Tours at the end of this year.[116]

These comments reveal that Montalto was perceived not only to hold sway with the powerful figures of the royal court, but to be willing to use this influence to assist the cause of his fellow Jews.[117] This in turn proves that Louis XIII's 1615 declaration was not an empty threat against the Concinis and their entourage, nor a hollow flexing of his political muscles. It had real and immediate consequences for Jews in Paris who were swiftly sent to the Châtelet, where not even Léonora's influential physician was able to help them. In addition to this and to Montalto's

114 'Déclaration qui expulse les juifs du royaume' (1615) in Isambert, *Recueil général*, XVI, p. 77.

115 *Mercure françois*, p. 45.

116 *Mercure françois*, pp. 45–6.

117 This assertion would later be corroborated by a deposition made by Alonso Lopez at the trial of Léonora Galigaï (see Pelorson, 'Carlos García', 533). The Jews imprisoned at the Châtelet were later released without apparent charge.

correspondence addressed to Jews in Rouen alluded to earlier, Cecil Roth has uncovered a number of letters written by Montalto between 1611 and 1612 to inhabitants of Saint-Jean-de-Luz—the main destination for refugees fleeing the Iberian Peninsula until 1619—in which he urged them to maintain their Jewish faith.[118] These sources suggest that Montalto clearly held some degree of political influence within and beyond the walls of Paris. His death on 19 February 1616 spared him the spectacle of Louis XIII's coup against the Concinis and the anti-Semitism that these events inspired, including the legal examinations of what remained of the royal Jewish entourage at Léonora's trial.[119]

The events surrounding the assassination of Concini on 24 April 1617 are well known. The subsequent trial of Concini's wife Léonora, however, has received less scholarly attention. Her trial can at first appear to be a less sensational act of removing the remaining traces of Italian influences at court, as well as of gaining access to the Concinis' considerable personal fortune. However, this event in fact has some bearing on Fontanier's trial. Its records offer valuable, first-hand accounts of the Jewish circle which had surrounded Marie de Médicis, as well as an insight into the relationship between Judaism and the law courts just four years before Fontanier's judges contended with this same issue.[120] Although her trial is usually considered to have been based on dubious accusations of witchcraft, the very first line of the charges against Léonora is unequivocal:

> Le premier faict est le crime de Judaisme verifié par l'introduction des Juifs au Royaume faict par Conchine et Léonora Galigaï sa femme [...] et d'icelle Galigaï pour la recherche de Montalto juif afin de le faire venir en France, ou il est parlé d'iceluy Montalto, qui est qualifié un grand hebrieu et vray juif.
>
> The first charge is the crime of Judaism, proved by the introduction of Jews into the kingdom by Concini and his wife Léonora Galigaï [...] and by the fact that Galigaï sought out Montalto the Jew in order to bring him to France, where it is said that this Montalto is a great Hebrew and a true Jew.[121]

There was much more. The second charge against Léonora was that a book entitled *Machazor*, 'à l'usage des juifs hespaignols, imprimé à Venise' ('for the use of Hispanic Jews and printed in Venice') was found at the Concinis' residence, along with

[118] Cecil Roth, 'Quatre Lettres d'Elie de Montalte', *Revue des Études Juives*, 87 (1929), 137–65; Zink, 'Une niche juridique', 649. On the freedoms of the Jews in this city prior to 1619, see Carsten L. Wilke, 'Le rapport d'un espion du Saint-Office sur sa mission auprès des crypto-juifs de Saint-Jean-de-Luz (1611)', *Sigila*, 16 (2006), 127–41. The Spanish Inquisition also monitored the Jews of St-Jean-de-Luz, going as far as attempting to infiltrate their ranks.

[119] Montalte's tomb, at the Beth Haim cemetary at Ouderkerk just outside of Amsterdam, was subsequently painted as one of the central images in Jacob van Ruisdael's *The Jewish Cemetery* (1650s). See Seymour Slide, *Jacob van Ruisdael: A Complete Catalogue of his Paintings, Drawings and Etchings* (New Haven, CT, and London: Yale University Press, 2001), p. 536; Steven Nadier, *Rembrandt's Jews* (Chicago, IL: University of Chicago Press, 2012), p. 212.

[120] See BNF Cinq cents de Colbert 221; BNF MS Fr 16536.

[121] BNF MS Fr 16536, fol. 470^{r}.

the *Cheinuc*, described as a form of catechism 'pour apprendre et accoustumer à l'hebrieu' ('to learn and familiarise the reader with Hebrew').[122] The Concinis were accused of sacrificing cockerels in Parisian churches as part of Jewish worship. Finally, it was alleged that after Montalto's death they were responsible for bringing his replacement Francisco d'Alvarez to Paris, who happened to be the nephew of the royal perfumer Manuel Mendéz.[123] Remarkably, it was not until the *fifth* charge that the Concinis were accused of something other than their relationship with the Parisian Jewish community: *sortilege* (sorcery).[124] Later interrogations and confrontations at Léonora's trial involving four Jewish witnesses—Mendéz, Alvarez, Lopez, and García—reveal that there had been a disagreement within the Jewish circle at court. Although the precise details of this quarrel are beyond the scope of the present study, it is noteworthy that the dispute centred on García accusing Montalto of dabbling in magic and necromancy.[125] Given the common conflation of Jews with witches, and of medical experts with occult rituals, such accusations suited Léonora's accusers irrespective of their veracity. As such, the interrogation records of Concini's wife Léonora are abound with questions pertaining to Judaism and littered with the name 'Montalte'. Although she was eventually convicted of *lèse-majesté divine* (potentially for the convenience of ambiguity or for financial incentives), Léonora Galigaï's trial produced a strong, sensational, and exemplary link between the Jewish community, the occult, and crimes against the state.[126]

In the wake of this trial, even former bastions of tolerance towards the Jews fell prey to anti-Semitism, reaching fever pitch in the very town which had welcomed the Jews so openly: Saint-Jean-De-Luz. Here, according to the *Mercure françois*, Jewish refugees 'vivent Chrestiennement en apparence; et toutesfois on a descouvert depuis, qu'ils faisoient leurs conventicules et synagogues en ses caves, contre les Ordonnances du Roy' ('live outwardly as Christians, and yet recently

[122] BNF MS Fr 16536, fol. 470^v. The Concinis were also found to be in possession of Hebrew books which had previously belonged to Montalto: Jacob ben Asher's *Arba Turim* (first published in 1475) and Johannes Buxtorf's *Synagoga Judaica* (Basel: S. Henricpetri, 1603). See Friedenwald, 'Montalto', 141. Both Léonora's and Fontanier's trials reveal how owning Hebrew texts acquired from the Montalto family could lead to burning at the stake.

[123] BNF MS Fr 16536, fol. 470^v – 171^v; Jean-François Dubost, *Marie de Médicis: La reine dévoilée* (Paris: Payot et Rivages, 2009), p. 551.

[124] Pierre de Lancre draws a comparison between courtiers and witches in the *advertissemens* to his *Le Livre des Princes, contenant plusieurs notables discours, pour l'instruction des Roys, Empereurs & Monarques* (Paris: Nicolas Buon, 1617), n.p. I am grateful to Jan Machielsen for pointing me towards this comparison.

[125] On this rupture between the Jews at court see especially Pelorson, 'Carlos García', 528–41. See also Duccini, *Concini*, p. 80.

[126] The pope had claimed the right to the Concini's wealth, much of which was held in Italy, as the crimes of Judaism and witchcraft were within Church jurisdiction. For Pelorson, this led the French royal authorities to play down the crime of Judaism at her trial in favour of lese-majesty, which was within their jurisdiction (Pelorson, 'Carlos García', 541).

they have been discovered to hold their gatherings and synagogues in cellars, in contravention of the king's ordinances').[127] On 19 March 1619, Catherine Fernandez was observed bringing her right hand to her mouth immediately after receiving Holy Communion as if to dispose of the host. The locals became impatient with the length of her subsequent interrogation, suspecting that Jews had paid off the magistrates. They seized Catherine from the church, placed her in a barrel filled with straw and dry wood, and burned her alive before vowing to do likewise to any Jew or Portuguese native they found in Saint-Jean-de-Luz the following day. Between two and five thousand people heeded their warning and fled into the night.[128]

Our overview of the history of Jews in early seventeenth-century France reveals the true audacity (or even the foolhardiness) of Fontanier's activities, especially given that these took place after the fall of the Concinis and their Jewish entourage. Fontanier's choice of friends could scarcely have been worse. To summarise: he had collaborated with Daniel Montalto, the son of the former Portuguese doctor of the ousted Marie de Médicis and her confidante Léonora Galigaï: Elijah Montalto. Léonora in turn was an Italian who had recently been executed for *lèse-majesté divine*, following a trial for witchcraft in which Judaism was unquestionably the chief official accusation. Montalto had also been the dominant figure in a perceived nest of nefarious Jews at the very heart of the royal court, whose collective influence—of which tangible evidence survives—extended to witchcraft, necromancy, atheist abbots, and Concini himself. Just two years later in 1619, the vicious murder of a Jewish woman, in what had traditionally been one of the most popular destinations for Jewish refugees in France, proved to be a powerful litmus test for the intolerance towards Judaism ushered in by the personal reign of Louis XIII. It is inconceivable that these events would not have been on the minds of Fontanier's Parisian judges. Hearing his appeal in 1621, they were faced with a suspected Jewish proselyte, who openly admitted to interacting with Jews abroad, and whose explanations repeatedly included the same word which had so frequently appeared in the charges read against Léonora Galigaï in the very same Parlement: *Montalte*.[129] Whereas legal precedent was found to be lacking by his judges, there was certainly a wealth of sensational social and political events serving as a backdrop to Fontanier's *Trésor inestimable*.

[127] *Mercure françois*, 5 (1619), p. 66.

[128] See *Mercure françois*, pp. 66–8; De L'Ancre, *L'incredulité et mescreance*, pp. 492–7; Zink, 'Une niche juridique', 642–50.

[129] Bellièvre himself, for example, sought to demonstrate that Fontanier was the author of the *Trésor inestimable*, 'et que ce n'estoit Monalte frere ny le defunct medecin Montalte qui l'avoient faict' ('and that it was neither the Montalto brother [Isaac] nor the deceased doctor Montalto [the father, Elijah] who had written it': Bellièvre, fol. 220^{r}).

RESURRECTING THE MATERIAL EVIDENCE: A RECONSTRUCTION OF THE *TRÉSOR INESTIMABLE*

A striking attribute of the extant archival documentation from Fontanier's trial is that it describes a contest between two individuals. There are no documents attesting to the witnesses' views on Fontanier as have been recently brought to light for Vanini, or which can be found in abundance in Théophile's trial records. We cannot draw from the accounts of interested parties beyond those tasked with passing judgement on the case, such as the memoirs and letters of Molé and Garasse. The *président à mortier* Nicolas de Bellièvre was tasked by the *procureur général* with overseeing Fontanier's appeal. As he is keen to stress in his memoir, Bellièvre devoted some seven hours to examining the defendant's incriminating *Trésor inestimable* meticulously.[130] He both prepared the line of questioning and personally put these questions to the accused in front of the full complement of judges assigned to the case. Whereas Guillaume de Catel had proved to be an influential voice among several others at Vanini's trial (as well as serving as *rapporteur*), Fontanier's legal adversary had especial and unique roles to play throughout his appeal in addition to being a senior member of the Parlement. Bellièvre's task in preparing his questioning was essentially an exercise in literary analysis rather than in the interpretation of the law. Unfortunately for Fontanier, his interrogator demonstrated great skill in his analysis of both the language and the content of Fontanier's text. Bellièvre's early biography offers some clues as to how he had come to hone such critical faculties outside of the legal profession.

Nicolas de Bellièvre was born on 21 August 1583 into a family which had already produced several generations of magistrates. His father Pomponne de Bellièvre (1529–1607) was made a *président à mortier* in 1579, before serving as chancellor from 1599 to 1604. Yet Nicolas's journey to Fontanier's trial was a combination of family tradition and an accident of fortune. As the youngest of Pomponne's three sons, he was not originally intended to follow in his father's footsteps. After Henri III had relieved him of his duties, Pomponne allied himself ever closer to Henri IV as early as 1591. In recognition of his loyalty, Henri IV offered him the bishopric of Noyon for his eldest son Albert, though the disruption caused by the Wars of Religion led him to receive the Abby of Saint-Cybard d'Angoulême instead.[131] This lucrative gift caused Pomponne to disrupt family tradition by preparing his first son Albert for a life in the service of the Church, which entailed a solid literary education and a strong grasp of Latin and Greek. Received as Abbot of Joui in 1594, Albert went on to become the Archbishop of Lyon in 1599. By 1604, however, he had suffered severe brain damage from an unknown illness,

[130] Bellièvre, fol. 220^{r}.

[131] See Olivier Poncet, *Pomponne de Bellièvre (1529–1607): un homme d'État au temps des guerres de religion* (Paris: École des Chartes, 1998), pp. 164–5, 317.

causing him to resign his position in the Church in favour of his eldest sibling and to retire to Joui until his death in 1621. It is highly likely that Pomponne's second son Claude—who had originally been trained for the magistracy—also received a solid literary education after he switched to a career in the Church in order for Albert's office to be transferred to him.[132] Having resigned his post as a *conseiller au Parlement de Paris* (acquired in 1602), Claude became Archbishop of Lyon in 1605 until his death in 1612.

The consequences of these events for Nicolas de Bellièvre were twofold. First, it is likely that in addition to his legal studies, Nicolas would have received the same literary education as his two elder brothers. As well as being in keeping with an envisaged career in the Church, an education in ancient poetry and theatre was also used to hone the rhetorical skills of future magistrates to prepare them for their craft as orators.[133] Traces of Nicolas's interest in the arts can be seen in the education he subsequently organised for his son, the future *premier président* Pomponne II de Bellièvre. According to Charles Perrault, this included 'une connoissance universelle de tous les beaux arts' ('a universal knowledge of all the fine arts').[134] Second, the combination of Henri IV's gift of a position in the Church to Pomponne's first son, Albert's illness, and Claude's change in career path, all meant that despite being the third son, Nicolas was able to pursue a legal career as the heir to the chancellor of France. Upon Claude's installation as Archibishop of Lyon, Nicolas gifted him the Priory of Longueville (which he had received from Albert in 1599) in exchange for Claude's position in the Parlement. Nicolas was duly received as a *conseiller au Parlement de Paris* on 14 January 1605 with exemption from the minimum age requirement (*avec dispensation d'âge*). He went on to become *procureur général* in 1612, before replacing Édouard Molé as a *président à mortier* in 1614.[135] By the time he came to judge Fontanier's case in 1621, Bellièvre had risen to one of the highest ranks in the Parlement de Paris in a relatively short space of time. He had likely enjoyed a similar literary education to his two elder brothers, having completed his studies at around the same time that Claude abandoned his own legal career in order to become Archbishop of Lyon.[136] He was therefore a highly qualified magistrate for reading and interpreting the theological tenets of Fontanier's *Trésor inestimable*, as well as for detecting irreligious poetic verse in his later role as one of Théophile de Viau's judges in 1625.

[132] Poncet, *Pomponne de Bellièvre*, pp. 322–4.

[133] See Marie Houllemare, *Politiques de la parole: le Parlement de Paris au XVIe siècle* (Geneva: Droz, 2011), pp. 163–6.

[134] Charles Perrault, *Les hommes illustres qui ont paru en France pendant ce siècle: avec leurs portraits au naturel*, 2 vols (Paris: A. Dezallier, 1696–1700), II (1700), p. 53.

[135] A letter dated 6 January 1612, written in support of Nicolas's candidacy to replace Jacques de La Guesle as *procureur général*, can be found in BNF MS Dupuy 91, 251^{r} - 252^{r}. See also BNF Cinq Cents de Colbert 147, fol. 179.

[136] Poncet, *Pomponne de Bellièvre*, p. 327.

Bellièvre begins his account of the trial with a meticulous description of the text's contents followed by a brief summary. From this, we learn that the *Trésor inestimable* was a 94-page in-quarto, formed of booklets attached together rather than being bound, and was written in French. Its full title was:

> *Thresor inestimable ou Manserisme, c'est à dire description du Manser par Rabbi Isaac Montalte docteur Portugais medecin de la Royne et du Roy. Reveü par Daniel Montalte frere de l'auteur.*
>
> *The inestimable treasure or Manserism, that is to say description of Manser, by Rabbi Isaac Montalto, Portuguese doctor to the Queen and King. Revised by Daniel Montalto, brother of the author.*[137]

As mentioned earlier, the inclusion of Isaac's nationality was not fortuitous, but served as a further marker of his confessional identity. It is also noteworthy that Isaac, whom Fontanier did not meet in Cambrai, is designated as the author of the work whereas Daniel is presented as its editor or proofreader. The title page in no way links Fontanier to the work's composition or dissemination. This in itself is flimsy evidence to support Fontanier's claim that he did not author the text. The Montaltos could simply have offered to advertise the work as their own, due to their famous family name as well as the fact that they were no longer residing in France. Alternatively, Fontanier could have removed a previous title page bearing his name from this collection of unbound sheets. Neither Bellièvre nor Fontanier alluded to the title page during the two interrogations at the Parlement de Paris. Though it offered nothing to further Bellièvre's agenda, it is notable that Fontanier did not think to quote the wording of the title page when denying authorship of the text, whereas Théophile would go on to do precisely this in denying a specific level of authorship of his *Traicté de l'immortalité de l'âme* (*Treatise on the Immortality of the Soul*).[138]

An epistle to the reader next identified the target readership as 'Marrans, c'est a dire ceulx qui se sont revoltés de la vérite Judaique pour suivre la damnation Chrestienne' ('Marrans, that is to say, those who have revolted against the truth of Judaism in order to follow Christian damnation').[139] Although Fontanier's placards had attracted Catholics and Protestants to his lessons, the text in fact appears to have been written for those *conversos* who had abandoned Judaism for Christianity, and perhaps even those refugees who had arrived in France as Jews before either converting straight away or slowly slipping from being

137 Bellièvre, fol. 220v; Labrousse and Soman, 'Fontanier', 116. On the potential meanings of 'Manserisme', see Labrousse and Soman, 'Fontanier', 130, note 18, which refutes the arguments made in Lachèvre, *Mélanges*, pp. 75–81 (where the title of Fontanier's text is incorrectly transcribed as 'Mausérisme' as it appears in Fontanier's definitive sentence).

138 See Chapter 5, p. 299.

139 The following remarks on the contents of the text are taken from Bellièvre, fol. 220v; Labrousse and Soman, 'Fontanier', 116.

crypto-judaïsants to true Catholics. Again, Fontanier made no use of this stated aim of the text to appeal to readers who had prior involvements with Judaism. On folio 12, the subversion of the Christian faith began with the first of twenty-eight chapters which, for Bellièvre, aimed to 'contredire quasi verset pour autre l'Evangile St Mathieu. Lequel ayant pensé destruire il s'imagine que les autres le sont aussy' ('contradict the Gospel of St Matthew almost verse for verse, believing that in destroying this Gospel he would destroy the others too'). Next came refutations of the *Pater Noster*, the *Ave Maria*, the *Credo*, the *Confiteor*, and finally the Ten Commandments (fols. 61–73). Bellièvre notes that criticisms of the Commandments came at the end of refutations of a number of prayers, 's'imaginoit l'auteur qu'ayant monstré le foible fondement de ses prieres avec la destruction de l'Evangile St Mathieu le Christianisme estoit destruit' ('the author believing that having shown the weak foundations of these prayers through the destruction of the Gospel of St Matthew, he had also destroyed Christianity'). Beginning with the genealogy of Christ, the twenty-eight chapters of St Matthew's Gospel give several details on Jewish observance. It is thus unsurprising that Fontanier's text should have engaged heavily with 'the most semitic of the gospels', in which it is argued that 'the new people of God form the successors to the Israel of the old covenant who were first invited to the messianic feast but refused the invitation'.[140]

Following a two-page 'conclusions de l'auteur', as of fol. 76 the text expounds the supposed truths of the Jewish faith. According to Bellièvre's summaries of these, some of which are reproduced in Figure 4.2, the majority of this second half of the work does not seek to attack Christian beliefs through Judaism. Rather, it describes Jewish teachings and customs including the Jewish holy day and Jewish prayers, eating practices, social interactions with those outside of the Jewish community, the persecution of their people, and a defence of moneylending. However astute Bellièvre's observations may have been on the wider strategy of the work, it should be remembered that the *Trésor inestimable* was not written in order to participate in an intellectual debate between theologians. The text was instead intended to serve as a practical teaching manual containing arguments to convert its readers, potentially including Fontanier himself. As such, the second half of the work appears to have introduced the reader to Jewish life in a descriptive manner devoid of aggression towards Christianity.

By paying close attention to the extant documentation, it is possible to hypothesise as to how far Fontanier had progressed into his *Trésor inestimable* by the time of his arrest. To recap the chronology proposed earlier: Fontanier was denounced by Petit and Gaultier who claimed that he had taught three lessons. Given the text's strategic structure of stages leading to Jewish conversion, it is likely that Fontanier

[140] *The New Jerusalem Bible: Study Edition*, ed. by Henry Wansbrough (London: Darton, Longman & Todd, 1994), pp. 1606–7. I am grateful to Michael Moriarty and John O'Brien for these reflections.

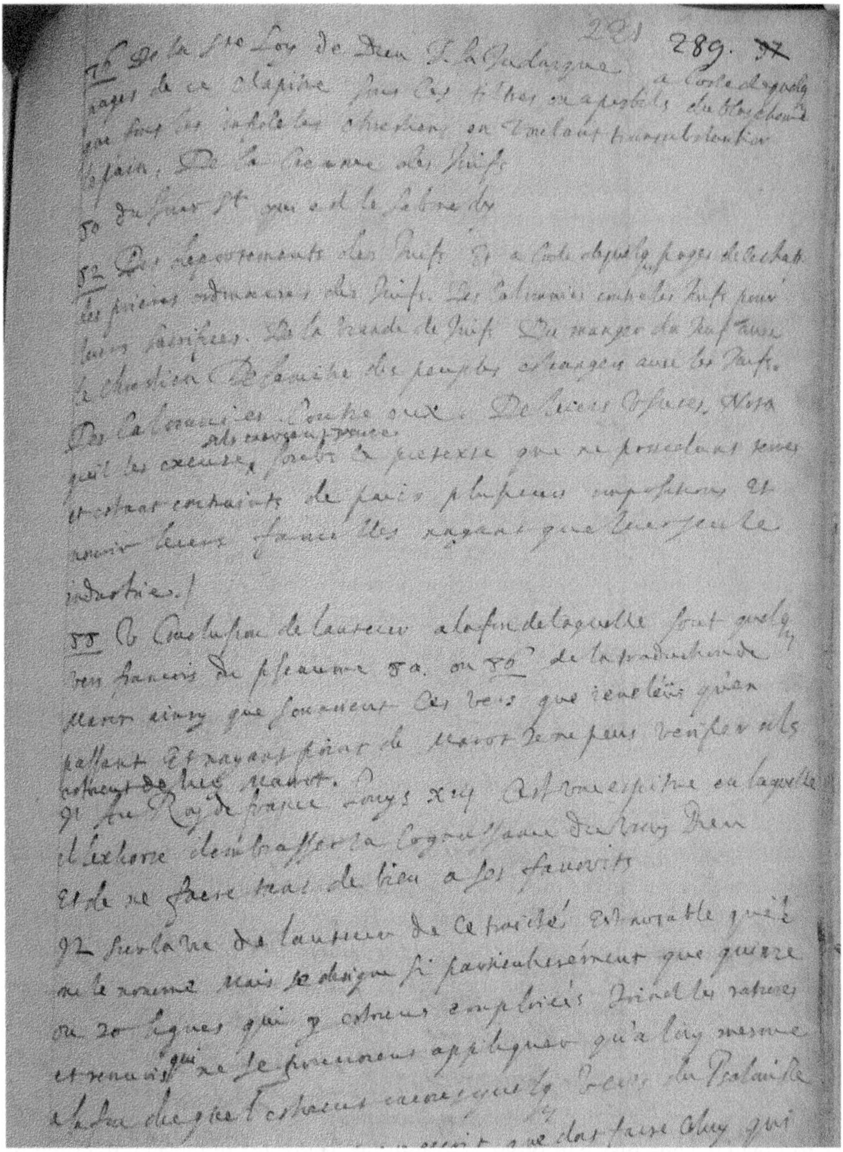

Figure 4.2 BNF MS Fr 18319: Nicolas de Bellièvre, *Remarques de monsieur le président de Bellièvre, sur ce qui s'est passé au Parlement de Paris (1607–1627)*, 2 vols, I, fol. 221r, which summarises the content of Jean Fontanier's *Trésor inestimable*.

would have worked through the chapters in the order in which they appeared in the text. One of Fontanier's defences at trial was to claim that 'ilz n'ont coppié que trois feuilletz' ('they [the students] had only copied out three pages').[141] Additionally, Bellièvre paraphrased one of the students who had claimed that it was 'a ceste derniere leçon que leur Maistre monstroit doctrine contraire au Christianisme' ('in this last lesson that their master was exposing them to a doctrine contrary to Christianity').[142] At first glance, this would suggest that the students had reached fol. 12 of the text, as it is here, according to Bellièvre, that the *Trésor inestimable* began its attack on Christianity. However, the previous twelve pages merely contained prefatory material, whereas fols. 12^{v} – 60 contained twenty-eight chapters which sought to contradict St Matthew's Gospel. Even if the students had indeed begun on fol. 12 in their first or even second lesson, and found text 'contrary to Christianity' some three pages later (*c.* fol. 15), they would surely have progressed further than this by the third lesson, whether through dictation or initial discussions in the first two lessons. Bellièvre's choice of words offers one possible solution here. He does not refer to attacks, scholarly refutations, or the mocking of Christianity as he did in describing the early section of Fontanier's text. Rather, his wording indicates the presentation of a *contrary doctrine* taught for its own sake, rather than as a weapon for dismantling Christian tenets. The *Trésor inestimable* progressed from critiquing elements of Catholicism to expounding the tenets of Judaism, and it was only on fol. 76 that the text began to introduce readers to Judaism thus:

> De la sainte loy de Dieu: I. la judaïque. A costé de quelques pages de ce chapitre sont ces tiltres ou apostiles du blaspheme que font les infideles chrestiens en voulant transubstantier le pain. De la creance des juifs.
>
> On God's Holy Law: I. The Jewish Law. Next to a few pages of this chapter are those titles or marginal notes on the blasphemies committed by Christian infidels in wishing to transubstantiate bread. On the belief of the Jews.[143]

The students' own notes recovered by d'Aguesseau offer further weight to this hypothesis. We know from multiple sources that at the moment of his arrest, Fontanier was expressing his desire to preach the Jewish faith, rather than denigrating Christianity. These remarks seem more likely to pertain to roughly fols. 76 to 88 of his *Trésor inestimable*. Given this, it is reasonable to propose that the passage summarised by Bellièvre as *la loi judaïque* exemplifying *la créance des juifs*, and the passage alluded to by Fontanier's students as a *doctrine*, were one and the same. Thus, it is plausible that at the moment of Fontanier's arrest, his students were copying from between fols. 76 and 88 of the *Trésor inestimable*, and most likely from fols. 78 or 79.

[141] AN X 2A 985, 10 December 1621 quoted in Lachèvre, *Mélanges*, p. 71.
[142] Bellièvre, fol. 219^{r}.
[143] Bellièvre, fol. 221^{r}; Labrousse and Soman, 'Fontanier', 116.

This leads us to consider how the text was used as a pedagogical resource. Given that the students' papers were seized during the arrest, it is doubtful that Fontanier would have lied about them having only copied out three pages. The fact that Bellièvre did not challenge this assertion in court or in his private memoirs suggests that this statement was true. Fontanier must have been alluding to the number of pages written on that particular day. It is also possible that the first two lessons may have been largely discursive in nature, which would explain how Fontanier could have reached fol. 76 and beyond by the third lesson. If this were the case, the *Trésor inestimable* would have first destabilised the students' Catholic faith through critical discussion. The second part of the text would subsequently have provided an education in Jewish beliefs and customs. Unlike the previous critiques of Catholicism, these more prescriptive regulations were written down by the students, either to be committed to memory or to be used in the private practice of Judaism. This would in turn explain why the arrest took place on the third lesson in particular. Assuming that Fontanier had outlined some form of teaching schedule to his students from the beginning, the third lesson was likely chosen by his denouncers as the first gathering where he could be caught in the act of teaching Jewish doctrine. According to his students, it was also the first lesson from which tangible proof of Fontanier's activities—the students' dictation—could be confiscated as physical evidence.

Bellièvre's summary ends by recording the supplementary material appearing at the end of the work, some of which he would go on to use against Fontanier during his interrogations. Fol. 88 gave the 'conclusions de l'auteur.'[144] Fol. 91 contained an epistle to Louis XIII urging him to embrace the true God 'et de ne faire tant de bien à ses favourits [sic]' ('not to be so generous towards his favourites').[145] It is easy to discern the voice of the Montalto brothers behind this request rather than that of Fontanier. Whereas their father Elijah had enjoyed great royal favour under Marie de Médicis as part of a wider network of Jews at the Louvre, Paris under the personal rule of Louis XIII was a far less hospitable place for Judaism, with royal favour channelled almost exclusively towards the duc de Luynes. Fol. 92 presented between fifteen and twenty lines on the life of the author without revealing his identity. Though no further comment is given on this section, Bellièvre suggested that it was a perfect match with Fontanier's own description of his life when interrogated on 10 December, the transcript of which has survived. Working backwards from Fontanier's statement in court thus allows us to make a broad guess as to the general contents of this passage.[146] Finally, fols. 93 and 94 gave the written oath and a copy of the placard, the latter of which

[144] Bellièvre, fol. 221ʳ; Labrousse and Soman, 'Fontanier', 116.
[145] Bellièvre, fol. 221ʳ; Labrousse and Soman, 'Fontanier', 116.
[146] Bellièvre, fol. 224ʳ; Labrousse and Soman, 'Fontanier', 121. For the transcription of Fontanier's description of his life see AN X 2A 985, 10 December 1621 quoted in Lachèvre, *Mélanges*, pp. 68–9.

included Fontanier's name. Bellièvre additionally remarks that a number of the pages bore marginal annotations, references, and crossed-out lines indicative of a working copy whose owner had engaged with the text as an author.[147]

Although the outline of the book ends here, we are able to complete our description of the *Trésor inestimable* using Bellièvre's paraphrasing of particular lines from the text, as well as from references to particular local customs and literature which will be discussed in the following section. He records how the text accused Christ of being born 'de l'accouplement d'un forgeron ou serrurier avec la Vierge laquelle, pour éviter la peine de l'adultère, feignit l'annonciation' ('from sexual relations between either a blacksmith or a locksmith and the Virgin Mary who, in order to avoid punishment for adultery, faked the Annunciation'), before adding in the margin of his memoir that 'encores disoit-il que ç'avoit esté comme par force, la surprenant une nuict depuis le 10 septembre jusques au 10 octobre, qu'en leur loy les hommes se levent à minuict pour aller au temple' ('he also added that she was raped, having been attacked in the night between 10 September and 10 October, during which time, according to their law, men awoke at midnight to go to worship').[148] The *Trésor inestimable* elsewhere asserted that the Messiah had yet to come, that Jews were Catholics as they had been dispersed across the Earth, and that Roman Catholics were the worst of the eight sects of Christians.[149]

These notes constitute all that remains of the *Trésor inestimable*.[150] Its tenets were so blatantly contrary to Catholic teaching that the trial did not at any point seek to confirm Fontanier's theological views on any of the issues it discussed. Rather, Bellièvre's aims were twofold. He and his fellow judges had to determine whether it was a crime for a Jew to preach their faith in France. During the main interrogation, however, his task was to demonstrate that Fontanier was guilty of the authorship, and therefore the ownership, of the text's blasphemous teachings. This second aim would require a subtle, erudite, and forensic approach to literary analysis. Fontanier appeared to lack any solid strategy for defending himself besides simply denying authorship of the text. In addition, both Bellièvre's memoir and the trial transcripts predominantly present the words of the magistrate rather than the defendant, as one would expect in a courtroom setting in which the interrogating judge had a greater degree of verbal licence than the responding

[147] Bellièvre, fol. 224^r; Labrousse and Soman, 'Fontanier', 120.

[148] Bellièvre, fol. 221^v; Labrousse and Soman, 'Fontanier', 117.

[149] See Bellièvre, fols. 221^v – 222^r; Labrousse and Soman, 'Fontanier', 118.

[150] It would be beyond the scope of this study to seek to identify this text and its potential circulation beyond France, not least as this question was not addressed at Fontanier's trial. At Léonora's trial, the Hebrew professor Philippe d'Aquin claimed that Montalto had spoken with him about the *Sefer Yetzirah* (see Friedenwald, 'Montalto', 141–2). Lachèvre suggests that the *Trésor inestimable* may have been inspired by this same text (*Mélanges*, p. 80). For Labrousse and Soman, the *Trésor inestimable* may simply have replicated pamphlets, which had circulated in Jewish communities for centuries, contradicting the biography of Jesus as told in the Gospels: the *Toledot Yeshu*. See Labrousse and Soman 'Fontanier', 127–8, 130 and Mothu, 'Pierre Petit', 262.

prisoner. As such, a strictly chronological analysis of the two court hearings would obscure the subtle and indeed fatal shifts in Fontanier's tactics under the weight of Bellièvre's considerable verbal and intellectual assault. Consequently, in order to explore Fontanier's defence fully, we will first consider Bellièvre's preparations for the trial and his subsequent questioning, before contrasting these with a separate focus on Fontanier's responses.

BELLIÈVRE'S STRATEGIES OF ACCUSATION: A FORENSIC LINGUISTIC APPROACH

Bellièvre's approach was more erudite and methodical than the literal readings of metaphors, or the pedantic clutching at religious vocabulary, which both featured in the literary analyses at Théophile's trial. Although it is difficult for the modern reader to set aside the abhorrent anti-Semitic prejudice of this case, Bellièvre's calculating tactics during his interrogation of the accused are nonetheless striking. As he coldly explains, his entire line of questioning was built around reaching his desired outcome:

> Ayant leü son livre et appliqué à son proces, je creu qu'il le falloit convaincre d'en estre l'auteur, et, pour y parvenir en l'interrogeant, de luy faire raconter sa vie en retrogradant, à commencer du jour qu'il fust constitué prisonnier, m'imaginant qu'il luy seroit plus facile de s'en resouvenir, et se doubteroit moins de la fin pour laquelle je le fesoy, m'enquerant pendant chaque sejour, voiage, employ ou estude, ce qu'il avoit faict, veu ou leü, afin qu'ayant tiré de luy ceste verité, naifvement ou pressé, je peusse inferer que ce n'estoit Montalte medecin, son frere ny autre, qui fust autheur de ce livre, mais que luy seul.
>
> Having read his book and worked on his trial, I thought it necessary to convict him of being the author of the text and, to arrive at this conclusion in his interrogation, to make him tell us about his life in reverse order, starting with the day of his arrest. I thought this would make it easier for him to remember these events, and would leave him less suspecting of the outcome I had in store for him. For each stay, journey, job, or period of study I would ask him what he had done, seen, or read, so that having extracted this truth from him, unwittingly or through coercion, I could infer that the author of this book was not the doctor Montalto, his brother, nor anyone else, but him [Fontanier] alone.[151]

We might therefore describe Bellièvre's strategy as reverse profiling. Constructing a profile of the author of the *Trésor inestimable* before seeking to fit it to Fontanier's biography would inevitably encourage the accused to be evasive and deceptive. Far better to allow him to describe his life in detail, guided imperceptibly by the line of questioning, before fitting this biography, described in

[151] Bellièvre, fol. 222^{r}; Labrousse and Soman, 'Fontanier', 118.

Fontanier's own words and under oath, to the authorial profile which Bellièvre had prepared in advance of the interrogation. It is also significant that Bellièvre sought not only to associate the text with Fontanier, his education, and his travels, but to *disassociate* it from those of Montalto. This presupposes that Bellièvre had at least some knowledge of Montalto's education and even his level of French. Fontanier's defence was that Montalto had authored the text, rather than an anonymous other with a limitless number of potential authorial and biographical characteristics. In this sense, the *président à mortier*'s task was somewhat simple. He had only to demonstrate beyond reasonable doubt that the text was written by a French Protestant with a limited level of legal training or wider education, rather than a Portuguese Jewish doctor who spoke several languages. The line of questioning was not the only weapon in the magistrate's arsenal. Anticipating the trajectory that the interrogation would take, he added in his memoir that on Friday morning, 'je commandé particulierement au greffier de la Tournelle de faire tenir prests les chirurgiens de la Conciergerie, si d'aventure on vouloit faire visiter cest accusé pour veoir s'il avoit esté circoncis' ('I asked the court scribe of the Tournelle in private to keep the Conciergerie surgeons on standby, just in case it was decided to have them confirm if the accused had been circumcised').[152]

The very next day, Saturday 4 December 1621, Fontanier underwent the first of his two interrogations. This brief first encounter between the two legal adversaries was of relatively little consequence for the trial. Its transcript—reproduced in full in Figure 4.3—occupies only a single page in the court records. Yet when read alongside Bellièvre's memoir, its darker purpose becomes clear. Having spent fifteen days in the Conciergerie, Fontanier had started to refuse food, though it is unclear whether this represented a defiant hunger strike or the prisoner's deteriorating mental health.[153] Although the *rapporteur* for the case was absent, Bellièvre suggested to his colleagues that Fontanier be interrogated in order to raise his spirits, and that they would then hear his appeal another day.[154] Lachèvre, who did not have access to Bellièvre's memoir, highlights the stark contrast between this apparent act of good will and the subsequent confirmation of the death sentence against Fontanier.[155] However, Bellièvre reveals that even at this early stage of the appeal his mind was already focussed on the potential of the trial to serve as a sobering example to others: 'car l'exemple estant attendu s'il

[152] Bellièvre, fol. 222^{r}; Labrousse and Soman, 'Fontanier', 118.

[153] See the *Histoire veritable*, p. 12: 'il n'eust pas demeuré huict jours en icelle [Conciergerie] que l'apprehension du supplice et la crainte de la mort luy avoient tellement esblouy le jugement, et porté a un tel desespoir, qu'il ne voulut point durant deux jours quasi boire ny manger' ('he had not spent eight days in the Conciergerie before the apprehension of his punishment, and the fear of death, had so clouded his judgement and brought him to such despair that he could hardly eat or drink a thing for two days').

[154] Bellièvre, fols. 219^{v} – 220^{r}. The designated *rapporteur* was Pierre Broussel.

[155] Lachèvre, *Mélanges*, p. 71–2.

meritoit la mort, il estoit plus expedient que ce fust en public que, par longueur en l'expedition, l'avoir laissé mourir en nos Cachots' ('given that an example was expected to be made of him if he were found to be deserving of death, it was more expedient to do so in public rather than by leaving him to die in our cells during a lengthy trial').[156] During this first interrogation Fontanier gave his name, age, profession, a brief summary of his employment history, and claimed to have converted to Catholicism in Rome. He was asked a single question: 's'il n'a pas doubté que la Catholique fut vraye' ('whether he had doubted the truth of the Catholic faith'), to which he replied:

> Dit que non et ne doubte. Et qu'un Espagnol, parent de Montalte, est l'autheur de son mal et ne se veirent qu'une fois à souper y a 4 mois et se sont veuz quelquefois du depuis et a conféré seul avec luy et ne se souvient des argumentz qu'il luy donnoit.
>
> Said no and that he does not doubt it. And that a Spanish relative of Montalto is the author of his troubles, that they only saw each other once at supper four months ago, and have seen each other a few times since. Has conversed alone with him and does not remember the arguments that he gave him.[157]

Fleeting though it was, this first interrogation had drawn the battle lines for the true contest which was to follow. Bellièvre's prisoner had assured him that he was a good, recently converted Catholic who had neither written the offending text nor remembered anything from his conversations with Daniel Montalto. The *président à mortier*'s plan had worked: the court scribe informed Bellièvre that Fontanier had eaten just one hour after his first interrogation, and that he now 'sembloit avoir quelque esperance de la vie' ('seemed to have some hope of living').[158] Fontanier's new-found optimism betrays his apparent ignorance of the imposing obstacle that Bellièvre was preparing for him. Having considered Broussel's *rapport* and the passages from the *Trésor inestimable* to which it referred on 9 December, Bellièvre took the offending text home in order to prepare the summary of its contents as outlined earlier. He also prepared detailed line of questioning for the final appeal hearing which took place the next day, on 10 December.

It would of course be inaccurate to claim that Bellièvre adopted a modern forensic linguistic approach in his interrogation, and anachronistic to suggest that he had such a concept in mind. A modern forensic linguist consulted by a police

156 Bellièvre, fol. 220^{r}. As prisoners under the protection of the king, it was also imperative for guilty parties to die as a result of an *arrêt* by the Parlement rather than in prison. See Bercé and Soman, 'Archives du Parlement', 265.

157 AN X 2A 985, 4 December 1621 quoted in Lachèvre, *Mélanges*, p. 67. Here Fontanier recalls Daniel's more famous father Elijah.

158 Bellièvre, fol. 220^{r}. See also the *Histoire veritable*, p. 13, which claims that after the Parlement 'luy donna quelque Esperance de salut' ('gave him some hope of salvation'), 'ces paroles luy augmenterent tellement le courage et la force qu'il perdit aucunement ces fortes apprehensions et imaginations de la mort qu'il avoit auparavant conceuës' ('these words raised his spirits and strength so much that he somewhat lost his great fears and thoughts of death that he had previously had').

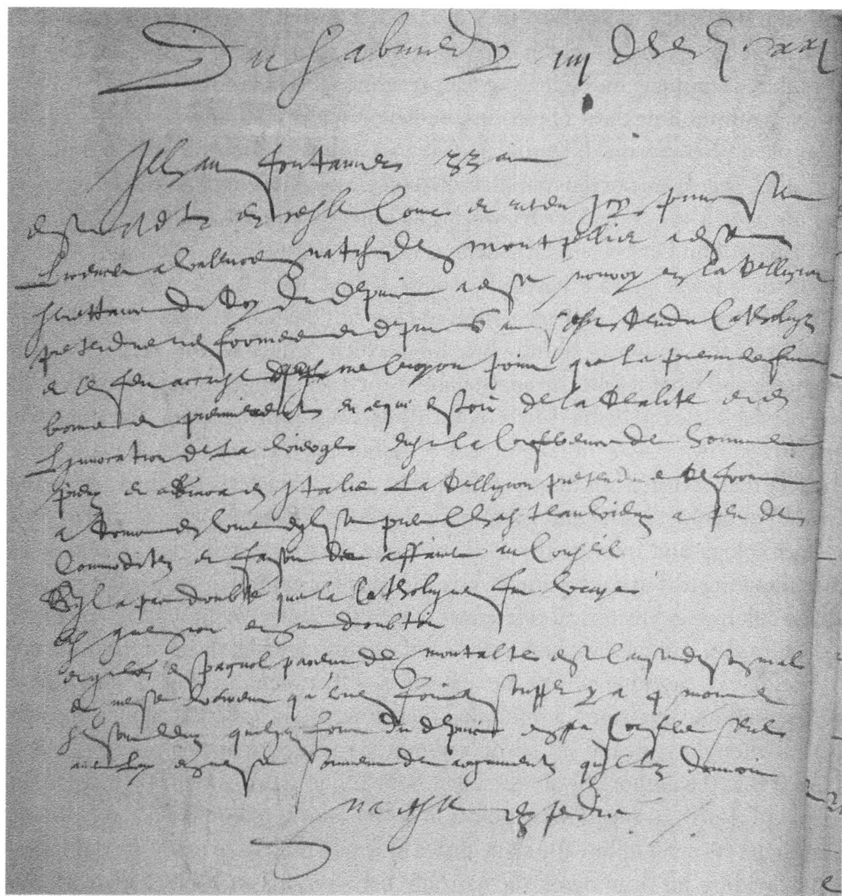

Figure 4.3 AN X 2A 985: the complete record of the Parlement's first interrogation of 'Jehan Fontanier, 33ans', Saturday 4 December 1621. On the first line of the last paragraph Fontanier asserts: 'Et qu'un espagnol, parent de Montalte, est l'autheur de son mal' ('and that a Spanish relative of Montalto is the author of his troubles').

force or a legal team, for example, does not seek to prove the innocence or guilt of a given party, but merely to establish the likelihood of a text being written by a potential author. Methodologically speaking, a forensic stylistic analysis would require a considerable corpora of linguistic choices from a potential author to compare with the text whose authorship is in dispute. Bellièvre had no such sample data at his disposal beyond Fontanier's single-page placard and the oath to be signed by his students which, having appeared at the end of the *Trésor inestimable*, may not have been authored by Fontanier alone if at all. Furthermore, modern forensic linguistic analyses often draw upon vast databases of phrases along with the frequency with which they are used, allowing the authorship analyst to determine the extent to which a given word or turn of phrase in a text can be considered a unique, individuating feature admissable in court.

Notwithstanding these objections, Bellièvre's wider method was surely an early example of these forms of textual analyses according to their broader definitions and aims. There is an obvious parallel with Douglas A. Kibbee's definition of forensic linguistics as a 'very broad term covering all aspects of the intersection of language and law'.[159] John Olsson similarly defines forensic linguistics as 'the application of linguistic knowledge to a particular social setting, namely the legal forum' and 'the interface between language, crime and law'.[160] Of equal relevance to Bellièvre's strategy is the notion of author profiling, which 'relates to the author's use of language and what it tells the analyst about the writer linguistically'.[161] Moreover, forensic stylistics is defined by Gerald R. McMenamin as using 'the linguistic analysis of writing style for the purpose of authorship identification', drawing from the fact that 'stylistic variation is reflected as class characteristics observed in the writing of distinct social and geographical groups'.[162] Despite obvious differences in technology and impartiality, Bellièvre was clearly engaging with Fontanier's incriminating text in a very similar way. He used the grammar, vocabulary, as well as the cultural and historical references within the *Trésor inestimable* to construct a profile of an author whose education and origins matched those of the accused.

Bellièvre's arguments can be categorised between an initial barrage of accusations and questions, a refutation that either Daniel or Isaac Montalto could have written the text, and six 'points' (numbered as such in his manuscript) which proved that the author could have been none other than Fontanier.[163] Given that Bellièvre clearly arranged these points in such a way as to construct a convincing argument, we shall follow the same order in which they were made at trial rather than dividing his arguments thematically between, for example, linguistic and chronological markers. After Fontanier had spoken at some length about his life, his religion, and his travels, Bellièvre began by undermining Fontanier's purported Catholic faith following his conversion:

[159] Douglas A. Kibbee, 'Forensic Linguistics and French', in *Studies in French Applied Linguistics*, ed. by Dalila Ayoun (Amsterdam and Philadelphia: John Benjamins, 2008), pp. 295–316 (p. 296).

[160] John Olsson, *Forensic Linguistics* (London and New York: Continuum, 2008), p. 3.

[161] Olsson, *Forensic Linguistics*, p. 98.

[162] Gerald R. McMenamin, 'Forensic Stylistics: Theory and Practice of Forensic Stylistics', in *The Routledge Handbook of Forensic Linguistics*, ed. by Malcolm Coulthard and Alison Johnson (London and New York: Routledge, 2010), pp. 487–507 (pp. 487, 489). For a general introduction to modern forensic linguistics, see Malcolm Coulthard and Alison Johnson, *An Introduction to Forensic Linguistics: Language in Evidence* (London and New York: Routledge, 2007).

[163] The transcripts of this final interrogation from the Archives Nationales are much more succinct than Bellièvre's manuscript, and even leave out certain points put to the accused entirely. As such, our reading of this hearing will be based on Bellièvre's text, with the relevant corresponding lines from the trial records given in footnotes for the sake of comparison.

> Qu'il avoit advoüé n'avoir esté à confesse que 4 mois avant, à un prestre de St-Eustache, duquel il ne sçait le nom, qu'il n'y avoit esté à Pasques parce qu'il n'estoit en bon estat. Qu'il n'avoit pas bien resolument et déterminément respondu du lieu de sa conversion à la religion catholique, si entre les mains de l'archevesque, son vicaire ou de religieux il avoit abjuré; qu'il n'en avoit aucunes lettres attestatoires.
>
> That he admitted that he last went to confession four months ago, to a priest at St. Eustache whose name he does not know, that he did not go there for Easter because he was not well. That he had not given a resolute or concrete answer as to where he converted to Catholicism, whether he had done so at the hands of the archbishop, his curate or a priest, and that he had no papers confirming this.[164]

Whereas evidence of the sincerity of Fontanier's Catholic faith was vague or non-existent, Bellièvre presented the court with much more tangible evidence of the defendant's Judaism:

> Qu'il avoit appris l'hebreu, c'estoit depuis ses estudes. Qu'il avoit esté par tous les lieux où il y avoit des synagogues en l'Europe, ou la pluspart, s'estoit servy de juifs à Constantinople, trouvé saisy de tables de Moïse, de prières hébraïques et de ce livre, de serments à luy prestés pour guarder le secret, livre escrit et signé de sa main. Qu'il eüst à recognoistre la verité s'il n'estoit pas prepucié, circonciz.
>
> That he had learned Hebrew, and had done so after his studies. That he had been to every place in Europe where there were synagogues, or most of them. That he employed the services of Jews in Constantinople. That the Laws of Moses and Hebrew prayers were seized from his property as were this book, the oaths of secrecy sworn to him, the book being written and signed in his hand. That he would have to answer whether or not he has been circumcised.[165]

Bellièvre records Fontanier's response to this onslaught thus: 'lors l'accusé, comme surpris, dict (touttesfois fort lentement) que non, et qu'il estoit chrestien et non l'auteur du livre' ('the accused then answered no (albeit very slowly), as if surprised, and that he was a Christian and was not the author of the book').[166] The trial transcript does not record any of this first hostile exchange between judge and defendant, but instead moves from Fontanier's account of his life to the Montalto brothers. The fact that Bellièvre records Fontanier's reply, and even the startled manner with which he delivered his verbal defence, proves that his memoir did not consist of preparatory notes which were not subsequently used in the interrogation, and that he did indeed put these points to Fontanier.[167]

Having called the sincerity of Fontanier's Catholic conversion into doubt, Bellièvre next had to eliminate the Montaltos as potential suspects, thereby

[164] Bellièvre, fol. 223^{r}; Labrousse and Soman, 'Fontanier', 119.
[165] Bellièvre, fol. 223^{r}; Labrousse and Soman, 'Fontanier', 119.
[166] Bellièvre, fol. 223^{r}; Labrousse and Soman, 'Fontanier', 119.
[167] As the next chapter will show, some of the questions prepared by Mathieu Molé for the interrogation of Théophile de Viau were not used in the trial hearings.

discrediting the major part of Fontanier's defence strategy. Isaac Montalto had spent only a short period of time in France. As such, Bellièvre suggested that even if Isaac had been the author of the *Trésor inestimable*, the text found in Fontanier's possession would necessarily have been a translation, as it had been written by 'un François qui sçavoit touts les quolibets dicts vulgaires, proverbs des carefours, berlans, cabarets et lieux infames' ('a Frenchman who knew all the so-called vulgar jibes, as well as sayings from the streets, gambling houses, inns, and odious places').[168] Not only was the text lacking any linguistic errors which might betray the authorship of a non-native French speaker, but it also lacked any reference to:

> touttes les langues et sciences que sçavoit excellement Montalte: hebreu, grec, latin, espagnol, italien; un seul traict d'humanité, d'antiquité, d'histoire, de philosophie, de medicine, en quoy excelloit Montalte, mais pas une seule conception d'un Portugais ou gentil esprit, ny pas mesmes une histoire des pais qu'il avoit habités.
>
> all the languages and sciences that Montalto knew very well: Hebrew, Greek, Latin, Spanish, Italian; [there was not] a trace of the humanities, Antiquity, history, philosophy, medicine, all of which Montalto excelled in. Not a single conception of a Portuguese national or a fine spirit, or even a story from the countries in which he had lived.[169]

If the text lacked the hallmarks of Isaac Montalto's erudition, its subjects and the very languages in which they were presented were equally beyond the capabilities of his brother Daniel who, according to Fontanier's own remarks at the opening of this hearing, 'estoit un marchant. Or cestuy qui l'a faict sçait le latin quelque peu. [...] Il y a une ligne escritte en grec dedans ce livre' ('was a merchant, yet the person who wrote this book knows a little Latin [...] there is a line written in Greek in this book').[170] In sum, the text could not have been written by a non-native speaker of French, 'eust-il esté nourry 40 ans en France' ('even if he had spent forty years in France').[171] These remarks are just one example of the potential disparity between the spoken word within the courtroom and the interrogation records. The trial transcripts only state that the *Trésor inestimable* was devoid of Portuguese and references to medicine, and omit all of the other disciplines quoted above.[172]

[168] Bellièvre, fol. 223^{v}; Labrousse and Soman, 'Fontanier', 120.
[169] Bellièvre, fol. 223^{v}; Labrousse and Soman, 'Fontanier', 120.
[170] Bellièvre, fol. 224^{r}; Labrousse and Soman, 'Fontanier', 120. Fontanier had claimed that the man who had given him the *Trésor inestimable* was 'Portugais, parle bon français et se melse de marchandises, qu'il a estudié en sa religion et aux humanitez et disoit que ce livre estoit de son frere' ('Portuguese, spoke French well, and dabbled in trading, that he has studied his faith and the humanities, and said that the book was by his brother': AN X 2A 985, 10 December 1621 quoted in Lachèvre, *Mélanges*, p. 69).
[171] Bellièvre, fol. 224^{r}; Labrousse and Soman, 'Fontanier', 120.
[172] 'Interrogé que Montalte ne l'a fait, qui estoit portugais et ne sçavoit que sa langue et un peu de françois, et qu'il n'y en a un seul mot ny de médecine comme Montalte estoit médecin. Dit que ça donc esté son parent' ('was put to the accused that Montalto did not write it, who was Portuguese and spoke only his own language and a little French, and that there was not a word of Portuguese or of medicine, whereas Montalto was a doctor. [Fontanier] said that it was therefore a relation of Montalto's': AN X

The memoir furthermore reveals that Bellièvre had in fact put a false assertion to Fontanier of which no trace is to be found in the trial records. He claimed that the text had been written 'depuis la mort de Montalte, décédé à Tours au grand voyage de Baione lors du mariage du roy' ('after Montalto had died at Tours during a great journey to Bayonne for the king's marriage'), citing as his evidence the arrival of Discalced Carmelites (*carmes déchaussées*) and the sieges of St-Jean-d'Angély, Clairac, and Montauban.[173] Bellièvre made two errors here. First, he mistook Daniel for his father Elijah, who was mentioned neither by Fontanier nor on the titlepage of the *Trésor inestimable*. Second, Elijah had indeed died on his return journey from celebrating the marriage between Louis XIII's sister Elizabeth and Philip IV of Spain, after Alvarez had failed to secure this honour for himself in order to ingratiate himself with the Spanish court. Yet these festivities took place not in Bayonne but Bordeaux, where Elijah would have been able to enter into direct contact with the city's Jewish community.[174]

Bellièvre had proved to his satisfaction that the Montaltos could not have written the *Trésor inestimable*, and was now ready to demonstrate that only Fontanier could have been its author. He could not have known precisely which biographical details Fontanier would give and in what order. Nevertheless, Fontanier's previous interrogation at the Parlement, potentially coupled with the now-lost records from his trial at the Châtelet, would have allowed Bellièvre to prepare a convincing line of questioning. He was therefore able to predict Fontanier's responses before his final interrogation had even begun. With a palpable sense of vengeance on behalf of the faith he sought to defend, the magistrate recorded how his strategy consisted in the same two-stage process with which the *Trésor inestimable* had sought to sweep away the supposed truths of Christianity, before moving on to construct arguments in favour of Judaism in their place:

> En guardant par ceste demonstration le mesme ordre qu'il avoit tenu en son livre, premierement de destruire la faulse creance qu'il vouloit donner que ce fust Montalte, et puis establissant la certitude et verité que c'estoit luy qui l'avoit composé.
>
> This demonstration respected the same order that Fontanier had adopted in his book: first by disproving the false belief that he wanted to give—that it was Montalto [who wrote the book]—and then by establishing as certain truth that he was the one who had written it.[175]

2A 985, 10 December 1621 quoted in Lachèvre, *Mélanges*, p. 69).

[173] Bellièvre, fol. 223^{v}; Labrousse and Soman, 'Fontanier', 120. The trial transcripts make no mention of these sieges appearing in the *Trésor inestimable* and only refer to the Discalced Carmelites (AN X 2A 985, 10 December 1621, quoted in Lachèvre, *Mélanges*, p. 70).

[174] Such is the explanation for this voyage proposed in Pelorson, 'Carlos García', 539. See also Friedenwald, 'Montalto', 144.

[175] Bellièvre, fol. 223^{v}; Labrousse and Soman, 'Fontanier', 120.

Again, given the potential importance of the order in which Bellièvre presents his points, we shall respect this same order in the following analyses. The first two indicators of Fontanier's guilt were material. He had been arrested in possession of the offending book, which was written and signed in his hand. Moreover, the presence of marginal annotations, references, and scored-out lines alluded to earlier were interpreted by Bellièvre as disproving the text to be a mere copy, 'car l'omission eust esté remplacée plus naifvement' ('as the omission of the original text would not have remained so visible').[176] In his third point, Bellièvre reclaimed the Gospel of St Matthew, critiqued so extensively in the *Trésor inestimable*, as a weapon with which to condemn the prisoner in front of him:

> Son parler [et] son stil s'y remarquoit evidemment *nam et loquela tua manifestum*. Il faict: fust esté, fussent esté, allarent, et caet—desquels termes de parler pour ~~disent~~ dire eust esté, eussent esté, allerent—usent ordinairement ceulx de son païs.
>
> His manner of speaking [and] his style are clearly visible, *for thy speech bewrayeth thee*. He writes: *fust esté, fussent esté, allarent* etc., which are terms commonly heard spoken where he is from to mean *eust esté, eussent esté, allerent*.[177]

Here, Bellièvre noted that certain errors in verb conjugation found in the incriminating text were typically observed amongst those living in Montpellier and the surrounding region. The pluperfect subjunctive of *être* (to be) is mistakenly conjugated by giving the auxiliary verb *être* in the imperfect subjunctive, rather than *avoir* (to have); whereas *aller* (to go) is conjugated incorrectly in the third-person plural of the past historic. Although this argument exemplifies the advanced erudition that Fontanier found himself up against, the language of the court records is somewhat less creative, giving no indication of Bellièvre's impressive eye for detail in this particular forensic linguistic analysis: 'interrogé que le stile est françois' ('put to him that the style is French').[178] If we were to rely on the court records alone, it would appear curious that Fontanier nervously responded to this bried insinuation by asserting 'dict ne l'avoir faict et qu'il est bon chrestien et y veult mourir et reclame la grâce de la Cour de prier Dieu' ('said that he did not do it, and that he is a good Christian and wishes to die as such, and begs the court to pray to God').[179] When read alongside Bellièvre's memoir, however, it becomes clear that Fontanier's outburst was intended to distance himself from Bellièvre's thinly veiled comparison between the defendant and St Peter as deniers of Christ, and that the magistrate's account is a true recollection of this exchange.

[176] Bellièvre, fol. 224r; Labrousse and Soman, 'Fontanier', 120. See AN X 2A 985, 10 December 1621, quoted in Lachèvre, *Mélanges*, p. 70: 'Interrogé qu'il a adjousté des lignes et partant qu'il ne l'a point coppié' ('asked whether he had added lines to the text, and that he had not simply copied it').

[177] Bellièvre, fol. 224r; Labrousse and Soman, 'Fontanier', 120. The Latin quotation is taken from Matthew 26:73, in which a female servant recognises St Peter as a Galilean by his accent.

[178] AN X 2A 985, 10 December 1621, quoted in Lachèvre, *Mélanges*, p. 70.

[179] AN X 2A 985, 10 December 1621, quoted in Lachèvre, *Mélanges*, p. 70.

Bellièvre's fourth point merely reiterated that Fontanier's life bore a strong resemblance to the life of the *Trésor inestimable*'s author as described in the text. In points five and six, the geographic identification of its author through linguistic markers was coupled with an analysis of the author's apparently limited learning. The text was written:

> par un homme de la capacité et incapacité desquelles il se venoit de depeindre, destitüé de bien dire, d'art de Rhetorique, d'argument concluant ou sophistiqué; nuls traicts de Poetes ou historiens, nulles marques de Philosophie, Medecine, Theologie ou Jurisprudence Mathematiques.
>
> by a man with the same abilities and inabilities which he has just shown himself to have: devoid of eloquent expression, of the art of rhetoric, of conclusive or sophisticated arguments. There are no traces of the poets or historians, no signs of philosophy, medicine, theology, jurisprudence, or mathematics.[180]

Far from being mere denigrations of the accused, these comments (particularly on Fontanier's lack of jurisprudential knowledge) feed back into Bellièvre's earlier interrogation strategies. As the magistrate rightly concludes here, Fontanier had betrayed his surprising lack of learning for a well-travelled teacher earlier on in the interrogation:

> Avoit peu estudié en grec dans la grammaire d'Antesig[nan]; peu en hebreu dans la grammaire de Bellarmin. [...] De touttes ses responces ayant sceu qu'il sçavoit peu de latin, qu'il sçavoit quelque mot de grec, avoit estudié en hebreu, qu'il n'avoit leu qu'un livre latin qui s'appelle Tite Live, quelque peu Plutarque, qu'il ne sçavoit rien en philosophie ny en droit, sur lequel interrogé il se souvint d'une regle de droit: *favorabiliores sunt rei quam actores*, qu'il ignorait les mathematiques, la medecine et la theologie, avoit leü quelques historiens françois seulement, à ce qu'il disoit.
>
> [He] had learned a little Greek in Antesignan's grammar book, a little Hebrew in Bellarmino's grammar book. [...] All of his answers revealed that he knew a little Latin, the odd word of Greek, that he had studied Hebrew, that he had only read one book in Latin entitled Livy, [and] a little Plutarch, that he knew nothing about philosophy or law, and when interrogated on the latter he recalled one law of jurisprudence: *defendants are treated more favourably than complainants*. He was ignorant of mathematics, medicine and theology, had read only a few French historians, so he said.[181]

As Labrousse and Soman observe, Fontanier's quotation from the *Digest* on the treatment of defendants and complainants was a common and elementary phrase in the learning of the law. As such, his recollection of this particular adage would in no way given the impression of legal expertise, thereby adding to the concordant

[180] Bellièvre, fol. 224r; Labrousse and Soman, 'Fontanier', 121.
[181] Bellièvre, fol. 222v–223r; Labrousse and Soman, 'Fontanier', 119. See also AN X 2A 985, 10 December 1621, quoted in Lachèvre, *Mélanges*, p. 69, where Fontanier recalled 'favorabiliores tali quam actori'.

profiles of Fontanier and the *Trésor inestimable*'s author.[182] In apparently referring to Livy's *History of Rome*, Fontanier committed a further blunder by mistaking the author's name, which appeared on the first line of the title page in most early modern editions, for the book's title (*Titi Livii Historiarum romanarum*, or *Titi Livii Historiarum ab urbe condita*). If Bellièvre demonstrated a knack for in-depth literary analysis, Fontanier gave the impression that he struggled even to judge a book by its cover. It is striking that this particular argument is entirely absent from the trial records. Whereas Bellièvre's first mention of these supposed proofs of guilt are given retrospectively in his manuscript, its subsequent repetition in his fifth argument confirms that it formed part of the oral interrogation, as shown by the magistrate's concluding remark on his six 'reasons': 'a touttes ces raisons l'accusé comme vaincu respondoit ou doucement, foiblement, ou rien' ('in response to all of these reasons the accused, as if defeated, spoke quietly or weakly, or said nothing at all').[183]

Finally, Bellièvre examined the *Trésor inestimable*'s sociocultural anecdotes as well as its discordant treatment of Catholics and Huguenots, all of which appear variously in points five and six of his arguments. The author had referred to the priest Louis Gaufridy's trial and execution for witchraft at the hands of the Parlement de Provence in 1611. Mention was made of a legal custom in Rouen, Venice, and other great cities (*bonnes villes*) of releasing a prisoner at Easter or on Ascension Day in imitation of the freeing of Barrabas, as well as the fact that a similar tradition was observed in Constantinople during Ramadan. These points, combined with the particular cities alluded to in the text, were presented by Bellièvre as being 'touttes choses, lieux, et non autres que ce qu'il nous avoit advoué avoir lëus ou véüs' ('all of the things and places that he [Fontanier] had admitted to having read or seen to us, and nothing else').[184] On this occasion, Bellièvre's arguments are less convincing, as they assume that the Montaltos could not have gained knowledge of these facts due to their foreign extraction. By Bellièvre's own insinuation, however, Daniel and Isaac Montalto were educated and well-travelled. Moreover, their father Elijah was in France in the early 1610s, had travelled beyond Paris during his stay there, and had corresponded with Jews in other cities including Rouen. It is thus entirely possible that the two generations of Montaltos could have gained knowledge of the details given above, and subsequently incorporated these into the *Trésor inestimable*—whatever the extent of their authorship—in order to make their text appear relevant to the lives of their intended French readers. On the subject of religion, Bellièvre alleged that

[182] Labrousse and Soman, 'Fontanier', 130, note 25. The adage is taken from the *Digest*, L, XVII (De diversis regulis juris antiqui [Concerning different rules of ancient law]), 125 (Gaius, Book 5 Ad Edictum Provinciale [On the Provincial Edict]).

[183] Bellièvre, fol. 225^{r}; Labrousse and Soman, 'Fontanier', 122.

[184] Bellièvre, fol. 224^{v}; Labrousse and Soman, 'Fontanier', 121.

Fontanier had retained the intellectual and rhetorical imprint of his Protestant upbringing in spite of his subsequent conversions to Catholicism and Judaism:

> Car de page en page il ne se presentoit aucun subject ou Controverse entre nous Catholiques et eux, ou de parler de N. St. Pere le Pape, des Cardinaux, Patriarches, Arch Evesques, evesques, Abbes, Religieux, Religieuses—bref, de touts prestres, ordre hierarchique, Ceremonies de l'Eglise Romaine, que l'auteur ne s'estendit—plongeast en injures atroces, derisions touttes tells que les Ministereaux et ignorans passionnés d'entr'eux ont accoustumé de vomir. Et puis, quand il n'en pouvoit ou vouloit plus dire, il renvoioit les Romains à Calvin et Luther et autres leurs adversaires, mais disoit-il: ces misérables-là sont encores trompés, toutesfois il ne leur disoit aulcunes injures, et disoit tousjours que la plus impertinente des 8 sectes du christianisme estoit la catholique.
>
> For on page after page he never presented a subject or controversy between we Catholics and them [the Protestants], nor did he speak of our Holy Father the pope, of cardinals, patriarchs, archbishops, bishops, abbots, monks or nuns, of any priest, hierarchical order, ceremony of the Roman Catholic Church (which the author did not expand upon), without descending into terrible insults, into the same mockeries habitually vomited by the ministers and the ignorant fanatics amongst them. Furthermore, when he was no longer willing or able to say more, he recommended that Catholics consult works by Calvin, Luther and other adversaries of theirs, but he says: 'these wretches are also wrong', yet he threw no insult at them, and always said that the most impertinent of the eight sects of Christianity was the Catholic one.[185]

Unlike Fontanier, the Montaltos had no first-hand experience of living as Protestants. In concluding his 'reasons', Bellièvre could not resist a further use of St Matthew's Gospel against the man who, in his view, had sought to destroy the Catholic faith of his five students by undermining this very same biblical text. Once again, in putting this assertion to Fontanier, Bellièvre innately linked the defendant to the persecution of Jesus through an association with the ancient Jews: 'Il falloit qu'il eust perdu le sens d'aveuglement, son livre criant *sanguis eius super me* et renonçant de bon cœur comme avoient faict autrefois les juifs' ('he must have taken leave of his sense through such blindness, as his book cries out *his blood be upon me*, gladly renouncing [Christ] as the Jews had once done').[186]

Before returning Fontanier to his cell, Bellièvre concluded his interrogation by giving four 'remarks' suggesting that divine providence had led to his arrest. Although these shed little light on the trial from a modern perspective, they nonetheless complete Bellièvre's strategy for condemning the accused. Fontanier had been staying at a house 'au Nom de Jesus, il avoit pensé prendre ce Jesus, mais

[185] Bellièvre, fols. 224^{v} – 225^{r}; Labrousse and Soman, 'Fontanier', 121.

[186] Bellièvre, fol. 225^{v}; Labrousse and Soman, 'Fontanier', 122. Bellièvre gives a slightly modified quotation from Matthew 27:25, which describes the crowd emphatically demanding that Pontius Pilate put Jesus to death: 'Sanguis eius super nos' ('his blood be upon us').

qu'il l'avoit pris' ('with the name of Jesus as its ensign. He had thought to attack Jesus, but it was Jesus who attacked him').[187] Second, Fontanier's arrest had taken place on Saturday, the Jewish Sabbath day: 'jour qu'il n'eüst pas pensé, comme luy debvant estre favorable au judaïsme' ('on a day he would not have suspected, as it should have been favourable to Jews like him'). Third, as alluded to at the beginning of this chapter, moments before his arrest Fontanier had dictated to his students 'la main me tremble, la plume me tombe des mains' ('my hand trembles, the quill falls from my hands'). Finally, the fact that Fontanier was standing trial on a Friday and at the age of thirty-three, 'jour et age auxquels Nostre Seigneur avoit operé le salut du monde que luy accusé avoit voulu destruire' ('the same day and age as Our Lord when he had brought about the salvation of the world that the accused had wished to destroy') was an extraordinary parallel, and 'n'estoit sans decret de la providence divine' ('was not without decree by divine providence'). These remarks might well recall the more tenuous arguments made in Garasse's diatribes against the libertines. However, one has only to recall the role afforded to the divine and the supernatural in trials for witchcraft of the period—such as floating defendants in rivers, seeking out the devil's mark, or locating parts of the body impervious to pain—to recognise that such parallels must have carried some weight in the minds of at least some of the judges. Bellièvre even goes as far as to allude to this link to witch trials implicitly. As Labrousse and Soman remark, in observing that Fontanier did not cry during his entire interrogation ('l'accusé ne plore'), Bellièvre recalled the belief held by certain demonologists that those who did not shed tears when standing trial for witchcraft were guilty, as 'les sorciers ne peuvent jetter des larmes en la presence du Juge' ('witches cannot shed tears in the presence of the judge').[188]

Such was Nicolas de Bellièvre's interrogation of Fontanier and, by extension, his reading of the now lost *Trésor inestimable*. His questioning was not flawless, and contained a small number of inaccuracies, points of confusion, and relatively tenuous arguments. Unfortunately for Fontanier these were relatively rare, and the vast majority of Bellièvre's questioning was intelligent, informed, and convincing. Having anticipated what Fontanier would say in his opening statement, Bellièvre led him to provide much of the biographical details that the magistrate had planned to use against him in subsequent questioning. Furthermore, there is evidence to suggest that much of Bellièvre's critical reading of the *Trésor inestimable* bears some resemblance to the aims and even techniques of modern forensic linguistics, notwithstanding the obvious limitations to such a comparison. Unlike our other two authors, however, Fontanier proved to be no match for his interrogator.

[187] Bellièvre, fol. 225^{v}; Labrousse and Soman, 'Fontanier', 122. The following 'remarks' are taken from Bellièvre, fols. 225^{v} – 226^{r}; Labrousse and Soman, 'Fontanier', 122–3.

[188] Bellièvre, fol. 225^{v}; Labrousse and Soman, 'Fontanier', 122, 131 (note 31); Henri Boguet, *Discours exécrable des sorciers* (Paris: Denis Binet, 1603), p. 100.

FONTANIER'S STRATEGIES OF SELF-DEFENCE

At the beginning of the interrogation of 10 December, Fontanier was first given the freedom to describe his life story in considerable detail. Given that Bellièvre based much of his authorial attribution of the *Trésor inestimable* on Fontanier's geographical movements and his education, it was essential to Bellièvre's plan that the accused be allowed to give as much autobiographical detail as possible at the beginning of this final hearing. Fontanier, however, could not have known this, and was instead likely to have seen the beginning of the interrogation as an opportunity to present the judges with a favourable image of his intellectual, religious, and moral character. For Lachèvre, Fontanier's reading was a 'trait de son caractère' ('one of his character traits'): 'Fontanier est fier de son érudition; il s'étend complaisamment sur ses études' ('Fontanier was proud of his learning and complacently spoke at some length about his studies').[189] Lachèvre's accusation of complacency or even arrogance is entirely out of keeping with what we know about Fontanier. Unlike the many aristocrats who toured the universities, studios, and courts of Europe for intellectual or artistic edification, there is no evidence that Fontanier undertook his various travels across Europe in order to study. Rather, his geographical movements represented a spiritual quest for answers, or at least for an end to the religious doubts with which he so openly admitted to having grappled at various points in his life. In vaunting his in fact limited reading and linguistic capabilities, Fontanier instead sought to emphasise his learning as much as possible in order to present himself as a respectable individual. Nevertheless, he was undeniably short-sighted in describing his engagement with the world of letters in a way that so closely matched the contents of the *Trésor inestimable*.

Fontanier provided two defences against the charges against him. The first was to deny authorship of the offending text. Although this issue was not raised directly in the first interrogation of 4 December, it is notable that Fontanier implied Daniel Montalto's authorship in describing their interactions: 'un espagnol, parent de Montalte, est *l'auteur* de son mal [...] a conféré seul avec luy et ne se souvient des *argumentz qu'il luy donnoit*' ('a Spanish relative of Montalto is the *author* of his troubles [...] talked alone with him and does not remember *the arguments that he gave him*').[190] In the main interrogation of 10 December, Fontanier ended his autobiographical opening statement with the same assertion on the subject of the Montaltos: 'disoit que ce livre estoit de son frère et croyt que c'est Montalte et que ce n'est pas de luy et que Montalte l'a faict' ('said that this book was by his brother and thinks that it was Montalto, and that it was not by him and that Montalto wrote it').[191] The *greffier* was tasked with recording the words of the defendant as

[189] Lachèvre, *Mélanges*, p. 67.

[190] AN X 2A 985, 4 December 1621, quoted in Lachèvre, *Mélanges*, p. 67, my emphasis.

[191] AN X 2A 985, 10 December 1621, quoted in Lachèvre, *Mélanges*, p. 69.

accurately as possible. It is easy to see that at this early stage of the interrogation Fontanier had already started to panic, and to give rambling, repetitious answers. On the other hand, this first defence was at least consistent: Fontanier explicitly denied that he had written the offending text on six separate occasions in the final interrogation. Bellièvre's recollection of this hearing fails to mention any of these denials, and presents Fontanier as a much weaker and more passive recipient of the magistrate's reasoned arguments than he actually was. Significantly, no clear distinction was made between the authorship of the work as a theological and intellectual exercise and the production of the physical text. Although Fontanier repeatedly asserted that the work was *de Montalte* (by Montalto) and that *Montalte l'a fait* (literally: that Montalto made it), he also admitted to having contributed to the production of the placard which had accompanied him into the chamber for the judges to scrutinise:

> Interrogé qu'il a adjousté des lignes et partant qu'il ne l'a point coppié.
> Dit qu'en copiant on met tout comme il y a de la radiation. [...]
> Interrogé que ses affiches ont relacion au corps de son livre et qu'il y a force radiations audit livre. Interrogé qu'il a change quelque chose. Lecture a luy faicte de l'affiche.
> Dit qu'il y a changé et adjousté.
>
> Asked whether he had altered some lines and that therefore he had not merely copied it.
> Said that in copying out a text one includes everything including crossings out. [...]
> Put to him that his placards were related to the main body of his book and that there are a large number of crossings out in this book. Asked whether he had changed anything. The placard was read out to him.
> Said that he had changed and modified parts of it.[192]

In this exchange, Fontanier muddied the waters by at the same time denying that he had written the *Trésor inestimable* whilst admitting that he had authored the placard. Later on, when asked if he was a Christian or a Jew, he gave a confused response which alluded to his writing of the incriminating text: 'a dit qu'il est bon chrestien et qu'au mois d'aoust dernier, il l'estoit et a escript le livre en 10 ou 12 jours' ('said that he is a good Christian, and that he was one last August, and that he wrote the book in ten or twelve days').[193] When added to the fact that he did not deny writing the oaths signed by his students, it is clear that Fontanier undermined his refutation of authorship through his inconsistent and unconvincing accounts of how the *Trésor inestimable* came into being.

[192] AN X 2A 985, 10 December 1621, quoted in Lachèvre, *Mélanges*, p. 70. On the distinctions between the writing (*écrire*) and production (*faire* or *faire imprimer*) of texts in early modern legislative acts, see Chapter 2, pp. 64–66.
[193] AN X 2A 985, 10 December 1621, quoted in Lachèvre, *Mélanges*, p. 70.

Fontanier's second defence, which we have already seen on several occasions in piecing together his biography, was that he had been plagued by doubts and had fallen victim to his own curiosity. If he had taken receipt of Montalto's dangerous book, for example, 'il a esté porté seulement de trop grande curiosité' ('he had only been driven by excessive curiosity').[194] For his part, Bellièvre reproached Fontanier for his highly irregular method of dispelling such doubts:

> S'il avoit des doubts, ce n'estoit le moien d'en estre esclaircy que de n'en conferer avec les docteurs chrestiens, puisqu'il conferoit avec les Juifs; ni mesme d'en estre esclaircy avec quatre escholiers de l'age qu'ils estoient et de leur ignorance à la loy sainte, mais bien resolution de les pervertir. L'accusé ne pouvoit que respondre.
>
> If he had doubts, the way to dispell these was not to have failed to discuss them with Christian doctors, as he discussed them with Jews. Nor was it right to dispel them with his four students, given their age and their ignorance of Holy Law, but rather [he] resolved to pervert them. The accused could not answer.[195]

Although Fontanier remained silent in the face of this unfair criticism, he could in fact have used Bellièvre's own strategy of relying on Fontanier's biography against him. After all, he had not only sought assistance in Paris from theologians at the Sorbonne, but had also taken up residence with the Capuchins in Toulouse. Later on, he would only confirm his brief stay in Toulouse having been prompted to do so by Bellièvre. Fontanier thus failed to capitalise on his opening statement to the court, in which he could have presented himself as a sincere Christian who had sought help from multiple Catholic institutions in France and potentially abroad.

The shortcomings of Fontanier's defence did not end there, but were exacerbated by a number of erroneous statements and further self-contradictions. In the first interrogation of 4 December, for example, he had asserted that '[il] abjura en Italie la Relligion prétendue réformée à Rome en une église près Chasteauvieux' ('in Italy he abjured the Protestant faith in Rome, in a church near Châteauvieux').[196] Yet in the second interrogation, Fontanier's rambling opening statement contradicted this assertion entirely: 'n'a esté à Rome mais bien à Venise, a esté 2 fois en Italie et la première fois avec le Cappitaine de Goulen [...] n'a jamais esté à Rome, auparavant demeuroit à Paris' ('has not been to Rome but has been to Venice, has been to Italy twice and the first time was with Captain de Goulen [...] has never been to Rome, previously lived in Paris').[197] This was no small detail in deciding the veracity of his supposed Catholic faith: not only was Fontanier

[194] AN X 2A 985, 10 December 1621, quoted in Lachèvre, *Mélanges*, p. 69. As Neil Kenny reminds us, early modern church discourse condemned curiosity as a sin (Neil Kenny, *The Uses of Curiosity in Early Modern France and Germany* (Oxford: Oxford University Press, 2004), pp. 99–100).

[195] Bellièvre, fol. 225^{r}; Labrousse and Soman, 'Fontanier', 122. Once again, Fontanier's enigmatic fifth student is not mentioned here.

[196] AN X 2A 985, 4 December 1621, quoted in Lachèvre, *Mélanges*, p. 67.

[197] AN X 2A 985, 10 December 1621, quoted in Lachèvre, *Mélanges*, p. 69.

unable to provide papers proving that he had converted to Catholicism, but he had also failed to give a clear and consistent account of where this alleged conversion had taken place.

There appears to have been no such town as Châteauvieux in Italy. Although there is no evidence with which to identify the town that Fontanier had in mind, a reference in Samuel Guichenon's *Histoire de Bresse* does allow us to propose one potential match: the 'Château de Chasteauvieux', known today as the Château de Duingt.[198] Overlooking Lake Annecy, it is close to the Genevan, Swiss, and Italian borders. It is also relatively close to L'Hôpital-sous-Conflans (incorporated into modern-day Albertville), which served as a pilgrimage hostel similar to those that Fontanier was likely to have visited during his travels across Europe. Finally, Labrousse and Soman note that native speakers of Occitan in the Languedoc region of France (including Fontanier's native Montpellier) were able to converse in Italian quite easily.[199] Could it be that Fontanier passed through the roughly seventy miles between this château and the modern Italian border ('*near* to Chasteauvieux'), where he heard enough Italian spoken to have mistakenly believed he was in Italy? Fontanier's anxious and restless state of mind at that time, and the fact that he was recalling these events whilst fighting for his life against the intense scrutiny of a senior magistrate of the Parlement, invites us at least to entertain the possibility. If this were the case, his error in placing this castle near Rome would certainly have done little to enhance his credibility.

He fared no better in accouting for Daniel Montalto's movements. When confronted with Bellièvre's judgement that the *Trésor inestimable* was written with a level of French beyond the abilities of a non-native speaker such as Montalto, Fontanier claimed that 'Montalte avoit demeuré toute sa vie en France' ('Montalto had lived in France his whole life').[200] Fontanier repeatedly referred to Montalto as *Portugais* which, as we saw earlier, was a byword for 'Jewish' at the time. The Montaltos were not only Jews, but famous Jews of foreign extraction with links to the royal court of Marie de Médicis. It would therefore have been futile for Fontanier to attempt to downplay their faith, especially given that he sought to deny his authorship of the *Trésor inestimable* rather than to challenge the undeniably Jewish nature of its contents. Given the notoriety of the Montalto family, this fleeting defence, which in fact represented a crucial element for Bellièvre's interrogation, was unlikely to have convinced the assembled chamber of judges.

[198] Samuel Guichenon, *Histoire de Bresse et de Bugey* (Lyon: Antoine Huguetan and Marc Ant. Ravaud, 1650), p. 36.

[199] Labrousse and Soman, 'Fontanier', 132, note 60. Savoie was known for its relatively permissive climate for free speech, as well for the genre of controversial pamphlet literature to which the *Trésor inestimable* belonged. See *Moqueries savoyardes: Monologues polémiques et comiques en dialecte savoyard de la fin du XVIe siècle*, ed. by Anne-Marie Vurpas (Lyon: La Manufacture, 1986). I am grateful to Mark Greengrass and John O'Brien for this information.

[200] AN X 2A 985, 10 December 1621, quoted in Lachèvre, *Mélanges*, p. 70.

At the end of his second interrogation, Fontanier attempted to mirror Bellièvre's strategy by proposing the following five 'reasons' of his own, this time demonstrating his innocence. He had not written the incriminating text; there was nothing to suggest that he had from his interrogation, 'mesmes qu'il la dict à ceulx qui escripvoient soubz luy' ('he even said so to those who were writing beneath him'); only three or four people had heard his lessons; these students had not spread them further; and he had not been accused of any specific crime.[201] The first two points were for the judges to decide, whilst the third point had no bearing on the ascertainment of his guilt. The fifth point is somewhat stronger. On the one hand, defendants were not automatically informed of the specific crime for which they stood accused prior to their trials, in the same way that they were not able to hear witness testimony against them before deciding if and how to propose *reproches* against the witnesses. However, the interrogation sought not to find him guilty of a specific crime (such as blasphemy or atheism), but to determine his authorship of the *Trésor inestimable*. As we will see in the following section, if Fontanier was not accused of any specific crimes during the interrogations, this was because the contents of this text and the question of his religious beliefs posed a delicate question of law for the magistrates. It would therefore be difficult to dismiss Fontanier's objection were it not for the fact that this was not his first trial. Fontanier had appeared before the Parlement in order to appeal the death sentence passed against him by the Châtelet. Whatever the contents of these now-lost trial documents may have been, the *arrêt* from the Châtelet had explicitely found him guilty of *lese-majesté divine*. Hence, the Parlement had only to follow a line of questioning which alluded to or informed this prior legal decision. Fontanier betrayed both his sense of fear and his ineffective self-defence by the end of the second interrogation:

> C'est que la déclaration de l'onnête [sic] profession qu'il fera en la relligion catholique fera plus de proffict que la mort qu'il souffrira et a recours à la miséricorde de Dieu qui a dict qu'il ne veult la mort du pescheur mais qu'il se convertisse et espère en la mort de la passion de nostre sauveur Jesus-Crist que par vostre volonté luy sera procuré une mort doulce affin qu'on ne mécognoisse la vraye proffession qu'il fera.
>
> Is that the sincere declaration he will make of his Catholic faith will do more good than the death he will suffer, and he invokes the mercy of God who said that he did not wish for the death of the sinner but that he should convert, and places his hope in death in the Passion of our saviour Jesus Christ, that by your will he will have a gentle death so that no-one will fail to be aware of the true profession that he will make.[202]

[201] AN X 2A 985, 10 December 1621, quoted in Lachèvre, *Mélanges*, p. 71. Fontanier was likely referring to the *greffier* writing the trial transcripts from the bench below him. This response paints a tragic picture of the accused, who desperately asserted his innocence indiscriminately to the agents of justice surrounding him.

[202] AN X 2A 985, 10 December 1621 quoted in Lachèvre, *Mélanges*, p. 71.

Bellièvre's memoir plays down Fontanier's final defence in relatively few words, whilst adding that 'apres ces paroles il se jecta à genoux. Je le fis réassoir' ('after these words he threw himself down on his knees. I had him sit down again').[203] The small wooden stool used for *interrogatoires sur la sellette* was designed to present the accused as cowering humbly before his or her judges.[204] In kneeling before the magistrates, Fontanier temporarily disrupted the power dynamic within the courtroom by adopting the posture of religious repentence, thereby performing in accordance with his assertions of sincere Catholic faith. Far from a courtesy for his prisoner's physical comfort, Bellièvre's invitation for Fontanier to resume his seat was an instruction to reprise the habitual position of subordination before the agents of royal justice. Fontanier had tried desperately to convince his judges that he had not authored the *Trésor inestimable* and that he was a sincere convert to Catholicism. However, he had in some instances admitted to authoring at least part of the text which he had arguably intimated in certain parts of his defence. He could scarcely have conceived of a worse closing statement: he would undertake an exemplary conversion to Catholicism if his judges first declared him to be an innocent Catholic convert. The two surviving accounts of the interrogations reveal that Fontanier had defended himself in a clumsy and confused manner, and that he failed to disprove the accusations of authorship and of Judaism made against him. As he was led back to his cell, the judges now had a number of points of law to consider.

DELIBERATIONS, QUESTIONS OF LAW, AND SENTENCING

Towards the end of the final interrogation, Bellièvre had threatened Fontanier with a medical examination to determine whether he had been circumcised:

> [Enquis] s'il est prépucié.
> A dict que non, fort bas.
> Remonstré qu'on le verra maintenant.
>
> [Asked] if he was circumcised.
> Said that he was not, very quietly.
> Was warned that they were about to find out.[205]

As Lazare Du Crot explains in his guide to criminal procedure at the Châtelet, 'le rapport des Barbiers faict partie de l'information, pourveu qu'il soit fait de l'Ordonnance du Juge, et qu'ils ayent presté le serment' ('the report of Barbers [i.e.

[203] Bellièvre, fol. 226r; Labrousse and Soman, 'Fontanier', 123. Bellièvre summarises Fontanier's fifth reason thus: 'qu'il feroit une si austere penitence qu'il seroit en plus grand exemple que par une mort rigoureuse et ignominieuse' ('that he would do such austere penance that he would serve as a greater example than if he were to suffer a rigorous and shameful death').

[204] Bastien, *Histoire de la peine de mort*, p. 72.

[205] AN X 2A 985, 10 December 1621, quoted in Lachèvre, *Mélanges*, p. 71.

surgeons] forms part of the *information*, as long as this is undertaken following an ordinance from the judge, and that they have sworn the oath').[206] Bellièvre's account sheds further light on this practice, and shows that despite being the judge in charge of the appeal case, he did not have the authority to order this examination without the consent of the majority of his fellow judges. Whilst these ultimately decided that the examination should take place straight away, their decision was not unanimous. As the working day was drawing to an end ('l'heure allait sonner'), the judges had the choice between coming to a definitive judgement that same day—a Saturday—or suspending the trial until Monday: 'nous estions quinze juges. Il passa que nous le jugerions et passerions l'heure' ('there were fifteen judges, and we decided that we would judge Fontanier and work past the hour').[207] With the judges quite literally working overtime on Fontanier's case, the *rapporteur* began his report, 'qui fust bien d'une bonne demie heure et plus, et dict choses belles' ('which lasted a good half an hour or more, and said fine things').[208] It is difficult to imagine that Fontanier's responses would have sparked a legal discussion lasting for more than half an hour. Rather, it seems more likely that much of the *rapporteur*'s speech would have pertained to the tenets of the *Trésor inestimable*, to Bellièvre's meticulous critical reading of these, and to the legal status of Jews. An interruption from the surgeons revealed that Fontanier had in their opinion been circumcised, 'parce qu'ayant voulu recouvrir le gland, la peau estoit courte et cicatrisée comme si le fer y eust passé il y avoit jà longtemps' ('because when they tried to cover the head of his penis, the skin was short and scarred as if the iron had already been passed over it some time ago'). The defendant had furthermore tried to explain this scar away by claiming that this procedure had been performed in order to cure him of an illness, 'mais que ce n'estoit la circoncision' ('but that it was not circumcision').[209] Remarkably, Bellièvre's memoir omits what was surely a crucial detail in the surgeons' report found in the official trial records:

> Fut visité, sçavoir s'il estoit préputié, par La Noue et Guibert, chirurgiens juréz, et après serment ont dit qu'il y a une cicatrice blanche et que mal aisément on a pu couvrir le gland, et qu'il y a longtemps pour le moins dix ans et ne reste qu'une blancheur sans dureté.
>
> Was visited by the surgeons La Noue and Guibert in order to determine if he was circumcised. After they had been sworn in, the surgeons said that there was a white

[206] Lazare Du Crot, *Le vray styl du Chastelet de Paris* (Paris: Jean Richer, 1623), p. 637. An almost identical explanation, though with reference to surgeons rather than barbers, is given in Jean Le Pain, *Le Practicien françois* (Paris: Jean Gesselin, 1624, p. 227.

[207] Bellièvre, fol. 226^r; Labrousse and Soman, 'Fontanier', 123.

[208] Bellièvre, fol. 226^r; Labrousse and Soman, 'Fontanier', 123.

[209] Bellièvre, fol. 226^r; Labrousse and Soman, 'Fontanier', 123. In arguing that Fontanier died unrepentantly, Bellièvre subsequently recalled (and underlined in his manuscript) how eight days before his sentence Fontanier 'recognust qu'il avoit esté circoncis' ('admitted that he had been circumcised': fol. 229^r; Labrousse and Soman, 'Fontanier', 126).

> scar and that it was difficult to cover the head of the penis; and that the scar had been there for some time, at least ten years, and was now no more than a soft white mark.[210]

It is not for the present study to evaluate the competence of the early modern surgeons in giving their professional opinion on the origins of Fontanier's scar, but to consider their testimony within the context of the words of both judge and defendant during the interrogations. The surgeons' report gives a crucial detail that has gone unnoticed in the few modern studies on Fontanier. The court heard sworn testimony that Fontanier's circumcision—for that is what the surgeons concluded the scar to be—had been performed at least ten years ago. Significantly, this predated his encounter with Daniel Montalto considerably, and brings us roughly to 1611. This date coincides with the end of Fontanier's studies and his first known travels abroad to Venice and Constantinople. As we saw earlier, Fontanier had asserted on the subject of this journey 'qu'il avoit des juifs pour truchement, ne leur a rien demandé de leur croyance' ('that he had Jews as translators, and asked them nothing about their beliefs').[211] It would be short-sighted to reconstruct the history of Fontanier's beliefs based on a single piece of speculative evidence regarding his circumcision. This said, it is at least worth outlining an alternative hypothesis on his personal journey prior to his arrest, and the significant consequences that this would have on our understanding of Fontanier's motivations.

Assuming that the surgeons' appraisals were accurate, it is highly likely that Fontanier was circumcised during his first trip to Venice and Constantinople, during which time he found himself in the company of Jews. In this case, his insistence that he did not speak with them about their beliefs had less to do with distancing himself from the Jewish teachings for which he was standing trial in 1621, and more to do with concealing his much earlier conversion to Judaism. This leads us to the perennial question of Fontanier's 'doubts', expressed to the priests in Verona (if this conversion to Catholicism took place) and to the Capuchins in Toulouse. If he had indeed converted to Judaism in 1610 or shortly afterwards, then his doubts would not have pertained to the teachings of his Christian faith which he wished to strengthen, but to his recently acquired *Jewish* faith which he had come to doubt or even to regret. Having sought the help of Catholic instructors in vain, a subsequent journey then brought him into contact with Daniel Montalto. Unlike the French Christians who had refused to offer advice or even a friendly ear, Montalto was only too happy to discuss points of faith with Fontanier, who was *already* a fellow Jew, and to strengthen him in their shared faith. Offering reassurance to the vulnerable Jewish convert, Montalto

[210] AN X 2A 985, 10 December 1621, quoted in Lachèvre, *Mélanges*, p. 71.
[211] AN X 2A 985, interrogation of 10 December 1621, quoted in Lachèvre, *Mélanges*, p. 69.

then entrusted him with a mission to spread Jewish doctrine to students in Paris. Only this time, Fontanier would be the confident, learned, and assured teacher of students with their own theological doubts.[212] How much easier it would be to explain why Montalto tasked Fontanier with this mission if, rather than being a recent convert, Fontanier had in fact been a Jew for some ten years. Whether or not the surgeons' estimations were accurate will likely remain an insoluble issue. Yet if true, this alternative and entirely plausible scenario would cast Fontanier's seemingly weak excuse for offering his lessons—'pour s'esclaircir de ses doubtes' ('to dispell his doubts')—in a rather different and convincing light.[213]

For their part, the magistrates had a much clearer issue to discuss, and the surgeons' report in fact appears to have had little bearing on the deliberation or judgement. The *rapporteur* Broussel was unable to find legal precedent for the punishment of a Jew who taught their faith in France. Bellièvre committed a small error, in supposedly correcting this *rapport* by referring to the banishment of Jews by St Louis in 1235.[214] Broussel's opinion on the case did little to address this thorny point of law:

> Son opinion fust: soit comme juif (n'estant point permis à eux d'estre en France, moins d'y dogmatiser; fit aussy grand cas de ce serment qu'il tiroit, pouvant estre de consequence à l'Estat [...]) soit aussy qu'il fust chrestien, ayant faict ce dont estoit convaincu, il estoit d'advis de confirmer la sentence excepté d'estre brulé vif, estant d'advis qu'il fust estranglé avant.
>
> His opinion was that, whether he was a Jew (who did not have permission to be in France, let alone to preach here, and also making much of his oath, which he thought could be of consequence for the State [...]), or whether he was a Christian, having done what he had been convicted of, he was of the view that Fontanier's sentence should be upheld apart from being burned alive, as he was of the opinion that he should first be strangled.[215]

Broussel's view that Fontanier was breaking the law by teaching Judaism was an inference, rather than a reference to previous legislation. The next magistrate to speak, a *conseiller* from the Grand' Chambre named Le Coigneux, had a more blunt and quite extraordinary view on the case: 'dict seulement qu'au lieu d'examiner les preuves de ce proces, il estoit d'avis qu'à la postérité il y eüst exemple qu'en un tel faict l'on n'avoit opiné que du bonnet' ('said only that instead of examining the evidence in this trial, he was of the opinion to provide posterity

[212] The *Histoire veritable* echoes this apparently rapid elevation of Fontanier's status: 'ce miserable, d'Escollier qu'il estoit devinst tout aussi-tost Grand Maistre' ('this wretch, the student that he was, became a great master straight away', p. 6).

[213] Bellièvre, fol. 218ʳ.

[214] Bellièvre, fol. 226ᵛ; Labrousse and Soman, 'Fontanier', 123. As we saw earlier, Charles VI had enacted similar legislation much later in 1394.

[215] Bellièvre, fol. 226ᵛ; Labrousse and Soman, 'Fontanier', 123.

with an example where such a case was judged quickly and unanimously').[216] In trial deliberations, magistrates were expected to be brief and focussed in their interventions. As such, when a given judge concurred with a previously expressed opinion, he could simply raise his hat in order to indicate his agreement, from which the term *opiner du bonnet* (literally: to give an opinion by the hat) was coined.[217] Le Coigneux took the view that not only was it important to prioritise the creation of historical precedent for such crimes over lengthy debate, but that this negated the need to examine the evidence at all. Le Coigneaux's fellow judges did not share his rather economical take on the law, whilst at the same time having little else to add. Bellièvre provided a characteristically more detailed intervention which cut to the very heart of the difficult legal question at hand. His contribution to the deliberation is worth quoting at length:

> Je dis seulement que, puisque c'estoit un proces, il en falloit opiner si l'accusé se fust avoüé juif et que ce qu'il avoit faict estoit par zele de sa religion, il nous eust empesché davantaige [sic], encores bien que les juifs n'ayant demeuré en France, mesme en estant bannis par l'edict publié au Parlement au mois de mai de l'an 1615. En ce cas, dogmatisant, l'on pourroit conclurre à la mort. [...] Touttesfois il falloit confesser que nos histoires ne nous fournissoient aulcun exemple en cas pareil, et nos ordonnances ne portoient auculne chose de cela – j'entends de la peine de mort au juif ou chrestien judaïsant, ny de galeres, ny de fouet. Mais que cest accusé se disant chrestien opiniastrement, il ne se pouvoit excuser de la peine de la loy de Dieu, qui est la mort. [...] J'estois aussy d'advis, et de brusler tout le proces, et du decret de prinse de corps contre les 4 escholiers, quand ce ne seroit qu'*ad terrorem* pour tous ceulx qui à l'advenir pourroit [sic] avoir d'aussy mauvaises curiosités que ceulx-cy avoient eü.
>
> I only said that, given that this was a trial, we would have to conclude that if the accused had admitted to being a Jew, and had claimed that his actions were out of zeal for his religion, he would have made it even more difficult for us, given that Jews have remained in France, even though they have been banished by the edict published by the Parlement in the month of May 1615. In this case, having preached his faith, we could pass the death sentence. [...] Nevertheless, we had to concede that there was no historical precedent for such a case, and that our ordinances made no mention of such a thing—by which I mean the death penalty for a Christian or Jew teaching Judaism, nor the galleys, nor flogging. But as the accused stubbornly called himself a Christian, he could not escape punishment according to God's law, which is death. [...] I also took the view both to burn all of the trial records, and to order the arrest of the four students, if only to instil fear in all of those who might in the future have such a terrible curiosity as these students had.[218]

[216] Bellièvre, fol. 226^{v}; Labrousse and Soman, 'Fontanier', 123.
[217] See this expression under 'bonnet' in the *Dictionnaire de l'Académie française* (Paris: Jean-Baptiste Coignard, 1694): 'se déclarer de l'advis d'un autre sans dire le sien [...] c'est-à-dire, tout d'une voix' ('declare oneself for the view of another without revealing one's own [...] that is to say, as one voice').
[218] Bellièvre, fols. 226^{v} – 227^{r}; Labrousse and Soman, 'Fontanier', 123–4.

Bellièvre's learned opinion reveals the true nature of Fontanier's cruel fate. Despite Louis XIII's *déclaration* of 1615, the fact that Jews had apparently remained in France after this date, as well as the lack of legal precedent, meant that the judges could not reasonably impose the death penalty or indeed corporal punishment. Though Bellièvre would doubtless have had a range of legal manuals and other relevant sources to consult, the end of his memoir reveals that he had meticulously consulted Nicolas Vignier's *Bibliothèque historiale* (Paris: Abel L'Angelier, 1587) in vain search of historical precedents which might suit his agenda. Despite finding a number of legislative acts against the Jews in this text, he was forced to concede that 'en tout ce qui dessus il n'y a peine de mort' ('but none of the above included the death sentence').[219] Fontanier, however, fatally misjudged his situation. Perceiving Bellièvre's attempts to identify him as a Jew, as well as the attention paid to his travels and his doubts, he chose to do all that he could to prove that he was a good Catholic with no other ambition than to strengthen his faith. What appeared to be a wise strategy of self-defence both logically and in terms of the society of his time was in fact fatally flawed from a legal perspective. Tragically, in desperately trying to disprove his Jewish identity, Fontanier had denied the one fact which, both legally and in Bellièvre's view, could have saved his life.

The Châtelet's death sentence was upheld by the Parlement de Paris on 10 December 1621, and on that same day Jean Fontanier was burned at the stake along with the *Trésor inestimable* and the original trial records from the Châtelet. An annotation at the bottom of the interrogation transcript reveals that the magistrates concurred with the *rapporteur* Broussel's suggestion that Fontanier be strangled to death before burning (Figure 4.4).[220] Even this apparent act of mercy was linked to the prisoner's weak forms of self-defence and his poor understanding of legal procedure. In striking contrast with the previous chapter, Fontanier's remarks following his sentencing have little in common with Vanini's famously proud and memorable exclamations on his way to the stake. As his sentence was read out to him, he simply commented: 'voilà un cruel jugement. [...] Dieu vous punisse aussy rigoureusement que vous me faictes' ('what a cruel judgement [...] may God punish you as harshly as you are punishing me').[221] Two doctors of theology from the Sorbonne were assigned to attend to the condemned prisoner until three

[219] Bellièvre, fol. 230^r. For other texts consulted by Bellièvre, see also fol. 230^v.

[220] For this second *arrêt de mort*, see AN X 2A 985, quoted in Lachèvre, *Mélanges*, p. 72; AN X 2B 330. A key figure in the next chapter, the *procueur général* Mathieu Molé, included a copy of the Parlement's *arrêt* against Fontanier in his memoirs. Molé inexplicably records this as being pronounced against 'Jehan Fontaine' in 1615, which leads us to surmise whether he mistakenly saw Fontanier's trial as a direct consequence of Louis XIII's expulsion of the Jews that same year. The editor of these memoirs, Aimé Champollion-Figeac, does not identify these remarks as pertaining to Jean Fontanier. See Mathieu Molé, *Mémoires de Mathieu Molé*, ed. by Aimé Champollion-Figeac, 4 vols (Paris: Jules Renouard, 1855), I, p. 104.

[221] Bellièvre, fol. 227^v; Labrousse and Soman, 'Fontanier', 124.

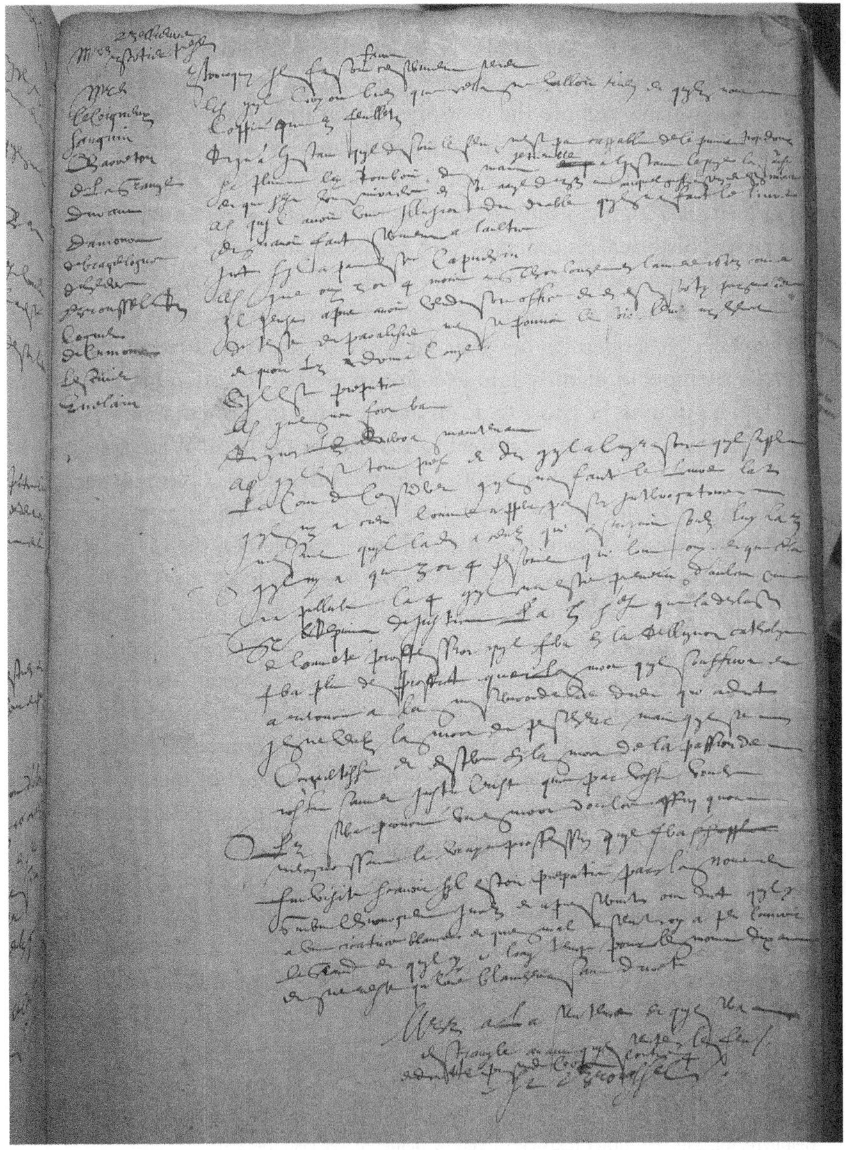

Figure 4.4 AN X 2A 985, 10 December 1621: the end of Fontanier's second interrogation which discusses his possible circumcision. The final paragraph concurs with the rapporteur 'qu'il sera estranglé avant qu'il sente le feu et decretté prise corps contre 4. Broussel' ('that he will be strangled before he feels the fire and the order is given for the arrest of the 4 [students]. Broussel'). The list in the top left-hand corner names Fontanier's judges from the Parlement: 'MM. Bellièvre, Potier présidents; MM Le Coigneux, Sanguin, Charreton, de La Grange, Durant, Damours, de Bragelongne, de Heere, Broussel R[apporteur], Coquet, de Crismont, Lescuier, Quelain.'

o'clock in the afternoon. They reported that Fontanier was terrified and that he still claimed that his punishment was too harsh. At the doctors' suggestion the *lieutenant criminel* paid a visit to Fontanier in order to calm him in advance of his execution:

> Se presentant au condamné, lequel luy demanda: que pouvés-vous faire pour moy? Respondit: addoucir la rigueur du supplice que vous ne sentirés point le feu. Il repart: mais j'en mourray tousjours. Et sur cela, recommença à dire qu'on le traittoit trop rigoureusement, puisqu'il s'estoit repenti.
>
> He presented himself to the condemned man, who asked him 'what can you do for me?' The *lieutenant* answered 'reduce your torment so that you will not feel the fire.' 'But I will still die', he answered, and then began once again to claim that he was being treated too harshly because he had repented.[222]

In exchange for his quiet compliance, Fontanier was offered a quicker and less painful death than the flames. As we saw earlier, strangulation in advance of being burned at the stake had already been afforded to him by both the official trial documents and the judges' deliberations. What is more, this act of mercy was in fact to be expected. As Soman has shown, the majority of *arrêts* condemning criminals to the stake included a *retentum* ordering them to be strangled to death before they were burned.[223] D'Aguesseau's attempt to strike a deal with Fontanier was thus nothing short of an opportunistic deception—one which capitalised on Fontanier's limited legal knowledge, and on his quite understandably fragile mental and emotional state. Whereas Fontanier was unable to overcome the erudite arguments of his persecutors, he made some attempt to resist their plans to present him to the crowds as a repentant sinner. For as with Vanini's execution, Fontanier's final hours constituted a series of highly political and spiritual acts of verbal and physical performance which aimed to display the power of royal justice to the public.[224] After two final acts of resistance, and a final disavowal of having written the *Trésor inestimable*, Fontanier conformed to the expected performative act of repentance.

222 Bellièvre, fols. 228^r – 228^v; Labrousse and Soman, 'Fontanier', 125. This account of Fontanier's conversation with d'Aguesseau was a subsequent addition to the bottom of fol. 228^r.

223 Alfred Soman, 'Criminal Jurisprudence in Ancien-Régime France: The Parlement of Paris in the Sixteenth and Seventeenth Centuries', in *Crime and Criminal Justice in Europe and Canada*, ed. by Louis A. Knafla (Waterloo, Ontario: Wilfrid Laurier University Press, 1981), pp. 43–75 (p. 51); Alfred Soman, 'Sorcellerie, justice criminelle et société dans la France moderne (l'ego-histoire d'un Americain à Paris)', *Histoire, économie et société*, 12: 2 (1993), 177–217 (200). Soman elsewhere suggests that this was in order to prevent the victims from screaming out blasphemies in the pain of their dying moments (Alfred Soman, 'La justice criminelle, vitrine de la monarchie française', *Bibliothèque de l'école des chartes*, 153: 2 (1995), 291–304 (300)).

224 See Bastien, *Histoire de la peine de mort*, p. 160: 'Pour la justice du roi, l'exécution capitale visait à convaincre la foule de la présence, de la puissance et de la légitimité de son pouvoir. […] Le rituel judiciaire fut une technique de persuasion et de communication' ('For the king's justice, capital punishment aimed to convince the crowd of the presence, the extent, and the legitimacy of its power. […] The judicial ritual was a technique of persuasion and of communication').

This was quickly announced to the crowds, who in turn responded by conforming to the Catholic performance of prayer expected of them:

> Conduit devant la grande porte de l'eglise de Paris, où estant, il ne vouloit prononcer ces mots: pour avoir faict et composé. Et neantmoins on le pressa de le faire, ce qu'il fit; ne vouloit demander pardon; pressé, il le fit aussy. De là, mené à Grève, où il fut une bonne heure, les docteurs requerant tousjours luy lieutenant criminel de superseder l'exécution, esperant toujours qu'il se convertiroit. Enfin le commandement faict de le faire descendre de la charrette. Voyant le condamné qu'il alloit estre exécuté, il dit qu'il vouloit bien se confesser au prestre. Ce qui fust à l'instant faict et, tost apres, celuy qui l'avoit confessé dit au peuple qu'il estoit converty et repentant. Et alors furent chantées les prières accoustumées. Lors l'image du crucifix luy fust mis es mains, car, auparavant, il ne l'avoit voulu prendre. A l'instant faict executer.
>
> Once he had been brought before the great door to the Church of Paris, he did not want to say these words: 'for having made and written'. Yet he was pressured into doing so, which he did. He did not want to ask for forgiveness, but once pressured, he did this too. From there he was taken to the Place de Grève, where he remained for a good hour. The doctors tried to ask the *lieutenant criminel* to halt the execution in the hope that he still might yet convert. Finally the order was given to bring him down from the cart. Seeing that he was going to be executed, the condemned man said that he wanted a priest to hear his confession, which was done straight away. Soon after this, the priest who had heard his confession told the people that he had converted and repented. And so the usual prayers were then sung. The image of the crucifix was then placed in his hands as, prior to this, he had not wanted to take it. He was then immediately executed.[225]

THE MEMORY OF JEAN FONTANIER

The records from the Parlement de Paris have survived for the trials of both Jean Fontanier and Théophile de Viau, both of which have been published by Frédéric Lachèvre. Both men were included in Garasse's *Doctrine curieuse*, both were the subject of pamphlets published immediately after their respective trials, and both

[225] Bellièvre, fol. 228[v] – 229[r]; Labrousse and Soman, 'Fontanier', 125. The *Histoire veritable* paints an unflattering image of the priests' methods: 'tantost par des moyens humains taschent à le remettre luy remonstrans qu'il feroit un grand tort à sa famille et à sa mémoire et laisseroit à tout le peuple subject de la maudire s'il mouroit en ceste abominable croyance, tantost ils se servent de menaces, quelquesfois de douceur et de promesses qu'on ne luy feroit point sentir l'ardeur du feu s'il vouloit mourir Chrestien' ('sometimes they tried through human means to persuade him to convert, reminding him that he would do a great disservice to his family and his memory and give everyone cause to curse them if he died in this abominable belief. In other instances they used threats, sometimes with gentleness and promises that he would not feel the flames if he wished to die a Christian': *Histoire veritable*, p. 14). Bellièvre goes on to discuss at some length whether or not Fontanier really had died a converted and repentant Catholic. He relates subsequent debates he had on this matter with the two doctors from the Sorbonne, Messier and Bernard, the latter of whom served as Fontanier's confessor (see Bellièvre, fol. 228[r]; Labrousse and Soman, 'Fontanier', 125–7). Bellièvre resolutely argued in these discussions that Fontanier had died unrepentant.

were subsequently mentioned as notorious examples of libertine authors. Why then has Théophile's trial enjoyed a large amount of modern scholarly attention, whilst Fontanier's has inspired only three previous dedicated studies? On the one hand, the large number of texts engendered by Théophile's trial in his own day, coupled with its status as a watershed moment in the history of policing literature, inevitably earned his trial a prominent place in *libertinage* studies. However, a more uncomfortable truth may simply be that as an author whose actions at trial evoke pity rather than admiration, Fontanier fails to measure up to the lauded images of the intelligent, articulate, and audaciously unrepentant Vanini and Théophile. Even contemporary descriptions were keen to stress his relative mediocrity:

> [Il était un] homme d'un Jugement commun, d'un esprit lent et tardif, et d'une nature fort pusillanime et craintifve [sic], de stature commune, de teint basanne de poil noir.
>
> [He was a] man of average judgement, of a slow and underdeveloped mind, and of a most cowardly and timid nature, of average stature, with tanned skin and black hair.[226]

> C'estoit un homme plustost petit que grand, bien faict, de poil fort noir, de couleur bazané, la barbe en pointe comme la portoit le monde de la Cour et de Paris: ce que je remarque pour monstrer qu'il estoit faict comme un autre.
>
> He was more of a short man than a tall one, shapely, with very black hair, tanned skin, his beard in a point as was popular at Court and in Paris, which I say to show that he looked like any other man.[227]

If we are tempted to see libertine authors as precursors to modern notions of tolerance, reason, and resistance, then Fontanier's wanderings across Europe, his limited education, and his ineffective self-defence at trial all render him a poor champion against religious oppression in early modern France.

This chapter has made some progress in reassessing the case of Jean Fontanier. His trial is a notable and tragic example of free-thinkers meeting their deaths at the hands of the legal system, after he had changed his defence on multiple occasions in a desperate attempt to escape with his life. On this level alone, his persecution serves to emphasise further the comparatively strong defences of Vanini and Théophile. Yet Fontanier is more than just a convenient point of comparison. Foolhardy though his conduct may have been, he brought a theological text imported from abroad to the streets of Paris, and undoubtedly made some level of contribution to its composition. He boldly wrote and displayed placards advertising an esoteric treasure through private lessons, coercing students into swearing before God to maintain the absolute secrecy of his text. He was judged—by his denouncers, by Bellièvre, and by two law courts—to have actively preached

[226] *Histoire veritable*, p. 4.
[227] Bellièvre, fol. 222^{r}; Labrousse and Soman, 'Fontanier', 118.

against Christianity in favor of Judaism. He did so shortly after the disgrace of Jewish members of the Concinis' entourage, with which he shared an indirect link through the Montaltos. When Fontanier's actions are considered independently from their legal consequences, they were arguably far more subversive and courageous than his limited posthumous reputation has recognised.

Fontanier's trial deserves our attention as much for the strategies of its principal judge as for the tragic story of its defendant. Nicolas de Bellièvre's memoir is an extremely rare account of a leading magistrate's views on a case, the psychology behind his preparation for a criminal interrogation, and the interactions between judges during a deliberation. These professional reflections go perhaps a small way towards nuancing the Revolutionary image of the magistrates as bloodthirsty precursors to modern criminal justice.[228] To be sure, there is strong evidence to suggest that Bellièvre had already decided his view on the case before the interrogations had begun. Yet as the presiding magistrate in possession of the records from Fontanier's first trial at the Châtelet, he could hardly have opened an appeal hearing without having already formed a professional judgement on the case. And professional it was. Doubtless disgusted by Fontanier's teachings against Catholic doctrine—which furthermore took place on the same road as the Hôtel de Bellièvre, the rue de Béthisy—Bellièvre showed himself to be much more focussed on the interpretation and application of the law than the colleagues he mentions in his memoir.[229] He thus put into action an effective legal and rhetorical strategy during the interrogations in order to achieve his aims. Bellièvre's actions were undeniably influenced by anti-Semitism, a pitiless intolerance of free-thinking, and a personal desire to pass the death penalty against Fontanier. Nevertheless, over the course of the trial he restricted himself to the application of the law; from his research into possible legal precedent in preparing his questions, to his contribution to the judges' deliberations. Fortunately for Bellièvre, Fontanier's refusal to identify himself as a Jew in fact spared the magistrates having to navigate uncertain legal territory.

This in turn leads us to ask whether Fontanier's trial went on to serve as a legal precedent for future such cases, either within the Parlement de Paris (potentially as a court of appeal) or in other courts, both royal and provostial, throughout the kingdom. Bellièvre explicitly claims that he recorded his memoir on Fontanier's case for this very purpose, albeit for his own private use: 'pour servir au Jugement de pareils proces s'il s'en presentoit a ladvenir' ('to aid in judging similar trials if the occasion presented itself in the future').[230] It would require considerable research

[228] On this point see Soman, 'Criminal Jurisprudence'. p. 44; Soman, 'L'ego-histoire', 197; and Julian Swann, *Exile, Imprisonment, or Death: The Politics of Disgrace in Bourbon France, 1610–1789* (Oxford: Oxford University Press, 2017), p. vii.

[229] Labrousse and Soman, 'Fontanier', 129, note 9.

[230] Bellièvre, fol. 220^r.

as part of a separate study to identify comparable trials in archival records. Even if these were to be found, they would not offer us the same glimpse into the judicial anthropology of the criminal chamber as Bellièvre's manuscript. Nevertheless, despite the progress made in this study, it is possible that future research on the prosecution of Jews in early modern France may yet add more to the historical and legal significance of Fontanier's trial.

Finally, Bellièvre's critical reading of the *Trésor inestimable* is surely an early precursor to forensic linguistics. He presented linguistic and stylistic choices in the offending text as convincing and legally admissable individuating features. He then linked the resultant author profile to the accused, whilst also excluding both of the Montalto brothers as potential authors. Despite relying on a very small selection of linguistic choices, Bellièvre nonetheless undertook a stylistic analysis of the likely national, intellectual, and spiritual identity of the text's author between two very different possible candidates. As such, Fontanier's case deserves its place in the prehistory of this discipline of authorship identification which, according to one of its modern scholars, is officially recognised as beginning in the eighteenth century.[231]

Bellièvre's mastery of the written and spoken word, however, was not absolute. In 1623, Marin Mersenne made the connection between Vanini and Fontanier, whom he describes as an impious man:

> quem nuper ob eandem ferme impietatem supremus *Parisiensis* Senatus extinxit, qui, licet Atheismum proseminare minime videretur, sed potius Judaismum inculcare et Evangelium *D. Matthaei*, atque adeo Christianam religionem [...] evertere.

> who has recently been put to death by the supreme court of Paris, even though he seemed not to spread atheism, but rather to teach Judaism and to overturn the Gospel of St Matthew and, in other words, Christianity itself.[232]

Mersenne's brief and at first glance unremarkable comment in fact contains one highly intriguing detail. We have already seen from Bellièvre's manuscript how the *Trésor inestimable* sought to undermine the Gospel of St Matthew. Yet neither Garasse nor the two pamphets published shortly after Fontanier's execution mention this particular feature of the incriminating text, whereas there is no evidence to suggest that Mersenne corresponded with Bellièvre. Between 1624

[231] For Olsson, 'the earliest known [authorship] controversy related to the authorship of the Bible, and was voiced by a German priest, H.B. Witter, who in 1711 pointed out that the different names for the Pentateuch could indicate that several authors had contributed to it' (Olsson, *Forensic Linguistics*, p. 17).

[232] 'Lettre de Mr. D.D. à Mr. D.L.C. contenant plusieurs Particularitez curieuses, qui ont été supprimées dans le *Commentaire* du Père Mersenne sur la Genese', in *Bibliotheque Britannique, ou histoire des ouvrages des sçavans de la Grande-Bretagne*, XVIII: 2 (1752), pp. 406–21. The English translation given above is based on Mothu's translation into French: 'que la Cour suprême de Paris avait récemment fait mourir, bien qu'il ne semblât nullement propager l'athéisme, mais plutôt enseigner le judaïsme et renverser l'Evangile de S. Matthieu et, pour mieux dire, le christianisme lui-même' ('Pierre Petit', 265).

and 1625, however, he did exchange letters and indeed collaborate with the future king's engineer and geographer: Fontanier's former student and denouncer Pierre Petit.[233] Old habits appear to have died hard for the loose-lipped Petit, who is the only known source from whom Mersenne could have learned this specific detail from Fontanier's text. The contents of Fontanier's destroyed *Trésor inestimable* did not therefore remain exclusively within Bellièvre's private memoirs as he had self-assuredly believed. The *président à mortier* had proved to be a formidable force within the Parlement de Paris. Within the Republic of Letters, however, not even the calculating Nicolas de Bellièvre could control everything.

[233] See De Waard, *Mersenne*, pp. 243–4, 248, 491. Claude Bredeau also mentions Fontanier's trial briefly in a letter to Mersenne dated 1622 (p. 110).

5

A Last Stand: The Trial of Théophile de Viau (1623–25)

Sachez donc, monsieur, que le Parlement ne trompe ni ne joue personne et qu'il rend à chacun ce qui lui est dû.

Know then, sir, that the Parlement neither cheats nor toys with anyone, and that it gives to each what they deserve.

[*Premier président* Jean Le Maistre[1]]

Sy je vays au Parlement, je suis perdu.

If I go to the Parlement, it will be the end of me.

[Théophile de Viau[2]]

The trial of the poet Théophile de Viau occupies a central place in the history of French libertinism. As one of the century's most sensational trials, its consequences were far reaching and immediate. It attracted an extraordinary level of public interest during its almost two-year duration from 4 October 1623 to 1 September 1625. At least seventy-four pamphlets were written for or against Théophile, without counting references to the trial in the letters and printed texts of other authors.[3] Théophile's trial centred on his alleged contribution to an audacious

[1] Quoted in E. Fayard, *Aperçu historique sur le Parlement de Paris*, 3 vols (Lyon: N. Scheuring; Paris: A. Picard, 1876), I, p. 442. I am grateful for permission to reproduce in this chapter work previously published in Adam Horsley, 'Strategies of Accusation and Self-defence at the Trial of Théophile de Viau (1623–25)', *Papers on French Seventeenth-Century Literature*, 44: 85 (2016), 157–77.

[2] AN X 2B 1185, fourth interrogation (3 June 1624) in Frédéric Lachèvre, *Le Libertinage devant le parlement de Paris: Le Procès du poète Théophile de Viau*, 2 vols (Paris: Honoré Champion, 1909), I, p. 431. All quotations from Lachèvre's *Procès* are taken from this first volume unless otherwise stated.

[3] A figure given in Stéphane Van Damme, *L'épreuve libertine: Morale, soupçon et pouvoirs dans la France baroque* (Paris: CNRS Éditions, 2008), p. 7. For a bibliography of contemporary pamphlets

poetic anthology, *Le Parnasse des poètes satyriques* (most commonly referred to in modern scholarship as *Le Parnasse satyrique*), as well as wider manifestations of his irreligious conduct, evinced both in his published poetry and according to witness testimony. An earlier conviction handed down *in absentia* on 18 August 1623 had found him guilty of *lèse-majesté divine*. In the subsequent trial which forms the main subject of this chapter, however, the poet was acquitted of all previous charges against him. With a considerable wealth of surviving documentation, Théophile's case is an exceptional lens through which to observe the relationship between subversive literature and the law.

Given that Théophile died shortly after his release, the outcome of his trial has predominantly been seen as a victory for the Catholic cause. For Antoine Adam, the libertine movement was defeated in 1625.[4] Joan DeJean posits that the fictional literary Théophile, emphasised by the prosecution in early interrogations, eclipsed the memory of Théophile the man who was ultimately eliminated by his persecutors.[5] Jacqueline Marchand, whilst conceding that Théophile escaped with his life, nonetheless claims that one of Théophile's main persecutors—the Jesuit Father François Garasse—emerged victorious from the trial.[6] More recently, Laurence Tricoche-Rauline has described Théophile's defence at his trial as clumsy, belated, and ineffective, whereas Laurence Giavarini has claimed that Garasse's *Doctrine curieuse* (Paris: Sebastien Chappelet, 1623), and its invention of Théophile as a seditious social deviant, were victories for the Jesuit's cause.[7] There is therefore a tendency to consider the verdict in relation to Théophile's persecutors and accusers, with relatively little engagement with his own agency in defending his texts and his person at trial.

This is not to say that Théophile's self-defence has remained entirely unexplored. DeJean has analysed in depth the notions of autobiographical writing and the *je poétique* (the poetic 'I') at his trial.[8] This fictionalisation of the defendant has also

and literary criticism on Théophile, see Guido Saba, *Fortunes et infortunes de Théophile de Viau* (Paris: Klincksieck, 1997), pp. 314–18.

[4] Antoine Adam, *Théophile de Viau et la libre pensée française en 1620* (Geneva: Slatkine Reprints, 1966), p. 404.

[5] Joan DeJean, 'Une autobiographie en procès: l'affaire Théophile de Viau', *Poétique*, 48 (November 1981), 431–48 (431). See also Joan DeJean, *The Reinvention of Obscenity. Sex, Lies, and Tabloids in Early Modern France* (Chicago, IL, and London: The University of Chicago Press, 2002), p. 30: 'In the end, the state eliminated the man widely considered the leading freethinker of his generation.'

[6] Jacqueline Marchand, 'Apologie du Père Garasse (1585–1631): Le Jésuite et les Libertins', *Cahiers laïques*, 173 (1980), 92–106 (105).

[7] Laurence Tricoche-Rauline, *Identité(s) libertine(s): L'écriture personnelle ou la création de soi* (Paris: Honoré Champion, 2009), p. 54; Laurence Giavarini, 'Le libertin et la fiction-sorcière à l'âge classique: Remarques sur Dom Juan et Théophile', in *Usages et théories de la fiction: le débat contemporain à l'épreuve des textes anciens (XVI–XVIIIe siècles)*, ed. by Françoise Lavocat (Rennes: Presses Universitaires de Rennes, 2004), pp. 185–218 (pp. 188, 200).

[8] DeJean, 'Autobiographie.' The question of identity and intent in a small corpus of Théophile's poems is also addressed in Leonard Hinds, '"Honni soit qui mal y pense" I: Avowals, Accusations, and Witnessing in the Trial of Théophile de Viau', *Papers on French Seventeenth-Century Literature*, 27: 53 (2000), 435–44.

been explored by Van Damme, who proposes a more favourable account of the poet's defence within the public literary sphere.[9] For Van Damme, Théophile's trial demonstrates the shifting political landscape in the early days of absolutism under Louis XIII's personal rule. Focussing on the perceived need to expose Théophile's *libertinage* to the public in order to justify its persecution,[10] and to define a collective libertine menace through the fictitious *porte-parole* embodied by Théophile, he highlights that the increased persecution of writers mirrored a growing intolerance towards witchcraft, Protestantism, and blasphemy.[11] Other critics have identified Théophile's trial as a symptom of wider divisions in French society between men of letters, as well as between the Church and state, for political and judicial dominance.[12]

Despite this range of modern critical approaches and the heavy focus on those responsible for the poet's persecution, a significant aspect of the trial proceedings has been almost entirely overlooked: the judges themselves. Lachèvre—the only scholar to have offered brief comment on those who judged Théophile's case—does not even provide their full names, and focusses predominantly on Garasse as the poet's chief persecutor. There is a persistent tendency in subsequent studies to employ the term 'Théophile's judges' casually, as if these were a unified, anonymous political entity serving as a mere legal extension of the more personal motives for persecuting Théophile held by Garasse, father Voisin, and the *procureur général du roi* (king's attorney general) Mathieu Molé. As will soon become clear, the truth of the matter was quite different. One of the aims of this chapter is to elucidate where possible the personal and professional identity of Théophile's judges, their values, and the precise role that several of them had in the trial proceedings. Drawing on previously neglected sources as well as a number of archival discoveries, it offers new insights into the machinations that led to Théophile's arrest. It will also be the first study to situate the trial within the regulations and mechanics of the Parlement de Paris itself, as well as a number of legal texts embodying its theoretical conduct, thereby demystifying the specialist and often unclear terms that can be found in the extant trial records.

[9] Van Damme speaks of Théophile's final victory in 1625 (Van Damme, *Épreuve*, p. 141).

[10] Van Damme, *Épreuve*, p. 10–16. This view contrasts with that of DeJean, for whom the rendering public of previously private immoralities and subversions was the cause, rather than the tool, of persecution. See DeJean, *Obscenity*, pp. 3–4, 14–15, 37, 46.

[11] On these points, see also Jean Delumeau, *La peur en occident: XIV*e*–XVII*e* siècles* (Paris: Fayard, 1978), pp. 390–1; Daniel Christiaens, 'Nouvelles considérations sur la disgrâce de Théophile de Viau', *Revue de l'Agenais* 139: 3 (2012), 507–18; Alain Cabantous, *Histoire du blasphème en Occident: XVI*e*–XIX*e* siècle* (Paris: Albin Michel, 2015), pp. 67–9, 94–5.

[12] Christian Jouhaud, *Les Pouvoirs de la littérature: histoire d'un paradoxe* (Paris: Gallimard, 2000), pp. 27–95; Marc Fumaroli, *L'Âge de l'éloquence: Rhétorique et «res literaria»* de la Renaissance au seuil de l'époque classique (Geneva: Droz, 2002), pp. 233–46. For a history of the Church's and state's control of the book trade in sixteenth and seventeenth-century France and their shortcomings, see Roger Chartier and Henri-Jean Martin, *Histoire de l'édition française*, 4 vols (Paris: Fayard, 1989), I — 'Le livre conquérant', pp. 330–72; DeJean, *Obscenity*, pp. 12–13, 39; and Van Damme, *Épreuve*, pp. 134–5.

In accordance with the codified rhythms of the Parlement, Théophile would not have encountered his judges until the very end of his trial, and was instead interrogated on numerous occasions by two magistrates in private. A study of Théophile's judges and their potential views on the case is therefore given after our analyses of the interrogations.

The scope of this chapter does not include the wider implications of this trial for other early modern authors, which has largely been addressed in the works mentioned earlier. Nor will it focus on the numerous texts that Théophile addressed to men of letters during his incarceration seeking support for his cause. Rather, this chapter offers a close reading of the trial exchanges themselves, grounded where appropriate in early modern legal theory and custom. Many of Lachèvre's transcriptions—the basis for all subsequent studies on this trial—are not referenced with the corresponding records at the Archives Nationales (AN). I have therefore provided references both to the original, unpaginated archival records and to the corresponding pages in Lachèvre. Additionally, in order to facilitate future studies based on the original documents, the following footnote brings together the classmarks for interrogations, depositions, and confrontations from this trial for the first time.[13]

The present study also proposes a close reading of another overlooked area of the trial—Théophile's defence of his texts inspired by the works of Antiquity, particularly his *Traicté de l'immortalité de l'âme* (*Treatise on the Immortality of the Soul*)—rather than approaching the trial solely from the perspective of the history of obscenity. By focussing on the legal and rhetorical strategies deployed by the defendant and his judges, I wish to avoid the tendency, observed in the works of Lachèvre and Adam, to follow in the magistrates' footsteps in 'judging' Théophile's texts.[14] In particular, I shall argue that the consistency and effectiveness of Théophile's defence was in stark contrast to the varied strategies of the prosecution, which failed to use the incriminating evidence at its disposal to full effect. In doing so, the present study assesses Théophile's self-defence from the perspective of the trial itself, and with a greater emphasis on the effective

[13] The relevant documents from the *minutes d'instruction* (the *interrogatoires*) can be found in AN X 2B 1184: four witness depositions (4 October – 23 November 1623); AN X 2B 1185: Théophile's first six interrogations (22 March – 15 June 1624) and seven witness depositions (24 April – 11 May 1624); AN X 2B 1186: Théophile's confrontations with twelve witnesses, including three resulting from *monitoires* (21 October 1624 – 22 August 1625). AN X 2B 1186 holds records from July to December 1624. However, at the time of writing this chapter the depositions and confrontations at Théophile's trial from 1625 (with the exception of Sepaus) also appear in this series, instead of their logical location under AN X 2B 1187 (January – June 1625). AN X 2A 988 (*plumitifs du conseil de la Tournelle*) holds Théophile's final interrogation before his full panel of judges (his *interrogatoire sur la sellette*, 27 August 1625), as well as the last-minute testimony of Jean Sepaus and the ensuing confrontation (29 August 1625).

[14] See on this point DeJean, 'Autobiographie', 342; Mathilde Bombart, '"Des vers méchants et impies?" Questions sur une poésie en procès', in *Lectures de Théophile de Viau*, ed. by Guillaume Peureux (Rennes: Presses Universitaires de Rennes, 2008), pp. 63–77 (pp. 63–5).

agency of the accused, rather than adopting a retrospective angle informed by the subsequent self-censorship and strategies of dissimulation adopted by free-thinking authors.[15]

THE *RECUEILS SATYRIQUES* AND A PREVIOUS TRIAL *IN ABSENTIA*

Between November and December 1622, a collection of obscene and irreligious poetry was published entitled *Le Parnasse des poètes satyrique*, along with its sister publication *La Quint-essence satyrique*. These were to be the last titles in a popular trend of *recueils satyriques* (satirical anthologies). Fifteen such anthologies of irreligious, obscene, and pornographic verse were published between 1599 and 1625, in addition to numerous reprints, totalling some four thousand poems.[16] As Michel Jeanneret reminds us, far from being a mere collection of impudent and irreverent poems, the erotic nature of these texts was an insubordinate act of rebellion against political, intellectual, and religious oppression.[17] These texts were first published with a degree of caution, as evidenced by the following address to the readers of *La Muse folâtre*:

> Diverses considérations (amy lecteur) m'ont retenu une longue espace de temps avant que me resoudre à faire voir le jour à ce petit Recueil. [...] Si je cognoy que ce coup d'essay te soit agréable, je te promets dans peu de jours te le rendre amplifié de beaucoup.
>
> A number of considerations (dear reader) have held me back for a long period of time before I resolved to show this little collection the light of day [...] If I learn that this first attempt is agreable to you, I promise you that within a few days I will give it to you in a considerably expanded form.[18]

The *recueils satyriques* had begun to attract criticism as early as 1617. The editor of the *Recueil des plus excellans vers satyriques de ce temps* attacks 'quelques visages severes ou hypocrites censeurs (qui semblent des Curies, peut-estre vivent

[15] On this subject, see in particular Jean-Pierre Cavaillé, *Dis/simulations. Jules-César Vanini, François La Mothe Le Vayer, Gabriel Naudé, Louis Manchon et Torquato Accetto: Religion, morale et politique au XVII*[e] *siècle* (Paris: Honoré Champion, 2008); see also Sophie Gouverneur, *Prudence et Subversions Libertines: La Critique de la raison d'État chez François de la Mothe le Vayer, Gabriel Naudé et Samuel Sorbière* (Paris: Honoré Champion, 2005); and Isabelle Moreau, *«Guérir du sot»: Les Stratégies d'écriture des libertins à l'âge classique* (Paris: Honoré Champion, 2007).

[16] Although not fully established terms during the period in question, *obscène* and *obscénité* had already experienced a developmental stage in the Renaissance. See the essays in *Obscénités renaissantes*, ed. by Hugh Roberts, Guillaume Peureux and Lise Wajeman (Geneva: Droz, 2011); particularly Emily Butterworth, 'Defining Obscenity' (pp. 31–8) and Emily Butterworth and Hugh Roberts, 'From Word to Thing' (pp. 87–92).

[17] Michel Jeanneret, *L'Éros rebelle: Littérature et dissidence à l'âge classique* (Paris: Seuil, 2003), p. 17. On the subversive nature of these poems, see also pp. 26–39.

[18] 'Le libraire au lecteur', in *La Muse folastre* (Rouen: Claude Morel, 1600), fol 2[r].

en Epicuriens)' ('a few stern faces or hypocritical censors (who seem to be curiae, and perhaps live as Epicureans)').[19] The *Cabinet satyrique* goes further, and refers to those who object to its publication as 'estant pour la pluspart esprits faibles, ils ont pour proprieté d'estre opiniatres en leurs opinions, et autant incapables de raison que de legitime vertu' ('being for the most part weak-minded, it is their property to be stubborn in their opinions, and just as incapable of reason as of true virtue').[20] The publishers of these texts hinted at their sulphurous content. Readers of the *Cabinet satyrique* were assured, with evident irony, that 'tout impiété en est hors, le respect aux choses divines y est exactement gardé' ('all impiety has been thrown out, respect for divine things is strictly adhered to here').[21] Claude d'Esternod offers a similar defence against possible accusations of impiety in his anonymous *L'Espadon satyrique*:

> Je cherche les hommes à la lanterne, comme Diogene, mais je n'attaque point les Dieux, comme Momus: n'osant mesme entreprendre la paranymphe de leurs loüanges, de peur que blasonnant sur elles, l'on ne m'accuse de curiosité, ou qu'en doutant, je ne sois declaré profane, et sacrilege.
>
> I search for men by lantern, like Diogenes, but I do not attack the Gods like Momus, daring not even to attempt to lead their praises, through fear that in describing them I should be accused of curiosity, or that in doubting them, I should be declared to be profane and sacrilegious.[22]

The precautions taken to avoid the type of criticism mentioned by d'Esternod were apparently effective, as none of the *recueils satyriques* suffered condemnation or censorship prior to the *Parnasse satyrique*. This text does not represent a major departure in tone or obscenity from the corpus of *recueils satyriques*. In a recycling of verse common for the genre, 176 poems out of the 385 poems in the *Parnasse* are taken from the *Délices Satyriques* (Paris: Antoine Estoc; Antoine de Sommaville, 1620) alone.[23] The *Parnasse* opens with a sonnet (the only poem in the work that bears Théophile's name) which graphically describes the final stages of syphilis, and ends with what could be interpreted as a vow to commit sodomy.[24]

19 'Au lecteur', in *Recueil des plus excellents vers satyriques de ce temps* (Paris: Antoine Estoc, 1617), n.p.

20 'Avertissement au Lecteur', in *Le Cabinet satyrique, ou recueil parfait des vers piquants et gaillards de ce temps* (Paris: Antoine d'Estoc, 1618), p. 5.

21 'Avertissement', in *Cabinet satyrique*, p. 5.

22 'Epistre', in [Claude d'Esternod], *L'Espadon satyrique, par le sieur de Franchere, gentilhomme Franc-comtois* (Lyon: Jean Lautret, 1619), n.p.

23 Lachèvre, *Procès*, p. 115. Théophile was far from the major contributor to the *Parnasse*. Of the at least twenty individual contributors to this anthology, seventeen had more poems published in the *Parnasse* than Théophile. Many of the poets with the largest number of poems in this title—including Motin, Régnier, Ronsard, and Sigogne—were all dead at the time of the *Parnasse*'s publication. This shows the publisher's attempt to increase sales by including well-established poets, whilst also suggesting that living poets may have been reluctant to see their names printed in such collections.

24 'Phillis, tout est foutu, je meurs de la vérole', in *Le Parnasse des poètes satyrique* ([n.p.]: [n. pub.], 1622), p. 1. The last line of the poem—'Je fais veu desormais de ne …tre qu'en cu' ('I vow that from

Théophile consistently denied having authored this poem, and indeed having any involvement in the *Parnasse satyrique*. He claimed that:

> Il n'a faict fayre ladite composition ny composé ledit sonnet et que au contraire ayant veu ledit livre entre les mains d'un librayre qui tient boutticque devant le Pallays et leu ledit sonnet, il deschira le feuillet où il estoit escript.
>
> He did not have the aforementioned collection of poems printed, nor did he compose the aforementioned sonnet. On the contrary, having seen the aforementioned book in the hands of a bookseller who keeps his shop in front of the Palace, and having read the aforementioned sonnet, he tore the page on which it appeared.[25]

Shortly afterwards, Garasse began to send chapters of his *Doctrine curieuse* to the printers as soon as their drafts were complete. One such draft came into Théophile's possession. Sensing the approaching danger to his person, he approached the *Prévôt de Paris* (Paris Provost), the Jesuit College, and the *procureur général* Mathieu Molé in order to censor Garasse's text, and to report the printer of the *Parnasse satyrique*—Antoine Estoc—for falsely attributing its opening poem to him.[26] Following Théophile's efforts, the *Parnasse satyrique* was banned from sale on 21 February 1623. Although the *Doctrine curieuse* was banned on 1 April, the Jesuits quickly had the decision reversed. Having failed to defend himself in the legal sphere, Théophile resorted to writing. In May 1623 he published the *Seconde partie* of his *Œuvres,* in which he defends himself against the *Doctrine curieuse* and those who sought his condemnation:

> Ceux qui veulent ma perte en font courir de si grands bruits que j'ai besoin de me montrer publiquement, si je veux qu'on sache que je suis au monde. [...] On a suborné des imprimeurs pour mettre au jour, en mon nom, des vers sales et profanes, qui n'ont rien de mon style ni de mon humeur.
>
> Those who are seeking my downfall are spreading so many rumours about it that I need to show myself publicly, if I want people to know that I am still here. [...] The printers have been suborned into producing, under my name, dirty and profane poems that are far removed from my style and my humour.[27]

On 11 July 1623 Molé issued a warrant for Théophile's arrest, as well as those of three other contributors to the *Parnasse*: Nicolas Frenicle, Guillaume Colletet, and Pierre Berthelot. The Parlement de Paris was unable to apprehend these men, and

---

now on I will only ...ck in the ass') was described as a vow to commit sodomy by Garasse in *La Doctrine curieuse des beaux esprits de ce temps* (Paris: Sebastien Chappelet, 1623), p. 782 and in [François Garasse], *Apologie du père François Garassus, de la Compagnie de Jésus, pour son Livre contre les Athéistes & Libertins de notre siècle* (Paris: Sebastien Chappelet, 1624), p. 252.

25 AN X 2B 1185, first interrogation (22 March 1624), in Lachèvre, *Procès*, p. 373.

26 Lachèvre, *Procès*, pp. 118–21. For a revised and definitive dating of Théophile's actions here, see p. 324–5 of the present chapter.

27 'Au lecteur', in Théophile de Viau, *Œuvres*, ed. by Guido Saba (Paris: Classiques Garnier, 1990), p. 187. All references from Théophile's *Œuvres* are taken from this edition unless otherwise stated.

tried them *in absentia* on 18 August 1623. The verdict of this first trial was reached in just one morning (see Figure 5.1). The *arrêt* (final judgement) found them:

> Convaincus du crime de lèze-majesté divine, et pour réparation les a condamnez et condamne [...] ledit Theophille bruslé vif, son corps réduict en cendres, icelles jectées au vent et lesdictz livres aussy bruslez [...] sy pris et aprehendez peuvent estre en leurs personnes, sinon ledit Theophille par figure et représentation et ledict Berthelot en effigye.
>
> Convicted of the crime of divine lese-majesty, and as punishment has condemned and condemns them [...] Théophile to be burned alive, his body reduced to ashes and then thrown to the wind, and the aforementioned books also burned [...] if they can be seized and apprehended in person, otherwise Théophile by figure and representation and the aforementioned Berthelot in effigy.[28]

Théophile and Berthelot were burned in effigy later that day, and the following day Garasse's *Doctrine curieuse* was finally published. Colletet was banished from Paris for nine years, whereas Frenicle was not pursued further.[29]

Lachèvre has published the relevant court documents for this case which have informed all subsequent studies on this early stage of Théophile's dealings with the law courts.[30] My own exploration of the archives has uncovered a previously unknown document which sheds new light on the final stages of Théophile's first prosecution: his entry in the *Registre des Conclusions de Monseigneur le Procureur General du Roy Molé*. These records provide Molé's views on both criminal and civil cases in the first person, which were subsequently used to assist judges in reaching a verdict.[31] The *conclusions* for Théophile's first trial are dated 14 August 1623.[32] This reveals that the judges took four days after receiving this document before reaching their verdict on 18 August. Théophile's protector, the duc de Montmorency, had written to Molé asking him to look upon the poet's case favourably ('de le favoriser en ses affaires') on 15 August.[33] Lachèvre claims that Molé ignored Montmorency's

[28] AN X 2B 342; AN X 2A 217, in Lachèvre, *Procès*, p. 143. As we saw in Chapter 2, *lèse-majesté divine* referred to crimes committed against God, whereas crimes of *lèse-majesté humaine* were committed against the sovereign. An *arrêt* from the Parlement de Paris could not be appealed, whereas *sentences* from lower courts could. See Roland Mousnier, *Les Institutions de la France sous la monarchie absolue*, 2 vols (Paris: Presses Universitaires de France, 1980), II, p. 374.

[29] On Colletet's involvement see Hugh Roberts, 'Obscenity and the Politics of Authorship in Early Seventeenth-century France: Guillaume Colletet and the *Parnasse des poètes satyriques* (1622)', *French Studies*, 68: 1 (2014), 18–33.

[30] These are AN X 2B 341: the arrest warrant against Théophile, Frenicle, Colletet, and Berthelot (11 July 1623); AN X 2A 986, AN X 2B 342, and AN X 2A 217: the first brief *arrêt* (18 August) and the lengthier *arrêt* (19 August, variants only). See Lachèvre, *Procès*, pp. 132, 141–3.

[31] Beginning in 1611, this register was a relatively new addition to the Parlement's records by 1623. See Madeleine Dillay, 'Conclusions du procureur général au Parlement de Paris relatives à la vérification et à l'enregistrement des lettres patentes (quelques exemples du commencement du règne de Louis XIII)', *Revue historique de droit français et étranger*, 4: 32 (1955), 255–66 (255).

[32] AN X 1A 8870, *Registre des Conclusions de Monseigneur le Procureur General du Roy Molé*.

[33] BNF Cinq Cents de Colbert, 2, p. 68; Lachèvre, *Procès*, p. 140. Théophile and Montmorency had

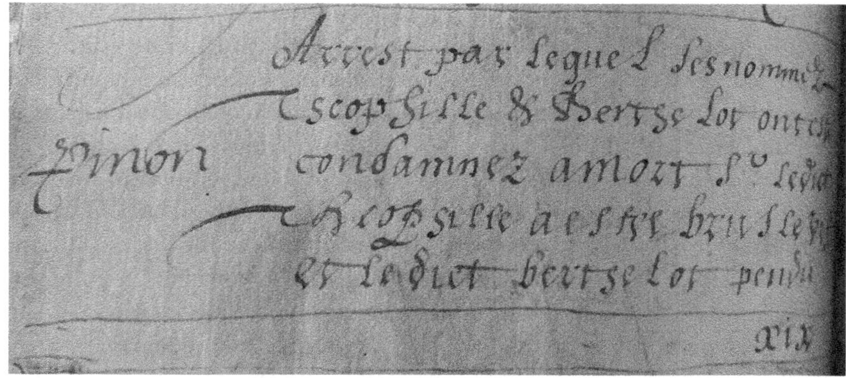

Figure 5.1 AN X 2A 1384: *Table d'arrêts* recording the death sentences against Théophile and Berthelot (19 August 1623) following their first trial *in absentia*, reproduced here for the first time. Jacques Pinon served as *rapporteur* for this trial, and as a *commissaire* entrusted with the instruction of Théophile's second, main trial. A further unpublished record of the registering of this judgement (*Registre d'entablement d'arrêt*) is given in a single line of AN X 2A 1373.

letter in order to pursue his agenda against Théophile.[34] However, it is now clear from the *conclusions* that the *procureur général* simply did not receive this letter until *after* he had already presented his *conclusions* to the Parlement – an act which ended his official role in the trial proceedings.

The *conclusions* furthermore present a number of variants to the subsequent, longer *arrêt* of 19 August for which it clearly served as a template (the *arrêt* of 18 August being an abbreviated version). Both documents show that the trial was instigated by Molé as public prosecutor ('sur la plaincte faicte par le Procureur général du roy'). However, Molé's version does not include the line given in the *arrêt* revealing that he brought copies of Théophile's offending texts to the Parlement to trigger a criminal investigation ('et livres par luy représentez').[35] Molé describes the three poets as 'autheurs de sonnets et vers contenans les impietés brutalités et blasphemes mentionnés au livre tres pernitieux intitulé Le Parnasse Satirique' ('authors of sonnets and verses containing the impieties, brutalities, and blasphemies mentioned in the very pernicious book entitled *Le Parnasse satyrique*'). Pronounced just five days later, the *arrêt* omits 'brutalités' and adds 'abominations'. Similarly, Molé suggested that prior to their execution, the criminals should declare in public that 'meschamment ils avoient faict, composé,

visited Molé in person to assert the poet's innocence in April 1623 (see Lachèvre, *Procès*, p. 120–1).

[34] Lachèvre, *Procès*, p. 140.

[35] AN X 2B 342, quoted in Lachèvre, *Procès*, p. 142. All subsequent references to the *arrêt* in this section are taken from this page.

faict imprimer et exposé en vente [...] Le Parnasse Satirique' ('wickedly they had made, written, had printed and displayed for sale [...] *Le Parnasse satyrique*'). This is rendered 'très meschamment et très abominablement' ('most wickedly and most abominably') in the *arrêt*, which also replaced 'brutalités' with 'abominations' a third time later on in the document. Thus, the judges removed the vocabulary of brutality which, as seen in Chapter 1, was often used in the anti-*libertin* polemics of the late sixteenth century and by Garasse, who directly influenced Molé's involvement in Théophile's second trial. The notion of brutality was not directly descriptive of an actual crime, whilst the lexicon of 'abomination' given in the *arrêt* was more closely linked with crimes against the established religion.

A description of the *Parnasse* as being 'imprimé par les nommez Estoc et Sommaville' ('printed by Estoc and Sommaville') is also absent in the *arrêt*, whilst the printers of Théophile's *Œuvres*—Pierre Billaine and Jacques Quesnel—appear in both sources. Notably, Molé found the poets to be guilty of 'lèse-majesté divine et humaine', whilst the final *arrêt* convicted them only for *lèse-majesté divine*. As we saw in Chapter 2, specific examples of *lèse-majesté humaine* included crimes against the sovereign or his councillors of state and treason.[36] Théophile's judges therefore took the view that his poems may well have constituted crimes against God such as blasphemy—a crime of *lèse-majesté divine*—but that they were insufficient proof of crimes against the king or the state.

Finally, this series has also proved useful in navigating other areas of the archives. In the early 1970s, Alfred Soman was able to identify the Conciergerie's *registres d'écrou* (registers of incarceration) as a research tool for gaining information on a prisoner's identity, their date of arrest, their crime, their final interrogation, as well as the verdict and the date of the reading of the *arrêt*.[37] Whilst I do not claim to have developed a comparable innovation, the *conclusions du procureur general* nevertheless offer researchers an extremely valuable (and relatively legible) summary of the various stages of a given trial. Though they do not give the final verdict or the date of the definitive sentence, they nonetheless give dates for a number of specific hearings besides the prisoner's final interrogation, not all of which are given in the four sources identified by Soman.[38] As we will see shortly, it is thanks to these *conclusions* that the present chapter includes previously unseen witness testimony from Théophile's trial which is not to be found in other sources beyond the interrogation records themselves.

[36] See Chapter 2, p. 92.

[37] Alfred Soman, 'Sorcellerie, justice criminelle et société dans la France moderne (l'ego-histoire d'un Americain à Paris)', *Histoire, économie et société*, 12: 2 (1993), 177–217 (186–90).

[38] These are the *écrous*, the *arrêts* as preserved in the register of *arrêts* and in the *minutes*, and the final *interrogatoires sur la sellette*, listed in the archives as the *plumitifs du conseil de la Tournelle*. See Alfred Soman, 'Petit guide des recherches dans les archives criminelles du Parlement de Paris à l'époque moderne', *Histoire et Archives*, 12: 1 (2002), 61–79 (63).

The Jesuits had emerged victorious from this first confrontation between Théophile and the defenders of Catholicism. Not only had he failed in his efforts to have the *Doctrine curieuse* permanently censored, but he had also failed to distance himself from the danger surrounding the authorship of the *Parnasse satyrique.* Though ordered by Montmorency to cross the northern border on 26 August, Théophile remained in France. At the same time, intricate collusions between Molé, Garasse, and the Jesuit Father Voisin were about to lead to the poet's arrest.

CONSPIRACIES LEADING TO THÉOPHILE'S ARREST AND HIS SECOND TRIAL

Théophile's second trial (1623–5) was not a sudden reaction to his poetry or to the *Parnasse satyrique*, but the culmination of a plot that had been conceived two years previously. In 1613, the Jesuit Father Voisin took in and converted a young Protestant, Louis Forest Sageot, who had been disowned by his father for 'd'estranges rebellions qu'il luy avoit faites dés l'aage [sic] de seize à dix-sept ans' ('strange rebellions that he had made against his father since the age of sixteen or seventeen').[39] Although Sageot was later expelled from the Jesuit order for spreading vice amongst the male pupils at La Flèche, Voisin continued to pay for Sageot's lodgings. Théophile and Sageot had met at Saumur in 1611. At trial, Théophile revealed that he had discovered Sageot 'en une action très sale' ('committing a very dirty act'), and that he had physically assaulted Sageot on numerous occasions.[40] Voisin thus had at his disposal a vulnerable young man who had repeatedly been humiliated by Théophile, making him an ideal and willing witness for the poet's eventual trial. Théophile's protector and royal favourite the duc de Luynes would provide Voisin with the opportunity he had been waiting for, by dying of fever during a military campaign against the Protestants in December 1621. Just days after Luyne's death, Sageot reported Théophile's unspecified abominations to Garasse during Advent. According to Garasse's memoirs, he was the first person to whom Sageot reported Théophile's blasphemies, before later repeating his accusations to Voisin.[41] Considering the relationship between Voisin and Sageot,

[39] Théophile de Viau, *Apologie au Roy* (Paris: [n. pub.], 1626), p. 13. Théophile was likely referring to homosexuality, having previously hesitated to describe Voisin's state of mind to the king thus: 'Je dirois à vostre Majesté les secrettes maladies de cet esprit, si ce n'estoit une incivilité criminelle que de vous en entretenir' ('I would tell your Majesty of the secret illnesses of this man's mind, were it not a criminal incivility to discuss them with you', p. 10. See also pp. 22–3). The following account of the conspiracy against Théophile prior to the 1623 trial draws on biographical information given in Adam, *Pensée*, pp. 257–362 and Lachèvre, *Procès*, pp. 113–30.

[40] AN X 2B 1186, confrontation between Théophile and Sageot (21 October 1624), in Lachèvre, *Procès*, p. 464.

[41] Adam, *Pensée*, p. 266. Adam has convincingly demonstrated that Garasse's account of this denunciation (see Charles Nisard, *Mémoires de Garasse (François) de la Compagnie de Jésus* (Paris:

it is far more likely that Sageot was sent to Garasse by Voisin. Garasse instructed Sageot to repeat his claims to the Cardinal de La Rochefoucauld, who had been ordered to survey Théophile's conduct by Louis XIII himself.[42]

After this event, almost certainly due to the collusion between Garasse and Voisin, Théophile was subjected to an increased level of suspicion and surveillance by the *Compagnie de Jésus.* The publication of the *Parnasse satyrique* shortly afterwards therefore provided further ammunition, but not a first motive, for Théophile's enemies to condemn him. A superficial reading of Garasse's *Doctrine curieuse,* which describes the *Parnasse satyrique* as 'le plus horrible que les siecles les plus Payens et les plus desbordez enfanterent jamais' ('the most horrible that the most pagan and excessive centuries ever engendered'), might lead us to believe that this anthology was Garasse's motivation for writing his lengthy text.[43] Yet as early as page seven Garasse attacks Théophile's reputation in particular.[44] Despite being a minor contributor to the *Parnasse,* Théophile is targeted repeatedly over the course of Garasse's text. The index gives seven entries for 'Théophile Autheur du Parnasse Satyrique', and eight entries for 'Un je ne sais qui autrement appelé Viau' ('an I don't know who otherwise called Viau'). As the *Parnasse* set no real precedent in terms of its obscene or irreligious content, why did this text in particular attract Garasse's scorn? The only plausible answer is that rather than the *Parnasse* provoking hostilities towards Théophile, it was in fact the prior conspiracy against Théophile by Garasse and Voisin (and later, Molé) which led to the *Parnasse*'s condemnation.[45] Théophile may have been a convenient scapegoat with which to launch an offensive against excessive freedom of expression and thought. In a similar way, the *Parnasse satyrique* presented an opportunity to justify the persecution of Théophile in particular, rather than inspiring his persecution outright. In this chain of causality—beginning with conspiracies against Théophile, followed by the publication of the *Parnasse,* then the publication of the *Doctrine curieuse,* and finally the poet's arrest—the collusion of Théophile's enemies was of crucial importance. Central to this conspiracy was the

Amyot, 1860), pp. 55–7), according to which Sageot approached Garasse of his own free will, is false (Adam, *Pensée*, pp. 265–8).

[42] The king's instruction to La Rochefoucauld appears to relate to a different incident of which we know very little. This incident led to Théophile's banishment in 1619, as announced in *Le Mercure françois, ou suite de l'histoire de notre temps*, 25 vols (Paris: Jean Richer, 1613–43), V - 1617–19 (1619), p. 65. Though the reasons for Théophile's banishment are unknown, he would later deny having received a royal order to leave France (AN X 2B 1185, first interrogation (22 March 1624), in Lachèvre, *Procès*, p. 370).

[43] Garasse, *Doctrine*, p. 781. See also p. 38, which links atheists and the impious to the *Parnasse satyrique*.

[44] Garasse, *Doctrine*, pp. 7–18.

[45] Notably, the *Parnasse* is not the only source text that Garasse used against Théophile. The *Doctrine curieuse* (and the prosecution at Théophile's subsequent trial) also refers to poems that had appeared in the *Première partie* of Théophile's *Œuvres* (first published by Pierre Billaine in 1621). From the *Première partie*, the *Doctrine curieuse* quotes 'Mon frère je me porte bien', 'Qui voudra pense à des empires', 'Au Roi sur son exil', and 'Je pensais au repos, et ce céleste feu'. This further suggests that the *Parnasse* was not Garasse's sole motivation for writing the *Doctrine curieuse*.

Jesuits' man on the inside of the legal system by which Théophile would be tried: the *procureur général du roi* Mathieu Molé.

Molé's sole modern biography focusses heavily on his later career as *premier président* and his role in the *Fronde*, and says little of his career in the 1620s.[46] Continuing his family's long history of service to the kings of France, he was received as a *conseiller* (councillor) in 1606, a *président aux requêtes* in 1610, before becoming *procureur général du roi* in 1614.[47] Molé had obtained this office following an agreement between his father Édouard and another of Théophile's judges whom we have already seen in the previous chapter: Nicolas de Bellièvre. Bellièvre agreed to vacate the office of *procureur général du roi* in favour of Mathieu Molé, and quickly went on to become *président à mortier* in time to judge Fontanier's case on appeal.[48]

Beyond his functions in the Parlement, Molé was also recognised for his wider role in calming the troubles of the early seventeenth century following the Wars of Religion.[49] Though a man of his position was inevitably involved with a range of legal affairs, it is worth noting that Molé had played a part in another trial for subversive literature shortly before Théophile's arrest. In 1618, the Florentine brothers François and André Sity were tried and executed, along with the Parisian poet Étienne Durand, for having composed and produced seditious texts including the now-lost and potentially apocryphal *Riparographie*. This trial, which Théophile curiously celebrated in his 'Sur la mort de Durand, et des deux Siti frères',[50] was instigated according to the *arrêt* 'à la requête du procureur général du roy, demandeur en crime de lèze-majesté' ('upon the request of the king's attorney general, complainant for the crime of lese-majesty').[51] Unsurprisingly given his role in the Parlement, Molé's interest in crimes related to *lèse-majesté*

[46] Le Baron de Barante, *Parlement et la Fronde: La vie de Mathieu Molé* (Paris: Didier, 1859).

[47] Guillaume Molé had opened the gates of Troyes to Charles VII and Joan of Arc in their journey to crown Charles at Reims in the early fifteenth century, and later drove the English out of Troyes in 1459. Molé's father Édouard was responsible for proposing the preservation of Salic law which allowed Henri IV to be crowned king of France. See Michel Popoff, *Prosopographie des gens du Parlement de Paris (1266–1743)* (Paris: Le Léopard d'or, 2003), p. 29; Barante, *Vie de Molé*, p. 19. The official *lettres de provision* for Molé's entry into the Parlement as a *conseiller* can be found in BNF MS Dupuy 468, p. 54: 'Lettres de provision de l'état de conseiller au Parlement de Paris, octroyées à Mathieu Molé, 9 juillet 1606'. For his nomination to the position of *procureur général* by the king, see BNF MS Cinq Cents de Colbert 147, fol. 189.

[48] BNF MS Cinq Cents de Colbert 147, fol. 189.

[49] Barante, *Vie de Molé*, pp. xii–xiii; Aubert de La Chenaye-Desbois and Jacques Badier, *Dictionnaire de la noblesse*, 19 vols (Paris: Schlesinger frères, 1864), XIII, p. 903.

[50] This poem had first appeared in *Le Second livre des delices de la poesie francaise, ou dernier recueil des plus beaux vers de ce temps* (Paris: Toussaint du Bray, 1620), p. 333.

[51] The *arrêt* is reproduced in Édouard Tricotel, 'Sur un poëte peu connu, Estienne Durand (1590–1618)', *Bulletin du bibliophile et du bibliothécaire*, (October 1859), 656–62 (657–9). The contents of this *arrêt* disprove DeJean's assertion that Durand 'was executed without any type of trial' (DeJean, *Obscenity*, p. 140). I am currently preparing a dedicated study on the trial of the Sity brothers and Durand which elucidates the political stakes in their condemnation.

and subversive literature is also demonstrated in surviving archival sources. For instance, he collated a four-volume archive of 'Procedures and *arrêts* against those accused of the crime of lese-majesty' dating back to 1442,[52] whereas another source belonging to Molé contains a manuscript entitled *De superstitione et Religione*.[53] Molé's memoirs provide early indications of his intolerance towards the Huguenots. Théophile was linked to Protestantism by religion (he was born into a Protestant family, and only converted to Catholicism in 1622), whereas Garasse uses the term *libertin* to refer to Protestants.[54] In a letter dated 24 September 1619, Molé expresses his fears that:

> Messieurs de la religion prétendue réformée ont acquis une maison au faubourg et prétendent y bâtir un hôpital pour loger leurs malades: c'est-à-dire que le prêche est dedans Paris et non plus à sept lieus ni deux de Paris.
>
> Those of the so-called reformed faith have acquired a house in the area and intend to build a hospital there to house their patients. In other words, the Protestant Church is inside of Paris and no longer seven or two leagues from Paris.[55]

Following the siege of Montpellier in October 1622, Louis XIII had ordered Molé to register letters patent granting the Huguenot leader, Henri de Rohan, the duchy of Valois as part of the peace settlement. Uncharacteristically, Molé appears to have deliberately delayed the execution of this order, much to the irritation of the sovereign:

> Nous ne pouvons approuver les difficultés que vous faites de requérir et poursuivre pour nous l'enregistrement, en notre cour de Parlement, de nos lettres patentes octroyées à notre cousin le duc de Rohan pour la jouissance de notre duché de Valois, après tant de commandements que nous vous en avons faits et réitérés.
>
> We cannot approve of the difficulties that you are causing in requesting and following up for us the registering, in our court of the Parlement, of our letters patent granted in favour of our cousin the duc de Rohan for our duchy of Valois, after so many commands that we have given and reiterated to you.[56]

Louis XIII was not the only correspondent anxiously awaiting news from the *procureur général* in October 1622. On 17 October—less than a year before Théophile's trial—Louis Lefèvre de Caumartin wrote his first letter to Molé since

[52] BNF MS Cinq Cents de Colbert 218–221: 'Procédures et arrests contre des accusés de crime de leze-majeste (1440–1652), recueillis par Matthieu Molé.' The fourth tome is concerned exclusively with Concini's execution, whereas the first volume includes the trial of Jean Fontanier (mistakenly dated 1615).

[53] BNF MS Baluze 209, fols 123^r - 125^r.

[54] Van Damme highlights this link between the Huguenots and libertines in explaining the increased intolerance towards *libertinage* during the military campaigns against the Huguenots in the 1620s (Van Damme, *Épreuve*, p. 11).

[55] 'Lettre du Roi à Molé', in Mathieu Molé, *Mémoires de Mathieu Molé*, ed. by Aimé Champollion-Figeac, 4 vols (Paris: Jules Renouard, 1855), I, p. 224.

[56] 'Lettre du Roi au même', in Molé, *Mémoires*, p. 291.

being named keeper of the Seals by the king. Caumartin's request was simple: he asked Molé to nominate judges to serve a rotation in the Chambre de l'Édit, which was created in 1576 to judge cases involving Protestants. Incredibly, Caumartin wrote three letters to Molé between 17 and 30 October with this same request, in which his sense of urgency and panic becomes increasingly evident.[57] It is tempting to speculate that Molé—usually known for his work ethic and his vigilance—may have neglected these administrative duties in order to focus on forming a case against Théophile.[58]

From a legal perspective, Molé's involvement in Théophile's case was threefold. First, he was named as Théophile's legal accuser in the longer *arrêt* for the first trial *in absentia* on 19 August 1623. This was instigated 'sur la plaincte faicte par le Procureur général du roy et livres par luy représentez' ('on the legal complaint made by the king's attorney general and on books provided by him'), whereas Molé is later described as 'demandeur et accusateur' ('plaintiff and accuser') during the early stages of the criminal investigation.[59] Second, since Chancellor Poyet's famous ordinance of Villers-Cotterêts in 1539, each trial was theoretically conceived as a contest between the accused and either a lord or the *procureur général,* and balanced between the *procureur* who asked for justice in the name of the king, and the judge tasked with investigating the criminal case.[60] Third, the concept of a *cas royal*—whereby a crime fell within royal jurisdiction and therefore that of legal representatives of the king's person—had by this time extended to cover all crimes of extreme gravity. These were commonly identified as crimes pertaining to *lèse-majesté* as described earlier, for which Théophile was convicted in his first trial.[61] This evolution coincided with the expansion of the king's interest to include the public interest, thereby allowing the *procureur général* to exercise his competences in matters broadly encroaching into this territory, including Théophile's alleged morally corrupting, irreligious, and obscene poetry sold publicly in the *Parnasse satyrique*.[62]

Molé is habitually described as having waged a personal campaign of persecution against Théophile; a claim first made by the poet himself on 7 June

[57] See BNF MS Cinq Cents de Colbert 6, fols 29–32. The letters have been collated in reverse chronological order.

[58] De La Chenaye-Desbois and Badier, *Dictionnaire de la noblesse*, p. 909.

[59] AN X 2B 342; AN X 2A 217, *arrêt* of 19 August 1623 against Théophile, Berthelot, Colletet, and Frenicle, in Lachèvre, *Procès*, p. 142; AN Y 136, fol. 212, in Lachèvre, *Procès*, p. 211.

[60] Adhémar Esmein, *Histoire de la procédure criminelle en France, et spécialement de la procédure inquisitoire* (Paris: L. Larose et Forcel, 1882), pp. 139–40.

[61] Adhémar Esmein, *Cours élémentaires d'histoire du droit français, à l'usage des étudiants de première année* (Paris: L. Larose, 1898), pp. 420–1. On *lèse-majesté* see Chapter 2, pp. 92–3.

[62] Esmein, *Cours élémentaires*, p. 400; J.H. Shennan, *The Parlement of Paris* (Stroud: Sutton, 1998), p. 43; Fr. Olivier-Martin, *Histoire du droit français des origines à la Révolution* (Paris: Éditions du CNRS, 1984), pp. 330–5, 514. This is another reason why Théophile was tried by the Tournelle and the Grand' Chambre, as the Grand' Chambre judged all cases in which the *procureur général* defended the interests of the king including crimes of *lèse-majesté* (see Mousnier, *Les Institutions*, p. 298).

1624 when he asked his interrogators 'n'avoyr aucun esgard aux accusations dudit procureur général à cause de la hayne particullyère qu'il a contre luy accusé' ('to disregard the accusations made by the attorney general due to the personal hatred he has for him the accused').[63] Although likely true, this claim should be balanced against Molé's legal function within the Parlement with regards to the broad domains of the king's interest and public order.[64]

There is a great deal of evidence demonstrating an alliance between Molé, Voisin, and Garasse against Théophile. Since the assassination of Henri IV in 1610, the Jesuits had sought to gain a tighter control over the University and the Parlement de Paris which, as we saw in Chapter 2, blamed the Jesuits for encouraging doctrines of justifiable regicide.[65] Although Garasse is remembered chiefly for his anti-*libertin* diatribes and his earlier quarrels with religious adversaries such as Pierre Du Moulin, little-known sources attest to his connections to the legal classes beyond his collaboration with Molé. It was Garasse who delivered the eulogy at the funeral of André de Nesmond de Chezac, the *premier président* of the Parlement de Bordeaux and *conseiller* to Henri IV, on 7 January 1617.[66] The lost 1623 edition of Garasse's *Apologie* contained an epistle to Nicolas de Verdun, the *premier président du Parlement de Paris* at Théophile's trial, whose initial openness to the Jesuits gradually gave way to the dominant Gallicanism of the Parlement.[67]

When Sageot eventually retracted his depositions—accusing Garasse and Voisin of deceiving him and breaking the oath of confession—the judges examined Sageot's confession and found it to have been written in two hands, one of which was undoubtedly Garasse's.[68] Furthermore, Garasse makes several allusions in the *Doctrine curieuse* to visits paid to Voisin by one of his former students: Théophile's close friend and likely lover Des Barreaux.[69] Garasse could not have known about the conversations between these two men unless one of them was keeping him informed. He was still actively involved in plots against Théophile at the time of his trial, despite the fact that he was no longer in Paris to witness

[63] AN X 2B 1185, fifth interrogation (7 June 1624), in Lachèvre, *Procès*, p. 434.

[64] Mousnier, *Les Institutions*, p. 370.

[65] See Lachèvre, *Procès*, pp. xxxix–xlvi.

[66] The eulogy appears in the *Remonstrances, ouvertures de palais, et arrestz prononcés en Robes Rouges, par Messire André de Nesmond, etc.* (Poictiers: A. Mesnier, 1617), pp. 1–26.

[67] Lachèvre, *Procès*, p. 276. The existence of two editions of the *Apologie* is alluded to in [Antoine Rémy], *Défense pour Estienne Pasquier vivant conseiller du Roy, et son Avocat Général en la Chambre des Comptes de Paris, contre les impostures et Calomnies de François Garasse* (Paris: Th. La Ruelle, 1624), pp. 42, 490.

[68] Sageot retracted his statements at some point between April and May 1625 (see Lachèvre, *Procès*, pp. 481–2). Confronted with his own handwriting in Sageot's written statement, Garasse claimed to have merely helped the elderly Cardinal de La Rochefoucauld with the task of writing (Garasse, *Mémoires*, pp. 76).

[69] An account of Des Barreaux's numerous meetings with his former tutor, the questions he asked Voisin, and the descriptions of these given in the *Doctrine curieuse* are detailed in Adam, *Pensée*, pp. 341–2.

events personally.[70] In a letter addressed to Molé on 6 November 1623, Garasse suggests specific poems for the Parlement to use to incriminate Théophile and the resultant charges that could be brought against him.[71] Many of these questions, repeated in Molé's own memoirs, were reproduced with little or no modification during the poet's trial.[72] Garasse was still actively examining Théophile's literary output, as his correspondence to Molé refers to three of Théophile's texts printed after both the *Première partie* of his *Œuvres* and the *Doctrine curieuse*.[73] Finally, in the same correspondance Garasse expresses his hatred of Théophile based on what he has learned 'par le fidelle rapport d'une infinité de deposans' ('from the reliable accounts from an infinite number of deponents').[74] The use of the legal term *deposans* is striking, and suggests that Garasse is referring to evidence heard at the trial rather than rumour or private conversations. Considering that at the time of this text's composition (6 November 1623) the trial had only heard the depositions of Jacques Trousset, René Le Blanc, and Gabriel Dange, it is likely that Garasse was aware of a forthcoming 'infinity' of testimony arranged by Voisin and Molé. The claim that the trial of Théophile de Viau took place as a reaction to the publication of the *Parnasse satyrique* is thus in need of nuance if not revision: it was in fact the culmination of a plan that had been years in the making.[75] In this sense, Théophile's trial constitutes far more than a verdict on one man's deportment, his alleged blasphemous speech in private, or his wider literary production. Between 1623 and 1625—a period identified by René Pintard as 'la grande crise' for libertinage—a certain way of writing, of living, and of thinking was also put on trial before the Parlement de Paris through the mouthpiece of Théophile.[76]

[70] Garasse had already been sent to Poitiers as early as 14 November 1623 to distance him from the polemic caused by his *Doctrine curieuse* (see Frédéric Lachèvre, 'Un mémoire inédit de François Garassus adressé à Mathieu Molé, procureur général, pendant le procès de Théophile', *Revue d'Histoire Littéraire de la France*, 18 (1911), 900–40 (905)).

[71] Lachèvre, 'Mémoire'. Garasse begins to give quotations of specific poems, and to expand on their blasphemous implications, on p. 929.

[72] See the *projet d'interrogatoire* in Molé, *Mémoires*, pp. 295–315. Due to the significance of variants and annotations not included in the *Mémoires*, this chapter will quote the original manuscript from BNF MS Cinq Cents de Colbert 2.

[73] These are Théophile's 'Première journée' and 'Cher Isis, tes beautés' (from the *Seconde partie* of Théophile's *Œuvres*, first published in May 1623); and the 'Plainte de Théophile à son amis Tircis', which was first published in pamphlet form after the poet's imprisonment in September 1623, roughly one month after the publication of the *Doctrine curieuse*.

[74] Lachèvre, 'Mémoire', 926.

[75] Such is the view expressed in Georges Mongrédien, *La Vie littéraire au XVIIe siècle* (Paris: Éditions Jules Tallandier, 1947), p. 102. Rather, the *Parnasse* was the pretext for Théophile's trial, which was in turn catalysed by Garasse's publication, as described in Michèle Rosellini, 'Le libertinage du roman comique à l'épreuve du procès de Théophile de Viau', in *Libertinism and Literature in Seventeenth-century France*, ed. by Richard G. Hodgson (Tübingen: Narr, 2009), pp. 37–69 (p. 39). Jeanneret ponders whether the *Parnasse satyrique* was the cause or catalyst for Théophile's trial, but stops short of a conclusion (*L'Éros rebelle*, p. 124).

[76] René Pintard, *Le Libertinage érudit dans la première moitié du XVIIe siècle* (Geneva: Slatkine, 2000),

As these conspiracies came to a head, Théophile remained in hiding, penning his *Maison de Sylvie* from the tranquil gardens of Montmorency's residence at Chantilly. Once his whereabouts had been discovered, Théophile began his slow journey into exile on 26 August, arriving at Le Catelet—a commune close to the northern border some fifty miles east of Amiens and roughly twelve miles north of Saint-Quentin—on 2 September. The authorities became aware of his location and were able to arrest him on 17 September in Le Catelet. He was then taken to the Paris Conciergerie prison on 28 September where he awaited his second, monumental trial in person, which began on 4 October 1623. Théophile would later paint a stark picture of his incarceration:

> Je n'y avois de la clarté que d'une petite chandelle à chaque repas; le jour y esclaire si peu qu'on ne sçauroit discerner la voûte d'avec le plancher, ny la fenestre d'avec la porte. Je n'y ai jamais eu de feu: aussi la vapeur de moindre charbon, n'ayant là dedans par où s'exhaler, m'eust esté du poison. Mon lict était de telle disposition que l'humidité de l'assiette et la pourriture de la paille y engendroit des vers et autres animaux qu'il me falloit escraser à toute heure.
>
> I had no other light than a little candle with each meal; there was so little daylight shining in that one could not tell the vault from the floor, nor the window from the door. I never had a fire, whereas the smoke from burning the smallest piece of coal, with nowhere to escape from the room, would have poisoned me. My bed was arranged in such a way that the humidity of its base and the rotten straw attracted worms and other animals that I had constantly had to squash.[77]

Figure 5.2 shows the *registre d'écrou* recording Théophile's arrival at the Conciergerie, and is published here for the first time. The right-hand column details the arrival of Théophile and 'Ysaac La Pause son serviteur' ('Isaac La Pause his servant') at the Conciergierie on 28 September 1623.[78] The left-hand column, which details the fate of the Conciergerie's prisoners, provides two new details. First, in recording Théophile's lifelong banishment on 1 September 1625 (despite being found innocent of the charges against him), it adds that the *arrêt* was read aloud by 'Mr Pierre Caluze' in order to make the verdict official. More significantly, it reveals that La Pause was not released a matter of days after his incarceration as Lachèvre surmises.[79] Instead, he remained imprisoned for almost

---

p. 34. The trials of Vanini, Fontanier, and Théophile also constituted a crisis according to J.S. Spink, *French Free-thought from Gassendi to Voltaire* (London: The Athlone Press, 1960), pp. 5, 27–47. For Françoise Charles-Daubert, Théophile's trial instigated a crisis between libertine thought and the Church (Françoise Charles-Daubert, 'La Bible des Libertins', in *Le Grand Siècle et la Bible*, ed. by Jean-Robert Armogathe (Paris: Beauchesne, 1989), pp. 667–89 (pp. 670, 676)).

[77] Théophile, *Apologie au Roy*, p. 16

[78] According to Théophile, this was no small event in the capital: 'estant arrivé à la Conciergerie, dont la presse du peuple m'empeschoit l'entrée' ('having arrived at the Conciergerie, where the jostling of the crowds prevented me from entering': *Apologie au Roy*, p. 15).

[79] Lachèvre, *Procès*, p. 197, note 1.

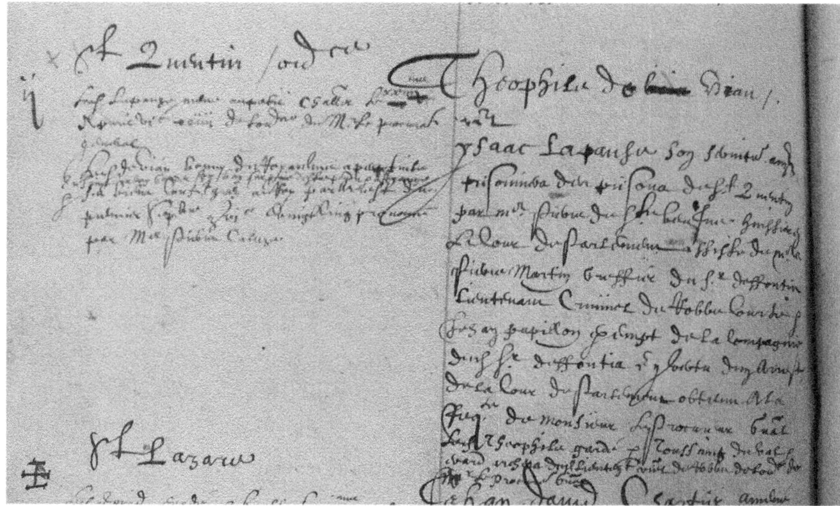

Figure 5.2 APP AB 26: *Registre d'écrou de la Conciergerie* (register of incarceration), fol. 158[r], showing the imprisonment of 'Theophile de Viau et Ysaac La Pause son serviteur' (28 September 1623). By permission of the Archives de la Préfecture de Police.

seven months, after which he was sent to the Petit Châtelet on 24 April 1624 'de l'ordonnance de Monsieur le procureur général' ('following an ordinance by the king's attorney general').

This apparently minor detail invites a number of questions. Why did La Pause remain in prison for so long? He did not write any incriminating texts, he was not mentioned in the *arrêt* for Théophile's arrest, and he did not participate in the trial proceedings. Moreover, why was he eventually transferred from the Conciergerie on Molé's orders? The answer can be found in what at first appears to be a mere coincidence: La Pause was released on the same day that two witnesses at Théophile's trial were interrogated (Claude d'Anisy and Pierre Rocolet, 24 April 1624). This correlation, along with a separate finding which we will explore later, has led me to discover that Lachèvre's dossier of interrogations is incomplete, and that Théophile's servant was in fact a participant in his master's trial.[80] La Pause's four-page interrogation from 24 April 1624 shows that he was a 'parent de Théophile poursuivy' ('a relative of Théophile the pursued') and a fellow native of Clairac (Figure 5.3).[81] His interrogation provided evasively vague answers to the questions put to him in order to deny his own involvement, whilst also starving his sole interrogator—Jacques Pinon—of any new incriminating information

[80] For the separate archival find which led to my discovery of La Pause's testimony, see pp. 322–6.

[81] AN X 2B 1185, interrogation of Isaac La Pause (24 April 1624). I am extremely grateful to Robin Briggs for helping me to transcribe the particularly difficult hand in this document.

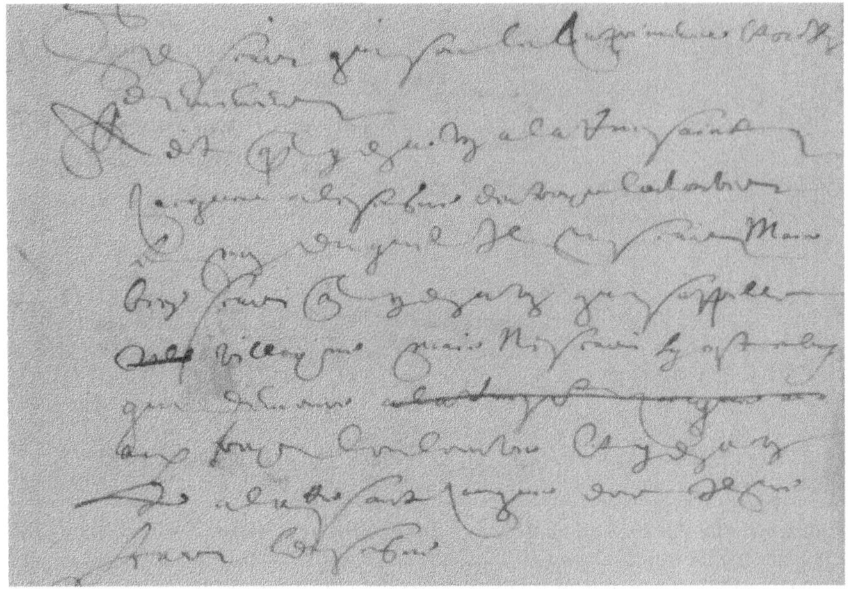

Figure 5.3 AN X 2B 1185: part of the lost interrogation of Isaac La Pause (24 April 1624). Here, La Pause is asked to give the names and locations of those responsible for printing Théophile's 'livres de poeysies' ('books of poetry'), to which he responds that he can only vaguely remember their emblems ('enseignes'), but not their names. For a transcription of this passage, see p. 325.

against his master. As such, his testimony contributes little to our understanding of how Théophile's poems or sexual relations were examined by the Parlement. It does, however, provide valuable new information on Théophile's arrest found neither in the poet's *Apologie au roy* nor in two contemporary pamphlets which describe the event.[82]

Théophile's movements from Chantilly on 26 August, up to his arrest in Le Catelet on 17 September, were previously unclear. Adam suggests that he slowly progressed north, stopping briefly at properties owned by those loyal to Montmorency and potentially at the residence of one of his patrons, Liancourt. Lachèvre focusses less on the journey than the destination, and proposes that Théophile hid on a farm on the outskirts of Le Catelet as of 2 September.[83] The *Procès-verbal de Théophile* recounts how on 16 September a certain Louis

[82] The arrest is recounted in *La Prise de Théophile par un prévost des maréchaux dans la citadelle du Castellet en Picardie, amené prisonnier en la Conciergerie du Palais, le jeudi 28 de ce mois* (Paris: Antoine Vitray, 1623); and the *Procès-verbal de l'emprisonnement de Théophile, présenté à la cour par le prévost des mareschaux* (Paris: Pierre Bamier, 1623). See Lachèvre, *Procès*, pp. 199–203.

[83] Adam, *Pensée*, p. 359; Lachèvre, *Procès*, p. 191.

Brocard, a resident of the village of Lempire, brought information on the poet's whereabouts to the *lieutenant criminel de robe court de Saint Quentin* Jacques Trousset. Théophile had asked a number of locals whether there was a secluded route to Le Catelet, and planned to avoid detection on the main road by traversing a wood close to Lempire. Having spotted Théophile outside of the village of Bony, Trousset followed him to Le Catelet and made his arrest.[84] By 28 September, Théophile had been taken to the Paris Concergerie to await trial.

La Pause's interrogation finally allows us to pinpoint the location of Théophile's hideout: '[il] partit de Chantilly et ils s'en allerent en une maison du sieur duc d'Aluin appellée Le Ronssoy en Picardie' ('he left Chantilly and they both went to a house belonging to the duc d'Aluin called Le Ronssoy in Picardie').[85] One of Théophile's protectors, Henri de Nogaret, seigneur de la Valette and duc de Candale, had obtained the title of duc d'Halluin from his marriage to Anne d'Halluin. By 1624, however, this marriage had been annulled and Anne had married Charles de Schomberg. As noble titles could not be lost due to divorce, there were unhelpfully two living ducs d'Halluins at the time of La Pause's interrogation.

Candale was without doubt one of Théophile's protectors and the addressee of several of his poems. However, Théophile had left Candale's entourage in favour of Montmorency in the first half of 1619, whilst Candale's lands were situated close to Toulouse. The Schombergs, on the other hand, could well have owned property some sixty miles north of their Château de Nanteuil in the area surrounding Le Catelet. Théophile's links to the Schombergs, though less evident, date much closer to the time of his arrest. Henri de Schomberg had served as commander of the artillery during the siege of Théophile's native Clairac in July 1623. On Louis XIII's orders, Théophile had attended this siege in order to persuade the inhabitants to surrender. Henri's daughter Anne had married Théophile's protector, Liancourt, in 1620. Henri's son Charles de Schomberg (the 'second' duc d'Halluin) had a long history of frequenting libertine authors. He was the young lord whose nose had suffered at the hands of Tristan L'Hermite during a childhood fistfight as recounted in *Le Page disgracié*, though Tristan would later write an ode celebrating Schomberg's victory at Leucate in 1637.[86] More compellingly, the playwright Alexandre Hardy dedicated the volumes of his *Œuvres* to patrons of his and Théophile's mutual literary circle: Montmorency, 'le duc d'Aluyn' (in 1625), and Liancourt.[87] La Pause's account thus shows that

[84] *Procès-verbal de l'emprisonnement de Théophile*, quoted in Lachèvre, *Procès*, p. 202. Trousset's deposition concurs with this sequence of events.

[85] AN X 2B 1185, interrogation of Isaac La Pause (24 April 1624).

[86] Tristan L'Hermite, *Le Page disgracié*, in *Libertins du XVIIe siècle*, ed. by Jacques Prévot, 2 vols (Paris: Gallimard, Bibliothèque de la Pléiade, 1998), I, pp. 381–595 (pp. 400, 588); 'A Monseigneur Le Mareschal de Schomberg, sur le Combat de Locate', in Tristan L'Hermite, *Les vers heroiques du sieur Tristan L'Hermite* (Paris: Jean Baptiste Loyson and Nicolas Portier, 1648), pp. 97–106.

[87] Adam, *Pensée*, p. 318.

Théophile's relations with Charles de Schomberg duc d'Halluin were closer than scholars have previously realised, to the extent that he offered the poet refuge on his way into exile abroad.

Ronssoy, where La Pause claims to have stayed with Théophile for fourteen or fifteen days, fits perfectly with the information outlined earlier from printed sources. Situated less than a mile south of Lempire and some three miles west of Bony, it was flanked by a sizeable patch of woodland. With no other woods in the area encompassing Lempire and Le Catelet, this was surely the same woodland which Théophile aimed to cross on his meandering route to avoid being recognised on the main road to Le Catelet.[88] Finally, La Pause claims that Trousset:

> pendant troys jours apres la capture dudit Théophile aurait aussy tost poursuivy ledit respondant sans autre subject ny occasion et depuis amené en cette ville et auparavant que ledit Théophile fust arresté iceluy bailla une lettre audit respondant pour prendre audit Sieur duc de Chaune [...] en la ville d'Amiens.
>
> pursued the respondant [La Pause] for three days after Théophile's capture, without other reason or pretext, before bringing him to this city. Before the aforementioned Théophile was arrested, he gave a letter to the respondant to take to the duc de Chaulnes [...] in the city of Amiens.[89]

Honoré d'Albret, duc de Chaulnes was the *lieutenant général du gouvernement de Picardie*, *maréchal de France*, and the brother of Théophile's former protector, the duc de Luynes. Théophile evidently knew that Chaulnes was in Amiens at the time. Furthermore, *lettres monitoires* were published against the poet in this same city over the course of his trial, suggesting that the Parlement was aware that he may have recently visited Amiens. La Pause's remarks thus allow us to propose the following plausible hypothesis. Théophile headed north from Montmorency's residence at Chantilly to meet Chaulnes in Amiens or the surrounding area—a route which would notably have taken him through Liancourt—before turning east towards Ronssoy. Rather than taking the north-east road leading to Le Catelet from the south, Théophile opted to travel either through the bois de Ronssoy or from this general direction, passing Lempire. The final leg of his journey saw him approaching Le Catelet through countryside from the west, during which he was recognised, followed to Le Catelet, and arrested. Although Théophile did not make it across the border, La Pause reveals that his master benefitted from

[88] Adam was therefore correct in assuming that Théophile's rural hideout was not on the road between Saint-Quentin and Le Catelet, but towards the west on the road between Hervilly and Le Catelet (Adam, *Pensée*, p. 359). The bois de Ronssoy is mapped alongside Bony in Guillaume Sanson, *Le comté d'Artois suivant qu'il est presentement divisé en François et Espagnol, dressé sur les Memoires les plus nouveaux* (Paris: H. Jaillot, 1674), and was still included on the *Carte de Cassini* in 1758. Rather than taking the road leading to Le Catelet, Théophile seems to have taken a route through the bois de Ronssoy, past Lempire, before approaching Le Catelet from the west.

[89] AN X 2B 1185, interrogation of Isaac La Pause (24 April 1624).

refuge offered by a number of patrons. Moreover, he was clearly corresponding with these in order to prepare either for his eventual return to France, or for his trial in the event of his arrest. Whereas Théophile's journey into exile has hitherto been seen as a period of nonchalant dithering, his final weeks of freedom in fact comprised a number of strategic manoeuvres.

Once Théophile had been imprisoned at the Conciergerie, two strands of preparations were made for his trial at the Parlement de Paris. On the one hand, the gathering of initial witnesses and evidence—the *instruction*—was conducted by the *commissaires* who would also interrogate the accused. On the other hand, Molé, who had initiated the trial proceedings against Théophile, busied himself by reading Théophile's works and by drafting questions for his two *commissaires* to put to Théophile in the opening interrogations. Before turning to the trial hearings, let us first move from those involved in collusions against the poet to a brief consideration of Théophile's first legal opponents during the *instruction* of his case.

THÉOPHILE'S INTERROGATORS

Given the supremacy and renown of the Parlement de Paris in the legal and political spheres, there is an exceptional wealth of surviving documentation on its magistrates. Théophile was initially investigated by the *commissaires* André Charton and Gabriel Damours who were responsible for recording the first witness statements. Damours was replaced by Jacques Pinon on 23 November 1623 for unknown reasons, though possibly due to the system of rotation in the Tournelle. Charton died in 1623, and had been replaced by François de Verthamon on 11 October 1623 after having conducted only one witness interrogation. The main *commissaires*, then, and the only ones to have interrogated the poet, were Pinon and Verthamon. The elder of Théophile's two interrogators, Jacques Pinon, was an experienced magistrate who had been received as a *conseiller* in the enquêtes chamber on 28 June 1584, before entering the Grand' Chambre on 13 August 1618.[90] He was also a poet. According to Pierre Bayle, Pinon was 'un grand juge de toutes choses' ('a great judge of all things'), whose poetry (published in 1615 and 1630) was well received in its time.[91] Writing after the fact, Moréri further asserts that Pinon:

[90] Jean Baptiste De L'Hermite-Souliers and François Blanchard, *Les eloges de tous les premiers presidens du Parlement de Paris* (Paris: Cardin Besongne, 1645), p. 101; Popoff, *Prosopographie*: 1991.

[91] Pierre Bayle, *Dictionnaire historique et critique*, 16 vols (Paris: Desoer, 1820–4), 12 (1820), p. 94. The Jacques Pinon who instructed Théophile's trial, and who died doyen of the Parlement on 25 April 1641, should not be confused with his son: another Latin poet and *conseiller* unhelpfully named Jacques Pinon.

> se distingua beaucoup dans cette charge par ses lumieres et son intégrité. [...] On voit par les éloges que les sçavans de son temps lui ont donné, et par ses poësies, surtout par son poëme *De anno Romano*, et le commentaire en prose qui l'accompagne, qu'il avoit beaucoup d'érudition.
>
> distinguished himself greatly in this role by his understanding and his integrity. [...] Both the praise offered to him by the learned men of his time, and his poetry—especially his poem *De anno Romano*, and the prose commentary that accompanies it—show that he was a man of great erudition.[92]

Moréri also claims that one of his poems—'Jacobi Pinonis senatoris Parisiensis de anno Romano carmen'—was dedicated to Louis XIII, who knew Pinon and regarded him highly.[93] In Pinon, then, Théophile faced an older, experienced magistrate who potentially enjoyed the favour of the king and his first minister. At the same time, Pinon was a fellow poet who even found time to write at least two poems during the course of Théophile's trial.[94]

The second interrogator, François de Verthamon, has suffered from a case of mistaken identity. In his edition of Marin Mersenne's letters, Cornelis de Waard claims that Verthamon, seigneur de Bréau and a *conseiller* in the Parlement since 17 August 1618, was the same man involved in Théophile's trial.[95] The junior status of this *conseiller* compared to Pinon would seem to adhere to the parliamentary norm of an *instruction* being conducted by a younger and older magistrate. However, it should be remembered that despite the magistrates' proud observance of the Parlement's traditions, such technicalities were not always observed with equal stringency in practice. The selection of the *commissaires* to investigate Théophile's case proves this. His second interrogator was in fact François de Verthamon sieur du Mas-du-Puy, the *father* of François de Verthamon seigneur de Bréau identified by De Waard. Théophile tells us so in his poem addressed to Verthamon. An unjustly overlooked poem combining the melancholic beauty of the 'Maison de Sylvie' and the alchemical synaesthesia of 'Un corbeau devant moi croasse', the text in question is entitled 'Remontrance de Théophile à Monsieur de Verthamont conseiller en la Grand-chambre'. Having only been admitted as a *conseiller* in 1618, François de Verthamon the son could not have risen to the ranks of the Grand' Chambre, the most senior chamber of the Parlement, by 1623. At this time, he was a *conseiller*

[92] Louis Moréri, *Nouveau supplément au grand dictionnaire historique, généalogique, géographique, etc.*, 2 vols (Paris: Jacques Vincent and others, 1749), II, p. 276. The prose commentary, Moréri continues, 'est rempli d'érudition, et montre beaucoup de lecture' ('is filled with erudition and demonstrates a large amount of reading').

[93] Moréri, *Nouveau supplement*, p. 277.

[94] A poem addressed to Richelieu in 1624, and a consolation to Bochard de Champigny on the death of his wife in 1625. The poem to Richelieu—'Ad illustrissimum virum Harmandum Plessaeum cardinalem Richelaeum'—can be found in BNF MS Baluze 326, fol. 98.

[95] See Marin Mersenne, *Correspondance du P. Marin Mersenne, religieux Minime*, ed. by Cornelis de Waard, 17 vols (Paris: Presses Universitaires de France, 1945), I (1617–27), p. 165.

in the fourth Chambre des Enquêtes. He would go on to become a *maistre des requestes* in 1626, but would never join the ranks of the Grand' Chambre. His father, however, was received as a *conseiller* on 17 August 1588, and joined the Grand' Chambre less than a year before the start of Théophile's trial on 18 February 1623.[96]

It seems highly unlikely that Théophile would have mistaken the son for the father in addressing his poem to one of his interrogators, especially given the influence he had over the poet's treatment. Théophile's complaint that 'l'an a fait plus de la moitié / Que tous les jours votre pitié / Me doit faire changer de place' ('It has been more than half a year / Since every day, your pity / Should have made me change place'), links the addressee directly to the trial, ruling out the possibility that he is appealing to the father to influence his son's lines of interrogation.[97] Finally, this theory is strengthened when compared to the two *conseillers* who were initially entrusted with the instruction, whose identities are happily less complicated to ascertain. Gabriel Damours was admitted as a *conseiller* in 1594 whilst the Parlement resided at Tours, and died in 1632. The other *commissaire* André Charton was received as a *conseiller* in 1587—the same year as one of Théophile's judges, Ursin Durant—and died in 1623.[98] The original pairing of Théophile's *commissaires* did not therefore respect the theoretical requirement for a junior and significantly more senior judge to carry out an *instruction*, and neither did the pairing of Verthamon and Pinon.

Verthamon's service to the Parlement had a colourful history. He had stayed in Paris to serve in the Parlement of the Catholic League—allegedly under duress—though it should be acknowledged that this was not a simple decision between *ligueur* or *politique* sympathies.[99] Whereas most magistrates were reintegrated into a single Parisian parlement 'sans enquête ni délai' ('immediately and without investigation'), Verthamon's actions during the time of the League were not the stuff of heroic legend, and led to an investigation into his conduct lasting roughly a year. Verthamon claimed that he had managed to escape Paris in disguise, before heading first to Dieppe and then to Tours on 2 December 1589. Upon investigation, however, evidence was uncovered proving that he had not dutifully headed straight to the king's parlement residing at Tours, but had gone to Châteaudun, and from Dieppe

[96] De L'Hermite-Souliers and Blanchard, *Les eloges*, p. 119; Popoff, *Prosopographie*, p. 2448. A number of the Verthamon family's legal manuscripts can be found in BNF MS NAF 2103–477 and BNF MS NAF 122.

[97] Théophile, *Œuvres*, p. 297.

[98] De L'Hermite-Souliers and Blanchard, *Les eloges*, p. 104. His name is often given as 'Charreton' in later sources.

[99] As Michel De Waele has convincingly argued, magistrates often saw the Parlement de Paris as synonymous with the king's authority and as an authority in its own right. Certain magistrates therefore stayed in Paris in order to defend the French crown, rather than abandon their duty and their sovereign by fleeing the battlefield of Paris. See Michel De Waele, *Les Relations entre le Parlement de Paris et Henri IV* (Paris: Publisud, 2006), pp. 158–64.

to Limoges rather than to Tours.[100] Yet by 1596 all appears to have been forgiven. When Henri IV arranged the Grands Jours at Lyon from 16 August to 10 November of that year—where the backlog of cases accrued outside of the Parlement de Paris's jurisdiction during the Wars of Religion were finally dealt with—Verthamon was one of the 'honnestes hommes et habilles' ('honourable and adept men') despatched from the Parlement de Paris to dispense the king's justice.[101] The men selected to interrogate Théophile were therefore two experienced judges and firm Catholics. The poet himself praised his interrogators' professionalism and impartiality to the king: 'messieurs mes Commissaires estoient bien aises que j'evitasse les surprises, et se monstrerent tousjours aussi prompts à me justifier qu'à me convaincre' ('my interrogators were pleased to see that I avoided making mistakes, and they always showed themselves to be just as quick to defend me as to convict me').[102]

In examining Théophile's literary engagement with the trial—both through his poetry and through texts written about the trial following his release—a striking disparity emerges. At no point did Théophile attempt to engage with Pinon through his writing beyond his implicit inclusion in texts addressed to the Parlement as a whole. Nor did he leave any comment on Pinon's actions during the trial exchanges apart from the first interrogation, in which Pinon reproached Théophile for his conversion to Catholicism: 'Monsieur de Pinon me remonstra que j'avois mal fait mon profit des instructions de ces bons Peres, et que j'estois tenu pour un homme qui ne croyoit autre Dieu que la nature' ('Mr de Pinon reproached me for having made little use of my education at the hands of these good priests, and that I was known for being a man who did not believe in any other God than nature').[103] Verthamon and the *premier président du Parlement de Paris* Nicolas de Verdun, on the other hand, were both addressed directly in Théophile's prison poetry. Verdun clearly held obvious sway in the Parlement and its deliberations over the final verdict. The decision to address a poem to Verthamon and not to Pinon, however, cannot be explained so easily.

There is one small clue in Théophile's *Apologie au Roy*. Here, Théophile recalls a confrontation with Claude d'Anisy on 21 October 1624. A lawyer with a far from convincing tale to tell the court, d'Anisy was not taken terribly seriously by Verthamon if Théophile is to be believed: '[Il] se fit luy mesme tant de reproches, et se couppa si souvent, que Monsieur de Verthamond ne se peut tenir de rire de

[100] See Édouard Maugis, *Histoire du parlement de Paris: De l'avènement des rois Valois à la mort d'Henri IV*, 3 vols (Paris: Auguste Picard, 1916), III, p. 289.

[101] *Journal de Nicolas-Edouard Olier, conseiller au Parlement 1593–1602* (Paris: Henri Menu, 1876), p. 25. See also Fayard, *Aperçu historique*, pp. 460–1.

[102] Théophile, *Apologie au Roy*, p. 20.

[103] Théophile, *Apologie au Roy*, p. 19. Théophile's recollection closely matches the trial records: 'remonstré qu'il a mal fait son prouffict de l'instruction qu'il peult avoyr recue desditz Pères' ('reproached for having made little use of the education that he might have received from the aforementioned priests': AN X 2B 1185, first interrogation (22 March 1624), in Lachèvre, *Procès*, p. 370).

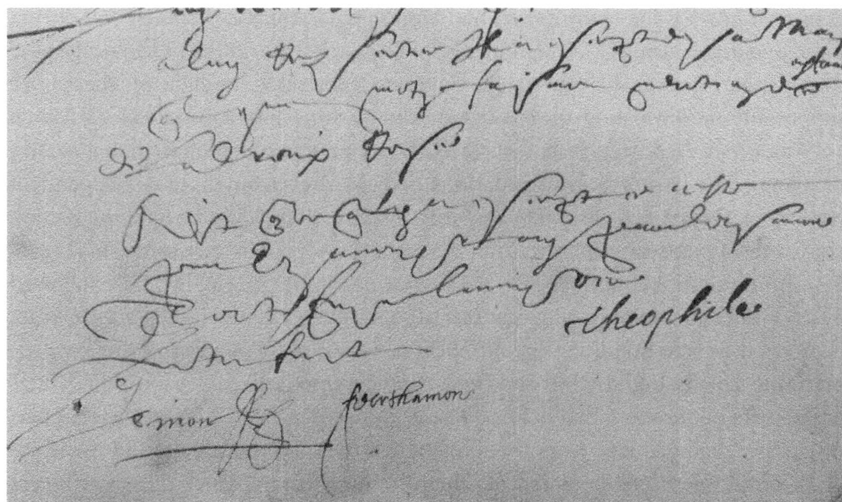

Figure 5.4 AN X 2B 1185: sixth interrogation (15 June 1624), signed by Jacques Pinon, François de Verthamon, and Théophile.

ses absurditez' ('he provided so many *reproches* against himself, and he tripped over his own words so often, that Mr Verthamon could not stop himself from laughing at his absurdities').[104] Could Théophile have interpreted this incident as a sign that Verthamon was a weak link to be exploited, and had a similar idea crossed his mind as a result of an earlier hearing, leading him to pen his poem to Verthamon in March 1624?[105] Although a lack of further evidence does not permit a definitive answer, the 'Remontrances de Théophile à Monsieur de Verthamon', the notes of sympathy Théophile observed from this magistrate, and the fact that Verthamon was not selected to judge the case in the final deliberation, all suggest that Théophile saw Verthamon as the more sympathetic of his two interrogators.

THE EARLY INTERROGATIONS: A TRIAL FOR OBSCENITY OR PHILOSOPHY?

Pinon and Verthamon did not have free rein to interrogate Théophile as they saw fit in the early hearings. Rather, their line of questioning was the final link in a chain of textual preparation. Garasse's letter to Molé and his *Doctrine curieuse* allowed the *procureur général* to complete a draft of questions which has survived in manuscript form. The extreme similarity between this document and questions put to the poet

104 Théophile, *Apologie au Roy*, p. 22.
105 Lachèvre convincingly dates this poem to the first half of March 1624 in *Procès*, p. 347.

demonstrates that the *commissaires* had Molé's preparations at their disposal during these opening hearings.[106] The influence of Garasse's texts on the *procureur général* should not, however, be overstated. Garasse's letter refers to eight of Théophile's supposedly incriminating texts, whereas the opening interrogation of 22 March 1624 alone covered twenty-six texts. Molé was therefore much more than a passive recipient of the Jesuit's recommendations, and also drew from his own independent reading of Théophile's works. Divided into three sections, with the opening section consisting of three columns, this draft is a veritable work of literary criticism (Figure 5.2). In the central column, Molé gives questions to be put to Théophile followed by a considerable number of quotations from his poetry. In the right-hand column, he notes the corresponding page numbers in Théophile's *Œuvres* and the *Parnasse satyrique*. Finally, both the left and right-hand columns give Molé's critical readings of the texts in question, that is to say the criminal ideas which he, inspired in part by Garasse, had deduced from them. Although the *commissaires* did not make use of all of the questions prepared for them by Molé, those which were used were replicated almost exactly, as the following comparison demonstrates:[107]

> Si c'est traiter de l'Imortalité [sic] de l'ame que descrire que les ames ont esté auparavant le corps, et qu'il devoit sçavoir que c'est l'Erreur d'Origène condamné par l'Eglise. Que mettre en avant que les ames apres leur separation d'avec le corps, si elles ont été méchantes, s'en vont en des d'animaux, et qu'il devoit sçavoir que c'est l'erreur de Pythagore, condamné par la commune créance de l'Esglise.
>
> If it is treating the theme of the immortality of the soul to state that souls existed before [their] bodies, and that he should know that this is the error for which Origen was condemned by the Church. That to put forward that once they are separated from the body, those souls which have been wicked go into animals, and that he should know that this is Pythagoras's error, condemned by the common belief of the Church.[108]
>
> d'avoir escript que les âmes ont esté auparavant les corps, qui est une erreur d'Origène condamnée par l'Esglize et qu'après leur séparation d'avec le corps, sy elles ont esté meschantes, elles vont au corps des animaux suivant l'erreur de Pitagore aussy condamnée par la creance de l'Esglize.
>
> having written that souls existed before [their] bodies, which is an error for which Origen was condemned by the Church and that after their separation from the body, if they have been wicked, they go into the bodies of animals following Pythagoras's error, also condemned by the belief of the Church.[109]

[106] BNF MS Cinq Cents de Colbert 2, fols. 94–105. Many of Garasse's assertions in his letter to Molé were reproduced without alteration in his *Apologie*.
[107] Lachèvre provides those questions put to Théophile which had appeared in Molé's draft in italics. He also gives the questions drafted by Molé which were not used at trial, 'volontairement ou par lassitude' ('intentionally or out of weariness'), in a separate section. See Lachèvre, *Procès*, pp. 402–6.
[108] BNF MS Cinq Cents de Colbert 2, fol. 95^{r}.
[109] AN X 2B 1185, first interrogation (22 March 1624), in Lachèvre, *Procès*, p. 374.

The questions and corresponding quotations are followed by a series of nine numbered 'propositions' and 'propositions meslees' ('mixed propositions') in Molé's manuscript. These give a wider perspective of Théophile's beliefs which Molé claims to have extrapolated from the texts, followed by his own brief observations. When read together, these summaries allow us to shed new light on the initial prosecution strategies of the *procureur général*.

Théophile's trial is understandably synonymous with early modern obscenity. It appears to have been triggered by the appearance of an obscene poem attributed to Théophile in the *Parnasse satyrique*, whereas Garasse certainly accuses the poet of obscenity and much more besides. The initial preparations in Molé's manuscript, however, tell a different story. The fourth proposition focusses on Théophile's *Première journée*, and links his appreciation of beautiful things exciting the senses to the sodomitic ending to his sonnet in the *Parnasse satyrique*. In his letter to Molé, Garasse had suggested that Théophile's passion for beautiful things was 'impie, et opposée directement à l'Evangile de Jésus-Christ, qui nous commande de brider nostre vue de peur de voir une femme par les yeux de convoytise' ('impious, and directly against the Gospel of Christ, which tells us to restrain our gaze through fear of seeing a woman through covetous eyes').[110] It was Molé, however, perhaps inspired by Garasse's wider condemnation of Théophile's sonnet, who first introduced the link between the *Première journée* and sodomy, describing Théophile's indulgence of the senses as a 'proposition d'autant plus abominable, que le vœu de Sodomie qu'a fait cet autheur au Parnasse' ('an even more abominable proposition than the vow to commit sodomy that this author made in the *Parnasse*').[111] Notably, Théophile's supposed vow to be the active partner in such sexual encounters situated him alongside the majority of those condemned for sodomy by the Parlement. Active sexual partners were depicted as the abusers, whilst passive homosexual partners often defended themselves as victims of sexual abuse—a power dynamic enforced by the fact that the passive partner was almost always the younger participant.[112]

This proposition is the one which most strongly suggests a trial for obscenity or sexual deviance, though the *commissaires* notably omitted the link made by Molé to sodomy and the *Parnasse satyrique* entirely.[113] However, this association

[110] Lachèvre, *Mémoire*, pp. 929–30. 'Impie' is replaced by 'brutale' in [François Garasse], *Apologie du pere François Garassus, de la Compagnie de Jésus, pour son Livre contre les Atheistes & Libertins de nostre siecle* (Paris: Sebastien Chappelet, 1624), p. 242.

[111] BNF MS Cinq Cents de Colbert 2, fol. 102v. Responding to Garasse, Théophile offered a defence of his text in [Théophile de Viau], *Apologie de Théophile* (Paris: [n. pub.], 1624), pp. 13–15.

[112] See Tom Hamilton, 'Sodomy and Criminal Justice in the Parlement of Paris: c.1540–c.1700', *Journal of the History of Sexuality*, 29: 3 (2020), 303–34, (323). Given the strong correlation between age and criminal homosexual dominance in trials for sodomy, it is worth adding that Théophile was ten years older than his likely lover Jacques Vallée Des Barreaux, who was twenty-three at the time of Théophile's arrest.

[113] See AN X 2B 1185, second interrogation (26 March 1624), in Lachèvre, *Procès*, p. 389.

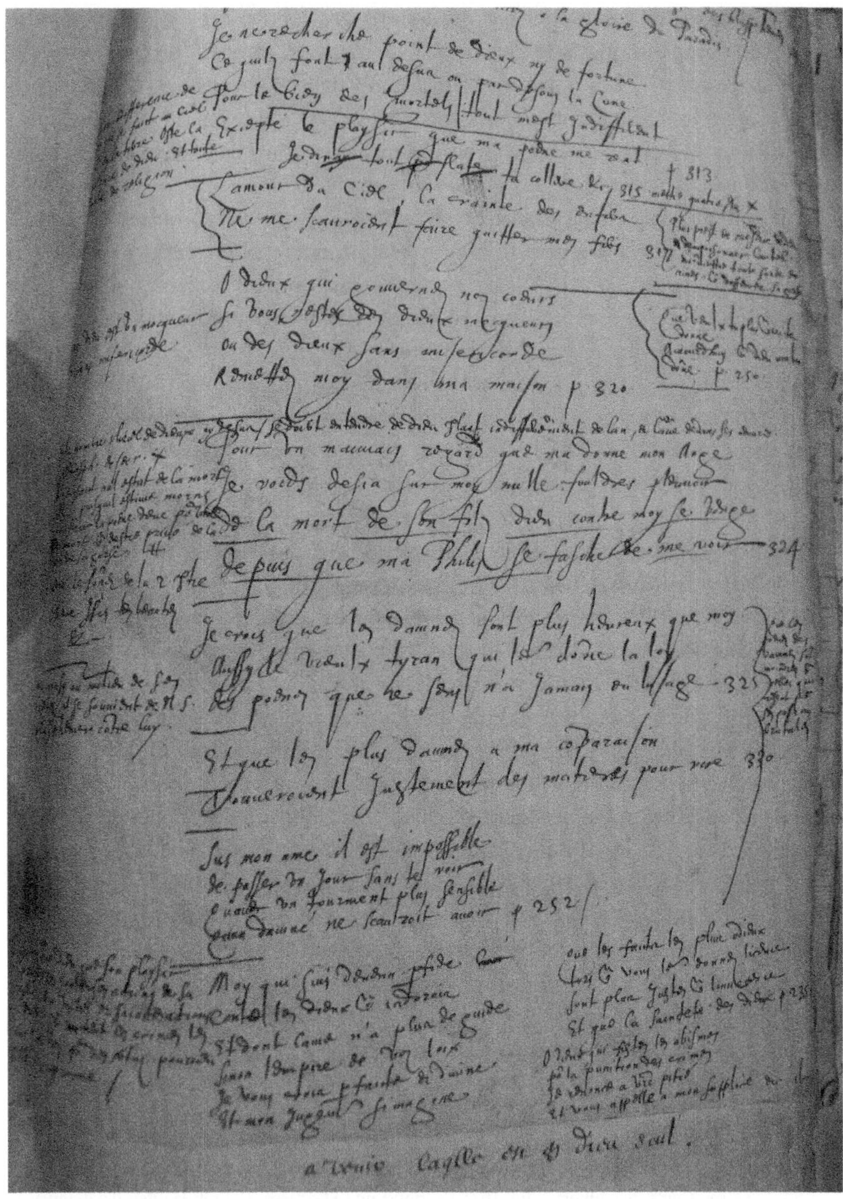

Figure 5.5 BNF MS Cinq Cents de Colbert 2, fol. 97r: Molé's draft of questions to be asked at Théophile's trial.

is in fact an exception rather than the rule in Molé's questions. Notwithstanding the obvious overlap between the obscene and the irreligious, seven of Molé's nine propositions associate Théophile with irreligion rather than obscenity, as do eleven of the fifteen *propositions meslees* at the end of the text. This primary objective is further evidenced by the prominent place of Théophile's *Traicté de l'immortalité de l'âme* and his *Première journée* in these questions and propositions. Molé's preparations thus explored new lines of inquiry beyond the undeniable role of the *Parnasse satyrique* as an obscene catalyst for Théophile's arrest. The minor variants found throughout Garasse's and Molé's texts also suggest a predominant concern with intellectual questions rather than with obscenity, supporting Rosellini's claim that Molé considered Théophile's bawdy poetry to be insufficient proof of his atheism.[114] Referring to Théophile's assertion in his *Première journée* that the soul is subject to the desires of the body, Garasse suggests to Molé that:

> Il commet non seulement une hérésie mais prononce un dogme d'impiété lorsqu'il dit *que les temperamens du corps forcent les mouvemens de l'ame* quoy qu'on puisse faire, c'est-à-dire en bon discours que qui est par son tempérament sujet à l'yvrognerie ou à l'impudicité, il est forcé de suivre ses appétits [...] voylà une proposition très abominable et prise formellement de l'escole d'Epicure.

> He not only commits heresy but pronounces impious dogma when he says *that the temperaments of the body force the movements of the soul* no matter what we do, that is to say that whoever is of the temperament to be subject to drunkenness or to impudicity is forced to follow his appetites [...] this is a most abominable proposition taken straight from the school of Epicurus.[115]

Remarkably, Molé modifies this accusation by removing the references to drunkenness, impudicity, appetites, and the association with Epicurus. In their place, and independent of Garasse's recommendations, he stresses that there is no amount of reason, will or discourse—all philosophically loaded terms—which can prevent such an obedience to one's desires, as well as adding a direct reference to God:

> Que puisque le tempérament du Corps force absolument les mouvements de nostre ame, et nos passions nous emportent si puissamment là où elles veulent, qu'il n'y a aucun discours qui puisse estre opposé à ceste necessité, ny aucun effort de raison ny de volonté qui puisse y résister, non plus qu'aux accès d'une fièvre, puisque nostre naissance nous fait voir si clairement que tant s'en faut que nostre Ame tienne de Dieu comme on dit, en son essence, qu'au contraire, nous naissons et sommes encore plus bas que les bestes ...

114 Michèle Rosellini, 'Théophile devant ses juges ou l'œuvre en procès', *L'immoralité littéraire et ses juges*, ed. by Jean-Baptiste Amadieu (Paris: Hermann, 2019), pp. 43–66 (pp. 52, 55).

115 Lachèvre, *Mémoire*, p. 929. This proposition is condemned even more strongly as 'tres-Epicurienne et atheiste tout à fait' ('very epicurean and completely atheistic') in Garasse, *Apologie*, pp. 240–1.

> That as the temperament of the body forces absolutely the movements of our soul, and our passions take us wherever they will with such strength, that there is no discourse that can be opposed to this necessity, nor any effort of reason or will capable of resisting it, no more than a bout of fever, as our birth so clearly shows us that our soul is far from being dependent on God as they say, in its essence, that on the contrary, we are born and are still lower than the beasts ...[116]

The *commissaires* repeated this interpretation on the futility of resistance to natural appetites (though omitting Molé's reference to fever and the beasts), and added that Théophile encouraged his readers 'tenyr toutes choses indifférantes sans mectre en considération ce qui est des vertus moralles et chrestiennes et mectre au mespris tous les commendementz de Dieu' ('to be indifferent towards all things without considering what might be moral or Christian virtues, and to hold all of God's commandments in contempt').[117] This example of a textual chain of trial preparation—from Garasse, through to Molé, and ending with the poet's interrogators—demonstrates that even lines of questioning which had originally pertained to Théophile's comments on obeying physical appetites were construed within an increasingly religious context, rather than being interpreted as obscene.

Molé's neglected pre-trial preparations show that he did not merely replicate Garasse's accusations. Not only did the *procureur général* both develop and edit out some of Garasse's arguments, but he also prepared an independent line of questioning, supported by meticulous bibliographical research, in a multi-layered draft of questioning to be passed on to the *commissaires*. Besides being remembered as another of Théophile's persecutors, Molé also merits recognition as one of his early literary critics; especially considering the detail of his draft questions which, irrespective of their ideological leanings, were certainly thorough and in parts original. More strikingly, and of greater significance for the wider strategies of accusation and defence at the trial to which we will now turn, Théophile's was not only a trial for obscenity. The nature of Molé's accusations, the thematic order in which these appear in his draft questioning, the texts on which they were based, and the variants in these questions between sources, all paint a picture that is strikingly different to that of later interrogations and confrontations. Théophile was first questioned not as an obscene culprit of a *crime contre nature* as his sonnet in the *Parnasse satyrique* would suggest, but as a theologically subversive philosopher poet. This said, the fluid boundaries between criminal sexuality and irreligion (for example masturbation, extra-marital sex, and sodomy), the nature of the corpus of texts at the judges' disposal, and Théophile's own responses, meant that the poet's crimes of irreligious thought did not remain the primary focus throughout the trial.

[116] BNF MS Cinq Cents de Colbert 2, fol. 103v.

[117] AN X 2B 1185, second interrogation (26 March 1624), in Lachèvre, *Procès*, p. 388.

THE USE OF LITERARY ANALYSIS AND THÉOPHILE'S DEFENCE OF HIS TEXTS

The proceedings of Théophile's trial can be roughly divided into interrogations of the accused and witness testimonies. For the latter, we can further distinguish between instances where the witness gave a statement (*déposition*) and those where Théophile was made to confront his accusers directly. Eighteen witnesses were called to testify against the poet in total, whilst seventy-five texts were selected to incriminate him. These include at least five that have since been identified as the works of other poets, and five that were not used in the trial hearings.[118] It is clear from the chronology of events that the appearance of Théophile's name in the *Parnasse satyrique* played a crucial role in his case. The opening hearings, however, do not reflect this. The two initial depositions, made by Jacques Trousset and René Le Blanc on 4 October and 15 October 1623 respectively, do not refer to the *Parnasse satyrique* or Théophile's literary output, but to the poet's admission to his lack of Christian faith in private conversations.[119] Trousset had been the *lieutenant de robe courte* at the prison of Saint-Quentin, where Théophile was held between his arrest and his escorted journey to Paris. It was at Saint-Quentin that Trousset met Le Blanc on 14 September 1623.[120] Le Blanc had first met Théophile in 1615 at Castelnau-Barbarens where, as part of the entourage of the comte de Candale, Théophile had reportedly spoken irreverently of the existence of God and immortal souls. With René Le Blanc we encounter something of an ancilliary collusion in which Voisin once again appears. As Théophile claims in his *Apologie au Roy*:

> Un homme qui fait profession de Religieux [...] avoit à sa devotion un Lieutenant du Prevost de la Connestablie nommé le Blanc, son confident particulier. [...] Ce Religieux qui disposa si absolument de cet officier de Justice, et qui trouva le gouverneur de vostre Citadelle si facile, c'est SIRE, le Père Voisin Jesuite.
>
> A man professing to be a priest [...] had the allegiance of a lieutenant of the provost constabulary named Le Blanc, his private confidant. [...] This priest who had this officer of justice at his absolute disposal, and who found the governor of your fortress so willing, Sire, is the Jesuit Father Voisin.[121]

[118] I use the phrase 'poetic verse' to include lines of poetry that appeared in Théophile's prose *Traicté de l'immortalité de l'âme* (counted as six separate poems), as well as in the *Vers pour le ballet des Bacchanales* (1623) and his tragedy, *Pyrame et Thisbée* (1623). These texts are provided in Lachèvre, *Procès*, pp. 307–419.

[119] See AN X 2B 1184 in Lachèvre, *Procès*, pp. 211–17. This *lieutenant* is mistakenly identified as Louis Le Blanc in Théophile de Viau, *Œuvres complètes*, ed. by Guido Saba, 3 vols (Paris: Honoré Champion, 1999), I, p. xxvi.

[120] On this meeting, see AN X 2B 1184, in Lachèvre, *Procès*, pp. 212–16.

[121] Théophile, *Apologie au Roy*, p. 9–10. It is notable that Théophile insists upon Voisin's Jesuit identity here.

The court next heard the depositions of Gabriel Dange (21 November) and Louis Forest Sageot (23 November). In addition to these, in late November attempts were made by the court to gather more incriminating evidence against Théophile in the provinces through *lettres monitoires*. These notices were given at churches inviting the faithful, on pain of excommunication, to come forward with information pertaining to the contents of the letter.[122] Following these events the trial was halted for four months, and it was only after this period of inactivity that Théophile was interrogated on his authorship of a large corpus of poetry, as well as the intended meaning of some of his compositions in prose, after he had been on hunger strike.[123] At this stage, the prosecution had clearly decided to condemn Théophile by associating him with the most subversive poems of the *Parnasse satyrique* and his early prose compositions.[124] On 22 March in particular, Théophile was repeatedly asked to confirm his authorship of a large corpus of texts. Molé thus hoped to consolidate Théophile's reputation as a composer of impious verse and to cement his links to the *Parnasse satyrique* that had been highlighted in Garasse's *Doctrine curieuse*. The *procureur général* would not have to rely solely on his own reading of the poems, or indeed Garasse's *Doctrine curieuse*, in order to inform his strategy. More than two months passed between the publication of Garasse's second attack on Théophile—the *Apologie du pere François Garassus*, which bears a privilege dated 10 January—and Théophile's first interrogation of 22 March, affording Molé both the time and the inspiration for his lines of questioning.

In the first encounter between the poet and his interrogators on 22 March 1624, Théophile was repeatedly asked to confirm his authorship of a significant number of supposedly subversive poems. Yet of the twenty-three poems mentioned on 22 March, only one would be used against Théophile in a subsequent hearing.[125] The short-lived strategy of attributing a large body of poetry to Théophile suggests a certain disorganisation, or perhaps even uncertainty, on the part of the prosecution. This is also apparent from the ways in which different texts were used at the trial, in which a clear distinction can be observed. Théophile's non-poetic works—his prose compositions and his tragedy *Pyrame et Thisbé*—were used to expose the weakness or even the nonexistence of his Catholic faith, whereas the majority of

[122] See Jacques Eveillon, *Traité des excommunications et monitoires* (Angers: P. Avril, 1651), to which the author later added *La Manière de publier, fulminer et exécuter toutes sortes de monitoires et excommunications* (Angers: P. Avril, 1654).

[123] Lachèvre, *Procès*, p. 362. These interrogations took place on 22, 26, and 27 March 1624 (see AN X 2B 1185, in Lachèvre, *Procès*, pp. 363–401).

[124] This decision had to an extent been made collectively, as the correspondence between Garasse and Molé demonstrates. See Lachèvre, 'Mémoire', 900–40, in which Garasse advised Molé on how to conduct his interrogations of the poet. As early as 1588, the États de Blois had stated plainly that 'ni le Clergé, ni le Tiers ne s'occupèrent de l'instruction criminelle' ('neither the clergy nor the Third Estate took part in criminal investigations': Esmein, *Histoire de la procedure*, p. 171).

[125] 'Ode' (Heureux, tandis qu'il est vivant), in Théophile, *Œuvres*, p. 70.

his poetry was used to suggest his supposed sexual immorality. Théophile therefore appears to have been tried for religious and social (including sexual) dissidence; a duality that aptly demonstrates the vague nature of the accusation of *libertinage* made against Théophile in *La Doctrine curieuse* and explored in Chapter 1. On 26 March 1624, for example, Théophile was questioned on the following scene from *Pyrame et Thisbe*:

> Mais mon Pyrame est mort sans espoir qu'il retourne
> De ces pasles manoirs où son esprit séjourne.
> Depuis que le Soleil nous void naistre, et finir,
> Le premier des deffuncts est encore à venir.
>
> But my Pyrame is dead without hope of return
> From those pale lands where his spirit dwells.
> Since the Sun bore witness to our birth and our end,
> The first of the dead has yet to return.[126]

According to the *commissaires*, in this passage Théophile:

> veult fayre croyre qu'il n'y a aucune résurrection des mortz, ayant dict par mocquerye que le premier des hommes deceddez est encore à venyr, dont il a voulu inférer que n'y ayant point d'espérance de retourner il ne falloit poinct attendre de résurrection.
>
> wants to make us believe that there is no resurrection of the dead, having said mockingly that the first man to have died has yet to return, from which he wished to infer that having no hope of returning, one should not await resurrection.[127]

Similar objections were made to Théophile's *Traicté de l'immortalité de l'âme* and his semi-autobiographical *Première journée*, which describes a number of conversations with his friends as well as containing an example of the poet's literary manifesto.[128] On 27 March 1624, for example, the trial focussed on the third chapter of the *Première journée* in which Théophile describes visiting a girl believed by the locals to be possessed:

> Je luy parlay latin le plus distinctement qu'il m'estoit possible, mais je ne vis jamais aucune apparence qu'elle l'entendit; je luy dis du grec, de l'anglois, de l'espagnol et de l'italien, mais à tout cela le diable ne trouva jamais à respondre un son articulé; pour du gascon, elle ne manqua point d'injures à me repartir. [...] Je ne pouvois me tenir de me mocquer, protestant que ce diable estoit ignorant pour les langues et qu'il n'avoit point voyagé.

126 *Pyrame et Thisbé*, Act V Scene 2, quoted in Lachèvre, *Procès*, p. 391.

127 AN X 2B 1185, second interrogation (26 March 1624), in Lachèvre, *Procès*, p. 391. On the denial of Christ's ressurection from the dead, see also 1 Corinthians 15:12–18.

128 For an analysis of autobiographical readings of this text, see DeJean, 'Autobiographie'; Martine Debaisieux, '*Première journée* de Théophile ou l'exorcisme de la tradition', *Cahiers du Dix-Septième siècle*, 7: 1 (1997), 179–92; Moreau, *Guérir*, pp. 98–100; Van Damme, *Épreuve*, pp. 158–64.

> I spoke to her in the clearest Latin that I could, but I never saw any sign that she understood it. I spoke to her in Greek, English, Spanish and Italian, but the Devil never found a single utterance to say in response. As for Gascon, she had no lack of insults with which to answer me. [...] I could not stop myself from mocking her, and from arguing that this devil did not know his languages and was not well travelled.[129]

Théophile was asked whether he had visited the girl 'pour aler veoyr les diables' ('to go and see devils'), and 's'il n'a pas dit publicquement que c'estoit risée et sottise de croyre qu'il y eut des diables et que ce que l'on disoit n'estoit que pour abuser le monde' ('if he had not said publicly that it was laughable and stupid to believe in devils and that what was said about them was only to deceive people') in order to suggest his irreligion and *libertinage*.[130] Théophile's prose fiction was therefore selected as a means of condemning him for blasphemy and atheism through an autobiographical reading, despite the fact that the poet was never asked to identify the poetic 'I' in his texts.[131] Théophile's poetry offers a wealth of potential evidence of his materialist, unorthodox views on Nature and the human condition, as attested by his subsequent reputation in literary criticism as a daring, subversive, and modern poet. It is difficult to explain why the prosecution should have abandoned attempts to prove Théophile's lack of Christian faith through his poetry, given that its objections to Théophile's texts were not, by contemporary standards, entirely unfounded. Despite affirming his innocence, it seems highly likely that Théophile held many of the irreligious views of which he was accused through quotations from his poetry at trial.

The prosecution's logic in its choice of poetic quotations throughout the trial is also unclear, as these were almost exclusively used to attack the poet's moral and social character in both interrogations and witness statements. Once again, the

[129] Quoted in Lachèvre, *Procès*, pp. 49–50. It is possible to use the *Première journée* to date the composition of part of the *Doctrine curieuse*. Sections seven to eleven of book VII of this text speak at length of libertine unbelief in the devil, demons, and their powers without alluding to Théophile's *Première journée* at all. Considering the strength of Théophile's criticism of demonic possession given above, it is unlikely that Garasse had read this text at the time of writing book VII. As the *Première journée* was first published in the *Seconde partie* of Théophile's *Œuvres* in late June 1623, Garasse is likely to have written book VII of the *Doctrine* prior to this date. This would be in accordance with Adam's estimated time of writing of this book, derived from another piece of textual evidence, of late April 1623 (see Adam, *Pensée*, p. 333).

[130] AN X 2B 1185, third interrogation (27 March 1624), in Lachèvre, *Procès*, p. 397. For Garasse, 'dire qu'il n'y a point de Diables au monde, c'est une proposition qui a son passe-port parmy les Libertins' ('to say that there are no devils in the world is a proposition which has credit amongst the libertines': Garasse, *Doctrine curieuse*, p. 843). On the perceived utility of exorcisms to convert atheists and libertines, see Laura Verciani, *Le moi et ses diables: Autobiographie spirituelle et récit de possession au XVIIe siècle*, trans. by Arlette Estève (Paris: Honoré Champion, 2001), p. 19.

[131] DeJean, 'Autobiographie', 436. For Peureux, Théophile evoked the question of the identity of the poetic *I* in his texts more than any writer of his day (Guillaume Peureux, 'Avertissements aux lecteurs', in *Lectures de Théophile de Viau*, ed. by Guillaume Peureux (Rennes: Presses Universitaires de Rennes, 2008), 9–22 (10)).

first hearing of 22 March 1624 stands apart from the others. This interrogation—unique in terms of the large number of poems cited—is the only instance in which the prosecution tried to use Théophile's poetry to discredit his image as a Catholic convert, thereby demonstrating a shift in its strategic objectives after this time. The very first question put to Théophile regarding a specific poem during this hearing was framed as follows: 'sy, sachant qu'il y a plusieurs espèces d'atéismes, il n'a pas cru le pouvoyr establyr plus aysément par sa poysie' ('if, given that there are several degrees of atheism, he did not think that he could establish it more easily through his poetry').[132] All of the twenty-three poems examined in this hearing pertain to Théophile's deviations from the Catholic faith. Ten claim that Man should pursue an epicurean obedience to natural impulses;[133] four present either a God indifferent to human suffering and supplication, or a predeterminism over which Man is powerless;[134] and seven replace God with a woman as the object of the poet's adoration.[135] Yet after this hearing, the prosecution would only make one further significant attempt to use Théophile's poetry to incriminate him on a theological level, and this with only a single poem.[136] Subsequent references to Théophile's poetry instead sought to cast his sexual morality in a poor light.

There is no obvious reason for this clear shift in the trial's focus. Although the hearing of 22 March had not yielded any conclusive evidence of Théophile's culpability, there was still ample poetic material on which the prosecution could have interrogated the defendant further.[137] Furthermore, the Parlement in fact rarely prosecuted defendants for sodomy, whereas the crimes of blasphemy and lese-majesty provided several notable and recent precedents upon which the magistrates could have drawn.[138] The decision to use Théophile's poetry in order to seek his condemnation for sodomy becomes all the more peculiar when compared to the wider corpus used in the trial as a whole. Of the fifty-

[132] AN X 2B 1185, first interrogation (22 March 1624), in Lachèvre, *Procès*, p. 375.

[133] See in Théophile, *Œuvres*: 'Ode' (Heureux tandis qu'il est vivant, p. 70); 'Stances' (S'il est vrai, Cloris, que tu m'aimes, p. 86); 'Désespoirs Amoureux, stances', p. 90; 'Consolation à M. D. L., stances', p. 97; 'Satire première', p. 126; 'Élégie' (Aussi souvent qu'Amour fait penser à mon âme, p. 143); 'Sonnet' (Les Parques ont le teint plus gai que mon visage, p. 158); 'Sonnet' (L'autre jour, inspiré d'une divine flamme, p. 164); 'Sonnet' (Si quelquefois Amour permet que je respire, p. 165); À Monsieur de L. sur la mort de son père', p. 376.

[134] 'Élégie' (Si votre doux accueil n'eût consolé ma peine, p. 102); 'Satire Seconde', p. 132; 'Epigramme à son frère', p. 184; 'Sonnet' (Chère Isis, tes beautés ont troublé la nature, p. 212).

[135] 'Ode' (Cloris, ma franchise est perdue, p. 67); 'Désespoirs Amoureux, stances', p. 90; 'Élégie' (Chère Philis, j'ai bien peur que tu meures, p. 135); 'Élégie' (Enfin guéri d'une amitié funeste, p. 140); 'Élégie' (Aussi souvent qu'Amour fait penser à mon âme, p. 143); 'Sonnet' (Si j'étais dans un bois poursuivi d'un lion, p. 157); 'Sonnet' (L'autre jour, inspiré d'une divine flamme, p. 164).

[136] AN X 2B 1185, third interrogation (26 March 1624), in Lachèvre, *Procès*, pp. 386–95, which examined Théophile's 'Élégie' (Cloris, lorsque je songe, p. 203).

[137] As DeJean notes, 'Had the prosecution stuck to its alleged mission and concentrated on presenting evidence of impiety and blasphemy, the magistrates could have had a field day with Théophile, whose poetry is at times as dangerously irreverent as they could have wished' (DeJean, *Obscenity*, p. 50).

[138] See Hamilton, 'Sodomy and Criminal Justice', 307.

nine poems used by the prosecution, at least seven include lines of an overtly sexual nature, and a further three refer to sodomy. Compared to these ten 'sexual' poems, the prosecution's corpus of incriminating texts also included thirty-three poems deemed philosophically and theologically suspect. Five of these prescribe obedience to the law of nature, whilst twenty-eight are of overtly irreligious content.[139] Once again, the prosecution's division between the types of accusations made against the poet, and the texts used to support their claims, appears to have been largely ineffective and illogical. The authorities thus confused irreligion and sexual immorality, both of which had been alluded to in Garasse's diatribe against the libertines. This may also have been due at least in part to Théophile's own defence in the early interrogations.

Unlike his persecutors, Théophile remained steadfast in both the simplicity and consistency of his approach during the early interrogations. In these as in later confrontations with witnesses, he simply denied authorship of forty-five of the texts quoted to him by the prosecution. This was despite the fact that seventeen of these had already been published in his *Œuvres* in 1621, and two in the *Seconde partie* of 1623. As Peureux has recently remarked, even if we assume that Théophile really was the author of the numerous texts used against him at trial, an autobiographical reading of these fails to allow critical scope for the numerous alternative uses of the poetic 'I'. Instead, a biased literal reading is privileged according to which the accuser wilfully conflates the real world with the one presented in satirical poems.[140]

On 22 March 1624, as the prosecution made its greatest and apparently final attempt to condemn the accused primarily as a subversive writer, Théophile claimed that the printer Pierre Billaine had added poems to the third edition of his *Œuvres* that were not of his composition, and that the officers who had arrested him had planted incriminating texts amongst his possessions.[141] This initial claim allowed Théophile to deny authorship of explicit or subversive poems subsequently attributed to him at trial—even those printed in his *Œuvres*—whilst acknowledging his authorship of other works, as the following exchange plainly demonstrates:

> Demandé: Luy avons remonstré que puisqu'il recognoist avoyr composé et faict imprimer la pluspart desditz livres, il ne peult desnyer le surplus.

[139] I borrow the phrase 'the law of nature' ('la règle de la nature') from Théophile's 'Ode' (Heureux tandis qu'il est vivant). See Théophile, *Œuvres*, p. 70.

[140] Guillaume Peureux, *La Muse satyrique (1600–1622)* (Geneva: Droz, 2015), p. 119. On the problematics of the first person, intentionality, and selfhood in early modern poetry, see James Helgeson, *The Lying Mirror: The First-person Stance and Sixteenth-century Writing* (Geneva: Droz, 2012).

[141] See AN X 2B 1185, first interrogation (22 March 1624), in Lachèvre, *Procès*, pp. 371–6. Neither Billaine nor any of the other printers implicated in the publication of the *Parnasse satyrique* were tried by the authorities.

> Répondu: A dit que puisqu'il n'en recognoist qu'une partye on ne luy doibt pas attribuer le surplus.
>
> Asked: Put to him that as he recognised having composed and had printed the majority of the aforementioned books, he cannot deny the rest.
> Responded: Said that as he recognised only a part of it, the rest should not be attributed to him.[142]

The five most frequently mentioned poems across the trial are all of a sexual rather than irreligious nature, and feature far more prominently in witness testimonies than in interrogations.[143] Significantly, none of the poems pertaining to Théophile's religious beliefs or supposed verbal professions of unbelief is mentioned by any of those called to testify against him. If we leave to one side the initial depositions made by Dange and Le Blanc—who had both come into contact with Théophile during his arrest—the project of incrimination by witness testimony was uniquely concerned with denouncing Théophile as a sexual deviant.[144] Many of the most frequently mentioned poems, however, can be attributed to other poets. The sonnet 'Multiplier le monde en votre accouplement' was almost certainly written by Malherbe prior to 1611.[145] 'La chambre du débauché' and 'la débauche' were written by Saint-Amant. 'Fureur d'amour' was written by Maynard and had even appeared under his name in the *Cabinet satyrique* of 1618 and its 1621 reprint. Furthermore, one of the most frequently cited poems—'A un marquis'—had appeared in the *Délices satyriques* of 1620 without attracting condemnation. The use of poetry to condemn Théophile as a sexual deviant was therefore a flawed strategy on two levels. First, it depended on a limited corpus of obscene texts used against the poet whilst neglecting a comparatively rich corpus of irreligious poems. Second, it represented an unprecedented condemnation of a genre of poetry which had appeared for some time in the *recueils satyriques* anthologies of salacious and bawdy poetry.

By denying authorship and by assuring the *commissaires* of his Christian faith, Théophile's early self-defence provided him with a solid strategic base upon which he could subsequently deny authorship of incriminating works attributed to him.[146] Combined with the ambiguity of his crimes derived from his association

142 AN X 2B 1185, first interrogation (22 March 1624), in Lachèvre, *Procès*, p. 372. On the status of earlier *brouillons* of poems as valid evidence, see Van Damme, *Épreuve*, p. 80.

143 These are, in descending order of frequency, 'Philis, tout est foutu, je meurs de la vérole', 'Chanson' (Approche, approche ma dryade), 'A un Marquis', 'Fureur d'Amour', and 'Multiplier le monde en votre accouplement'.

144 Théophile would later allude to his arrest by these 'deux méchants prévôts, / Fort grands voleurs, et très dévots' ('two wicked provosts, / Very great thieves / and very devout') in his 'Requête de Théophile au Roi' in 1625 (Théophile, *Œuvres*, p. 266).

145 See Lachèvre, *Procès*, p. 409; François de Malherbe, *Poésies*, ed. by Antoine Adam (Paris: Gallimard, 1971), p. 209.

146 Such as his affirmation of his conversion to Catholicism at the hands of the personal confessor of Louis XIII, the Jesuit Father Séguiran. See AN X 2B 1185, first interrogation (22 March 1624), in

with *libertinage,* Théophile's successful self-defence led the prosecution to turn its attention to his *Traicté de l'immortalité de l'âme* before relying increasingly on witness testimony. The early hearings had constituted an illogical and unsuccessful attempt by Théophile's interrogators to use his poetry against him. Their comments on his prose *Traicté de l'immortalité de l'âme*, however, reveal a more competent line of questioning which is best appreciated when viewed in terms of rhetoric and the question of literary identity.

WEAPONISING RHETORIC: TRANSLATION, IMITATION, PEDAGOGY, AND AUTHORIAL CULPABILITY

Despite Théophile's numerous assertions of his literary independence from 'la sotte antiquité' ('stupid Antiquity'), both his poetry and his trial records betray a debt to ancient Greek and Roman authors.[147] Given that the debates on a nascent literary modernism in the 1620s were based, for Jean-Louis Bailly, on the notion of a correct use of the ancients, references to texts from Antiquity within the context of Théophile's trial have much to tell us about the kind of modernity that was at stake.[148] In particular, references to translation and imitation show that Théophile made use of the tools of rhetoric, as given in contemporary teaching manuals, in order to defend himself during his trial.

Théophile is often credited with hiding behind the ancients as a libertine strategy for disseminating subversive ideas, recalling Montaigne's criticism of the act of 'se couvrir des armes d'autruy, jusques à ne montrer pas seulement le bout de ses doigts' ('hiding behind the shield of the other, to the point of not even showing one's fingertips').[149] Within the corpus of seventeenth-century libertine literature, imitation can often be seen to serve as a means of deflecting potential criticism and even prosecution for subversive ideas. La Mothe Le Vayer, for example, published numerous *Dialogues faits à l'imitation des Anciens,* albeit under a pseudonym and with false dates and places of publication, in order to give voice to his scepticism.[150] Théophile appears at first glance to have harnessed this same potential of the ancients for *dissimulatio.* During his first interrogation, he was asked about his *Traicté de l'Immortalité de l'âme*, based on Plato's *Phaedo*, which had appeared in the *Première partie* of the poet's *Œuvres*:

Lachèvre, *Procès*, p. 370.

[147] 'A Monsieur du Fargis', in Théophile, *Œuvres*, p. 123. On this issue see Alain Lanavère, 'Théophile de Viau, imitateur des anciens', *XVIIe siècle*, 251: 2 (2011), 397–422 (419).

[148] Jean-Louis Bailly, 'Modeles chez Théophile de Viau prosateur', in *Le Modèle à la renaissance*, ed. by Claudie Balavoine, Jean Lafond and Pierre Laurens (Paris: Vrin, 1986), p. 141–50 (p. 141).

[149] 'De l'institution des enfants', in Michel de Montaigne, *Essais*, ed. by Pierre Villey and V.L. Saulnier (Paris: Presses Universitaires de France, 2004), p. 148.

[150] See in particular Cavaillé, *Dis/simulations*.

Dem: s'il n'a pas fait imprimer le livre de l'*Immortallitté de l'Ame* pour tesmoigner à un chacun ce qui estoit de sa créance.
Rep: A dit [...] que c'est un discours qu'il a faict en parafrasant le *Phédon* de Platton et estoit bien ayse de monstrer qu'en l'esprit d'un payen il y avoit des sentimentz d'un homme qui croyoit un Dieu et l'immortallitté de l'Ame.

Asked: whether he had the book on the *Immortalty of the Soul* printed to demonstrate to everyone what he believed.
Responded: Said [...] that it was a discourse that he had written by paraphrasing Plato's *Phaedo* and that he was very glad to demonstrate that the spirit of a pagan could have the sentiments of a man who believed in God and the immortality of the soul.[151]

Later on in the same hearing, the judges again attempted to identify Théophile with the views expressed in this text:

Dem: [il] semble qu'il s'est contenté d'ymitter un payen soubz le nom du *Phédon* de Platton pour soubz telz noms authoriser les mauvaises maximes qui sont dans ledit livre.
A dit qu'il n'a jamais entrepris de traicter des mattyères de théollogye et ne s'est esloigné du sens de l'autheur et n'avoit intention d'establyr aucune creance non plus que ceux qui lysent les auteurs prophanes dans leurs classes.

Asked: it seems that he was happy to imitate a pagan under the name of Plato's *Phaedo*, so that under this guise he could give authority to the terrible maxims in the aforementioned book.
Said that he has never attempted to deal with theological matters and did not go beyond the author's meaning, and had no intention to establish any belief system any more than those who read prophane authors in the classroom.[152]

Finally, in the 1626 *Apologie au Roy*, Théophile recalled this trial hearing thus:

Je respondis que je n'avois point composé ce livre-là, que c'estoit un ouvrage de Platon; que je l'avois traduit sans m'esloigner du sens de l'autheur. [...] Sainct Augustin, qui ne parle jamais de Platon sans admiration, m'a fourny de quoy faire approuver la peine que j'ai prise en cette traduction.

I answered that I had not written that book, that it was a work by Plato; that I had translated it without going beyond the author's meaning. [...] St Augustin, who only ever speaks of Plato with admiration, gave me enough reason to make the effort to write this translation.[153]

Both Théophile and his interrogators made a striking and vital distinction between imitation and translation. Théophile's defence, as well as the subsequent

[151] AN X 2B 1185, first interrogation (22 March 1624), in Lachèvre, *Procès*, p. 373. For an overview of Théophile's *Traicté*, see Richard A. Mazzara, 'The *Phaedo* and Théophile de Viau's "Traicté de l'immortalité de l'âme"', *The French Review*, 40: 3 (1966), 329–40.
[152] In Lachèvre, *Procès*, p. 373.
[153] Théophile, *Apologie au Roy*, pp. 19–20.

questions put to him, suggest that the translation of texts running contrary to the teachings of the Catholic Church is unproblematic from a theological and legal perspective. If impiety remains lurking between the lines, this is an admissible by-product of the process of translation; a process which, according to these trial records at least, affords very little if any literary agency to the translator. The poet's interrogators, however, do not use the vocabulary of translation in their questioning. Instead, Théophile is accused of imitation. In responding that he has translated Plato's text, he refutes this accusation whilst at the same time acknowledging that imitation would indeed render him guilty.[154] This distinction between imitation and translation, and the reference to the classroom environment, point towards a more complicated strategy than the simple borrowing from impious works of Antiquity in order to hide behind their original authors. I want to argue that these exchanges derived from a shared learning experience of the teaching of rhetoric, or at least from a mode of textual engagement in the wider world of letters which this teaching had engendered.[155]

Imitatio was one of the essential categories of rhetoric from the Greco–Roman world which had been revived by humanists in the sixteenth century. The *Ratio studiorum*, a Jesuit teaching manual published in 1599, allows us to see not only how Latin and Greek were taught, but how this pedagogical experience subsequently coloured the way in which writers perceived their art and that of others. As Shennan remarks, the vast majority of children of the Parisian magistrate class were educated by the Jesuits (though not between 1594 and 1618 following Jean Châtel's attempt on the king's life). The Jesuit syllabus was particularly orientated towards rhetoric, thereby facilitating alliances with the court aristocracy through a shared educational background,[156] as well as promoting a certain communal spirit—an *esprit de corps*—through this experience.[157] Finally, Jesuit colleges also provided a solid literary education which, as early as 1546, was necessary for those wishing to enter into the legal profession—the very social class that often encouraged the creation and flourishing of colleges.[158] Traces of this classical

[154] On this text as translation, see Melaine Folliard, 'Le *Traicté de l'immortalité de l'âme* de Théophile de Viau, ou les voix du traducteur', *Libertinage et philosophie au XVII*e *siècle*, 11—*Le Libertinage et l'éthique â l'âge classique*, (2009), 71–116.

[155] For a similar view on contemporary material which has inspired the following comments on the *Ratio studiorum*, see Emmanuel Bury, 'De l'imitation scolaire à l'imitation adulte: le cas de la *Ratio studiorum* et son influence sur Guez de Balzac', *Littératures classiques*, 1: 74 (2011), 11–30.

[156] Shennan, *The Parlement*, pp. 127–8. Houllemare notes that the magistrates shared the same schooling characterised by the increasing importance of rhetoric (Houllemare, *Le Parlement*, pp. 131, 163, 166). See also Catherine Holmès, *L'Éloquence judiciaire de 1620 à 1600: reflet des problèmes sociaux, religieux et politiques de l'époque* (Paris: Nizet, 1967), pp. 18–19, 23–4.

[157] See Mousnier, *Les Institutions*, p. 331. On the potential of this *esprit de corps* as a weapon against the king's authority, see Julian Swann, *Exile, Imprisonment, or Death: The Politics of Disgrace in Bourbon France, 1610–1789* (Oxford: Oxford University Press, 2017), pp. 170–223, 342–77.

[158] In August 1546, François I decreed that as well as being God-fearing, judges should also be 'instruits en bonnes lettres' ('learned in high literature': E. Girard, *Trois livres des offices de France* (Paris: Estienne

education were evident in the magistrates' speeches in the Parlement, and can also be found in their surviving private letters.[159] It may at first seem improbable that the methods of the Jesuit *Ratio studiorum* would have been known to Théophile who, after all, studied at the Protestant academy of Saumur. Nevertheless, in all likelihood he would have followed a similar curriculum.

Saumur was largely interested in the teaching of ancient languages. Though still Protestant territory under the governorship of Duplessis-Mornay since April 1589, it had a large Catholic population which was never entirely subjugated by the Reformer and which was even allowed to teach in a communal college. Though it is natural to assume that the educational institutions of the two religions would have competed with each other, surviving sources on everyday life at Saumur point to a more nuanced relationship. The Catholic collège des Ardilliers was founded close to the Protestant academy in 1619, and prior to this Catholics were permitted to teach in primary and secondary schools.[160] Such was Saumur's reputation as a centre of academic excellence that even a number of Catholic students were sent to study there.[161]

Surviving documents from the academy attest to a surprisingly fluid boundary between the two institutions. The Catholics at Ardilliers enjoyed a relationship of emulation and fraternity with the Protestants. This sense of brotherhood was also seen in the students, who were known to attend classes held at the opposing institution and to applaud their teaching.[162] A practice of emulation also extended into the very structure of the two institutions. The Jesuits, for example, adopted the division of classes into groups of ten known as *décuries*—whose leaders were decided by their performance in written composition tasks, and who were given real privilege and responsibility in the classroom—based on the success of this practice in Protestant classrooms.[163] The Protestants at Saumur were in turn willing to offer boarding to their students, despite this going against their belief

Richer, 1638), p. 20). On the link between the development of Jesuit colleges and the magistrate class within the context of the history of humanism, see François de Dainville, *L'éducation des jésuites (XVIe-XVIIIe siècles)* (Paris: Éditions de Minuit, 1978), p. 25. According to Dainville, the *Ratio* was the dominant manual used by the Jesuits for the teaching of rhetoric for the first half of the seventeenth century (pp. 190–4).

[159] Louis Servin, for example, mentions Pliny the Younger, Gaius Ateius Capito, and Marcus Cornelius Negrinus in the space of a single letter to Chancellor Pomponne de Bellièvre, in which he details the progress he has made in writing up his parliamentary speeches (BNF MS Fr 15898, pp. 23–7).

[160] Roughly half of Saumur's population was Catholic at this time (L.-J. Méteyer, *L'Académie Protestante de Saumur* (Paris: La Cause, 1933), p. 18). As early as August 1614, Louis XIII had published *Lettres-patentes qui donnent aux jésuites établis à Paris la chapelle N.-D. des Ardilliers, près Saumur*, some ten years after his father Henri IV had recalled the Jesuits from their exile imposed by the *arrêt* of 28 December 1594 (*Recueil général des anciennes lois françaises, depuis l'an 420, jusqu'à la révolution de 1789*, ed. by François-André Isambert and others, 29 vols (Paris: Belin-Leprieur, 1822–33), XVI (1829), p. 52).

[161] Méteyer, *L'Académie*, p. 32.

[162] Méteyer, *L'Académie*, p. 103.

[163] Méteyer, *L'Académie*, p. 37.

that the family environment was essential for the development of a child's faith, following the increased demands from parents which could only have stemmed from a knowledge of Catholic institutional practices.[164]

The crossover between the two religions is also evident in the classroom teaching itself, and again hints towards a shared awareness of the expectations and successful methods of the time. Saumur was particularly specialised in its teaching of Latin and Greek. Pierre-Daniel Bourchenin notes that the *Ratio* is typical of the curricula found in academies and colleges, due in part to the fact that teaching methods were designed to respond to the needs of their time and that the same authors were studied by both confessions.[165] Even if we are to consider the issue in terms of competition between the two faiths and their institutions, this nonetheless necessitated the study of the ancients at Saumur in order to interpret Holy Scripture.[166] Beyond this, finally, Duplessis-Mornay was well aware of the Protestant students' need to know their enemy through an awareness of what the Catholics were reading, which required the teachers at Saumur 'de leur faire rafraischir la lecture des anciens, mesmes des scholastiques et que chacun en prinst sa part à lire' ('to refresh their reading of the ancients, even the scholastics, and to ensure that each took their turn to read').[167] These considerations suggest that the teaching methods in the Jesuit and Protestant traditions were closely related, that Théophile was at least aware of the kind of rhetorical learning prescribed in the *Ratio*, and that he may have experienced this first-hand.[168]

The *Ratio* repeatedly emphasises the use of imitation as a means of acquiring grammatical knowledge and of attaining eloquence, itself intrinsically linked to a certain resemblance to the ancients. The application of grammar began with simple translation:

> Its aim should be practised in applying the rules of grammar. Sometimes the pupils should be required to add to it the translation of a short passage from Cicero or some expression illustrating the rules of syntax.[169]

Later on however, in the middle class, an examination of grammar rules and translation progressed to one of imitation, and more advanced students were

[164] D. De Chavigny, *L'Eglise & l'Académie Protestantes de Saumur* (Saumur: Paul Godet, 1914), pp. 25–6.

[165] Pierre-Daniel Bourchenin, *Étude sur les académies protestantes en France au XVIe et au XVIIe siècle* (Paris: Grassart, 1882), pp. 449, 451.

[166] See Joseph Prost, *La philosophie à l'académie protestante de Saumur (1606–1685)* (Paris: Henry Paulin, 1907), pp. 7–8.

[167] Duplessis-Mornay, *Mémoires*, quoted in Prost, *La philosophie*, pp. 10–11.

[168] François Gomar had left the University of Leyde in order to take up the position of first rector at Saumur, which he then modelled on his previous place of work. See Chavigny, *L'Eglise & l'Académie*, p. 11. Prost, however, cites a letter from 3 April 1593 which suggests that Duplessis-Mornay himself had sought information on the University of Leydn (Prost, *La Philosophie*, p. 7).

[169] *The Jesuit Ratio Studiorum of 1599*, ed. and trans. by Allan P. Farrell, S.J. (Washington: Conference of Major Superiors of Jesuits, 1970), p. 94.

encouraged to emancipate themselves to some extent from the models of Antiquity. When addressing what students should be asked to do whilst teachers corrected this written work, the *Ratio* describes how translation became less important as students progressed.[170] Imitation is not introduced until the middle classes, though the exercise is still largely concerned with syntax.[171] Then, by the higher class, imitation and the rules of syntax are presented as equal options for the teacher.[172] Finally, in the instructions for teachers on how to correct this work, grammar becomes gradually less important through the classes, and imitation is only included in the higher class.[173]

These comparisons demonstrate that grammar was first learned through translation before being practised through imitation. This reflects a hierarchy of linguistic aptitude following the increasingly independent literary production of the writer, itself evident by the higher students' freedom to write original content whilst imitating the linguistic style or form of an ancient writer.[174] In his *Ciceronianus*, Erasmus offers a similar condition to the use of imitation: 'J'approuve l'imitation, mais celle qui procède d'un modèle qui convienne à ton propre génie, et surtout qui ne s'y oppose pas' ('I approve of imitation, but one which comes from a model in accordance with your own genius, and which above all is not in opposition to it').[175] Here, Erasmus rejects a degree of imitation in which the proximity to the object of imitation is so close that no space is afforded to the imitator's own authorial identity, texts in which the distinction between imitation and translation can appear blurred, as well as imitations which do not reflect the *propre génie* of the imitator. These were clearly crucial distinctions at Théophile's trial, for as Jacques Pelletier had briefly remarked in his *Art poétique* in 1555, 'un Traducteur n'a jamais le nom d'Autheur' ('a translator is never called an author').[176] Théophile's contemportaries seem to have maintained these distinctions. Balzac's literary adversary Jean Goulu writes in his *Lettres de Phyllarque à Ariste*:

> Imiter, s'entend faire quelque chose de semblable, mais copier veut dire ne faire que la mesme chose. [...] Je n'entens pas que pour imiter Ciceron, tu mettes simplement

[170] *Ratio*, pp. 86–93.
[171] 'Turn into Latin passages dictated in the vernacular either in imitation of the author and especially as an exercise in the rules of syntax, translate a passage of Cicero into the vernacular and retranslate the same into Latin' (*Ratio*, pp. 89–90).
[172] *Ratio*, p. 86.
[173] *Ratio*, pp. 86, 93.
[174] On early modern concepts of translation, see Terence Cave, *The Cornucopian Text: Problems of Writing in the French Renaissance* (Oxford: Clarendon Press, 1979), part I chapters 1 ('Copia') and 2 ('Imitation'); Glyn P. Norton, 'Translation Theory in Renaissance France: Étienne Dolet and the Rhetorical Tradition', *Renaissance and Reformation*, 10: 1 (1974), 1–13; and Armand Colin, 'Théories et pratiques de la traduction littéraire en France', *Le français aujourd'hui*, 3: 42 (2003), 5–17.
[175] Erasmus, *Ciceronianus* (Basel: Johannes Froben; Paris: Simon de Colines, 1528) quoted in Fumaroli, *Éloquence*, p. 103.
[176] Quoted in *Traités de poétique et de rhétorique de la Renaissance*, ed. by Francis Goyet (Paris: Librairie Générale Française, 1990), p. 263.

> en François ce qu'il a dit élegamment en Latin, cela s'appelle traduire et non pas imiter.
>
> To imitate means to do something similar, but to copy means only to do the same thing. [...] I do not mean that to imitate Cicero, you simply put into French what he has said elegantly in Latin, that is called translation and not imitation.[177]

From this perspective too, a good imitation surpasses the skills of translation acquired early in language learning by incorporating the ideas and identity of the imitator, thereby demonstrating a higher degree of linguistic competence. A good imitation is one which also surpasses the original text, or adds something to the object of imitation, in order for the imitator's identity and his ideas to be visible. For as Théophile asserts, 'Demosthene et Virgile, n'ont point escript en nostre temps, et nous ne sçaurions escrire en leur siecle' ('Demosthenes and Virgil did not write in our time, and we would not know how to write in their age').[178] It is noteworthy that Théophile should mention Demosthenes and Virgil in particular, as both of these writers were prescribed for teaching rhetoric to Protestants during his time as a student.[179]

These observations permit a fresh consideration of Théophile's trial exchanges on the subject of his *Traicté* and his recollection of these in his *Apologie au Roy*. They also allow us to address the complex question of whether Théophile's text was in fact a translation or an imitation, which surprisingly has yet to form the subject of a dedicated critical study. The interrogators Pinon and Verthamon, adopting Molé's *projet d'interrogatoire* almost word for word in the opening interrogation, accused Théophile of imitation. In doing so, they suggested that he was not only able to authorise certain maxims in Plato's dialogue, but to author them; to contribute something of his own character and ideas to the work, as both the pedagogical manuals as well as men of letters from Petrarch to Balzac suggest. Théophile, however, claimed not to have *eloigné du sens de l'auteur*. On the one hand, as commentators have long acknowledged, this remark serves as a potential mask behind which the poet can hide his sympathies for Plato's ideas. On the other, it also denigrates Théophile's supposed imitation as translation. This would have been viewed as an exercise devoid of Théophile's own agency and ideas, due to a distinction observed in the theories of rhetoric to which he himself alludes in mentioning the classroom environment.

[177] Père Goulu, *Lettres de Phyllarque à Ariste* (II, XVI), quoted in Roger Zuber, *Les émerveillements de la raison: Classicismes littéraires du XVIIe siècle français* (Paris: Klincksieck, 1997), p. 171.

[178] *Première journée* in *Seconde partie*, pp. 18–19.

[179] Bourchenin, *Les académies*, p. 196. Bourchenin also notes how translation was taught in the first year of study (p. 192). In 1592, Antoine Arnauld alluded to the political writings of Demosthenes by naming his own work the *Antiespagnol, autrement les Philippiques d'un Demosthene François*, attesting to an appreciation for this author of Antiquity amongst the legal class (quoted in Houllemare, *Politiques*, p. 281). On Demosthenes and Cicero as aesthetic and political models for the jurists, see also Houllemare, *Politiques*, p. 354–5.

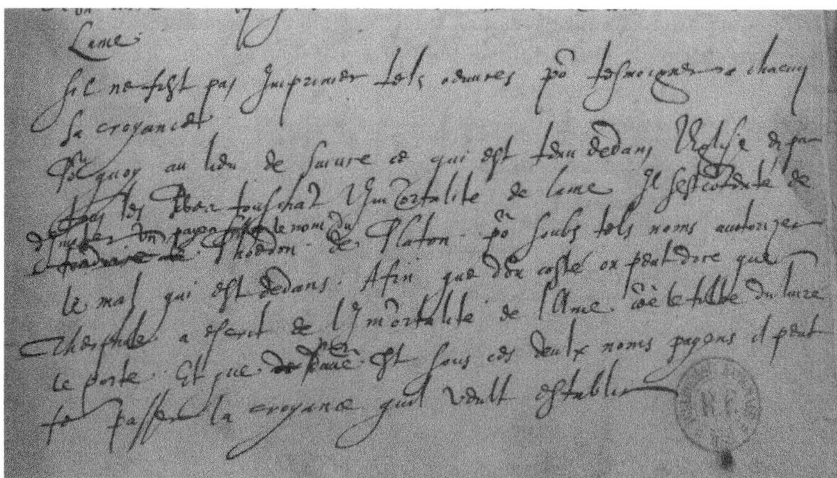

Figure 5.6 BNF MS Cinq Cents de Colbert 2, fol. 94^{r}: Part of Molé's draft of questions to be asked at Théophile's first interrogation. 'Traduire' is replaced with 'imiter' on the centre-left.

Molé's draft of questions also shows an awareness of these distinctions. He insists on the insidious nature of the text, 'quand ce ne seroit qu'une traduction (que non)' ('whether it is merely a translation or not'), thereby conceding that a translation would indeed diminish Théophile's responsibility.[180] He furthermore instructed the interrogators to ask Théophile:

> Pourquoy au lieu de suivre ce qui est tenu dedans l'Eglise et par tous les Pères touschant l'immortalité de l'âme, il s'est contenté d'imiter un païen, sous le nom du Phaedon de Platon pour, soubs tels noms, autoriser le mal qui est dedans. Afin que, d'un costé, on pût dire que Théophile a escrit de l'immortalité de l'âme, comme le tiltre du livre le porte, et que, d'autre part, sous ces deulx noms payens, il peut faire passer la croyance qu'il veult establir.
>
> Why, rather than following the views of the Church and all the Fathers on the immortality of the soul, he was happy to imitate a Pagan, under the name of Plato's *Phaedo*, so that under such names, he can give authority to the evil contained within the work. So that on the one hand it could be said that Théophile wrote this text, as the title of the book shows, and on the other hand, under these two Pagan names, he can expound the belief system that he wishes to establish.[181]

Finally, a close examination of Molé's manuscript reveals that he had originally claimed that Théophile was 'contenté de traduire le *Phedon* de Platon' ('happy to translate Plato's *Phaedo*'), before scoring this out and then adding more weight to the accusation: 'd'imiter un payen' ('to imitate a Pagan') (Figure 5.6).

[180] BNF MS Cinq Cents de Colbert 2, fol. 95.
[181] BNF MS Cinq Cents de Colbert 2, fol. 94.

Théophile's description of his first interrogation also demonstrates that both parties were aware of these differences. In the 1625 *Apologie au Roy,* Théophile recalls the first interrogation thus:

> Monsieur de Verthamond, contribuant peut estre un advis à ma justification, répartit qu'il n'y avoit point d'apparence que je fusse un athée, puis que, pour faire voir au public que j'avois des sentimens de la divinité tels qu'un chrestien les doit avoir, j'avois fait un livre de l'Immortalité de l'âme qui rendoit raison de ma créance.
>
> Mr de Vertamon, perhaps contributing to my defence, answered that there was nothing to suggest that I was an atheist given that, in order to show the public that I had views on the divine that a Christian should have, I had written a book on the immortality of the soul which gave an account of my beliefs.[182]

Yet the defendant's ears were keenly sensitive to the underlying implication of a criminal voice in this apparently benign but in fact insidious remark by Verthamon:

> Cela estoit dangereux pour un estourdi ou pour un meschant; mais moy, qui [...] n'avois autre chemin à suivre que celui de la vérité, je respondis que je n'avois point composé ce livre-là; que c'estoit un ouvrage de Platon; [...] que, pour monstrer que j'estois chrestien, j'allois à la messe, je communiois, je me confessois.
>
> This would be dangerous for an absent-minded or wicked person. But as for me, [...] having no other path to follow than that of the truth, I answered that I had not written that book, that it was a work by Plato [...] that, to show that I was a Christian, I went to Mass, I took Communion, I confessed my sins.[183]

Théophile was well aware that Verthamon was attempting to extract an admission of authorial agency from him, by blinding his judgement with a rare glimmer of sympathy. In response, Théophile nimbly stepped over the trigger wires by refuting the magistrate's association of the text with *mes sentiments* and *ma créance.* This strategy nonetheless had its limitations. When Théophile was confronted with the impious facets of purportedly pagan influences appearing in his poetry, such as references to gods in the plural, he defended himself by claiming that 'quand il avoit parlé de dieux en pluriel se a esté à la façon des poettes et que quand il a parlé de Dieu au singulyer il n'en a jamais parlé qu'au terme d'un bon chrestien' ('when he had spoken of the gods in the plural, it had been in the manner of the poets of Antiquity, and that when he spoke of God in the singular he had only done so as a good Christian').[184] Such a refutation appears problematic for the rhetorical distinctions he had made earlier. The idea that within the space of a single text he could write in the mindset of the ancients, as well as in that of an early modern Catholic, clearly left him open to the charge, which had previously been read

[182] Théophile, *Apologie au Roy*, p. 19.
[183] Théophile, *Apologie au Roy*, p. 19. Théophile repeats here an assertion he had made in his *Apologie de Théophile*, p. 17: 'je vay à la Messe, je communie, je me confesse'.
[184] AN X 2B 1185, first interrogation (22 March 1624), in Lachèvre, *Procès*, p. 380.

against him, of including his own views in his texts. Théophile's assertion that he wrote gods in the plural à la *façon des poettes* surely hints not towards translation, but imitation.

A little later in the *Apologie au Roy*, Théophile seeks to offer further assurances of his Catholic faith by stressing that in his translation of Plato, 'il y a plusieurs endroicts que j'ay en quelque façon desguisez pour les tourner à l'advantage de nostre créance' ('there are several parts that I have in some way disguised to turn them to the advantage of our faith').[185] Here again, Théophile deviates from his adopted position of what Jean-Pierre Chauveau terms 'la modestie du traducteur'.[186] In accordance with his assertion that the writers of Antiquity did not write in our times, Théophile has adapted the text, supposedly in order to meet the expectations of Catholic readers, thereby exposing his own identity above the proverbial parapet of translation. The interrogators pushed Théophile further over the authorship of this text in the first interrogation:

> Dem: Luy avons remonstré qu'il a faict intituller ledit livre non en forme de traduction ny de paraphrase, mais comme un traicté de sa composition.
> Rép: — A dit qu'il n'est pas simplement intitullé *L'Immortallitté de l'Ame,* mais *la Mort de Socrate* et *Phédon* et ne se peult entendre que du *Diallogue* de Platon.
>
> Asked: Suggested to him that he entitled the aforementioned book not as a translation nor as a paraphrase, but as a treatise of his composition.
> Responded: Said that he did not only entitle it *The Immortality of the Soul,* but *the Death of Socrates* and *Phaedo,* which could only mean Plato's *Dialogue*.[187]

Although imitation is not mentioned explicitly here, Théophile is accused of deliberately avoiding the genre of translation, thereby suggesting that a mere translation would be beyond reproach in accordance with the poet's own strategy of defence seen earlier.

Finally, when the defence of translation was not available to him, Théophile tellingly chose to admit authorship of a text and to defend it as its sole creator, rather than to claim imitation as a means of diminishing his culpability. On more than one occasion, the *commissaires* reproached Théophile's ode 'Heureux tandis qu'il est vivant' for prescribing obedience to one's natural appetites.[188] The poem in question is inspired by the second epode of Horace (Beatus ille qui procul negotiis), which may have been one of many poems memorised from his school days.[189] Again, modern scholarship on Théophile's trial and indeed his poetry treat translation and

[185] AN X 2B 1185, first interrogation (22 March 1624), in Lachèvre, *Procès*, p. 369.
[186] Jean-Pierre Chauveau, 'Le *Traicté de l'Immortalité de l'Ame, ou la Mort de Socrate*', in *Théophile de Viau: Actes du Colloque du CMR 17 offerts en hommage à Guido Saba*, ed. Roger Duchêne (Paris, Seattle, WA, and Tübingen: Biblio 17, 1991), p. 45–61 (p. 48).
[187] AN X 2B 1185, first interrogation (22 March 1624), in Lachèvre, *Procès*, p. 374.
[188] AN X 2B 1185, second interrogation (26 March 1624), in Lachèvre, *Procès*, p. 395.
[189] Lanavère, 'Théophile imitateur', 403.

imitation as interchangeable terms, both of which can be understood as literary inspiration and as a shield against accusations of impious literary composition.[190] According to this rather simplistic notion, Théophile should surely have been able to defend himself by claiming that this poem was written *à la façon d'Horace*. Yet these distinctions clearly *mattered* to the world of letters and to Théophile's judges. At no point in his trial did Théophile deny having written his poem. He did not defend himself as only having imitated Horace, nor did he attempt to explain any impious interpretations of the poem as stemming from its pagan inspiration. This is because 'Heureux tandis qu'il est vivant' is very much written in imitation of Horace rather than as a translation. From the point of view of the literary world as well as that of the practitioners of rhetoric, this afforded ample space for the poet's own ideas and agency for which he was challenged at trial. Rather than recognise his imitation, Théophile avoided the distinction between translation and imitation that he had used earlier to his advantage, and claimed instead, somewhat less convincingly, that 'il n'a jamais parlé qu'il fallût s'abandonner à la nature ny oublier le crestianisme et vivre comme les bestes et a tousjours fait profession de chrestien' ('he has never said that one must give in to nature nor forget Christianity and live like the beasts, and has always professed to be a Christian').[191]

Théophile's defence of his texts inspired by Antiquity is much more complex than a simple appropriation of a text containing unorthodox views, which the poet then spread from behind the mask of the ancients. Both Théophile and his judges drew upon a shared knowledge of rhetoric originating in the classroom. Théophile defended his texts on a subtle and subsequently overlooked rhetorical level, by denigrating his text as a less advanced writing exercise which did not include space for his own ideas. Although he poured scorn over the act of imitation as a lesser form of writing, within the courtroom setting both Théophile and his interrogators recognised that he was more likely to be condemned by admitting to imitation than to translation, as the former exposed his own views to scrutiny. There is thus a tension between Théophile's 'modern' rationalist literary desire, and his pressing personal need for a legal defence. Translation is frowned

[190] Folliard, for example, overlooks the distinctions between translation and imitation outlined in this study by asserting that the *Traicté* is both a translation and a paraphrase, despite conceding that Théophile adds to the original and gives free reign to *inventio*. For Cavaillé, the text is a 'paraphrase en prose et en vers' ('a paraphrasing in verse and in prose'). Rosellini has emphasised Théophile's definition of his work as a translation rather than an original work, but does not explore the tension with imitation. She furthermore highlights how this strategy allowed Théophile to present himself as a fellow transmitter of ideas from Antiquity (alongside the Jesuits themselves) rather than as a theologian. See Folliard, 'Traducteur', pp. 75–6, 83; Jean-Pierre Cavaillé, *Les Déniaisés: Irréligion et libertinage au début de l'époque moderne* (Paris: Classiques Garnier, 2013), p. 225; Rosellini, 'Théophile devant ses juges', pp. 58–9. For a comparative study of several texts by Théophile and Plato's *Phaedo*, see Hugh Roberts, 'An Exiled Poet adapts Plato: Théophile de Viau's *Traité de l'immortalité de l'âme* and the *Phaedo*', *International Journal of the Classical Tradition* (forthcoming, 2021).

[191] AN X 2B 1185, first interrogation (22 March 1624), in Lachèvre, *Procès*, p. 375.

upon by men of letters, and considered a more basic writing process for teachers of rhetoric, yet it is a useful tool for libertine dissimulation. Liberal imitation, conversely, is an advanced and respected literary endeavour, yet dangerous at a trial in which Théophile's adversaries sought to recognise the criminal voice of the accused in the work of the imitated. It is perhaps this final assertion which both Théophile and his judges had in mind when considering the poet's texts inspired by Antiquity: the extent to which the ancient inspirations for Théophile's libertine poetry, and his modern philosophy for writing and living as expounded in his poetry, were in fact one and the same.

Given that the *commissaires* spent only a short while on these particular texts before moving on to discuss his alleged sexual immorality and disreputable behaviour, Théophile's strategy of defence appears to have been successful. He therefore seems to have played an active part in shifting the focus of the trial from his ideas expressed in literature to alleged speech crimes in his private life. By denigrating his philosophical capabilities, by depicting himself as a translator rather than a disciple of pagan values, and by denying authorship of many of the poems quoted to him, Théophile was able to thwart the prosecution's attempts to present him as an impious philosopher poet with considerable success. Perhaps sensing that he had defended himself effectively, the prosecution no longer attempted to incriminate him through direct quotations from his supposedly irreligious texts. Instead, the interrogators focussed on incriminating the poet's character through licentious poetry. When this strategy had also proved unsuccessful, the trial's focus shifted once again, this time to witness depositions attesting to Théophile's blasphemous speech and his purported homosexuality.[192]

THE USE OF WITNESS TESTIMONY

As far as we can tell, witness testimony was the sole basis upon which Vanini was sent to his death. The depositions made by witnesses during Théophile's trial were evidently considered to be of equally high importance by his judges, either to validate or to inspire the questions posed during interrogations. A defendant would typically be unaware of the content of the witness's deposition

[192] I am therefore of a different opinion to DeJean on this point, for whom Théophile's persecutors 'se bornèrent à faire état de faits qu'on pourrait qualifier de «littéraires»: faits tirés de ses écrits ou liés à leur effet. Ils se servirent de ses œuvres littéraires comme uniques pièces à conviction, et déchaînèrent toute l'autorité de leur discours judiciaire pour soumettre à la question les intentions que Théophile y avait mis' ('restricted themselves to reporting on facts that can be qualified as "literary": facts taken from his writings or linked to them. They made use of his literary works as the sole pieces of incriminating evidence, and unleashed the authority of their entire judiciary discourse to examine the intentions that Théophile had put in them': DeJean, 'Autobiographie', 431). Many of the witnesses did indeed quote Théophile's texts in their depositions in order to question both his Christian faith and his sexuality. Yet they also recounted events that they had witnessed and rumours they had heard about the poet.

before it was read out to them. They could only object to the credibility of the testimonial evidence before this reading, and any subsequent *reproches* would not be entertained. There would then be an opportunity for the accused to 'confront' the witness. The witnesses themselves, though faced with harsh punishment for false testimony, were permitted to make limited alterations to their testimony over the course of the trial, and could also be granted a *salvation* in which they could justify contradictions in their statements that emerged during the hearings.[193]

Witness depositions and confrontations were heard throughout Théophile's trial from clerics, lawyers, prisoners, officials, and people working within the book trade, although few of these appear to have known him personally. The prosecution thus hoped to complete the revelation of Théophile's vices through his lewd poetry in the *recueils satyriques*, so as to leave little doubt as to the poet's true character and conduct as evidenced through testimony. The early depositions focussed on Théophile's religious unbelief. René Le Blanc, for example, recalls an encounter in which he witnessed the accused:

> tenyr pluzieurs discours d'impietez contre Dieu, la Vierge et les sainctz: luy a veu prandre une bible pluzieurs foys de laquelle il rechercheoit les motz les plus sacrosainctz, lesquelz ledit Theophille tournoyt en risée et impietez.
>
> say many impious things against God, the Virgin and the saints; saw him take a Bible several times from which he looked for the most sacrosanct words, which Théophile then distorted into jokes and impieties.[194]

Gabriel Dange's deposition attempts to link Théophile to the *Parnasse satyrique* via a quotation from the anonymous 'Approche, approche ma Dryade', in which the poet supposedly expresses his extraordinary powers of masturbation:

> [Dange] avoit des vers dudit Theophille escriptz de la main dudit Theophille sur le sujet du branlement de pique et qu'il avoit des vers dudit Theophille par lesquelz il disoit que en branlant la pique il feroit resussitter les mortz.
>
> [Dange] had lines of Théophile's poetry written in Théophile's hand on the subject of masturbation, and he had poems by Théophile which said that by masturbating he would resurrect the dead.[195]

[193] Van Damme's assertion that criminal procedure confers 'un caractère irréversible' upon interrogations and oral depositions (Van Damme, *Épreuve*, p. 72) is contestable. On the presentation of witness testimony, the legal restrictions on the witness and the accused before and during confrontations, and the possible objections the defendant could make against witnesses, see Esmein, *Histoire de la procedure*, pp. 139–51. For discussions of these points in early modern legal texts, see Jean Imbert, *La Pratique Judiciaire, tant civile que criminelle*, enrichie par M. Pierre Guénois et M. Bernard Automne (Paris: Robert Foüet, 1616), pp. 284–5, 638–46; Claude Le Brun de La Rochette, *Le Procès civil, et criminel, contenans la methodique liaison du droit, et de la practique judiciaire, civile et criminelle* (Lyon: Pierre Rigaud, 1622), I—*Le Procès civil*, pp. 84–9, II—*Le Procès criminel*, pp. 81–141; and [Johannes Masuer], *La Pratique de Masuer*, trans. by Antoine Fontanon (Paris: Denis Binet, 1610), p. 310.

[194] AN X 2B 1184, deposition by René Le Blanc (11 October 1623), in Lachèvre, *Procès*, p. 215.

[195] AN X 2B 1184, deposition by Gabriel Dange (21 November 1623), in Lachèvre, *Procès*, p. 251.

The strategy of using poetry to cast suspicion on Théophile's sexual conduct remains present throughout all subsequent depositions. It was at this point that Théophile affirmed his social identity as Théophile de Viau by signing his full name, thus abandoning his earlier strategy of insisting on the vague and unstable nature of 'Théophile' as a literary *je* in his corpus.[196] Though a notable lapse in the consistency of the poet's defence, this might also suggest that Théophile realised that the mask of literary abstraction was no longer sufficient to disprove accusations pertaining to his sexual identity.

The depositions varied in credibility. On 29 April 1624, Pierre Guibert recalled eighteen lines of poetry from four separate poems that Théophile had supposedly recited to him 'il y a sept ou huict ans' ('seven or eight years ago').[197] Though Guibert's supposedly incredible powers of recollection would surely have been unlikely to convince, it is worth noting that this may not have appeared as suspect as it might to a modern reader. As Lenman and Parker note, the high costs of trials, and the uncertainty of their outcome in early modern Europe, often caused people to avoid settling their grievances through the legal system for many years, resulting in a backlog of incriminating evidence and testimonies.[198] Théophile's reaction to Guibert's testimony also reveals much about both his strategy of defence and his readership. As DeJean observes, Théophile corrected Guibert's initial claim to be a bourgeois informing the court that he was in fact the son of a butcher, thereby evidencing the non-elite readership of his poetry.[199] This also demonstrates how Théophile wished to denigrate the social position of those who testified against him at a time when, as we saw earlier in Vanini's trial, the perceived validity of testimonial evidence could be influenced by a witness's social status.

Théophile's strategy of defence during witness confrontations is strikingly consistent compared to that of his accusers. First, as with the authorship of many of the poems quoted to him, Théophile denied knowing eleven of the witnesses with whom he was confronted at trial. In doing so, he was able to cast doubt upon their testimony by suggesting that these were merely based on 'ouy dire' ('hearsay').[200]

The act of masturbation may in itself have strengthened the argument that Théophile had committed sodomy. Le Brun de La Rochette lists 'corruption de soi-même' ('corruption of oneself') as one of four forms of sodomy in his legal treatise (La Rochette, *Le Procès civil*, p. 8).

[196] DeJean notes that after his confrontation with Pierre Galtier on 18 August 1625, Théophile began to sign with his full name (DeJean, 'Autobiographie', 438).

[197] AN X 2B 1184, deposition by Pierre Guibert (29 April 1624), in Lachèvre, *Procès*, p. 413.

[198] 'This explains the curious fact that, when the case was eventually tried, aggravations and incidents from years—even decades before—were adduced as evidence' (Bruce Lenman and Geoffrey Parker, 'The State, the Community and the Criminal Law in Early Modern Europe', in *Crime and the Law: The Social History of Crime in Western Europe since 1500*, ed. by V.A.C. Gatrell, Bruce Lenman and Geoffrey Parker (London: Europa Publications, 1980), p. 11–48 (p. 19)).

[199] DeJean, *Obscenity*, p. 51–2.

[200] A claim the poet made during his confrontation with Antoine Vitré (AN X 2B 1186 (21 October 1624), in Lachèvre, *Procès*, p. 467). On 22 November 1624, he also claimed that Pierre Bonnet 'se trompe de ce qu'il dit avoir ouy dire les impietez et atéismes' ('is mistaken in saying that he had heard about

This may have served to discredit testimonial evidence at his trial, as rumour and gossip were valid objections to testimony at this time.[201] The witnesses themselves often debased the authenticity of their depositions by situating these within the context of gossip. On 22 August 1625, Jean Raveneau told the court that:

> Dimanche dernyer il ouyt dire à Françoys Hervé [...] que, s'estant trouvé en la compaignie d'un nommé Gastelyer à présent Capuchin, ledict Gastelyer avoit dict audit Hervé qu'en sa présence [...] Theophille avoit dict que ceux qui prenoyent le corps de Jesus Christ le vendredy estoyent pires que les bougres parce qu'ilz ne sçavoyent s'ilz menjoient de la chayr ou du poysson.
>
> Last Sunday he heard from François Hervé [...] that, having found himself in the company of a certain Gastelier, now a Capuchin, Gastelier had said to Hervé that in his presence [...] Théophile had said that those who took the body of Christ on a Friday were worse than buggers as they did not know if they were eating flesh or fish.[202]

These aspersions would also have echoed a chronic problem in the early modern legal world: the bearing of false testimony. As early as 1555, Guillaume Jaudin had described false testimony as 'le vice le plus commun que l'on voye' ('the most common vice that we come across').[203] In 1600 Philbert Boyer, a prosecutor of the Parlement de Paris, remarked that:

> Le temps est venu que les faux tesmoins sont en grande abondance, n'ont aucune crainte de Dieu, ny de la punition du diable, executeur de sa justice, pourveu qu'ils ayent de l'argent pour deposer faux.
>
> We have reached a point where there is a great abundance of false witnesses, who have no fear of God, nor of punishment by the devil as the executor of his justice, as long as they receive money for giving false testimony.[204]

In a subsequent edition of this text published ten years later, Boyer revealed that the situation had far from improved:

> Cela se voit ordinairement et journellement, tellement, que l'on faict autant et plus d'exécutions de faux tesmoins que de tous autres crimes. Ce que j'en dis n'est que pour l'horreur et détestation de cet abominable crime de faux tesmoins.

---

impieties and atheisms': AN X 2B 1186, confrontation with Pierre Bonnet, in Lachèvre, *Procès*, p. 472).

[201] The accused was permitted to make *reproches de droit* and *reproches de fait* against the witness. One such *reproche de droit* was that the testimony 'n'est fondé que sur ouyr dire' ('is only founded on hearsay'), whereas a valid *reproche de fait* was that the witness 'n'a cognoissance du faict, ny des personnes' ('had no knowledge of the fact or of the people involved': La Rochette, *Le Procès civil*, p. 85).

[202] AN X 2B 1186, confrontation with Jean Raveneau (20 August 1625), in Lachèvre, *Procès*, p. 494. On early modern slander and gossip, see Emily Butterworth, *Poisoned Words. Slander and Satire in Early Modern France* (Oxford: Legenda, 2006); Nicholas Hammond, *Gossip, Sexuality and Scandal in France (1610–1715)* (Oxford: Peter Lang, 2011); and Mathilde Bombart, 'When Writers Gossip: Authorial Reputation in the Literary Polemics of the French 1620s', *Renaissance Studies*, 30: 1 (2016), 137–51.

[203] Guillaume Jaudin, *Traité de tesmoings et d'enquestes* (Paris: Françoys Regnault, 1555), fols. 16^r – 16^v.

[204] Philbert Boyer, *Le Stille de la cour et justice des requestes du palais* (Paris: Jean Richer, 1600), fol. 88^r.

> This is such an ordinary and daily occurrence, that as many if not more executions are carried out for bearing false testimony as for all other crimes. I speak of this purely out of horror and abhorrence for this abominable crime of bearing false witness.[205]

A number of early modern legal texts assert that false witnesses were punished with the same sentence that the accused would have faced if found guilty,[206] and it was for this reason that one of the first questions asked of witnesses and defendants was whether the two parties knew each other.[207] Despite the fact that the witnesses were able to corroborate each other's claims that Théophile was the author of certain poems, the individuals chosen to carry out this task proved to be both unconvincing and unreliable. The final witness to be called, Jean Sepaus, had been taken from his cell at the Conciergerie on 29 August 1625. His testimony, surely a culmination of the prosecution's failure to procure effective witnesses, again demonstrates the extent to which Théophile's objections to rumour were well-founded:

> A dit ne congoistre Theophille, et dit avoir entendu parler de luy. [...] estant aux Carmes, il y eut ung homme qui parla à luy qui luy recitta ung sonnet, et dit lors qu'il croyoit que c'estoit Theophille, mais, l'ayant veu à cette heure, croit que ce n'est luy, mais ung nommé Amanuelli. [...] ledit tesmoin a dit ne congoistre l'accusé et ne croit pas que ce soit luy. [...] Ledit tesmoin a dit qu'un jour Amanuelli au faulxbourg Saint Germain avec La Taille, Amanuelli luy monstra des vers qu'il disoit que Theophille avoit faictz.
>
> Said that he does not know Théophile, and says he has heard of him. [...] Whilst at the Carmelite monastery, there was a man who spoke to him and recited a sonnet to him, and said that he thought it was Théophile, but having now seen him, does not think that it was him, but someone called Amanuelli. [...] the witness said that he does not know the accused and does not believe that it is him. [...] The witness said that one day at the Faubourg Saint Germain Amanuelli, along with La Taille, showed him poetry that he said had been written by Théophile.[208]

Théophile's self-defence also included invalidating testimonies by suggesting that they were coloured by hatred or other personal motives, which again had a

[205] Quoted in Esmein, *Histoire de la procédure*, pp. 152–3.

[206] See for example La Rochette, *Le Procès civil*, p. 141; Jean Duret, *Traicté des peines et amendes* (Lyon: François Arnoullet, 1610), pp. 67ᵛ – 68ʳ; and article 10 of Henri III's 1585 ordinance quoted in Bernard Automne, *La Conference du droict François avec le droict romain* (Paris: Nicolas Buon, 1610), p. 461, which also gives a number of historic examples of this punishment from the fifteenth and sixteenth centuries.

[207] See, for instance, Imbert, *Pratique judiciaire*, p. 643; La Rochette, *Le Procès civil*, p. 137.

[208] AN X 2A 988, deposition by Jean Sepaus (29 August 1625), in Lachèvre, *Procès*, pp. 503–4. Beyond the context of Théophile's trial, these examples of gossip in court records are precious accounts allowing 'for tremendous insight into the mental and social world' of the non-elites (Suzannah Lipscomb, 'Crossing Boundaries: Women's Gossip, Insults and Violence in Sixteenth-century France', *French History*, 25: 4 (2011), 408–26 (413).

basis in contemporary legal theory.[209] As well as highlighting the personal hatred and machinations of Garasse and Voisin throughout the trial, Théophile also made similar accusations against three witnesses. In literary and intellectual debate, personal interest and slander were often used to deride the arguments and even the credibility of a given party, as Garasse's literary polemic amply demonstrates. Théophile's objections show that he was well aware of this. He accused Louis Forest Sageot of 's'en voulant prendre à luy accusé' ('wishing to attack him the accused'),[210] Jean Millot of having 'déposé par animosité et passion' ('given his statement out of animosity and passion'),[211] and Pierre Guibert of continuing his brother's vendetta against him.[212] The tone of these *reproches* could differ somewhat from our previous examples of the finer distinctions between imitation and translation. When confronted with Pierre Rocolet, for example, the poet 'ayant ouy le nom du tesmoin, a dit qu'il est sans honneur et prostitute sa femme et le consant' ('having heard the name of the witness, said that he is a man without honour who prostitutes his wife and consents to it').[213] Despite the defendant's disadvantages against witnesses in criminal trials, such claims appear to have been acceptable discourse in the Parlement if Bernard Automne is to be believed: 'Reproches injurieuses et diffamatoires sont bonnes et recevables en jugement' ('insulting and defamatory *reproches* are sound and admissible evidence in judging a case').[214] Théophile's use of *reproches* also served to steer his eventual judges away from sentencing him to death, as an example from a separate trial led by his most senior judge demonstrates. In a letter to Louis XIII, the *premier président* Nicolas de Verdun describes his eagerness to condemn a defendant to death for blasphemy. However, not all of his colleagues shared this view, and appear to have countered Verdun's opinion with mutually recognised legal justifications including that:

> les tesmoings n'estoient pas entiers, l'accusé ayant bailli quelques reproches contre eux; [...] qu'on ne condamne jamays au dernier supplice, un prevenu qu'il ne soit conviancu du crime dont on l'accuse par deux ou troys tesmoings entiers, et non reprochez.

> the witnesses did not constitute full proofs, as the accused had made a number of *reproches* against them; [...] that a defendant is never condemned to death unless

[209] Boyer, for example, notes that witnesses must swear as part of their oath 'que pour amitié, haine, or, ou argent, ils ne diront autre chose que la verité' ('that they will not say anything other than the truth, irrespective of friendship, hatred, or money': Boyer, *Le Stille*, p. 87ᵛ).

[210] AN X 2B 1186, confrontation with Louis Forest Sageot (21 October 1624), in Lachèvre, *Procès*, p. 464.

[211] AN X 2B 1186, confrontation with Jean Millot (27 August 1625), in Lachèvre, *Procès*, p. 499.

[212] AN X 2B 1186, confrontation with Pierre Guibert (18 January 1625), in Lachèvre, *Procès*, p. 478.

[213] AN X 2B 1186, confrontation with Pierre Rocolet (21 October 1624), in Lachèvre, *Procès*, p. 468.

[214] Automne, *La Conférence*, p. 691. Automne quotes an *arrêt* from 10 December 1584 in this instance. For further context, see Natalie Zemon Davis, *Fiction in the Archives: Pardon Tales and their Tellers in Sixteenth-century France* (Stanford, CA: Stanford University Press, 1987), Chapter 2: 'Angry Men and Self-defence' (pp. 36–76).

> he is convicted of the crime of which he is accused by two or three reliable witnesses that have not been the subjects of *reproches*.[215]

When this is considered alongside accusations of rumour-mongering, as well as personal and emotional motivations which were all well-founded by witness depositions, it is clear that Théophile consistently maintained the upper hand during confrontations with witnesses who were unable to cast reasonable doubt over the poet's religious or sexual conduct. The credibility of the prosecution was further damaged on 22 August 1625. As the magistrates assembled to judge Théophile, one of the judges presented his colleagues with Voisin's memoirs, who had apparently been entrusted with them by their author. These memoirs are now lost, but even Garasse was forced to acknowledge the devastating effect of this revelation on the prosecution: 'à la lecture de ces écrits il y eut deux présidents qui s'alarmèrent fort, et dirent avec grande colère que le Père Voisin méritait mieux la mort que Théophile' ('at the reading of these writings two *présidents* were greatly alarmed, and said in great anger that Father Voisin was more deserving of death than Théophile').[216]

The strategies of the prosecution and the accused, with regards to both literary quotation and witness testimony, show that Théophile's interrogators committed a crucial error in shifting their focus from Théophile's impiety to his sexuality, thereby neglecting the majority of the poems selected (in part by Garasse, as demonstrated by his correspondence with Molé), to condemn him. The inconsistency of their line of questioning, and the desperation with which they relied upon unconvincing depositions late in the trial, suggest their frustration and fear of losing control of proceedings. This would explain why, having failed to incriminate the poet as a thinker, witness testimonies became increasingly important to the authorities in presenting Théophile as a sexually deviant author of the *Parnasse satyrique*. Despite this change of approach, Théophile's consistent and convincing tactics during witness confrontations were sufficiently effective to secure his freedom.

On 27 August Théophile was interrogated briefly in front of the full complement of judges in an *interrogatoire sur la sellette* prior to their deliberation (Figure 5.7). The interrogation began with questions pertaining to the poet's religious education and his *Traicté*. This was either in order to sum up the contents of the wider trial, which had begun with questions on this very text on 22 March 1624, or to make a last-minute attempt to bring the focus of the trial back to Théophile's impious philosophical views. The subsequent questions were short, vague, and focussed on poems in the *Parnasse satyrique*, Théophile's supposed homosexuality, and his blasphemous speech acts in an

[215] BNF MS Dupuy 63, p. 170^{v}.
[216] Garasse, *Mémoires*, p. 72.

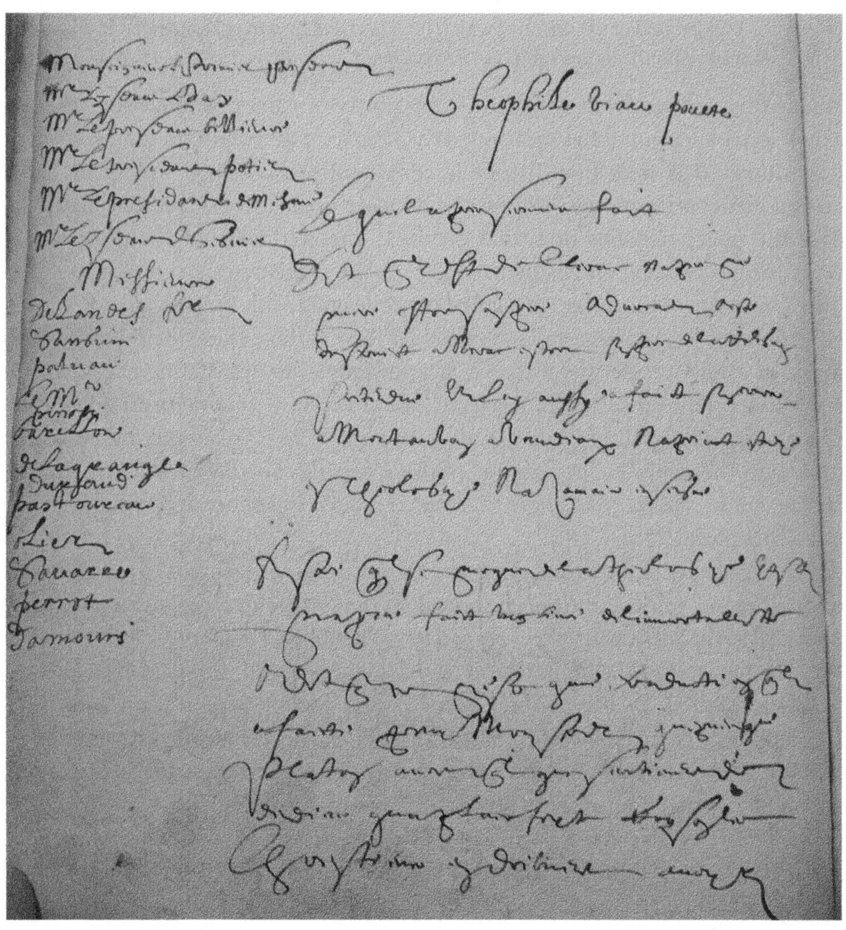

Figure 5.7 AN 2 XA 988: Théophile is interrogated *sur la sellette* before his judges, whose names are given in the left-hand margin (27 August 1625). The list begins with the *premier président* Verdun, before giving the *présidents*, Deslandes (identified in shorthand as *rapporteur*), and the other judges.

incoherent order.[217] Théophile continued to refute that he had intended to write as a theologian, and again denied authorship of the poems quoted to him. In a final effort to regain the upper hand, the magistrates heard the last-minute testimony of Sepaus, another prisoner of the Parlement, on 29 August. The scant evidence from Sepaus's deposition marked the end of the trial, and the judges reached their verdict later that day. The following day, on 1 September 1625, the

[217] See AN X 2A 988, Théophile's final *interrogatoire sur la sellette* before his judges (27 August 1625), in Lachèvre, *Procès*, pp. 500–2.

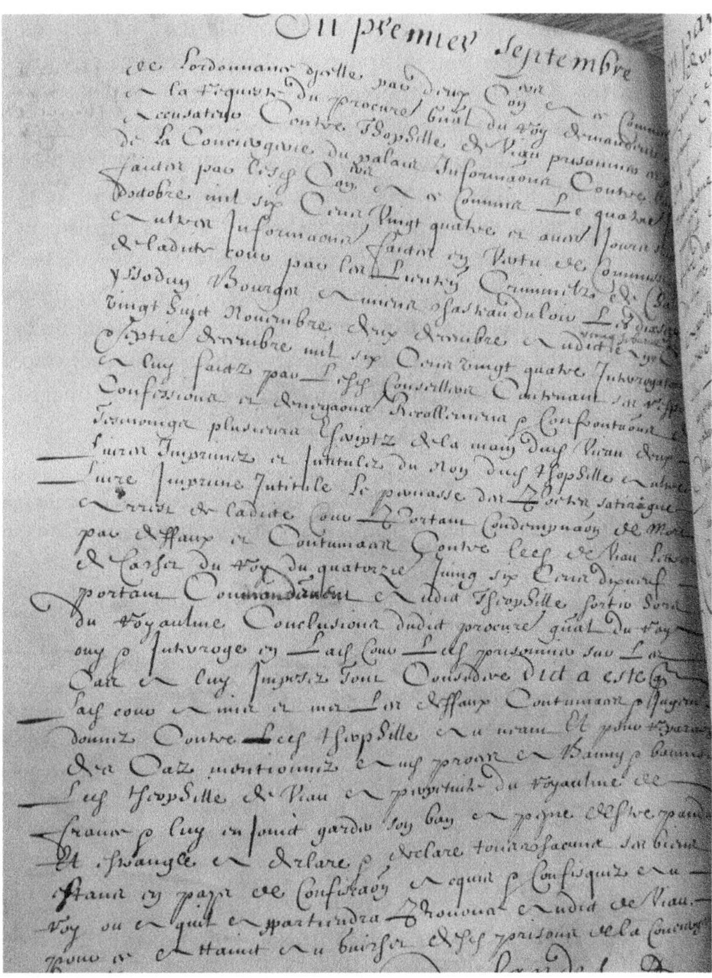

Du premier Septembre

Figure 5.8 AN X 2A 224: Copy of the *arrêt* from Théophile's trial which quashed his previous conviction from 19 August 1623 (1 September 1625).

Parlement's *arrêt* quashed Théophile's previous conviction from 19 August 1623. As if to save face or to satisfy supporters of the Jesuits, the Parlement nonetheless added that 'pour réparation des cas mentionnez audict procès' ('as punishment for the offences mentioned in this trial'), Théophile was sentenced to permanent banishment from France, which in reality constituted an order prohibiting him from returning to Paris (Figure 5.8).[218]

[218] AN X 2B 357 and AN X 2A 224 (both quoted in Lachèvre, *Procès*, p. 505); AN X 2A 224. A copy of the *arrêt* can also be found in BNF MS Dupuy 93, fol. 62. Théophile was finally pardoned and

The collapse of the legal case against Théophile may be seen as a final consequence of failed interrogation strategies, of a poor choice of witnesses, or a testament to the defendant's ultimately successful strategies of self-defence. Another aspect of the verdict, however, has yet to be considered in critical studies of this trial: the views of the judges. This is doubtless due in part to the fact that the votes of individual judges were not written down in trial records at this time, and were supposed to be kept in absolute secrecy.[219] This is intrinsically linked to the image of the Parlement as a single, unified entity. Houllemare has argued that magistrates were reluctant to publish their reflections on the law through fear of undermining the collective legal voice and the perceived 'unité de corps' ('a united body') of official documents such as *arrêts* with an individual voice. It was essential, she adds, for the magistrates to maintain a positive public image through collective ritual:[220]

> Le silence sur le contenu des délibérations renforce l'unité symbolique du corps judiciaire, en affichant une unanimité du jugement. Cette façade unie maintient la fiction d'une concorde dans l'État, à travers une institution ne parlant que d'une seule voix.
>
> The silence surrounding the contents of deliberations reinforces the symbolic unity of the judicial body by showing unanimity in its judgements. This united façade maintains the fiction of agreement within the State, through an institution consistently speaking with a single voice.[221]

Théophile's trial is but one example of how this unity was a fictional façade. The following study of the poet's judges allows us to shed new light on his acquittal, and is the first to propose how individual judges may have voted on this case.

THE *CORPS JUDICIAIRE* DISMEMBERED: THÉOPHILE'S JUDGES AND THE FINAL DELIBERATIONS

Théophile was judged on 29 August 1625 in a joint assembly of the Grand' Chambre, the Tournelle, and the Chambre de l'Édit. This final chamber had not previously formed part of Théophile's trial. It was likely to have been involved

permitted to return to Paris in August 1626.

[219] This said, Soman has nonetheless uncovered a rare account of how individual judges voted during the deliberation of an arson case which led to a death in 1554. See Soman, 'Sorcellerie, justice criminelle et société', 199–200.

[220] Houllemare, *Parlement*, pp. 369, 379.

[221] Houllemare, *Parlement*, p. 124. On this *esprit de corps*, see also A. Lloyd Moote, *The Revolt of the Judges: The Parlement of Paris and the Fronde 1643-1652* (Princeton, NJ: Princeton University Press, 1971), pp. 13–16; Mousnier, *Les Institutions*, pp. 257, 331–3; Sylvie Daubresse, *Le Parlement de Paris ou la voix de la raison (1559–1589)* (Geneva: Droz, 2005), pp. 46–53, 247–311; Houllemare, *Parlement*, p. 162; and Swann, *Exile, Imprisonment, or Death*, p. 353. For Mousnier, this collective identity stemmed from the shared learning experience of the Jesuits discussed earlier (Mousnier, *Les Institutions*, p. 331).

in the final deliberation due to the scale of the trial by this time, rather than any doubts concerning Théophile's conversion to Catholicism which, as Jouhaud observes, meant that the poet could not use his Huguenot identify as a defence of his texts and beliefs.[222] Eighteen judges gathered to reach a verdict, with a majority of two votes required for the judgement to be passed.[223] Lachèvre's study only gives the ranks and surnames of the judges, thereby leaving the faces of those who stared down at the defendant in almost total shadow. Though any attempt to deduce the decision of a given judge must remain hypothetical, the identification of the judges allows for a more nuanced picture of the so-called *corps judiciaire* that held Théophile's fate in the balance. It also permits us to appreciate the extent to which his implicit acquittal—itself inseparable from his strategies of self-defence—constituted a remarkable feat given the backgrounds of some of his judges. Thanks largely to the invaluable work conducted by Michel Popoff, I have also been able to identify many of Théophile's judges, and to offer comment on the composite members of the assembled chambers, for the first time. Depending on the criteria used, there were arguably three hearings in which Théophile was judged. The judges first assembled on 21 and 22 August 1625, but were interrupted by the mysterious yet damning revelations regarding Voisin. On 27 August, Théophile was interrogated *sur la sellette* by the entire panel of judges, most of whom would not have previously met him. Finally, the judges assembled on 29 August and reached their verdict, which was made official in an *arrêt* on 1 September.[224]

The following list of judges at the final deliberation of 29 August gives the full names of those that I have been able to identify with confidence. For others, the presence of more than one magistrate of a given family name in different chambers of the Parlement (a common occurrence throughout the Parlement's history) does not allow for definite identification. The final deliberation was attended by the *premier président du Parlement de Paris* Nicolas de Verdun; *présidents* Nicolas Le

[222] Jouhaud, *Pouvoirs de la littérature*, p. 47. Lebigre has argued that the Chambre de l'Édit was competent in this trial as Théophile was a Protestant (Arlette Lebigre, 'Les procès de Théophile de Viau', in *Quelques procès criminels des XVIIe et XVIIIe siècles*, ed. by Jean Imbert (Paris: Presses Universitaires de France, 1964), pp. 29–43 (p. 42)). There is no evidence that Théophile's interrogators still considered him to be a Huguenot. This chamber was on the other hand included in trials for extremely grave crimes. One such example is the trial of the regicide François Ravaillac, who was certainly not a Protestant. Finally, the Chambre de l'Édit only contained a single Huguenot judge, and was expected to defend Catholic parties against Huguenot litigants, rather than to provide Huguenots with an arena for trial by peers. See Diane C. Margolf, *Religion and Royal Justice in Early Modern France: The Paris Chambre de l'Édit, 1598–1665* (Kirksville, MO: Truman State University Press, 2003), pp. 33–5.

[223] As stipulated in Charles VII's ordinance of 1451 (see Charles Desmaze, *Le Parlement de Paris* (Paris: Cosse, Marchal et Billard, 1860), p. 55) and later confirmed in article 17 of Charles IX's declaration of 10 July 1566 (Isambert, *Recueil général*, XIV ii, p. 216).

[224] Lachèvre, *Procès*, pp. 495–505 gives the names of judges present at these individual concluding hearings.

Jay, Nicolas de Bellièvre, André Potier, Henri II de Mesmes, and Pierre Séguier; *conseillers* Guillaume Deslandes, Denis Paluau, Le Mercier, Jacques Sanguin, Jacques Pinon, Ursin Durant, de La Grange, François Pastoureau, Nicolas-Edouard Olier, Jules Savarre, Perrot, and Gabriel Damours.[225] The *présidents* Nicolas Chevalier and Hierosme (also referred to as Jérôme) d'Hacqueville d'Onsembray, as well as *conseillers* Bouchet,[226] Jean-Jacques Barillon, and Delanauve, had attended the previous sessions but were absent from the 29 August hearing.

Molé was not present for the vote, as confirmed by the court records which state that during the deliberations, 'Monsieur le Procureur général est entré en la Chambre et dict à la cour...' ('the king's attorney general came into the Chamber and said to the court...') to propose Sepaus as a new witness.[227] It is also noteworthy that one of Théophile's interrogators, François de Verthamon, was not selected to judge the case, whereas both his partner in the *instruction* Jacques Pinon, and his surviving original interrogator Gabriel Damours, were. Given the required majority of at least two votes, there could therefore have been no more than seven of the eighteen names at the final hearing (and possibly fewer) who judged Théophile worthy of the stake, and the machinations of Garasse and Molé worthy of credence.

Working together for an institution as prestigious as the Parlement de Paris inevitably led to professional rivalries. Richelieu recounts a scene in 1617 in which two *conseillers* were despatched as *commissaires* to seize papers from a suspect's residence. The majesty of the Parlement supposedly embodied by the magistrates, however, did not last long outside of the Palais de justice:

> Ils entrèrent en contestation dès la porte du logis et se donnèrent quelques coups de poing à qui entreroit le premier, soit d'affection qu'ils avoient à faire leur charge ou par vanité de leur rang.
>
> As soon as they were at the door of the lodgings, they began to disagree as to who should enter first and threw a few punches at each other, either out of a desire to carry out their work or out of vanity for their rank.[228]

One of the most obvious divisions in the Parlement was that of age and experience. Youth was long considered to be a problem for the Parlement. An

[225] Lachèvre, *Procès*, p. 502.

[226] Most likely Antoine du Bouchet, a *conseiller* since 14 December 1583 who entered the Grand' Chambre on 26 March 1616. This judge could also have been Antoine's son Henry du Bouchet, who had been a *conseiller* since 1622. However, a deputation from the Parlement to the new Chancellor Étienne d'Aligre in 1624 included Antoine, along with several magistrates involved with Théophile's trial—Hierosme de Hacqueville, Guillaume Deslandes, Jacques Sanguin, Ursin Durant, and François de Verthamon—leading us to surmise that Antoine was likely one of Théophile's judges. See Jean Feron and Claude Collier, *Histoire des Connestables: Chanceliers, et Gardes Des Seaux, etc.* (Paris: l'Imprimerie royale, 1658), p. 146.

[227] AN X 2A 988, deposition by Jean Sepaus (29 August 1625), in Lachèvre, *Procès*, p. 503.

[228] Armand Jean du Plessis, Cardinal de Richelieu, *Mémoires du Cardinal de Richelieu*, ed. by Horric de Beaucaire and others, 10 vols (Paris: Librairie Renouard, 1907–31), II (1909), pp. 1616–19, 188–9.

ordinance from May 1579 on the general policing of the realm had stated that no one under the age of twenty-five could obtain judicial office. *Présidents* had to be at least forty years old in order to command the respect of their younger colleagues.[229] Both in 1524 and 1525, the *gens du roi* (the king's men) had insisted on these standards, and that those entering the Parlement should not do so without having first undertaken the required training.[230] As early as 1566 there were complaints that the examination for entry into the Parlement had become too easy.[231] Royal letters of dispensation show that many of those involved in Théophile's trial, including Molé himself, had been able to circumvent these rules.[232] The evident concern with the age of certain members of the Parlement becomes all the more relevant to Théophile's trial when considered in terms of their extra-parliamentary lives. Many magistrates frequented academic circles or salons.[233] Achille de Harlay, the former *premier président du Parlement de Paris,* appears to have been particularly concerned with magistrates who did not take their roles seriously. Some kept company unbefitting of their social and professional rank, some swore, whilst others preferred to cast off their professional attire outside of the Parlement in order to partake in the delights of Paris more inconspicuously.[234] Furthermore, as Henri-Jean Martin notes, the social groups most likely to be influenced by the book trade were the clergy, financers, and magistrates, whereas for Folliard the legal class was one of the largest customer bases for editions of poetry.[235] All things considered, it is not difficult to imagine some of these young magistrates frequenting the same bookshops or taverns in which Théophile's texts were circulating.

Théophile's judges represent a range of age and experience. Jean-Jacques Barillon was received as a *conseiller* on 17 August 1623,[236] Nicolas-Edouard Olier

[229] 'Ordonnance sur les états généraux de Blois' (1579), article 105, quoted in Isambert, *Recueil général*, XIV, p. 407. These sentiments were echoed in further legislation passed on 9 March 1602 (Isambert, *Recueil général*, XV, p. 169). In 1547, Henri II had fixed the minimum age at thirty (Shennan, *The Parlement*, p. 137).

[230] Shennan, *The Parlement*, p. 137.

[231] A candidate would open a random page in an anthology of Roman law. He would then be given a matter of hours to prepare for an interrogation on the laws and ordinances selected by the *présidents*, and for a debate with the *conseillers*. See the 'Ordonnance de Moulins' (1566), article 10, quoted in Desmaze, *Le Parlement*, p. 101. On recruitment into the magistracy and the magistrates' financial situations, see especially François Bluche, *Les Magistrats du parlement de Paris au XVIIIe siècle* (Paris: Economica, 1986).

[232] Shennan, *The Parlement*, p. xvi. Molé was received as a *conseiller* on 29 July 1606 'avec dispense d'âge' aged twenty-two (see Maugis, *Histoire du parlement*, p. 322).

[233] Robert Mandrou, *Magistrats et sorciers en France au XVIIe siècle* (Paris: Plon, 1968), p. 316.

[234] See De Waele, *Les Relations*, pp. 74, 85–9; Houllemare, *Parlement*, pp. 511–14.

[235] See Henri-Jean Martin, *Le Livre français sous l'ancien régime* (Paris: Promodis, 1987), p. 154; Melaine Folliard, 'Les intermittences du nom d'auteur dans les premiers recueils collectifs (1597–1607)', *Littératures classiques*, 80: 1 (2013), 35–62 (43).

[236] De L'Hermite-Souliers and Blanchard, *Les eloges*, p. 121; Popoff, *Prosopographie*, p. 505. Barillon was also a member of Mersenne's circle (Mersenne, *Correspondance*, p. xxxvii).

had risen to the Grand' Chambre on 15 January 1624,[237] and the future chancellor Pierre Séguier had only inherited the title of *président à mortier* from his uncle Antoine in November 1624.[238] At the other end of the spectrum, Théophile's interrogator Jacques Pinon had been a *conseiller* since 1584 and a member of the Grand' Chambre since 1618.[239] Nicolas de Bellièvre had been made a *conseiller* aged just nineteen on 21 August 1602. Despite legislation on minimum age requirements, he had risen to this office due to 'sa capacité plutost que la faveur de son père' ('his abilities rather than due to his father's position').[240] He was Mathieu Molé's predecessor as *procueur général du roi* (1612–14), and had been a *président à mortier* since the resignation of Molé's father Édouard on 13 March 1614.[241] Nicolas Chevalier, *président des enquêtes,* had been a *conseiller* since 1602 and would die as the doyen of the Grand' Chambre in 1633.[242] Finally, Théophile was judged by two previous *lieutenants civils du Châtelet* who were the *de facto* heads of this exceptional *prévôté* court: Nicolas Le Jay (1609–13) and his successor Henri II de Mesmes (1613–21, whose tenure ended shortly before Fontanier's initial trial at the Châtelet). Those whose roles afforded them particular influence over the outcome of the trial were the magistrates charged with instructing the case as *commissaires* (Pinon and Verthamon), the *premier président* Nicolas de Verdun, and the *rapporteur* Guillaume Deslandes.

Deslandes was one of the most experienced judges at Théophile's trial. Born into a family whose service to the crown could be traced back to the fourteenth century, he brought to bear over fifty years of legal experience beginning with his nomination as a *conseiller* in July 1572.[243] Garasse's description of Deslandes as 'un vieillard à l'âge de quatre-vingt-douze ans' ('an old man of ninety-two') is only a slight exaggeration: he died the doyen of the Grand' Chambre on 20 May 1630, aged ninety.[244] Surviving records show that he played a role, and was often a key participant, in a number of important affairs of state in which he demonstrated competence in a variety of fields, from rights to succession to the personal execution of royal edicts.[245] In January 1595, Deslandes had reacted angrily to

[237] Olier, *Journal*, p. 6; Popoff, *Prosopographie*, p. 1880.

[238] De L'Hermite-Souliers and Blanchard, *Les eloges*, p. 367; Popoff, *Prosopographie*, p. 150.

[239] De L'Hermite-Souliers and Blanchard, *Les eloges*, p. 101.

[240] Popoff, *Prosopographie*, p. 1991.

[241] De L'Hermite-Souliers and Blanchard, *Les eloges*, p. 381; Popoff, *Prosopographie*, p. 58; Maugis, *Histoire du parlement*, p. 320.

[242] De La Chenaye-Desbois and Badier, *Dictionnaire de la noblesse*, p. 584; Maugis, *Histoire du Parlement*, p. 301.

[243] De L'Hermite-Souliers and Blanchard, *Les eloges*, pp. 88–9; Popoff, *Prosopographie*, p. 1522.

[244] Garasse, *Mémoires*, pp. 242–3.

[245] *Sommaires réponses aux moyens proposés par madame de Longueville pour empêcher la mise en possession requise par M. de Nemours, en exécution de l'arrêt donné, au rapport de M. Deslandes, le 13 août 1605* ([n.p.]: [n.pub.], [1605?]); *Édict du Roy de l'erection en tiltre d'offices de receveurs des consignations en main tierce, etc.* (Paris: F. Morel & P. Mettayer, 1618), p. 19, in which Henri IV tasks Deslandes, along with other experienced magistrates, with proclaiming in person letters patent from 7

the admission of Huguenot magistrates into the sovereign courts following the verification of the 1577 Edict of Pacification, warning the Parlement that 'un Juge Hérétique pouvoit faire plus de mal qu'une armée entiere de Gens d'armes' ('a heretical judge could do more damage than an entire army of men at arms').[246] When the Parlement came to debate the burning of Jesuit texts in 1610, Deslandes showed himself to be a staunch though slightly forgetful Catholic:

> M. Deslandes entr'autres se roidissant contre cette opinion, dit que si nous bruslions les Livres des Jesuites, il faloit [sic] à plus forte raison brusler ceux de Luther et de Calvin: Auquel repliqua fort plaisamment (mais pertinemment et à propos) un Conseiller d'Eglise qui estoit près de lui, que les Livres de Calvin avoient esté bruslez il y avoit long-temps, et qu'on n'avoit pas accoustumé de brusler les Livres deux fois.
>
> Mr Deslandes was among several judges hardened against this view, and said that if we burned books written by the Jesuits, there would be even greater reason to burn books by Luther and Calvin. A councillor of the Church sitting near to him replied most agreeably (yet pertinently and rightly) that Calvin's books had been burned some time ago, and that it was not customary to burn books twice.[247]

Deslandes was not invariably disposed towards harsh punishments. He was one of the two *rapporteurs* at the trial of the wife of the assassinated royal favourite Concino Concini, Léonora Galigaï. Whereas his co-*rapporteur* Courtin judged Léonora to deserve death by hanging for witchcraft, Deslandes was inclined towards banishment.[248] Garasse's memoirs offer evidence of Deslandes's Jesuit sympathies, describing him as 'notre unique support en la Grand chambre' ('our sole support in the Grand' Chambre'), a 'personnage très-vénérable par sa sainteté et par son âge' ('a most venerable person for his sanctity and his age') who spent half an hour with the body of the Jesuit confessor Pierre Coton in 1626, and one of Garasse's 'intimes amis' ('intimate friends') along with Mathieu Molé.[249] It therefore seems highly likely that Deslandes would have been predisposed towards recommending the death sentence in his report to the assembled chambers at Théophile's trial. This would concur with Garasse's evidently biased account of the verdict, in which he claims that Deslandes and Pinon 'qui sont reconnus pour être des saints du monde, et des juges de l'antique probité, concurrent un si grand déplaisir, qu'ils en furent malades à la mort' ('who are known as being saints in this world, and judges with the integrity of ancient times, were so displeased with the verdict that they fell deathly ill').[250]

February 1609 in cities across the kingdom.

[246] Pierre de L'Estoile, *Journal du règne de Henri IV*, 4 vols ([Paris]: [n. pub.], 1732), I, p. 85.

[247] L'Estoile, *Journal*, II, p. 173.

[248] *Journal inédit d'Arnaud d'Andilly (1614–1620)*, ed. by Achille Halphen (Paris: J. Techner, 1857), p. 308.

[249] Garasse, *Mémoires*, pp. 204, 244–3, 283.

[250] Garasse, *Mémoires*, p. 86.

Unfortunately for Théophile, Deslandes was not the biggest obstacle to his release. Other experienced judges at the trial had specific experience in the policing of subversive texts and speech acts, including two of its most senior magistrates: Henri de Mesmes and Nicolas de Verdun. Henri II de Mesmes, whose family can be traced back to 1279, had been received as a *conseiller* on 28 June 1608. He then rose through the ranks of *lieutenant civil* of the Châtelet and the *prévôté* (provostship) of Paris (1613). He served as a deputy of the Third Estate at the Paris Estates General (1614) and at the Assembly of Notables at Rouen (1617). He later became provost of the merchants of the city of Paris (1618), before becoming a *président à mortier* on 26 February 1621 and eventually the second *président* of the Parlement in 1627.[251] Contemporary accounts suggest that de Mesmes was sometimes a little too eager to serve justice. At the Estates General of 1614, a certain Barrilliere had criticised François I's provisions for French naval vessels. De Mesmes had Barrilliere seized and removed by two bailiffs for his impertinence, leaving several shocked observers to remind the magistrate:

> que ledit sieur n'estoit là comme Lieutenant Civil et Magistrat, ains comme particulier Deputé, et que c'estoit blesser l'authorité des Estats, qu'un particulier entreprist de constituer prisonnier, un homme qui estoit venu sous la foy et sauf-conduit des Estats.
>
> that he was not there as the *lieutenant civil* or as a magistrate, but as a specific deputy, and that it was an offence to the authority of the Estates for such a man to attempt to inprison a man who had come trusting in the faith and safe passage of the Estates.[252]

His impressive legal career, particularly his time as *lieutenant civil,* brought with it first-hand experience in the persecution of subversive texts and speech acts. In a fascinating letter to Louis XIII dated 18 September 1615, de Mesmes refers to a previous letter from the king in which the sovereign 'me comende de proceder extraordinairement contre les autheurs, Imprimeurs, et colporteurs des livretz et libelles diffammatoires qui s'impriment et se vendent a Paris' ('commanded me to proceed extraordinarily against authors, printers and hawkers of defamatory booklets and pamphlets which are being printed and sold in Paris').[253] De Mesmes worked hard yet unsuccessfully to penetrate the ring of printers and distributors of these texts. Having been told by the pedlars under interrogation that the texts had been delivered to their doors by strangers for almost no money, he chillingly informed the king of the progress he had made with his informants:

[251] De L'Hermite-Souliers and Blanchard, *Les eloges*, pp. 387–8; Popoff, *Prosopographie*, p. 121. The father of the libertine poet and purported 'widow' of Théophile—Des Barreaux—was chosen to be admitted as a *conseiller* on 10 May 1595 over Jean-Jacques de Mesmes (see Maugis, *Histoire du Parlement*, p. 309).
[252] *Recueil tres exact et curieux de tout ce qui s'est faict & passé de singulier & memorable en l'Assemblée generale des Estats tenus à Paris en l'année 1614* (Paris: Au Palais, 1651), pp. 407–8.
[253] BNF MS Dupuy 91, p. 212^{r}.

> Nonobstant ces responces et deffences des colporteurs, ceux d'entr'eux qui se sont trouvés les plus coupables ont esté condamnés à endurer toutes les peines qu'un corps mortel peult souffrir sans mourir.
>
> Notwithstanding the hawkers' answers and attempts to defend themselves, those of them found to be the guiltiest have been condemned to endure all the pains that a mortal body can suffer without dying.[254]

Finally de Mesmes admitted defeat, and confessed that he was unable to condemn the printers and authors 'comme j'ay faict par le passé' ('as I have done in the past').[255] For those willing to conform to the exigencies of orthodoxy, Henri de Mesmes could be a friend and even a patron. Mandrou has observed that de Mesmes was a regular attendee of private academic and scientific gatherings, and had a fixed day for receiving guests including Louis Servin, the erudite libertine Gabriel Naudé, and even one of Garasse's critics, François Ogier.[256] De Mesmes's father Henri I had amassed an impressive library including a number of ancient texts, which Henri II expanded further with Greek and oriental manuscripts. Naudé even dedicated his *Advis pour dresser une bibliothèque*, as well as his 1626 work of libertine scepticism, the *Apologie pour tous les grand personnages qui ont été faussement soupçonné de magie*, to this same judge who had previously hunted down illegal and subversive texts in person.[257] Similarly to Verthamon, de Mesmes had connections with intellectual and even literary circles. These demand a more nuanced view of the legal anthropology governing social boundaries between members of the Parlement on the one hand, and members of high society and the Republic of Letters on the other. In de Mesmes, Théophile was faced with a judge who was at the same time a high-ranking royal servant, a man of obvious learning in his father's footsteps, and an experienced, unflinching enemy of purportedly subversive literature.

The most imposing figure during the final deliberations was the *premier président* Nicolas de Verdun. Verdun had been a *conseiller* in the Parlement since 1583, a member of Catherine de Médicis's private council, and a *président* first in the requêtes then the enquêtes chambers.[258] He was sent to Toulouse in order to serve as the *premier président* of its Parlement on 9 April 1602, before returning to replace Achille de Harlay as *premier président du Parlement de Paris* in either 1611 or 1616.[259] Verdun was a staunch Catholic, and had been one of the magistrates

[254] BNF MS Dupuy 91, pp. 212^r – 212^v.
[255] BNF MS Dupuy 91, p. 212^r.
[256] Mandrou, *Magistrats et sorciers*, pp. 315–16; Fumaroli, *Éloquence*, p. 545.
[257] *Mémoires inédits de Henri de Mesmes*, ed. by Édouard Fremy (Geneva: Slatkine, 1970), pp. 109–11. De Mesmes's patronage of Naudé was also a continuation of his father's association with the authors of his day. Philippe Girard dedicated his translation of Jean Passerat's *Rien* to Henri I in 1597, who was also a patron of Pierre de Ronsard.
[258] Houllemare, *Parlement*, p. 85.
[259] De L'Hermite-Souliers and Blanchard, *Les eloges*, p. 81; Popoff, *Prosopographie*, p. 49; Fayard, *Aperçu*

to stay in Paris and swear allegiance to the Catholic League's Parlement. This decision caused him some difficulty both immediately after the event and later on in his career.[260] Nevertheless, he was known for his great piety, and was described by his contemporaries as a *président* 'qui congois que l'impiete est justement deceu' ('who knows that impiety is justly left disappointed');[261] a man who declared war on vice, who donated money to ruined churches and monasteries,[262] and who was appreciated for 'son subtil jugement, sa divine eloquence, / Sa saincte pieté, sa douceur, sa prudence' ('his subtle judgement, his divine eloquence, / his saintly piety, his calmness, his prudence').[263] It was furthermore claimed that Verdun echoed the patron saint of lawyers—St Ivo of Kermartin—in that his judgements were so wise that even defeated parties approved of them.[264]

Given his position in the Parlement, it is not surprising that Verdun saw a number of legal texts dedicated to him in the years leading up to Théophile's trial.[265] The death of his wife Charlotte du Gué in 1622 provoked a strong reaction from men of letters. At least twenty-eight authors penned works of poetry and prose in her memory, with some contributing multiple texts.[266] These included texts by Malherbe, Jean Grangier—the teacher of rhetoric whose pedantry would later be ridiculed in Cyrano de Bergerac's *Le Pédant joué* (completed in late 1651)—Jean Boucher, and Claude Garnier, who would go on to attack Théophile during his incarceration in his 'Atteinte contre les impertinences de Théophile, enemy des bons esprits.'[267] Ironically, Verdun even received a poem of consolation from Guillaume Colletet, whose arrest warrant and subsequent nine-year banishment he would sign just one year later in connection with the *Parnasse satyrique*.

---

historique, p. 14. Popoff dates Verdun's installation at the Parlement de Paris to 1616, whereas account of this event dated 9 April 1611 is given in BNF MS Dupuy 90, p. 66[r].

[260] See Maugis, *Histoire du Parlement*, p. 268.

[261] *L'Adieu à Monseigneur de Verdun conseiller du Roy en ses conseils d'Estat & privé, & premier president au Parlement de Tholose* ([n.p.]: [n. pub], 1616), p. 2.

[262] [Le Père Boucher], *Oraison funebre sur le trespass de Madame M. Charlotte du Gué, en son vivant Espouse de Monseigneur M. Messire Nicolas de Verdun, etc.* (Paris: Denys Moreau, 1622), pp. 51–2.

[263] D.L.N, *Elegie, ou chant pitoyable, sur la mort de tres illustre seigneur, messire Nicolas de Verdun, etc.* (Paris: Jacques Dugast, 1627), p. 5.

[264] *La vie et mort de messire Nicolas de Verdun, etc.* (Paris: Jean Bessin, 1627), p. 7. Malherbe also praises Verdun's judgements in 'À Monsieur le Premier Président, sur la mort de Madame sa femme', in Malherbe, *Poésies*, pp. 203–5.

[265] Including the *Plaidoyez de Mr Jacques de Puymisson, advocate au Parlement de Tolose* (Tolose: Jacques and R. Colomiés, 1612); Guillaume de Segla, *Histoire tragique, et arrests de la cour de Parlement de Toulouse* (Paris: Nicolas la Caille, 1613); Gabriel Cayron, *Stil et forme de proceder, tant en la cour de Parlement de Tolose, et chambre des requestes d'icelle, etc.* (Tolose: Jean Boude, 1611); and Jean Boucher, *L'Olympe francoys* (Paris: Denis Moreau, 1621).

[266] See *Tombeaux, oraisons funèbres, consolations et poèmes divers* ([n.p]: [n.pub], 1621).

[267] I have provided a more accurate dating of Cyrano's comedy and argued that a third, now lost version of the play was in circulation in Cyrano's lifetime in Adam Horsley, '"Ne l'as-tu point vu passer, mon garde?" Towards a Third Version of Cyrano de Bergerac's *Le Pédant joué*', *French Studies Bulletin*, 123 (2012), 28–31. On Théophile and Garnier see Lachèvre, *Procès*, II, pp. 135–47.

Owing to his piety and his sense of professional duty, Verdun shared de Mesmes's enthusiasm for the hunting down of subversive authors and blasphemers. In a letter to Henri IV catalogued as dating from 1602 (but more likely written in 1606), he details his investigation into the Bishop of Castres—a supporter of the League—for publishing a defamatory text.[268] In May 1603, Verdun wrote an unusually long letter to the king on the subject of a clerk from Castelnau named Blaise Vitalis who had been accused of blasphemy.[269] There are numerous instances in the letter in which Verdun betrays his emotional involvement in the case, as well as his irritation at being unable to secure the death penalty against the defendant. He also reveals himself to be more generally concerned by the high levels of licentious speech in public places and the lack of harsh punishments for such crimes. Remarkably, Verdun even goes as far as to lament the lack of punishment for a certain blasphemer—Father Gaspard de Séguiran—who would go on to be the personal confessor of Louis XIII and to convert Théophile to Catholicism![270] Théophile's *requête* to the *premier président* alone, then, was unlikely to have done much to dissuade Verdun from his habitual zeal against blasphemous tongues and quills.[271]

Other factors, however, might have fared better in persuading Verdun to rule in Théophile's favour. Given the ongoing conflict between the Jesuits and the Parlement de Paris, as well as the continued hostilities towards the Jesuits from a broad spectrum of opponents, Marie de Médicis had appointed Verdun *premier président du Parlement de Paris* in 1611 due to his reputed sympathy for the Jesuits to whom he owed his education.[272] This appointment was at first promising for the Jesuit cause. As one contemporary remarked, after his arrival in Paris Verdun was quick to give orders against the printing of texts against the pope or the Church of Rome.[273] Yet far from calming the conflict as the queen had hoped, Verdun

[268] BNF MS Dupuy 63, pp. 162–3. On p. 163 reference is made to the king's accident at the Port de Neuilly. This seems likely to refer to an incident which occured on 9 June 1606, when Henri IV's carriage fell into the water whilst returning home from Saint-Germain-en-Laye.

[269] BNF MS Dupuy 63, pp. 170–4. I have examined this case in detail in Adam Horsley, 'Blasphemy Hunters: Nicolas de Verdun and the Punishment of Criminal Speech in Early Bourbon France', *French Studies*, 75: 2 (2021), 145–62.

[270] BNF MS Dupuy 63, p. 172^r.

[271] As Lebigre notes, Théophile's 'extra-juridical' poems addressed to Verdun and the Parlement as a whole had no legal basis or consequence. See Lebigre, 'Les procès de Théophile de Viau', p. 41.

[272] As Joseph Bergin remarks on the Jesuits' loyalty to Rome, 'controversy clung to them in France from the beginning, and no good Gallican, Catholic or Protestant could stomach what seemed to be their political allegiance' (Joseph Bergin, *Church, Society and Religious Change in France, 1580–1730* (New Haven, CT, and London: Yale University Press, 2009), p. 112).

[273] Borghese to Ubaldini (24 May 1611) quoted in Alfred Soman, 'Press, Pulpit and Censorship in France before Richelieu', *Proceedings of the American Philosophical Society*, 120: 6 (1976), 439–63 (457–8). On the rivalry between Gallican and Jesuit factions, see Fumaroli, *Éloquence*, pp. 223–57, 326–42; Eric Nelson, *The Jesuits and the Monarchy: Catholic Reform and Political Authority in France (1590–1615)* (Aldershot: Ashgate 2005), pp. 189–90; Jean-François Dubost, *Marie de Médicis: La reine dévoilée* (Paris: Payot et Rivages, 2009), pp. 453–6.

soon converted to the predominant Gallicanism of the Parlement. He encouraged Edmond Richer to publish his Gallican *Libellus de Ecclesiastica et politica potestate* (Paris: [n. pub.], 1611) which, as seen in Chapter 2, was censored in 1612 for being in conflict with the doctrine of absolute monarchy. Both Verdun's ambitions and his hostility towards the Jesuits were exacerbated when, during the course of Théophile's trial in October 1624, he was overlooked to replace Nicolas Brulart de Sillery as Chancellor in favour of the Jesuit Étienne Aligre. Garasse's memoirs make the *premier président*'s feelings quite clear:

> Le Premier président, qui n'était pas de nos meilleurs amis, et auquel on avait ouï dire cette parole, le jour de la promotion de M. d'Aligre à la charge de garde-des-sceaux, à laquelle il aspirait depuis longtemps: *qu'il se vengerait des Jésuites un jour de sa vie*.
>
> The *premier président*, who was not one of our best friends, and who was heard to have said, on the day that Mr d'Aligre was promoted to the role of keeper of the Seals, which he had long aspired to: *that he would have his revenge on the Jesuits one day*.[274]

Shortly after Théophile's trial, in 1626 the Parlement debated possible sanctions against the Jesuits for Antonio Santarelli's *Tractaus de haeresi, schismatic, apostasia, etc.* (Rome: Bartholomæ Zannetti, 1625). The Parlement decided on a relatively lenient punishment despite, according to Garasse, 'quelque chaleur que M. le Premier président témoignât du contraire' ('certain heated words of the *premier président* in favour of the contrary'). Verdun even went so far as to order the medieval clock of the Palais de justice to be wound back in order to allow more time to vent his anger in the chamber.[275] The *premier président* therefore harboured anti-Jesuit sentiments directly before, during, and after he and his fellow judges deliberated a verdict on Théophile's case.

Could Théophile de Viau's trial have been Nicolas de Verdun's opportunity for vengeance against the Jesuits?[276] According to Garasse, the stakes for the Jesuits in the trial outcome were also clear to another magistrate of the Parlement: 'afin qu'il ne fût pas dit que la cause des Jésuites prévalait dans la cour; car cette parole fut avancée publiquement par un président' ('so that it would not be said that the Jesuit cause had prevailed in the court, as this phrase was put forward

[274] Garasse, *Mémoires*, p. 30. Garasse later describes a sodomy case involving a Jesuit priest judged by Verdun. The accuser retracted his accusation against the priest in a written statement taken shortly before his own execution, which Verdun promptly tore up. Garasse's account of this event reveals his own personal animosity towards him: 'Dieu permit que le Premier Président s'aveuglât grandement en cette affaire, car il condamna par précipitation ce méchant prêtre sodomiste, et le fit brûler' ('God allowed the *premier président* to be most blinded in this affair, as he condemned the wicked sodomite priest to be burnt at the stake in great haste': Garasse, *Mémoires*, p. 32).

[275] Garasse, *Mémoires*, pp. 203–4.

[276] A theory supported by Adam, *Pensée*, p. 395 and Van Damme, *Épreuve*, p. 153, which mistakenly refers to the *premier président* as Nicolas de Verdier.

in public by a *président*').[277] As both the well-known Santarelli affair and my own recent discovery of Blaise Vitalis's trial demonstrate, the strong views of the *premier président* were not always enough to prevent the collective voice of the Parlement from voting against him, and it is perfectly conceivable that such a situation presented itself at Théophile's trial. On the other hand, is it doubtful that Garasse would have failed to acknowledge the *premier président*'s support in the final deliberations had he judged Théophile to be guilty, especially given the striking change of allegiances that this would have represented. Given his personal animosity, it seems unlikely that Verdun could have brought himself to voice his support for what was so obviously and so publicly a campaign led by the Jesuits. Similarly, political allegiances with regards to the Jesuits may also have influenced Henri de Mesmes. Despite his enthusiastic pursuit of illegal pamphlet printers, De Mesmes was very much a Gallican magistrate and would not therefore have found it easy to vote in line with Jesuit expectations.[278]

Théophile's letters written after his release permit us to deduce the decisions of two other judges with greater confidence. Our previous chapter on Fontanier's trial did little to depict Nicolas de Bellièvre as a lenient judge. Surprisingly, when Théophile wrote to him asking for more time to prepare for his exile, he recalled: 'vous m'avez retiré de la mort [...] puis que vous m'avez laissé la vie, ne m'ostez point la liberté d'en user. Je dois l'un à vostre justice, et je tiendray l'autre de vostre bonté' ('you have pulled me away from death [...] given that you have spared my life, do not take away my freedom to enjoy it. I owe the one to your justice, and I will take the other from your goodness').[279] Garasse furthermore alludes to a *président* who sought to avoid a Jesuit victory in this trial, identified by Lachèvre as Bellièvre.[280] This leads us to the perhaps unexpected conclusion that whatever his motives may have been, the magistrate who had so ruthlessly pursued Fontanier's death sentence in 1621 proved to be an ally for Théophile in 1625. A similar request for extra time to Olier (who happened to be Molé's cousin) also implies the judge's sympathies for the poet:

> Ce qui me fait plus esperer vostre faveur, c'est la longueur de ma persecution: Cela me donne la hardiesse de vous offrir cette requeste à presenter, pour obtenir autant de delay qu'il en faut à mon esprit pour un travail qui marque au moins l'obligation que j'ay à tous ceux qui ont pris soin de ma delivrance. Je ne sçaurois vous rien promettre que les ressentimens d'une personne incapable d'ingratidude.

[277] Garasse, *Mémoires*, pp. 72–3.

[278] On De Mesmes and Gallicanism, see [Louis Séguier], *Sententia praetoris praefecturae Parisiensis, etc.* (Paris: P. Durand, 1614), p. 7; Frédéric Gabriel, 'Libertinage et gallicanisme', *Littératures classiques*, 55: 3 (2004), 69–75 (69).

[279] 'A Monseigneur le Président de Bellièvre', in *Nouvelles œuvres de feu Mr Théophile, composées d'excellentes Lettres Françoises & Latines*, ed. by [Jean] Mayret (Paris: Antoine de Sommaville, 1648), p. 57.

[280] Garasse, *Mémoires*, pp. 72–3; Lachèvre, *Procès*, p. 496.

> It is the length of my persecution which gives me the greatest hope for your favour. It gives me the boldness to offer you this appeal to present, in order to obtain as long a delay as is necessary for my spirit to undertake a task that at least marks the duty I have towards all those who have worked for my deliverance. I can only promise you the deepest feelings of someone incapable of ingratitude.[281]

There is one final element of judging a criminal case which has been entirely ignored in scholarship on Théophile's case. The trial was instigated by Molé, who lodged a legal complaint to the Parlement and brought copies of Théophile's published works to substantiate his claims. Given this, and given the serious nature of the accusations made against the poet, it is surprising that modern studies should present the influence of the *gens du roi* as ending with Molé's draft of questions for the opening hearing, as if Molé played no further part in the trial after March 1624. The *registres d'écrou*, for example, show that Molé had ordered La Pause to be transferred from the Conciergerie and interrogated on 24 April 1624—a manoeuvre which Molé would later mirror in bringing Sepaus from his cell on 29 August 1625. As seen earlier with Théophile's first trial *in absentia*, the *procureur général* or one of his *substituts* could propose their views on the case. Alongside the opinion of the *rapporteur*, these *conclusions* were intended to guide the other judges in deliberating their verdict.

Figure 5.9 reproduces one of the four pages from Molé's *conclusions* on Théophile's second trial, which are presented here for the first time. Although signed by one of Molé's *substituts* 'Acari'—either due to Molé's need to distance himself from his lost cause or because of genuine commitments elsewhere—Molé's involvement in the trial leaves little doubt that the contents of this document were prepared with his approval.[282] The *conclusions* grant us new insights into Molé's views on Théophile's case at the end of the trial, thus completing the picture painted by his pre-trial preparations. Not surprisingly, Molé had remained unconvinced by Théophile's performance in interrogations and confrontations, and undeterred by the dubious witness testimony produced against him. As the case against Théophile began to fall apart in the summer of 1625, Molé pursued the death sentence to the very end. His recommendations to the judges, as the king's representative in the Parlement, almost read as a document from an alternative timeline in which Théophile was ultimately found guilty and executed:

> Je requiers pour le roy led. Theophile Viau estre declaré atteinct et convaincu des cas mentionnés au proces et pour reparation condamne a faire amende honorable devant la principalle porte de l'eglise Nostre Dame de cette ville de Paris et illec a genou teste pieds nuds en chemise, la corde au col, tenant en sa main une

[281] 'A Monsieur Olier', in *Nouvelles œuvres*, pp. 64–5. On Olier's family link with Molé, see *Journal de Nicolas-Edouard Olier*, p. 13.

[282] The *substitut* 'Acari' could well have been one of the sons of Pierre Acari, a fervent *ligueur* and husband of the future Marie de l'Incarnation: Nicolas, Jean, or most likely Pierre.

torche ardente du poids de deux livres, dire et declarer que tres meschamment et abominablement, il a escript, composé, faict imprimer et deposer en vente lesd. livres et escriptes remplis d'impuretés, b[r]outalités, impietés, et atheismes contenans en iceux, dict et proferé les blasphemes contre l'honneur de Dieu et son eglise, mentionnés aud. cas dont il se repent, en demande pardon a dieu au roy, et a [la] justice, ce faict mené et conduict en la place de greve, et la pandu et estranglé a une potence laquelle pour cet effect y sera dressé son corps, lesd. livres et son proces jetté en ung feu ardens, mis et reduicts en cendres, icelle jettés au vent.

In the name of the king I apply for the aforementioned Théophile Viau to be declared accused and convicted of the cases mentioned in the trial, and as punishment to be condemned to perform the *amende honorable* before the main door of the church of Notre-Dame in this city of Paris. There, on his knees, wearing only a shirt with his feet and head bare, a rope around his neck, holding in his hand a burning torch weighing two pounds, he is to say and declare that most wickedly and abominably he has written, composed, had printed and delivered for sale the aforementioned books and writings filled with impurities, brutalities, impieties, and atheisms contained within them; said and pronounced blasphemies against the honour of God and his Church mentioned in the aforementioned case of which he repents, and asks forgiveness from God, the king, and the judiciary. Once this is done, he is to be brought and driven to the Place de Grève, where he is to be hanged and strangled on gallows erected there for that purpose. His body, the aforementioned books, and his trial are to be thrown into a raging fire, put and reduced to ashes, which are to be thrown to the wind.[283]

As with his previous *conclusions*, Molé maintains the accusation of 'brutalities' which had been omitted from the death sentence carried out in effigy in 1623. The document also begins with a useful summary of the various stages of the trial and their corresponding dates, including reference to La Pause's previously unknown interrogation. These details elucidate a further stage of Théophile's legal manoeuvres for which Frédéric Lachèvre and Antoine Adam have proposed conflicting hypotheses. According to Lachèvre, who erroneously claims that the *Parnasse satyrique* was published in 1623, Théophile obtained a sentence banning Estoc from selling copies of the anthology in April that year. Despite the fact that other contemporary sources prove Théophile's actions, Lachèvre continues, there is no evidence of his legal complaint in the archives.[284] In Lachèvre's scenario, Théophile adroitly took matters into his own hands shortly after the offending text appeared in print. However, in convincingly demonstrating that the *Parnasse satyrique* was printed in November or (most likely) December 1622, Adam's authoritative hypothesis solves one problem whilst creating another. For Adam,

[283] AN X 1A 8874: *Registre des Conclusions de Monseigneur le Procureur General du Roy Molé*, 4 August 1625.

[284] Lachèvre, *Procès*, p. 119: 'il ne reste aucune trace aux Archives Nationales de cette instance'.

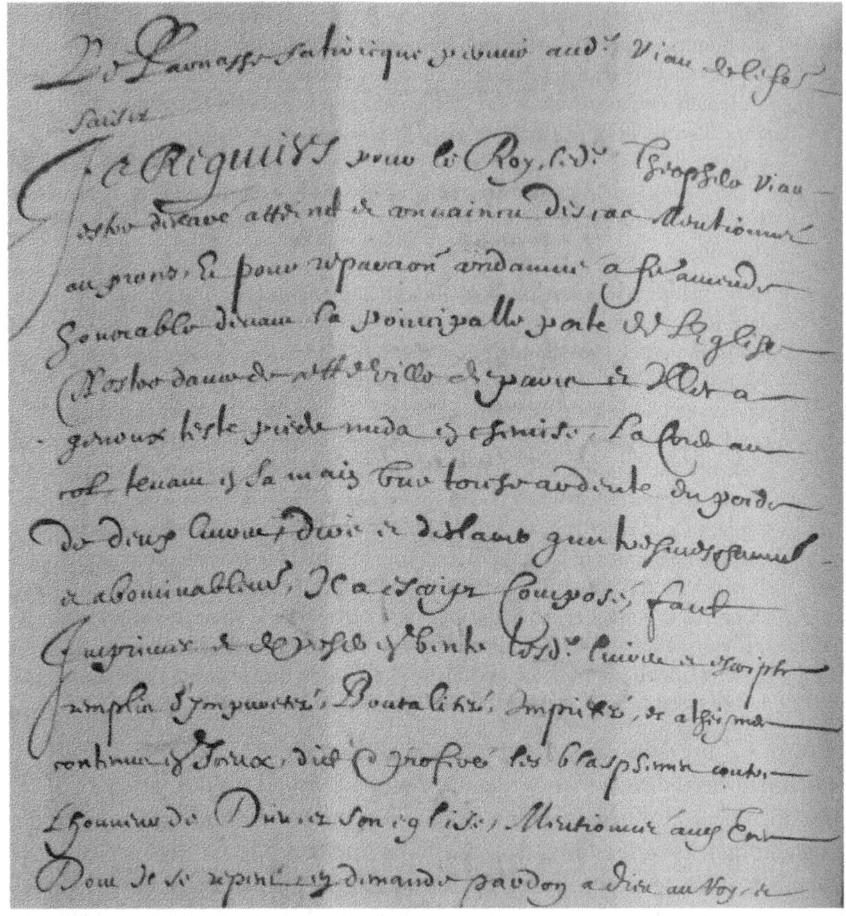

Figure 5.9 AN X 1A 8874: *Registre des Conclusions de Monseigneur le Procureur General du Roy Molé* (4 August 1625).

Théophile took up to six months to realise the danger that the *Parnasse satyrique* placed him in before reporting Estoc to the authorities in April 1623.[285] The *conclusions* offer the first confirmation of Théophile's complaint in a legal archive and definitively put this particular scholarly debate to rest:

> Requete presenté au prevost de Paris par led. Theophile le 30 janvier 1623 et sentence par luy obtenue sur icelle le 21 febvrier ensuivant, par laquelle deffences ont esté faictes au nommé Estoc marchant libraire et tous autres d'exposé en vente led. livre intitulé Le Parnasse satiricque permis aud. Viau de le faire saisir.

[285] Adam, *Pensée*, pp. 333–7.

> Appeal presented to the Paris Provost by the aforementioned Théophile on 30 January 1623 and sentence obtained by him on this matter on the following 21 February, according to which the book merchant Estoc and all others have been banned from displaying for sale the aforementioned book entitled *Le Parnasse satyrique*, [and according to which] the aforementioned de Viau is permitted to have it seized.[286]

Leaving to one side the three weeks taken by the *prévôt de Paris* to rule on this matter, and taking into account that Théophile may not have seen the *Parnasse satyrique* on sale in the first few days of its publication, Théophile took roughly two months to mount his legal challenge to the anthology which would eventually lead to his arrest, in January 1623. As already clear from the interrogations and Molé's draft of questions, the *conclusions* furthermore show that the arrest did not centre on the *Parnasse satyrique* alone, but involved:

> Deux livres imprimés chez Pierre Bilayne es années 1622 et 1623 intitulés Les Oeuvres dud. Theophile autre livre imprimé chez Anthoine Estoc aud. an 1622 intitulé Le Parnasse des poetes satiricques.

> Two books printed by Pierre Billaine in the years 1622 and 1623 entitled the *Œuvres* of the aforementioned Théophile, and another book printed by Antoine Estoc in the year 1622 entitled *Le Parnasse des poètes satyriques*.[287]

These remarks present an interesting contrast to another new document revealed earlier: the forgotten interrogation of the poet's servant. When asked to give the names and locations of those responsible for printing Théophile's broadly termed 'livres de poeysies' ('books of poetry'), La Pause was careful to allude only to the printers of the *Œuvres* and not those of the *Parnasse*:

> A dict qu'il y en a un à la rue Saint Jacques à l'enseigne des Trois Colombiers le nom duquel il ne scait mais bien scait qu'il y a un qui s'appelle Villoyne mais ne scait sy c'est celuy qui demeure aux Trois Colombiers et qu'il y a ung aultre a la rue Saint Jacques dont il ne scait l'enseigne.

> Said that one of them is on the rue Saint Jacques under the emblem of the Three Dovecotes [Jacques Quesnel] whose name he does not know, but does know that there is one called Villoyne [sic, Pierre Billaine] but does not know if it is the one at the Three Dovecotes, and that there is another on the rue Saint Jacques but does not know his emblem [Toussaint Du Bray?].[288]

Finally, the *conclusions* are signed 4 August 1625. This means that a further five witnesses were hastily presented *after* the representative of the Crown prosecution

[286] AN X 1A 8874.
[287] AN X 1A 8874.
[288] AN X 2B 1185, interrogation of Isaac La Pause (24 April 1624). Like his servant, Théophile had pointed the finger at Du Bray in his third interrogation (27 March 1624) for having published Maynard's 'L'autre jour je vis dans un temple' in the *Délices de la poésie Françoise*, which was attributed to Théophile at trial. See AN X 2B 1185, third interrogation (27 March 1624), in Lachèvre, *Procès*, p. 399.

had already submitted his recommendations on the case; the last of whom, Sepaus, has been presented at the request of Molé himself.

Théophile's panel of judges was far from the image of a single and united *corps judiciaire* that the Parlement so carefully cultivated. The poet's fate was decided by young men and old, with disparate levels of legal experience and services to the Crown. To venture hypotheses on the votes of judges other than those mentioned above would be to indulge in educated speculation. What can be said with more certainty, however, is that the backgrounds of many of Théophile's judges lead us to surmise that they would not have looked favourably upon his plight.

From a modern perspective, it is all too easy to view Théophile as an intelligent, articulate victim who was able to thwart the at times risible efforts of religious zealots to put him to death. Without wishing to detract from his considerably effective self-defence, this study equally invites us to appreciate just how lucky Théophile was to escape the Parlement de Paris alive. We have already seen the effect of Voisin's memoirs on two *présidents* who 's'alarmèrent fort, et dirent avec grande colère que le P. Voisin méritait mieux la mort que Théophile' ('were greatly alarmed, and said in a great rage that Father Voisin was more deserving of death than Théophile').[289] Nevertheless, many of those who played particularly influential roles in the trial thought otherwise. It is likely that the *rapporteur* Deslandes and one of the two *commissaires* (Pinon) were in favour of sentencing Théophile to death, and we now know that the *conclusions* of the *procureur général* Molé recommended nothing less. Two of the more senior judges were seasoned veterans in persecuting libertine literature and speech acts, though their relations with the Jesuits hinder our efforts to deduce how they might have voted. With so many influential judges against him, it is difficult to account for Théophile's eventual and non-lethal punishment without another authoritative magistrate spearheading the vote for clemency along with Bellièvre. This was most probably the magistrate who had a record of acting against the Jesuits in the Parlement, who had manifested personal hatred towards them immediately before, during, and following Théophile's trial, and who was addressed personally in one of Théophile's poems written during his captivity: the *premier président* and head of the Parlement, Nicolas de Verdun.[290]

[289] Garasse, *Mémoires*, p. 80.

[290] Although an encomiastic poem in which hyperbole is often privileged over accuracy, in his 'Très humble requête de Théophile à Monseigneur le Premier Président' Théophile nonetheless describes Verdun as his best hope for securing his freedom: 'C'est de vous sur tous que j'attends / A voir retrancher la licence / Qui fait habiter trop longtemps / La crainte avec l'innocence' ('It is by your hand especially that I wait / To see the licence removed / Which for too long has allowed / Fear to dwell alongside innocence'(Théophile, *Œuvres*, p. 283).

THE VERDICT: A VICTORY FOR CATHOLIC ORTHODOXY?

The question of who emerged victorious from Théophile's trial is a complex one. On the one hand, Théophile had initially been condemned and burned in effigy on 18 August 1623 for having contributed to the authoring of 'des sonnetz et vers contenant les impietez et blasphèmes et abominations mentionnez au livre très pernitieux intitulé le *Pernasse satiricque*' ('sonnets and poems containing the impieties, blasphemies, and abominations mentioned in the very pernicious book entitled the *Parnasse satyrique*').[291] Pascal Debailly notes that the *Seconde partie* of Théophile's *Œuvres* only contained gallant and romantic poetry devoid of any polemical content, demonstrating the significant effect of the trial on his ability to express his libertine ideas through literature.[292]

The trial might also suggest in part the weakness of Théophile's writing as a means of self-defence. As early as the 'Au lecteur' found in the *Seconde partie* of his *Œuvres* in May 1623, he addressed the accusations made against him through literature. This defence was a precursor to the substantial corpus of texts he would later write during his imprisonment. Eventually allowed ink and paper in his cell, Théophile wrote several texts between 23 November 1623 and 22 March 1624 in which he sought to gain support for his cause.[293] He defended his Catholic faith, described the appalling conditions of his captivity, responded to texts written against him, and rebuked those courtiers who had deserted him. He furthermore implored powerful men for support, addressing his appeals to the Parlement, to judges, to his protectors, and to the king. In his moment of peril, Théophile abandoned the traditional themes of nature, love, and liberty typical of his earlier works in order to secure his release through strengthening his relationships with men of power. The hyperbolic praise given to officials and men of state —'chers lieutenants des dieux qui gouvernez mon sort, / [...] Mes juges, mes dieux tutélaires,' ('dear lieutenants of the gods who govern my fate, / My judges, my guardian gods'),[294]—contrasts with the poet's aversion to flattering those other than the king which he had so often expressed in his poetry.[295] His flattering of influential men in his hour of need, as well as the life

[291] AN X 2B 342, *arrêt* against Théophile, Berthelot, Colletet, and Frenicle (19 August 1623), in Lachèvre, *Procès*, p. 142. This second, longer *arrêt* provides more detail than the first *arrêt* passed the previous day (AN X 2A 986).

[292] Pascal Debailly, 'Théophile de Viau et le déclin de l'*éthos* satirique', in *La Parole polémique*, ed. by Gilles Declerq, Michel Murat and Jacqueline Dangel (Paris: Honoré Champion, 2003), pp. 149–71 (p. 165).

[293] These are 'La Pénitence de Théophile', 'Requête de Théophile au Roi', 'Theophilus in carcere', 'Apologie de Théophile', 'Requête de Théophile à Nosseigneurs de Parlement', 'Très humble requête de Théophile à Monsieur le Premier Président de Verdun', 'Remerciement à Coridon', and the 'Prière de Théophile aux poètes de ce temps'.

[294] 'Requête de Théophile à Nosseigneurs de Parlement', in Théophile, *Œuvres*, p. 276.

[295] Such as 'Quand la Divinité, qui formait ton essence', in Théophile, *Œuvres*, p. 111, addressed to his former protector Candale in 1619. Théophile had previously acknowledged that subservience to Louis

of theological study that replaced his amusements of court, are of an altogether different nature to the earlier texts for which Théophile had at the same time become so famous and so relentlessly persecuted.[296] Following his second trial, Théophile complained of his need to hide from fame and, perhaps, the potential gaze of the authorities.[297] When released from the miserable conditions of his prison cell 'avec des incommoditez et de corps et de fortune' ('with troubles of the body and of fortune'), he remained in poor health and died roughly one year after his release.[298] Together with the abrupt end to the trend of *recueils satyriques* following the trial, it is clear that from a literary perspective at least, the defenders of Catholic orthodoxy had been successful in vanquishing their perceived enemies.

On the other hand, the new archival material presented in this chapter reveals that Théophile was neither as slow in his efforts to remove the *Parnasse satyrique* from sale, nor as nonchalant in the weeks prior to his arrest, as previously thought. Although his journey into exile was far from a speedy one, he spent his time close to the northern border visiting and writing to his protectors in order to prepare either for his imminent arrest or eventual return, rather than idling on French soil in the hope of a change of fortune. After two years of intense interrogation, Théophile was acquitted of the crime of *lèse-majesté divine* for which he had been convicted *in absentia* in 1623. His accusers had failed to prove the poet's irreligious or sexually immoral nature through textual analysis. Coupled with increasingly dubious witness testimonies, this failure allowed him to maintain the upper hand in a performative struggle for dominance in the construction of authoritative reality within the courtroom setting. It is also worth stressing that Théophile's success at trial was not entirely due to the failings of his accusers. He responded to the prosecution's tactics in an adroit and intelligent manner, as evidenced in particular through the efforts of both parties to capitalise on the distinctions between translation and imitation. Finally, he maintained his strategies of self-defence throughout the trial proceedings in contrast with the shifting focus of his interrogators.

XIII was such a pleasure 'que les plus libertins ont plaisir à vous craindre' ('that the most libertine men enjoy fearing you': 'Au Roi, Etrenne', in Théophile, *Œuvres*, p. 19).

[296] 'Mon jeu, ma danse et mon festin / Se font avec saint Augustin / [...] Je maudis mes jours débauchés' ('My games, my dancing and my feasts / Are with St Augustin / I curse my debauched days': 'La Pénitence de Théophile', in Théophile, *Œuvres*, p. 261).

[297] 'Vous desirez me voir en un temps où le Soleil mesme n'a pas cette liberté. Une reputation de bon esprit qui fait aujourd'hui tant promener mon nom par les ruës, contraint ma personne de se cacher' ('You wish to see me at a time when even the Sun does not have this freedom. My reputation as a fine wit, which now causes my name to be spoken in public so frequently, forces me to hide myself': 'Lettre XVI' (A Monsieur le Comte de Rieux), in *Nouvelles œuvres*, pp. 71–2).

[298] 'A Monseigneur le Président de Bellièvre', in Théophile, *Nouvelles œuvres*, p. 56.

This feat is all the more remarkable given the severe though far from unanimous opposition he faced in his final judgement by the Parlement de Paris.[299] This mixed group of ages, social circles, levels of seniority, and previous experiences in dealing with the threat of subversive literature and its authors, was a formidable reactionary force which would not have given its verdict lightly. Despite the fact that one of his two *commissaires*, the *rapporteur*, and the *procureur général du roi* had all likely voted for the death sentence, Théophile was able to win the day, and was surely right in interpreting his banishment as a mere act of appeasement towards his enemies.[300] His poetry, much of which is today recognised for the irreligious and daring sexual content for which it was condemned, continued to be reprinted at an average rate of more than one new edition per year for the remainder of the century.[301] The catalyst to his ordeal—*Le Parnasse satyrique*—went through at least three reprints in 1660, 1668, and 1684. The ongoing trial even led Peter Paul Rubens to request a copy from Peiresc's brother in December 1624, precisely because it was the text which 'fut cause de son désastre, et a esté condamné et exécuté si cruellement' ('was the cause of his disaster and has been condemned and executed so cruelly').[302]

Théophile's enemies, however, had unquestionably suffered a less triumphant fate. Voisin was banished permanently from France.[303] Garasse's anti-*libertin* texts had embroiled him in several rhetorical and theological battles against men of letters, the Church, and the Sorbonne. Disgraced, he retired from the literary world to Poitiers on the instructions of the Jesuits, where he cared for plague victims until succumbing to the illness in 1631. As Garasse himself had almost prophetically remarked on his supposed third order of libertine books: 'c'est la peste

[299] Given these points, Spink surely denies Théophile his due credit in claiming that the poet was merely a passive pawn in the battle between the Jesuits and the Parlement: 'in the end the opponents of the Jesuits were strong enough to prevent a burning at the stake' (Spink, *French Free-thought*, p. 42).

[300] 'Après avoir rendu mon innocence claire à tout le monde, encore a-il fallu donner à la fureur publique un arrest de banissement contre moy' ('After having shown my innocence clearly to all, it was still necessary to banish me for the sake of public furore': 'Au Duc de Montmorency', in *Nouvelles œuvres*, p. 21).

[301] Ninety-three editions of Théophile's poetry were printed in the seventeenth century according to Antoine Adam (*Histoire de la littérature française au XVIIe siècle*, 5 vols (Paris: Albin Michel, 1997), I, p. 88); eighty-eight editions according to Jean-Pierre Chauveau ('Situation de Théophile', in *Lectures de Théophile de Viau*, ed. by Guillaume Peureux (Rennes: Presses Universitaires de Rennes, 2008), 27–41 (27); and seventy-nine according to Van Damme (*Épreuve*, p. 7). These compare with just sixteen editions of Malherbe's poetry.

[302] Peter Paul Rubens to Palamède Fabri de Valvarez (12 December 1624), in *Codex diplomaticus Rubenianus: documents relatifs à la vie et aux œuvres de Rubens*, ed. by Max Rooses and Charles Louis Ruelens, 6 vols (Anvers: Jos Maes, 1887–1909), III (1900), p. 309. Given the date of this letter, Rubens is likely referring to the condemnation and burning of the *Parnasse satyrique* rather than the poet. I am grateful to Christine Göttler for this reference.

[303] Lachèvre, *Procès*, p. 506. Upon hearing of an accusation of sodomy against Voisin by Des Barreaux, Louis XIII is reported to have called Voisin 'le plus méchant homme de mon royaulme' ('the most wicked man in my kingdom': Garasse, *Mémoires*, pp. 77–80).

et la gangrene de la devotion' ('it is the plague and gangrene of devotion').[304] The multiple connotations of the term *libertin*—so amply demonstrated in the works of Garasse which, along with their author, had an undeniable influence on the trial proceedings—are clearly reflected in the prosecution's interrogation strategy. Its abrupt and often irrational changes in tactics reveal that the authorities struggled to define what exactly the defendant's crime was. Did Théophile merit the death sentence for being an atheist, a *bon vivant*, a bisexual, or to quote Garasse 'un certain composé de toutes ces qualités'?[305] Butterworth and Roberts allude to this problematic in their evaluation of Garasse's polemic:

> For Garasse, obscenity is a sin of the tongue that implies heresy of thought as well as immorality of action. [...] The very term 'obscénité' crystallizes this confusion between thought, word and action.[306]

For DeJean, this uncertainty regarding Théophile's crimes had been present as early as his initial banishment in 1619.[307] The changes in focus from the poet's philosophical works to his irreligious poetry, from his unbelief to his sexual immorality, and from his literature to witness accusations, are prime examples of the difficulties posed in attempting to pin down a libertine identity in the early modern period. Inheriting this problematic of definition from Garasse and other writers of texts against *libertins*, Théophile's persecutors ultimately failed to link him with any of these perceived dangers to the established order. What the trial did achieve was to modify irrevocably the way in which free-thinkers expressed themselves through literature in the seventeenth century. After the trial, there were no new *recueils satyriques* titles. The printers, who had so eagerly capitalised on the popular taste for this literary genre, became aware of the dangers associated with publishing licentious poetry. The authorities succeeded, with hindsight, in curbing literary and religious licence in France.[308] Yet they were unsuccessful in condemning the accused who emerged as the dominant rhetorical force at his trial. Still only in his mid-thirties, in the months between his release and his death Théophile still had many more years ahead of him in the eyes of his contemporaries. Had his health not been ruined by the poor conditions of his cell, by other natural causes, and ultimately by the medical care of his time, the relatively negative judgements made on Théophile's performance at trial may well have been quite different.[309]

[304] Garasse, *Doctrine*, p. 1016. For fascinating recent discoveries in Italian archives detailing the Jesuits' internal communications and critical readings of the *Doctrine curieuse*, see Van Damme, *Épreuve*, pp. 152–5.

[305] François Garasse, *Les Recherches des Recherches et autres œuvres de Me Etienne Pasquier* (Paris: Sébastien Chappelet, 1622), p. 681.

[306] Butterworth and Roberts, 'Word to Thing', p. 89.

[307] DeJean, *Obscenity*, p. 32.

[308] See DeJean, *Obscenity*, pp. 29, 46, 53, 55.

[309] Though Théophile is traditionally said to have died as a result of his captivity, *Le Mercure françois*

Théophile's persecution was in many ways a means of stifling the growing popularity of subversive and obscene literature. Though many critics believe that a first wave of libertinism was defeated following Théophile's trial, these judgements reflect the fate of Théophile as an individual rather than that of *libertinage*.[310] It is therefore in terms of the wider implications for *libertinage* that one must judge the success or failure of the defenders of Catholic orthodoxy at Théophile's trial. The *libertinage* of Théophile de Viau evidenced by his poetry was one of nonchalance towards social and literary conventions, of simple pleasures provided by nature's bounty, and an aversion to any form of regulation that was more stifling than nurturing to the spirit. A central component of this outlook was friendship.[311] In his early theatrical career under Alexandre Hardy, in his friendships with Boisrobert, Saint-Amant, and Des Barreaux, and in the numerous objects of his love poetry, the cult of pleasure prescribed by Théophile is one which is augmented by agreeable (that is to say, like-minded) company. Leading up to Théophile's arrest, Des Barreaux's 'Réponse de Tircis' reveals both his doubts over Théophile's protested innocence and his indifference to the latter's fate:

> Je crains que tant de vers exécrables qui portent ton nom si dévot, ne résonnent si fort aux oreilles de tes Juges, que la petite voix de ta deffense n'y trouve aucune entrée. Quelle innocence pourra vaincre tant de tesmoignages d'impiété!
>
> I fear that so many appalling poems, bearing your so devout name, might have such a resonance in the ears of your judges that they may not hear the small voice of your defence. What kind of innocence can overcome so much evidence of impiety![312]

Des Barreaux appears to abandon his friend to his fate, and even goes on to advise Théophile to embrace the devouring fires lit for him by Parlement in imitation of the saints.[313] During his captivity Théophile provided a valuable account of those whom he both esteemed and considered to be his peers: the 'Prière de Théophile aux poètes de ce temps.' Addressed to seven writers—including his former literary mentor Hardy as well as fellow writers of licentious verse Boisrobert, Saint-Amant, and Maynard—Théophile encourages these men to continue his fight in the event of his execution:

---

presents the conditions of his cell as but one of several contributing factors to his death. Not only does it state that he died of a fever which began shortly after his release, but it also attributes Théophile's death to an incompetent doctor whose remedy led to the fever spreading to the brain: 'Mais le malheur voulut qu'un Chimiste eut le premier le soin de Theophile en ceste maladie, lequel luy donna d'une pouldre pour luy faire perdre ceste fiévre' ('Sadly an alchemist was the first to care for Théophile in his illness, who gave him a powder to cure him of his fever': *Mercure françois*, pp. 12, 474–5).

310 In addition to the sources cited at the beginning of this chapter, see, for instance, Adam, *Pensée*, pp. 404, 434; Claude Reichler, *L'Âge libertin* (Paris: Éditions de minuit, 1987), p. 16.

311 Guido Saba, *Théophile de Viau: un poète rebelle* (Geneva: Slatkine Reprints, 2008), p. 32.

312 Quoted in Lachèvre, *Procès*, p. 225.

313 Lachèvre, *Procès*, p. 226.

S'il arrive que mon naufrage
Soit la fin de ce grand orage
Dont je voy mes jours menacez,
Je vous conjure, ô trouppe saincte!
Par tout l'honneur des trepassez,
De vouloir achever ma plainte.

If it comes to pass that my shipwreck
Should be the end of this great storm
Which I see is threatening my days,
I implore you, oh saintly troupe,
On the honour of all those who went before us,
To carry on my fight.[314]

Neither Des Barreaux nor any of the other poets mentioned in this text responded to Théophile's call to arms.[315] Saint-Amant no longer counted himself among Théophile's friends and aligned himself, following Boisrobert's example, with another of the poet's former friends, Balzac.[316] Maynard restricted the circulation of his future libertine poetry to friends, before subsequently attempting to present a more polished side of his poetic verve in his 1646 *Œuvres*.[317] Théophile was shocked at having been abandoned by his closest friends and allies, and lamented in a letter to Montmorency that it was considered an abomination to support his cause during the trial.[318] As he put it to the king, though he had managed to avoid a guilty verdict at trial, 'mes amis changèrent de face / ils furent tous muets et sourds' ('my friends changed their countenance / they were all mute and deaf).[319] Théophile's trial isolated a recognised head of the libertines and put

[314] 'Prière de Théophile aux poètes de ce temps', in Théophile, *Œuvres*, p. 291. It is notable that Théophile chose the same imagery of *naufrage* to describe his situation as Des Barreaux.

[315] Godard de Donville notes that even those texts that oppose Garasse's polemical ideas—Naudé's *Instruction à la France,* La Brosse's *Traité sur la médisance*, and Ogier's *Jugement et censure de la Doctrine Curieuse*—do not defend Théophile. See Louise Godard de Donville, 'Théophile, les «Beaux Esprits» et les Rose-Croix: un insidieux parallèle du P. Garasse', in *Correspondances*, ed. by W. Leiner and P. Ronzeaud (Tübingen and Aix-en-Province: Narr, 1992), pp. 143–54 (p. 153).

[316] Adam, *Pensée*, p. 363. For Adam, Balzac was responsible for Théophile's abandonment by his friends and was largely motivated by politics at court (pp. 364–6).

[317] I have explored these themes in more detail in Adam Horsley, '*Le Président libertin:* The Poetry of François Maynard after the Trial of Théophile de Viau', *Early Modern French Studies*, 37: 2 (2015), 93–107; 'The Good Times and the Bad: François Maynard's Reflections on his Past and Future', in *Managing Time: Literature and Devotion in Early Modern France*, ed. by Richard Maber and Joanna Barker (Oxford: Peter Lang, 2017), pp. 107–31; ''Mon livre, je ne peux m'empescher de te plaindre': Reflections on the Compilation of François Maynard's 1646 *Œuvres*', in *'A qui lira': Littérature, livre et librairie en France au XVIIe siècle*, ed. by Mathilde Bombart and others (Tübingen: Nar – Biblio 17, 2020), 633–42; and 'Secret Cabinets, Scribal Publication and the *Satyrique*: François Maynard and Libertine Poetry in Public and Private Spaces', *The Sixteenth Century Journal*, 51: 1 (2020), 55–78.

[318] 'A Monsieur le Duc de Montmorency' in *Nouvelles œuvres*, p. 22: 'sur le poinct de mon jugement il a semblé que me secourir estoit une infamie'.

[319] 'Requête de Théophile au Roi', in Théophile, *Œuvres*, p. 265. There is a striking parallel here with a line from Théophile's incriminating poem in *Le Parnasse satyrique*, which could well allude to the poet's desertion by his friends as much as to the sympoms of syphilis: 'Mes amis plus secrets ne m'osent

an end to his libertine poetry as early as the second edition of the poet's *Œuvres*. It was successful in silencing more than just one of the *beaux esprits* targeted by Garasse. It created an atmosphere of suspicion and fear that led to a reorganisation of alliances and groups of friends who intentionally displayed their aversion to Théophile in order to distance themselves from his prosecution.

Théophile's last stand deserves to be judged on a more complex axis than a polarised contest between the wills of the poet and the agents of royal justice. The latter in turn merit a more granular political, professional, ideological, and cultural analysis, rather than their identities being restricted to the generic and homogenising label of 'Théophile's judges'. As this chapter has shown, the trial can be considered in terms of strategies of accusation and self-defence, or in terms of the ability of either party to control the direction of the court proceedings. From a literary perspective, the question of a victorious party at the trial may be answered in terms of its effect on so-called libertine literature, or its impact on Théophile's specific, first wave of libertine literature and the resultant rise in dissimulated scepticism. The verdict can in turn be viewed in terms of the legal process, of Théophile's premature death, or as a contest between Gallican and Jesuit factions within the assembled chambers in which Théophile's personal fate was viewed to be of little consequence. The repercussions for his adversaries within the legal sphere, however, were notably less severe than those of the Jesuits and men of letters embroiled in Théophile's trial. For contrary to what we might expect from such a public failure, the magistrates who had sided with Théophile's enemies, including the *procureur général* Mathieu Molé, emerged from this legal contest spectacularly defeated yet with their lives and authority intact.

---

approcher' ('my closest friends dare not come near me': 'Phillis, tout est foutu, je meurs de la vérole', in *Le Parnasse satyrique*, p. 1).

Conclusion

> J'ai toujours ouï dire, que c'est une méchante raillerie, que de se railler du Ciel, et que les libertins ne font jamais une bonne fin.
>
> I have always heard it said that it's a terrible mockery to mock Heaven, and that libertines never come to a good end.
>
> [Molière, *Dom Juan* (1665)[1]]

In the second scene of Molière's *Dom Juan* the titular character's servant, Sganarelle, reveals to his master that he is scandalised 'de vous voir tous les mois vous marier' ('to see you marry on a monthly basis').[2] For Dom Juan, his actions form part of the pursuit of pleasure, of beauty, and of a means to thwart Time itself in its efforts to restrict his womanising to a single, linear chronology.[3] As the ineffective defender of religion, Sganarelle couches his master's lasciviousness somewhat differently, abhorring instead that he should 'jouer ainsi d'un mystère sacré' ('play with a sacred mystery in such a way').[4] These views on marriage thus echo the word history of the term *libertin* which, as we have seen, encompasses an excessive satisfaction of sensual desires, a lack of respect for the Christian faith, and conceptions of freedom whose origins can be traced back to ancient Roman law. During our first encounter with Dom Juan, his womanising is presented to us as a backstory; a summary of his life philosophy and a catalogue of his previous, unnamed female conquests whose fates predict the action of the ensuing play. Sganarelle's remarks, and the ambivalent chastisements which will subsequently typify his performance, are thus turned as much towards his and Dom Juan's shared past as towards the

[1] Molière, *Dom Juan*, Act I Scene 2, in Molière, *Œuvres complètes*, ed. by Georges Couton, 2 vols (Paris: Gallimard, Bibliothèque de la Pléiade, 1971), 2, p. 37.
[2] Molière, *Dom Juan*, Act I Scene 2, p. 36.
[3] 'Toutes les belles ont droit de nous charmer, et l'avantage d'être rencontrée la première, ne doit point dérober aux autres les justes prétentions qu'elles ont toutes sur nos cœurs' ('All beautiful women have the right to charm us, and the advantage of being found first should not rob the others of the just claims which they all have to our hearts': Molière, *Dom Juan*, Act I Scene 2, p. 35.
[4] Molière, *Dom Juan*, Act I Scene 2, p. 37.

ensuing plot, which famously culminates with his master's descent into Hell. In other words, if Sganarelle has learned that libertines never come to a good end, his instructor has not, for once, been the so far unscathed Dom Juan teaching at his 'Escole du Libertinage' ('School of *Libertinage*').[5] Rather, Sganarelle recalls the examples of others who ran the risk of being labelled libertines, and who trod the path leading from a plethora of possible permutations of ungodly living to punishing and purifying flames.

This study began by exploring the word history of the term *libertin*. Its apparently uncertain and even contradictory definitions in the seventeenth century are in fact part of its etymological, cultural, and social history—in which it was increasingly used as an accusation against theological adversaries—rather than the linguistic abuses of a term which lost all practical use. An appreciation of the libertine phenomenon thus requires us to suspend an instinctive desire for linguistic cogency from which historical usage emanates outwards. Instead, we must embrace the diverse contexts in which the word is to be found, and treat these as tributaries feeding into the image of a social, religious, and political Other whose fluid lexical boundaries presented no apparent obstructions to the word's use in the early modern period.

These boundaries are broadly related to questions of freedom and religion. Both are first to be found in Antiquity; whether it be freed Roman slaves, or the freedmen of the *synagoga quae appellatur Libertinorum* in Acts 6:9, who were among the first to reject the teachings of Christ's Church. These two potential meanings are present in pre-seventeenth-century texts. Authors in this period used *libertin* to refer to freed slaves as recounted in ancient texts, or to equate them with contemporaries whom they identified with a form of slavery. In theological texts such as those of Calvin, it was also used to denote adversaries whose beliefs were seen to pertain to those of the synagogue of Acts 6:9. Contrary to the claims of some critics, Calvin did not 'invent' the term *libertin*.[6] What he does appear to have pioneered (as far as our non-exhaustive word history has been able to discern) is the use of the term as an accusation in French. Rather than limit himself to a description of his theological adversaries, Calvin added his own derogatory comments to the supposed beliefs of his *libertins* with a strong emphasis, for example, on the supposedly bestial nature of their lifestyle. As early as Farel's *Glaive de la parole véritable*, the accusations made against Anabaptists became more numerous and expanded beyond Calvin's initial descriptions. In building upon the images of the *libertin* provided by Calvin, Farel demonstrated the unstable nature of the term when used as an accusation, even in instances

[5] Le sieur de Rochemont [Jean Barbier d'Aucour], *Observations sur une comédie de Molière, intitulée* Le Festin de Pierre (Paris: N. Pepingué, 1665), p. 8.

[6] For a further example see Walter H. Lemke, '"Libertin": from Calvin to Cyrano', *Studi Francese*, 58 (1976), 58–60 (58).

where two writers addressed the same theological opponent. The resurgence of *libertins* in Calvin's and Farel's polemics, in which the word's meaning could be altered between two authors who knew each other and who were writing in the same period, did not discourage others from using the term.

Branching out from the initial duality of the term between a freedman and a rejecter of Christ, the meanings of the word *libertin* in the seventeenth century included a social outsider, a glutton, an atheist, and even a Huguenot. Its use to denote the Huguenots is particularly significant for the history of the term as an accusation, as Calvin himself was labelled a *libertin* due to his perceived estrangement from the Catholic faith. More significant still are those examples in which *libertin* is given as a synonym alongside other crimes against Christianity, such as atheism, heresy, and Epicureanism. In certain cases, the use of *libertin* as an adjective clearly demonstrates that as well as being an accusation of irreligion in its own right, *libertin* could be used to enhance descriptions of other forms of impiety, as was also the case for the crime of blasphemy.[7]

The vague and contradictory nature of François Garasse's definitions of *libertin* has already been the subject of modern scholarly criticism, yet remains integral to any study of the term *libertin* in the 1620s. Despite the outcome of Théophile's trial and the Jesuit's rambling hyperbole, Garasse found a degree of success in his literary polemic. His *Doctrine curieuse* did, after all, have the desired effect of perpetuating a sullied image of the recently executed Vanini and Fontanier, and he actively participated in bringing Théophile to trial. It was only once Théophile was in the hands of the Parlement that his persecution began to lose momentum. In deploring the lack of clarity in Garasse's accusation, there has perhaps been a tendency to assume that Garasse and Marin Mersenne *required* a cogent definition of a *libertin,* or that they even sought such clarity.[8] Their libertine accusation seems to have served to maximise the extent of a perceived threat, and ultimately to present the same form of *surdramatisation* to which Jean Delumeau refers in his study on fear: 'le pouvoir politico-religieux, qui se sent fragile, est entraîné à une surdramatisation et multiplie comme à plaisir le nombre de ses ennemis de l'intérieur et de l'extérieur' ('the political and religious powers, sensing their own fragility, were drawn into over-dramatisation, and wilfully expanded the number of their enemies within and without').[9]

The effect of indiscriminate and even reciprocal accusations of *libertinage* along a paradigmatic axis may well be to the detriment of those readers of Garasse

[7] Alfred Soman notes that blasphemy was often included alongside other criminal charges. See Alfred Soman, 'Press, Pulpit and Censorship in France before Richelieu', *Proceedings of the American Philosophical Society*, 120: 6 (1976), 439–63 (450).

[8] On the accuracy of descriptions of Théophile as a *libertin* in *La Doctrtine curieuse* and the merits of this text in attempting to define the term, see Isabelle Moreau, *«Guérir du sot»: Les Stratégies d'écriture des libertins à l'âge classique* (Paris: Honoré Champion, 2007), p. 51.

[9] Jean Delumeau, *La peur en occident: XIVe–XVIIe siècles* (Paris: Fayard, 1978), p. 391.

and Mersenne, both past and present, 'cherchant à définir une essence libertine' ('seeking to define an essence of libertinism').[10] However, it was also effective in fuelling a culture of fear and suspicion amongst a public still recovering from the experience of the Wars of Religion and the political events following Henri IV's assassination. We might therefore place less emphasis on the parameters of the accusation—that is to say, who should and should not be called a *libertin* according to the term's meanings established by these apologists—and to privilege instead the individual being accused, the identity of their accuser, and the intended effect of that accusation, on a case-by-case basis. As such, it is difficult to agree completely with Godard de Donville's assertion that the figure of the *libertin* is purely literary, devoid of a relationship with the history of ideas or events in which it appears.[11] It seems impossible to attribute the polemics of writers such as Garasse and Mersenne exclusively to the literary contexts of the time. Rather, if authors felt at liberty to write increasingly subversive and audacious works, it was because the relative absence of a stable reign under a male sovereign, and internal conflict between those in positions of political power, had at first resulted in a relatively ineffective policing of the print market.[12]

The fact that some of the first books to be censored by the king and his royal parlements discussed the temporal power of kings, the extent of papal authority in French affairs of state, as well as justifiable regicide, demonstrates that the printing press and public opinion were considered potential threats in the wake of the pamphlet wars of the 1610s. In the spirit of the Counter-Reformation, conservative readers such as Garasse were able to ride the prevailing winds of censorship to curtail a level of literary licence which, in their eyes, had gone unchecked for too long. On the other hand, this book has emphasised the value of criminal trials as spaces of cultural and intellectual debate, as well as of the critical readership of texts tarred vaguely by Garasse with the accusation of *libertinage*. Unlike in the literary world of anti-*libertin* polemical texts, within the courtroom setting those who were accused of crimes pertaining to *libertinage* were physically present, and able to offer responses to the critical readings of their subversive texts which have survived in trial records. This makes such criminal procedures all the more valuable for the study of libertine literature given that, as Peter Rushton notes in

[10] Stéphane Van Damme, *L'épreuve libertine: Morale, soupçon et pouvoirs dans la France baroque* (Paris: CNRS Éditions, 2008), p. 91. On the paradigmatic axis of synonyms and antonyms for 'curiosity', see Neil Kenny, *Curiosity in Early Modern Europe: Word Histories* (Wiesbaden: Harrassowitz Verlag, 1998), p. 111.

[11] Louise Godard de Donville, *Le Libertin des origines à 1665: un produit des apologètes* (Paris, Seattle and Tübignen: Papers on French Seventeenth-Century Literature (Biblio 17), 1989), p. 405.

[12] Roger Chartier and Henri-Jean Martin note, for example, that Sully did not include the publication of books in the list of administrative sectors that he chose to reorganise with an aim to monitor them more closely (Roger Chartier and Henri-Jean Martin, *Histoire de l'édition française*, 4 vols (Paris: Fayard, 1989–91), I — 'Le livre conquérant' (1991), p. 367).

his study of witch trials, 'the meaning of archival texts, far more than that of the printed word, is bound up with the context of their production and use'.[13]

Our authors of study were rumoured to have engaged in some form of *libertinage*—be it irreligion, sexual deviance, or a combination of the two—whilst their ordeals before the criminal justice system ultimately sought to ascertain the sincerity of their Catholic faith. In another trait held in common with the persecution of witches, Vanini was *reported* to have uttered irreverent views on the Church and to have corrupted the youth of Toulouse. Numerous witness statements *reported* that Théophile had made impious jokes, whereas Fontanier's teachings were first reported to the authorities by his private students. To quote Rushton again:

> Judicial decisions resulted from public performances of narrative accounts, which, by being accepted, became authoritative versions of reality. In this sense, truth was 'constructed' in what was called courts of record, those with final authority.[14]

In this way, the criminal trial is more than a mechanism leading to punishment. It seizes creative agency from the subversive author, and places it in the hands of magistrates who had quite different intentions towards the contemporary public and, as we saw in Fontanier's trial deliberations, wider posterity. Rather than inadvertently promulgating free-thinking through sensational trials, or simply punishing literary deviance after the fact, the magistrates consolidated what some critics have referred to as the juridical, social, and cultural reality of *libertinage*.[15] The libertine phenomenon risked existing almost exclusively within the pages of apologists such as Garasse, and within the minds of a limited readership of theological treatises or irreverent poems. It was therefore just as important that the libertine menace be made flesh within the courtroom as it was for these subsequent embodiments of free-thinking to be displayed, punished, and destroyed within the public, ritualistic performance of an execution.

The similarities between witchcraft and *libertinage* do not end here. Vanini was reputed to be a sorcerer, whereas Fontanier's Judaism linked him to a strong historic conflation between Jews and witches. Van Damme has drawn a parallel between the fights against *libertinage* and witchcraft in the 1620s, whereas Laurence Tricoche-Rauline has suggested that the fear of demonic possession represented 'une pathologie religieuse symétrique à celles des libertins' ('a religious pathology

[13] Peter Rushton, 'Texts of Authority: Witchcraft Accusations and the Demonstration of Truth in Early Modern England', in *Languages of Witchcraft: Narrative, Ideology and Meaning in Early Modern Culture*, ed. by Stuart Clark (Hampshire and London: Macmillan, 2001), pp. 21–39 (p. 22).

[14] Rushton, 'Authority', p. 24.

[15] Melaine Folliard, Pierre Ronzeaud and Mathilde Thorel, *Théophile de Viau, la voix d'un poète. Poésies 1621, 1623, 1625* (Paris: Presses Universitaires de France, 2008), p. 39 (which refers specifically to Vanini, Fontanier, and Théophile); Jean-Pierre Cavaillé, *Les Déniaisés: Irréligion et libertinage au début de l'époque moderne* (Paris: Classiques Garnier, 2013), p. 389.

consistent with that held towards the *libertins*').[16] These parallels were also recognised by contemporary observers. The heroes of both Cyrano de Bergerac's and Tristan L'Hermite's novels face accusations of witchcraft, and Gabriel Naudé's *Apologie pour tous les grands personnages qui ont esté faussement soupçonnez de magie* (Paris: François Targa, 1625) seeks to distinguish between great men of the mathematical sciences and the occult. Descriptions of the practices of these satanic others can even appear strikingly similar to Garasse's characterisation of the *libertins*:

> Dancer indecemment, festiner ordement, s'accoupler diaboliquement, sodomiser execrablement, blasphemer scandaleusement, se venger insidieusement, courir après tous desirs horribles, sales et desnaturez brutalement.
>
> Dancing indecently, celebrating filthily, copulating diabolically, sodomising execrably, blaspheming scandalously, avenging insidiously, brutally running after all horrible, dirty and unnatural desires.[17]

These similarities were even perceived in the legal sphere. Commenting to Louis XIII on the tendency of the Parlement de Paris to quash convictions for witchcraft on appeal, Théophile openly compares himself to those convicted of sorcery. In doing so, he adroitly critiques the persistent belief in witches and those who condemned accused witches to death, whilst at the same time lauding other magistrates—those of the royal parlements—for sharing his own more rational world view:

> Les mieux sensez et les plus Chrestiens du siècle, qui sont instruits des faussetez de mes accusations, accomparent mon accident aux Arrests qui souvent interviennent aux procez de sortilege, lors que vos premiers Juges ont condamné à mort des pauvres idiots, le Parlement qui est l'azile de l'innocence, justifie ces miserables, et neantmoins sur la diffamation les bannit du lieu de leur demeure. C'est une necessité de Police, contre laquelle je ne murmure point.
>
> The most sensible and Christian people of our time, who are aware of the falseness of the accusations against me, compare my plight to the *arrêts* which often intervene in trials for sorcery. When your first judges have condemned poor idiots to death, the Parlement, which is the sanctuary of innocence, finds in favour of these wretches, and yet banishes them from their place of abode for defamation. It is a necessity for civil order, against which I mutter not a word.[18]

[16] Van Damme, *Épreuve*, p. 52; Laurence Tricoche-Rauline, *Identité(s) libertine(s): L'écriture personnelle ou la création de soi* (Paris: Honoré Champion, 2009), p. 565. Sophie Houdard and Roger Aubenas have furthermore shown that Calvinists were also labelled witches. See Sophie Houdard, *Les Sciences du Diable: Quatre discours sur la sorcellerie (XVe–XVIIe siècle)* (Paris: Les Éditions du cerf, 1992), p. 139; Roger Aubenas, *La Sorcière et l'Inquisiteur* (Aix-en-Province: La Pensée Universitaire, 1956), p. 3.

[17] Jacques Fontaine, *Discours des marques des sorciers* (Paris: Denis Langlois, 1611) quoted in Houdard, *Sciences*, p. 167.

[18] Théophile de Viau, *Apologie au Roy* (Paris: [n. pub.], 1626), p. 7. On the small number of original sentences for witchcraft upheld by the Parlement de Paris on appeal, see Alfred Soman, 'Aux origines

The uses of *libertin* and *sorcière* as terms of accusation may well therefore have shared common origins, circumstances, and objectives regarding individuals who, to quote one poet of the time, had 'tourn[é] en libertin le dos à Dieu' ('turned their back on God like a libertine').[19] Whereas the study of early modern witchcraft almost inevitably entails that of the prosecution of those perceived to be dangerous, irreligious, and sexualised others, the critical reading sphere created by a criminal trial does not hold such a prominent place in the study of libertine literature. The courtrooms are officialising environments in which rumour, speculation, and slander are transformed into clear and convincing manifestations of truth as interpreted by the dispensers of royal justice. The trials of our subversive authors are thus a crucial part of the history of free-thinking and subversive literature in terms of readership, critical reception, and the subsequent authoring of the intellectual and legal afterlives of their text in archival records.

One of the aims of this study has been to explore how covert libertine writing strategies operated within a legal arena when they had failed to protect their authors from prosecution. Were libertine authors able to replicate the sophisticated strategies of simulation from their written texts in court, and if so, to what extent did these performances themselves constitute a subversive threat to the established order? Vanini's case can only be appreciated as an author trial with the benefit of hindsight and information unknown to his judges. Fontanier's trial constituted, in essence, a debate on whether or not the accused was the author of a text attacking Christianity. Finally, Théophile's judges knew that he was the author of at least the majority of the numerous incriminating texts quoted to him in his interrogations. This final trial was a contest of willpower, in which the poet had the rhetorical skill to deny authorship of poems printed in his name as well as drafts found in his possession. Théophile furthermore mounted intelligent arguments pertaining to the distinctions and limits of various literary and social identities, including the finer nuances of the poetic 'I' and the difference between imitation and translation.

From the perspective of criminal procedure, Chapters 3–5 have similarly explored a range of legal engagements with subversive authors. Vanini was condemned based on testimonial evidence of irreverent private conversations. His irreligious speech seemed to have had strong parallels with his views as expressed in his texts, although the judges were unaware that he was the author of these.

de l'appel de droit dans l'Ordonnance criminelle de 1670', *XVII*^{e} *siècle*, 32 (1980), 21–35 (24).

19 'Le Poète—douzième satyre', in Robert Angot de l'Éperonnière, *Les Exercises de ce temps*, ed. by Frédéric Lachèvre (Paris: Société des textes Français Modernes, 1997), p. 117. A key difference, of course, is that in most witch trials the defendant had not actually committed the acts of which they had been accused. Rather, as Christine Larner defines witch-hunting, such trials formed 'the process whereby the politically powerful pursue a group of persons selected for their beliefs or supposed attributes rather than for anything they have done' (Christina Larner, *Enemies of God: The Witch-hunt in Scotland* (Edinburgh: John Donald, 2000), p. 1).

Having been denounced by his students, whose testimony does not appear to have fed into the ensuing trial beyond his initial arrest, Fontanier was condemned largely as a result of Bellièvre's forensic readings of the *Trésor inestimable*, in which he disproved Fontanier's denials of having authored the text to devastating effect. Théophile's trial relied on both textual and testimonial evidence. In both cases, he was able to present considerable (though variably convincing) refutations of the claims put to him by his interrogators. Although we have considered a small corpus of three authors, their notoriety as *libertins* in the seventeenth century, the central place of Vanini and Théophile in modern scholarship on *libertinage*, and the depth of our three case studies, nonetheless allow us to propose conclusions from these monumental trials and to offer reflections for future work.

So much of Vanini's story was and remains fiction. Often alluded to as an Italian philosopher and author, Vanini was not tried by the authorities in Toulouse as an author at all. The myth of a helpless libertine languishing in his cell, whilst the Parlement de Toulouse seemed uninterested or at least unhurried in advancing his case, has very recently been dispelled by Didier Foucault's discovery of Marguerite de Senaux's memoirs. These reveal that Vanini's servants were coerced into testifying against him, and that his long period of incarceration encompassed a more active criminal investigation into his conduct than was previously thought. The two figures most often associated with his trial—Guillaume de Catel and 'Francon'—present us with a number of difficulties. I have argued that there is compelling evidence to suggest that although Francon certainly existed, his role as the star witness at Vanini's trial is a complete fabrication, intended to provide a convenient scapegoat to hide the identities of those members of influential families who wished to conceal their associations with a suspected blasphemer. Catel, for his part, undoubtedly played a pivotal role in Vanini's downfall. However, having paid close attention to the mechanics of legal procedure it seems either unlikely that he was both the *rapporteur* (reporter) and the *substitut du procureur général* (a substitute for the king's attorney general) for the case, or that if he was, this constituted an unusual and potentially problematic anomaly in what was already quite an extraordinary trial. Just as Jean de Rudèle raided the bookshops of Toulouse in search of Vanini's texts, having realised exactly who had been burned alive in the Place du Salin eight months previously, so too do modern researchers continue to learn more about this most enigmatic of authors. An author who whether in the streets of Toulouse, in Lambeth Palace, or in the preface to a modern edition of Cyrano, continues to delight in hiding in plain sight.

Whilst archival evidence from his trial proceedings is lacking, there is sufficient literary evidence pertaining to Vanini's execution to appreciate why he has been recognised by some as the prince of atheists and libertines.[20] There is a clear

[20] Jean-Pierre Cavaillé, 'Le 'prince des athées': Vanini et Machiavel', in *L'enjeu Machiavel*, ed. by Gérald

parallel between the simulation and dissimulation in Vanini's texts, and those he exercised in person during his stays in England and Toulouse. Additionally, both in England and in France Vanini was a man who knew when he was beaten. He did not continue to profess his innocence or repentance to the bitter end when under interrogation by George Abbot or by the Parlement de Toulouse. Rather, when his mask of conformity had slipped firmly to the floor, he seized the opportunity to enjoy the freedom that this total exposure afforded him in the knowledge that he had already been identified as a dangerous thinker. The distinction between Vanini the man and the author again seems pertinent here. As Vanini was not tried as an author, and as *De admirandis* was only condemned by the Sorbonne a month after its publication, his trial is not an evident tool with which to evaluate his authorial strategies of dissemination.

Vanini repeatedly made the mistake of getting himself into trouble for things that he said in private company and not for what he had written, with the exception of the eventual censorship of *De admirandis*. Even this condemnation seems to have had no major consequence on Vanini other than potentially motivating him to flee Paris. The writing strategies Vanini used to protect himself as a literary figure were thus more successful than those of Vanini the travelling teacher and philosopher. To put it another way: Vanini's unorthodox views were less of a danger to him when available to a public readership in print, the circulation of which he had no control over, than they were in a private conversational sphere of trusted interlocutors where Vanini had full control over who heard his views. Vanini's trial might well be considered as a separate chapter in his biography to his career as an author, not least as there is no evidence that he was preparing further works for publication whilst in Toulouse. By this time he had begun a career as a private tutor, and was later arrested, tried, and executed for his spoken blasphemies. Even at his execution, Vanini disrupted the expected legal and spiritual public performance of repentance through his words and actions, until the very instrument for his subversive words was physically torn from his body. As Cavaillé has recently remarked, this final act of nonconformity, staged within a gruesome judicial theatre in which a criminal was expected to repent, shattered the traditional image of both saints and sinners; serving as an 'alternativa radicale alle figure del santo o del martire, ma anche a quella dell'eretico, ossia di colui che devia in materia di religione' ('a radical alternative to the figures of the saint or the martyr, but also to that of the heretic, that is, one who deviates in matters of religion').[21] This inability

Sfez and Michel Senellart (Paris: Presses Universitaires de France, 2001), pp. 59–74; Émile Namer, *La Vie et l'œuvre de J.C. Vanini: Prince des Libertins* (Paris: Vrin, 1980).

21 Jean-Pierre Cavaillé, 'L'incarnazione delle false libertà: Vanini nella letteratura apologetica del Seicento', in *Giulio Cesare Vanini: Filosofia della libertà e libertà del filosofare. Atti del terzo convegno internazionale di studi Vaniniani (Lecce – Taurisano, 7–9 febbraio 2019)*, ed. by Francesco Paolo

to maintain the outward mask of conformity informs and nuances our reading of his texts, whilst also allowing us to appreciate the audacity and efficacy of their rhetorical strategies further. When we think of Vanini's place alongside well-known examples of *libertin* authors, we would do well to remember that his imprudence and lack of self-control were manifested in his social rather than literary activities; and that it was his tongue, not his quill, that was symbolically destroyed at the request of the magistrates.

Couched unflatteringly between the trials of Vanini and Théophile, in which the defendants held forth with strong rebuttals of the magistrates' accusations, Jean Fontanier's appeal hearings before the Parlement de Paris are in many ways characterised by absence. Unlike our other two authors, he did not enjoy the benefits of a family legal tradition or an aristocratic patron. The one mentor who did not tire of Fontanier's doubts, Daniel Montalto, was nowhere to be found when his protégé needed assistance which, in any case, he would have been unable to provide. Fontanier seemed oblivious to the fact that attitudes towards Jews had hardened since the fall of the Concinis, and that he was associating himself with the very same family who, according to Léonora Galigaï's trial records, was instrumental in fanning the flames of intolerance towards the Jewish community. There was an absence of any form of covert writing strategy in the *Trésor inestimable* as far as we can tell from Bellièvre's memoir. It was as if Fontanier, with a striking similarity to Vanini's private conversations with those he trusted, believed that his anti-Catholic teachings would be safe from reproach if disseminated within a private reading space, thereby negating any need for the irony or dissimulation exemplified in Vanini's texts. Even the placards advertising his lessons gave their author's true name and address, betraying a lack of any thought to the potential danger in which he was placing himself.

At trial, Fontanier was consistent in his strategy of denying authorship of the incriminating text attributed to him. This is by no means a hollow or charitable remark in his favour, for this very same strategy would after all serve Théophile well some three years later. Yet as Bellièvre so clinically observed, Fontanier's written and spoken words were devoid of the literary expertise, the rhetorical fineness, and the strategic foresight needed to convince his judges. The modern critic is further confronted with an absence of proof. The *Trésor inestimable* and witness interrogations contained within the initial trial records from the Châtelet were all destroyed, and it is only thanks to Bellièvre's manuscript that we are able to gain an insight into the contents of Fontanier's text. His interrogations reveal that Fontanier was almost always on the back foot, and that his ripostes led to a number of incriminating omissions, contradictions, and ultimately, an accidental admission of guilt.

Raimondi (Rome: Aracne, 2019), pp. 185–97 (p. 194).

In addition to adopting the same strategy of denying authorship that Théophile would later utilise successfully, it is also worth highlighting that Fontanier attempted to conceal the true nature of his teachings to a small degree. The contents of his placards bore little resemblance to the subject matter of his private lessons, and even these were protected with a vow of secrecy made by his initiates. Nevertheless, this oath—whose importance is made clear by the fact that it was reproduced in multiple contemporary sources condemning Fontanier's crimes—clearly drew more attention to the subversive nature of his text. Since his death, Fontanier's trial has been absent from a large number of authoritative studies on libertine literature. He was, to use Pintard's popular distinction, neither a *libertin érudit* nor a writer of sexually explicit or obscene texts, nor did he belong to a network of writers or thinkers. If Fontanier were to be included in a work on popular religious belief, it is unclear whether he would be most at home in a section on Catholic or Protestant doubt, on Protestant or Jewish conversion, or on Jewish or sceptical teaching.[22] He left behind neither a corpus of texts from which to deduce a social or theological philosophy, nor an exemplary record of clever self-defence or audacious unrepentance at trial. If a distinct lack of court records hinders yet encourages scholarship on Vanini's case, one has to concede that there is much to discourage studies of the extant documents from Fontanier's trial.

The neglect of Fontanier's case in modern scholarship has been both unfortunate and unjust. Appearing in the same year as the four-hundredth anniversary of his trial, this book has sought to consolidate Fontanier's place in the histories of free-thinking, of writing practices, of forensic linguistics, and of anti-Semitism. To this end, it has afforded the space to bring together the surviving material relevant to his life and trial, and has proposed new theories regarding his witnesses, his lost text, and his motivations. I have posited that Fontanier may have been overlooked in *libertinage* studies because he cuts a poor figure of a champion for modern notions of free-thinking. Moreover, Fontanier embarked on multiple geographical and spiritual journeys in search of a solid, theological belief system to settle what he described as his doubts. As such, he does not fit naturally into a field of academic study typically concerned with unbelief or with irreverence towards religious dogma. Nevertheless, Fontanier holds this trait in common with other authors in libertine studies who expressed their 'doubts' through erudite scepticism, whilst both Vanini's and Théophile's cases demonstrate that outward religious conversion did not exclude private unbelief. These considerations, along with Fontanier's fate as a condemned author and the accusation of *libertinage* made against him by

[22] Fontanier's belief system continues to evade concise definition in modern studies. Recently, Richard Watson has asserted that Fontanier was a 'deist', whereas Robert A. Schneider has classed him as 'a mystic'. See Richard Watson, *Cogito, Ergo Sum: The Life of René Descartes* (Boston, MA: David R. Godine, 2007), p. 152; Robert A. Schneider, *Dignified Retreat: Writers and Intellectuals in the Age of Richelieu* (Oxford: Oxford University Press, 2019), p. 127.

multiple contemporaries, surely earn him a place in *libertinage* studies. For when considered separately from his trial, his actions as an author and teacher show that in some respects, he was arguably the most audacious of our three libertines. When Fontanier's legal performance is measured against the brave and articulate paragons of defiance embodied by Vanini and Théophile, however, his trial perhaps makes for uncomfortable reading not because his self-defence was the least effective of the three, but because his foibles were the most human.

With Théophile de Viau's trial, we move from the respective enigma and tragedy of our previous case studies to the sensational. The value of this trial from the perspective of literary studies is obvious. It brought an end to an entire genre of publication—the *recueils satyriques* poetic anthologies—as well as signalling the need for subversive authors to adopt covert writing strategies to avoid emulating Théophile's exemplary ordeal. A milestone, then, 'both in the reinvention of obscenity and in the history of censorship'.[23] His trial also presents us with a wealth of legal and historical sources which, for the most part, have survived as court records in manuscript form. An indispensable resource for researchers unfamiliar with criminal archives, Lachèvre's two-volume study brings together transcriptions of the complete corpus of interrogations, witness statements, and confrontations with the exception of my recent discovery of Isaac La Pause's interrogation.[24] These records are precious accounts of how Théophile's works were read critically by his contemporaries, both as material objects and in relation to the poet's speech in private conversation as reported by witnesses.

This said, the convenience of such transcripts comes at the price of an estrangement from the source material, as well as potential distortion from Lachèvre's own writing practices. How do these original documents differ from Lachèvre's edition? Are his transcriptions accurate, reliable, or even complete, or was this conservative apologist for Ancien Régime absolutism guilty of a similar act of selective reading to Théophile's judges?[25] It is all too easy to leave these questions unanswered when faced with the very difficult handwriting in which the interrogation records were written, and to discard the original documents as 'impossible to decipher' and 'indecipherable' in favour of Lachèvre's more accessible transcriptions.[26] The research conducted with original sources for the present

[23] Joan DeJean, *The Reinvention of Obscenity. Sex, Lies, and Tabloids in Early Modern France* (Chicago, IL, and London: The University of Chicago Press, 2002), p. 29. For Schneider, this trial 'marked a turning point in the attitudes and latitude of expression for a generation of writers, inducing them to see the wisdom of caution, discretion, and conformism' (Schneider, *Dignified Retreat*, p. 127).

[24] Frédéric Lachèvre, *Le Libertinage devant le parlement de Paris: Le Procès du poète Théophile de Viau*, 2 vols (Paris: Honoré Champion, 1909).

[25] Lachèvre's political sympathies and his resultant hostility to the very subject matter of his books are well-known. For a recent defence of Lachèvre, see Aurélie Julia, *Frédéric Lachèvre (1855–1943): Un érudit à la découverte du XVIIe siècle libertin* (Paris: Honoré Champion, 2019).

[26] DeJean, *Obscenity*, p. 148, note 41. I am in part indebted to DeJean's comments here for arousing my curiosity and encouraging me to grapple with these archival sources. I do not claim to have entirely

study has proved illuminating. For practical reasons, it has not been possible to reproduce a representative photographic sample of the full corpus of trial records in this volume. Yet it is hoped that the images included in this book will encourage engagement with the original primary sources in future studies. My own efforts have revealed Lachèvre's transcriptions of Théophile's trial records to be accurate, complete, and as the images in the present study show, no small palaeographical feat. For the most part, the trial transcripts do not run words together for the purpose of conserving ink, though there certainly are ample examples of this practice.[27] Lachèvre's only omissions are variants in the court records, which are usually scored out and rarely exceed a few words in length. Though one can never predict the future research interests of other scholars, these small variants are not, as far as I have been able to discern, of any apparent consequence for the study of Théophile's trial.

This is not to say that the original sources are otherwise devoid of interest. They reveal, for example, that the scribes recorded lines of poetry quoted against the accused in a noticeably neater hand than spontaneous verbal exchanges, as demonstrated in Figure 6.1. The scribes could well have been provided with an edition of Théophile's poetry to copy from in court, as the page numbers for poems were provided in Molé's draft of questions. Alternatively, the scribes might simply have transcribed these poetic quotations after the trial hearing. Furthermore, whilst all hearings relative to Théophile's trial were recorded in the same hand, the confrontations with three witnesses on 22 and 29 November were manifestly recorded in a different hand altogether (Figure 6.2). The original copy of Molé's draft of questions reveals some more significant variants, including crucial evidence demonstrating the *procureur général*'s awareness of the distinction between imitation and translation. Through the arrangement of various columns and references on its pages, this same document allows us to learn more about Molé's critical reading practices than is possible with a modern linear transcription with footnotes. Finally, this study has revealed that from previously overlooked variants, to documents entirely new to scholarship, to forgotten characters in the story of Théophile's prosecution, the archives have not yet given up all of their secrets on even this most famous of author trials.

Théophile was not only able to replicate his libertine writing strategies in court, but to articulate these in responses which almost form micro literary manifestos similar to those present in several of his poems. In both arenas, he adroitly distinguished between the Christian God in the singular and the pagan gods in

answered her call for 'a very courageous scholar indeed to tackle this case [...] with extensive training in palaeography' (p. 148, note 41). Nevertheless, the images, arguments, and critical comments included in Chapter 5, as well as in the present conclusion, will at least go some way towards dispelling the myths of both the impenetrability of the archival sources and the unreliability of Lachèvre's transcriptions.

[27] A claim made in DeJean, *Obscenity*. p. 148, note 41.

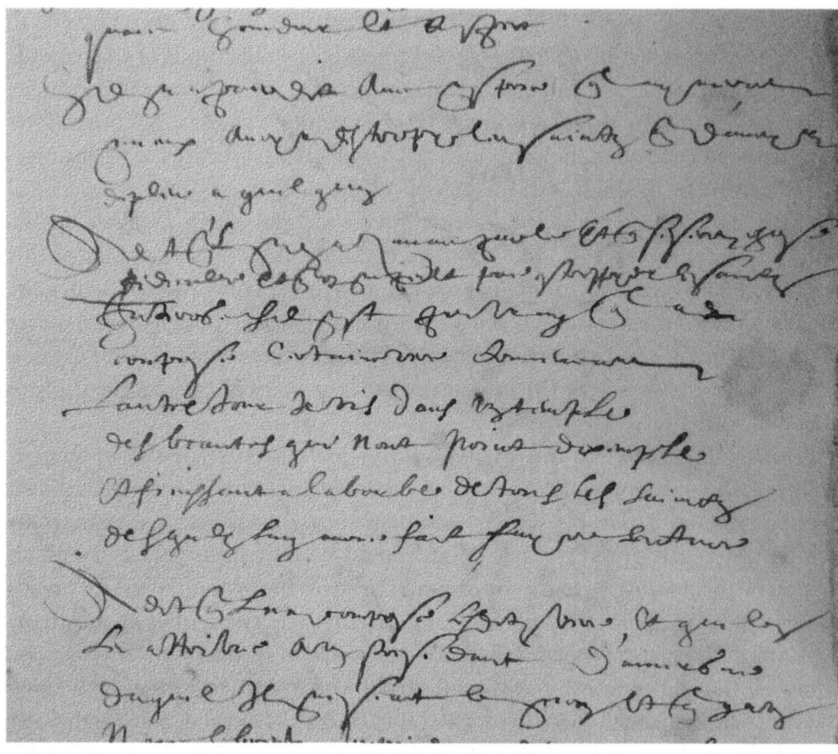

Figure 6.1 AN X 2B 1185: Théophile's third interrogation (27 March 1624). This image shows lines of quoted poetry recorded in less hurried, more legible handwriting than the transcripts of oral exchanges, as well as examples of both adjoined words and spacing between words. Here, the court falsely attributed a modified version of Francois Maynard's 'Pour une jeune dame' to Théophile, who responds 'qu'il n'a composé lesditz vers et que l'on les attribue à un Président d'Auvergne duquel il ne sçait le nom' ('that he did not write these verses and that they are attributed to a *président* in Auvergne, whose name he does not know').

the plural. The subversive messages behind many of the lines of poetry quoted to him were defended with literal readings—*n'a jamais dit* ([I] never said)—over the inferred readings of the magistrates, who had adopted the position of the target readership of these texts in order to demonstrate their author's culpability. Perhaps the most striking strategy to emerge from Chapter 5 is the poet's shared understanding with his interrogators of the distinctions between imitation and translation, and the potential consequences of these when used as weapons within a legal context. There is a distinct shift in the comparatively inconsistent strategy of the magistrates who, in observing how Théophile was able to refute their critical readings convincingly, moved the focus of the trial to spoken blasphemies and

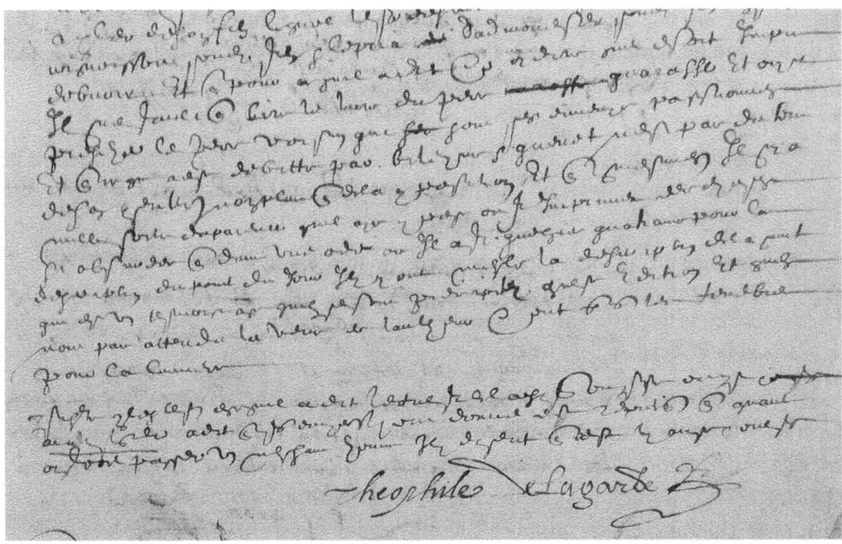

Figure 6.2 AN X 2B 1186: The signed confrontation between Théophile and Charles Le Caron (29 November 1624). This confrontation, along with those of Pierre Bonnet and Étienne Delagarde (22 November), was transcribed in a different hand to the other records for Théophile's trial as exemplified in Chapter 5 and in Figure 6.1.

sexual misdemeanour. In marked contrast to Fontanier's trial, at no point did the judges appear to have the upper hand over the confident and steadfast Théophile. With more experience as a published writer than Vanini, and with a more advanced command of linguistic subtlety than Fontanier, Théophile mounted an impressive defence of his conduct. This defence was ultimately convincing for his judges, and surely worthy of its posthumous reputation as a last stand for the first wave of libertine literary production.

There is however tension in Théophile's relationship to his art at trial, similar to that of the emancipated poetic 'I' writing (albeit grudgingly) for the benefit of patrons.[28] This same writer who in so many of his poems expressed a desperation for freedom, and a militant despair in the face of the social, religious, and literary climate of his time, denied authorship of forty-five of his texts including seventeen which had been printed bearing his name. This leads us to ask to what extent this disavowal of his poems—undertaken specifically in order to dissociate himself from the ideas they contained—affected the authenticity of their message, not least as there is no textual evidence to suggest that Théophile returned to old

[28] See, for example, 'À Monsieur du Fargis', in Théophile de Viau, *Œuvres*, ed. by Guido Saba (Paris: Classiques Garnier, 1990), pp. 123–5.

habits after his release. It was quite extraordinary that after having survived his ordeal at the Parlement de Paris, this leading figure in libertine literature boasted that he was the first author to participate in the censorship of such texts:

> J'apportay pour ma deffence la sentence du Prevost de Paris, obtenuë contre les imprimeurs [du *Parnasse satyrique*], et suppliay la Cour de considerer que j'estois le premier de ma profession, qui par une affection aux bonnes mœurs, et pour oster le scandale public, avoit fait supprimer de telles œuvres.
>
> I brought in my defence the sentence by the *Prévôt de Paris*, which I obtained against the printers [of the *Parnasse satyrique*], and begged the court to consider that I was the first of my profession, out of affection for moral decency and to avoid public scandal, to have had such works banned.[29]

It goes without saying that this is an easy criticism to make from a vantage point far from the foreboding Parisian Grand' Chambre, and Théophile's prevailing sense of self-preservation would be flimsy evidence indeed with which to criticise his character. Yet this book has considered libertine authors at the intersection of legal history and literary scholarship, and Théophile's defence shows that the consequences of any given act within the courtroom arena can be viewed differently depending on disciplinary perspective. It is difficult to construe precisely what Fontanier's views were at the moment of his alleged conversion to Catholicism under the shadow of the stake. Once Vanini's mask of conformity had been irrevocably discredited, he was prepared to die for his beliefs. Ultimately, Vanini revealed himself to be one with the literary 'J-C' who so skilfully dissimulated religious scepticism in *De admirandis*. Théophile, on the other hand, recognised that the attitudes and belief systems prescribed in his poetry struck a very different note when echoed within the walls of the Conciergerie than they had inside Montmorency's *Maison de Sylvie*. When faced with the choice between his literature or his life, he understandably decided to disassociate himself from the purportedly libertine views expressed by his poetic 'I' for the sake of his own personal safety.

These legal struggles were contests between two parties. Another aim of this study has been to consider the roles of the magistrates, and to evaluate the efforts during the early years of Louis XIII's reign to police literature. Rather than facing a monolithic state apparatus, seditious and subversive authors could be tried by a variety of different law courts. This was further reflected by a given court's composite diversity of opinion. A panel of judges included variations in age, seniority, professional experience, and ideological sympathies. As Fontanier's and Théophile's trials make clear, not all magistrates (or indeed, all Catholics) came to the same conclusions when passing judgement on a purportedly libertine author. As I have argued throughout, in assembling to judge a defendant for their writings,

[29] Théophile, *Apologie au Roy*, pp. 20–1.

the judges formed a gathering of learned men engaged in the critical readership of texts in a similar way to other readers, such as Garasse, in the theological and literary spheres. It is worth remembering that in doing so, the magistrates were not working as far outside of their routine judgement of cases as we might first think. Given that the evidence in criminal cases was written down (such as interrogations and witness depositions), and given that the full complement of judges would usually only assemble for the final interrogation and deliberation, it was in fact the normal function of the judges to serve as critical readers. Only the oral intervention of the *rapporteur*—and, if required, the *procureur général*—served as lenses through which the content of these transcribed oral exchanges could be refracted.

Marie Houllemare has shown how the Parlement de Paris was steeped in orality; from the hearing of witnesses and interrogations, to deliberations and the reading out of *arrêts* (final judgements), to the gossip which swirled around the market stalls outside of the chambers, blending colloquial and legal French with the languages of Antiquity through learned quotation.[30] This was only one side of the judicial process. On the other, the oral statements made by defendants, witnesses, and the interrogators themselves were transformed into written texts, often forming such large corpora that the very purpose of the *rapporteur* was to save his fellow judges from having to wade through often considerable material evidence themselves. The trial of a subversive author therefore constituted a two-way interchange between written and oral cultures. First, it gave a voice to an incriminating text, and a human form to the ideas it contained. This allowed the law courts to punish and eradicate these human embodiments of dangerous ideas, alongside the offending literary objects that they had created, from God-fearing society. Second, it gave physical, textual form to the critical reading of those texts, to related verbal testimonies and defences, to the mechanics of criminal procedure, and by extension to the mentalities of censorship against which illegal literature was often written. The magistrates were perfectly aware of this paradox, which they sought to counteract in part by attempting to impose differences in legal practice between public and private spheres. For example, *arrêts* for particularly unpleasant or scandalous crimes were worded in vague terms—sometimes restricting their printed, publicly available counterparts to describing the generic stages of criminal procedure and the verdict—lest the public at large be disturbed (or worse, inspired) by the Devil in the detail.[31]

The memoirs of Molé and Bellièvre serve as fine examples of this ironic potential for criminal procedure to immortalise dissident voices. These precious

[30] Marie Houllemare, *Politiques de la parole: le Parlement de Paris au XVI*[e] *siècle* (Geneva: Droz, 2011), p. 131.

[31] Pierre de L'Estoile, for example, relates that court clerks were banned from disseminating copies of an *arrêt* for a bestiality case on 15 October 1601. See Soman, 'Press, Pulpit and Censorship', 450.

accounts, along with the extant archival documentation, have also allowed us a glimpse into the psychology of dispensing justice in the early modern period. Having sent defendants to their deaths for exploring their spirituality or their sexuality, for giving voice to their sense of humour or their frustrations, it is perhaps instinctive for us to adopt the default view of these judges as Catholic zealots, as political absolutists, and as unpitying tormentors unperturbed by the blood on their hands. This becomes all the more natural when, as with Fontanier's persecution for Judaism, the object of study bears uncomfortable parallels with more recent historical events. Unsurprisingly, this book has not found the judges of our authors to have been hesitant dispensers of harsh and exemplary justice. Rather, it has found their actions to be more nuanced. The case for using these trials as examples of literary engagement has already been made in the preceding chapters. Yet the court records have also exposed the practical limitations of the dispensing of justice. It was previously believed that Vanini was thrown into prison without subsequent event, and that a witness was produced only when he was on the verge of being released.[32] We now know, however, that he was detained whilst sufficient testimonial evidence was gathered against him, and that the Parlement de Toulouse was not therefore prepared to execute him on the basis of rumour, accusation, and interrogation alone. Zealous intolerance and excessive violence were one thing, but failing to ensure due diligence was quite another.

Bellièvre was all too mindful of the thorny legal issues presented by a potential Christian convert to Judaism teaching his new faith. His manuscript reveals that the need for consensus in the deliberations, as well as an openness to debating different courses of action, was respected when judging what was considered to be one of the worst possible crimes: lese-majesty. The *président à mortier*'s account leads us to conclude, with justifiable hesitation, that the strong anti-Semitism of Fontanier's judges was not entirely unbridled. Bellièvre's preparations for the trial, his interrogation method, and his instructions to have Fontanier's body examined by surgeons, may be abhorrent to the modern reader. According to the standards of the time, however, Bellièvre operated within both the law and the boundaries of cold, methodical logic, as epitomised by his forensic linguistic approach to proving Fontanier's authorship of the *Trésor inestimable*. That the magistrates should have paid such attention to questions of formality, to procedure, and to historical and legal precedent, despite being faced with a wealth of incriminating evidence and a self-contradicting defendant, points to this same conclusion. Despite their abhorrence of Fontanier's actions, they were mindful that unlike the

[32] To recall Gramond's claim, 'il étoit même sur le point d'être élargi, à cause de l'ambiguité des preuves' ('he [Vanini] was even on the verge of being released, due to the ambiguous nature of the evidence against him': Gabriel-Barthélemy de Grammond, *Historiarum Galliae ab excessu Henrici IV libri XVIII* (Toulouse: Arnald Colomerium, 1643) translated in David Durand, *La Vie et les œuvres de Lucilio Vanini* (Rotterdam: Gaspar Fritsch, 1717), pp. 187–8).

zealous Catholics of Saint-Jean-de-Luz in 1619, they could only manifest their intolerance within the confines of the law. Their manipulation of legal customs regarding Fontanier's hunger strike and his strangulation prior to being burned, however, tragically show that modern preconceptions of early modern criminal procedure are nonetheless often justified.

The verdict at Théophile's trial demonstrates that even when presented with a notorious author of irreverent and obscene poetry (including poems alleged to pertain to the poet's own non-heterosexual tendencies), not to mention a large number of witnesses, the magistrates of the highest court in the land were not always inclined to find the defendant guilty. As voluminous as the evidence was, and despite the considerably premeditated nature of Théophile's prosecution by Molé, Garasse, and Voisin, the judges were unconvinced by what they had heard. The attempts made in Chapter 5 to deduce how individual judges may have voted are not intended to be irrefutable assertions. Rather, they serve as a means of illustrating the types of personalities that Théophile was up against, as well as his considerable success in beating the odds to win over the majority of his judges. Without wishing to detract from his accomplishment, the very public nature of the Jesuits' involvement in this trial does not discount the possibility that for many of his judges, finding Théophile innocent was a lesser evil (and perhaps even an intentional affront to the Jesuit order) than allowing Garasse's and Voisin's plans to come to fruition.

It is remarkable that amongst the charges against our authors—blasphemy, impiety, lese-majesty, and the various stages of the material production of texts—the term *libertin* does not appear, although it does occur very occasionally within the trial records themselves. On the one hand, there was no legal ordinance, edict, or declaration designating *libertinage* as a crime. On the other, as Chapter 1 has amply shown, the term *libertin* as an accusation became so vague (yet no less potent) that it was perhaps unfit for purpose in a legal arena which sought to clarify truth. The accusation of *libertinage*—so famously typified by Garasse's polemic but also by other contemporary writers—was translated into the crimes mentioned above for which there was both legal status and precedent. This process allows us to speak of the trials *of* libertine authors, but not of trials *for* libertine authorship. What proves difficult for neat compartmentalisation is in fact enriching from the perspectives of the histories of writing, the law, and ideas. As Frédéric Tinguely remarks on the broad range of individuals targeted by Garasse's accusations: 'il produit une sorte d'inflation polémique d'autant plus difficile à contrôler que les termes mis en relation sont toujours plus que deux' ('it produces a kind of polemical inflation which is even more difficult to control as there are always more than two terms being related to one another').[33] A problematically

[33] Frédéric Tinguely, 'Garasse et les altérités croisées', in *Libertin! Usage d'une invective aux XVI*[e] *et*

ambiguous term for the outcome of a trial, then, *libertinage* nonetheless served to fuel the fear, the literary polemics, and the subsequent arrests of those found to have committed infractions for which it was an appropriate term of opprobrium.

The trials of Giulio Cesare Vanini, Jean Fontanier, and Théophile de Viau stand as remarkable testaments to their audacity and to their progressive thinking. Their judges proved themselves to be highly competent critical readers, though nonetheless subjects and indeed proponents of the predominant ideologies, intolerance, and prejudices of their age. Although harsh in their judgements, they were not inflexible towards persuasion, moderation, or the restrictions placed on them by the habitual workings of a criminal justice system which nonetheless stacked the odds firmly (but not absolutely) against the defendant. The unhappy endings of these contests between libertines and the law should not cloud our evaluation of the legal and personal journeys that our authors were forced to embark upon, and their failings in court ought not to detract from their other victories great and small; neither from their audacity which attracted the attention of the law courts, nor from their reputations consolidated only shortly after their deaths. For it is through their perilous ordeals related in this book, under the unflinching gaze of the royal parlements, that these authors have been sympathetically remembered by the same posterity whose judgement the magistrates themselves so feared.

XVIIe siècles, ed. by Thomas Berns, Anne Staquet and Monique Weis (Paris: Classiques Garnier, 2013), pp. 117–31 (p. 131).

Select Glossary of Legal Terms Used

CONTENTS*

* Some of the terms and procedures outlined in this Glossary are still present in the modern French legal system.

Monitoire
Parlement
Persister
Premier Président
Président
Président à mortier
Prévôt
Prévôté
Procès
Procureur général du roi
Rapport
Rapporteur
Registres d'écrou
Reproche
Sac
Sentence
Substitut du procureur général du roi
Tournelle

Amende honorable

In passing a death sentence, a court could order a prisoner to perform a highly choreographed act of repentance to the crowd immediately prior to their execution, which was termed making 'honourable amends'. The prisoner would typically be dressed in only a shirt, given a candle to hold, and loaded into a cart. They would then be paraded in public, stopping outside the main doors of Notre-Dame Cathedral (for prisoners tried in Paris) to ask forgiveness from God, the king, and the judiciary ('la justice') for their crimes. This custom demonstrates the significance of Vanini's and Fontanier's deviations from their expected performance prior to their executions.

Arrêt

An *arrêt* can refer to legislation enacted by the king which was then ratified by the royal **parlements.** In the context of this study, however, an *arrêt* most frequently refers to a decision or verdict reached by a law court. Where this decision was made in a court of the first instance (for example, the **Châtelet's** initial decision against Fontanier prior to his appeal), I have translated the *arrêt* as the **sentence**. When this decision was reached in a **parlement** (whether as a final court of appeal as for Fontanier's trial, or as the first court to hear the case as in Théophile's trial), I have translated *arrêt* as a final judgement.

Capitole

The building which housed the municipal court of Toulouse (the **Capitoulat**) and its magistrates (the ***capitouls***).

Capitoul

A magistrate of the municipal court of Toulouse (the **Capitoulat**).

Capitoulat

The municipal court of Toulouse, whose jurisdiction covered the day-to-day running of the city and its amenities, as well as a number of crimes including capital offences. It fell within the appellate jurisdiction of the Parlement de Toulouse.

Cas royal

A 'royal case' was originally a crime which could only be judged by the royal law courts (the **parlements**). In our period of study, it referred to infractions against the king's person, property, rights, and interests. Given that these covered those of the king's subjects, a *cas royal* came to refer to any serious crime which was deemed to threaten the public interest.

Chambres assemblées

A joint hearing in a **parlement** of the **Grand' Chambre** and **Tournelle** chambers. This was reserved for particularly serious crimes or for trying defendants of high social rank.

Châtelet

The provostship (***prévôté***) for the region of Paris of the same level as a bailiwick (*bailliage*). The Châtelet also served as a court of appeal for cases judged in seigneurial courts, whilst its own judgements in the first instance were within the appellate jurisdiction of the Parlement de Paris, as was the case in Fontanier's trial.

Commissaire

A magistrate commissioned with the ***instruction*** of a case. This was not an office, but a temporary role assigned to a magistrate for a specific trial.

Conciergerie

The name given to the prisons of the Parlement de Paris and the Parlement de Toulouse.

Conclusions

The remarks made on a case by the ***procureur général*** or his ***substitut***, which highlighted any questions of law arising from a case as well as the ***procureur général***'s recommendations for the final judgement. This document was available to judges when deliberating their verdict alongside the ***rapport***.

Confrontation

A hearing in which a defendant was confronted with a witness who had testified against them. The accused was first asked whether they had any ***reproches*** to make against their witness before their deposition was read out to them. The accused was then effectively able to cross-examine the witness in an attempt to invalidate their testimony.

Conseiller

The councillors were the regular magistrates of a **parlement**. They served in a specific chamber and could also be drafted to serve on rotation in the **Tournelle**.

Entier

If a sufficient amount of proof was found to construct a case against a defendant, or if a single given piece of evidence was considered to be admissible in court, these were described as *entiers* (whole). This furthermore explains why certain documents refer to half-proofs (*demi-preuves*), whose fractional evidence could sometimes be used cumulatively to construct a case.

Gens du roi

The king's men were a group of magistrates serving in a **parlement** or a ***prévôté*** who represented the king and his interests. They consisted of the ***procureur général du roi***, his ***substituts***, and the *avocat général du roi* (assistant public prosecutor).

Grand' Chambre (also written as Grand'chambre, Grande Chambre, Grand chambre or Grande-Chambre)

The senior chamber of a ***parlement*** staffed by its most experienced magistrates. Those with the rank of ***président*** who sat in the Grand' Chambre were known as ***présidents à mortier***. The Grand' Chambre judged trials for particularly serious crimes, as well as those committed by high-ranking defendants including princes of the blood and certain magistrates. It also hosted plenary sessions and *lits de justice* held by the king.

Greffier

The court scribe tasked with recording transcripts of interrogations, witness depositions, and ***confrontations***.

Information

A body of evidence collected during the investigation (***instruction***) of a trial by ***commissaires***.

Instruction

The act of gathering evidence for a trial. Two magistrates were named ***commissaires*** to carry out this task, which included the collation of witness testimony, interrogating a prisoner, and bringing the accused face to face with their witnesses in ***confrontations***. The resultant body of evidence was known as the ***information***.

Instruire

The act of carrying out the ***instruction*** of a trial in order to present the court with the resultant ***information***.

Interrogatoire

The interrogation of a defendant or witness by one or both of the ***commissaires*** assigned to the case in question. Whereas statements by witnesses were usually referred to as *dépositions*, witnesses were said to be interrogated (*interrogé*), including at the scene of a potential crime as was the case during Fontanier's arrest.

Interrogatoire sur la sellette

The interrogations of a defendant, of witnesses, and any ***confrontations*** between the two parties usually took place in private. The judges would only see the written records of these which had been synthesised by the ***rapporteur***. Before the judges deliberated a verdict, however, the defendant could be brought before their judges for an *interrogatoire* (or *audience*) *sur la sellette*, in order to undergo a final interrogation whilst sitting on a small wooden stool (*la sellette*).

Lèse-majesté divine

A capital offence against God. Such crimes included sorcery, simony, heresy, apostasy, and blasphemy.

Lèse-majesté humaine

A capital offence against the king or his councillors of state. Such crimes included treason, counterfeiting, and sedition through the carrying of firearms or through illicit gatherings. Due to the king's status as God's representative on Earth, and in particular the French king's title of first son of the Catholic Church, there could be a certain degree of overlap between these two forms of *lèse-majesté*.

Lieutenant civil du Châtelet

A magistrate who presided over the policing of the city of Paris. Whilst this office was rivalled by the ***lieutenant criminel*** for supremacy within the jurisdiction of Paris, in our period of study the *lieutenant civil* was the *de facto* head of the **Châtelet**.

Lieutenant criminel du Châtelet

A magistrate who presided over the criminal chamber of the **Châtelet**.

Monitoire

The practice of using churches to seek evidence or witnesses for a trial. *Lettres monitoires* were read out by priests to their parishioners, or nailed to the entrances of churches, imploring anyone with relevant information to come forward on pain of excommunication.

Parlement

A royal court of justice and the highest court within its given jurisdiction. The oldest of these was the Parlement de Paris on which all subsequent parlements were modelled. A parlement could hear cases in the first instance (such as Théophile's trial) or as a final court of appeal (as for Fontanier's trial). The Parlement de Paris additionally served a political purpose, registering legislation such as ***arrêts*** in order to legitimise the king's decrees.

Persister

At the end of an interrogation, witness deposition or ***confrontation***, the transcript of the hearing would be read out to the defendant or witness. If they agreed that this written record was an accurate account of what had been said, they were said to have *persisté*.

Premier Président

The leading magistrate of a **parlement** who was selected for office by the king. Besides his many judicial and political duties, a *premier président* presided over the most serious of criminal cases tried in his **parlement**, as was the case for the trials of Vanini and Théophile.

Président

The senior rank in the chamber of a **parlement** other than its **Grand' Chambre**.

Président à mortier

The name given to a ***président*** who sat in the most senior chamber of a **parlement**: the **Grand' Chambre**. These were visually distinguished from the ***présidents*** of other chambers by their mortarboards from which they derived their name. Any of the *présidents à mortier* were able to take the place of an absent ***premier président***, including in order to preside over ***chambres assemblées***.

Prévôt

The provost of a provostship (***prévôté***). The *prévôt* of the **Châtelet** was considered the first *prévôt* of the kingdom, but was a largely ceremonial role in terms of criminal justice in our period.

Prévôté

A provostship, presided by a ***prévôt***. A *prévôté* dealt with the public order of its jurisdiction and could try certain cases as a court of first instance. Its judgements were under the appellate jurisdiction of a **parlement**.

Procès

A legal trial. Unlike some modern justice systems, where evidence is first gathered before a suspect is arrested, charged, and brought to trial, early modern French magistrates understood a *procès* to include the preliminary interrogations of witnesses and of the accused. In modern trials, a panel of judges or a jury is often present to observe defendants being questioned in court. In our case studies however, the only event analogous to these modern hearings came at the end of a *procès* in which the judges could attend a final interrogation of the accused: the ***interrogation sur la sellette***.

Procureur général du roi

The king's attorney general and head of the ***gens du roi***. The *procureur général* was a representative of the king serving as his political agent in the Parlement de Paris, as well as being one of the Parlement's leading magistrates. As a result of the wide and flexible definitions of the king's interests (and therefore of crimes which could be considered a ***cas royal***), the *procureur général* served as chief public prosecutor. One of the ways in which an ***instruction*** could be initiated was at the request of the *procureur général* or one of his ***substituts***. Whilst he did not sit in judgement for criminal trials, the *procureur général* or one of his ***substituts*** could offer his opinion (***conclusions***) based on the points of law relevant to the case in question, which would subsequently be considered in the judges' final deliberations.

Rapport

The report of a ***rapporteur***, which was delivered during the deliberations over a verdict. The large amount of trial documents and written evidence collated in a trial's ***sac*** was synthesised so that cases could be judged more swiftly. The resulting synthesis was the *rapport* which organised the significant documents, guided judges through the ***information***, and offered a view on each piece of evidence. The *rapport* was read out to the judges assigned to a case by the ***rapporteur*** before the other judges volunteered their own views.

Rapporteur

The term used to describe the reporter designated to prepare and deliver the ***rapport*** for a trial. This was not an office, but a temporary role assigned to a magistrate for a specific trial. The wider legal competencies of a magistrate were often judged by how well he performed when called to serve as *rapporteur*, which also influenced his wider professional reputation. By the seventeenth century, the *rapporteur* spoke first in deliberations, as seen in Fontanier's trial.

Registres d'écrou

The records of incarceration of the Paris **Conciergerie.** These detail the arrival of the prisoner in the right-hand column, and the outcome of their trial in the left-hand column.

Reproche

Before hearing witness testimony, a defendant was permitted to present *reproches* in order to discredit the witness and to invalidate their deposition. The numerous forms of valid *reproches* included claims pertaining to the mental capacities of the witness, their character, their economic condition, their social or familial situation, the reliability of their statements, their impartiality, and their conduct in the chamber.

Sac

The sack containing evidence pertaining to a trial. Initially collated by the ***commissaires*** during the ***instruction***, the sack would then be examined in detail by the ***rapporteur***. During the deliberations leading to the judging of a case, the magistrates would normally rely on a ***rapport*** of the evidence rather than inspecting every piece of evidence themselves.

Sentence

When speaking of ***arrêts*** in criminal trials, it is necessary to distinguish between the judgement of a court of the first instance and that of a **parlement** hearing the case on appeal (as in Fontanier's case). In this study, the 'sentence' refers to a judgement or ***arrêt*** from a court of the first instance, whereas ***arrêts*** from a royal **parlement** have been translated as 'final judgements'.

Substitut du procureur général du roi

A member of the ***gens du roi***, a *subsitut* could be asked to stand in for the ***procureur général du roi*** in a trial due to the number of cases dealt with by a **parlement**. As such, investigations and trials could be instigated at the request of the *substitut du procureur général du roi* as recorded in the final ***arrêts***. The *substitut* offered his ***conclusions*** (also termed *opinion*) in the closing stages of a trial. Unlike the roles of ***rapporteur*** or ***commissaire***, a *substitut* was an official and permanent role within a **parlement**.

Tournelle

The criminal chamber of a **parlement** competent in judging crimes carrying corporal punishment (including relatively small crimes), and the final court for the criminal cases of the unprivileged. There were no fixed magistrates assigned to the Tournelle as was the case for other chambers such as the **Grand' Chambre**. Instead, judges from other chambers served in the Tournelle on a rotation basis. In certain instances, the Tournelle and the **Grand' Chambre** judged cases together as ***chambres assemblées***.

Bibliography

ARCHIVE AND MANUSCRIPT SOURCES

Archives Nationales de France, Paris (AN)

X 1A 8870: *Registre des Conclusions de Monseigneur le Procureur General du Roy Molé* (18 mai – 27 octobre 1623).
X 1A 8874: *Registre des Conclusions de Monseigneur le Procureur General du Roy Molé* (9 mai – 18 août 1625).
X 2A 217: 'Registre d'arrêts transcrits' (3 mai – 27 octobre 1623).
X 2A 224: 'Registre d'arrêts transcrits' (1 août – 31 décembre 1625).
X 2A 985: 'Plumitifs du conseil de la Tournelle' (12 novembre 1621 – 26 octobre 1622).
X 2A 986: 'Plumitifs du conseil de la Tournelle' (12 novembre 1622 – 27 octobre 1623).
X 2A 988: 'Plumitifs du conseil de la Tournelle' (13 novembre 1624 – 25 octobre 1625).
X 2A 1373: 'Registre d'entablement d'arrêts de la Tournelle criminelle' (13 novembre 1615 – 25 octobre 1625).
X 2A 1384: 'Table d'arrêts' (12 novembre 1620 – octobre 1627).
X 2B 78: 'Minutes d'arrêts' (janvier – février 1574).
X 2B 330: 'Minutes d'arrêts' (octobre – décembre 1621).
X 2B 341: 'Minutes d'arrêts' (juin – juillet 1623).
X 2B 342: 'Minutes d'arrêts' (août – septembre 1623).
X 2B 357: 'Minutes d'arrêts' (septembre – octobre 1625).
X 2B 1184: 'Minutes d'instruction' (1623).
X 2B 1185: 'Minutes d'instruction' (janvier – juin 1624).
X 2B 1186: 'Minutes d'instruction' (juillet – décembre 1624).
X 2B 1187: 'Minutes d'instruction' (janvier – juin 1625).

Archives de la Préfecture de Police, Paris (APP)

AB 25: 'Registre d'écrou de la Conciergerie du Palais de Justice' (1621).
AB 26: 'Registre d'écrou de la Conciergerie du Palais de Justice' (1623).

Archives départementales de la Haute-Garonne (ADHG)

MS 1 B 3548 (1603): 'Arrêt de mort de Blaise Vitalis'.
MS B 382 (1619): 'Arrêt de mort de Pompée Ucilio [Vanini]'.

Archives Municipales de Toulouse (AMT)

BB 278: *Annales des capitouls de la ville de Toulouse*, vol. VI, 'chronique 290' (Nicolas de Saint-Pierre, 1618).

BB 278: *Annales des capitouls de la ville de Toulouse*, vol. VI, 'chronique 291' (Pierre de Carrière, 1619).

Bibliothèque Municipale de Toulouse (BMT)

696: 'Extrait des Annales de Toulouse de 1295 à 1633' (1618–1619).

Monastère de la Croix (Évry)

Vie de Mère Marguerite de Jésus de Senaux o.p. Fondatrice des Monastères de Saint-Thomas et de la Croix à Paris, 1589–1667.

Bibliothèque Nationale de France, Paris (BNF)

BNF MS Baluze 209: 'Correspondances et pièces diverses (XVIe–XVIIe siècle)'.

BNF MS Baluze 212: 'Mélanges — notes de Sauval. Documents concernant la Bibliothèque de Colbert'.

BNF MS Baluze 326: 'Recueil des pièces concernant principalement les Protestants au XVIIe siècle — papiers divers du cardinal de Richelieu'.

BNF MS Cinq Cents de Colbert 2: 'Recueil de lettres et mémoires, en originaux, imprimés et copies, concernant l'Histoire de France (1278–1665)' (1617–45).

BNF MS Cinq Cents de Colbert 6: 'Recueil de lettres et mémoires, en originaux, imprimés et copies, concernant l'Histoire de France (1278–1665)' (1232–1640).

BNF MS Cinq Cents de Colbert 147: 'Recueil de pièces, contrats, procès, lettres patentes, comptes, concernant particulièrement de grandes familles françaises, Armagnac, La Tour d'Auvergne, Concressault, Laval, etc. (1202–1660)' (1597–1618).

BNF MS Cinq Cents de Colbert 218: 'Procédures et arrests contre des accusés de crime de leze-majeste recueillis par Matthieu Molé (1440–1652)', 4 vols, I (1453–1626).

BNF MS Cinq Cents de Colbert 219: 'Procédures et arrests contre des accusés de crime de leze-majeste recueillis par Matthieu Molé (1440–1652)', 4 vols, II (1627–1652).

BNF MS Cinq Cents de Colbert 220: 'Procédures et arrests contre des accusés de crime de leze-majeste recueillis par Matthieu Molé (1440–1652)', 4 vols, III (1440–1632).

BNF MS Cinq Cents de Colbert 221: 'Procédures et arrests contre des accusés de crime de leze-majeste recueillis par Matthieu Molé (1440–1652)', 4 vols, IV (1617).

BNF MS Dupuy 63: 'Lettres de plusieurs grands et autres emploiez dans les affaires d'Estat, escrites au Roi [Henri IV], ès années 1596, 1597, 1598, 1599, 1600, 1601, 1602, 1603, 1604, 1605 et 1606, 3 vols, III'.

BNF MS Dupuy 90: 'Recueil de pièces concernant la fin du règne de Henri IV et le règne de Louis XIII', 5 vols, I (1610–13).

BNF MS Dupuy 91: 'Recueil de pièces concernant la fin du règne de Henri IV et le règne de Louis XIII', 5 vols, II (1614–15).

BNF MS Dupuy 93: 'Recueil de pièces concernant la fin du règne de Henri IV et le règne de Louis XIII', 5 vols, IV (1625–30).

BNF MS Dupuy 468: 'Recueil de documents concernant l'histoire de l'Allemagne, du Danemark, de la Hongrie, de la Pologne et de la Suède, et les relations de ces différents pays avec la France, de 1447 à 1633 environ'.

BNF MS Dupuy 498: 'Recueil de pièces concernant les parlements de Paris, de Toulouse, de Dijon, de Rouen, d'Aix, de Navarre et de Metz, de 1464 à 1637 environ'.

BNF MS Dupuy 558: 'Recueil de traités et de mémoires juridiques, relatifs aux cas royaux'.

BNF MS Dupuy 688: 'Recueil de lettres, françaises, italiennes et latines, pour la plupart autographes, de Charles-Quint, de Rubens et de divers savants du XVIIe siècle.'

BNF Est., Ed 30: Abraham Bosse, *Les Métiers* (1632–33): 'L'Étude du procureur'.

BNF MS Fr 4745: 'Recueil de documents concernant l'histoire de France dans ses rapports avec celles d'Italie et d'Espagne, au XVIe et au XVIIe siècle', 10 vols, VI: Memoires et discours sur divers matieres'.

BNF MS Fr 15734: 'Censures d'un certain nombre d'ouvrages, principalement d'ouvrages de Jésuites du XVIIe siècle'.

BNF MS Fr 15898: 'Papiers et correspondance de Pompone Ier de Bellièvre (1566–1607)', 22 vols, IX: 'Lettres originelles adressées au chancelier de Bellièvre par divers présidents et conseillers aux Parlements, etc. (1599–1606)'.

BNF MS Fr 16536: 'Recueil de pièces diverses, manuscrites et imprimées, lettres de rois de France, arrêts de Parlements, interrogatoires, mémoires, factums, etc., concernant un grand nombre de Procès criminels, des XIVe, XVe et XVIe siècles (1202–1657)', 2 vols, II (1202–1631).

BNF MS Fr 18319: 'Remarques de monsieur le président de Bellièvre, sur ce qui s'est passé au Parlement de Paris (1607–1627)', 2 vols, I (1607–1622).

BNF MS Fr 22087: 'Collection Anisson — Du Perron sur la Librairie et l'Imprimerie', 133 vols, XXVII: 'Libelles diffamatoires et livres prohibés (1413–1680)'.

BNF MS Fr 22115: 'Collection Anisson — Du Perron sur la Librairie et l'Imprimerie', 133 vols, LV: 'Librairie, Colporteurs et afficheurs (1560–1783)'.

BNF NAF 122: 'Institution du droit François et romain'.

BNF NAF 2103–2477: 'Collection de copies et extraits des registres du Parlement de Paris, des principaux procès criminels, etc., formée en grande partie par MM. De Verthamon, puis par le procureur-général Joly de Fleury', 375 vols.

PRINTED PRIMARY SOURCES

L'Adieu à Monseigneur de Verdun conseiller du Roy en ses conseils d'Estat & privé, & premier president au Parlement de Tholose ([n.p.]: [n. pub], 1616).

Advertissement a la France touchant les libelles qu'on seme contre le gouvernement de l'Estat ([n.p.]: [n.pub], 1615).

Angot de L'Éperonnière, Robert, *Les Exercises de ce temps*, ed. by Frédéric Lachèvre (Paris: Société des textes Français Modernes, 1997).

Appian Alexandrin, Historien Grec, *Des Guerres des Romains, livres XI, traduicts en Francoys par feu M. Claude de Seyssel* (Lyon: A. Constantin, 1544).

[Arnaud d'Andilly, Robert], *Journal inédit d'Arnaud d'Andilly (1614–1620)*, ed. by Achille Halphen (Paris: J. Techner, 1857).

Automne, Bernard, *La Conference du droict François avec le droict romain* (Paris: Nicolas Buon, 1610).

Auvray, Jean, *Le Banquet des Muses, ou les divers satires du sieur Auvray* (Rouen: David Ferrand, 1628).

Bayle, Pierre, *Dictionnaire historique et critique*, 16 vols (Paris: Desoer, 1820–1824).

Bellarmino, Roberto, *Tractatus de potestate summi pontificis in rebus temporalibus adversus Gulielmum Barclaium* (Rome: B. Zannetti, 1610).

Benedicti, Jean de, *La Somme des péchés et des remèdes d'iceux* (Paris: Guillaume de la Noue, 1601).

Bisselius, Joannes, *Ætatis nostrae eminentium septenii III* (Hamburg: J. Burger, 1677).

Boguet, Henri, *Discours exécrable des sorciers* (Paris: Denis Binet, 1603).

Boiceau, Jean, *Traité de la preuve par témoins en matière civile*, ed. by M. Danty (Paris: Guillaume Cavelier, 1697).

Bonarscii, Clari [Scribani, Charles], *Amphitheatrum honoris* (Palæopoli Advaticorum [Anvers]: Alexandrum [Plantin Moretus], 1605).

Bouchard, Jean-Jacques, *Confessions*, ed. by Patrick Mauriès (Paris: Le Promeneur, 2003).

Bouchel, M. L., *Recueil des status et reglemens des marchands, libraires, imprimeurs, & relieurs de la ville de Paris* (Paris: François Julliot, 1620).

Boucher, Jean, *L'Olympe francoys* (Paris: Denis Moreau, 1621).

[Boucher, Jean], *Oraison funebre sur le trespass de Madame M. Charlotte du Gué, en son vivant Espouse de Monseigneur M. Messire Nicolas de Verdun, etc.* (Paris: Denys Moreau, 1622).

Boyer, Philbert, *Le Stille de la cour et justice des requestes du palais* (Paris: Jean Richer, 1600).

Bruscambille [Jean Gracieux], 'Les Pitagoriens', in *Œuvres complètes*, ed. by Hugh Roberts and Annette Tomarken (Paris: Honoré Champion, 2012).

Budé, Guillaume, *De l'Institution du Prince, revue, enrichi, d'Arguments par Messire Jean de Luxembourg, abbé d'Ivry* (Paris: Nicole l'Arrivour, 1547).

Budé, Guillaume, *Le Livre de l'institution du Prince* (Paris: J. Foucher, 1547).

Buxtorf, Johannes, *Synagoga Judaica* (Basel: S. Henricpetri, 1603).

Le Cabinet satyrique, ou recueil parfait des vers piquants et gaillards de ce temps (Paris: Antoine d'Estoc, 1618).

Calvin, Jean, *Brieve instruction pour armer tous les bons fidèles contre les erreurs de la secte commune des Anabaptistes* (Geneva: Jehan Girard, 1544), in Jean Calvin, *Œuvres*, ed. by Françis Higman and Bernard Roussel (Paris: Gallimard, Bibliothèque de la Pléiade, 2009), pp. 623–724.

Calvin, Jean, *Contre la secte fantastique et furieuse des libertins, qui se nomment spirituels* (Geneva: Jehan Girard, 1545), in Jean Calvin, *Œuvres*, ed. by Françis Higman and Bernard Roussel (Paris: Gallimard, Bibliothèque de la Pléiade, 2009), pp. 725–830.

Camus, Jean-Pierre, *La Sixième partie de l'Alexis de Monseigneur l'Evêque de Belley* (Paris: Claude Chapelet, 1623).

Camus, Jean-Pierre, *Les Diversités*, 10 vols (Paris: Claude Chappelet, 1609–18).

Catel, Guillaume, *Histoire des comtes de Tolose* (Tolose: P. Bosc, 1623).

Catel, Guillaume, *Mémoire de l'histoire du Languedoc* (Tolose: P. Bosc, 1633).

Cayron, Gabriel, *Stil et forme de proceder, tant en la cour de Parlement de Tolose, et chambre des requestes d'icelle, etc.* (Tolose: Jean Boude, 1611).

Chevillier, André, *L'Origine de l'imprimerie de Paris: Dissertation historique et critique* (Paris: Jean de Laulne, 1694).

Coste, Hilarion de, *La Vie du R. P. Marin Mersenne, théologien, philosophe et mathématicien de l'Ordre des Pères Minimes* (Paris: Sébastien Cramoisy et Gabriel Cramoisy, 1649).

Cotgrave, Randle, *Dictionary of the French and English Tongues* (London: Adam Islip, 1611).

[Coton, Pierre], *Le Théologien dans les conversations avec les sages et les grands du monde* [ed. by Michel Boutauld] (Paris: Sebastien Marbre-Cramoisy, 1683).

Cyrano de Bergerac, Savinien, *Les États et Empires de la Lune et du Soleil*, ed. by Madeleine Alcover (Paris: Honoré Champion Classiques, 2004).

Damhouder, Joos de, *Practique judiciaire des causes criminelles* (Anvers: Jehan Bellere, 1564).

Declaration du roy, sur l'arrest fait de la personne de Monseigneur le Prince de Condé, & sur l'eslongnement des autres Princes, Seigneurs & Gentils-hommes. Publiée en Parlement le Roy y seant le septiesme jour de Septembre 1616 (Paris: Fed. Morel & P. Mettayer, 1616).

Declaration et Manifeste de Monsieur le Prince de Condé présenté au Roy, etc., de Coucy, 9 août 1615 ([n.p.]: [n. pub.], 1615).

Delamare, Nicolas, *Traité de la police,* 4 vols (Paris: Michel Brunet, 1722).

Les Délices Satyriques (Paris: Antoine Estoc; Antoine de Sommaville, 1620).

De L'Hermite-Souliers, Jean Baptiste and Blanchard, François, *Les eloges de tous les premiers presidens du Parlement de Paris* (Paris: Cardin Besongne, 1645).

Delrio, Martin, *Investigations into Magic,* ed. and trans. by P.G. Maxwell-Stuart (Manchester and New York: Manchester University Press, 2000).

Dictionnaire de l'Académie française (Paris: Jean-Baptiste Coignard, 1694).

Dictionnaire en théologie contenant entière déclaration des mots, phrases et manières de parler de la sainte Écriture tant du vieil que du nouveau Testament (Geneva: Jean Crespin, 1560).

Dictionnaire français–allemande et allemande–français (Nuremberg: Levinus Hulsius, 1602).

Dictionnaire ou promptuaire français–flamand (Rotterdam: I. Waesbergue, 1602).

Diodati, Jean, *La Saincte Bible* (Geneva: Pierre Aubert, 1644).

Discours sur la vie et mort de Jean Fontanier natif de Montpellier, etc. (Paris: Isaac Mesnier, 1621).

Discours sur les mariages de France & l'Espagne contenant les raisons qui ont meu Monseigneur le Prince à en demander la surséance ([n.p.]: [n. pub.], 1614).

D.L.N, *Elegie, ou chant pitoyable, sur la mort de tres illustre seigneur, messire Nicolas de Verdun, etc.* (Paris: Jacques Dugast, 1627).

Du Crot, Lazare, *Le vray styl du Chastelet de Paris* (Paris: Jean Richer, 1623).

Du Moulin, Pierre, *De la Vocation des Pasteurs* (Sedan: Jean Jannon, 1618).

Dupleix, Scipion, *Mémoires des Gaules* (Paris: Laurent Sonnius, 1619).

Duret, Claude, *Histoire admirable des plantes et herbes émerveillables et miraculeuses en nature* (Paris: Nicolas Buon, 1625).

Duret, Jean, *Traicté des peines et amendes* (Lyon: François Arnoullet, 1610).

Édict du Roy de l'erection en tiltre d'offices de receveurs des consignations en main tierce, etc. (Paris: F. Morel & P. Mettayer, 1618).

Effroyables pactions faictes entre le diable & les pretendus invisibles. Avec leurs damnables Instructions, perte déplorable de leurs Escoliers, & leur miserable fin ([n.p]: [n. pub], 1624).

Erasmus, Desiderius, *Ciceronianus, sive de optimo genere dicendi* (Basel: Johannes Froben; Paris: Simon de Colines, 1528).

Escalopier, Pierre de l', *M.T. Ciceronis de natura Deorum libri tres, cum Petri Lescaloperii argumentis, expositionibus et illustrationibus* (Paris: Sebastien Cramoisy, 1660).

[Esternod, Claude d'], *L'Espadon satyrique, par le sieur de Franchere, gentilhomme Franc-comtois* (Lyon: Jean Lautret, 1619).

Eveillon, Jacques, *La Manière de publier, fulminer et exécuter toutes sortes de monitoires et excommunications* (Angers: P. Avril, 1654).

Eveillon, Jacques, *Traité des excommunications et monitoires* (Angers: P. Avril, 1651).

Examen sur l'inconnue et nouvelle caballe des freres de la Rozee-Croix, habituez depuis peu de temps en la ville de Paris (Paris: [n. pub], 1623).

Farel, Guillaume, *Le Glaive de la parole véritable, tiré contre le Bouclier de défense: duquel un Cordelier Libertin s'est voulu servir, pour approuver ses fausses et damnables opinions* (Geneva: Jean Girard, 1550).

Farrell, Allan P. S. J. (ed.), *The Jesuit Ratio Studiorum of 1599* (Washington: Conference of Major Superiors of Jesuits, 1970).

Feron, Jean and Collier, Claude, *Histoire des Connestables: Chanceliers, et Gardes Des Seaux, etc.* (Paris: l'Imprimerie royale, 1658).

Ferrand, Jacques, *Traicté de l'essence et guérison de l'amour ou de la mélancholie érotique* (Tolose: Jacques Colomiex et Raymond Colomiez, 1610).

Ferrière, Claude-Joseph de, Dictionnaire de droit et pratique, 2 vols (Paris, V. Brunet, 1769).

Figon, Charles de, *Discours des estats et offices, tant du gouvernement, que de la justice & des finances de France* (Paris: Galiot Corrozet, 1608).

Fludd, Robert, *Sophiae cum moria certamen* ([Frankfurt (?)]: [n. pub.], 1629).

Fontaine, Jacques, *Discours des marques des sorciers* (Paris: Denis Langlois, 1611).

Fontanon, Antoine and Michel, Gabriel, *Les édicts et ordonnances des rois de France*, 4 vols (Paris: [n. pub.], 1611).

Foscarini, Paolo Antonio, *Lettera sopra l'opinione de' Pittagorici e del Copernico* (Naples: Lazaro Scoriggio, 1615).

Fournier, Édouard and Le Roux de Lincy, Antoine, (eds.), *Les Caquets de l'Accouchée* (Paris: P. Jannet, 1855).

Frizius, Joachim [Robert Fludd], *Summum Bonum* ([Frankfurt (?)]: [n. pub.], 1629).

Furetière, Antoine, *Dictionnaire universel*, 3 vols (The Hague and Rotterdam: Arnoud et Reinier Leers, 1690).

Garasse, François, *L'Abus découvert en la censure prétendue des textes de l'Ecriture sainte* (Paris: [n. pub.], 1626).

[Garasse, François], *L'Anti-Joseph* ([n.p]: [n. pub.], 1615).

[Garasse, François], *Apologie du Père François Garassus, de la compagnie de Jesus, pour son Livre contre les Atheistes & Libertins de nostre siecle* (Paris: Sebastien Chappelet, 1624).

[Garasse, François], *Elegiarum de funesta morte Henrici magni liber singularis* (Poitiers: Antoine Ménier, 1611).

[Garasse, François], *Elixir Calvinisticum* (In Ponte Charentonio [Paris (?)]: Joannem Molitorem, 1615).

[Garasse, François], *Horoscopus Anticotonis* ([Antwerp (?)]: Ex officina Hieronymi Verdussii, 1614).

Garasse, François, *La Doctrine curieuse des beaux esprits de ce temps* (Paris: Sebastien Chappelet, 1623).

Garasse, François, *La Somme théologique des vérités capitales de la Religion Chrétienne* (Paris: Sébastien Chapelet, 1625).

L'Esponoeil, Charles de [Garasse, François], *Le Banquet des sages* ([n.p]: [n. pub], 1617).

[Garasse, François], *Le Rabelais reformé par les Ministres* (Brussels: Christophe Girard, 1619).

Garasse, François, *Les Recherches des Recherches et autres œuvres de Me Etienne Pasquier* (Paris: Sébastien Chappelet, 1622).

[Garasse, François], *Sacra Rhemensia Carolina Heroica nomine Collegii Pictavensis oblata Ludov. XIII. Regi Christianissimo in sua inauguration* (Poitiers: Antoine Ménier, 1611).

Garnier, Claude, *Le Te Deum, Contre les Atheistes Libertins* (Paris: Daniel Guillemot, 1623).

Gaultier, Jacques, *Table chorographique de l'état du christianisme* (Lyon: Pierre Rigaud, 1626).

Gibert, Jean-Pierre, *Usages de l'Eglise Gallicane, concernant les censures et l'irregularité* (Paris: Jean Mariette, 1724).

Girard, Étienne, *Trois livres des offices de France* (Paris: Estienne Richer, 1638).

Goyet, Francis (ed.), *Traités de poétique et de rhétorique de la Renaissance* (Paris: Librairie Générale Française, 1990).

Gramond, Gabriel-Barthélemy de, *Historia prostratae Ludovico XIII sectariorum in Gallia rebellionis* (Toulouse: Petrum Bosc, 1623).

Gramond, Gabriel-Barthélemy de, *Historiarum Galliae ab excessu Henrici IV libri XVIII* (Toulouse: Arnald Colomerium, 1643) translated in David Durand, *La Vie et les œuvres de Lucilio Vanini* (Rotterdam: Gaspar Fritsch, 1717).

Le Grand dictionnaire français-latin (Lyon: C. Larhot, 1625).

[Guay, Geoffrey?], *Nouveau jugement de ce qui a été dit et écrit pour et contre le livre de la Doctrine Curieuse des beaux esprits de ce temps* (Paris: Jacques Quesnel, 1624).

[Guénois, Pierre], *Le corps du droict françois* (Geneva: Pour Jean de Laon, 1600).

Guichenon, Samuel, *Histoire de Bresse et de Bugey* (Lyon: Antoine Huguetan and Marc Ant. Ravaud, 1650).

Histoire prodigieuse nouvellement arrivée à Paris: D'une jeune fille agitée d'un Esprit fantastique et invisible (Paris: Ducarroy, 1625).

Histoire veritable de la vie de Jean Fontanier (Paris: Melchior Mondiere, 1621).

Histoire véritable de tout ce qui s'est faict et passé depuis le premier Janvier 1619 jusques à present, tant en Guyenne, Languedoc, Angoulmois, Rochelle, qui Limousin & autres lieux circonvoisins (Paris: Nicolas Alexandre, 1619).

Holbach, Paul-Henri Thiry, Baron d', 'Prêtres', in *Encyclopédie, ou dictionnaire raisonné des sciences, des arts et des métiers, etc.*, ed. by Denis Diderot and Jean le Rond d'Alembert, 28 vols (Paris: Briasson, David, Le Breton et Durand, 1751–1772), XIII (1751).

Imbert, Jean, *La Pratique Judiciaire, tant civile que criminelle*, enrichie par M. Pierre Guénois et M. Bernard Automne (Paris: Robert Foüet, 1616).

Isambert, François-André and others (eds.), *Recueil général des anciennes lois françaises, depuis l'an 420, jusqu'à la révolution de 1789*, 29 vols (Paris: Belin-Leprieur, 1822–33).

Jaudin, Guillaume, *Traité de tesmoings et d'enquestes* (Paris: Françoys Regnault, 1555).

La Guesle, Jacques de, *Les Remontrances de Messire Jaques de La Guesle Procureur General du Roi* (Paris: Pierre Chevalier, 1611).

Laistner, Ludwig and Brost, Eberhard (eds.), *Carmina Burana: Lieder der Vaganten* (Heidelberg: Verlag Lambert Schneider, 1961).

L'Ancre, Pierre de, *Le Livre des Princes, contenant plusieurs notables discours, pour l'instruction des Roys, Empereurs & Monarques* (Paris: Nicolas Buon, 1617).

L'Ancre, Pierre de, *L'incredulité et mescreance du sortilege plainement convaincue* (Paris: Nicolas Buon, 1622).

L'Ancre, Pierre de, *Tableau de l'inconstance et instabilité de toutes choses* (Paris: Abel l'Angelier, 1610).

La Noue, François de, *Discours Politiques et Militaires* (Basle: François Forest, 1587).

La Roche Flavin, Bernard de, *Treize livres des parlemens de France* (Geneva: Mathieu Berjon, 1621).

Laurent, R.P.F., *Le Palais de l'amour divin entre Jésus et l'âme chrétienne* (Paris: Denys de la Noüe et Charles Chastellain, 1614).

Le Bret, Cardin, *De la souveraineté du roy* (Paris: Toussaint Du Bray, 1632).

Le Brun de La Rochette, Claude, *Les Procès civil, et criminel, contenans la methodique liaison du droit, et de la practique judiciaire, civile et criminelle* (Rouen: Pierre l'Oyselet, 1619).

Le Brun de La Rochette, Claude, *Les Procès civil, et criminel, contenans la methodique liaison du droit, et de la practique judiciaire, civile et criminelle* (Lyon: Pierre Rigaud, 1622).

Le Loyer, Pierre, *Discours, et histoires des spectres, visions et apparitions des esprits, anges, démons, et âmes, se montrant visible aux hommes* (Paris: Nicolas Buon, 1605).

Le Pain, Jean, *Le Practicien françois* (Paris: Jean Gesselin, 1624).

Le Petit, Claude, *Les Œuvres libertines de Claude Le Petit*, ed. by Frédéric Lachèvre (Geneva: Slatkine Reprints, 1968).

Le Roy, Louys, *Exhortation aux Francois pour vivre en concorde, et jouir du bien de la paix* (Paris: Jacques du Puis, 1570).

L'Estoile, Pierre de, *Journal du règne de Henri IV*, 4 vols ([Paris]: [n. pub.], 1732).

L'Estoile, Pierre de, *Journal de L'Estoile pour le règne de Henri IV*, ed. by André Martin, 3 vols (Paris: Gallimard, 1958).

Lettre de Monseigneur le Prince de Condé à la reine ([n.p.]: [n. pub.], 1614); *Response de la Reyne Régente, Mère du Roy à la lettre escrite à sa Majesté par Monseigneur le Prince de Condé* ([n.p.]: [n. pub.], 1614).

Lettre de Monsieur le prince de Condé au Parlement de Paris, présentée par le sieur de Fiefbrun, le vingt-deuxiesme février 1614 ([n.p]: [n. pub.], 1614).

Lettre du Roy à Monsieur le Prince de Condé [n.p.]: [n. pub], 1615).

Leys, Lenaert, *De providentia numinis et animi immortalitate* (Antwerp: Ex officina Plantiniana, 1613).

L'Hermite, Tristan, *Les vers heroiques du sieur Tristan L'Hermite* (Paris: Jean Baptiste Loyson and Nicolas Portier, 1648).

L'Hermite, Tristan, *Le Page disgracié*, in *Libertins du XVIIe siècle*, ed. by Jacques Prévot, 2 vols (Paris: Gallimard, Bibliothèque de la Pléiade, 1998), I, pp. 381–595.

Loyseau, Charles, *Cinq livres du droit des offices* (Paris: Abel d'Angelier, 1614).

Lublinskaya, A.D., *French Absolutism: The Crucial Phase, 1620–1629*, trans. by Brian Pearce (Cambridge: Cambridge University Press, 1968).

Macho, Julien, *Le vray Exposition et Declaration de la Bible, tant du Vieil que du Nouvel Testament* (Lyon: [n.pub.], [c. 1480?]).

[Malherbe, François de], *Lettres de Malherbe* (Paris: J. J. Blaise, 1822).

Malherbe, François de, *Poésies*, ed. by Antoine Adam (Paris: Gallimard, 1971).

[Malingre, Claude], *Traicté des Atheistes, Deistes, Illuminez d'Espagne et nouveaux pretendus Invisibles, dits de la Confrairie de la Croix-Rosaire*, in Raemond Florimond, *Histoire générale du progrèz et décadence de l'hérésie moderne*, 3 vols (Paris: Pierre Chevalier, 1624), II, pp. 13–55.

Mariana, Juan de, *De rege et regis institutione* (Toledo: Petrum Rodericum, 1598).

[Masuer, Johannes], *La Pratique de Masuer*, trans. by Antoine Fontanon (Paris: Denis Binet, 1610).

Mayerne, Louis Turquet de, *La monarchie aristodémocratique* (Paris: J. Berjon and J. le Bouc, 1611).

Maynard, Géraud de, *Notables et singulieres questions du droit escrit*, 4 vols (Paris: Robert Foüet, 1628).

Le Mercure françois, ou suite de l'histoire de notre temps, 25 vols (Paris: Jean Richer, 1613–43).

Mersenne, Marin, *Correspondance du P. Marin Mersenne*, ed. by Cornelis de Waard, 18 vols (Paris: Presses Universitaires de France, 1945).

Mersenne, Marin, *La Vérité des sciences*, ed. by Dominique Descotes (Paris: Honoré Champion, 2003).

Mersenne, Marin, *La Vérité des sciences, contre les Sceptiques ou Pyrrhoniens* (Paris: Toussaint Du Bray, 1625).

Mersenne, Marin, *L'Impiété des déistes*, ed. by Dominique Descotes (Paris: Honoré Champion, 2005).

Mersenne, Marin, *L'Impiété des déistes, athées, et libertins de ce temps* (Paris: Pierre Bilaine, 1624).

Mersenne, Marin, *Quaestiones celeberrimae in Genesim* (Paris: Sebastien Cramoisy, 1623).

Mesmes, Henri I de, *Mémoires inédits de Henri de Mesmes*, ed. by Édouard Fremy (Geneva: Slatkine, 1970).

Milhard, Pierre, *La Grande guide des curés, vicaires, et confesseurs* (Lyon: François Arnoullet, 1619).

Milhard, Pierre, *La Vraie guide des curés, vicaires, et confesseurs* (Rouen: Robert de Roues, 1610).

Molé, Mathieu, *Mémoires de Mathieu Molé*, ed. by Aimé Champollion-Figeac, 4 vols (Paris: Jules Renouard, 1855).

Molière, *Œuvres complètes*, ed. by Georges Couton, 2 vols (Paris: Gallimard, Bibliothèque de la Pléiade, 1971).

Montaigne, Michel de, *Essais*, ed. by Pierre Villey and V.L. Saulnier (Paris: Presses Universitaires de France, 2004).

Montalto, Elijah, *Optica, Intra Philosophia* (Florence: Cosmum Juntam, 1606).

Montalto, Elijah, *Optica, Intra Philosophia* (Colonia Allobrogum: P. M. Marceau, 1613).

Montlyart, Jean de, *Les Hiéroglyphiques de Jean-Pierre Valérian* (Lyon: Paul Frellon, 1615).

Mornay, Philippe de, sieur Du Plessis, *Mystère de l'iniquité, c'est à dire, l'Histoire de la papauté* (Saumur: T. Portau, 1611).

Morteira, Saul Levi, *Arguments Against the Christian Religion in Amsterdam*, trans. and ed. by Gregory Kaplan (Amsterdam: Amsterdam University Press, 2017).

La Muse folastre (Rouen: Claude Morel, 1600).

[Mussart, Vincent], *Le Fouet des jureurs et blasphemateurs du nom de Dieu* (Troye: Nicolas Oudot, 1614).

Muyart de Vouglans, Pierre François, *Institutes au droit criminal, etc.* (Paris: Le Breton, 1757).

Naudé, Gabriel, *Apologie pour tous les grands personnages qui ont esté faussement soupçonnez de magie* (Paris: François Targa, 1625).

Naudé, Gabriel, *Instruction à la France sur la verité de l'histoire des Freres de la Roze-Croix* (Paris: François Julliot, 1623).

[Naudé, Gabriel Parisien] G.N.P., *Le Marfore ou discours contre les libelles* (Paris: Louis Boulenger, 1620).

[Naudé, Gabriel and Patin, Guy], *Naudaeana et Patiniana* (Paris: Florentin et Pierre Delaulne, 1701).

Nicot, Jean, *Thrésor de la langue françoyse* (Paris: David Douceur, 1606).

Nisard, Charles (ed.), *Mémoires de Garasse (François) de la Compagnie de Jésus* (Paris: Amyot, 1860).

Ogier, François, *Jugement et censure du livre de la Doctrine Curieuse, de François Garasse* (Paris: [n. pub.], 1623).

Olier, Nicolas-Edouard, *Journal de Nicolas-Edouard Olier, conseiller au Parlement 1593–1602* (Paris: Henri Menu, 1876).

Papon, Jean and others, *Recueil d'arrests notables des cour souveraines de France* (Paris: Robert Fouet, 1621).

Le Parnasse des poètes satyrique ([n.p.]: [n. pub.], 1622).

Perrault, Charles, *Les hommes illustres qui ont paru en France pendant ce siècle: avec leurs portraits au naturel*, 2 vols (Paris: A. Dezallier, 1696–1700).

Petit, Pierre, *Dissertation sur la nature des cometes [...] par P. Petit, Intendant des Fortifications* (Paris: Louis Billaine, 1664).

[Petit, Pierre], *Petri Petiti, philosophi & doctoris medici, Miscellanearum observationum libri quatuor* (Trajecti ad Rhenum: Typis Rudolphi a Zyll, 1682).

Plaidoyez de Mr Jacques de Puymisson, advocate au Parlement de Tolose (Tolose: Jacques and R. Colomiés, 1612).

Porete, Marguerite, *A Mirror for Simple Souls*, ed. by Charles Crawford (Dublin: Gill and Macmillan, 1981).

La Prise de Théophile par un prévost des maréchaux dans la citadelle du Castellet en Picardie, amené prisonnier en la Conciergerie du Palais, le jeudi 28 de ce mois (Paris: Antoine Vitray, 1623).

Procès-verbal de l'emprisonnement de Théophile, présenté à la cour par le prévost des mareschaux (Paris: Pierre Bamier, 1623).

La Quint-essence Satyrique, ou Seconde partie du Parnasse des Poètes Satyriques de notre temps (Paris: Antoine de Sommaville, 1622).

Reboul, Guillaume de, *Apologie de Reboul sur la cabale des reformez* ([n.p.]: [n. pub.], 1597).

Reboul, Guillaume de, *La cabale des reformez* (Montpellier: chez le Libertin, 1597).

Recueil des plus excellents vers satyriques de ce temps (Paris: Antoine Estoc, 1617).

Recueil tres exact et curieux de tout ce qui s'est faict & passé de singulier & memorable en l'Assemblée generale des Estats tenus à Paris en l'année 1614 (Paris: Au Palais, 1651).

Relation de ce qui s'est passé à Toulouse le 3.10. & 11. Février; pour le mariage de Madame sœur du Roy avec le Prince de Savoye (Toulouse: Raymond Colomiez, 1619).

Remonstrances, ouvertures de palais, et arrestz prononcés en Robes Rouges, par Messire André de Nesmond, etc. (Poictiers: A. Mesnier, 1617).

Remonstrances présentées au roy par noseigneurs du parlement le vingt-uniesme may 1615 ([n.p.]: [n. pub.], 1615).

[Rémy, Antoine], *Défense pour Etienne Pasquier vivant conseiller du Roi, et son Avocat Général en la Chambre des Comptes de Paris, contre les impostures et Calomnies de François Garasse* (Paris: Thomas de la Ruelle, 1624).

Response de Monsieur le Prince de Condé au Roy, de Coucy, 27 juillet 1615 ([n.p.]: [n. pub], 1615).

Richelieu, Armand Jean du Plessis, Cardinal de, *Mémoires du Cardinal de Richelieu*, ed. by Horric de Beaucaire and others, 10 vols (Paris: Librairie Renouard, 1907).

Richer, Edmond, *Libellus de Ecclesiastica et Politica Potestate* (Paris: [n. pub.], 1611).

Roche-Flavin, Bernard de la and Graverol, François, *Arrests notables du parlement de Toulouse* (Toulouse: Guillaume-Louis Colomiez & Jerôme Posuel, 1682).

Rochemont, le sieur de [Jean Barbier d'Aucour], *Observations sur une comédie de Molière, intitulée* Le Festin de Pierre (Paris: N. Pepingué, 1665).

Rooses, Max, and Ruelens, Charles Louis (eds.), *Codex diplomaticus Rubenianus: documents relatifs à la vie et aux œuvres de Rubens*, 6 vols (Anvers: Jos Maes, 1887–1909).

Rosset, François de, *Les Histoires mémorables, et tragiques de ce temps* (Paris: Pierre Chevalier, 1619).

Sá, Manuel de, *Aphorismi confessariorum* (Venice: [n. pub.], 1595).

Saint-Cyran, Jean du Vergier de Hauranne de, *La Somme des fautes et faussetés capitales, contenues en la Somme théologique du Père François Garasse de la Compagnie de Jésus* (Paris: J. Boüillerot, 1626).

Sanchez, Thomas, *Disputationum de Sancto Matrimonii Sacramento Tomi Tres* (Antwerp: M. Nutium, 1607).

Sanson, Guillaume, *Le comté d'Artois suivant qu'il est presentement divisé en François et Espagnol, dressé sur les Memoires les plus nouveaux* (Paris: H. Jaillot, 1674).

Santarelli, Antonio, *Tractaus de haeresi, schismatic, apostasia, etc.* (Rome: Bartholomæ Zannetti, 1625).

Schoppe, Caspar, *Ecclesiasticus auctoritati Jacobi regis oppositus* (Hartberg: [n. pub.], 1611).

Le Second livre des delices de la poesie francaise, ou dernier recueil des plus beaux vers de ce temps (Paris: Toussaint du Bray, 1620).

Le Second volume de la Bible en français (Paris: [n. pub.], 1541).

Segla, Guillaume de, *Histoire tragique, et arrests de la cour de Parlement de Toulouse* (Paris: Nicolas la Caille, 1613).

[Séguier, Louis], *Sententia praetoris praefecturae Parisiensis, etc.* (Paris: P. Durand, 1614).

Sommaires réponses aux moyens proposés par madame de Longueville pour empêcher la mise en possession requise par M. de Nemours, en exécution de l'arrêt donné, au rapport de M. Deslandes, le 13 août 1605 ([n.p.]: [n.pub.], [1605?]).

[Sonnet de Courval, Thomas], *Les Œuvres satyriques du Sieur de Courval-Sonnet gentilhomme virois* (Paris: Rolet Boutonne, 1622).

Suárez, Francisco, *Defensio fidei* (Conimbriga: Gomez de Loureyro, 1613).

Tallemant des Réaux, Gédéon, *Historiettes*, ed. by Antoine Adam, 2 vols (Paris: Gallimard, Bibliothèque de la Pléiade, 1960), I.

Tesoro de las dos lengua francese y espanola (Paris: Orry, 1607).

Thuillier, Renato, *Diarium partum et sororum ordinis minimorum provinciae Franciae sive Parisiensis qui religiose abierunt ab anno 1506 ad annum 1700*, 2 vols (Paris: Petrus Gissart, 1709).

Tombeaux, oraisons funèbres, consolations et poèmes divers ([n.p]: [n.pub], 1621).

Vallée, Geoffroy, *La béatitude des chrestiens, ou Le fléo de la foy* ([Paris (?)]: [n. pub.], 1572).

Vanini, Giulio Cesare, *Amphiteatrum aeternae providentiae* (Lyon: Antoine de Harsy, 1615).

Vanini, Giulio Cesare, *L'anfiteatro dell'eterna provvidenza*, ed. by Francesco Paolo Raimondi and others (Galatina: Congedo, 1981).

Vanini, Giulio Cesare, *De admirandis nature regine deaeque mortalium arcanis* (Paris: Adrien Perier, 1616).

Vanini, Giulio Cesare, *I meravigliosi segreti della natura*, ed. by Francesco Paolo Raimondi (Galatina: Congedo, 1990).

Vanini, Giulio Cesare, *Œuvres philosophiques de Vanini*, ed. by Xavier Rousselot (Paris: Charles Gosselin, 1842).

Vanini, Giulio Cesare, *Tutte le opere*, ed. by Francesco Paolo Raimondi and Mario Carparelli (Milan: Bompiani, 2010).

Viau, Théophile de, *Apologie au Roy* (Paris: [n. pub.], 1626).

[Viau, Théophile de], *Apologie de Théophile* (Paris: [n. pub.], 1624).

Viau, Théophile de, *Nouvelles œuvres de feu Mr Théophile, composées d'excellentes Lettres Françoises & Latines*, ed. by [Jean] Mayret (Paris: Antoine de Sommaville, 1648).

Viau, Théophile de, *Œuvres*, ed. by Guido Saba (Paris: Classiques Garnier, 1990).
Viau, Théophile de, *Œuvres complètes*, ed. by Guido Saba, 4 vols (Paris: Nizet, 1987).
Viau, Théophile de, *Œuvres complètes*, ed. by Guido Saba, 3 vols (Paris: Honoré Champion, 1999).
La vie et mort de messire Nicolas de Verdun, etc. (Paris: Jean Bessin, 1627).
Vignier, Nicolas, *Bibliothèque historiale* (Paris: Abel L'Angelier, 1587).
Wolff, Étienne (ed.), *Carmina Burana* (Paris: Imprimerie Nationale, 1995).

SECONDARY SOURCES

Abraham, Claude Kurt, *Gaston d'Orléans et sa cour: étude littéraire* (Chapel Hill, NC: The University of North Carolina Press, 1964).
Adam, Antoine, *Histoire de la littérature française au XVIIe siècle*, 5 vols (Paris: Albin Michel, 1997).
Adam, Antoine, *Les Libertins au XVIIe siècle* (Paris: Buchet-Chastel, 1964).
Adam, Antoine, *Théophile de Viau et la libre pensée française en 1620* (Geneva: Slatkine Reprints, 1966).
Addante, Luca, 'Radicalismes politiques et religieux', in *Libertin! Usage d'une invective aux XVIe et XVIIe siècles*, ed. by Thomas Berns, Anne Staquet and Monique Weis (Paris: Classiques Garnier, 2013), pp. 29–50.
Albert, Luce, 'Jean Calvin et le libertin spirituel — de l'archétype à l'alter ego', in *Libertin! Usage d'une invective aux XVIe et XVIIe siècles*, ed. by Thomas Berns, Anne Staquet and Monique Weis (Paris: Classiques Garnier, 2013), pp. 83–99.
Alcover, Madeleine, *Cyrano relu et corrigé* (Geneva: Droz, 1990).
Armogathe, Jean-Robert, 'Giulio Cesare Vanini: una retorica della sovversione', in *Giulio Cesare Vanini: Dal testo all'interpretazione*, ed. by Giovanni Papuli (Taurisano: Edizioni di Presenza, 1996), pp. 31–44.
Aubenas, Roger, *La Sorcière et l'Inquisiteur* (Aix-en-Province: La Pensée Universitaire, 1956).
Bailly, Jean-Louis, 'Modeles chez Théophile de Viau prosateur', in *Le Modèle à la renaissance*, ed. by Claudie Balavoine, Jean Lafond and Pierre Laurens (Paris: Vrin, 1986), pp. 141–50.
Bakhtin, Mikhail, *Rabelais and His World*, trans. by Hélène Iwolsky (Bloomington, IN: University of Indiana Press, 1984).
Bannister, Mark, 'Vanini and the development of seventeenth-century thought', *Seventeenth-Century French Studies*, 19 (1997), 25–36.
Barante, Le Baron de, *Parlement et la Fronde: La vie de Mathieu Molé* (Paris: Didier, 1859).
Baraude, Henri, *Lopez: Agent financier et confident de Richelieu* (Paris: Éditions de la Revue Mondiale, 1933).
Barni, Jules, *Les Martyrs de la libre pensée* (Geneva: Les Principaux Libraires, 1862).
Barthas, Jérémie, 'Retour sur la notion de libertin à l'époque moderne. Les politiques libertins à Florence, 1520–1530', *Libertinage et philosophie*, 8 (2004), 181–99.
Bastien, Pascal, *Une histoire de la peine de mort: Bourreaux et supplices 1500–1800* (Paris: Seuil, 2011).
Bastien, Paul, 'La parole du confesseur auprès des suppliciés (Paris, XVIIe–XVIIIe siècle)', *Revue Historique*, 2: 634 (2005), 283–308.

Beaulieu, Armand, *Mersenne: Le Grand Minime* (Brussels: Fondation Nicolas-Claude Fabri de Peiresc, 1995).

Benbassa, Esther, *The Jews of France: A History from Antiquity to the Present*, trans. by M. B. DeBevoise (Princeton, NJ: Princeton University Press, 1999).

Bercé, Yves-Marie and Soman, Alfred, 'Les archives du Parlement dans l'histoire', *Bibliothèque de l'école des chartes*, 153: 2 (1995), 255–73.

Bergin, Joseph, *Church, Society and Religious Change in France, 1580–1730* (New Haven, CT, and London: Yale University Press, 2009).

Bergin, Joseph, *The Politics of Religion in Early Modern France* (New Haven, CT and London: Yale University Press, 2014).

Berkovitz, Jay R., 'The Jews of France', in *The Cambridge History of Judaism*, ed. by Jonathan Karp and Adam Sutcliffe (Cambridge: Cambridge University Press, 2017), pp. 923–48.

Berriot, François, *Athéismes et athéistes au XVIe siècle en France*, 2 vols (Lille: Cerf, 1984).

Biet, Christian, *Droit et littérature sous l'Ancien Régime: Le jeu de la valeur et de la loi* (Paris: Honoré Champion, 2002).

Bilis, Hélène E., *Passing Judgement: The Politics and Poetics of Sovereignty in French Tragedy from Hardy to Racine* (Toronto, Buffalo, NY, and London: University of Toronto Press, 2016).

Bimbenet-Privat, Michèle, 'Série Y: Châtelet de Paris, répertoire numérique détaillée' [accessed 10 October 2019]: http://www.archivesnationales.culture.gouv.fr/chan/chan/pdf/sa/Y-0-Intro.pdf

Bitsch, Caroline, *Vie et carrière d'Henri II de Bourbon, Prince de Condé (1588–1646)* (Paris: Honoré Champion, 2008).

Bluche, François, *Les Magistrats du parlement de Paris au XVIIIe siècle* (Paris: Economica, 1986).

Bombart, Mathilde, '"Des vers méchants et impies?" Questions sur une poésie en procès', in *Lectures de Théophile de Viau*, ed. by Guillaume Peureux (Rennes: Presses Universitaires de Rennes, 2008), pp. 63–77.

Bombart, Mathilde, 'Un antijésuitisme «littéraire»? La polémique contre François Garasse', in *Les Antijésuites: Discours, figures et lieux de l'antijésuitisme à l'époque moderne*, ed. by Pierre-Antoine Fabre and Catherine Maire (Rennes: Presses Universitaires de Rennes, 2010), pp. 179–96.

Bombart, Mathilde, 'When Writers Gossip: Authorial Reputation in the Literary Polemics of the French 1620s', *Renaissance Studies*, 30: 1 (2016), 137–51.

Bondois, Paul M., *Le Maréchal de Bassompierre* (Paris: Albim Michel, 1925).

Bourchenin, Pierre-Daniel, *Étude sur les académies protestantes en France au XVIe et au XVIIe siècle* (Paris: Grassart, 1882).

Bourdrel, Phillipe, *Histoire des juifs de France*, 2 vols (Paris: Ablin Michel, 2004).

Boutcher, Warren, *The School of Montaigne in Early Modern Europe*, 2 vols (Oxford: Oxford University Press, 2017).

Boxel, Piet van, 'Robert Bellarmine, Christian Hebraist and Censor', in *History of Scholarship: A Selection of Papers from the Seminar on the History of Scholarship Held Annually at the Warburg Institute*, ed. by Christopher Ligota and Jean-Louis Quantin (Oxford: Oxford University Press, 2006), pp. 251–75.

Briggs, Robin, *The Witches of Lorraine* (Oxford: Oxford University Press, 2007).

Bury, Emmanuel, 'De l'imitation scolaire à l'imitation adulte: le cas de la *Ratio studiorum* et son influence sur Guez de Balzac', *Littératures classiques*, 1: 74 (2011), 11–30.

Busson, Henri, *La Pensée Religieuse Française de Charron à Pascal* (Paris: Librairie Philosophique J. Vrin, 1933).

Busson, Henri, *Le Rationalisme dans la Littérature Française de la Renaissance (1533–1601)* (Paris: Librairie Philosophique J. Vrin, 1957).

Butterworth, Emily, 'Defining Obscenity', in *Obscénités renaissantes*, ed. by Hugh Roberts, Guillaume Peureux and Lise Wajeman (Geneva: Droz, 2011), pp. 31–8.

Butterworth, Emily, *Poisoned Words: Slander and Satire in Early Modern France* (Oxford: Legenda, 2006).

Butterworth, Emily and Roberts, Hugh, 'From Word to Thing', in *Obscénités renaissantes*, ed. by Hugh Roberts, Guillaume Peureux and Lise Wajeman (Geneva: Droz, 2011), pp. 87–92.

Cabantous, Alain, *Histoire du blasphème en Occident: XVIe–XIXe siècle* (Paris: Albin Michel, 2015).

Carmona, Michel, *Richelieu* (Paris: Tallandier, 2013).

Carparelli, Mario, *Il più bello e il più maligno spirito che io abbia mai conosciuto. Giulio Cesare Vanini nei documenti e nelle testimonianze* (Padova: Il Prato, 2013).

Cassan, Michel, *La Grande peur de 1610: Les français et l'assassinat d'Henri IV* (Paris: Champ Vallon, 2010).

Cavaillé, Jean-Pierre, 'Adrien de Monluc, dévot ou libertin?', *Les Dossiers du Grihl*, online since 10 November 2011. http://dossiersgrihl.revues.org/1362 [accessed 15 May 2019].

Cavaillé, Jean-Pierre, *Dis/simulations. Jules-César Vanini, François La Mothe Le Vayer, Gabriel Naudé, Louis Manchon et Torquato Accetto. Religion, morale et politique au XVIIe siècle* (Paris: Honoré Champion, 2008).

Cavaillé, Jean-Pierre, 'Le 'prince des athées': Vanini et Machiavel', in *L'enjeu Machiavel*, ed. by Gérald Sfez and Michel Senellart (Paris: Presses Universitaires de France, 2001), pp. 59–74.

Cavaillé, Jean-Pierre, *Les Déniaisés: Irréligion et libertinage au début de l'époque moderne* (Paris: Classiques Garnier, 2013).

Cavaillé, Jean-Pierre, 'Les Usages polémiques des termes «*libertine*», «*libertinism*» en Grande-Bretagne aux XVIe et XVIIe siècles', in *Libertin! Usage d'une invective aux XVIe et XVIIe siècles*, ed. by Thomas Berns, Anne Staquet and Monique Weis (Paris: Classiques Garnier, 2013), pp. 51–79.

Cavaillé, Jean-Pierre, 'L'histoire des «libertins» reste à faire', *Les Dossiers du Grihl*, online since 18 October 2010. http://dossiersgrihl.revues.org/4498?lang=en [accessed 20 September 2011].

Cavaillé, Jean-Pierre, 'L'incarnazione delle false libertà: Vanini nella letteratura apologetica del Seicento', in *Giulio Cesare Vanini: Filosofia della libertà e libertà del filosofare. Atti del terzo convegno internazionale di studi Vaniniani (Lecce — Taurisano, 7–9 febbraio 2019)*, ed. by Francesco Paolo Raimondi (Rome: Aracne, 2019), pp. 185–97.

Cavaillé, Jean-Pierre, 'Pierre Charron, "disciple" de Montaigne et "patriarche des prétendus esprits forts"', *Les Dossiers du Grihl* (2009). http://journals.openedition.org/dossiersgrihl/280 [accessed 4 March 2020].

Cavaillé, Jean-Pierre, 'Une pensée de la transgression. Politique, religion et morale chez Jules-César Vanini', in *Kairos*, 12 (1998): *Vanini: Libertinage et philosophie à l'époque moderne*, ed. by Jean-Pierre Cavaillé and Didier Foucault (Toulouse: Presses Universitaires du Mirail, 1998), pp. 99–141.

Cavaillé, Jean-Pierre and Foucault, Didier, 'Introduction', in *Kairos*, 12 (1998): *Vanini: Libertinage et philosophie à l'époque moderne*, ed. by Jean-Pierre Cavaillé and Didier Foucault (Toulouse: Presses Universitaires du Mirail, 1998).

Cave, Terence, *The Cornucopian Text: Problems of Writing in the French Renaissance* (Oxford: Clarendon Press, 1979).

Caye, Pierre, 'Libertinisme et théologie: considérations sur une expérience de pensée singulière et perdue', in *La Question de l'athéisme au dix-septième siècle*, ed. by Pierre Lurbe and Sylvie Taussig (Turnhout: Brepols, 2004), pp. 11–29.

Chalmers, Alexander, *The General Biographical Dictionary*, 32 vols (London: J. Nichols and Son and Bentley, 1812–17).

Charles-Daubert, Françoise, 'La Bible des Libertins', in *Le Grand Siècle et la Bible*, ed. by Jean-Robert Armogathe (Paris: Beauchesne, 1989), pp. 667–89.

Charles-Daubert, Françoise, *Les Libertins érudits en France au XVIIe siècle* (Paris: Presses Universitaires de France, 1998).

Chartier, Roger, *The Order of Books: Readers, Authors, and Libraries in Europe between the Fourteenth and Eighteenth Centuries*, trans. by Lydia G. Cochrane (Cambridge: Polity Press, 1994).

Chartier, Roger and Martin, Henri-Jean, *Histoire de l'édition française*, 4 vols (Paris: Fayard, 1989–91).

Chauveau, Jean-Pierre, '*Le Traicté de l'Immortalité de l'Ame, ou la Mort de Socrate*', in *Théophile de Viau: Actes du Colloque du CMR 17 offerts en hommage à Guido Saba*, ed. Roger Duchêne (Paris, Seattle and Tübingen: Bibkio 17, 1991), pp. 45–61.

Chauveau, Jean-Pierre, 'Situation de Théophile', in *Lectures de Théophile de Viau*, ed. by Guillaume Peureux (Rennes: Presses Universitaires de Rennes, 2008), pp. 27–41.

Chiffoleau, Jacques, 'Le crime de lèse-majesté, la politique et l'extraordinaire. Note sur les collections érudites de procès de lèse-majesté du XVIIe siècle français et sur leurs exemples médiévaux', in *Les procès politiques (XIVe–XVIIe siècle)*, ed. by Yves-Marie Bercé (Rome: École française de Rome, 2007), pp. 577–657.

Christiaens, Daniel, 'Nouvelles considérations sur la disgrâce de Théophile de Viau', *Revue de l'Agenais* 139: 3 (2012), 507–18.

Christie, Richard Copley, 'Vanini in England', *The English Historical Review*, 10 (1895), 238–65.

Clarke, Jack Alden, *Huguenot Warrior: The Life and Times of Henri de Rohan, 1597–1638* (The Hague: Martinus Nijhoff, 1966).

Cohen, Richard I. and others (eds.), *Jewish Culture in Early Modern Europe* (Pittsburgh, PA, and Cincinnati, OH: University of Pittsburgh Press and Hebrew Union College Press, 2014).

Cohn, Norman, *Europe's Inner Demons. An Enquiry Inspired by the Great Witch-hunt* (London: Sussex University Press, 1975).

Colin, Armand, 'Théories et pratiques de la traduction littéraire en France', *Le français aujourd'hui*, 3: 42 (2003), 5–17.

Como, David and Atherton, Ian, 'The Burning of Edward Wightman: Puritanism, Prelacy and the Politics of Heresy in Early Modern England', *English Historical Review*, 120: 489 (2005), 1215–50.

Constant, Jean-Marie, *Gaston d'Orléans: Prince de la liberté* (Paris: Perrin, 2013).

Conzelmann, Hans, *Acts of the Apostles: A Commentary on the Acts of the Apostles*, ed. by Eldon Jay Epp and Christopher R. Matthews, trans. by James Limburg, A. Thomas Kraabel and Donald H. Juel (Philadelphia, PA: Fortress Press, 1987).

Cook, Harold J., *The Young Descartes: Nobility, Rumour, and War* (Chicago, IL: The University of Chicago Press, 2018).

Cottret, Bernard, *Calvin: A Biography*, trans. by M. Wallace McDonald (Edinburgh: T&T Clark, 1995).

Coulthard, Malcolm and Johnson, Alison (eds.), *The Routledge Handbook of Forensic Linguistics* (London: Routledge, 2010).

Cousin, Victor, *Fragments de philosophie cartésienne—Vanini ou la philosophie avant Descartes* (Paris: Didier, 1856).

Crouzet, Denis, *Dieu en ses royaumes: une histoire des guerres de religion* (Paris: Champ Vallon, 2008).

Dainville, François de, *L'éducation des jésuites (XVI*[e]*-XVIII*[e] *siècles)* (Paris: Éditions de Minuit, 1978).

Dana, Charles A. and Ripley, George, *The New American Cyclopaedia*, 16 vols (New York: D. Appleton and Company, 1858–1866), VII (1864).

Davidson, Nicholas S., '"Le plus beau et le plus meschant esprit que ie aye cogneu": Science and Religion in the Writings of Giulio Cesare Vanini, 1585–1619', in *Heterodoxy in Early Modern Science and Religion,* ed. by John Brooke and Ian Maclean (Oxford: Oxford University Press, 2005), pp. 59–79.

Daubresse, Sylvie, *Le Parlement de Paris ou la voix de la raison (1559–1589)* (Geneva: Droz, 2005).

Debailly, Pascal, 'Le Père Garasse, critique et disciple de Mathurin Régnier', *XVII*[e] *siècle*, 188 (1995), pp. 431–45.

Debailly, Pascal, 'Théophile de Viau et le déclin de l'*éthos* satirique', in *La Parole polémique,* ed. by Gilles Declerq, Michel Murat and Jacqueline Dangel (Paris: Honoré Champion, 2003), pp. 149–71.

Debaisieux, Martine, '*Première journée* de Théophile ou l'exorcisme de la tradition', *Cahiers du Dix-Septième siècle*, 7: 1 (1997), 179–92.

Debbagi Baranova, Tatiana, *A coups de libelles: Une culture politique au temps des guerres de religion (1562–1598)* (Geneva: Droz, 2012).

De Chavigny, D., *L'Eglise & l'Académie Protestantes de Saumur* (Saumur: Paul Godet, 1914).

DeJean, Joan, *Libertine Strategies: Freedom and the Novel in Seventeenth-century France* (Columbus, OH: Ohio State University Press, 1981).

DeJean, Joan, *The Reinvention of Obscenity. Sex, Lies, and Tabloids in Early Modern France* (Chicago, IL, and London: The University of Chicago Press, 2002).

DeJean, Joan, 'Une autobiographie en procès: l'affaire Théophile de Viau', *Poétique*, 48 (November 1981), 431–48.

Delumeau, Jean, *La peur en occident: XIV*[e]*–XVII*[e] *siècles* (Paris: Fayard, 1978).

Denis, Philippe, *Edmond Richer et le renouveau du conciliarisme au XVII*[e] *siècle* (Paris: Éditions du Cerf, 2014).

Dennequin, Marjorie, *Les 'Dévotieuses': dévotion et préciosité à Grenoble au XVIIe siècle: la Congrégation de la Purification* (unpublished doctoral thesis, Université Grenoble Alpes, 2015).

Desmaze, Charles, *Le Châtelet de Paris: son organisation, ses privilèges* (Paris: Didier, 1870).

Desmaze, Charles, *Le Parlement de Paris* (Paris: Cosse, Marchal et Billard, 1860).

Dethier, Hubert, 'J.-C. Vanini et *L'Amphitheatrum* de Heinrich Khunrath', in *Giulio Cesare Vanini dal Tardo Rinascimento al Libertinisme érudit, Atti del Convegno di Studi (Lecce — Taurisano, 24–26 ottobre 1985)*, ed. by Francesco Paolo Raimondi (Galatina: Congedo, 2003), pp. 75–107.

De Waele, Michel, *Les Relations entre le Parlement de Paris et Henri IV* (Paris: Publisud, 2006).

Dickson, Donald R., *The Tessera of Antilia: Utopian Brotherhoods and Secret Societies in the Early Seventeenth Century* (Leiden: Brill, 1998).

Dillay, Madeleine, 'Conclusions du procureur général au Parlement de Paris relatives à la vérification et à l'enregistrement des lettres patentes (quelques exemples du commencement du règne de Louis XIII)', *Revue historique de droit français et étranger*, 4: 32 (1955), 255–66.

Dobiache-Rojdesvensky, Olga, *Les poésies des Goliards* (Paris: Rieder, 1931).

Dolan, Claire, *Les Procureurs du Midi sous l'Ancien Régime* (Rennes: Presses Universitaires de Rennes, 2012).

Donné, Boris, *Vanini: portrait au noir* (Paris: Allia, 2019).

Dotoli, Giovanni, *Temps de Préfaces—Le débat théâtral en France de Hardy à la Querelle du «Cid»* (Paris: Klincksieck, 1996).

Douais, Célestin, 'Le Testament de Guillaume de Catel', *Revue des Pyrénées*, 9 (1897), 497–507.

Doyle, John P., *Collected Studies on Francisco Suárez*, ed. by Victor M. Salas (Leuven: Leuven University Press, 2010).

Dubédat, Jean Baptiste, *Histoire du Parlement de Toulouse*, 2 vols (Paris: Arthur Rousseau, 1885).

Dubost, Jean-François, *La France italienne: XVI*[e]*–XVII*[e] *siècles* (Paris: Aubier, 1997).

Dubost, Jean-François, *Marie de Médicis: La reine dévoilée* (Paris: Payot et Rivages, 2009).

Duccini, Hélène, *Concini: Grandeur et misère du favouri de Marie de Médicis* (Paris: Ablin Michel, 1991).

Duccini, Hélène, *Faire voir, faire croire: l'opinion publique sous Louis XIII* (Seyssel: Champ Vallon, 2003).

Duccini, Hélène, 'Regard sur la littérature pamphlétaire en France au XVIIe siècle', *Revue historique*, 260: 2 (1978), 313–39.

Duggan, Anne E., 'Epicurean Cannibalism, or France Gone Savage', *French Studies*, 67: 4 (2013), 463–77.

Dulieu, Louis, 'Le chancelier François Ranchin', *Revue d'histoire des sciences*, 28: 3 (1974), 223–39.

Dunkelgrün, Theodor, 'The Christian Study of Judaism in Early Modern Europe', in *The Cambridge History of Judaism*, ed. by Jonathan Karp and Adam Sutcliffe (Cambridge: Cambridge University Press, 2017), pp. 316–48.

Elliot, J. H., *Richelieu and Olivares* (Cambridge: Cambridge University Press, 1984).

Erlanger, Philippe, *Richelieu* (Paris: Perin, 2004).

Esmein, Aldémar, *Cours élémentaires d'histoire du droit français, à l'usage des étudiants de première année* (Paris: L. Larose, 1898).

Esmein, Aldémar, *Histoire de la procédure criminelle en France* (Paris: Larose et Forcel, 1882).

Farge, Arlette, *The Allure of the Archives*, trans. by Thomas Scott-Railton, with a foreword by Natalie Zemon Davis (New Haven, CT: Yale University Press, 2013).

Faure, Claire, *La justice criminelle des capitouls de Toulouse (1566–1789)* (Toulouse: Presses de l'Université Toulouse 1 Capitole, 2017).

Fayard, E., *Aperçu historique sur le Parlement de Paris*, 3 vols (Lyon: N. Scheuring; Paris: A. Picard, 1876).

Febvre, Lucien, *Le Problème de l'incroyance au 16*[e] *siècle: La Religion de Rabelais* (Paris: Albin Michel, 1968).

Folliard, Melaine, 'Les intermittences du nom d'auteur dans les premiers recueils collectifs (1597–1607)', *Littératures classiques*, 80: 1 (2013), 35–62.

Folliard, Melaine, 'Le *Traicté de l'immortalité de l'âme* de Théophile de Viau, ou les voix du traducteur', *Libertinage et philosophie au XVIIe siècle*, 11—*Le Libertinage et l'éthique â l'âge classique*, (2009), 71–116.

Folliard, Melaine, Ronzeaud, Pierre and Thorel, Mathilde, *Théophile de Viau, la voix d'un poète. Poésies 1621, 1623, 1625* (Paris: Presses Universitaires de France, 2008).

Foucault, Didier, *1619: Vanini, un libertin sur le bûcher* (Portet-sur-Garonne: Éditions Midi-Pyrénéennes, 2018).

Foucault, Didier, *Histoire du libertinage* (Paris: Perrin, 2010).

Foucault, Didier, 'Jacques Ferrand, la 'mélancolie érotique' et la censure des théologiens toulousains', *Cahiers du Centre d'étude d'histoire de la médecine*, 17 (2009), 39–61.

Foucault, Didier, *Un Philosophe libertin dans l'Europe baroque: Giulo Cesare Vanini (1585–1619)* (Paris: Honoré Champion, 2003).

Foucault, Michel, *Surveiller et punir* (Paris: Gallimard, 1975).

Fouqueray, Henri, *Histoire de la Compagnie de Jésus en France*, 5 vols (Paris: Bureaux des Études, 1910–25).

Franceschi, Sylvio Hermann de, *La Crise théologico-politique du premier âge baroque. Antiromanisme doctrinal, pouvoir pastoral et raison du prince: le Saint-Siège face au prisme français (1607–1627)* (Rome: École française de Rome, 2009).

Friedenwald, Harry, 'Montaigne's Relation to Judaism and the Jews', *The Jewish Quarterly Review*, 31: 2 (1940), 141–8.

Friedenwald, Harry, 'Montalto: A Jewish Physician at the Court of Marie de Médicis and Louis XIII', *Bulletin of the Institute of the History of Medicine*, 3:2 (1935), 129–58.

Friedland, Paul, *Seeing Justice Done—The Age of Spectacular Capital Punishment in France* (Oxford: Oxford University Press, 2012).

Frisch, Andrea, *The Invention of the Eyewitness: Witnessing and Testimony in Early Modern France* (Chapel Hill, NC: The University of North Carolina Press, 2004).

Fuller, Thomas, *The Church History of Britain from the Birth of Jesus Christ Until the Year 1648*, ed. by J.S. Brewer, 6 vols (Oxford: Oxford University Press, 1845).

Fumaroli, Marc, *L'Âge de l'éloquence: Rhétorique et «res literaria» de la Renaissance au seuil de l'époque classique* (Geneva: Droz, 2002).

Gabriel, Frédéric, 'Libertinage et gallicanisme', *Littératures classiques*, 55: 3 (2004), 69–75.

Garrigues, Véronique, *Adrien de Monluc (1571–1646)—d'encre et de sang* (Limoges: Presses Universitaires de Limoges, 2006).

Garrigues, Véronique, 'Adrien de Monluc et l'académie des Philarètes', *Bulletin de la Société archéologique du Gers*', 3ème trimestre (1999), 285–97.

Gérard, Constantin, *Histoire du Châtelet et du Parlement de Paris* (Paris: Cognet, 1847).

Giavarini, Laurence, 'Le libertin et la fiction-sorcière à l'âge classique: Remarques sur Dom Juan et Théophile', in *Usages et théories de la fiction: le débat contemporain à l'épreuve des textes anciens (XVI–XVIIIe siècles)*, ed. by Françoise Lavocat (Rennes: Presses Universitaires de Rennes, 2004), pp. 185–218.

Giesey, Ralph E., Haldy, Lanny and Millhorn, James, 'Cardin Le Bret and Lese Majesty', *Law and History Review*, 4 (1986), 23–54.

Gilby, Emma, *Descartes's Fictions: Reading Philosophy with Poetics* (Oxford: Oxford University Press, 2019).

Godard de Donville, Louise, *Le Libertin des origines à 1665: un produit des apologètes* (Paris, Seattle and Tübignen: Papers on French Seventeenth-Century Literature (Biblio 17), 1989).
Godard de Donville, Louise, 'Théophile et son milieu dans les années précédant son procès', in *Théophile de Viau: Actes du colloque du CMR 17 offerts en hommage à Guido Saba*, ed. by Roger Duchêne (Paris, Seattle and Tübingen: Biblio 17, 1991), pp. 31–44.
Godard de Donville, Louise, 'Théophile, les «Beaux Esprits» et les Rose-Croix: un insidieux parallèle du P. Garasse', in *Correspondances*, ed. by W. Leiner and P. Ronzeaud (Tübingen and Aix-en-Province: Narr, 1992), pp. 143–54.
Gouverneur, Sophie, *Prudence et Subversions Libertines: La Critique de la raison d'État chez François de la Mothe le Vayer, Gabriel Naudé et Samuel Sorbière* (Paris: Honoré Champion, 2005).
Grantham Turner, James, *Schooling Sex: Libertine Literature and Erotic Education in Italy, France and England 1534–1685* (Oxford: Oxford University Press, 2009).
Greengrass, Mark, 'The Calvinist and the Chancellor: The Mental World of Louis Turquet de Mayerne', *Francia. Forschungen zur Westeuropäischen Geschichte*, 34 (2007), 1-23.
Hamilton, Tom, *Pierre de L'Estoile and His World in the Wars of Religion* (Oxford: Oxford University Press, 2017).
Hamilton, Tom, 'Sodomy and Criminal Justice in the Parlement of Paris: c.1540–c.1700', *Journal of the History of Sexuality*, 29: 3 (2020), 303–34.
Hammond, Nicholas, *Gossip, Sexuality and Scandal in France (1610–1715)* (Oxford: Peter Lang, 2011).
Hammond, Nicholas, *The Powers of Sound and Song in Early Modern Paris* (University Park, PA: Pennsylvania State University Press, 2019).
Helgeson, James, *The Lying Mirror: The First-person Stance and Sixteenth-century Writing* (Geneva: Droz, 2012).
Hildesheimer, Françoise and Morgat-Bonnet, Monique, *Le Parlement de Paris: Histoire d'un grand corps de l'État monarchique, XIIIe–XVIIIe siècle* (Paris: Honoré Champion, 2018).
Hinds, Leonard, '"Honni soit qui mal y pense" I: Avowals, Accusations, and Witnessing in the Trial of Théophile de Viau', *Papers on French Seventeenth-Century Literature*, 27: 53 (2000), 435–44.
Hine, William L., 'Mersenne and Vanini', *Renaissance Quarterly*, 29: 1 (1976), 52–65.
Holland, Susan, 'Archbishop Abbot and the problem of puritanism', *The Historical Journal*, 37:1 (1994), 23–43.
Holland, Susan, 'George Abbot: The Wanted Bishop', *Church History*, 56: 2 (1987), 172–87.
Holmès, Catherine, *L'Éloquence judiciaire de 1620 à 1660: reflet des problèmes sociaux, religieux et politiques de l'époque* (Paris: Nizet, 1967).
Höpfl, Harro, *Jesuit Political Thought: The Society of Jesus and the State, c.1540–1630* (Cambridge: Cambridge University Press, 2004).
Horsley, Adam, 'Blasphemy Hunters: Nicolas de Verdun and the Punishment of Criminal Speech in Early Bourbon France', *French Studies*, 75: 2 (2021), 145–62.
Horsley, Adam, '*Le Président libertin*: The Poetry of François Maynard after the Trial of Théophile de Viau', *Early Modern French Studies*, 37: 2 (2015), 93–107.
Horsley, Adam, '"Mon livre, je ne peux m'empescher de te plaindre': Reflections on the Compilation of François Maynard's 1646 Œuvres', in 'A *qui lira*': *Littérature, livre et librairie en France au XVIIe siècle*, ed. by Mathilde Bombart and others (Tübingen: Nar – Biblio 17, 2020), pp. 633–42.

Horsley, Adam, '"Ne l'as-tu point vu passer, mon garde?" Towards a Third Version of Cyrano de Bergerac's *Le Pédant joué*', *French Studies Bulletin*, 123 (2012), 28–31.

Horsley, Adam, 'Remarks on Subversive Performance at the Trial of Giulio Cesare Vanini (1618–1619)', *Modern Language Review*, 110: 1 (2015), 85–103.

Horsley, Adam, 'Secret Cabinets, Scribal Publication and the *Satyrique*: François Maynard and Libertine Poetry in Public and Private Spaces', *The Sixteenth Century Journal*, 51: 1 (2020), 55–78.

Horsley, Adam, 'Strategies of Accusation and Self-defence at the Trial of Théophile de Viau (1623–25)', *Papers on French Seventeenth-Century Literature*, 44: 85 (2016), 157–77.

Horsley, Adam, 'The Good Times and the Bad: François Maynard's Reflections on his Past and Future', in *Managing Time: Literature and Devotion in Early Modern France*, ed. by Richard Maber and Joanna Barker (Oxford: Peter Lang, 2017), pp. 107–31.

Houdard, Sophie, *Les Invasions mystiques: Spiritualités, hétérodoxies et censures au début de l'époque moderne* (Paris: Les Belles Lettres, 2008).

Houdard, Sophie, *Les Sciences du Diable: Quatre discours sur la sorcellerie (XVe–XVIIe siècle)* (Paris: Les Éditions du cerf, 1992).

Houllemare, Marie, *Politiques de la parole: le Parlement de Paris au XVIe siècle* (Geneva: Droz, 2011).

Huff, Peter A., 'Calvin and the Beasts: Animals in John Calvin's Theological Discourse', *JETS*, 42: 1 (March 1999), 67–75.

Huguet, Edmond, *Dictionnaire de la langue française du seizième siècle*, 7 vols (Paris: E. Champion; Didier, 1925–67).

Israel, Jonathan I., *Diasporas within a Diaspora: Jews, Crypto-Jews, and the World of Maritime Empires (1540–1740)* (Leiden: Brill, 2002).

Israel, Jonathan I., *European Jewry in the Age of Mercantilism, 1550–1750* (Oxford: Clarendon Press, 1985).

Jeanneret, Michel, *L'Éros rebelle: Littérature et dissidence à l'âge classique* (Paris: Seuil, 2003).

Joris, Freddy, *Mourir sur l'échafaud: Sensibilité collective face à la mort et perception des exécutions capitales du Bas Moyen Age à la fin de l'Ancien Régime* (Liège: Éditions du Céfal, 2005).

Jouhaud, Christian, 'La méthode de François Garasse', in *Les Jésuites à l'âge baroque (1540–1640)*, ed. by Luce Giard and Louis de Vaucelles (Grenoble: Jérôme Millon, 1996), pp. 243–60.

Jouhaud, Christian, *Les Pouvoirs de la littérature, histoire d'un paradoxe* (Paris: Gallimard, 2000).

Julia, Aurélie, *Frédéric Lachèvre (1855–1943): Un érudit à la découverte du XVIIe siècle libertin* (Paris: Honoré Champion, 2019).

Kahn, Didier, 'The Rosicrucian Hoax in France (1623–24)', in *Secrets of Nature: Astrology and Alchemy in Early Modern Europe*, ed. by William R. Newman and Anthony Grafton (Cambridge, MA, and London: The MIT Press, 2006), pp. 235–344.

Kelley, Donald R., *Foundations of Modern Historical Scholarship: Language, Law, and History in the French Renaissance* (New York and London: Columbia University Press, 1970).

Kelly, G.A., 'From Lèse-Majesté to Lèse-Nation: Treason in Eighteenth-century France', *Journal of the History of Ideas*, 42: 2 (1981), 269–86.

Kenny, Neil, *Born to Write: Literary Families and Social Hierarchy in Early Modern France* (Oxford: Oxford University Press, 2020).

Kenny, Neil, *Curiosity in Early Modern Europe: Word Histories* (Wiesbaden: Harrassowitz Verlag, 1998).

Kenny, Neil, *The Uses of Curiosity in Early Modern France and Germany* (Oxford: Oxford University Press, 2004).
Kibbee, Douglas A., 'Forensic linguistics and French', in *Studies in French Applied Linguistics*, ed. by Dalila Ayoun (Amsterdam and Philadelphia, PA: John Benjamins, 2008), pp. 295–316.
Krynen, Jacques, 'De la représentation à la dépossession du roi: les parlementaires «prêtres de la justice»', *Mélanges de l'école française de Rome* 114: 1 (2002), 95–119.
Labrousse, Elisabeth and Soman, Alfred, 'Un bûcher pour un judaïsant: Jean Fontanier (1621)', *XVII*[e] *siècle*, 39: 2 (1987), 113–32.
La Chenaye-Desbois, Aubert de and Badier, Jacques, *Dictionnaire de la noblesse*, 19 vols (Paris: Schlesinger frères, 1864).
Lachèvre, Frédéric, *Le Libertinage devant le parlement de Paris: Le Procès du poète Théophile de Viau*, 2 vols (Paris: Honoré Champion, 1909).
Lachèvre, Frédéric, *Mélanges sur le libertinage au XVII*[e] *siècle* (Paris: Honoré Champion, 1920).
Lachèvre, Frédéric, 'Un mémoire inédit de François Garassus adressé à Mathieu Molé, procureur général, pendant le procès de Théophile', *Revue d'Histoire Littéraire de la France*, 18 (1911), 900–40.
Lanavère, Alain, 'Théophile de Viau, imitateur des anciens', *XVII*[e] *siècle*, 251: 2 (2011), 397–422.
Langbein, John H., *The Origins of Adversary Criminal Trial* (Oxford: Oxford University Press, 2005).
Langlois, Monique, 'Parlement de Paris', in Michel Antoine and others, *Guide des recherches dans les fonds judiciaires de l'ancien régime* (Paris: Imprimerie Nationale, 1958), pp. 67–139.
Lanhers, Yvonne, 'Châtelet', in Michel Antoine and others, *Guide des recherches dans les fonds judiciaires de l'ancien régime* (Paris: Imprimerie Nationale, 1958).
Larner, Christina, *Enemies of God: The Witch-hunt in Scotland* (Edinburgh: John Donald, 2000).
Lebigre, Arlette, *La Justice du Roi: La vie judiciaire dans l'ancienne France* (Paris: Albin Michel, 1988).
Lebigre, Arlette, 'Les procès de Théophile de Viau', in *Quelques procès criminels des XVII*[e] *et XVIII*[e] *siècles*, ed. by Jean Imbert (Paris, Presses Universitaires de France, 1964), pp. 29–43.
Lemke, Walter H., '"Libertin": from Calvin to Cyrano', *Studi Francese*, 58 (1976), 58–60.
Lenman, Bruce and Parker, Geoffrey, 'The State, the Community and the Criminal Law in Early Modern Europe', in *Crime and the Law: The Social History of Crime in Western Europe Since 1500*, ed. by V.A.C. Gatrell, Bruce Lenman and Geoffrey Parker (London: Europa Publications, 1980), pp. 11–48.
Lenoble, Robert, *Mersenne ou la naissance du mécanisme* (Paris: Librairie Philosophique J. Vrin, 1943).
Leopizzi, Marcella, *Les Sources documentaires du courant libertin français—Giulio Cesare Vanini* (Fasano: Schena; Paris: Presses de l'université de Paris-Sorbonne, 2004).
Leopizzi, Marcella, 'Vanini en France: perspectives de recherche', *Studi Francesi*, 168 (2012), 505–12.
Lerner, Robert E., *The Heresy of the Free Spirit in the Later Middle Ages* (Berkeley, Los Angeles, CA, and London: University of California Press, 1972).

Lever, Maurice, *Les bûchers de Sodome* (Paris: Fayard, 1985).
Lipscomb, Suzannah, 'Crossing Boundaries: Women's Gossip, Insults and Violence in Sixteenth-century France', *French History*, 25: 4 (2011), 408–26.
Lough, John, *Writer and Public in France: from the Middle Ages to the Present Day* (Oxford: Clarendon, 1978).
Love, Harold, *Scribal Publication in Seventeenth-century England* (Oxford: Clarendon Press, 1993).
Maclean, Ian, *Interpretation and Meaning in the Renaissance: The Case of Law* (Cambridge: Cambridge University Press, 1992).
Magne, Émile, *Le Plaisant Abbé de Boisrobert, fondateur de l'Académie Française* (Paris: Mercure de France, 1909).
Mandrou, Robert, *Magistrats et sorciers en France au XVIIe siècle* (Paris: Plon, 1968).
Marchand, Jacqueline, 'Apologie du Père Garasse (1585–1631): Le Jésuite et les Libertins', *Cahiers laïques*, 173 (1980), 92–106.
Margolf, Diane C., *Religion and Royal Justice in Early Modern France: The Paris Chambre de l'Édit, 1598–1665* (Kirksville, MO: Truman State University Press, 2003).
Margolin, Jean-Claude, 'Libertins, libertinisme et «libertinage» au XVIe siècle', in *Aspects du Libertinisme au XVIe siècle*, ed. by André Stegmann (Paris: Librairie Philosophique J. Vrin, 1974), pp. 1–34.
Martin, Henri-Jean, *Le Livre français sous l'ancien régime* (Paris: Promodis, 1987).
Martin, Henri-Jean, *Livre, pouvoirs et société à Paris au XVIIe siècle*, 2 vols (Geneva: Droz, 1999).
Martin, Henri-Jean, *The History and Power of Writing*, trans. by Lydia G. Cochrane (Chicago, IL, and London: The University of Chicago Press, 1994).
Martin Peterson, Nora, *Involuntary Confessions of the Flesh in Early Modern France* (Newark, DE: University of Delaware Press, 2016).
Matthews, Shelly, *Perfect Martyr: The Stoning of Stephen and the Construction of Christian Identity* (Oxford: Oxford University Press, 2010).
Maugis, Édouard, *Histoire du parlement de Paris: De l'avènement des rois Valois à la mort d'Henri IV*, 3 vols (Paris: Auguste Picard, 1916).
Mazzara, Richard A., 'The *Phaedo* and Théophile de Viau's "Traicté de l'immortalité de l'âme"', *The French Review*, 40: 3 (1966), 329–40.
McGowan, Margaret M. (ed.), *Dynastic Marriages 1612/1615: A Celebration of the Habsburg and Bourbon Unions* (Farnham: Ashgate, 2013).
McKenna, Antony and Moreau, Pierre-François (eds.), *Libertinage et philosophie au XVIIe siècle, 12: Le libertinage est-il une catégorie philosophique?* (Saint-Étienne: Presses Universitaires de Saint-Étienne, 2010).
McMenamin, Gerald R., 'Forensic Stylistics: Theory and Practice of Forensic Stylistics', in *The Routledge Handbook of Forensic Linguistics*, ed. by Malcolm Coulthard and Alison Johnson (London and New York: Routledge, 2010), pp. 487–507.
Melammed, Renée Levine, *A Question of Identity: Iberian Conversos in Historical Perspective* (Oxford: Oxford University Press, 2004).
Méteyer, L.-J., *L'Académie Protestante de Saumur* (Paris: La Cause, 1933).
Metro, Antonino, 'Unus testis, nullus testis', in *Critical Studies in Ancient Law, Comparative Law and Legal History: Essays in Honour of Alan Watson*, ed. by John Cairns and Olivia Robinson (Oxford and Portland, OR: Hart Publishing, 2001), pp. 108–16.
Mongrédien, Georges, *La Vie littéraire au XVIIe siècle* (Paris: Éditions Jules Tallandier, 1947).

Moote, A. Lloyd, *The Revolt of the Judges: The Parlement of Paris and the Fronde 1643–1652* (Princeton, NJ: Princeton University Press, 1971).

Moreau, Isabelle, *«Guérir du sot»: Les Stratégies d'écriture des libertins à l'âge classique* (Paris: Honoré Champion, 2007).

Moreau, Isabelle, 'Sceptics and Free-thinkers', in *The Cambridge History of French Thought*, ed. by Michael Moriarty and Jeremy Jennings (Cambridge: Cambridge University Press, 2019), pp. 110–23.

Moréri, Louis, *Le Grand dictionnaire historique*, 10 vols (Paris: Les libraires associés, 1759).

Moréri, Louis, *Nouveau supplément au grand dictionnaire historique, généalogique, géographique, etc.*, 2 vols (Paris: Jacques Vincent and others, 1749).

Mothu, Alain, '*L'Antibigot* ou les «Quatrains du Déiste»', *La Lettre clandestine*, 21 (2013), 23–68.

Mothu, Alain, 'Pierre Petit à l'école antichrétienne de Jean Fontanier (1621)', *La Lettre clandestine*, 23 (2015), 261–70.

Mothu, Alain, 'Pour en finir avec les *libertins*', *Les Dossiers du Grihl*, online since 9 September 2010: http://dossiersgrihl.revues.org/4490?lang=en [accessed 20 September 2011].

Mousnier, Roland, *L'Assassinat d'Henri IV: 14 mai 1610* (Paris: Gallimard, 1964).

Mousnier, Roland, *Les Institutions de la France sous la monarchie absolue*, 2 vols (Paris: Presses Universitaires de France, 1980).

Muchnik, Natalia, 'La conversion en héritage. Crypto-judaïsants dans l'Europe des XVIe et XVIIe siècles (Espagne, France, Angleterre)', *Histoire, économie & société*, 4: 33 (2014), 10–24.

Nadier, Steven, *Rembrandt's Jews* (Chicago, IL: The University of Chicago Press, 2012).

Namer, Émile, *Documents sur la vie de Jules-César Vanini de Taurisano* (Bari: Adriatica Editrice, 1965).

Namer, Émile, *La Vie et l'œuvre de J.C. Vanini: Prince des Libertins* (Paris: Vrin, 1980).

Nelson, Eric, *The Jesuits and the Monarchy: Catholic Reform and Political Authority in France (1590–1615)* (Aldershot: Ashgate 2005).

Nisard, Charles, *Les Gladiateurs de la république des lettres aux XVe, XVIe, et XVIIe siècles*, 2 vols (Paris: Michel Lévy Frères, 1860).

Norton, Glyn P., 'Translation Theory in Renaissance France: Étienne Dolet and the Rhetorical Tradition', *Renaissance and Reformation*, 10: 1 (1974), 1–13.

Oliel-Grausz, Evelyne, 'Juifs, judaïsme et affrontements religieux (XVIe siècle – milieu XVIIe siècle', in *L'Europe en conflits: Les affrontements religieux et la genèse de l'Europe moderne vers 1500 – vers 1650*, ed. by Wolfgang Kaiser (Rennes: Presses Universitaires de Rennes, 2008), pp. 363–409.

Olivier-Martin, Fr., *Histoire du droit français des origines à la Révolution* (Paris: Éditions du CNRS, 1984).

Olsson, John, *Forensic Linguistics* (London and New York: Continuum, 2008).

Patterson, Jonathan, *Villainy in France (1463–1610): A Transcultural Study of Law and Literature* (Oxford: Oxford University Press, 2021).

Patterson, Jonathan and Wilton-Godberfforde, Emilia (eds.), *Early Modern French Studies*, 39: 2 (2017)—'Variations of Vileness'.

Pelorson, Jean-Marc, 'Le docteur Carlos García et la colonie hispano-portugaise de Paris (1613–1619)', *Bulletin Hispanique*, 71: 3–4 (1969), 518–76.

Pervo, Richard, *Acts: A Commentary*, ed. by Harold W. Attridge (Minneapolis, MN: Fortress Press, 2009).

Petitfils, Jean-Christian, *Fouquet* (Paris: Perrin, 2005).

Petitfils, Jean-Christian, *Louis XIII*, 2 vols (Paris: Perrin, 2014).

Peureux, Guillaume, 'Avertissements aux lecteurs', in *Lectures de Théophile de Viau*, ed. by Guillaume Peureux (Rennes: Presses Universitaires de Rennes, 2008), pp. 9–22.

Peureux, Guillaume, *La Muse satyrique (1600–1622)* (Geneva: Droz, 2015).

Pfister, Laurent, 'Author and Work in the French Print Privileges System: Some Milestones', in *Privilege and Property: Essays on the History of Copyright*, ed. by Ronan Deazley and others (Cambridge: Open Book Publishers, 2010), pp. 115–36.

Picot, Émile, *Théâtre Mystique de Pierre du Val et des Libertins Spirituels de Rouen au XVIe siècle* (Paris: Damascène Morgand, 1882).

Pintard, René, *Le Libertinage érudit dans la première moitié du XVIIe siècle* (Geneva: Slatkine, 2000).

Pollack, Samuel J., *The Crown and Judicial Venality in the Parlement of Toulouse, c.1490–1547* (unpublished doctoral thesis, Christ Church Oxford, 2016).

Poncet, Olivier, *Pomponne de Bellièvre (1529–1607): un homme d'État au temps des guerres de religion* (Paris: École des Chartes, 1998).

Popkin, Richard, 'Father Mersenne's War Against Pyrrhonism', *The Modern Schoolman*, 34 (1957), 61–78.

Popkin, Richard, *The History of Scepticism: From Savonarola to Bayle* (Oxford: Oxford University Press, 2003).

Popoff, Michel, *Prosopographie des gens du Parlement de Paris (1266–1743)* (Paris: Le Léopard d'or, 2003).

Prost, Joseph, *La philosophie à l'académie protestante de Saumur (1606–1685)* (Paris: Henry Paulin, 1907).

Racaut, Luc, *Hatred in Print. Catholic Propaganda and Protestant Identity During the French Wars of Religion* (Aldershot: Ashgate, 2002).

Raimondi, Francesco Paolo, 'Filosofia della libertà e libertà del filosofare in Vanini. Dal Rinascimento all'Età moderna', in *Giulio Cesare Vanini: Filosofia della libertà e libertà del filosofare. Atti del terzo convegno internazionale di studi Vaniniani (Lecce – Taurisano, 7–9 febbraio 2019)*, ed. by Francesco Paolo Raimondi (Rome: Aracne, 2019), pp. 157–83.

Raimondi, Francesco Paolo (ed.), *Giulio Cesare Vanini dal Tardo Rinascimento al Libertinisme érudit, Atti del Convegno di Studi (Lecce – Taurisano, 24–26 ottobre 1985)* (Galatina: Congedo, 2003).

Raimondi, Francesco Paolo, *Giulio Cesare Vanini Nell'Europa del Seicento, seconda edizione aggiornata* (Rome: Aracne, 2014).

Raimondi, Francesco Paolo, 'L'arrêt "de mort" contro Vanini: un documento enigmatico', *Bruniana & Campanelliana*, 17: 2 (2011), 585–96.

Raimondi, Francesco Paolo, 'Le Retour de Vanini dans le monde catholique à la lumière de nouveaux documents londoniens', *La Lettre clandestine*, 11 (2001), 135–55.

Raimondi, Francesco Paolo, '*Simulatio* e *dissimulatio* nella ecnica vaniniana della composizione del testo', in *Giulio Cesare Vanini e il libertinimso*, ed. by Francesco Paolo Raimondi (Galatina: Congedo, 2000), pp. 77–126.

Raimondi, Francesco Paolo, 'Vanini et Mersenne', in *Kairos*, 12 (1998): *Vanini: Libertinage et philosophie à l'époque moderne*, ed. by Jean-Pierre Cavaillé and Didier Foucault (Toulouse: Presses Universitaires du Mirail, 1998), pp. 181–253.

Ramet, Henri, *Le Capitole et le Parlement de Toulouse* (Cressé: Éditions des Régionalismes, 2008).

Raphaël, Freddy, 'Juifs et sorcières dans l'Alsace médiévale', *Revue des sciences sociales*, 3 (1974), 69–106.

Ratel, Guillaume, *Between Facts and Faith: The Judicial Practices of the Conseillers of the Parlement de Toulouse (1550–1700)* (unpublished doctoral thesis, Cornell University, 2017).

Reichler, Claude, *L' Âge libertin* (Paris: Éditions de minuit, 1987).

Rieger, Dietmar, '"Histoire de loi – Histoire tragique". Authenticité et structure de genre chez F. de Rosset', *XVIIe siècle*, 46: 184 (1994), pp. 461–77.

Roberts, Hugh, 'An Exiled Poet adapts Plato: Théophile de Viau's *Traité de l'immortalité de l'âme* and the *Phaedo*', *International Journal of the Classical Tradition* (forthcoming, 2021).

Roberts, Hugh, '"Au Diable soient donnez les Comediens": La haine dans les apologies du théâtre au début du XVIIe siècle', *Littératures classiques*, 98 (2019), 65–75.

Roberts, Hugh, 'Obscenity and the Politics of Authorship in Early Seventeenth-century France: Guillaume Colletet and the *Parnasse des poètes satyriques* (1622)', *French Studies*, 68: 1 (2014), 18–33.

Roberts, Hugh, Peureux, Guillaume and Wajeman, Lise, *Obscénités renaissantes* (Geneva: Droz, 2011).

Roche, Bruno, *Le Rire des libertins dans la première moitié du XVIIe siècle* (Paris: Honoré Champion, 2011).

Rosellini, Michèle, 'Le libertinage du roman comique à l'épreuve du procès de Théophile de Viau', in *Libertinism and Literature in Seventeenth-century France*, ed. by Richard G. Hodgson (Tübingen: Narr, 2009), pp. 37–69.

Rosellini, Michèle, 'Risques et bénéfices de la publication d'un "mauvais livre": la stratégie commerciale des libraires-éditeurs du Parnasse satyrique (1622–1625)', in *Les arrière-boutiques de la littérature: auteurs et imprimeurs-libraires aux XVIe et XVIIe siècles*, ed. by Edwige Keller-Rahbé (Toulouse: Presses Universitaires du Mirail, 2010), pp. 185–208.

Rosellini, Michèle, 'Théophile devant ses juges ou l'œuvre en procès', *L'immoralité littéraire et ses juges*, ed. by Jean-Baptiste Amadieu (Paris: Hermann, 2019), pp. 43–66.

Roth, Cecil, 'Les Marranes à Rouen. Un chapitre ignoré de l'histoire des Juifs de France', *Revue des Études Juives*, 88 (1929), 113–55.

Roth, Cecil, 'Quatre Lettres d'Elie de Montalte', *Revue des Études Juives*, 87 (1929), 137–65.

Roy, Émile, *La Vie et les œuvres de Charles Sorel, sieur de Souvigny (1602–1674)* (Geneva: Slatkine reprints, 1970).

Rushton, Peter, 'Texts of Authority: Witchcraft Accusations and the Demonstration of Truth in Early Modern England', in *Languages of Witchcraft: Narrative, Ideology and Meaning in Early Modern Culture*, ed. by Stuart Clark (Basingstoke and London: Macmillan, 2001), pp. 21–39.

Saba, Guido, *Fortunes et infortunes de Théophile de Viau* (Paris: Klincksieck, 1997).

Saba, Guido, *Théophile de Viau: un poète rebelle* (Geneva: Slatkine Reprints, 2008).

Sanchez, Jean-Christophe, 'Deux nobles commingeois dans l'entourage de Vanini: le baron de Montaut et le sieur Francon', in *L'esprit de liberté à Toulouse au temps du parlement (1443–1790), actes du colloque de Toulouse à l'occasion du 400e anniversaire du bûcher de Vanini (18–19 avril 2019)*, ed. by Didier Foucault, Olivier Guerrier and Yves Le Pestipon (Toulouse: Presses universitaire du Midi, forthcoming).

Saperstein, Marc, *Exile in Amsterdam. Saul Levi Morteira's Sermons to a Congregation of New Jews* (Cincinnati, OH: Hebrew Union College Press, 2005).

Sawyer, Jeffrey K., *Printed Poison: Pamphlet Propaganda, Faction Politics, and the Public Sphere in Early Seventeenth-century France* (Berkeley, Los Angeles, CA, and Oxford: University of California Press, 1990).

Schmidt, Charles, *Traités mystiques écrits dans les années 1547 à 1549, publiés d'après le manuscrit original* (Paris: Sandoz et Fischbacher, 1876).

Schneider, Gerhard, *Der Libertin, Zur Geistes- und Sozialgeschichte des Bürgertums im 16. und 17. Jahrhundert* (Stuttgart: J.B. Metzlert, 1970).

Schneider, Robert A., *Dignified Retreat: Writers and Intellectuals in the Age of Richelieu* (Oxford: Oxford University Press, 2019).

Schneider, Robert A., *Public Life in Toulouse 1463–1789: From Municipal Republic to Cosmopolitan City* (Ithaca, NY, and London: Cornell University Press, 1989).

Scholar, Richard, *Montaigne and the Art of Free-thinking* (Oxford: Peter Lang, 2010).

Scholar, Richard, *The 'Je-Ne-Sais-Quoi' in Early Modern Europe: Encounters with a Certain Something* (Oxford: Oxford University Press, 2005).

Schreiber, Jean-Philippe, 'La criminalisation du péché', in *Le blasphème: du péché au crime*, ed. by Alain Dierkens and Jean-Philippe Schreiber (Brussels: Éditions de l'université de Bruxelles, 2012).

Scott, James C., *Domination and the Arts of Resistance* (New Haven, CT, and London: Yale University Press, 1990).

Secret, François, 'Notes sur quelques alchimistes', *Bibliothèque d'Humanisme et Renaissance*, 33 (1971), 625–40.

Senning, Calvin F., 'Vanini and the Diplomats, 1612–1614: Religion, Politics, and Defection in the Counter-Reformation Era', *Historical Magazine of the Protestant Episcopal Church*, 54: 3 (1985), 219–39.

Shear, Adam, 'Science, Medicine, and Jewish Philosophy', in *The Cambridge History of Judaism*, ed. by Jonathan Karp and Adam Sutcliffe (Cambridge: Cambridge University Press, 2017), pp. 522–49.

Shennan, J.H., *The Parlement of Paris* (Stroud: Sutton, 1998).

Silverman, Lisa, *Tortured Subjects: Pain, Truth, and the Body in Early Modern France* (Chicago, IL: The University of Chicago Press, 2001).

Skinner, Quentin, 'Meaning and Understanding in the History of Ideas', *History and Theory*, 8: 1 (1969), 3–53.

Slide, Seymour, *Jacob van Ruisdael: A Complete Catalogue of his Paintings, Drawings and Etchings* (New Haven, CT, and London: Yale University Press, 2001).

Soltau, Roger, 'La Monarchie aristo-démocratique de Louis Turquet de Mayerne', *Revue du seizième siècle*, 13 (1926), 78–94.

Soman, Alfred, 'Aux origines de l'appel de droit dans l'Ordonnance criminelle de 1670', *XVIIe siècle*, 32 (1980), 21–35.

Soman, Alfred, 'Criminal Jurisprudence in Ancien-Régime France: The Parlement of Paris in the Sixteenth and Seventeenth Centuries', in *Crime and Criminal Justice in Europe and Canada*, ed. by Louis A. Knafla (Waterloo, Ontario: Wilfrid Laurier University Press, 1981), pp. 43–75.

Soman, Alfred, 'Deviance and Criminal Justice in Western Europe, 1300–1800: An Essay in Structure', *Criminal Justice History*, 1 (1980), 3–28.

Soman, Alfred, 'La Décriminalisation de la sorcellerie en France', *Histoire, économie et société*, 4 (1985), 179–203.

Soman, Alfred, 'La justice criminelle, vitrine de la monarchie française', *Bibliothèque de l'école des chartes*, 153: 2 (1995), 291–304.

Soman, Alfred, 'Les procès de sorcellerie au Parlement de Paris (1565–1640)', *Annales: Économies, Sociétés, Civilisations*, 32 (1977), 790–814.

Soman, Alfred, 'Petit guide des recherches dans les archives criminelles du Parlement de Paris à l'époque moderne', *Histoire et Archives*, 12: 1 (2002), 61–79.

Soman, Alfred, 'Press, Pulpit and Censorship in France before Richelieu', *Proceedings of the American Philosophical Society*, 120: 6 (1976), 439–63.

Soman, Alfred, 'Sorcellerie, justice criminelle et société dans la France moderne (l'ego-histoire d'un Américain à Paris)', *Histoire, Économie et Société*, 12: 2 (1993), 177–217.

Spink, J.S., *French Free-thought from Gassendi to Voltaire* (London: The Athlone Press, 1960).

Stegmann, André, *Aspects du libertinisme au XVIe siècle* (Paris: Librairie Philosophique J. Vrin, 1974).

Stokes, Laura, *Demons of Urban Reform: Early European Witch Trials and Criminal Justice, 1430–1530* (Basingstoke: Palgrave Macmillan, 2011).

Storez-Brancourt, Isabelle, 'A l'ombre de Messieurs les Gens du Roi: le monde des substituts', in *Histoire du Parquet*, ed. by Jean-Michel Carbasse (Paris: Presses Universitaires de France, 2000), pp. 157–204.

Swann, Julian, *Exile, Imprisonment, or Death: The Politics of Disgrace in Bourbon France, 1610–1789* (Oxford: Oxford University Press, 2017).

Taylor, Helena, *The Lives of Ovid in Seventeenth-century French Culture* (Oxford: Oxford University Press, 2017).

Tinguely, Frédéric, 'D'un usage pervers de l'analogie: libertins et protestants dans la *Doctrine curieuse* du Père Garasse', *Libertinage et philosophie*, 8 (2004), 31–46.

Tinguely, Frédéric, 'Garasse et les altérités croisées', in *Libertin! Usage d'une invective aux XVIe et XVIIe siècles*, ed. by Thomas Berns, Anne Staquet and Monique Weis (Paris: Classiques Garnier, 2013), pp. 117–31.

Tricoche-Rauline, Laurence, *Identité(s) libertine(s): L'écriture personnelle ou la création de soi* (Paris: Honoré Champion, 2009).

Tricotel, Édouard, 'Sur un poëte peu connu, Estienne Durand (1590–1618)', *Bulletin du bibliophile et du bibliothécaire*, (October 1859), 656–62.

Trooz, Charles de, 'Le Père Garasse et *La Doctrine curieuse*', *Lettres Romanes*, 1: 2 (1947), 113–34.

Van Damme, Stéphane, *L'épreuve libertine: Morale, soupçon et pouvoirs dans la France baroque* (Paris: CNRS Éditions, 2008).

Van Damme, Stéphane, 'Libertine Paris', in *The Cambridge Companion to the Literature of Paris*, ed. by Anna Louise Milne (Cambridge: Cambridge University Press, 2013), pp. 34–51.

Vaneigem, Raoul, *The Movement of the Free Spirit* (New York: Zone Books, 1994).

Van't Spijker, Willem, *Calvin: A Brief Guide to His Life and Thought*, trans. by Lyle D. Bierma (Louisville: Westminster John Knox Press, 2009).

Verciani, Laura, *Le moi et ses diables: Autobiographie spirituelle et récit de possession au XVIIe siècle*, trans. by Arlette Estève (Paris: Honoré Champion, 2001).

Vesperini, Pierre, *Lucrèce: Archéologie d'un classique européen* (Paris: Fayard, 2017).

Vigier, Fabrice, 'En quête de preuves! La publication de monitoires ecclésiastiques dans le diocèse de Poitiers à l'époque moderne', in *La Preuve en justice de l'antiquité à nos jours*, ed. by Bruno Lemesle (Rennes: Presses Universitaires de Rennes, 2003), pp. 171–89.

Vurpas, Anne-Marie (ed.), *Moqueries savoyardes: Monologues polémiques et comiques en dialecte savoyard de la fin du XVIe siècle* (Lyon: La Manufacture, 1986).

Waddell, Helen, *Songs of the Wandering Scholars*, ed. by Dame Felicitas Corrigan (London: The Folio Society, 1982).

Wagenvoort, Gerrit Harm, 'Le Rabelais reformé (1620) du P. François Garasse, S.J.: Une réaction au traité de Pierre du Moulin, De la Vocation des Pasteurs (Style, mentalité, controverse religieuse et emploi des sources)' (unpublished masters dissertation, Université Catholique de Nimègue, 1992).

Waite, Gary K., *Jews and Muslims in Seventeenth-century Discourse: From Religious Enemies to Allies and Friends* (London and New York: Routledge, 2019).

Wansbrough, Henry (ed.), *The New Jerusalem Bible: Study Edition* (London: Darton, Longman & Todd, 1994).

Watson, Richard, *Cogito, Ergo Sum: The Life of René Descartes* (Boston, MA: David R. Godine, 2007).

Wenzel, Eric, 'Forcer les témoignages: le délicat recours au monitoire sous l'Ancien Régime', in *Les témoins devant la justice: Une histoire des statuts et des comportements*, ed. by Benoit Garnot (Rennes: Presses Universitaires de Rennes, 2003), pp. 83–90.

Whicher, George F., *The Goliard Poets: Medieval Latin Songs and Satires* (Westport, CT: Greenwood Press, 1976).

Wilke, Carsten L., 'Le rapport d'un espion du Saint-Office sur sa mission auprès des crypto-juifs de Saint-Jean-de-Luz (1611)', *Sigila*, 16 (2006), 127–41.

Williams, Noel H., *A Gallant of Lorraine: François, Seigneur de Bassompierre, Marquis d'Harouel, Maréchal de France (1579–1646)*, 2 vols (London: Hurst and Blackett Ltd., 1921).

Wyneken, Karl H., 'Calvin and Anabaptism', in *Articles on Calvin and Calvinism*, ed. by Richard C. Gamble (New York and London, Garland Publishing, 1992), pp. 18–29.

Yates, Frances A., *Giordano Bruno and the Hermetic Tradition* (Chicago, IL: The University of Chicago Press, 1964).

Yates, Frances A., *The Rosicrucian Enlightenment* (London: Routledge and Kegan Paul, 1972).

Zemon Davis, Natalie, *Fiction in the Archives: Pardon Tales and their Tellers in Sixteenth-century France* (Stanford, CA: Stanford University Press, 1987).

Zemon Davis, Natalie, *Society and Culture in Early Modern France* (London: Duckworth, 1975).

Zink, Anne, 'Être juif à Bayonne en 1630', *Annales du Midi: revue archéologique, historique et philologique de la France méridionale*, 108: 2 (1996), 441–60.

Zink, Anne, 'Une niche juridique: L'installation des Juifs à Saint-Esprit-lès-Bayonne au XVIIe siècle', *Annales. Histoire, Sciences Sociales*, 49: 3 (1994), 639–69.

Zuber, Roger, *Les émerveillements de la raison: Classicismes littéraires du XVIIe siècle français* (Paris: Klincksieck, 1997).

Index*

* To avoid excessive references, page numbers have not been given here for each individual reference to Vanini, Fontanier, and Théophile within their respective dedicated chapters. Page ranges pertaining to events at their trials can be found in the table of contents.

9 780197 267004

Printed and bound by CPI Group (UK) Ltd, Croydon, CR0 4YY

31/08/2025

14726937-0002